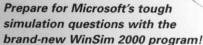

Prepare for Microsoft's tough simulation questions with the brand-new WinSim 2000 program!

✔ Use the simulators to guide you through real-world tasks step-by-step, or watch the movies to see the "invisible hand" perform the tasks for you.

Search through two complete books in PDF–MCSE: Windows 2000 Professional Study Guide *and* the Dictionary of Networking!

✔ Access the entire *MCSE: Windows 2000 Professional Study Guide*, complete with figures and tables, in electronic format.

✔ Search the *MCSE: Windows 2000 Professional Study Guide* chapters to find information on any topic in seconds.

✔ Look up any networking term in the *Dictionary of Networking*.

SYBEX

MCSE: Windows 2000 Professional Study Guide

Exam 70-210: Objectives

OBJECTIVE	PAGE

NOTE   Exam objectives are subject to change at any time without prior notice and at Microsoft's sole discretion. Please visit Microsoft's Training & Certification Web site (www.microsoft.com/Train_Cert) for the most current listing of exam objectives.

SYBEX

MCSE:
Windows® 2000 Professional
Study Guide

Lisa Donald
with James Chellis

San Francisco • Paris • Düsseldorf • Soest • London

SYBEX

Associate Publisher: Neil Edde
Contracts and Licensing Manager: Kristine O'Callaghan
Acquisitions & Developmental Editor: Dann McDorman
Editor: Marilyn Smith
Project Editor: Malka Geffen
Production Editor: Shannon Murphy
Technical Editors: Donald Fuller, Dan Renaud
Book Designer: Bill Gibson
Graphic Illustrator: Tony Jonick
Electronic Publishing Specialists: Judy Fung, Bill Gibson
Proofreaders: Leslie E. H. Light, Laurie O'Connell, Lindy Wolf, Nancy Riddiough, Camera Obscura, Andrea Fox
Indexer: Ted Laux
CD Coordinator: Kara Schwartz
CD Technician: Keith McNeil
Cover Designer: Archer Design
Cover Illustrator/Photographer: The Image Bank

SYBEX

To Our Valued Readers:

In recent years, Microsoft's MCSE program has established itself as the premier computer and networking industry certification. Nearly a quarter of a million IT professionals have attained MCSE status in the NT 4 track. Sybex is proud to have helped thousands of MCSE candidates prepare for their exams over these years, and we are excited about the opportunity to continue to provide people with the skills they'll need to succeed in the highly competitive IT industry.

For the Windows 2000 MCSE track, Microsoft has made it their mission to demand more of exam candidates. Exam developers have gone to great lengths to raise the bar in order to prevent a paper-certification syndrome, one in which individuals obtain a certification without a thorough understanding of the technology. Sybex welcomes this new philosophy as we have always advocated a comprehensive instructional approach to certification courseware. It has always been Sybex's mission to teach exam candidates how new technologies work in the real world, not to simply feed them answers to test questions. Sybex was founded on the premise of providing technical skills to IT professionals, and we have continued to build on that foundation, making significant improvements to our study guides based on feedback from readers, suggestions from instructors, and comments from industry leaders.

The depth and breadth of technical knowledge required to obtain Microsoft's new Windows 2000 MCSE is staggering. Sybex has assembled some of the most technically skilled instructors in the industry to write our study guides, and we're confident that our Windows 2000 MCSE study guides will meet and exceed the demanding standards both of Microsoft and you, the exam candidate.

Good luck in pursuit of your MCSE!

Neil Edde
Associate Publisher—Certification
Sybex, Inc.

SYBEX Inc. 1151 Marina Village Parkway, Alameda, CA 94501
Tel: 510/523-8233   Fax: 510/523-2373   HTTP://www.sybex.com

For Kevin. You are the best!

Acknowledgments

This book is the result of a great team. First, I'd like to thank Marilyn Smith, who did a tremendous job of translating my writing into a form that is very readable. Marilyn put in countless hours and worked through my many revisions as the book evolved. She is the hardest working and most professional editor I have ever had the privilege to work with.

I'd also like to thank the team that made this book possible. Thanks to James Chellis for allowing me to work on the MCSE series. James is a visionary and is my business idol. Neil Edde, the Associate Publisher for this series, has nurtured the MCSE since the early days. Dann McDorman, the Associate Developmental Editor, is always fun to work with. Malka Geffen, the Project Editor, somehow managed to keep this project on track, which was not always an easy task.

Donald Fuller and Dan Renaud worked as the Technical Editors. They did a great job of keeping me honest and minimizing any errors within the book. Shannon Murphy worked as the Production Editor and coordinated with Tony Jonick who developed the artwork from my drawings. Judy Fung worked as the Electronic Publishing Specialist. Keith McNeil worked as the CD Technician. Matthew Sheltz worked very hard on the CD content and is also very appreciated. Without the great work of the team, this book would not be possible.

On the local front, I'd like to thank Elisa Sands, my assistant, and Martina Fiserova, who keeps my life sane. Without these two, I'd never get anything done. I'd also like to thank my family for always supporting me.

Contents at a Glance

Contents

Table of Exercises

Introduction

Microsoft's new Microsoft Certified Systems Engineer (MCSE) track for Windows 2000 is the premier certification for computer industry professionals. Covering the core technologies around which Microsoft's future will be built, the new MCSE certification is a powerful credential for career advancement.

This book has been developed, in cooperation with Microsoft Corporation, to give you the critical skills and knowledge you need to prepare for one of the core requirements of the new MCSE certification program for Windows 2000 Professional. You will find the information you need to acquire a solid understanding of Windows 2000 Professional, to prepare for Exam 70-210: Installing, Configuring, and Administering Microsoft Windows 2000 Professional, and to progress toward MCSE certification.

Why Become Certified in Windows 2000?

As the computer network industry grows in both size and complexity, the need for *proven* ability is increasing. Companies rely on certifications to verify the skills of prospective employees and contractors.

Whether you are just getting started or are ready to move ahead in the computer industry, the knowledge, skills, and credentials you have are your most valuable assets. Microsoft has developed its Microsoft Certified Professional (MCP) program to give you credentials that verify your ability to work with Microsoft products effectively and professionally. The MCP credential for professionals who work with Microsoft Windows 2000 networks is the new MCSE certification.

Over the next few years, companies around the world will deploy millions of copies of Windows 2000 as the central operating system for their mission-critical networks. This will generate an enormous need for qualified consultants and personnel to design, deploy, and support Windows 2000 networks.

Windows 2000 is a huge product that requires professional skills of its administrators. Consider that Windows NT 4 has about 12 million lines of code, while Windows 2000 has more than 35 million! Much of this code is needed to deal with the wide range of functionality that Windows 2000 offers.

Windows 2000 actually consists of several different versions:

Windows 2000 Professional The client edition of Windows 2000, which is comparable to Windows NT Workstation 4, but also includes the best features of Windows 98 and many new features.

Windows 2000 Server/Windows 2000 Advanced Server   A server edition of Windows 2000 for small to mid-sized deployments. Advanced Server supports more memory and processors than Server does.

Windows 2000 Datacenter Server   A server edition of Windows 2000 for large, wide-scale deployments and computer clusters. Datacenter Server supports the most memory and processors of the three versions.

With such an expansive operating system, companies need to be certain that you are the right person for the job being offered. The MCSE is designed to help prove that you are.

As part of its promotion of Windows 2000, Microsoft has announced that MCSEs who have passed the Windows NT 4 core exams must upgrade their certifications to the new Windows 2000 track by December 31, 2001, to remain certified. The Network Press MCSE Study Guide series, published by Sybex, covers the full range of exams required for either obtaining or upgrading your certification. For more information, see the "Exam Requirements" section later in this Introduction.

Is This Book for You?

If you want to acquire a solid foundation in Windows 2000 Professional, this book is for you. You'll find clear explanations of the fundamental concepts you need to grasp.

If you want to become certified as an MCSE, this book is definitely for you. However, if you just want to attempt to pass the exam without really understanding Windows 2000, this book is *not* for you. This book is written for those who want to acquire hands-on skills and in-depth knowledge of Windows 2000.

If your goal is to prepare for the exam by learning how to use and manage the new operating system, this book is for you. It will help you to achieve the high level of professional competency you need to succeed in this field.

What Does This Book Cover?

This book contains detailed explanations, hands-on exercises, and review questions to test your knowledge.

Think of this book as your complete guide to Windows 2000 Professional. It begins by covering the most basic concepts, such as the features of the operating system and how to install and configure it. Next, you will learn how to perform important tasks, including:

- Managing users and groups

- Managing access to files and folders

- Configuring local and network printing

- Managing network and dial-up connections

You will also learn how to tune your computer's performance, troubleshoot your system, and recover from system failures.

Throughout the book, you will be guided through hands-on exercises, which give you practical experience for each exam objective. At the end of each chapter, you'll find a summary of the topics covered in the chapter, which also includes a list of the key terms used in that chapter. The key terms represent not only the terminology that you should recognize, but also the underlying concepts that you should understand to pass the exam. All of the key terms are defined in the glossary at the back of the study guide.

Finally, each chapter concludes with 20 review questions that test your knowledge of the information covered. You'll find an entire practice exam, with 50 additional questions, in Appendix A. Many more questions, as well as multimedia demonstrations of the hands-on exercises, are included on the CD that accompanies this book, as explained in the "What's on the CD?" section at the end of this Introduction.

The topics covered in this book map directly to Microsoft's official exam objectives. Each exam objective is covered completely. Because Microsoft developed similar exam objectives for the Professional and Server exams, there is a degree of overlap between the Sybex books covering these exams. However, it is important to work through each book in its entirety, viewing any repeated material as a reminder and a chance to reinforce your understanding of Windows 2000.

How Do You Become an MCSE?

Attaining MCSE certification has always been a challenge. However, in the past, individuals could acquire detailed exam information—even most of the exam questions—from online "brain dumps" and third-party "cram" books or software products. For the new MCSE exams, this simply will not be the case.

To avoid the "paper-MCSE syndrome" (a devaluation of the MCSE certification because unqualified individuals manage to pass the exams), Microsoft has taken strong steps to protect the security and integrity of the new MCSE track. Prospective MSCEs will need to complete a course of study that provides not only detailed knowledge of a wide range of topics, but true skills derived from working with Windows 2000 and related software products.

In the new MCSE program, Microsoft is heavily emphasizing hands-on skills. Microsoft has stated that, "Nearly half of the core required exams' content demands that the candidate have troubleshooting skills acquired through hands-on experience and working knowledge."

Fortunately, if you are willing to dedicate time and effort with Windows 2000, you can prepare for the exams by using the proper tools. If you work through this book and the other books in this series, you should successfully meet the exam requirements.

This book is a part of a complete series of Sybex MCSE Study Guides, published by Sybex, that covers the five core Windows 2000 requirements as well as the new Design electives you need to complete your MCSE track. Titles include:

- MCSE: Windows 2000 Professional Study Guide

- MCSE: Windows 2000 Server Study Guide

- MCSE: Windows 2000 Network Infrastructure Administration Study Guide

- MCSE: Windows 2000 Directory Services Administration Study Guide

- MCSE: Windows 2000 Network Security Design Study Guide

- MCSE: Windows 2000 Network Infrastructure Design Study Guide

- MCSE: Windows 2000 Directory Services Design Study Guide

There are also study guides available from Sybex on additional MCSE electives.

Exam Requirements

Successful candidates must pass a minimum set of exams that measure technical proficiency and expertise:

- Candidates for MCSE certification must pass seven exams, including four core operating system exams, one design exam, and two electives.

- Candidates who have already passed three Windows NT 4 exams (70-067, 70-068, and 70-073) may opt to take an "accelerated" exam plus one core design exam and two electives.

If you do not pass the accelerated exam after one attempt, you must pass the five core requirements and two electives.

The following table shows the exams a new certification candidate must pass.

All of these exams are required

Exam #	Topic	Requirement Met
70-210	Windows 2000 Professional	Core (Operating System)
70-215	Windows 2000 Server	Core (Operating System)
70-216	Windows 2000 Network Infrastructure Administration	Core (Operating System)
70-217	Windows 2000 Directory Services	Core (Operating System)

One of these exams is required

Exam #	Topic	Requirement Met
70-219	Designing a Windows 2000 Directory Services Infrastructure	Core (Design)

70-220	Designing Security for Windows 2000	Core (Design)
70-221	Designing a Windows 2000 Network Infrastructure	Core (Design)

Two of these exams are required

Exam #	Topic	Requirement Met
70-219	Designing a Windows 2000 Directory Services	Elective
70-220	Designing Security for Windows 2000	Elective
70-221	Designing a Windows 2000 Network Infrastructure	Elective
Any current MCSE elective	Exams cover topics such as Exchange Server, SQL Server, Systems Management Server, Internet Explorer Administrators Kit, and Proxy Server (new exams are added regularly)	Elective

For a more detailed description of the Microsoft certification programs, including a list of current MCSE electives, check Microsoft's Training and Certification Web site at www.microsoft.com/train_cert.

The Windows 2000 Professional Exam

The Windows 2000 Professional exam covers concepts and skills required for the support of Windows 2000 Professional computers. It emphasizes the following areas of Windows 2000 Professional support:

- Installing Windows 2000 Professional

- Implementing and administering resources

- Implementing, managing, and troubleshooting resources

- Monitoring and optimizing system performance and reliability

- Configuring and troubleshooting the Desktop environment

- Implementing, managing, and troubleshooting network protocols and services

- Implementing, monitoring, and troubleshooting security

This exam can be quite specific regarding Windows 2000 Professional requirements and operational settings, and it can be particular about how administrative tasks are performed in the operating system. It also focuses on fundamental concepts relating to Windows 2000 Professional's operation. Careful study of this book, along with hands-on experience, will help you prepare for this exam.

Microsoft provides exam objectives to give you a very general overview of possible areas of coverage of the Microsoft exams. For your convenience, we have added in-text objectives listings at the points in the text where specific Microsoft exam objectives are covered. However, exam objectives are subject to change at any time without prior notice and at Microsoft's sole discretion. Please visit Microsoft's Training and Certification Web site (www.microsoft.com/Train_Cert) for the most current exam objectives listing.

Types of Exam Questions

In the previous tracks, the formats of the MCSE exams were fairly straightforward, consisting almost entirely of multiple-choice questions appearing in a few different sets. Prior to taking an exam, you knew how many questions you would see and what type of questions would appear. If you had purchased the right third-party exam preparation products, you could even be quite familiar with the pool of questions you might be asked. As mentioned earlier, all of this is changing.

In an effort to both refine the testing process and protect the quality of its certifications, Microsoft has introduced adaptive testing, as well as some new exam elements. You will not know in advance which type of format you will see on your exam. These innovations make the exams more challenging, and they make it much more difficult for someone to pass an exam after simply "cramming" for it.

Microsoft will be accomplishing its goal of protecting the exams by regularly adding and removing exam questions, limiting the number of questions that any individual sees in a beta exam, limiting the number of questions delivered to an individual by using adaptive testing, and adding new exam elements.

Exam questions may be in multiple-choice, select-and-place, simulation, or case study-based formats. You may also find yourself taking an adaptive format exam. Let's take a look at the exam question types and adaptive testing, so you can be prepared for all of the possibilities.

Multiple-Choice Questions

Multiple-choice questions include two main types of questions. One is a straightforward type that presents a question, followed by several possible answers, of which one or more is correct.

The other type of multiple-choice question is more complex. This type presents a set of desired results along with a proposed solution. You must then decide which results would be achieved by the proposed solution.

You will see many multiple-choice questions in this study guide and on the accompanying CD, as well as on your exam.

Select-and-Place Questions

Select-and-place exam questions involve graphical elements that you must manipulate in order to successfully answer a question. For example, a question could present a diagram of a computer network, as shown below.

The diagram shows several computers next to boxes that contain the text "Place here." The labels represent different computer roles on a network, such as print server and file server. Based on information given for each computer, you are asked to drag and drop each label to the correct box. You need to place *all* of the labels correctly. No credit is given if you correctly label only some of the boxes.

Simulations

Simulations are the kinds of questions that most closely represent and test the actual skills you use while working with Microsoft software interfaces. These types of exam questions include a mock interface on which you must perform certain actions according to a given scenario. The simulated interfaces look nearly identical to what you see in the actual product, as shown in the example below.

Simulations are by far the most complex element introduced into Microsoft exams to date. Because of the number of possible errors that can be made on simulations, it is worthwhile to consider the following recommendations from Microsoft:

- Do not change any simulation settings that don't pertain to the solution directly.

- Assume that the default settings are used when related information has not been provided.

- Make sure that your entries are spelled correctly.

- Close all of the simulation application windows after completing the set of tasks in the simulation.

The best way to prepare for the simulation questions is to spend time working with the graphical interface of the product on which you will be tested.

We recommend that you study with the Edge Test WinSim 2000 product, which is included on the CD that accompanies this study guide. By completing the exercises in this study guide and working with the WinSim 2000 software, you can greatly improve your level of preparation for simulation questions.

Case Study–Based Questions

Case study–based questions first appeared in the Microsoft Certified Solution Developer program (Microsoft's certification program for software programmers). Case study–based questions present a scenario with a range of requirements. Based on the information provided, you need to answer a series of multiple-choice and ranking questions. The interface for case study–based questions has a number of tabs, each of which contains information about the scenario. At present, this type of question appears only in the Design exams.

Adaptive Exam Format

Microsoft presents many of its exams in an *adaptive* format. This format is radically different from the conventional format previously used for Microsoft certification exams. Conventional tests are static, containing a fixed number of questions. Adaptive tests change, or "adapt," depending on your answers to the questions presented.

The number of questions presented in your adaptive test will depend on how long it takes the exam to ascertain your level of ability (according to the statistical measurements on which the exam questions are ranked). To determine a test-taker's level of ability, the exam presents questions in increasing or decreasing order of difficulty.

Unlike the previous test format, the adaptive format will *not* allow you to go back to see a question again. The exam only goes forward. Once you enter your answer, that's it—you cannot change it. Be very careful before entering your answer. There is no time limit for each individual question (only for the exam as a whole.) Your exam may be shortened by correct answers (and lengthened by incorrect answers), so there is no advantage to rushing through questions.

How Adaptive Exams Determine Ability Levels

As an example of how adaptive testing works, suppose that you know three people who are taking the exam: Herman, Sally, and Rashad. Herman doesn't know much about the subject, Sally is moderately informed, and Rashad is an expert.

Herman answers his first question incorrectly, so the exam presents him with a second, easier question. He misses that, so the exam gives him a few more easy questions, all of which he misses. Shortly thereafter, the exam ends, and he receives his failure report.

Sally answers her first question correctly, so the exam gives her a more difficult question, which she answers correctly. She then receives an even more difficult question, which she answers incorrectly. Next, the exam gives her a somewhat easier question, as it tries to gauge her level of understanding. After numerous questions of varying levels of difficulty, Sally's exam ends, perhaps with a passing score, perhaps not. Her exam included far more questions than were in Herman's exam, because her level of understanding needed to be more carefully tested to determine whether or not it was at a passing level.

When Rashad takes his exam, he answers his first question correctly, so he is given a more difficult question, which he also answers correctly. Next, the exam presents an even more difficult question, which he also answers correctly. He then is given a few more very difficult questions, all of which he answers correctly. Shortly thereafter, his exam ends. He passes. His exam was short, about as long as Herman's test.

Benefits of Adaptive Testing

Microsoft has begun moving to adaptive testing for several reasons:

- It saves time by focusing only on the questions needed to determine a test-taker's abilities. An exam that might take an hour and a half in the conventional format could be completed in less than half that time when presented in adaptive format. The number of questions in an adaptive exam may be far fewer than the number required by a conventional exam.

- It protects the integrity of the exams. By exposing a fewer number of questions at any one time, it makes it more difficult for individuals to collect the questions in the exam pools with the intent of facilitating exam "cramming."

- It saves Microsoft and/or the test-delivery company money by reducing the amount of time it takes to deliver a test.

We recommend that you try the Edge Test Adaptive Exam, which is included on the CD that accompanies this study guide.

Exam Question Development

Microsoft follows an exam-development process consisting of eight mandatory phases. The process takes an average of seven months and involves more than 150 specific steps. The MCP exam development consists of the following phases:

Phase 1: Job Analysis Phase 1 is an analysis of all of the tasks that make up a specific job function, based on tasks performed by people who are currently performing that job function. This phase also identifies the knowledge, skills, and abilities that relate specifically to the performance area to be certified.

Phase 2: Objective Domain Definition The results of the job analysis provide the framework used to develop objectives. The development of objectives involves translating the job-function tasks into a comprehensive set of more specific and measurable knowledge, skills, and abilities. The resulting list of objectives—the *objective domain*—is the basis for the development of both the certification exams and the training materials.

Phase 3: Blueprint Survey The final objective domain is transformed into a blueprint survey in which contributors are asked to rate each objective. These contributors may be past MCP candidates, appropriately skilled exam development volunteers, or Microsoft employees. Based on the contributors' input, the objectives are prioritized and weighted. The actual exam items are written according to the prioritized objectives. Contributors are queried about how they spend their time on the job. If a contributor doesn't spend an adequate amount of time actually performing the specified job function, his or her data is eliminated from the analysis. The blueprint survey phase helps determine which objectives to measure, as well as the appropriate number and types of items to include on the exam.

Phase 4: Item Development A pool of items is developed to measure the blueprinted objective domain. The number and types of items to be written are based on the results of the blueprint survey.

Phase 5: Alpha Review and Item Revision   During this phase, a panel of technical and job-function experts reviews each item for technical accuracy, then answers each item, reaching a consensus on all technical issues. Once the items have been verified as technically accurate, they are edited to ensure that they are expressed in the clearest language possible.

Phase 6: Beta Exam   The reviewed and edited items are collected into beta exams. Based on the responses of all beta participants, Microsoft performs a statistical analysis to verify the validity of the exam items and to determine which items will be used in the certification exam. Once the analysis has been completed, the items are distributed into multiple parallel forms, or *versions*, of the final certification exam.

Phase 7: Item Selection and Cut-Score Setting   The results of the beta exams are analyzed to determine which items should be included in the certification exam based on many factors, including item difficulty and relevance. During this phase, a panel of job-function experts determines the *cut score* (minimum passing score) for the exams. The cut score differs from exam to exam because it is based on an item-by-item determination of the percentage of candidates who answered the item correctly and who would be expected to answer the item correctly.

Phase 8: Live Exam   As the final phase, the exams are given to candidates. MCP exams are administered by Sylvan Prometric and Virtual University Enterprises (VUE).

 Microsoft will regularly add and remove questions from the exams. This is called item *seeding*. It is part of the effort to make it more difficult for individuals to merely memorize exam questions passed along by previous test-takers.

Tips for Taking the Windows 2000 Professional Exam

Here are some general tips for taking the exam successfully:

- Arrive early at the exam center so you can relax and review your study materials. During your final review, you can look over tables and lists of exam-related information.

- Read the questions carefully. Don't be tempted to jump to an early conclusion. Make sure you know *exactly* what the question is asking.

- Answer all questions. Remember that the adaptive format will *not* allow you to return to a question. Be very careful before entering your answer. Because your exam may be shortened by correct answers (and lengthened by incorrect answers), there is no advantage to rushing through questions.

- On simulations, do not change settings that are not directly related to the question. Also, assume default settings if the question does not specify or imply which settings are used.

- Use a process of elimination to get rid of the obviously incorrect answers first on questions that you're not sure about. This method will improve your odds of selecting the correct answer if you need to make an educated guess.

Exam Registration

You may take the exams at any of more than 1,000 Authorized Prometric Testing Centers (APTCs) and VUE Testing Centers around the world. For the location of a testing center near you, call Sylvan Prometric at 800-755-EXAM (755-3926), or call VUE at 888-837-8616. Outside the United States and Canada, contact your local Sylvan Prometric or VUE registration center.

You should determine the number of the exam you want to take, and then register with the Sylvan Prometric or VUE registration center nearest to you. At this point, you will be asked for advance payment for the exam. The exams are $100 each. Exams must be taken within one year of payment. You can schedule exams up to six weeks in advance or as late as one working day prior to the date of the exam. You can cancel or reschedule your exam if you contact the center at least two working days prior to the exam. Same-day registration is available in some locations, subject to space availability. Where same-day registration is available, you must register a minimum of two hours before test time.

You may also register for your exams online at www.sylvanprometric.com or www.vue.com.

When you schedule the exam, you will be provided with instructions regarding appointment and cancellation procedures, ID requirements, and information about the testing center location. In addition, you will receive a registration and payment confirmation letter from Sylvan Prometric or VUE.

Microsoft requires certification candidates to accept the terms of a Non-Disclosure Agreement before taking certification exams.

What's on the CD?

With this new book in our best-selling MCSE study guide series, we are including quite an array of training resources. On the CD are numerous simulations, practice exams, and flashcards to help you study for the exam. Also included are the entire contents of the study guide. These resources are described in the following sections.

The Sybex Ebook for Windows 2000 Professional

Many people like the convenience of being able to carry their whole study guide on a CD. They also like being able to search the text to find specific information quickly and easily. For these reasons, we have included the entire contents of this study guide on a CD, in PDF format. We've also included Adobe Acrobat Reader, which provides the interface for the contents, as well as the search capabilities.

Sybex WinSim 2000

We developed WinSim 2000 to allow you to experience the multimedia and interactive operation of Windows 2000 Professional. The WinSim 2000 product provides both audio/video files and hands-on experience with key features of the Windows 2000 Professional operating system. Built around the exercises in this study guide, WinSim 2000 can give you the knowledge and hands-on skills that are invaluable for understanding Windows 2000 (and passing the exam). A sample screen from WinSim 2000 is shown below.

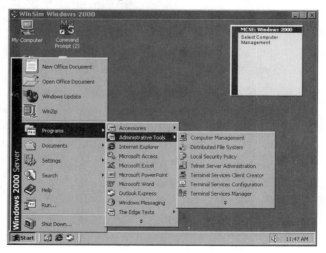

The Sybex MCSE Edge Tests

The Edge Tests are a collection of multiple-choice questions that can help you prepare for your exam. There are three sets of questions:

- Bonus questions specially prepared for this edition of the study guide, including 50 questions that appear only on the CD

- An adaptive test simulator that will give the feel for how adaptive testing works

- All of the questions from the study guide presented in a test engine for your review

A sample screen from the Sybex MCSE Edge Tests is shown below.

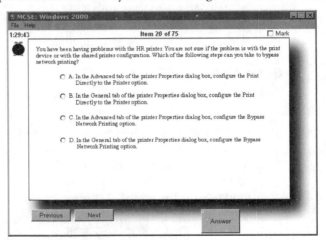

Sybex MCSE Flashcards for PCs and Palm Devices

The "flashcard" style of exam question offers an effective way to quickly and efficiently test your understanding of the fundamental concepts covered in the Windows 2000 Professional exam. The Sybex MCSE Flashcards set consists of more than 150 questions presented in a special engine developed specifically for this study guide series. The Sybex MCSE Flashcards interface is shown below.

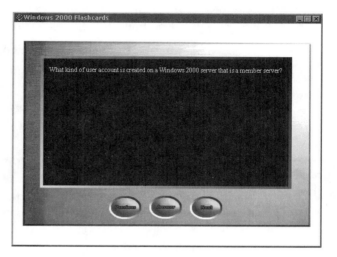

Because of the high demand for a product that will run on Palm devices, we have also developed, in conjunction with Land-J Technologies, a version of the flashcard questions that you can take with you on your Palm OS PDA (including the PalmPilot and Handspring's Visor).

How Do You Use This Book?

This book can provide a solid foundation for the serious effort of preparing for the Windows 2000 Professional exam. To best benefit from this book, you may wish to use the following study method:

1. Study each chapter carefully. Do your best to fully understand the information.

2. Complete all hands-on exercises in the chapter, referring back to the text as necessary so that you understand each step you take. If you do not have access to a lab environment in which you can complete the exercises, install and work with the exercises available in the Win-Sim 2000 software included with this study guide.

3. Answer the review questions at the end of each chapter. If you would prefer to answer the questions in a timed and graded format, install the Edge Tests from the CD that accompanies this book and answer the chapter questions there instead of in the book.

4. Note which questions you did not understand and study the corresponding sections of the book again.

5. Make sure you complete the entire book.

6. Before taking the exam, go through the training resources included on the CD that accompanies this book. Try the adaptive version that is included with the Sybex MCSE Edge Test. Review and sharpen your knowledge with the MCSE Flashcards.

NOTE In order to complete the exercises in this book, your hardware should meet the minimum hardware requirements for Windows 2000. See Chapter 1 for the minimum and recommended system requirements.

To learn all of the material covered in this book, you will need to study regularly and with discipline. Try to set aside the same time every day to study and select a comfortable and quiet place in which to do it. If you work hard, you will be surprised at how quickly you learn this material. Good luck!

Contacts and Resources

To find out more about Microsoft Education and Certification materials and programs, to register with Sylvan Prometric or VUE, or to get other useful information, check the following resources.

Microsoft Certification Development Team   www.microsoft.com/ Train_Cert/mcp/examinfo/certsd.htm

Contact the Microsoft Certification Development Team through their Web site to volunteer for one or more exam development phases or to report a problem with an exam. Address written correspondence to:

Certification Development Team
Microsoft Education and Certification
One Microsoft Way
Redmond, WA 98052

Microsoft TechNet Technical Information Network
www.microsoft.com/technet/subscription/about.htm

(800) 344-2121

Use this Web site or number to contact support professionals and system administrators. Outside the United States and Canada, contact your local Microsoft subsidiary for information.

Microsoft Training and Certification Home Page
www.microsoft.com/train_cert

This Web site provides information about the MCP program and exams. You can also order the latest Microsoft Roadmap to Education and Certification.

Palm Pilot Training Product Development: Land-J   www.land-j.com

(407) 359-2217

Land-J Technologies is a consulting and programming business currently specializing in application development for the 3Com PalmPilot Personal Digital Assistant. Land-J developed the Palm version of the Edge Tests, which is included on the CD that accompanies this study guide.

Sylvan Prometric   www.sylvanprometric.com

(800) 755-EXAM

Contact Sylvan Prometric to register to take an MCP exam at any of more than 800 Sylvan Prometric Testing Centers around the world.

Virtual University Enterprises (VUE)   www.vue.com

(888) 837-8616

Contact the VUE registration center to register to take an MCP exam at one of the VUE Testing Centers.

Assessment Test

1. By default, what extension is applied to custom consoles that are created for the MMC?

    A. .mmc

    B. .msc

    C. .con

    D. .mcn

2. Which users are able to manage mandatory profiles on Windows 2000 Professional computers?

    A. The user who uses the profile

    B. Server Operators

    C. Power Users

    D. Administrators

3. Which MMC snap-in would you load to access System Monitor?

    A. System Monitor

    B. Performance Monitor

    C. ActiveX Control

    D. Performance Logs and Alerts

4. Which group would you assign permissions to if you wanted only users with valid usernames and passwords to have access to a specific resource?

    A. Domain Users

    B. Users

    C. Everyone

    D. Authenticated Users

5. Which of the following options *cannot* be configured as a part of an answer file?

    A. Display settings

    B. Network settings

    C. Time zone

    D. Screen saver

6. Which of the following print permissions are applied to the Power Users group by default on shared Windows 2000 Professional printers? Choose all that apply.

    A. No permissions are granted

    B. Print

    C. Manage Printers

    D. Manage Documents

7. Which accessibility utility is used to read aloud screen text, such as the text in dialog boxes, menus, and buttons?

A. Read-Aloud

B. Orator

C. Dialog Manager

D. Narrator

8. Which option within the Windows 2000 Professional upgrade process summarizes likely problems with the upgrade?

A. The Troubleshooting Guide

B. The Compatibility Issues Report

C. The Upgrade Report

D. The Professional Upgrade Status Report

9. Which utility is used to track performance in Windows 2000?

A. Performance Monitor

B. System Monitor

C. Event Viewer

D. Process Manager

10. What utility is used to set processor affinity if you have multiple processors installed on your Windows 2000 Professional computer?

A. Control Panel, Processors

B. System Monitor

C. System Manager

D. Task Manager

11. What icon do you use in Control Panel in Windows 2000 Professional to set locale settings?

A. Regional Options

B. Locale Settings

C. Geographical Settings

D. Multinational Support

12. Susan is a member of the Sales and Managers groups. The Managers group has been allowed the Full Control permission to the D:\DATA folder. The Sales group has been allowed the Read & Execute permission, but has been denied the Full Control permission to the D:\DATA. What are Susan's effective rights?

A. Full Control

B. Read & Execute

C. Read

D. No permissions

13. Which utility can you use to install a non-Plug-and-Play network adapter in Windows 2000 Professional?

    A. Control Panel, Network icon

    B. Control Panel, Network and Dial-up Connections icon

    C. Control Panel, Network Adapters icon

    D. Control Panel, Add/Remove Hardware icon

14. You want Linda to be able to create users and groups on your Windows 2000 Professional computer. Linda says when she logs on she is not able to create new users. When you check Linda's group membership, which group memberships would allow her the necessary permissions to create new users? Choose two answers.

    A. Admins

    B. Administrators

    C. Power Users

    D. Server Operators

15. Which option allows you to configure Windows 2000 Professional computers to use a hardware profile?

    A. Hardware Profile Editor

    B. Control Panel, System

    C. Computer Management utility

    D. MMC Computer Manager utility

16. Which separator page file would you use if you wanted to use a separator page on a Windows 2000 Professional computer and were using a PostScript print device that did not support dual-mode printing?

    A. pcl.sep

    B. pscript.sep

    C. sysprint.sep

    D. sysprintj.sep

17. Which option would you use if you wanted to access network files from your laptop while traveling and then have the file resynchronize with the network when you reattached to the network?

    A. Synchronized folders

    B. Managed folders

    C. Roaming folders

    D. Offline files and folders

18. Which command can you use to verify the IP configuration that your computer is using?

    A. IPCONFIG

    B. TESTIP

    C. PING

    D. GROPE

19. What information must be configured on a VPN client so that it can access a VPN server? Choose two answers.

    A. IP address

    B. MAC address

    C. Domain name

    D. Connection address

20. Which of the following statements is true regarding the creation of a group?

    A. Only members of the Administrators group can create users on a Windows 2000 Professional computer.

    B. Group names can be up to 64 characters.

    C. Group names can contain spaces.

    D. Group names can be that same as usernames, but not other group names on the computer.

21. Which of the following statements are true concerning spanned volumes? Choose all that apply.

    A. Spanned volumes can contain space from 2 to 32 physical drives.

    B. Spanned volumes can contain space from 2 to 24 physical drives.

    C. Spanned volumes can be formatted as FAT16, FAT32, or NTFS partitions.

    D. Spanned volumes can only be formatted as NTFS partitions.

22. Which of the following user rights is required to install computers through RIS? Choose two answers.

    A. Join a Computer to the Domain

    B. Remotely Install Windows 2000

    C. Log On as a Batch Job

    D. Authorize the RIS Server

23. What process would you use if you wanted to dual-boot you computer to Windows 2000 Professional and Window 98 and want to use the features of NTFS?

    A. You should install Windows 98 first and Windows 2000 Professional last. You should create two partitions. Install Windows 98 on the first partition and format the partition as FAT32. Put Windows 2000 on the second partition and format the partition as NTFS.

    B. You should install Windows 2000 Professional first and Windows 98 last. You should create two partitions. Install Windows 98 on the first partition and format the partition as FAT32. Put Windows 2000 on the second partition and format the partition as NTFS.

    C. You should install Windows 2000 Professional first and Windows 98 last. You should create two partitions. Install Windows 2000 on the first partition and format the partition as NTFS. Put Windows 98 on the second partition and format the partition as FAT.

    D. You cannot dual-boot between Windows 98 and Windows 2000 Professional.

24. How do you start the Windows 2000 Recovery Console if you cannot start your Windows 2000 Professional operating system?

    A. With the Windows 2000 Professional Setup Disks

    B. Through `WINNT32 /RC`

    C. Press F8 during the boot sequence

    D. Boot with the Windows 2000 boot disk, then type `WINNT /CMDCONS`

25. Which of the following options would keep a Windows 2000 Professional upgrade from successfully installing? Choose all that apply.

    A. A drive that was compressed with DoubleSpace

    B. A drive that was compressed with DriveSpace

    C. A computer that had only 64MB of RAM

    D. A computer that had only a Pentium 133MHz processor

26. Which of the following two utilities are used to manage Peer Web Services?

    A. Personal Web Manager

    B. PWS Manager

    C. Internet Web Manager

    D. Internet Services Manager

27. How do you access advanced startup options in Windows 2000 during the boot process?

    A. Press the spacebar

    B. Press F6

    C. Press F8

    D. Press F10

28. You want to install Windows 2000 Professional on a computer that has no operating system installed, but the computer will not boot to the CD-ROM drive. Which of the following options is the best solution to your problem?

    A. Create Windows 2000 Professional Setup Boot Disks using the Windows 2000 Professional CD on another computer. Use these disks on your computer, so you can start the installation process.

    B. Create the Emergency Startup disks using the Windows 2000 Professional CD on another computer. Use these disks on your computer, so you can start the installation process.

    C. Upgrade you computer.

    D. Install Windows 98 on the computer, then upgrade it to Windows 2000 Professional.

29. Which utility is used to upgrade a FAT16 or FAT32 partition to NTFS?

    A. UPFS

    B. UPGRADE

    C. Disk Manager

    D. CONVERT

30. Which of the following audit policy options allows you to track events related to file and print object access?

    A. File and Object Access

    B. Audit Object Access

    C. Audit File and Print Access

    D. Audit All File and Print Events

Answers to Assessment Test

1. B. When you create a custom console for the MMC, the default extension that is applied is `.msc`. See Chapter 4 for more information.

2. D. The only users who can manage mandatory profiles are members of the Administrators group. See Chapter 8 for more information.

3. C. You would load the ActiveX Control, System Monitor Control to access the System Monitor utility. See Chapter 14 for more information.

4. D. You would assign permissions to the Authenticated Users group if you wanted only users with valid usernames and passwords to access a specific resource. See Chapter 7 for more information.

5. D. You can't configure user preference items, such as a screen saver, in an answer file. See Chapter 2 for more information.

6. B, C, D. By default, the Power Users group is allowed Print, Manage Printers, and Manage Documents permissions. See Chapter 12 for more information.

7. D. The Narrator utility uses a sound output device to read text that is on the screen. See Chapter 5 for more information.

8. C. Sometimes the answer is so obvious that it doesn't appear to be correct. This is the case here. The report that shows you any potential problems with the upgrade process is simply named Upgrade Report. See Chapter 3 for more information.

9. B. In Windows NT 4, you used Performance Monitor to track performance. In Windows 2000, you use System Monitor to track system performance. See Chapter 14 for more information.

10. D. You can set processor affinity for Windows 2000 processes through the Task Manager utility. Processor affinity is the ability to assign a processor to a dedicated process (program). This feature is only available when multiple processors are installed. See Chapter 4 for more information.

11. A. Out of the four options, only Regional Options appears in Control Panel. Through Regional Options, you can configure multilingual support and locale information. See Chapter 5 for more information.

12. B. Susan would not be allowed the Full Control permission, since this was explicitly denied through her membership in the Sales group. She would be allowed the Read & Execute permission. See Chapter 10 for more information.

13. D. In Windows 2000, you add hardware through the Add/Remove Hardware option in Control Panel. You can manage existing network adapters through Network and Dial-up Connections. See Chapter 11 for more information.

14. B, C. On Windows 2000 Professional computers, members of the Administrators and Power Users groups are able to create new users. See Chapter 6 for more information.

15. B. You configure hardware profiles through the System icon in Control Panel. You could also access this dialog box by right-clicking My Computer and selecting Properties. There is no Hardware Profile Editor or MMC Computer Manager utility. The Computer Management utility is used to manage system tools, storage, services, and applications. See Chapter 8 for more information.

16. C. You would use the `sysprint.sep` separator page if you had a PostScript print device that did not support dual-mode printing. If you wanted to use separator pages on a print device that supported dual-mode printing, you would use the `pcl.sep` separator page. See Chapter 12 for more information.

17. D. You would use offline files and folders to take data offline and then resynchronize data when you reattached to the network. See Chapter 10 for more information.

18. A. The `IPCONFIG` command is used to display a computer's IP configuration. See Chapter 11 for more information.

19. A, C. When you configure a VPN connection, you see the Destination Address dialog box. You must specify the IP address or host domain name of the computer that you will connect to. See Chapter 13 for more information.

20. C. Administrators and members of the Power Users local groups can create new groups. Group names can contain up to 256 characters. Group names can contain spaces. Group names must be unique to the computer, different from all the other usernames and group names that have been specified on that computer. See Chapter 7 for more information.

21. A, C. You create a spanned volume from free space that exists on 2 to 32 physical drives. When the spanned volume is initially created, it can be formatted with FAT16, FAT32, or NTFS. If you extend a volume that already contains data, the partition must be NTFS. See Chapter 9 for more information.

22. A, C . In order to install an image through RIS, the user who is installing the RIS client must have the Join a Computer to the Domain user right and the Logon as a Batch Job right. See Chapter 2 for more information.

23. A. You should install Windows 98 first and Windows 2000 Professional last. If you installed Windows 2000 and then installed Windows 98, your boot loader menu would not work properly. You should create two partitions. Install Windows 98 on the first partition and format the partition as FAT32. Put Windows 2000 on the second partition and format the partition as NTFS. When you boot to Windows 2000, you will be able to see both partitions. When you boot to Windows 98, you will only see the first partition. If you made the second partition FAT32, Windows 98 would not be able to access it, since only the first partition is marked active. See Chapter 1 for more information.

24. A. You start the Recovery Console through the Windows 2000 Professional Setup Disks or by installing the Recovery Console by using the `WINNT32/ CMDCONS` command prior to failure. See Chapter 15 for more information.

25. A, B. You can upgrade a computer that only has 64MB of RAM or a Pentium 133MHz processor, but you can't upgrade drives that have DoubleSpace or DriveSpace installed. See Chapter 3 for more information.

26. A, D. After you install PWS, the Personal Web Manager and Internet Services Manager utilities are installed under Administrative Tools. See Chapter 13 for more information.

27. C. During the boot process, you are prompted to press F8 to access the Advanced Options menu. See Chapter 15 for more information.

28. Answer: A. The Windows 2000 Professional Setup Boot Disks can be used to start a Windows 2000 Professional installation on a computer that does not support booting to a CD-ROM drive. You could also upgrade your computer, but that is not the best solution. See Chapter 1 for more information.

29. D. The `CONVERT` utility is used to convert a FAT16 or FAT32 partition to NTFS. See Chapter 9 for more information.

30. B. While all options sound plausible, only Audit Object Access is an actual option. Audit Object Access is used to enable auditing of access to files, folders, and printers. Once you enable auditing of object access, you must enable file auditing through NTFS security, or enable print auditing through printer security. See Chapter 6 for more information.

Chapter 1

Getting Started with Windows 2000 Professional

MICROSOFT EXAM OBJECTIVES COVERED IN THIS CHAPTER

✓ Perform an attended installation of Windows 2000 Professional.

✓ Troubleshoot failed installations.

Windows 2000 Professional is not just an upgraded version of Windows 98 or Windows NT 4. Instead, it integrates the best features of both of those operating systems, and adds other features, such as more hardware support and reduced cost of ownership. You should evaluate the features that Windows 2000 Professional offers to determine if it meets your requirements.

After you decide that Windows 2000 Professional is the operating system for you, your next step is to install it. This process is fairly easy if you have prepared for the installation, know what the requirements are, and have met the prerequisites for a successful installation.

Preparing for an installation involves making sure that your hardware meets the minimum requirements and that Windows 2000 Professional supports your hardware. When you install Windows 2000 Professional, you should also decide if you are upgrading or installing a clean copy on your computer. An upgrade preserves existing settings; a clean install puts a fresh copy of the operating system on your computer. Installation preparation also involves making choices about your system's configuration, such as selecting a file system and a disk-partitioning scheme.

Once you've completed all the planning, you are ready to install Windows 2000 Professional. This is a straightforward process that involves running a Setup program, running a Setup Wizard, and installing Windows 2000 Networking.

If you have any problems with the installation, you will need to troubleshoot them. Some problems that you might encounter are media defects or hardware that doesn't meet the minimum requirements.

When you install Windows 2000, you should also consider if the computer will be used for dual-boot or multi-boot purposes. Dual-booting or multi-booting allows you to have your computer boot with operating systems other than Windows 2000 Professional.

The first section of this chapter covers the design goals of Windows 2000 Professional. Then you will learn how to prepare for Windows 2000 Professional installation, perform the installation, troubleshoot any installation problems, and set up for dual-booting or multi-booting.

The Design Goals of Windows 2000 Professional

In order to develop Windows 2000 Professional, Microsoft devised the following design goals:

- Integrate the best features of Windows 98

- Integrate the best features of Windows NT Workstation 4

- Provide a wide range of support for hardware

- Make the operating system easier to use

- Reduce the cost of ownership

The Windows 2000 Professional features associated with these design goals are covered in the following sections.

Features from Windows 98

Windows 98 offers a variety of features that were not integrated into Windows NT Workstation 4. The following Windows 98 features are included in Windows 2000 Professional:

- *Plug-and-Play* support, which allows the operating system to recognize and configure hardware without any user intervention.

- Added support for *the Advanced Configuration and Power Interface (ACPI)*, considered to be the next generation of power management for Plug-and-Play technology. Features of ACPI include:

  - The automatic and dynamic detection of hardware that is installed

- The ability to determine what hardware resources (such as IRQs and I/O ports) are required by the new device, and whether other devices need to be automatically reconfigured to accommodate the new device

- The ability to load the appropriate driver automatically (if the driver is available)

- Added support for the *Universal Serial Bus (USB)*, which is an external serial bus standard that allows a single USB port to support up to 127 devices. Common USB devices include mice, modems, and keyboards. USB supports hot-plug (which allows you to add devices to the computer without powering down the computer) and Plug-and-Play technology.

- New support for the *Institute of Electrical and Electronic Engineers (IEEE) 1394 standard*, which supports data transfer at speeds up to 400Mbps. Different trademark names for this standard are FireWire, I-link, and Lynx.

- The use of the Active Desktop, which integrates the user's browser and shell into a single integrated Desktop.

Features from Windows NT Workstation 4

Windows NT Workstation 4 is the foundation upon which Windows 2000 Professional is built. The features that made Windows NT Workstation 4 a powerful operating system are included in Windows 2000 Professional:

- An operating system with a high degree of reliability. Windows 2000 Professional is more robust and less likely to crash than Windows $9x$ operating systems.

- Local security that is built into the operating system. Windows 2000 Professional requires that users be authenticated with a valid logon name and password before they can access the computer. Support is also included for the NTFS file system, which allows you to set local security for the file system.

- A high-performance operating system, with true 32-bit processing.

Hardware Support

The ability to support a wide range of hardware was a major design goal for Windows 2000 Professional. The operating system provides drivers for many types of peripherals, such as monitors, sound cards, digital cameras, printers, scanners, DVD drives, CDRW (CD Read/Write) drives, and network cards.

Ease of Use

When you use Windows 2000 Professional for the first time, you will notice that the user interface is not exactly the same as the Windows 9x or NT 4 interface. The operating system was designed so that users who needed to perform a specific task can intuitively figure out how to accomplish that task. The following are some of the features that make Windows 2000 Professional easier to use:

- The installation process is simpler than the process for Windows NT installations and requires less user input.

- The user shell (interface) is more logically organized and offers more customization options.

- Users can easily add hardware. Windows 2000 Professional supports self-repairing applications, Plug-and-Play, and ACPI. These features reduce the possibility of system downtime when new hardware is installed.

Lower Cost of Ownership

Windows 2000 Professional reduces the cost of ownership by minimizing the maintenance and rollout costs associated with installing, upgrading, and maintaining the operating system. Windows 2000 Professional comes with many deployment options, such as support for remote installations and automated unattended installations. Through Remote Installation Services (RIS), you can easily install the Windows 2000 operating system and applications.

RIS and automated installations are covered in Chapter 2, "Automating the Windows 2000 Installation."

New Features of Windows 2000

There are a host of new features created for Windows 2000 Professional to set it aside from all of its competitors. The following are some of the new features:

- Disk quota support

- Inherited and uninherited permissions

- Internet printing support

- The ability to configure printer drivers for additional operating systems that will connect to your print server

- The Encrypting File System (EFS), which uses public and private encryption, allowing a user to transparently encrypt files

- A highly integrated Wizard technology to make configuration tasks easier

- Enhanced virtual private networking support (previous versions have VPN support, Win2k Pro adds IPSec and L2TP support)

Preparing to Install Windows 2000 Professional

As mentioned in the previous section, Windows 2000 Professional is easy to install. But this doesn't mean that you don't need to prepare for the installation process. Before you begin the installation, you should know what is required for a successful installation and have all of the pieces of information you'll need to supply during the installation process. In preparing for the installation, you should make sure you have the following information:

- What the hardware requirements are for Windows 2000 Professional

- How to use the Hardware Compatibility List to determine if your hardware is supported by Windows 2000 Professional

- The difference between a clean install and an upgrade

- What installation options are suitable for your system, such as which disk-partitioning scheme and file system you should select for Windows 2000 Professional to use

The following sections describe the hardware requirements and installation considerations.

Hardware Requirements

In order to install Windows 2000 Professional successfully, your system must meet certain hardware requirements. Table 1.1 lists the minimum requirements as well as the more realistic recommended requirements.

The minimum requirements specify the minimum hardware required before you should even consider installing Windows 2000 Professional. These requirements assume that you are installing only the operating system and not running any special services or applications. For example, you may be able to get by with the minimum requirements if you are just installing the operating system to learn the basics of the software.

The recommended requirements are what Microsoft suggests to achieve what would be considered "acceptable performance" for the most common configurations. Since computer technology and the standard for acceptable performance are constantly changing, the recommendations are somewhat subjective. However, the recommended hardware requirements are based on the standards at the time that Windows 2000 Professional was released.

The hardware requirements listed in Table 1.1 were those specified at the time this book was published. Check Microsoft's Web site at http://www.microsoft.com/windows2000/guide/professional/sysreq/default.asp for the most current information.

TABLE 1.1 Hardware Requirements

Component	Minimum Requirement	Recommended Requirement
Processor	Intel Pentium 133MHz or higher	Intel Pentium 133MHz or higher
Memory	64MB	64MB

TABLE 1.1 Hardware Requirements *(continued)*

Component	Minimum Requirement	Recommended Requirement
Disk space	2GB hard disk with 650MB of free disk space	1GB or more of free disk space
Network	None	Network card and any other hardware required by your network topology (if you want to connect to a network)
Display	Video adapter and monitor with VGA resolution	Video adapter and monitor with VGA resolution or higher

These requirements represent the operating system requirements. If you are running any processor-intensive or memory-intensive tasks or applications, factor these requirements separately. When determining disk-space requirements for add-on software and data, a good rule of thumb is to plan what you need for the next 12 months, then double that number.

Depending on the installation method you choose, other devices may be required, as follows:

- If you are installing Windows 2000 Professional from the CD, you should have at least a 12x CD-ROM drive.

- To start the installation locally and to create an Emergency Repair Disk, you need a high-density floppy drive.

- If you choose to install Windows 2000 Professional from the network, you need a network connection and a server with the distribution files.

Windows 2000 Professional supports computers with one or two processors.

Measurement Units Used in Hardware Specifications

Computer processors are typically rated by speed. The speed of the processor, or *central processing unit* (*CPU*), is rated by the number of clock cycles that can be performed in one second. This measurement is typically expressed in *megahertz* (*MHz*). One MHz is one million cycles per second.

Hard disks are commonly rated by capacity. The following measurements are used for disk space and memory capacity:

1*MB* (*megabyte*) = 1024KB (kilobytes)

1*GB* (*gigabyte*) = 1024MB

1*TB* (*terabyte*) = 1024GB

1*PB* (*petabyte*) = 1024TB

1*EB* (*exabyte*) = 1024PB

The Hardware Compatibility List (HCL)

Along with meeting the minimum requirements, your hardware should appear on the Hardware Compatibility List (HCL). The HCL is an extensive list of computers and peripheral hardware that have been tested with the Windows 2000 Professional operating system.

The Windows 2000 Professional operating system requires control of the hardware for stability, efficiency, and security. The hardware and supported drivers on the HCL have been put through rigorous tests to ensure their compatibility with Windows 2000 Professional. Microsoft guarantees that the items on the list meet the requirements for Windows 2000 and do not have any incompatibilities that could affect the stability of the operating system.

If you call Microsoft for support, the first thing a Microsoft support engineer will ask about is your configuration. If you have any hardware that is not on the HCL, you won't be able to get support from Microsoft.

To determine if your computer and peripherals are on the HCL, check the most up-to-date list at www.microsoft.com/hwtest/hcl.

As I learned from my own mistake, you shouldn't just assume that a hardware item is on the HCL. I recently purchased a computer manufactured by a well-known, brand-name company. Because it was a higher-end Pentium with all the bells and whistles and came with Windows 98 preinstalled, I assumed that it would support Windows NT and Windows 2000. The salesperson said it would. When I got home and opened the box, I couldn't find any documentation about loading Windows NT or Windows 2000. A check of the vendor's Web site and a call to their technical support hotline verified that the computer did not support either operating system. I had to return the computer and argue with the store manager to get my money back.

Clean Install or Upgrade?

Once you've determined that your hardware not only meets the minimum requirements but also is on the HCL, you need to decide whether you want to do a *clean install* or *upgrade*.

The only operating systems that can be upgraded to Windows 2000 Professional are Windows 95, Windows 98, and Windows NT 3.51 or 4. Any other operating system cannot be upgraded, but it may be able to coexist with Windows 2000 in a dual-boot environment. Dual-booting is covered in the "Supporting Multiple-Boot Options" section later in this chapter.

If you don't have an operating system that can be upgraded, or if you want to keep your previous operating system intact, you need to perform a clean install. A clean *install* puts Windows 2000 Professional operating system into a new folder and uses its default settings the first time the operating system is loaded. The process for a clean installation is described in the "Running the Windows 2000 Professional Installation Process" section later in this chapter.

Installation Options

There are many choices that you will need to make during the Windows 2000 Professional installation process. The following are some of the options that you will configure:

- How your hard disk space will be partitioned
- The file system your partitions will use

- Whether the computer will be a part of a workgroup or a domain
- The language and locale for the computer's settings

Before you start the installation, you should know which choices you will select. The following sections describe the options and considerations for picking the best ones for your installation.

Partitioning of Disk Space

Disk partitioning is the act of taking the physical hard drive and creating logical partitions. A *logical drive* is how space is allocated to the drive's primary and logical partitions. For example, if you have a 5GB hard drive, you might partition it into two logical drives: a C: drive, which might be 2GB, and a D: drive, which might be 3GB.

The following are some of the major considerations for disk partitioning:

- The amount of space required
- The location of the system and boot partition
- Any special disk configurations you will use
- The utility you will use to set up the partitions

These considerations are covered in detail in the following sections.

Size Matters

One important consideration in your disk-partitioning scheme is determining the partition size. You need to consider the amount of space taken up by your operating system, the applications that will be installed, and the amount of stored data. It is also important to consider the amount of space required in the future.

Just for Windows 2000, Microsoft recommends that you allocate at least 1GB of disk space. This amount of space allows room for the operating system files and for future growth in terms of upgrades and installation files that are placed with the operating system files.

The System and Boot Partition

When you install Windows 2000, files will be stored in two locations: the system partition and the boot partition.

The *system partition* contains the files needed to boot the Windows 2000 Professional operating system. The files stored on the system partition do not take any significant disk space. By default, the system partition uses the computer's active partition, which is usually the C: drive.

The *boot partition* contains the files that are the Windows operating system. By default, the Windows operating system files are located in a folder named WINNT. You can, however, specify the location of this folder during the installation process. Microsoft recommends that the boot partition be at least 1GB.

Special Disk Configurations

Windows 2000 Professional supports several disk configurations. Options include simple, spanned, and striped volumes. These configuration options are covered in detail in Chapter 9, "Managing Disks."

Windows 2000 Server also includes options for mirrored and RAID 5 volumes.

Disk Partition Configuration Utilities

If you are partitioning your disk prior to installation, you can use several utilities, such as the DOS or Windows FDISK program or a third-party utility such as PowerQuest's Partition Magic. You might want to create only the first partition where Windows 2000 Professional will be installed. You can then use the Disk Management utility in Windows 2000 to create any other partitions you need. The Windows 2000 Disk Management utility is covered in Chapter 9.

You can get more information about FDISK and other disk utilities from your DOS or Windows documentation. Also, basic DOS functions are covered in *MCSE 2000 JumpStart: Computer and Network Basics* by Lisa Donald (Sybex, 2000).

File System Selection

Another factor that determines your disk-partitioning scheme is the type of file system you use. Windows 2000 supports three file systems:

- *File Allocation Table (FAT16)*
- *FAT32*
- *New Technology File System (NTFS)*

The following sections briefly describe these three file systems. See Chapter 9 for more details about the features of FAT, FAT32, and NTFS.

FAT16

FAT16 (originally just FAT) is the 16-bit file system widely used by DOS and Windows 3.*x*. FAT16 tracks where files are stored on a disk using a file-allocation table and a directory-entry table. The disadvantages of FAT16 are that it only supports partitions up to 2GB and it does not offer the security features of NTFS. The advantage of FAT is that it is backward compatible, which is important if the computer will be dual-booted with another operating system, such as DOS, Unix, Linux, OS/2, or Windows 3.1. Almost all PC operating systems read FAT16 partitions.

FAT32

FAT32 is the 32-bit version of FAT, which was first introduced in 1996 with Windows 95, with OEM (original equipment manufacturer) Service Release 2 (OSR2). With FAT32, disk partitions can be as large as 2TB (terabytes). It has more fault-tolerance features than FAT16, and also improves disk-space usage by reducing the size of clusters. However, it lacks several of the features offered by NTFS for a Windows 2000 system, such as local security, file encryption, disk quotas, and compression.

If you choose to use FAT, Windows 2000 will automatically format the partition with FAT16 if the partition is less than 2GB. If the partition is over 2GB, it will be automatically partitioned as FAT32.

 Windows NT 4 and earlier releases of NT do not support FAT32.

NTFS

NTFS is a file system designed to provide additional features for Windows NT and Windows 2000 computers. Some of the features NTFS offers include the following:

- The ability to set local security on files and folders.

- The option to compress data. This feature reduces disk-storage requirements.

- The flexibility to assign disk quotas. Disk quotas are used to limit the amount of disk space a user can use.

- The option to encrypt files. Encryption offers an additional level of security.

Unless you are planning on dual-booting your computer to an operating system other than Windows NT, Microsoft recommends using NTFS.

Membership in a Domain or Workgroup

One Windows 2000 Professional installation choice is whether your computer will be installed as a part of a *workgroup* or as part of a *domain*.

You should install as part of a workgroup if you are a part of a small, decentralized network or if you are running Windows 2000 on a computer that is not part of a network. To join a workgroup, you simply choose that workgroup.

Domains are part of larger, centrally administered networks. You should install as part of a domain if any Windows 2000 servers on your network are configured as domain controllers with the Microsoft Active Directory installed. To join a domain, you must specify the name of a valid domain and provide the username and password of a user who has rights to add a computer to the domain. A domain controller for the domain and a DNS server must be available to authenticate the request to join the domain.

Language and Locale

Language and locale settings are used to determine the language the computer will use. Windows 2000 supports many languages for the operating system interface and utilities.

Locale settings are used to configure the locality for items such as numbers, currencies, times, and dates. An example of a locality is that English for United States specifies a short date as *mm/dd/yyyy* (month/day/year), and English for South Africa specifies a short date as *yyyy/mm/dd* (year/month/day).

Choosing Your Installation Method

You can install Windows 2000 Professional by using the distribution files on the Windows 2000 Professional CD or by using files that have been copied to a network share point. The following sections discuss each installation method.

Installing Windows 2000 from the CD

When you install Windows 2000 from the Windows 2000 Professional CD, you have several options for starting the installation:

- You can boot to another operating system, access your CD-ROM drive, and run `WINNT.EXE` or `WINNT32.EXE` (depending on the operating system you are using, as explained in the next section).

- If your computer is able to boot to the CD, you can insert the Windows 2000 Professional CD into its CD-ROM drive and restart your computer.

- If your computer has no operating system installed and does not support booting from the CD-ROM drive, you can use the Windows 2000 Professional Setup Boot Disks.

Installing from Another Operating System

If your computer already has an operating system installed and you want to upgrade your operating system or dual-boot your computer, you boot your computer to the operating system that is currently installed, then start the Windows 2000 Professional installation process. Depending on the operating system that is running, you start the installation by using one of the following commands from the I386 folder:

- From Windows 9*x* or Windows NT, use `WINNT32.EXE`.

- From any other operating system, use `WINNT.EXE`.

Installing by Booting from the Windows 2000 CD

If your computer can boot from the CD-ROM drive, then all you need to do is insert the Windows 2000 Professional CD and restart your computer. When the computer boots, the Windows 2000 Professional installation process will start automatically.

Installing from Setup Boot Disks

If your computer cannot boot from the CD-ROM drive, you can create floppy disks that can boot to the Windows 2000 Professional operating system. These disks are called the *Windows 2000 Professional Setup Boot Disks*. From these floppy disks, you can install or reinstall the Windows 2000 operating system. The Windows 2000 Professional Setup Boot Disks are not specific to a computer; they can be used by any computer running Windows 2000 Professional.

To create the Windows 2000 Professional Setup Boot Disks, you need four high-density floppy disks. They should be labeled Windows 2000 Professional Setup Boot Disk, Windows 2000 Professional Setup Disk #2, Windows 2000 Professional Setup Disk #3, and Windows 2000 Professional Setup Disk #4.

The command to create boot disks from Windows 2000, Windows NT, or Windows 9*x* is MAKEBT32.EXE. The command to make boot disks from a 16-bit operating system is MAKEBOOT.EXE. These utilities are located on the Windows 2000 Professional CD in the BOOTDISK folder.

The Windows 2000 Professional Setup Boot Disks are also used for the Recovery Console and the Emergency Repair Disk (disaster- recovery methods), which are covered in Chapter 15, "Performing System Recovery Functions." You will create Windows 2000 Professional Setup Boot Disks in an exercise in Chapter 15.

Installing Windows 2000 over a Network

If you are installing Windows 2000 Professional from the network, you need a *distribution server* and a computer with a network connection. A distribution server is a server that has the Windows 2000 Professional distribution files copied to a shared folder. The following steps are used to install Windows 2000 Professional over the network:

1. Boot the target computer.

2. Attach to the distribution server and access the share that has the \WINNT folder shared.

3. Launch WINNT or WINNT32 (depending on the computer's current operating system).

4. Complete the Windows 2000 Professional installation.

Running the Windows 2000 Professional Installation Process

This section describes how to run the Windows 2000 Professional installation process. As explained in the previous section, you can run the installation from the CD or over a network. The only difference in the installation procedure is the point where you start—from your CD-ROM drive or from a network share. The steps in the following sections assume that the disk drive is clean and that you are starting the installation using the Windows 2000 Professional CD.

Microsoft
Exam
Objective

Perform an attended installation of Windows 2000 Professional.

There are three main steps in the Windows 2000 Professional installation process:

- Run the Setup program. If you boot from DOS or Windows 9*x*, the Setup program will be DOS-based. If you boot from Windows NT, the Setup program will be GUI-based.

- Run the Setup Wizard.

- Install Windows 2000 Networking.

Each of these steps is covered in detail in the following sections.

The following sections give the details of the installation process to show how the process works. But you should not actually install Windows 2000 Professional until you reach Exercise 1.1. In that exercise, you'll set up your computer to complete the rest of the exercises in this book.

Running the Setup Program

The Setup program starts the Windows 2000 installation. In this stage of the installation, you start the installation program, choose the partition where Windows 2000 Professional will be installed, and then copy files.

The following steps are involved in running the Setup program:

1. On an Intel computer, access your CD-ROM drive and open the I386 folder. This folder contains all of the installation files for an Intel-based computer.

2. Start the Setup program.

   - If you are installing Windows 2000 from an operating system other than Windows 9*x* or Windows NT, launch WINNT.

   - If you are installing Windows 2000 from 32-bit mode Windows 9*x* or Windows NT, launch WINNT32.

3. The Windows 2000 Setup dialog box appears. Your first choice is to specify the location of the distribution files. By default, this is where you executed the WINNT program. Normally, you just accept the default path and press Enter.

4. The Setup files are copied to your disk. If the SMARTDRV program is not loaded on your computer, you will see a message recommending that you load SMARTDRV. This is a disk-caching program that speeds up the process of copying files. SMARTDRV ships with DOS and Windows.

With SMARTDRV, it usually takes a few minutes to copy the files. Without SMARTDRV, it can take more than an hour.

5. Once the files have been copied, you are prompted to remove any floppy disks and to restart the computer.

6. The opening Windows 2000 Setup dialog box appears. At this point, you can set up Windows by pressing Enter, repair a Windows 2000 installation by pressing R, or quit the setup process by pressing F3.

7. The Windows 2000 License Agreement dialog box appears. You can accept the License Agreement by pressing F8, or you can disagree by pressing Escape (or F3 if you are in DOS mode). If you press Escape, the installation program will terminate, and your name and address will be sent directly to Microsoft for further analysis (just kidding about that second part).

8. The next dialog box asks you which partition you want to use to set up Windows 2000. You can pick a partition that already exists, or you can choose free space and a partition will be created for you. Whichever partition you choose must have at least 1GB of free space. The default folder name will be WINNT. At this point, you can create or delete partitions and the file systems the partitions will use.

After you indicate the partition that will be used as the Windows 2000 boot partition, the Windows installation files will be copied to the installation folders. Then the computer automatically reboots.

Running the Windows 2000 Setup Wizard

Once your computer finishes with the Setup program, the computer will restart, and the Windows 2000 Setup Wizard will start automatically. The Setup Wizard begins by detecting and installing device drivers. This process will take several minutes, and your screen may flicker during this process.

Then the Setup Wizard will gather information about your locale, name, and product key, as follows (you click Next after completing each dialog box):

1. The Regional Settings dialog box appears. From this dialog box, you choose your locale and keyboard settings. Locale settings are used to configure international options for numbers, currencies, times, and dates. Keyboard settings allow you to configure your keyboard to support different local characters or keyboard layouts. For example, you can choose Danish or United States-Dvorak through this option.

2. In the Personalize Your Software dialog box, you fill in the Name and Organization boxes. This information is used to personalize your operating system software and the applications that you install. If you install Windows 2000 Professional in a workgroup, the Name entry here is used for the initial user.

3. The Product Key dialog box appears. In the boxes at the bottom of this dialog box, you type in the 25-character product key, which can be found on the back of your Windows 2000 CD case.

4. The Computer Name and Administrator Password dialog box appears. Here, you specify a name that will uniquely identify your computer on the network. Your computer name can be up to 15 characters. The Setup Wizard suggests a name, but you can change it to another name. Through this dialog box, you also type and confirm the Administrator password. An account called Administrator will automatically be created as a part of the installation process.

WARNING   Be sure that the computer name is a unique name within your network. If you are part of a corporate network, you should also verify that the computer name follows the naming convention specified by your Information Services (IS) department.

5. If you have a Plug-and-Play modem installed, you will see the Modem Dialing Information dialog box. Here, you specify your country/region, your area code (or city code), whether you dial a number to get an outside line, and whether the telephone system uses tone dialing or pulse dialing.

6. The Date and Time Settings dialog box appears. In this dialog box, you specify date and time settings and the time zone in which your computer is located. You can also configure the computer to automatically adjust for daylight savings time.

7. The Network Settings dialog box appears. This dialog box is used to specify how you want to connect to other computers, networks, and the Internet. You have two choices:

   - Typical Settings installs network connections for Client for Microsoft Networks, as well as File and Print Sharing for Microsoft Networks. It also installs the TCP/IP protocol with an automatically assigned address.

   - Custom Settings allows you to customize your network settings. You can choose whether or not you want to use Client for Microsoft Networks, File and Print Sharing for Microsoft Networks, and the TCP/IP protocol. You should use the custom settings if you need to specify particular network settings, such as a specific IP address and subnet mask (rather than using an automatically assigned address).

8. In the next dialog box, Workgroup or Computer Domain, you specify whether your computer will be installed as a part of a local workgroup or as a part of a domain. (See the "Membership in Domain or Workgroup" section earlier in this chapter for details about these choices.)

9. The computer will perform some final tasks, including installing Start menu items, registering components, saving settings, and removing any temporary files. This will take several minutes. After the final tasks are complete, you will see the Completing the Windows 2000 Setup Wizard dialog box. Remove the CD from your computer and then click the Finish button to restart your computer.

Installing Windows 2000 Networking

Once your computer finishes with the Setup Wizard and the computer restarts, the Network Identification Wizard starts automatically. The Network Identification Wizard is responsible for the network component installation.

Depending on your computer's configuration, you may see a dialog box that deals with how users will log on to the computer. This dialog box offers two choices:

- The Users Must Enter a User Name and Password to Use This Computer option does just what it says. If you select this option, users must enter a username and password to log on to the computer.

- The Windows Always Assumes the Following User Has Logged On option sets up Windows 2000 so that the user does not need to enter a username or password to use the computer. If you are the only person using the computer in a secure, non-networked environment, you might choose this option. However, in a networked, business environment, you do not want to allow such a security risk.

Next, the Network Identification Wizard prompts you to finish the Wizard. If you chose the Users Must Enter a User Name and a Password to Use This Computer option, you need to provide a valid Window 2000 username and password in the Windows logon dialog box. At this point, the only users defined on the system are Administrator and the *initial user* (which is the username you entered for identification).

The installation is complete. You are logged on and greeted with the Windows 2000 Professional Getting Started Wizard. This Wizard helps new users navigate the operating system.

Setting Up Your Computer for Hands-on Exercises

The exercises in this book assume that your computer is configured in a specific manner. Your computer should have at least a 3GB drive that is configured with the minimum space requirements and partitions. Other exercises in this book make assumptions that your computer is configured as follows:

- 2.5GB (about 2500MB) C: primary partition with the FAT file system

- 250MB D: extended partition with the FAT file system

- 250MB of free space

Of course, you can allocate more space to your partitions if it is available.

You are probably wondering why we are not using any NTFS partitions. The reason is that you will convert a FAT partition to NTFS and use the features of NTFS in Chapter 9. You will also use the features of NTFS in Chapter 10, "Accessing Files and Folders." You are probably also wondering about the free space requirement. You need free space because you will create partitions in Chapter 9. If no free space exists, you won't be able to complete that exercise.

Exercise 1.1 assumes that you are not currently running Windows NT and that you are performing a clean installation and not an upgrade. Your partitions should be created and formatted, and SMARTDRV should be loaded. Also, before you begin, make sure that you hardware meets the requirements listed in Table 1.1.

As noted earlier in this chapter, you can set up your partitions through the DOS or Windows FDISK utility or a third-party program. For example, if you have a Windows 98 computer, you can use it to create a Windows 98 boot disk. Set up the disk with FDISK and FORMAT and manually copy the SMARTDRV utility from the Windows folder on the Windows 98 computer to the Windows 98 boot disk. Then you will be able to boot your computer and see your CD-ROM drive.

You should make a complete backup of your computer before repartitioning your disk or installing new operating systems. All data will be lost during this process!

EXERCISE 1.1

Installing Windows 2000 Professional

In this exercise, you will install Windows 2000 Professional, which is a three-part process.

Running the Setup Program

1. Boot your computer and insert the Windows 2000 CD into your CD-ROM drive.

EXERCISE 1.1 *(continued)*

2. From the DOS prompt on your computer, access your CD-ROM drive. If you have configured your computer to our recommended specifications, your CD-ROM drive should be E:.

3. From the CD-ROM drive prompt, change directories to I386 by typing **CD I386** and pressing Enter.

4. From the \I386> prompt, type **WINNT** and press Enter.

5. From the Windows 2000 Setup dialog box, press Enter to accept the default path location for the Windows 2000 distribution files. It will take a few minutes to copy the files.

6. Remove any floppy disks from the computer and press Enter to restart the computer.

7. The computer restarts, and the Welcome to Setup screen appears. Press Enter to set up Windows 2000.

8. The License Agreement dialog box appears. Scroll down to the bottom of the page. Press F8 to agree to the license terms if you wish to continue.

9. In the next dialog box, specify the C: partition as the one you want to use to set up Windows 2000. Then press Enter.

10. In the next dialog box, choose to leave the current file system intact (no changes). Press Enter to continue.

Setup now examines your disks. The Windows installation files will be automatically copied to the installation folder, which will take a few minutes. After the files are copied, the computer will automatically reboot. After the computer reboots, the Welcome to the Setup Wizard dialog box will appear. You are prompted to click Next to continue. If you do not make a selection within 10 seconds, the installation will continue automatically. The Windows 2000 Professional Setup program will automatically detect and install drivers on your computer. This process will take a few minutes.

EXERCISE 1.1 *(continued)*

Running the Windows 2000 Setup Wizard

11. The Regional Settings dialog box appears. Click Next to accept the default settings and continue.

12. In the Personalize Your Software dialog box, type your name and organization. Click the Next button.

13. In the Product Key dialog box, type the 25-character product key (this key can be found on a sticker on the CD case). Click the Next button.

14. The Computer Name and Administrator Password dialog box appears. Type in the computer name. You can also specify an Administrator password (since this computer will be used for practice, you can leave the Password field blank if you want to). Click the Next button.

15. If you have a Plug-and-Play modem installed, the Modem Dialing Information dialog box appears. Specify the settings for your environment and click the Next button.

16. The Date and Time Settings dialog box appears. Verify that all of the settings are correct and click the Next button.

17. After the Networking component files are copied (which takes a few minutes), the Network Settings dialog box appears. Confirm that the Typical Settings button is selected. Then click the Next button.

18. In the Workgroup and Computer Domain dialog box, confirm that the No, This Computer Is Not on a Network, or Is on a Network without a Domain option is selected to indicate that you don't want to put the computer in a domain. In this dialog box, you can accept the default workgroup name, WORKGROUP, or you can specify a unique workgroup name. Since this is a practice computer, the workgroup name is not important. Click the Next button. The Setup components are installed, which takes several minutes.

19. When the Completing the Windows 2000 Setup Wizard appears, remove the CD from the drive and click the Finish button. The computer will restart.

EXERCISE 1.1 *(continued)*

20. When the computer reboots, choose Microsoft Windows 2000 from the boot selection options by pressing Enter. (This is the default selection if no choice is made.)

Running the Network Identification Wizard

21. Windows 2000 Professional starts and displays the Welcome to the Network Identification Wizard dialog box. Click the Next button to continue.

22. In the Users of This Computer dialog box, click the Users Must Enter a User Name and Password to Use This Computer option. Click the Next button to continue.

23. In the Completing the Network Identification Wizard dialog box, click the Finish button.

Windows 2000 Professional is now installed, and you should be logged on to Windows 2000 and see the Getting Started with Windows 2000 dialog box.

Troubleshooting Installation Problems

The Windows 2000 installation process is designed to be as simple as possible. The chances for installation errors are greatly minimized through the use of Wizards and the step-by-step process. However, it is possible that errors may occur.

Microsoft ✓ *Exam* *Objective*

Troubleshoot failed installations.

The following are some possible installation errors you might encounter:

Media errors   Media errors are caused by defective or damaged CDs. To check the CD, put it into another computer and see if you can read it. Also check your CD for scratches or dirt—it may just need to be cleaned.

Insufficient disk space   Windows 2000 needs at least 1GB of free space for the installation program to run properly. If the Setup program cannot verify that this space exists, the program will not let you continue.

Not enough memory   Make sure that your computer has the minimum amount of memory required by Windows 2000 Professional (64MB). Not having enough memory may cause the installation to fail or blue-screen errors to occur after installation.

Not enough processing power   Make sure that your computer has the minimum processing power required by Windows 2000 Professional (Pentium 133MHz). Not having enough processing power may cause the installation to fail or blue-screen errors to occur after installation.

Hardware that is not on the HCL   If your hardware is not on the HCL, Windows 2000 may not recognize the hardware, or the device may not work properly.

Hardware with no driver support   Windows 2000 will not recognize hardware without driver support.

Hardware that is not configured properly   If your hardware is Plug-and-Play compatible, Windows should configure it automatically. If your hardware is not Plug-and-Play compatible, you will need to manually configure the hardware per the manufacturer's instructions.

Incorrect CD key   Without a valid CD key, the installation will not go past the Product Key dialog box. Make sure that you have not typed in an incorrect key (check the back of your CD case for this key).

Failure to access TCP/IP network resources	If you install Windows 2000 with typical settings, the computer is configured as a DHCP client. If there is no DHCP server to provide IP configuration information, the client will be unable to access network resources through TCP/IP.
Failure to connect to a domain controller when joining a domain	Make sure that you have specified the correct domain name. If your domain name is correct, verify that your network settings have been set properly and that a domain controller and DNS server are available. If you still can't join a domain, install the computer in a workgroup, then join the domain after installation.

When you install Windows 2000 Professional, several log files are created by the Setup program. You can view these logs to check for any problems during the installation process. Two log files are particularly useful for troubleshooting:

- The action log includes all of the actions that were performed during the setup process and a description of each action. These actions are listed in chronological order. The action log is stored as *Windir*\setupact.log.

- The error log includes any errors that occurred during the installation. For each error, there is a description and an indication of the severity of the error. This error log is stored as *Windir*\setuperr.log.

In Exercise 1.2, you will view the Windows 2000 setup logs to determine if there were any problems with your Windows 2000 installation.

EXERCISE 1.2

Troubleshooting Failed Installations with Setup Logs

1. Select Start ➤ Programs ➤ Accessories ➤ Windows Explorer.

2. In Windows Explorer, double-click My Computer, double-click Local Disk (C:), and double-click WINNT (this is the default *Windir* folder, set up in Exercise 1.1).

3. Since this is the first time you have opened the WINNT folder, click the Show All Files option to display all the files that it contains.

4. In the WINNT folder, double-click the setupact file to view your action log in Notepad. When you are finished viewing this file, close Notepad.

5. Double-click the setuperr file to view your error file in Notepad. If no errors occurred during installation, this file will be empty. When you are finished viewing this file, close Notepad.

6. Close Windows Explorer.

Supporting Multiple-Boot Options

You may want to install Windows 2000 Professional but still be able to run other operating systems. *Dual-booting* or *multi-booting* allows your computer to boot multiple operating systems. Your computer will be automatically configured for dual-booting if there was a supported operating system on your computer prior to the Windows 2000 Professional installation (and you didn't upgrade from that operating system).

One reason for dual-booting is to test various systems. If you have a limited number of computers in your test lab, and you want to be able to test multiple configurations, you dual-boot. For example, you might configure one computer to multi-boot with Windows NT Workstation 4, Windows NT Server 4 configured as a primary domain controller (PDC), Windows 2000 Professional, and Windows 2000 Server.

Another reason to set up dual-booting is for software backward compatibility. For example, you may have an application that works with Windows 95 but not under Windows 2000 Professional. If you want to use Windows 2000 but still access your legacy application, you can configure a dual-boot.

Here are some keys to successful dual-boot configurations:

- Make sure you have plenty of disk space. It's a good idea to put each operating system on a separate partition, although this is not required.

- Put the simplest operating systems on first. If you want to support dual-booting with DOS and Windows 2000 Professional, DOS must be installed first. If you install Windows 2000 Professional first, you cannot install DOS without ruining your Windows 2000 configuration. This requirement also applies to Windows 9*x*.

- Never, ever, upgrade to Windows 2000 dynamic disks. Dynamic disks are seen only by Windows 2000 and are not recognized by any other operating system, including Windows NT.

- Do not convert your file system to NTFS if you are planning a dual-boot with any operating system except Windows NT or Windows 2000. These operating systems are the only ones that recognize NTFS.

- If you will dual-boot with Windows NT 4, you must turn off disk compression, or Windows 2000 will not be able to read the drive properly.

If you are planning on dual-booting with Windows NT 4, you should upgrade it to NT 4 Service Pack 4 (or higher), which provides NTFS version 5 support.

Once you have installed each operating system, you can choose the operating system that you will boot to during the boot process. You will see a boot selection screen that asks you to choose which operating system you want to boot.

Summary

In this chapter, you learned how to install Windows 2000 Professional. We covered the following topics:

- The design goals of Windows 2000 Professional, which include taking the best features of Windows 98 and Windows NT 4, providing a wide range of support for hardware, making the operating system easy to use, and lowering the cost of ownership.

- Installation preparation, which begins with making sure that your computer meets the minimum system requirements and that all of

‚ your hardware is on the Hardware Compatibility List (HCL). Then you need to decide whether you will perform a clean install or an upgrade. Finally, you should plan which options you will select during installation. Options include how to partition your disk space, how to select a file system, whether the computer will be installed as a part of a workgroup or a domain, and your language and locale settings.

- The methods you can use for installation, which include using the distribution files on the Windows 2000 Professional CD or using files that have been copied to a network share point. If you will be installing Windows 2000 from the CD, you can start the installation by booting from another operating system, booting from the CD, or using the Windows 2000 Professional Setup Boot Disks.

- How to install Windows 2000 Professional, which occurs in three main installation phases: running the Setup program, running the Setup Wizard, and installing Windows 2000 Networking.

- How to troubleshoot installation problems. Common errors are caused by media problems, lack of disk space or memory, and hardware problems. You can view Setup log files to check for problems that occurred during the installation.

- Information about supporting dual-boot or multi-boot environments. Dual-booting and multi-booting allow you to boot to a choice of two or more operating systems.

Key Terms

Before taking the exam, you should be familiar with the following terms:

Advanced Configuration and Power Interface (ACPI)

boot partition

central processing unit (CPU)

clean install

disk partitioning

distribution server

domain

dual-boot

EB (exabyte)

FAT32

File Allocation Table (FAT16)

GB (gigabyte)

Hardware Compatibility List (HCL)

Institute of Electrical and Electronic Engineers (IEEE) 1394 standard

logical drive

MB (megabyte)

multi-boot

NTFS (New Technology File System)

PB (petabyte)

Plug-and-Play

system partition

TB (terabyte)

Universal Serial Bus (USB)

Windows 2000 Professional Setup Boot Disks

workgroup

Review Questions

1. What is the minimum processor required for an Intel-based computer to install and run Windows 2000 Professional?

   A. 80486

   B. A Pentium with a 133MHz or better processor

   C. A Pentium II with a 166MHz or better processor

   D. A Pentium III with a 333MHz or better processor

2. What is the minimum memory required to install and run Windows 2000 Professional?

   A. 64MB

   B. 16MB

   C. 32MB

   D. 128MB

3. What is the minimum free disk space required to install Windows 2000 Professional?

   A. 500MB

   B. 650MB

   C. 1GB

   D. 1.2GB

4. What is the name of the list that shows the computers and peripheral hardware that have been extensively tested with the Windows 2000 Professional operating system?

   A. The Windows Compatibility List

   B. The W2K Compatibility List

   C. The Microsoft Compatibility List

   D. The Hardware Compatibility List

5. The boot partition contains the files that are the Windows 2000 Professional operating system. By default, where is this folder located?

   A. WIN2K

   B. WINNT

   C. WINDOWS

   D. WIN2.K

6. What three file systems does Windows 2000 Professional support?

   A. File Allocation Table (FAT16)

   B. HPFS

   C. FAT32

   D. NTFS

7. When you install your Windows 2000 Professional computer, what two options do you have for computer membership?

   A. Workgroup

   B. Active Directory

   C. Domain

   D. MDS

8. Which of the following is *not* a major step in the Windows 2000 Professional installation process?

   A. Running the Configuration Setup Wizard

   B. Running the Setup program

   C. Running the Setup Wizard

   D. Installing Windows 2000 Networking

9. You should run WINNT32 if you are installing Windows 2000 Professional from which operating system? Choose all that apply.

   A. DOS

   B. Windows 95

   C. Windows 98

   D. Windows NT

10. If you choose Typical Settings, which of the following configurations are made during the Network Settings component of the Windows 2000 Professional installation? Choose all that apply.

   A. Network connections for Client for Microsoft Networks

   B. File and Print Sharing for Microsoft Networks

   C. NetBEUI protocol with automatic addressing

   D. TCP/IP protocol with automatically assigned address

11. You have the following computers in your test lab. You want to install and test Windows 2000 Professional. Which of the following computers can be used? Choose two answers.

Computer	Processor	Memory	Available Hard Disk Space
Computer A	Pentium II 266MHz	32MB	1GB
Computer B	Pentium III 450MHz	64MB	650MB
Computer C	Pentium II 166MHz	64MB	500MB
Computer D	Pentium 133MHz	64MB	750MB

   A. Computer A

   B. Computer B

   C. Computer C

   D. Computer D

12. You are attempting to install a computer called WIN2Ksales1 into the TestCorp.com domain. When you attempt to join the domain, you get an error that the domain can't be located. Which of the following options must be configured and running in your domain? Choose two answers.

    A. A PDC

    B. A domain controller

    C. A DNS server

    D. A WINS server

13. Your computer is configured with two hard drives. On disk 0, you have decided to configure logical drive C:. On disk 1, you have decided to configure logical disk D:. You want to run Windows 98 for backward compatibility with some applications that will not run under Windows 2000. However, you also want to run Windows 2000 Professional to take advantage of the Windows 2000 features. On drive D:, you want to store files that should have a high level of security. You will install Windows 98 on drive C: and Windows 2000 Professional on drive D:. How should the drives on this computer be configured?

    A. Configure both logical drives as FAT32

    B. Configure both logical drives with NTFS

    C. Configure logical drive C: as FAT32 and logical drive D: as NTFS

    D. Configure logical drive C: as NTFS and logical drive D: as FAT32

14. You install Windows 2000 Professional using the typical settings. After you start the computer, you realize that you can't see any other computers on the network. The network is using the TCP/IP protocol. What is the most likely problem?

    A. You have not installed Client Services for Microsoft.

    B. You have not installed File and Print Sharing for Microsoft Networks.

    C. You have not installed the TCP/IP protocol stack.

    D. There was no DHCP server to allocate an IP address, and your IP settings have not been configured.

15. You have a computer that will dual-boot between Windows NT 4 and Windows 2000 Professional. Which of the following statements reflects proper configuration?

   A. You should turn off disk compression on the Windows NT 4 configuration.

   B. You should enable dynamic disks on the Windows 2000 Professional configuration.

   C. You should install both operating systems into the same *Windir* directory so you will be able to access applications under both operating systems.

   D. You should edit the Registry on the Windows 2000 computer for HKEY_LOCAL_MACHINE\DualBoot to a value of 1 so that you will be able to access applications under both operating systems.

16. You have a computer that is on the HCL. The hard drive was erased and you are unable to access the CD-ROM drive. Where can you find the 32-bit command to create the Windows 2000 Professional Setup Boot Disks on the Windows 2000 Professional CD? The computer that will create the disks is already running Windows 2000 Professional.

   A. \I386\MAKEBOOT

   B. \I386\MAKEBT32

   C. \BOOTDISK\MAKEBOOT

   D. \BOOTDISK\MAKEBT32

17. You want to be able to install Windows 2000 Professional over the network. What folder must be copied from the Windows 2000 Professional CD?

   A. \OEM

   B. \I386

   C. \Intel

   D. \$WINI386

18. What steps should you take if the computer does not recognize your network interface card? Choose three answers.

    A. Make sure the network card is on the HCL.

    B. Check to see if the network card is Plug-and-Play compatible or if it needs to be manually configured.

    C. Make sure the network card is compatible with the other network cards on the network.

    D. Make sure you have the latest driver for the network card.

19. You are in the process of troubleshooting a Windows 2000 Professional installation. You want to verify all of the actions that were taken during the Setup phase. Where can you find a log file that will tell you this information?

    A. *Windir*\\verify.log

    B. *Logfiles*\\verify.log

    C. *Windir*\\setupact.log

    D. *Logfiles*\\setup.log

20. You are in the process of troubleshooting a Windows 2000 Professional installation. You want to view any errors that occurred during the Setup phase. Where can you find a log file that will tell you this information?

    A. *Windir*\\error.log

    B. *Logfiles*\\error.log

    C. *Windir*\\setuperr.log

    D. *Logfiles*\\setuperr.log

Answers to Review Questions

1. B. The processor must be at least a Pentium 133MHz or better.

2. A. Your computer must have at least 64MB of memory for Windows 2000 Professional.

3. B. You must have a minimum of a 2GB drive, with at least 650MB of free space to install Windows 2000 Professional.

4. D. The Hardware Compatibility List (HCL) shows the computers and components that have been tested to work with Windows 2000.

5. B. The Windows 2000 Professional system files are stored in the WINNT folder by default. You can change this folder name or location during installation.

6. A, C, D. Windows 2000 supports the FAT16, FAT32, and NTFS file systems. Windows NT 3.51 was the last version of NT to support the HPFS file system.

7. A, C. You can install your computer as a part of a workgroup or as a part of the domain. Domains are part of the Active Directory, but you install computers into domains, not directly into the Active Directory. There is no such thing as MDS within the context of Windows 2000.

8. A. Option A does not exist.

9. B, C, D. You can run WINNT32 only from 32-bit operating systems such as Windows 9*x* and Windows NT.

10. A, B, D. The NetBEUI protocol is not installed by default if you install Windows 2000 using Typical Settings.

11. B, D. Computers B and D meet the minimum requirements of a Pentium 133MHz or higher processor, 64MB of memory, and at least 650MB of free disk space.

12. B, C. You must have a domain controller and a DNS server running in your domain in order to add a computer to the domain.

13. C. You should configure logical drive C: as FAT32 since Windows 98 will not read NTFS partitions. Logical drive D: should be configured as NTFS since you want to implement local security.

14. D. If you install Windows 2000 with the typical settings, the computer is configured as a DHCP client. If there is no DHCP server to provide IP configuration information, the client will be unable to access network resources through TCP/IP. By default, the typical settings will install Client for Microsoft Networks and File and Print Sharing for Microsoft Networks.

15. A. You should turn off disk compression before you dual-boot. Windows 2000 does not support the disk compression that was used by Windows NT 4. There is no way to configure the operating systems to recognize applications under both platforms.

16. D. If you are creating Windows 2000 Professional Setup Boot Disks from a computer that is running Windows 2000, Windows NT, or Windows 9*x*, you use the MAKEBT32.EXE command. If you are making the boot disks from a 16-bit operating system, you use the MAKEBOOT.EXE command. These commands can be found in the BOOTDISK folder on the Windows 2000 Professional CD.

17. B. You must copy the \I386 folder and share the folder to install Windows 2000 Professional over a network.

18. A, C, D. If your computer will not recognize your network card, you should ensure that the network card is on the HCL and make sure you have the latest driver. You can check for the latest driver on the vendor's Web site. Even if the card is not on the HCL and is not Plug-and-Play compatible, it may work if it is properly configured.

19. C. You can find the log file that details Setup actions in *Windir*\setupact.log.

20. C. You can find the log file that details any Setup errors in *Windir*\setuperr.log.

Chapter

2

Automating the Windows 2000 Installation

MICROSOFT EXAM OBJECTIVES COVERED IN THIS CHAPTER

✓ **Perform an unattended installation of Windows 2000 Professional.**

- Install Windows 2000 Professional by using Windows 2000 Server Remote Installation Services (RIS).

- Install Windows 2000 Professional by using the System Preparation Tool.

- Create unattended answer files by using Setup Manager to automate the installation of Windows 2000 Professional.

✓ **Install applications by using Windows Installer packages.**

You can automate the installation of Windows 2000 Professional in several ways: by using Remote Installation Services (RIS), disk imaging, or unattended installation. To help facilitate remote installations, you can also use answer files. Answer files are used with automated installation to provide answers to the questions that are normally asked during the installation process. After you've installed Windows 2000 Professional, you can automate the installation of applications by using Windows Installer packages.

This chapter begins with an overview of the three main automated deployment options. Next, it details the use of unattended answer files, RIS, and disk images. Finally, you will learn how to automate application installation through the use of Windows Installer packages.

Choosing Automated Deployment Options

If you need to install Windows 2000 Professional on multiple computers, you could manually install the operating system on each computer, as described in Chapter 1, "Getting Started with Windows 2000 Professional." However, automatic deployment will make your job easier, more efficient, and more cost effective.

You can use the following options for automated deployment:

- Remote installation
- Disk imaging (cloning)
- Unattended installation

The following sections provide an overview of each of these options.

An Overview of Remote Installation

Remote Installation Services (RIS) is a new technology that has been introduced with Windows 2000 to allow *remote installation* of Windows 2000 Professional.

An RIS server installs Windows 2000 Professional on RIS clients, as illustrated in Figure 2.1. The RIS server must have the RIS server software installed and configured. RIS clients are computers that have a *Pre-Boot Execution Environment (PXE)* network card or use an RIS boot disk with a PXE-compatible network card. No other software is required to connect to the RIS server. Remote installation is a good choice for automatic deployment when you need to be able to deploy large numbers of computers and your clients are PXE-compliant.

FIGURE 2.1 Remote Installation Services (RIS) uses an RIS server and RIS clients.

RIS Server

Stores:
RIS server software
Windows 2000 Professional
    CD-based or RIPrep image
Answer files (optional)

RIS Client

Requires a PXE-based boot
ROM, an RIS boot disk
with a network adapter that
supports PXE, or a NetPC computer

The RIS server can be configured with either of two types of images:

- A CD-based image contains only the Windows 2000 Professional operating system. You can create answer files for CD-based images to respond to the Setup program's configuration prompts.

- A Remote Installation Preparation (RIPrep) image can contain the Windows 2000 operating system and applications. This type of image is based on a preconfigured computer.

RIS installation is covered in detail in the "Using Remote Installation Services" section later in this chapter.

An Overview of Disk Imaging

Disk imaging, or disk duplication, is the process of creating a reference computer for the automated deployment. The reference, or source, computer has Windows 2000 Professional installed and is configured with the settings and applications that should be installed on the target computers. Disk imaging is a good choice for automatic deployment when you have the hardware that supports disk imaging and you have a large number of computers with similar configuration requirements. For example, education centers that reinstall the same software every week might use this technology.

You use the *System Preparation Tool (Sysprep)* utility to prepare the disk image, then you remove the drive with the disk image and insert it into a special piece of hardware, called a disk duplicator, to copy the images. The copied disks are inserted into the target computers. After you add the hard drive that contains the disk image to the target computers, you can complete the installation from those computers. Figure 2.2 illustrates the disk-imaging process. You can also copy disk images by using special third-party software.

FIGURE 2.2   Disk imaging uses a reference computer for configuring target computers.

Creating disk images is covered in detail in the "Using Disk Images" section later in this chapter.

An Overview of Unattended Installation

Unattended installation is a practical method of automatic deployment when you have a large number of clients to install and the computers are not PXE-compliant. With an unattended installation, you use a distribution server to install Windows 2000 Professional on a target computer.

The distribution server contains the Windows 2000 Professional operating system files and possibly an answer file to respond to installation configuration queries. The target computer must be able to connect to the distribution server over the network. After the distribution server and target computers are connected, you can initiate the installation process. Figure 2.3 illustrates the unattended installation process.

FIGURE 2.3   Unattended installation uses a distribution server and a target computer.

Distribution Server

Target

Stores:
Windows 2000 Professional
operating system files
Answer files (optional)

Requires enough software to
connect to the distribution server

The process for unattended installations is covered in *Mastering Windows 2000 Server*, by Mark Minasi (Sybex, 2000).

Using Setup Manager to Create Answer Files

*A*nswer files are automated installation scripts that are used to answer the questions that appear during a normal Windows 2000 Professional installation. You can use answer files with Windows 2000 unattended installations, Sysprep (disk images), or RIS installations. Setting up answer files allows you to easily deploy Windows 2000 Professional to computers that may not be configured in the same manner, with little or no user intervention.

Microsoft
Exam
Objective

Perform an unattended installation of Windows 2000 Professional.

- Create unattended answer files by using Setup Manager to automate the installation of Windows 2000 Professional.

You create answer files through the *Setup Manager (SETUPMGR)* utility. There are several advantages to using Setup Manager to create answer files:

- You can easily create answer files through a graphical interface, which reduces syntax errors.

- The utility simplifies the addition of user-specific or computer-specific configuration information.

- With Setup Manager, you can include application setup scripts within the answer file.

- The utility creates the distribution folder that will be used for installation files.

In order to access the Setup Manager utility, you must extract the Windows 2000 Deployment Tools from the Windows 2000 Professional CD. The following sections explain how to access the Setup Manager utility and how to use Setup Manager to create an unattended answer file.

Extracting the Windows 2000 Deployment Tools

The Windows 2000 Deployment Tools include the Setup Manager utility for creating unattended answer files, as well as the System Preparation Tool utility for creating disk images. The Deployment Tools are stored on the Windows 2000 Professional CD, in the \Support\Tools folder, in the Deploy.cab file. You can extract these files by using the File ➤ Extract command in Windows Explorer. The following steps are used to extract the Windows 2000 Deployment Tools:

1. Log on to your Windows 2000 computer as Administrator.

2. Use Windows Explorer to create a folder named **Deployment Tools** on the root folder of your C: drive.

3. Insert the Windows 2000 Professional CD. Using Windows Explorer, copy the \Support\Tools\Deploy file (the .cab extension is hidden by default) to the C:\Deployment Tools folder.

4. Double-click the Deploy.cab file to display its contents, as shown in Figure 2.4.

FIGURE 2.4   The Deploy.cab file contents

5. In Windows Explorer, select Edit ➢ Select All. Then select File ➢ Extract.

6. The Browse for Folder dialog box appears. Select Local Disk (C:) and then Deployment Tools. Click the OK button to extract the files to the specified folder.

7. Verify that the Deployment Tools were extracted to C:\Deployment Tools. There should be eight items (including the Deploy.cab file).

In Exercise 2.1, you will extract the Windows 2000 Deployment Tools.

EXERCISE 2.1

Extracting the Windows 2000 Deployment Tools

1. Log on to your Windows 2000 computer as Administrator.

2. Select Start ➢ Programs ➢ Accessories ➢ Windows Explorer.

3. In Windows Explorer, double-click My Computer, and then double-click Local Disk (C:). Select File ➢ New ➢ Folder. Type in **Deployment Tools** for the folder name.

4. Insert the Windows 2000 Professional CD into your computer (hold down the Shift key if you want to bypass the auto-play feature).

5. In Windows Explorer, double-click the CD drive (the E: drive if you configured your computer as specified in Exercise 1.1), double-click the Support folder, and then double-click the Tools folder.

6. Right-click DEPLOY and select Copy. Double-click the Local Disk (C:), and then double-click the Deployment Tools folder. Right-click and select Paste.

7. Double-click the Deploy.cab file. Select Edit ➢ Select All, and then select File ➢ Extract.

8. In the Browse for Folder dialog box, select Local Disk (C:) and then Deployment Tools. Click the OK button.

9. Check the C:\Deployment Tools folder in Windows Explorer to make sure that it contains the eight items.

10. Close Windows Explorer.

Using Setup Manager to Create Unattended Answer Files

After you have extracted the Windows 2000 Deployment Tools from the Windows 2000 Professional CD, you can run the Setup Manager utility to create a new answer file, create an answer file that duplicates the current computer's configuration, or edit answer existing answer files.

The following steps describe how to create a new installation script. In this example, the instructions describe how to create an answer file for an RIS installation that provides default answers, uses the default display configuration, configures typical network settings, and does not edit any additional options.

1. Select Start ➢ Run and click the Browse button in the Run dialog box. Double-click the Deployment Tools folder, double-click the Setupmgr program, and then click the OK button.

2. The Windows 2000 Setup Manager Wizard starts, as shown in Figure 2.5. Click the Next button.

FIGURE 2.5 The Welcome to the Windows 2000 Setup Manager Wizard dialog box

3. The New or Existing Answer File dialog box appears, as shown in Figure 2.6. This dialog box provides choices for creating a new answer file, creating an answer file that duplicates this computer's configuration, or modifying an existing answer file. Select the Create a New Answer file option and click the Next button.

FIGURE 2.6 The New or Existing Answer File dialog box

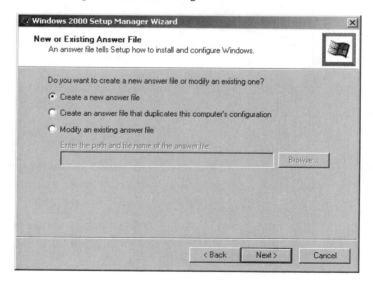

4. The Product to Install dialog box appears, as shown in Figure 2.7. You can choose Windows 2000 Unattended Installation, Sysprep Install, or Remote Installation Services. Select Remote Installation Services and click the Next button.

FIGURE 2.7 The Product to Install dialog box

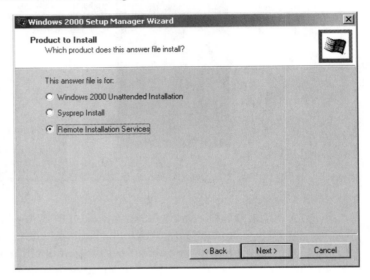

5. The User Interaction Level dialog box appears, as shown in Figure 2.8. This dialog box offers the following options:

- The Provide Defaults option allows you to configure default answers that will be displayed. The user is prompted to review the default answer and can change the answer if desired.

- The Fully Automated option uses all of the answers in the answer file and will not prompt the user for any interaction.

- The Hide Pages option hides the Wizard page from the user, if you have supplied all of the answers on the Windows Setup Wizard page.

- The Read Only option allows the user to see the Setup Wizard display page, but not to make any changes to it (this option is used if the Setup Wizard display page is shown to the user).

- The GUI Attended option allows only the text-mode portion of the Windows Setup program to be automated.

Select the Provide Defaults option and click the Next button to continue.

FIGURE 2.8 The User Interaction Level dialog box

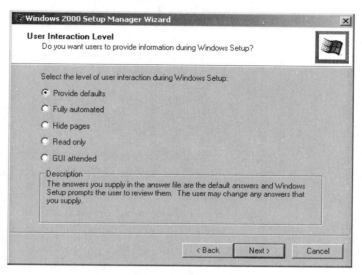

6. The Administrator Password dialog box appears, as shown in Figure 2.9. You can choose to prompt the user for a password, or you can specify the Administrator password in this dialog box. You can also specify that when the computer starts, the Administrator will automatically be logged on. Enter and confirm an Administrator password. Then click the Next button.

FIGURE 2.9 The Administrator Password dialog box

7. The Display Settings dialog box appears, as shown in Figure 2.10. From this dialog box, you can configure the following settings:

- The Colors option allows you to set the display color to the Windows default, 16 colors, 256 colors high color (16 bit), high color (24 bit), or high color (32 bit).

- The Screen Area option allows you to set the screen area to the Windows default, 640 × 480, 800 × 600, 1024 × 768, or 1280 × 1024, or 1600 × 1200.

- The Refresh Frequency option (the number of times the screen is updated) allows you to set the refresh frequency to the Windows default, 60Hz, 70Hz, 72Hz, 75Hz, or 85Hz.

- The Custom button displays a dialog box that allows you to further customize display settings for the color, screen area, and refresh frequency.

Click Next to accept the default configuration and continue.

FIGURE 2.10   The Display Settings dialog box

8. The Network Settings dialog box appears, as shown in Figure 2.11. You can choose Typical Settings (installs TCP/IP, enables DHCP, and installs Client for Microsoft Networks) or Custom Settings (allows you to customize the computer's network settings). Select the Typical Settings option and click the Next button.

FIGURE 2.11 The Network Settings dialog box

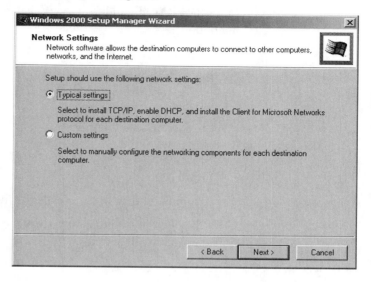

9. The Time Zone dialog box appears, as shown in Figure 2.12. Select your computer's time zone from the drop-down list and click the Next button.

FIGURE 2.12 The Time Zone dialog box

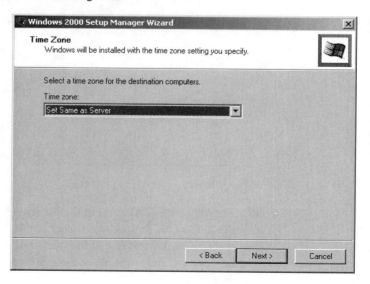

10. The Additional Settings dialog box appears, as shown in Figure 2.13. If you select to edit additional settings, you can configure the following options:

   - Telephony settings

   - Regional settings

   - Languages

   - Browser and shell settings

   - Installation folder

   - Install printers

   - A command that will run once the first time a user logs on

   Click the Next button to accept the default selection of No, Do Not Edit the Additional Settings.

FIGURE 2.13   The Additional Settings dialog box

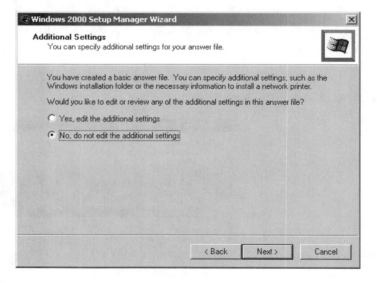

11. The Setup Information File Text dialog box appears, as shown in Figure 2.14. This dialog box allows you to give the answer file a descriptive name and help text. Enter the name in the Description String text box and the help text in the Help String text box. Then click the Next button.

FIGURE 2.14   The Setup Information File Text dialog box

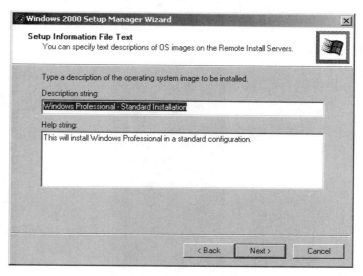

12. The Answer File Name dialog box appears, as shown in Figure 2.15.
Click the Browse button. Select Local Disk (C:) and click the Create
New Folder icon. Create a new folder for the answer files and click the
Open button. In the Save As dialog box, specify a filename (the default
is `remboot.txt`) and click the Save button. Then click the Next button.

FIGURE 2.15   The Answer File Name dialog box

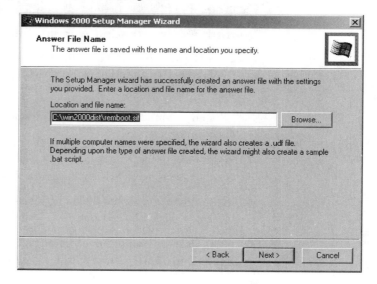

13. The Completing the Windows 2000 Setup Manager Wizard dialog box appears, as shown in Figure 2.16. Click the Finish button.

FIGURE 2.16 The Completing the Windows 2000 Setup Manager Wizard

In Exercise 2.2, you will create an automated answer file that can be used with an RIS installation.

EXERCISE 2.2

Creating an Unattended Answer File

1. Select Start ➢ Run and click the Browse button. Double-click the Deployment Tools folder, double-click the Setupmgr program, and then click the OK button.

2. When the Windows 2000 Setup Manager Wizard starts, click the Next button.

3. In the New or Existing Answer File dialog box, select the Create a New Answer file option and click the Next button.

4. In the Product to Install dialog box, select Remote Installation Services and click the Next button.

5. In the User Interaction Level dialog box, select the Provide Defaults option and click the Next button.

EXERCISE 2.2 *(continued)*

6. In the Administrator Password dialog box, select the Prompt the User for an Administrator Password option and click the Next button.

7. In the Display Settings dialog box, click Next to accept the default settings and continue.

8. In the Network Settings dialog box, select Typical Settings and click the Next button.

9. In the Time Zone dialog box, select the Set Same as Server option and click the Next button.

10. In the Additional Settings dialog box, select the No, Do Not Edit the Additional Settings option and click the Next button.

11. In the Setup Information File Text dialog box, click Next to accept the default settings and continue.

12. In the Answer File Name dialog box, click the Browse button. Select Local Disk (C:) and click the Create New Folder icon. Create a new folder named **Win2000Dist** and click the Open button. In the Save As dialog box, enter a filename or accept the default name (remboot.txt) and click the Save button. Then click the Next button.

13. When the Completing the Windows 2000 Setup Manager Wizard dialog box appears, click the Finish button. Your answer file will be created.

Using Remote Installation Services (RIS)

You can remotely install Windows 2000 Professional through RIS. For RIS installation, you need an RIS server that stores the Windows 2000 Professional operating system files in a shared image folder and clients that can access the RIS server. Depending on the type of image you will distribute, you may also want to configure answer files (as described in the previous section), so that users do not need to respond to any Windows 2000 Professional installation prompts.

Microsoft ✓ *Exam* *Objective*

Perform an unattended installation of Windows 2000 Professional.

- Install Windows 2000 Professional by using Windows 2000 Server Remote Installation Services (RIS).

The following are some of the advantages of using RIS for automated installation:

- You can remotely install Windows 2000 Professional.

- The procedure simplifies server image management by allowing you to access Windows 2000 distribution files and use Plug-and-Play hardware detection during the installation process.

- You can quickly recover the operating system in the event of a computer failure.

- Windows 2000 security is retained when you restart the destination computer.

The following sections describe how to set up the RIS server and the RIS clients, and how to install Windows 2000 Professional through RIS.

RIS is usually used for remote installation of Windows 2000 Professional. However, Microsoft has introduced support for Windows 2000 Server installation through RIS.

Preparing the RIS Server

The RIS server is used to manage and distribute the Windows 2000 Professional operating system to RIS client computers. As explained earlier in this chapter, RIS servers can distribute CD-based images or RIPrep images. A CD-based image contains the operating system installation files and can be customized for specific computers through the use of answer files. RIPrep images are based on a preconfigured computer and can contain applications as well as the operating system. RIPrep images are used to deploy Windows 2000 Professional to computers that are commonly configured.

Preparing the RIS server involves the following steps:

1. Make sure that the server meets the requirements for running RIS.

2. Install RIS.

3. Configure and start RIS.

4. Authorize the RIS server through DHCP Manager.

5. Grant users who will perform RIS installations the user right to create computer accounts.

6. Grant users who will perform the RIS installation the Log On as a Batch Job user right.

7. Configure the RIS server to respond to client computers (if this was not configured when RIS was installed).

The following sections describe these steps.

There is a hands-on exercise to create an RIS server in *MCSE: Windows 2000 Server Study Guide,* by Lisa Donald with James Chellis (Sybex, 2000).

Meeting the RIS Server Requirements

In order for RIS to work, the computer that is acting as the RIS server must be a Windows 2000 domain controller or member server. The server on which you will install RIS must meet the hardware requirements for RIS and be able to access the required network services.

Hardware Requirements

The RIS server must meet the following hardware requirements:

- It must have the minimum processor (Pentium 133MHz or higher) and memory (128MB) required for Windows 2000 Server.

- It must have at least two disk partitions, one for the operating system and one for RIS images. The partition that will hold the RIS images should be at least 2GB and be formatted as NTFS.

- It needs to have a network adapter installed.

Network Services

The following network services must be running on the RIS server or be accessible to the RIS server from another network server:

- A Dynamic Host Configuration Protocol (DHCP) server, which is used to assign DHCP addresses to RIS clients

- A Domain Name System (DNS) server, which is used to locate the Active Directory

- The Active Directory, which is used to locate RIS servers and RIS clients, as well as to manage RIS configuration settings and client installation options

Installing the RIS Server

To install RIS on the RIS server, take the following steps:

1. Select Start ➢ Programs ➢ Administrative Tools ➢ Configure Your Server.

2. The Windows 2000 Configure Your Server dialog box appears, as shown in Figure 2.17. Click the Advanced option and select Optional Components.

FIGURE 2.17 The Windows 2000 Configure Your Server dialog box

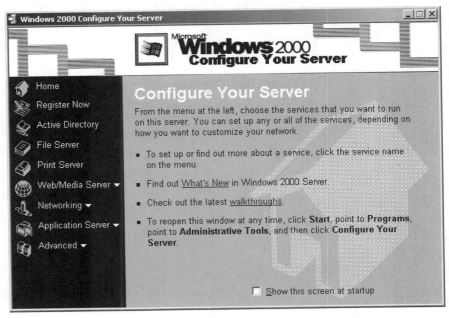

3. Click the Start the Windows Components Wizard option.

4. The Windows Components Wizard starts, as shown in Figure 2.18. Select the Remote Installation Services option and click the Next button.

FIGURE 2.18   The Windows Components Wizard

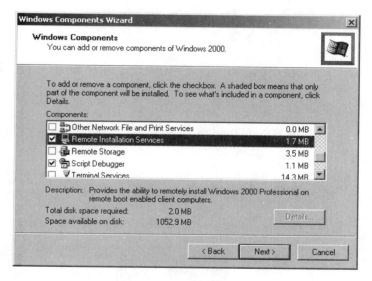

5. The Insert Disk dialog box prompts you to insert the Windows 2000 Server CD so that the proper files can be copied. Insert the CD and click the OK button.

6. After the process is complete, the Competing the Windows Components Wizard dialog box appears. Click the Finish button.

7. When you see the System Settings Change dialog box, click the Yes button to restart your computer.

As part of the RIS installation, the following services are loaded on the server:

- Boot Information Negotiation Layer (BINL), which is used to respond to client requests.

- Single Instance Store (SIS), which manages duplicate copies of images by replacing duplicate images with a link to the original files. The main purpose of this service is to reduce disk space.

- Trivial File Transfer Protocol (TFTP), which is the file transfer protocol that is used to download the Client Installation Wizard from the RIS server to the RIS clients.

These services are required for the RIS server to properly function.

Configuring and Starting RIS with a CD-Based Image

After you install RIS, you can configure the RIS server through the following steps:

1. Select Start ➢ Run, type **RISETUP** in the Run dialog box, and click the OK button.

2. The Remote Installation Services Setup Wizard starts, as shown in Figure 2.19. Click the Next button to continue.

FIGURE 2.19 The Welcome to the Remote Installation Services Setup Wizard dialog box

3. The Remote Installation Folder Location dialog box appears, as shown in Figure 2.20. This folder must be on an NTFS version 5 (or later) partition. This folder can't reside on the same partition as the system or boot partition. Specify the path of the remote installation folder and click the Next button.

FIGURE 2.20 The Remote Installation Folder Location dialog box

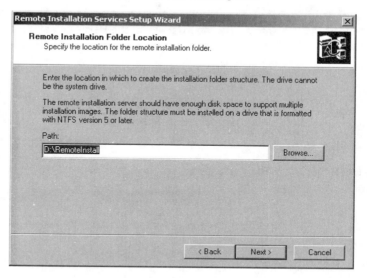

4. The Initial Settings dialog box appears, as shown in Figure 2.21. This dialog box allows you to configure client support during server configuration. You can specify that the server should respond to client computers requesting service and that it should not respond to unknown client computers. You can select one or both options, or leave them both unchecked and configure client support later. Make your selection(s) and click the Next button.

FIGURE 2.21 The Initial Settings dialog box

The instructions in this section describe how to use a CD-based image. To create an RIPrep image, run the Remote Installation Service Setup Wizard on a Windows 2000 Professional computer that has been configured to be used as an image.

5. The Installation Source Files Location dialog box appears, as shown in Figure 2.22. Specify the location of the Windows 2000 Professional distribution files and click the Next button.

FIGURE 2.22 The Installation Source Files Location dialog box

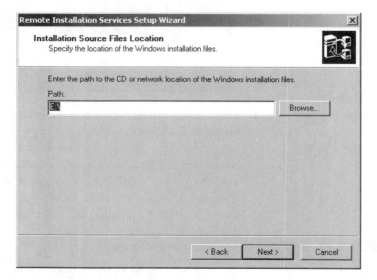

6. The Windows Installation Image Folder Name dialog box appears, as shown in Figure 2.23. Specify the name of the folder that will be used for the Windows 2000 Professional distribution files and click the Next button.

7. The Friendly Description and Help Text dialog box appears, as shown in Figure 2.24. This dialog box allows you to specify a friendly name and help text to help users select the Windows installation image. Enter a name and text, then click the Next button.

FIGURE 2.23   The Windows Installation Image Folder Name dialog box

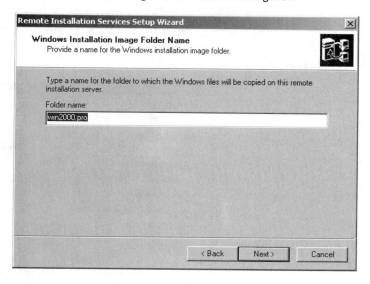

FIGURE 2.24   The Friendly Description and Help Text dialog box

8. The Review Settings dialog box appears, as shown in Figure 2.25. This dialog box allows you to confirm your installation choices. If all of the settings are correct, click the Finish button.

FIGURE 2.25 The Review Settings dialog box

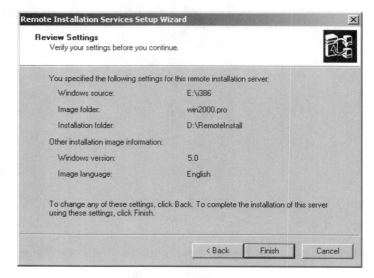

9. The installation files will be copied, which can take several minutes. When the process is complete, click the Done button.

Authorizing the RIS Server through DHCP Manager

In order for an RIS server to respond to client requests, the DHCP server must be authorized through the Active Directory. By authorizing DHCP servers, you ensure that rogue DHCP servers do not assign client IP addresses.

To authorize the DHCP server, take the following steps:

1. Select Start ➤ Programs ➤ Administrative Tools ➤ DHCP.

2. In the left pane of the DHCP window, right-click your DHCP server. From the pop-up menu, select Authorize, as shown in Figure 2.26.

FIGURE 2.26 Selecting to authorize a DHCP server

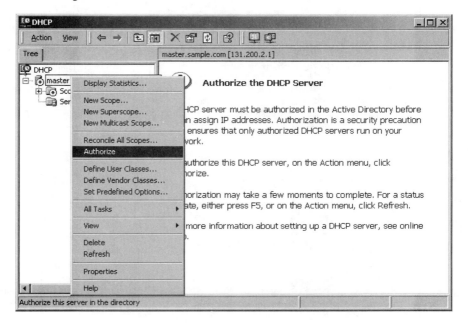

3. Close the DHCP console.

You'll learn more about DHCP in Chapter 11, "Managing Network Connections."

Granting the User Right to Create Computer Accounts

In order to install an image using RIS, users must have the user right to create a computer account in the Active Directory. You can specify that users can create accounts anywhere in the domain, or you can specify that users can create computer accounts only in specific organizational units.

To grant the user right to create computer accounts, take the following steps:

1. Select Start ➤ Programs ➤ Administrative Tools ➤ Active Directory Users and Computers.

2. The Active Directory Users and Computers window appears, as shown in Figure 2.27. Right-click the domain or organizational unit where you want to allow users to create computer accounts and select Delegate Control from the pop-up menu.

FIGURE 2.27 The Active Directory Users and Computers window

3. The Delegation of Control Wizard starts, as shown in Figure 2.28. Click the Next button.

FIGURE 2.28 The Welcome to the Delegation of Control Wizard dialog box

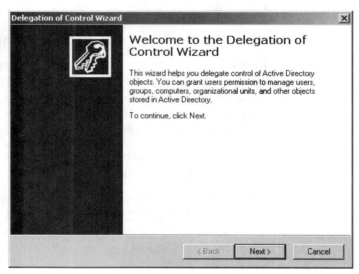

4. The Users or Groups dialog box appears, as shown in Figure 2.29. Click the Add button.

FIGURE 2.29 The Users or Groups dialog box

5. The Select Users, Computers, or Groups dialog box appears, as shown in Figure 2.30. Select the users or groups that will use RIS to install Windows 2000 Professional and click the Add button. Then click the OK button.

FIGURE 2.30 The Select Users, Computers, or Groups dialog box

6. You return to the Users or Groups dialog box. Click the Next button.

7. The Tasks to Delegate dialog box appears, as shown in Figure 2.31. Select the Join a Computer to the Domain check box and click the Next button.

FIGURE 2.31 The Tasks to Delegate dialog box

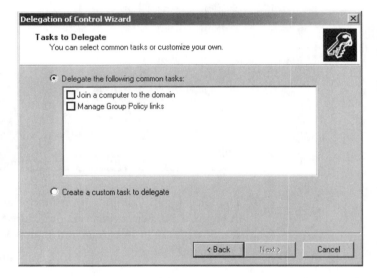

8. The Completing the Delegation of Control dialog box appears, as shown in Figure 2.32. If all of the configuration options are correct, click the Finish button.

9. Close the Active Directory Users and Computers window.

The Active Directory is covered in detail in *MCSE: Windows 2000 Directory Services Administration Study Guide,* by Anil Desai with James Chellis (Sybex, 2000).

FIGURE 2.32   The Completing the Delegation of Control Wizard dialog box

Granting the User Right to Log On as a Batch Job

The user account that will perform the remote installation must have the user right that allows logging on as a batch job. By default, the Administrators group does not have this user right. To assign the Log On as a Batch Job user right, take the following steps:

1. Add the Group Policy snap-in to the MMC administrator console. (The MMC and snap-ins are covered in Chapter 4, "Configuring the Windows 2000 Environment," and adding the Group Policy snap-in and assigning user rights are covered in Chapter 6, "Managing Users.")

2. Expand Local Computer Policy, Computer Configuration, Windows Settings, Security Settings,Local Policies, User Rights Assignment.

3. Double-click the Log On as a Batch Job user right.

4. The Local Security Policy Setting dialog box appears, as shown in Figure 2.33. Click the Add button.

FIGURE 2.33 The Local Security Policy Setting dialog box

5. The Select Users or Groups dialog box appears. Click the user or group you wish to assign this permission to and click the Add button. Click the OK button.

6. You will return to the Local Security Policy Setting dialog box. Click the OK button.

7. Close the MMC.

Configuring the RIS Server to Respond to Client Requests

The RIS server must be configured to respond to client requests. You can configure the server response as a part of the RIS server installation or later, after the RIS server is installed and ready for client requests. Take the following steps to configure the RIS server to respond to client requests:

1. Select Start ➤ Programs ➤ Administrative Tools ➤ Active Directory Users and Computers.

2. The Active Directory Users and Computers window appears (see Figure 2.27). Expand your domain and select Computers or Domain Controllers to access the computer that acts as your RIS server. Right-click the RIS server and select Properties from the pop-up menu.

3. The computer Properties dialog box appears. Select the Remote Install tab to see the dialog box shown in Figure 2.34.

FIGURE 2.34 The Remote Install tab of the computer Properties dialog box

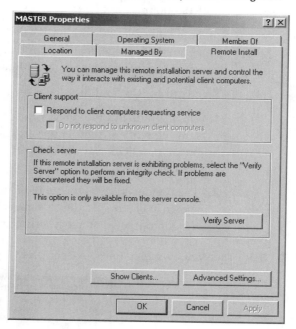

4. Check the Respond to Client Computers Requesting Service check box. Click the OK button.

5. Close the Active Directory Users and Computers window.

Preparing the RIS Client

The RIS client is the computer on which Windows 2000 Professional will be installed. RIS clients rely on a technology called PXE, which allows the client computer to remotely boot and connect to an RIS server.

In order to act as an RIS client, the computer must meet all of the hardware requirements for Windows 2000 Professional (see Chapter 1) and have a network adapter installed. In addition, the RIS client must support one of the following configurations:

- Use a PXE-based boot ROM (a boot ROM is a special chip that uses read-only memory) with a BIOS that supports starting the computer with the PXE-based boot ROM

- Have a network adapter that supports PXE that can be used with an RIS boot disk

- Follow the Net PC standard, which supports the ability to boot to the network, manage upgrades, and prevent users from changing hardware and operating system configurations

To create an RIS boot disk, take the following steps:

1. On a Windows 2000 Professional computer that is connected to the same network as the RIS server, select Start ➢ Run. In the Run dialog box, type **\\RIS_Server\Reminst\Admin\I386\Rbfg.exe** and click the OK button.

2. The Windows 2000 Remote Boot Disk Generator dialog box appears, as shown in Figure 2.35. Insert a blank floppy disk in your computer, select the appropriate destination drive, and click the Create Disk button.

FIGURE 2.35   The Windows 2000 Remote Boot Disk Generator dialog box

3. You see a message verifying that the boot floppy was created and asking whether or not you want to create another disk. Select Yes and repeat the procedure to create another boot disk, or click No. After you are finished creating RIS boot disks, click the Close button.

Installing Windows 2000 Professional through RIS

After the RIS server has been installed and configured, you can install Windows 2000 Professional on an RIS client that uses a PXE-compliant network card or an RIS boot disk with a network card that supports PXE.

To install Windows 2000 Professional on the RIS client, take the following steps:

1. Start the computer. When prompted, press F12 for a network service boot.

2. The Client Installation Wizard starts. Press Enter to continue.

3. The Windows 2000 Logon dialog box appears. Specify the domain you will log on to and enter a valid domain username and password.

4. A menu appears with the options Automatic Setup, Custom Setup, Restart a Previous Setup Attempt, or Maintenance and Troubleshooting. Select Automatic Setup.

5. If you have only one RIS image, it will automatically be installed. If you have multiple RIS images, the user will see a menu of RIS images to select from.

The remote installation process will start. What happens next depends on the image type and whether you have configured answer files.

Using Disk Images

You can use disk images to install Windows 2000 Professional on several computers that have the same configuration. Also, if a computer is having technical difficulties, you can use a disk image to quickly restore it to a baseline configuration.

Microsoft ✓ *Exam* *Objective*	**Perform an unattended installation of Windows 2000 Professional.** ▪ Install Windows 2000 Professional by using the System Preparation Tool.

In order to create a disk image, you install Windows 2000 Professional on the source computer with the configuration that you want to copy. The source computer's configuration should also include any applications that should be installed.

Once you have your source computer configured, you use the System Preparation Tool (Sysprep) to prepare the disk image for the disk duplication. After you've created the disk image, you can copy the image to destination computers through third-party software or through hardware disk duplication.

Preparing for Disk Duplication

In order to use a disk image, the source and target computers must meet the following requirements:

- The mass-storage controllers (SCSI or IDE) must be the same type on the source and destination computers.

- The HAL (Hardware Abstraction Layer) must be the same on the source and destination computers (this means that the processor type must be the same).

- The size of the destination computer's hard drive must be at least as large as the source computer's hard drive.

- Plug-and-Play devices on the source and destination computers do not need to match, as long as the drivers for the Plug-and-Play devices are available.

Using the System Preparation Tool

The System Preparation Tool is included on the Windows 2000 Professional CD in the \Support\Tools folder, in the Deploy.cab file. When you run this utility on the source computer, it strips out information from the master copy that must be unique for each computer, such as the security ID (SID).

After you install the copied image on the target computer, a Mini-Setup Wizard runs. This Wizard automatically creates a unique computer SID and then prompts the user for computer-specific information, such as the product ID, regional settings, and network configuration. The information that is required can also be supplied through an automated installation script. Some of the command switches that you can use to customize how the System Preparation Tool works include the following:

-quiet	Runs the installation with no user interaction
-pnp	Forces Setup to run Plug-and-Play detection of hardware
-reboot	Restarts the target computer
-nosidgen	Doesn't create an SID on the destination computer (used with disk cloning)

WARNING   After you run the System Preparation Tool on a computer, you need to run the Setup Manager Wizard to reconfigure all of the unique information for the computer. You should only run this utility on source reference computers that will be used for disk duplication purposes.

Creating a Disk Image

To run the System Preparation Tool and create a disk image, take the following steps:

1. Install Windows 2000 Professional on a source computer. (See Chapter 1 for instructions on installing Windows 2000 Professional.)

2. Log on to the source computer as Administrator, and if desired, install and configure any applications that also should be installed on the target computer.

3. Extract the Deploy.cab file from the Windows 2000 Professional CD. (See the "Extracting Windows 2000 Deployment Tools" section earlier in this chapter for instructions on extracting this file.)

4. Select Start ➢ Run and click the Browse button in the Run dialog box. Select Local Drive (C:), Deployment Tools, double-click Sysprep, and click the OK button.

5. The Windows 2000 System Preparation Tool dialog box appears, as shown in Figure 2.36. This dialog box warns you that the execution of this program will modify some of the security parameters of the computer. Click the OK button.

FIGURE 2.36 The Windows 2000 System Preparation Tool dialog box

6. You will be prompted to turn off your computer.

In Exercise 2.3, you will use the System Preparation Tool to prepare the computer for disk imaging. In Exercise 2.4, you will complete the Windows 2000 Professional installation on the target computer. This exercise assumes that you have completed Exercise 2.1.

EXERCISE 2.3

Using the System Preparation Tool

1. Log on to the source computer as Administrator, and if desired, install and configure any applications that also should be installed on the target computer.

2. Select Start ➤ Run and click the Browse button. Select Local Drive (C:), Deployment Tools. Double-click Sysprep and click the OK button.

3. In the Windows 2000 System Preparation Tool dialog box, click the OK button.

4. When prompted, turn off your computer.

Copying and Installing from a Disk Image

After you've run the System Preparation Tool on the source computer, you can copy the image and then install it on the target computer.

If you are using special hardware (a disk duplicator) to duplicate the disk image, shut down the source computer and remove the disk. Copy the disk and install the copied disk into the target computer. If you are using special software, copy the disk image per the software vendor's instructions.

After the image is copied, turn on the destination computer. The Mini-Setup Wizard runs and prompts the user as follows (if you have not configured an answer file):

- Accept the End User License Agreement

- Specify regional settings

- Enter a name and organization

- Specify your product key

- Specify the computer name and Administrator password

- Specify dialing information (if a modem is detected)

- Specify date and time settings

- Specify which networking protocols and services should be installed

- Join a workgroup or a domain

If you have created an answer file for use with disk images, as described in the "Using Setup Manager to Create Answer Files" section earlier in the chapter, the installation will run without requiring any user input.

In Exercise 2.4, you will use the stripped image that was created in Exercise 2.3 to simulate the process of continuing an installation from a disk image.

EXERCISE 2.4

Installing Windows 2000 Professional from a Disk Image

1. Turn on your computer. The Windows 2000 Setup Wizard will start. Click the Next button to continue (this will happen automatically if you don't click the Next button after about 10 seconds).

2. In the License Agreement dialog box, click the I Accept This Agreement option and click the Next button.

3. In the Regional Settings dialog box, click Next to accept the default settings and continue.

4. In the Personalize Your Software dialog box, enter your name and organization. Then click the Next button.

5. In the Your Product Key dialog box, type the 25-character product key and click the Next button.

6. In the Computer Name and Administrator Password dialog box, specify the computer name and an Administrator password (if desired). Then click the Next button.

7. If you have a modem installed, the Modem Dialing Information dialog box appears. Specify your dialing configuration and click the Next button.

8. In the Date and Time Settings dialog box, specify the date, time, and time zone. Then click the Next button.

9. In the Network Settings dialog box, verify that Typical Settings is selected and click the Next button.

10. In the Workgroup or Computer Domain dialog box, verify that the No, This Computer Is Not on a Network, or Is on a Network without a Domain Controller option is selected and click the Next button.

11. When the Completing the Windows 2000 Setup Wizard dialog box appears, click the Finish button.

12. When the computer restarts, start Windows 2000 Professional.

13. When the Network Identification Wizard starts, click the Next button.

14. In the Users of This Computer dialog box, select the Users Must Enter a User Name and Password to Use This Computer option and click the Next button.

15. When the Completing the Network Identification Wizard dialog box appears, click the Finish button.

16. Log on to the computer as Administrator.

Installing Applications with Windows Installer Packages

With Windows 2000, you can easily distribute new applications through *Windows Installer packages*, which are special application distribution files. In order to use Windows Installer packages, you must have a Windows 2000 server configured as a domain controller (so that the Active Directory is running).

Microsoft
✓ *Exam*
Objective

Install applications by using Windows Installer packages.

Windows Installer packages work with applications that are one of the following file types:

- *Microsoft Installer (MSI)* format files, which are usually provided by the software vendor and support features such as on-demand installation of features as users access those features.

- Repackaged applications (MSI files), which do not include the native Windows Installer packages. Repackaged applications are used to provide users with applications that can be easily deployed, perform self-diagnosis and repair, and can be cleanly installed.

- *ZAP* files, which are used if you do not have MSI files. ZAP files are used to install applications using their native Setup program.

If your application includes a modification tool, you can create customized application installations that include specific features of the application through the use of modification (.mst) files.

Windows Installer packages work as *published applications* or *assigned applications*. When you publish an application, users can choose whether or not they will install the application through the Control Panel Add/Remove Programs icon. When you assign an application to users or computers, the package is automatically installed when the user selects the application on the Programs menu or by document invocation (by the document extension).

The following are the main steps for using Windows Installer packages to distribute applications:

1. Copy the MSI application to a network share.

2. Create a Group Policy object (GPO) for the application.

3. Filter the GPO so only authorized users can access the application.

4. Add the package to the GPO.

5. If it is a published application, install it through the Control Panel Add/Remove Programs icon.

These steps are discussed in detail in the following sections.

Copying the MSI Application to a Share

As noted earlier, Windows Installer works with MSI applications. Applications that use the MSI standard will include a file with an .msi extension on the application's distribution media.

If you have applications that do not use MSI, you can still deploy them by creating your own MSI file. To help you create your own MSI file, Microsoft provides VERITAS Software Console and WinINSTALL Discover. This software is available in the *Microsoft Windows 2000 Server Resource Kit* (Microsoft Press, 2000).

You need to create a network share that will be used to store the application and copy the .msi file to the network share. As an example, we'll use Windows 2000 Server Administrative Tools as the sample application that we want to distribute. You would copy the application file named Adminpak.msi from the Windows 2000 Server CD \I386 folder to the D:\Packages\AdminTools folder on the Windows 2000 Server domain controller, as shown in Figure 2.37. In this example, the Packages folder is shared.

FIGURE 2.37   An MSI application copied to a network share

Creating a Group Policy Object

Your next step in preparing an application for distribution is to create a GPO on a Windows 2000 Server domain controller. To create a GPO, take the following steps:

1. Select Start ➤ Programs ➤ Administrative Tools ➤ Active Directory Users and Computers.

2. Right-click your domain name and select Properties from the pop-up menu. Click the Group Policy tab.

3. The Group Policy tab of the domain Properties dialog box appears, as shown in Figure 2.38. Click the New button.

FIGURE 2.38 The Group Policy tab of the domain Properties dialog box

4. A new Group Policy object will be created. Specify the new GPO name (in this example, **AdminTools**).

Filtering the Group Policy Object

After you've created the GPO, you need to filter it so that only authorized users will be able to install the application. To filter a GPO, take the following steps:

1. In the Group Policy tab of the domain Properties dialog box (see Figure 2.38), highlight the package you created and click the Properties button.

2. The Default Domain Policy Properties dialog box appears. Click the Security tab. Remove permissions from all groups except Domain Admins. For the Domain Admins group allow the Read, Write, Create All Child Objects, Delete All Child Objects, and Apply Group Policy permissions (by checking the Allow box), as shown in Figure 2.39.

FIGURE 2.39 The Security tab of the Default Domain Policy Properties dialog box

3. Click the OK button to close the Default Domain Policy Properties dialog box.

Adding the Package to the Group Policy Object

Finally, you need to add the package to the GPO you created for it. You can configure the package so that it is published or assigned to a user or a computer. Published applications are advertised through the Add/Remove Programs utility. Assigned applications are advertised through the Programs menu.

If you are configuring the package for a user, you add the package to the User Configuration\Software Settings\Software installation. If the package is for a computer, you add it to the User Configuration\Software Settings\ Software installation. In this example, the application will be published for users. To publish an application, take the following steps:

1. In the Group Policy tab of the domain Properties dialog box (see Figure 2.38), highlight the package and click the Edit button.

2. The Group Policy window appears, as shown in Figure 2.40. Expand User Configuration, then Software Settings. Right-click Software Installation and select New ➤ Package.

FIGURE 2.40 The Group Policy window

Specify the location of the software package and click the Open button.

3. The Deploy Software dialog box appears, as shown in Figure 2.41. Specify the deployment method. The options are Published, Assigned, or Advanced Published or Assigned. For this example, select Published. Then click the OK button.

FIGURE 2.41 The Deploy Software dialog box

If you have access to a Windows 2000 domain controller, you can complete the steps in Exercise 2.5 to publish an application. You will also need to have access to the Windows 2000 Server CD.

EXERCISE 2.5

Publishing an Application with Windows Installer

1. Select Start ➢ Programs ➢ Accessories ➢ Windows Explorer.

2. In Windows Explorer, double-click My Computer and double-click Local Disk (C:). Select File ➢ New ➢ Folder and type in the name **AdminTools**.

3. Insert the Windows 2000 Server CD and copy the application file named I386\Adminpak.msi from the CD to the C:\AdminTools folder. Right-click the AdminTools folder and select Sharing. Select the Share This Folder option and click the OK button.

4. Select Start ➢ Programs ➢ Administrative Tools ➢ Active Directory Users and Computers.

5. In the Active Directory Users and Computers window, right-click your domain name and select Properties. Click the Group Policy tab. Click the New button and enter the name **AdminTools**.

EXERCISE 2.5 *(continued)*

6. Highlight the AdminTools package and click the Properties button. Click the Security tab. Remove permissions from all groups except Domain Admins. For the Domain Admins group allow the Read, Write, Create All Child Objects, Delete All Child Objects, and Apply Group Policy permissions (by checking the Allow boxes). Click the OK button.

7. Highlight the AdminTools package and click the Edit button. Expand User Configuration, then Software Settings. Right-click Software Installation and select New ➢ Package.

8. Specify the network location (based on your computer name and the share name) of the software package and click the Open button.

9. In the Deploy Software dialog box, specify the deployment method Published, then click the OK button.

Installing a Published Application

After the application (package) has been published, users who have permission to access the application can install it on a Windows 2000 Professional computer that is a part of the same domain that contains the application. The published application is available through the Add/Remove Programs icon in the Control Panel. In the Add/Remove Programs utility, click the Add New Programs option, and you will see the published application listed in the dialog box. Select the application and click the Add button to install it.

If you completed Exercise 2.5, you can follow the steps in Exercise 2.6 to install the published application.

EXERCISE 2.6

Installing a Published Application

1. Log on to a Windows 2000 Professional computer that is a part of the domain that contains the published application. Log on as a user who has permission to access the application.

2. Select Start ➢ Settings ➢ Control Panel. Double-click the Add/Remove Programs icon, then click the Add New Programs option.

3. The published application (AdminTools) is listed in the dialog box. To install the application, highlight it and click the Add button.

Summary

In this chapter, you learned how to install Windows 2000 Professional through automated installation. We covered the following topics:

- An overview of the three common methods for automated installation, which include remote installation, disk imaging, and unattended installations

- How to use unattended answer files to automatically respond to the queries that are generated during a normal installation process

- How to use RIS, including how to install and configure the RIS server as well as the requirements for the RIS clients

- How to create disk images using the System Preparation Tool (Sysprep)

- How to install applications through Windows Installer packages

Key Terms

Before taking the exam, you should be familiar with the following terms:

answer file

assigned applications

disk imaging

Microsoft Installer (MSI)

Pre-Boot Execution Environment (PXE)

published applications

remote installation

Remote Installation Services (RIS)

Setup Manager (SETUPMGR)

System Preparation Tool (Sysprep)

unattended installation

Windows Installer packages

ZAP files

Review Questions

1. What are the two types of images that can be stored on an RIS server?

   A. CD-based

   B. ROM-based

   C. RIS-based

   D. RIPrep

2. Which of the following services is not required to be running in order to support the RIS server?

   A. DNS

   B. WINS

   C. DHCP

   D. Active Directory

3. What command is used to configure the RIS server?

   A. RIPREP

   B. RISCONFIG

   C. RISETUP

   D. The Control Panel, RIS icon

4. What requirement must be met on a client computer in order to install Windows 2000 Professional from an RIS server? Choose two answers.

   A. The computer must use a PXE-based boot ROM.

   B. The computer must use an RIPrep-based boot ROM.

   C. The computer must use an RIS boot disk with any network adapter that supports RIPrep.

   D. The computer must use an RIS boot disk with a network adapter that supports PXE.

5. What command is used to generate an RIS boot disk?

    A. RBFG

    B. PXEBOOT

    C. RIPREP

    D. RISBOOT

6. What program is used to create unattended answer files?

    A. UAF

    B. Answer Manager

    C. Setup Manager

    D. Sysprep

7. What utility is used to prepare a disk image that can be used to install Windows 2000 Professional?

    A. UAF

    B. Image Manager

    C. Setup Manager

    D. Sysprep

8. Where can you find the Windows 2000 Deployment Tools on the Windows 2000 Professional CD?

    A. \Support\Tools\Deploy.cab

    B. \Deployment\Deploy.cab

    C. \Support\Support.cab

    D. \Support\Tools\Support.cab

9. What standards are supported to install applications with the Windows Installer packages? Choose two answers.

    A. ZAP files

    B. APP files

    C. MSI files

    D. ISM files

10. Which of the following services is required in order to use Windows Installer packages?

    A. DHCP

    B. WINS

    C. Installer

    D. Active Directory

11. You want to install the Windows 2000 Deployment Tools and have accessed the appropriate `.cab` file. What command do you use to access the contents of the `.cab` file?

    A. Expand

    B. Unzip

    C. Extract

    D. Uncompress

12. Which of the following automated installation options use unattended answer files? Choose three answers.

    A. Unattended installations

    B. RIS installations

    C. Extracted installations

    D. System Preparation Tool disk images

13. Which of the following options is *not* an advantage of using an RIS automated installation?

    A. The Windows 2000 security is retained when you restart the computer.

    B. Plug-and-Play hardware detection is used during the installation process.

    C. Unique information is stripped out of the installation image so that it can be copied to other computers.

    D. You can quickly recover the operating system in the event of a system failure.

14. Which of the following options is *not* an advantage of using disk images with the System Preparation Tool?

   A. The Windows 2000 security is retained when you restart the computer.

   B. Plug-and-Play hardware detection is used during the installation process.

   C. Unique information is stripped out of the installation image so that it can be copied to other computers.

   D. You can quickly recover the operating system in the event of system failure.

15. You want to install an RIS server to be used to deploy Windows 2000 Professional. Which of the following options is *not* a requirement for configuring the RIS server?

   A. The remote installation folder must be NTFS version 5 or later.

   B. The remote installation folder must reside on the system partition.

   C. You need to configure the RIS server through the `RISETUP` command.

   D. The DHCP server must be authorized through the Active Directory.

16. Which utility would you use to configure the RIS server to respond to client requests?

   A. Active Directory Users and Computers

   B. Active Directory Users and Groups

   C. RIS Manager

   D. RISMAN

17. Which of the following options is *not* associated with using disk images with the Sysprep utility?

    A. Disk imaging requires that you have third-party software or hardware to complete the disk-duplication process.

    B. The System Preparation Tool is used to strip out unique information about the computer.

    C. When the computer with the duplicated disk starts, a Mini-Setup Wizard is run to finish the computer's configuration.

    D. You can configure the computer through an RIPrep image.

18. Which Sysprep command-line switch would you use if you did not want to create a new SID on the destination computer?

    A. `-nosid`

    B. `-nosidgen`

    C. `-skipsid`

    D. `-quiet`

19. What types of files are used with Windows Installer packages when you don't have vendor-supplied Microsoft Installer files and will install applications using their native setup program?

    A. ZAW files

    B. ZIP files

    C. ZAP files

    D. MSI files

20. What types of files can be used with Windows Installer packages to create customized application installations that include specific application features?

    A. MSI files

    B. ZAP files

    C. ZAW files

    D. MST files

Answers to Review Questions

1. A, D. You can store CD-based images, which contain the operating system installation files, and RIPrep images, which are fully configured images, on RIS servers.

2. B. DNS, DHCP, and the Active Directory must be properly configured and running in order for RIS to work.

3. C. The RISETUP command is used to configure the RIS server.

4. A, D. In order to act as an RIS client, the client computer must have a PXE-based boot ROM or an RIS boot disk with a network adapter that supports PXE.

5. A. You can create an RIS boot disk from any Windows 2000 computer by attaching to *RIS_Server*\reminst\admin\i386 and running the Rbfg.exe command.

6. C. Setup Manager (SETUPMGR) is used to create unattended answer files.

7. D. The Sysprep utility is used to prepare a disk image that can be used to install Windows 2000 Professional.

8. A. You can find the Windows 2000 Deployment Tools on the Windows 2000 Professional folder in \Support\Tools\Deploy.cab

9. A, C. In order to use Windows Installer packages, you must have a Microsoft Installer (MSI) file or a ZAP file.

10. D. You must have the Active Directory installed to use Windows Installer packages.

11. C. To access the contents of a .cab file, you use the Extract command on Windows Explorer's File menu.

12. A, B, D. When you run the Setup Manager to create unattended answer files, you have the option of creating answer files for unattended installations, Sysprep, or RIS installations.

13. C. Unique information is stripped out of the installation image when you use the System Preparation Tool to create a disk image.

14. A. Windows 2000 security is not retained when you use the System Preparation Tool. You actually see a dialog box warning you of this before the Sysprep program will proceed.

15. B. When you configure your RIS server, the remote installation folder can't be on the system partition.

16. A. You enable RIS servers to respond to client requests through the Active Directory Users and Computers utility. In the Remote Install tab of the RIS server Properties dialog box, check or uncheck the Respond to Client Computers Requesting Service check box.

17. D. RIPrep images are associated with an RIS server and are not used with disk duplication and the System Preparation Tool.

18. B. The -nosidgen switch prevents SID generation.

19. C. ZAP files are used if you don't have MSI files. ZAP files are used to install applications using their native setup programs.

20. D. MST (modification) files are used to customize Windows Installer packages that include specific application features.

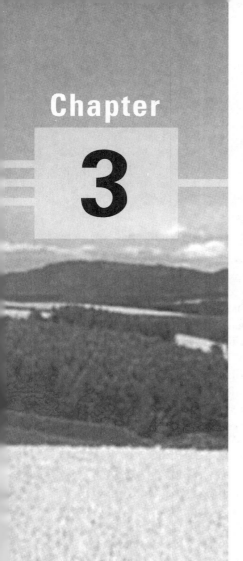

Chapter 3

Upgrading to Windows 2000 Professional

MICROSOFT EXAM OBJECTIVES COVERED IN THIS CHAPTER

✓ **Upgrade from a previous version of Windows to Windows 2000 Professional.**

- Apply update packs to installed software applications.
- Prepare a computer to meet upgrade requirements.

Before you attempt to upgrade Windows 2000 Professional, you need to understand the difference between an upgrade and a clean installation. If your previous operating system can be upgraded to Windows 2000 Professional and you want to retain your system settings, then you choose to perform an upgrade. If your operating system does not support a Windows 2000 upgrade or if you want to start from scratch, then you choose to perform a clean installation. Client upgrade paths and requirements are used to determine if your operating system can be upgraded to Windows 2000 Professional. In order to upgrade, you must be running Windows 9x or Windows NT 3.51 or 4, and your hardware must meet the minimum requirements. This chapter covers the requirements for upgrading to Windows 2000 Professional.

You also should consider possible upgrade problems or known issues. This is especially important if you are upgrading from Windows 9x, because the upgrading process is not as smooth as it is when you are starting from a Windows NT system. An example of an upgrade issue is lack of support in Windows 2000 for applications or utilities that use virtual device drivers. You'll find a discussion of these issues in this chapter.

There are several tasks you should perform to prepare your computer before you start the upgrade process. This chapter provides an upgrade checklist to help you plan your upgrade strategy. Some of the items in the upgrade checklist include deleting any unnecessary files or applications and taking an inventory of your computer's configuration.

Finally, after you've made your preparations, you are ready for the big moment. Here, you will learn about all of the steps involved in the Windows 2000 upgrade process.

Upgrade packs are used to make any changes to your Windows 9*x* or Windows NT applications that are required to make the application work properly in Windows 2000. The final section of this chapter describes how to apply upgrade packs.

The upgrade process for Windows 2000 Professional and Server is extremely similar. The major differences involve the client upgrade paths and hardware requirements.

Deciding Whether to Upgrade

An upgrade allows you to preserve existing settings. A clean install places Windows 2000 in a new folder. After a fresh install, you need to reinstall all of your applications and reset your preferences.

You should perform an upgrade if the following conditions are true:

- You are running Windows 9*x* or Windows NT Workstation 3.51 or 4.

- You want to keep your existing applications and preferences.

- You want to preserve any local users and groups you've created under Windows NT.

- You want to upgrade your current operating system with the Windows 2000 operating system.

You should perform a clean install if any of the following conditions are true:

- There is no operating system currently installed.

- You have an operating system installed that does not support an upgrade to Windows 2000 (such as DOS or Windows 3.*x*).

- You want to start from scratch, without keeping any existing preferences.

- You want to be able to dual-boot between Windows 2000 and your previous operating system.

Performing a clean install and dual-booting are covered in detail in Chapter 1, "Getting Started with Windows 2000 Professional."

Preparing to Upgrade to Windows 2000 Professional

Like any other major change to your computer, upgrading to Windows 2000 Professional requires some preparatory steps.

Microsoft ✓ *Exam* *Objective*

Upgrade from a previous version of Windows to Windows 2000 Professional.

- Apply update packs to installed software applications.
- Prepare a computer to meet upgrade requirements.

Getting ready to upgrade to Windows 2000 Professional involves the following steps:

- Make sure that your system meets the operating system and hardware requirements.
- Consider upgrade issues, particularly if you're upgrading from Windows 95 or 98.
- Use an upgrade checklist to plan for the upgrade.

These preparations are discussed in detail in the following sections.

Client Upgrade Paths and Requirements

In order to upgrade to Windows 2000 Professional, you must follow a particular path. Only the following operating systems can be directly upgraded to Windows 2000 Professional:

- Windows 95 (all releases)
- Windows 98 (all releases)
- Windows NT Workstation 3.51
- Windows NT Workstation 4

There is no upgrade path from Windows NT Server to Windows 2000 Professional.

If you are running a version of Windows NT Workstation prior to 3.51, you first need to upgrade to Windows NT Workstation 3.51 or Windows NT Workstation 4. Then you can upgrade to Windows 2000 Professional. You cannot upgrade to Windows 2000 Professional from any version of Windows NT Server.

The hardware requirements for upgrading are the same as those for a clean installation. In order to upgrade to Windows 2000 Professional, your computer hardware must meet the following requirements:

- Pentium 133MHz or higher processor

- 64MB of RAM (more memory is recommended)

- 2GB hard drive with at least 650MB of free disk space

- VGA or better resolution monitor

Along with meeting these requirements, your hardware should be listed on the Hardware Compatibility List (HCL). See Chapter 1 for more information about the HCL.

The hardware requirements listed here were those specified at the time this book was published. Check Microsoft's Web site at http://www.microsoft.com/windows2000/upgrade/ for the most current information.

Upgrade Considerations for Windows 9*x*

The upgrade to Windows 2000 Professional from Windows NT is a smoother process than it is from Windows 9*x*. This is because the Windows NT and Windows 2000 structures have more in common than the Windows 9*x* and Windows 2000 structures do. Therefore, upgrading from Windows 9*x* requires more planning and testing than upgrading from Windows NT.

Compatibility Problems

To assist you in the upgrade process, the Windows 2000 Setup program provides a "report-only" mode, which generates compatibility reports and stores them in a central location. You can then analyze these reports to determine whether your hardware or software applications port properly from Windows 9x to Windows 2000 Professional.

You can generate the Windows 2000 compatibility report in three ways:

- Run Winnt32 /checkupgradeonly, which will launch the Windows 2000 Setup program, but will only run enough of the setup procedure to generate the compatibility report.

- Run the Chkupgrd.exe program. This program can be downloaded from http://www.microsoft.com/windows/downloads/ default.asp.

- A compatibility report is automatically generated as part of the Windows 2000 upgrade process.

If any of your applications are not compatible with Windows 2000, you may be able to get software that the software vendor has written to make the application work. This software is in the form of a migration DLL (dynamic link library), which is implemented in an upgrade pack. Upgrade packs are discussed in more detail later in this chapter, in the "Applying Update Packs" section. If an upgrade pack is not available, you will need to get a version of the application that will work with Windows 2000 Professional.

Unsupported Options

Although Windows 9x can be upgraded to Windows 2000 Professional, you should be aware that the following options are not supported through the upgrade process:

Applications that use file-system filters, such as third-party anti-virus software and disk-quota management software These types of file-system filters won't work under Windows 2000. You should contact vendors who use file-system filters for upgraded software supported by Windows 2000 Professional.

Any custom power-management solutions or tools Custom power-management solutions are no longer used, because these features are added through Windows 2000 Advanced Configuration and Power Interface (ACPI) and Advanced Power Management (APM). You should remove any custom power-management solutions or tools prior to running the upgrade process. (The ACPI and APM are covered in Chapter 4, "Configuring the Windows 2000 Environment.")

Any custom Plug-and-Play solutions Custom Plug-and-Play solutions are no longer used, because Windows 2000 has a full set of Plug-and-Play features. You should remove any custom Plug-and-Play solutions before starting the upgrade process.

Third-party applications for Windows 9x that support compressed drives, disk defragmenters, and disk utilities These are not supported by Windows 2000 because it offers native support for disk compression and disk defragmentation (which are discussed in Chapter 9, "Managing Disks"). If you want to use third-party utilities, you should contact the vendor to get an upgrade of your application that has been written specifically for Windows 2000. If the application can't be upgraded to a Windows 2000–specific version, you should remove the utility prior to running the upgrade process.

Any applications or utilities that use virtual device drivers (VxDs) or 386 drivers Older 16-bit drivers for Windows 9x were based on VxDs. VxD drivers are not compatible with the Windows 2000 operating system. You can determine if you are using these drivers by checking the [386Enh] section of the System.ini file. Some device drivers use VxDs to provide property pages in property dialog boxes. If you want to continue to use these applications or utilities, you should contact the vendor to get an upgrade of your application or utility that has been written specifically for Windows 2000.

An Upgrade Checklist

Once you have made the decision to upgrade, you should develop a plan of attack. The following upgrade checklist (valid for upgrading from both Windows 9x and NT) will help you plan and implement a successful upgrade strategy.

- Back up all of your data and configuration files and verify that you can successfully restore your backup. Before you make any major changes to your computer's configuration, you should back up your data and configuration files. Chances are if you have a valid backup, you won't have any problems. Chances are if you don't have a valid backup, you will have problems.

- Delete any unnecessary files or applications, and clean up any program groups or program items you don't use. Theoretically, you want to delete all of the junk on your computer before you upgrade. Think of this as the spring-cleaning step.

- Perform a disk scan, a current virus scan, and defragmentation. These are also similar to spring-cleaning chores. This step just prepares your drive for the upgrade. You should verify that there are no problems with your drive prior to the upgrade.

- Uncompress any partitions that have been compressed with DriveSpace or DoubleSpace. You cannot upgrade partitions that are currently compressed.

- Verify that your computer meets the requirements for an upgrade. Be sure that your computer meets the minimum hardware requirements for Windows 2000 Professional and that all of your hardware is on the HCL.

- Take an inventory of your current configuration. This inventory should include documentation of your current network configuration, the applications that are installed, the hardware items and their configuration, the services that are running, and any profile and policy settings.

- Perform the upgrade. In this step, you upgrade from your previous operating system to Windows 2000 Professional.

- Verify your configuration. After Windows 2000 Professional has been installed, use your inventory to verify that the upgrade was successful.

Performing the Windows 2000 Upgrade

As you would expect, the process of upgrading to Windows 2000 is much simpler than performing a clean installation (as we did in Chapter 1). You pick the system from which you are upgrading, then follow the Setup Wizard's instructions to provide the information the Setup program needs. The final steps in the upgrade process are automatic.

The following steps are used in the Windows 2000 Professional upgrade process:

1. Start your current operating system, and insert the Windows 2000 Professional CD into your CD-ROM drive. If auto-play is turned on, you see an upgrade dialog box, as shown in Figure 3.1. If your computer does not automatically bring up the upgrade dialog box, select Start ➤ Run ➤ Browse. (From Windows NT Workstation 3.51, open Program Manager and choose File ➤ Run ➤ Browse.) Then select your CD-ROM drive, open the I386 folder, and launch WINNT32.

FIGURE 3.1 The Windows 2000 Professional upgrade dialog box

2. The Welcome to the Windows 2000 Setup Wizard dialog box appears, as shown in Figure 3.2. Click the Upgrade to Windows 2000 (Recommended) option, then click the Next button.

FIGURE 3.2 The Welcome to Windows 2000 Setup Wizard dialog box

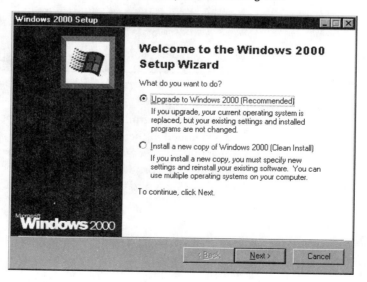

3. The License Agreement dialog box appears. Click the option to accept the agreement. (The upgrade will terminate if you do not accept the agreement.)

4. The Product Key dialog box appears. Type in the 25-character product key, which you can find on the back of the Windows 2000 Professional jewel case. Click the Next button.

5. You see the Preparing to Upgrade to Windows 2000 dialog box, as shown in Figure 3.3. This window informs you that Setup will prompt you for upgrade files, search for incompatible items, and generate an Upgrade Report. Click Next to continue.

FIGURE 3.3 The Preparing to Upgrade to Windows 2000 dialog box

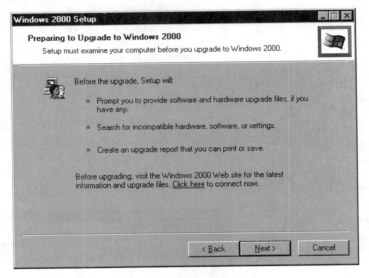

6. The Provide Upgrade Packs dialog box appears, as shown in Figure 3.4. As explained in the next section, upgrade packs are used with applications that worked with your previous operating system but need to be upgraded to work with Windows 2000. Select whether or not you have upgrade packs and click the Next button.

FIGURE 3.4 The Provide Upgrade Packs dialog box

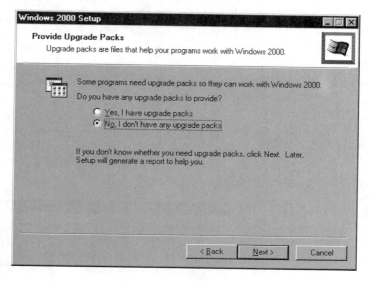

7. If your computer has FAT16 or FAT32 partitions, you see the Upgrading to the Windows 2000 NTFS File System dialog box, as shown in Figure 3.5. This dialog box allows you to convert your existing file system to NTFS. Chapter 1 contains information that will help you determine whether you should convert your file system. Make your selection and click the Next button.

FIGURE 3.5 Upgrading to the Windows 2000 NTFS File System dialog box

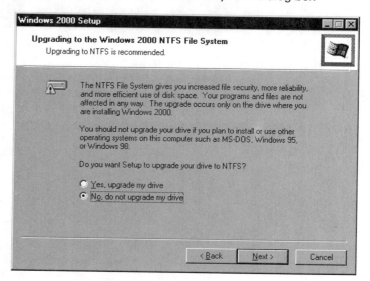

8. The Setup program now generates an *Upgrade Report*. This report summarizes any known compatibility issues that you might encounter during the upgrade. The purpose of this report is to help you minimize any errors that will occur from the upgrade process. If any errors are found, you can save the report as a file or print the report. If you are lucky, you will see the dialog box shown in Figure 3.6. You can click the Next button to continue. If the report indicates that there are problems that you might want to resolve prior to the upgrade, back out of the upgrade process. You can start over after you've resolved the problems.

FIGURE 3.6   The Upgrade Report dialog box

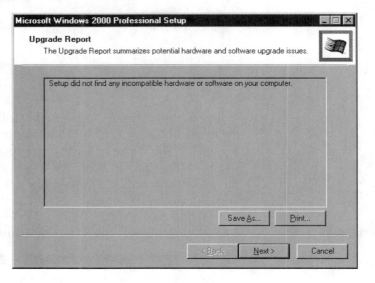

9. The next dialog box, Ready to Install Windows 2000, is shown in Figure 3.7. This dialog box informs you that the next part of the installation is automatic and will take 75 to 90 minutes with three restarts. Click the Next button to continue.

The actual amount of time the process takes varies with specific hardware and software configurations. For example, in my test lab, the installation took about 45 minutes.

FIGURE 3.7 The Ready to Install Windows 2000 dialog box

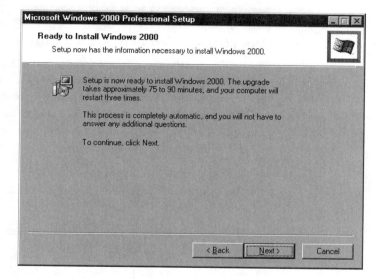

Now you can just sit back and relax while the Setup program performs the rest of the upgrade automatically. When the process is complete, Windows 2000 Professional will be installed on your computer. At this point, it's a good idea to verify that everything was upgraded properly. Using the inventory you made before upgrading (see the "Upgrade Checklist" section earlier in the chapter), check that your hardware and software has made it through the transition and are working properly.

Exercise 3.1 shows the steps for upgrading to Windows 2000 Professional. To set up your computer to be used for the exercises in this book, you installed Windows 2000 Professional from scratch in Chapter 1. You would follow the steps in Exercise 3.1 if you were upgrading from your current operating system, and you had not performed the clean install procedure outlined in Exercise 1.1.

NOTE For the purpose of studying for the MSCE exam with this book, it is recommended that you install Windows 2000 Professional as outlined in Exercise 1.1. If you perform an upgrade instead, you may not be able to successfully complete some of the other exercises in this book.

EXERCISE 3.1

Upgrading to Windows 2000 Professional

1. Insert the Windows 2000 Professional CD into your CD-ROM drive. When the upgrade dialog box appears, click Yes to upgrade. If necessary, select Start ➤ Run ➤ Browse (from Windows NT Workstation 3.51, open Program Manager and select File ➤ Run ➤ Browse), select your CD-ROM drive, open the I386 folder, and launch WINNT32 to bring up the upgrade dialog box.

2. In the Welcome to the Windows 2000 Setup Wizard dialog box, click the Upgrade to Windows 2000 (Recommended) option. Click the Next button to continue.

3. In the License Agreement dialog box, click the option to accept the agreement.

4. In the Product Key dialog box, type in your 25-character product key. Then click the Next button.

5. In the Preparing to Upgrade to Windows 2000 dialog box, click Next to continue.

6. In the Provide Upgrade Packs dialog box, select the Yes, I Have Upgrade Packs option if you have obtained upgrade packs for any third-party software applications. Otherwise, select No, I Don't Have Any Upgrade Packs. Then click the Next button.

7. The Upgrading to the Windows 2000 NTFS File System dialog box appears if your computer has FAT16 or FAT32 partitions. Select the No, Do Not Upgrade My Drive option. (You will upgrade to NTFS in an exercise in Chapter 9.) Then click the Next button.

> **EXERCISE 3.1** *(continued)*
>
> 8. The Upgrade Report dialog box appears. If the report shows that errors were found, click the Save As button and specify the filename and location. Click the Next button to continue.
>
> 9. In the Ready to Install Windows 2000 dialog box, click the Next button. The upgrade process continues automatically, and Windows 2000 Professional will be installed on your computer.

Applying Update Packs

Theoretically, any applications that you had installed on your previous operating system should work with the upgraded operating system. The upgrade process is supposed to keep all of the program groups, and you shouldn't need to reinstall applications to have them work.

Microsoft ✓ *Exam Objective*

Upgrade from a previous version of Windows to Windows 2000 Professional.

- Apply update packs to installed software applications.
- Prepare a computer to meet upgrade requirements.

In the real world, it's possible that some applications will not upgrade properly. In the worst case, the applications will disappear after the upgrade, and you will need to reinstall the application (as sometimes occurred with Windows NT upgrades). Some of the reasons that applications do not upgrade properly include the following:

- The configuration information needs to be stored in a different part of the Registry than the part that was used for Windows NT or Windows 9x.

- The Registry values used by Windows NT or Windows 9x are different from the Registry values that are required by Windows 2000.

- Different versions of files (for example, `.dll` or `.exe`) may be required for the application to work properly in Windows 2000.

- The application may make calls specific to the Windows 9*x* operating system that are not supported in Windows 2000.

If a Windows 9*x* application makes direct calls to the hardware, it may need to be rewritten to work properly with Windows 2000. Windows NT and Windows 2000 do not allow applications to directly access the hardware.

Microsoft recommends that application developers test their applications for Windows 2000 upgrade compatibility. Some applications will upgrade without any problems, but other applications will need help to upgrade smoothly. For third-party software, this help comes in the form of a migration DLL, which is implemented as an upgrade pack (called an update pack in the test objectives) in Windows 2000. Third-party vendors may supply migration DLLs through their company's Web site or by distributing disks or CDs to registered users of the applications.

When you run the upgrade process, Windows 2000 should detect any applications that are installed. If any migration DLLs have been installed, they will be applied automatically. You can also specify that upgrade packs be applied during the upgrade process (see Figure 3.4, shown earlier in this chapter).

Summary

In this chapter, you learned how to upgrade to Windows 2000 Professional. We covered the following topics:

- Guidelines for when you should upgrade and when you should install a fresh copy of Windows 2000 Professional

- The client upgrade paths that can upgrade to Windows 2000 Professional and the minimum hardware requirements to perform an upgrade

- Upgrade considerations and potential problems with the Windows 2000 Professional upgrade process

- An upgrade checklist with steps to help ensure a successful upgrade

- All of the steps in the Windows 2000 Professional upgrade process

- How to apply update packs to software applications so that they work under Windows 2000 Professional

Key Terms

Before you take the exam, be sure you're familiar with the following key terms:

clean install

upgrade

upgrade pack

Upgrade Report

Review Questions

1. Which of the following operating systems can be upgraded to Windows 2000 Professional? Choose all that apply.

   A. Windows NT Workstation 3.5

   B. Windows NT Workstation 3.51

   C. Windows NT Workstation 4

   D. Windows 95

2. Which of the following operating systems offers the smoothest upgrade to Windows 2000 Professional?

   A. Windows 95

   B. Windows 98

   C. Windows NT Workstation 4

   D. Windows NT Server 4

3. Which of the following options cannot be upgraded from Windows 95 to Windows 2000 Professional? Choose all that apply.

   A. Any applications that run under Windows 95 and are not specifically written for Windows 2000 Professional

   B. Third-party drivers that support compressed drives

   C. Third-party applications that use virtual device drivers (VxDs)

   D. Any custom power-management solutions or tools

4. Which command is used to start an upgrade to Windows 2000 Professional from a Windows 95 computer that does not have auto-run enabled?

   A. WIN2K

   B. INSTALL

   C. WINNT

   D. WINNT32

5. Which command is used to start an upgrade to Windows 2000 Professional from a Windows NT 4 computer?

   A. WIN2K

   B. INSTALL

   C. WINNT

   D. WINNT32

6. Which option is used to tell applications that were previously installed how to be configured so that they will work with Windows 2000 Professional after an upgrade?

   A. DLL packs

   B. Upgrade packs

   C. Application packs

   D. UPG packs

7. How much memory is required on a Windows 95 computer that will be upgraded to Windows 2000 Professional?

   A. 16MB

   B. 32MB

   C. 64MB

   D. 128MB

8. Which of the following partitions will Windows 2000 recognize during an upgrade? Choose all that apply.

   A. FAT16

   B. HPFS

   C. NTFS

   D. FAT32

9. Which of the following operating systems would most likely require the use of update packs during the upgrade to Windows 2000 Professional? Choose all that apply.

A. Windows 95

B. Windows 98

C. Windows NT Workstation 3.51

D. Windows NT Workstation 4

10. Which of the following steps do you skip during a Windows 2000 Professional upgrade that are normally done in a Windows 2000 Professional clean installation? Choose all that apply.

A. Provide a 25-character product key

B. Agree to the license agreement

C. Specify which networking components you want to install

D. Specify which networking services you want to install

11. In which of the following cases would you choose *not* to upgrade to Windows 2000 Professional?

A. You are currently running Windows 95 and want to take advantage of the new features of Windows 2000 Professional.

B. You want to keep your existing applications and preferences.

C. You want to preserve any local users and groups you have created with Windows NT Workstation.

D. You want your computer to be able to dual-boot between your current operating system and Windows 2000 Professional.

12. Which of the following computers can be upgraded to Windows 2000 Professional without any changes? Choose all that apply. You have the following computers installed in your workgroup:

Computer	Operating System	Processor	Memory	Available Disk Space
Computer A	Windows 95	Pentium 133MHz	32MB	750MB
Computer B	Windows NT Workstation 3.5	Pentium 433MHz	64MB	2GB
Computer C	Windows 95	Pentium 266MHz	64MB	1GB
Computer D	Windows 98	Pentium 133MHz	128MB	650MB

A. Computer A

B. Computer B

C. Computer C

D. Computer D

13. Which of the following tasks should *not* be completed prior to a Windows 2000 upgrade?

A. Back up all of your data and configuration files.

B. Perform a virus scan on your computer.

C. Compress any files that are not frequently used.

D. Take an inventory of your current configuration.

14. How would you upgrade from Windows NT Workstation 3.5 to Windows 2000 Professional?

   A. Run WINNT

   B. Run WINNT32

   C. Run Upgrade

   D. First upgrade to Windows NT 3.51 or Windows NT 4

15. Which of the following options are features found in Windows update packs? Choose three answers.

   A. Update packs can be used to modify the Registry so an application will work properly with Windows 2000.

   B. Update packs can be used with computers that dual-boot between different operating systems so that applications will be recognized by both operating systems.

   C. Update packs update files that need to be upgraded to work properly with Windows 2000.

   D. The application may need to be modified by an update pack so that it does not make direct calls to the system hardware.

16. How would you upgrade from Windows NT Server 3.5 to Windows 2000 Professional?

   A. Run WINNT

   B. Run WINNT32

   C. First upgrade to Windows NT 3.51 or Windows NT 4

   D. There is no option for this upgrade

17. Which program is used to check for compatibility problems prior to a Windows 2000 upgrade?

   A. Chkupgrd

   B. Upgrdrpt

   C. Upgradecomp

   D. Chkcomp

18. How can you tell if your Windows 95 computer is using VxDs prior to a Windows 2000 upgrade?

   A. Check the `System.ini` file

   B. Check the `Config.ini` file

   C. Check the `Report.ini` file

   D. Check the `Program.ini` file

19. You have Windows 95 installed in your C:\Windows folder. You install Windows 2000 Professional to the C:\WINNT folder. What is the result of this configuration?

   A. You have upgraded to Windows 2000 Professional and can also dual-boot to Windows 95.

   B. You have upgraded to Windows 2000 Professional and can't access your Windows 95 operating system.

   C. You have configured your computer to dual-boot and can access the Windows 95 settings since both installation folders are on the same partition.

   D. You have configured your computer to dual-boot but can't access the Windows 95 settings since the operating system files are in different installation folders.

20. You are considering upgrading your Windows 95 computer to Windows 2000 Professional. How much free disk space is required on the partition that will be used to upgrade the Windows 2000 operating system files?

   A. 500MB

   B. 650MB

   C. 750MB

   D. 1GB

Answers to Review Questions

1. B, C, D.   You can upgrade to Windows 2000 Professional from Windows 95, Windows 98, Windows NT 3.51, and Windows NT 4. If you want to upgrade from Windows NT 3.5, you must first upgrade to Windows NT 3.51 or Windows NT 4.

2. C.   Windows NT offers the smoothest upgrade path, but you cannot upgrade to Windows 2000 Professional from Windows NT Server 4.

3. B, C, D.   Applications that run under Windows 95 will probably work with Windows 2000. The exceptions are applications that use VxDs or disk filters.

4. D.   Windows 2000 does not use an Install program for the installation or upgrade. You use WINNT32 to start an upgrade from Windows 9x or Windows NT 3.51 or 4. There is no command called WIN2K.

5. D.   Windows 2000 does not use an Install program for the installation or upgrade. You use WINNT32 to start an upgrade from Windows 9x or Windows NT 3.51 or 4. There is no command called WIN2K.

6. B.   The Windows 2000 upgrade process will ask you if you want to provide any upgrade packs. Upgrade packs are used to specify how applications that are upgraded should be configured.

7. C.   The memory requirements for an installation and an upgrade are the same. Your computer must have a minimum of 64MB of memory to install or upgrade to Windows 2000 Professional.

8. A, C, D.   Windows 2000 will recognize only FAT16, FAT32, and NTFS partitions.

9. A, B.   Windows 95 and 98 are more likely to require the use of update packs than Windows NT because the Windows 2000 Professional and Windows NT configurations are much more compatible. This means that Windows NT applications will probably upgrade more successfully than Windows 95 and Windows 98 applications.

10. C, D.   During the installation and upgrade process, you must provide a valid 25-character product key and agree to the license agreement. Your networking components and services are upgraded from your previous configuration. If you want to select additional networking components or services, you can do that after the upgrade process is complete.

11. D.   If you want your computer to dual-boot, you should install a clean copy of Windows 2000 Professional instead of upgrading to Windows 2000 Professional.

12. C, D.   Computers C and D meet the minimum requirements of running Windows 95, Windows 98, Windows NT Workstation 3.51, or Windows NT 4 as the operating system. You must also have a Pentium 133MHz processor or higher, 64MB (or more) of memory, and at least 650MB of free disk space.

13. C.   You should not compress any files that were not frequently used since Windows 2000 will not upgrade a partition that is currently compressed.

14. D.   There is no direct upgrade path from Windows NT Workstation 3.5 to Windows 2000 Professional. If you want to upgrade from Windows NT 3.5, you must upgrade to Windows NT 3.51 or Windows NT 4 first.

15. A, C, D.   Windows update packs are used to upgrade applications so that they will work properly with Windows 2000. Windows update packs may modify the Registry, update application files, and update calls so that they do not directly access system hardware.

16. D.   Windows NT Server has no upgrade path to Windows 2000 Professional.

17. A. The Chkupgrd utility is used to check for compatibility problems prior to a Windows 2000 upgrade. This utility can be found at `http://www.microsoft.com/windows/downloads/default.asp`.

18. A. You can determine if you are using VxD or 386 drivers by checking the [386Enh] section of the `System.ini` file.

19. D. If you put the installation files in separate folders, you will create a computer that dual-boots. There will be no sharing of configuration information in this case.

20. B. You must have a minimum of 650MB of free space on the partition that will be used to upgrade the Windows 2000 operating system files.

Chapter 4

Configuring the Windows 2000 Environment

MICROSOFT EXAM OBJECTIVES COVERED IN THIS CHAPTER

✓ **Implement, manage, and troubleshoot disk devices.**

- Install, configure, and manage DVD and CD-ROM devices.
- Monitor and configure removable media, such as tape devices.

✓ **Implement, manage, and troubleshoot display devices.**

- Configure multiple-display support.
- Install, configure, and troubleshoot a video adapter.

✓ **Implement, manage, and troubleshoot mobile computer hardware.**

- Configure Advanced Power Management (APM).
- Configure and manage card services.

✓ **Implement, manage, and troubleshoot input and output (I/O) devices.**

- Monitor, configure, and troubleshoot I/O devices, such as printers, scanners, multimedia devices, mouse, keyboard, and smart card reader.
- Monitor, configure, and troubleshoot multimedia hardware, such as cameras.
- Install, configure, and manage Infrared Data Association (IrDA) devices.
- Install, configure, and manage wireless devices.
- Install, configure, and manage USB devices.

✓ **Update drivers.**

✓ **Manage and troubleshoot driver signing.**

✓ **Monitor and configure multiple processing units.**

✓ **Configure and troubleshoot fax support.**

After you've installed Windows 2000 Professional, you will need to install and configure your hardware. The easiest hardware devices to install are those that follow the Plug-and-Play standard. However, it's not that difficult to install non-Plug-and-Play hardware through the Add/Remove Hardware utility in Control Panel.

To configure your hardware, you generally use the Computer Management utility or Control Panel. You can also create custom administrative consoles through the Microsoft Management Console (MMC).

In this chapter, you will learn how to configure the Windows 2000 environment, beginning with an overview of the main configuration utilities. Then you will learn how to update drivers and manage driver signing. Next, you will learn how to configure many different types of hardware, including disk devices, display devices, mobile computer hardware, I/O devices, imaging devices, multiple processors, and fax support. Finally, you will learn how to configure and manage Windows 2000 services.

Windows 2000 Management Utilities

Windows 2000 Professional includes several utilities for managing various aspects of the operating system configuration:

- Control Panel allows you to configure a wide range of options, such as your display, mouse, and system properties.

- The Computer Management utility provides tools for managing common system functions, the computer's storage facilities, and the computer's services.

- The Microsoft Management Console (MMC) provides a common environment for administrative tools.

- The Registry Editor allows you to edit the Registry for advanced system configuration.

Each of these utilities is covered in detail in the following sections.

Control Panel

Control Panel is the main utility for configuring your computer's setup. You can access Control Panel by selecting Start ➤ Settings ➤ Control Panel or by opening My Computer and selecting Control Panel. The Control Panel window contains icons for its options, as shown in Figure 4.1. Table 4.1 provides brief descriptions of the Control Panel options.

FIGURE 4.1 The Control Panel window

TABLE 4.1 Control Panel Options

Option	Description
Accessibility Options	Allows you to configure options that make Windows 2000 more accessible to users with limited sight, hearing, or mobility
Add/Remove Hardware	Allows you to install, remove, and troubleshoot your hardware (primarily used for non-Plug-and-Play hardware)
Add/Remove Programs	Allows you to change or remove programs that are currently installed on your computer, add new programs, and add or remove Windows 2000 components
Administrative Tools	Provides access to Windows 2000 administrative utilities, including Component Services, Computer Management, Data Sources (ODBC), Event Viewer, Local Security Policy, Performance, Services, and Telnet Server Administration
Date/Time	Allows you to set the date, time, and time zone for your computer
Display	Allows you to configure your computer's display, including background, screen saver, appearance, Active Desktop, and visual effects
Folder Options	Allows you to configure folder options, such as general folder properties, file associations, and offline files and folders
Fonts	Allows you to manage the fonts installed on your computer
Game Controllers	Allows you to add, remove, and configure game controllers, including joysticks and game pads

TABLE 4.1 Control Panel Options *(continued)*

Option	Description
Internet Options	Allows you to configure Internet connection properties, including security, content settings, and Internet programs
Keyboard	Allows you to configure keyboard settings, including speed, input locales (language and keyboard layout), and the keyboard driver
Mouse	Allows you to configure mouse settings, including button configuration, mouse pointers, motion settings, and the mouse driver
Network and Dial-up Connections	Contains settings for network and dial-up connections and a Wizard to create new connections
Phone and Modem Options	Allows you to configure telephone dialing options and modem properties
Power Options	Allows you to configure power schemes, hibernation, APM, and UPS options
Printers	Allows you to install and manage printers
Regional Options	Allows you to set regional options, including numbers, currency, time, date, and input locales
Scanners and Cameras	Allows you to configure cameras and scanners
Scheduled Tasks	Allows you to configure tasks to be run at specific times or intervals
Sounds and Multimedia	Allows you to configure sound devices and to assign sounds to system events

TABLE 4.1   Control Panel Options *(continued)*

Option	Description
System	Allows you to configure system properties, including network identification, hardware, user profiles, and advanced settings
Users and Passwords	Provides a simple tool for managing users and passwords (the Local Users and Groups utility is used for more advanced user management, as described in Chapter 6, "Managing Users")

The Control Panel options for configuring hardware devices are described in this chapter. The other options are covered throughout this book. For example, you will learn how to use Accessibility Options, Regional Options, and Display settings in Chapter 5, "Managing the Desktop."

Computer Management

Computer Management provides a single, consolidated tool for managing common management tasks. The interface is organized into three main areas:

- *System Tools* provides access to utilities for managing the computer, such as Event Viewer and System Information.

- Storage provides access to utilities for managing the computer's storage, such as Disk Management and Disk Defragmenter.

- Services and Applications provides access to utilities for managing the computer's services, such as WMI (Windows Management Instrumentation) Control and Indexing Service.

You can access Computer Management by right-clicking the My Computer icon on your Desktop and selecting Manage from the pop-up menu. The main Computer Management window is shown in Figure 4.2.

FIGURE 4.2 The Computer Management window

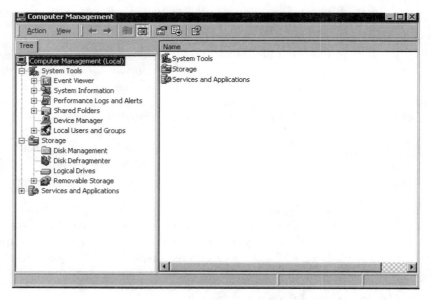

The following sections provide an overview of the utilities that can be accessed through Computer Management.

System Tools

System Tools includes six utilities that are used to manage common system functions:

- Event Viewer
- System Information
- Performance Logs and Alerts
- Shared Folders
- Device Manager
- Local Users and Groups

Event Viewer

The *Event Viewer* utility tracks information about your hardware and software. You can also monitor Windows 2000-related security events. As shown in Figure 4.3, Event Viewer tracks information through three log files:

- The Application log includes events related to applications that are running on the computer, such as SQL Server or Outlook Express application errors.

- The Security log includes events related to security, such as the success or failure of actions monitored through auditing.

- The System log includes events related to the operating system, such as failure to load a device driver.

FIGURE 4.3 The Event Viewer window

Using the Event Viewer utility is discussed in detail in Chapter 15, "Performing System Recovery Functions."

System Information

The *System Information* utility is used to collect and display information about the computer's current configuration. This information can be used to troubleshoot your computer's configuration. It can also be printed and kept for reference.

In System Information, the information is organized into five categories by default: System Summary, Hardware Resources, Components, Software Environment, and Internet Explorer 5. Figure 4.4 shows an example of the System Summary information.

FIGURE 4.4 The System Information window

Performance Logs and Alerts

Through the *Performance Logs and Alerts* utility, you can configure logs of performance-related data (called counter logs and trace logs) and generate alerts based on performance-related data. Figure 4.5 shows an example of counter logs created in Performance Logs and Alerts. You can view the logs through the Windows 2000 System Monitor utility or through database or spreadsheet applications.

FIGURE 4.5   The Performance Logs and Alerts window

Using the Performance Logs and Alerts utility is discussed in detail in Chapter 14, "Optimizing Windows 2000."

Shared Folders

Through the *Shared Folders* utility, you can create and manage shared folders on the computer. This utility displays the following information:

- All of the shares that have been created on the computer

- The user sessions that are open on each share

- The files that are currently open, listed by user

Figure 4.6 shows an example of shares listed in the Shared Folders utility.

FIGURE 4.6 The Shared Folders window

Using Shared Folders is covered in more detail in Chapter 10, "Accessing Files and Folders."

Device Manager

The *Device Manager* utility provides information about all of the devices that your computer currently recognizes. For each device, Device Manager shows the following information:

- Whether or not the hardware on your computer is working properly
- Settings for the device
- Resources used by the device

From Device Manager, you can load, unload, and update device drivers. You also can print a summary of all the device information for your computer. Figure 4.7 shows the Device Manager window.

FIGURE 4.7 The Device Manager window

Using the Device Manager utility is discussed in the "Installing Non-Plug-and-Play Hardware," "Updating Drivers," "Managing Disk Drives," and "Troubleshooting Devices" sections later in this chapter.

Using the Device Manager utility is discussed in the "Installing Non-Plug-and-Play Hardware," "Updating Drivers," "Managing Disk Drives," and "Troubleshooting Devices" sections later in this chapter.

Local Users and Groups

The *Local Users and Groups* utility is used to manage users and groups on a Windows 2000 Professional computer or a Windows 2000 Server running as a member server. Figure 4.8 shows an example of users listed in this utility.

FIGURE 4.8 The Local Users and Groups window

Using the Local Users and Groups utility is discussed in detail in Chapter 6, "Managing Users."

Storage

Storage contains four utilities that are used to manage the computer's storage facilities: Disk Management, Disk Defragmenter, Logical Drives, and Removable Storage.

Disk Management

Disk Management is the Windows 2000 graphical interface for managing disks, volumes, partitions, logical drives, and dynamic volumes. Figure 4.9 shows an example of the Disk Management window displaying information about a dynamic disk with three volumes.

FIGURE 4.9 The Disk Management window

Using the Disk Management utility is discussed in detail in Chapter 9, "Managing Disks."

Disk Defragmenter

The *Disk Defragmenter* utility is used to analyze and defragment your disk. The purpose of disk defragmentation is to optimize disk access by rearranging existing files so that they are stored contiguously. Figure 4.10 shows an example of an analysis display in this utility.

FIGURE 4.10 The Disk Defragmenter window

Using the Disk Defragmenter utility is discussed in detail in Chapter 9.

Logical Drives

The *Logical Drives* utility lists all of the logical drives that exist on your computer, as shown in Figure 4.11. Through this utility, you can manage the properties of each logical drive.

FIGURE 4.11 The Logical Drives window

Removable Storage

The *Removable Storage* utility provides information about your computer's removable storage media, as shown in Figure 4.12. Removable storage media include CD-ROMs, DVDs, tapes, and jukeboxes containing optical discs.

FIGURE 4.12   The Removable Storage window

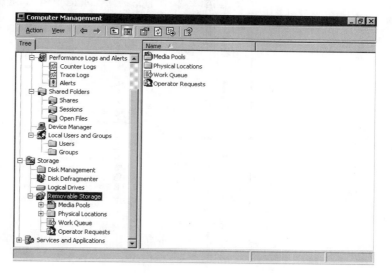

Services and Applications

Through the Services and Applications utility, you can manage all of the services installed on your computer. The services are grouped in three categories: WMI Control, Services, and Indexing Services.

WMI Control

WMI (Windows Management Instrumentation) Control provides an interface for monitoring and controlling system resources. Through WMI Control, you can view WMI status and manage Windows 2000 operations and configuration settings.

Services

Services lists all of the services on your computer, as shown in Figure 4.13. Through Services, you can manage general service properties, the logon account the service uses, and the computer's recovery response if the service fails. This utility also shows any dependencies that the service requires.

FIGURE 4.13 The Services window

Using the Services utility is covered in more detail in the "Managing Windows 2000 Services" section later in this chapter.

Indexing Service

The *Indexing Service* is used to create an index based on the contents and properties of files stored on your local hard drive. A user can then use the Windows 2000 Search function to search through or query the index for specific keywords. Figure 4.14 shows an example of an Indexing Service Query Form.

By default, the Indexing Service is not started on a Windows 2000 Professional computer. This service is required for successful indexing and query support.

FIGURE 4.14   A query in the Indexing Service

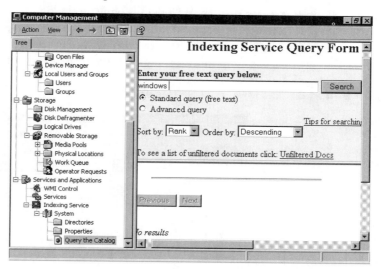

Using the Indexing Service is covered in more detail in Chapter 10, "Accessing Files and Folders."

Microsoft Management Console

The *Microsoft Management Console* (MMC) is the console framework for management applications. The MMC provides a common environment for snap-ins, which are administrative tools developed by Microsoft or third-party vendors.

The MMC offers many benefits, including the following:

- The MMC is highly customizable—you add only the snap-ins you need.

- Snap-ins use a standard, intuitive interface, so they are easier to use than previous versions of administrative utilities.

- MMC consoles can be saved and shared with other administrators.

- You can configure permissions so that the MMC runs in authoring mode, which an administrator can manage, or in user mode, which limits what users can access.

- Most snap-ins can be used for remote computer management.

As shown in Figure 4.15, the MMC console contains two panes: a console tree on the left and a details pane on the right. The console tree lists the hierarchical structure of all of the snap-ins that have been loaded into the console. The details pane contains a list of properties or other items that are part of the snap-in that is highlighted in the console tree.

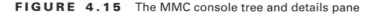

FIGURE 4.15 The MMC console tree and details pane

On a Windows 2000 Professional computer, there is no item created for the MMC by default. To open the MMC, select Start ➢ Run and type **MMC** in the Run dialog box. When you first open the MMC, it contains only the Console Root folder, as shown in Figure 4.16. The MMC does not have any administrative functionality by default. It is simply a framework that is used to organize administrative tools through the addition of snap-in utilities.

FIGURE 4.16 The opening MMC window

Configuring MMC Modes

You can configure the MMC to run in author mode, for full access to the MMC functions, or in one of three user modes, which have more limited access to the MMC functions. To set a console mode, select Console ➢ Options to open the Options dialog box. In this dialog box, you can select from the console modes listed in Table 4.2.

TABLE 4.2 MMC Console Modes

Console Mode	Description
Author mode	Allows use of all the MMC functions
User mode–full access	Allows users full access to window management commands, but they cannot add or remove snap-ins
User mode–limited access, multiple window	Allows users to create new windows, but they can access only the areas of the console tree that were visible when the console was last saved
User mode–limited access, single window	Allows users to access only the areas of the console tree that were visible when the console was last saved, and they cannot create new windows

Adding Snap-Ins

To add snap-ins to MMC and save your console, take the following steps:

1. From the main console window, select Console ➢ Add/Remove Snap-in to open the Add/Remove Snap-in dialog box.

2. Click the Add button to open the Add Standalone Snap-in dialog box.

3. Highlight the snap-in you wish to add and click the Add button.

4. If prompted, specify whether the snap-in will be used to manage the local computer or a remote computer. Then click the Finish button.

5. Repeat steps 3 and 4 to add each snap-in you want to include in your console.

6. When you are finished adding snap-ins, click the Close button.

7. Click the OK button to return to the main console screen.

8. After you have added snap-ins to create a console, you can save the console by selecting Console ➢ Save As and entering a name for your console. You can save the console to a variety of locations, including in a program group or on the Desktop. By default, custom consoles have an `.msc` extension.

In exercises in later chapters, you will add MMC snap-ins to create different custom consoles and save them in various locations. This will give you an idea of the flexibility of the MMC and how you can set up custom consoles for your administrative tasks.

Registry Editor

The *Registry* is a database that the operating system uses to store configuration information. The Registry Editor program is used to edit the Registry. This utility is designed for advanced configuration of the system. Normally, when you make changes to your configuration, you use other utilities, such as Control Panel.

 Only experienced administrators should use the Registry Editor. It is intended to be used to make configuration changes that can only be made directly through the Registry. For example, you might edit the Registry to specify an alternate location for a print spool folder. Improper changes to the Registry can cause the computer to fail to boot. You should use the Registry Editor with extreme caution.

Windows 2000 ships with two Registry Editor utilities:

- The *REGEDT32* program is the primary utility that you should use in Windows 2000. It supports full editing of the Registry. To use REGEDT32, select Start ➢ Run and type **REGEDT32** in the Run dialog box.

- The *REGEDIT* program is included with Windows 2000 because it has better search capabilities than REGEDT32. However, it is lacking some of the options that are available with REGEDT32. For example, you can't set security for Registry keys through REGEDIT, and REGEDIT does not offer the option of using the utility in read-only mode. To use REGEDIT, select Start ➢ Run and type **REGEDIT** in the Run dialog box.

The Registry is organized in a hierarchical tree format of keys and subkeys that represent logical areas of computer configuration. By default, when you open the Registry Editor, you see five Registry key windows, as shown in Figure 14.17. The five Registry keys are listed in Table 4.3.

FIGURE 4.17   The Registry Editor windows

TABLE 4.3   Registry Keys

Registry Key	Description
HKEY_CURRENT_USER	Contains the configuration information for the user who is currently logged on to the computer. This key is a subkey of the HKEY_USERS key.
HKEY_USERS	Contains the configuration information for all users of the computer.
HKEY_LOCAL_MACHINE	Contains computer hardware configuration information. This computer configuration is used, regardless of the user who is logged in.

TABLE 4.3 Registry Keys *(continued)*

Registry Key	Description
HKEY_CLASSES_ROOT	Contains configuration information that is used by Windows Explorer to properly associate file types with applications.
HKEY_CURRENT_CONFIG	Contains the configuration of the hardware profile that is used during system startup.

Installing Hardware

If you buy new hardware, it will probably be Plug-and-Play. If you use older hardware, you will most likely need to configure the hardware to be properly recognized by the operating system.

Installing Plug-and-Play Devices

Plug-and-Play technology uses a combination of hardware and software that allows the operating system to automatically recognize and configure new hardware without any user intervention. Windows 2000 Plug-and-Play support includes the following features:

- Automatic and dynamic recognition of hardware that is installed

- Automatic resource allocation (or reallocation, if necessary)

- Determination of the correct driver that needs to be loaded for hardware support

- Support for interaction with the Plug-and-Play system

- Support for power management features

To test Plug-and-Play device installation, I installed a second EIDE drive on my computer, upgraded my CD-ROM drive, and added a Zip drive. Each time I added a device, Windows 2000 Professional automatically recognized it, and I did not need to set any configuration options.

Installing Non-Plug-and-Play Hardware

Legacy or older hardware is also supported by Windows 2000 Professional. When you install this type of hardware, you need to configure it in the same manner you did before Plug-and-Play technology was introduced.

First, you need to configure the hardware device's resources manually on the device or through a software configuration program. Hardware resources include the device's interrupt request (IRQ), I/O port address, memory address, and Direct Memory Access (DMA) settings. Before you configure the resources for the new device, you should determine which resources are available. You can view a listing of the currently allocated resources in the Device Manager utility, as follows:

1. Right-click My Computer and select Manage. In the Computer Management window, select System Tools, then select Device Manager.

2. Select View ➢ Resources by Connection.

3. Device Manager displays a list of the current resources. Click a resource to see all of the resources of that type that have been allocated. Figure 4.18 shows an example of an IRQ listing in Device Manager.

FIGURE 4.18   Viewing resource allocation in Device Manager

After you've configured the hardware resources, you can use the Add/Remove Hardware utility in Control Panel to add the new device to Windows 2000 Professional and install the device driver. If the device is not listed, you will need to use a manufacturer-provided driver. Insert the disk that contains the driver and click the Have Disk button in Add/Remove Hardware.

Managing Device Drivers

A *device driver* is software that allows a specific piece of hardware to communicate with the Windows 2000 operating system. Most of the devices on the Microsoft Hardware Compatibility List (HCL) have drivers that are included on the Windows 2000 Professional distribution CD. Managing device drivers involves updating them when necessary and deciding how to handle drivers that may not have been properly tested.

Updating Drivers

Device manufacturers periodically update device drivers to add functionality or enhance driver performance. The updated drivers are typically posted on the manufacturer's Web site.

Microsoft   **Update drivers.**
✓ Exam
Objective

You can update device drivers through the Device Manager utility, as follows:

1. From the Desktop, right-click My Computer and select Manage from the pop-up menu.

2. The Computer Management window opens (see Figure 4.2 earlier in this chapter). Select System Tools, then Device Manager.

3. The right side of the window lists all of the devices that are installed on your computer (see Figure 4.7 earlier in this chapter). Select the device whose driver you want to update.

4. The device Properties dialog box appears, as shown in Figure 4.19. Click the Driver tab.

FIGURE 4.19 The device Properties dialog box

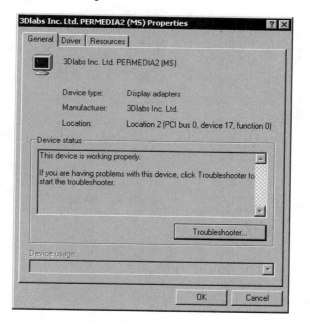

5. The Driver tab, shown in Figure 4.20, contains information about the driver, including the provider, date, version, and digital signer. The three buttons at the bottom of this dialog box allow you to see more details, uninstall the driver, or update the driver. Click the Update Driver button in the lower-right corner.

FIGURE 4.20 The Driver tab of the device Properties dialog box

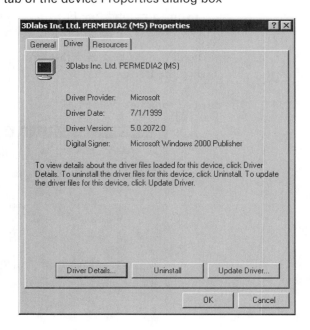

6. The Upgrade Device Driver Wizard starts, as shown in Figure 4.21.
   Click the Next button.

FIGURE 4.21 The Welcome to the Upgrade Device Driver Wizard dialog box

7. The Install Hardware Device Drivers dialog box appears, as shown in Figure 4.22. You can choose to have the Wizard search for a suitable driver, which is recommended, or you can have the Wizard display a list of known drivers for the device so you can choose a specific driver. Make your selection and click the Next button.

FIGURE 4.22 The Install Hardware Device Drivers dialog box

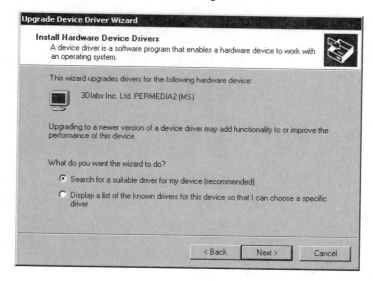

8. The Locate Driver Files dialog box appears, as shown in Figure 4.23. This dialog box allows you to specify the location of the driver files. You can have the Wizard look on your floppy disk or CD-ROM drive, specify a location, or use the Microsoft Windows Update utility. Once you make your selection, click the Next button.

The Microsoft Windows Update utility connects your computer to Microsoft's Web site and checks for driver and other updates. This utility is discussed in more detail in Chapter 14.

FIGURE 4.23 The Locate Driver Files dialog box

9. The Driver Files Search Results dialog box appears, as shown in Figure 4.24. Select the driver you wish to install and click the Next button.

FIGURE 4.24 The Driver Files Search Results dialog box

10. The files will be installed for your driver. Then you will see the Completing the Upgrade Device Driver Wizard dialog box, as shown in Figure 4.25. Click the Finish button to close this dialog box.

FIGURE 4.25 The Completing the Upgrade Device Driver Wizard dialog box

11. You may see a dialog box indicating that you must restart your computer before the change can be successfully implemented. If necessary, restart your computer.

In Exercise 4.1, you will update a device driver. In order to complete this exercise, you will need to have an updated driver for one of your hardware devices.

EXERCISE 4.1

Updating a Device Driver

1. From the Desktop, right-click My Computer and select Manage. In Computer Management, select System Tools, then Device Manager.

2. In the Device Manager listing, select the device for which you have an updated driver.

3. In the device Properties dialog box, click the Driver tab. Then click the Update Driver button.

> **EXERCISE 4.1** *(continued)*
>
> 4. In the opening Upgrade Device Driver Wizard dialog box, click the Next button.
>
> 5. In the Install Hardware Device Drivers dialog box, select the Search for a Suitable Driver for My Device (Recommended) option and click the Next button.
>
> 6. In the Locate Driver Files dialog box, select the option that describes where you want the Wizard to look for the driver files and click the Next button.
>
> 7. In the Driver Files Search Results dialog box, select the driver you wish to install and click the Next button.
>
> 8. When the Completing the Upgrade Device Driver Wizard dialog box appears, click the Finish button.
>
> 9. If you see a dialog box indicating that you must restart your computer before the change can be successfully implemented, select to restart the computer.

Managing Driver Signing

In the past, poorly written device drivers have caused problems with Windows operating systems. Microsoft is now promoting a mechanism called *driver signing* as a way of ensuring that drivers are properly tested before they are released to the public.

Microsoft ✓ *Exam Objective*

Manage and troubleshoot driver signing.

You can specify how Windows 2000 Professional will respond if you select to install an unsigned driver through the Driver Signing Options dialog box. To access this dialog box, right-click My Computer, select Properties from the pop-up menu, and click the Hardware tab in the System Properties dialog box. This tab has Hardware Wizard, Device Manager, and Hardware Profiles options, as shown in Figure 4.26. Clicking the Driver Signing button in the Device Manager section opens the Driver Signing Options dialog box, as shown in Figure 4.27.

FIGURE 4.26 The Hardware tab of the System Properties dialog box

FIGURE 4.27 The Driver Signing Options dialog box

In the Driver Signing Options dialog box, you can select from three options for file system verification:

- The Ignore option has Windows 2000 install all of the files, whether or not they are signed. You will not see any type of message about driver signing.

- The Warn option has Windows 2000 display a warning message before installing an unsigned file. You can then choose to continue with the installation or cancel it. This is the default setting.

- The Block option has Windows 2000 prevent the installation of any unsigned file. You will see an error message when you attempt to install the unsigned driver, and you will not be able to continue.

If you check the Apply Setting As System Default option, the settings that you apply will be used by all users who log on to the computer.

In Exercise 4.2, you will check the setting for driver signing.

EXERCISE 4.2

Managing Driver Signing

1. From the Desktop, right-click My Computer and select Properties.

2. In the System Properties dialog box, click the Hardware tab, then click the Driver Signing button.

3. In the Driver Signing Options dialog box, verify that the Warn radio button is selected and the Apply Setting As System Default check box is checked.

4. Click the OK button to close the dialog box.

Managing Disk Devices

You can manage disk devices through the Device Manager utility. The following sections describe how to manage CD-ROM, *DVD*, and removable media devices. Managing disks is covered in Chapter 9, "Managing Disks."

Microsoft ✓ *Exam* *Objective* | **Implement, manage, and troubleshoot disk devices.**

- Install, configure, and manage DVD and CD-ROM devices.

- Monitor and configure removable media, such as tape devices.

Managing DVD and CD-ROM Devices

DVDs and CD-ROMs are listed together under DVD/CD-ROM Drives in Device Manager. Double-click DVD/CD-ROM Drives, then double-click the CD-ROM or DVD device you wish to manage. This brings up the device Properties dialog box, which has three tabs:

- The General tab, shown in Figure 4.28, lists the device type, manufacturer, and location. It also shows the device status, which indicates whether or not the device is working properly. If the device is not working properly, you can click the Troubleshooter button in the lower-right area of the dialog box to get some help with resolving the problem.

FIGURE 4.28 The General tab of a CD-ROM Properties dialog box

- The Properties tab, shown in Figure 4.29, allows you to set options such as volume and playback settings.

FIGURE 4.29 The Properties tab of a CD-ROM Properties dialog box

- The Driver tab, shown in Figure 4.30, shows information about the currently loaded driver, as well as buttons that allow you to see driver details, uninstall the driver, or update the driver. (See the "Updating Drivers" section earlier in the chapter for details on updating a driver.)

FIGURE 4.30 The Driver tab of a CD-ROM Properties dialog box

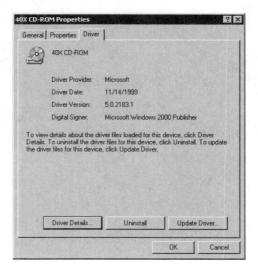

In Exercise 4.3, you will manage disk devices.

EXERCISE 4.3

Managing Disk Devices

1. From the Desktop, right-click My Computer and select Manage. In Computer Management, select System Tools, then Device Manager.

2. Double-click DVD/CD-ROM Drives, then double-click the DVD or CD-ROM device you wish to manage.

3. In the General tab of the device Properties dialog box, verify that your device is working properly. If the device is not working properly, click the Troubleshooter button. The Troubleshooter Wizard will ask you a series of questions and attempt to help you resolve the problem.

4. Click the Properties tab and configure the options to suit your personal preferences.

5. Click the Driver tab. Note the information about the currently loaded driver.

6. Click the OK button to save your settings and close the dialog box.

Managing Removable Media

Removable media are devices such as tape devices and Zip drives. Like DVD and CD-ROM devices, removable media devices can also be managed through Device Manager.

Removable media are listed under Disk Drives in Device Manager. Double-click Disk Drives, then double-click the removable media device you wish to manage. This brings up the device Properties dialog box. The General and Driver tabs are similar to those for CD-ROM and DVD devices, as described in the previous section. The Disk Properties tab contains options for the specific removable media device. For example, for an IOMEGA Zip 250, you can enable or disable the write cache, as shown in Figure 4.31.

FIGURE 4.31 The Disk Properties tab of a Zip disk Properties dialog box

Managing Display Devices

A *video adapter* is the device that outputs the display to your monitor. You install a video adapter in the same way that you install other hardware. This means that if it is a Plug-and-Play device, all you need to do is shut down your computer, add the video adapter, and turn on your computer. Windows 2000 Professional will automatically recognize the new device.

Microsoft ✓ **Exam Objective**

Implement, manage, and troubleshoot display devices.

- Configure multiple-display support.
- Install, configure, and troubleshoot a video adapter.

You can configure several options for your video adapters, and if you have multiple monitors with their own video adapters, you can configure multiple-display support. The following sections describe how to configure video adapters and configure your computer to support multiple monitors.

Configuring Video Adapters

The options for video adapters are on the Settings tab of the Display Properties dialog box, as shown in Figure 4.32. To access this dialog box, select the Display icon in Control Panel or right-click an empty area on your Desktop and select Properties from the pop-up menu.

 The other tabs in the Display Properties dialog box allow you to customize the appearance of your Desktop. These options are discussed in Chapter 5.

FIGURE 4.32 The Settings tab of the Display Properties dialog box

The Colors option in the Settings tab sets the color depth for your video adapter. The Screen Area option allows you to set the resolution for your video adapter.

To configure advanced settings for your video adapter, click the Advanced button in the lower-right corner of the Settings tab. This brings up the monitor Properties dialog box, as shown in Figure 4.33. This dialog box has five tabs with options for your video adapter and monitor:

- The General tab allows you to configure the font size for the display. You can also specify what action Windows 2000 will take after you change your display settings.

- The Adapter tab allows you to view and configure the properties of your video adapter.

- The Monitor tab allows you to view and configure the properties of your monitor, including the refresh frequency (how often the screen is redrawn).

A lower refresh frequency setting can cause your screen to flicker. Setting the refresh frequency too high can damage some hardware.

- The Troubleshooting tab allows you to configure how Windows 2000 uses your graphics hardware. For example, you can configure hardware acceleration settings.

- The Color Management tab allows you to select color profiles (the colors that are displayed on your monitor).

FIGURE 4.33   The monitor Properties dialog box

In Exercise 4.4, you will view the properties of your video adapter.

WARNING Normally, the video adapter is configured for typical use. Be careful if you change these settings, because improper settings may cause your display to be unreadable.

EXERCISE 4.4

Managing Your Video Adapter

1. Right-click an empty area on the Desktop, select Properties, and select the Settings tab.

2. Click the Advanced button at the bottom of the Settings tab. Note your current settings in the General tab.

3. Click the Adapter tab. Note your current settings.

4. Click the Monitor tab. Note your current settings.

5. Click the Troubleshooting tab. Note your current settings.

6. Click the OK button to close the monitor Properties dialog box.

7. Click the OK button to close the Display Properties dialog box.

Using Multiple-Display Support

Windows 2000 Professional allows you to extend your Desktop across a maximum of 10 monitors. This means that you can spread your applications across multiple monitors.

In order to set up multiple-display support, you must have a video adapter installed for each monitor, and you must use Peripheral Connection Interface (PCI) or Accelerated Graphics Port (AGP) video adapter cards. In order to use the video adapter that is built into the system board for multiple-display support, the chipset must use the PCI or AGP standard.

If your computer has the video adapter built into the system board, you should install Windows 2000 Professional before you install the second video adapter. This is because Windows 2000 will disable the video adapter that is built into the system board if it detects a second video adapter. When you add a second video adapter after Windows 2000 is installed, it will automatically become the primary video adapter.

Configuring Multiple-Display Support

To set up multiple-display support, take the following steps:

1. Turn off your computer and install the PCI or AGP adapters. Plug your monitors into the video adapters and turn on your computer. Assuming that the adapters are Plug-and-Play, Windows 2000 will automatically recognize your new adapters and load the correct drivers.

2. Open the Display Properties dialog box (right-click an empty area on your Desktop and select Properties) and click the Settings tab. You should see monitor icons for each of the monitors, as shown in Figure 4.34.

FIGURE 4.34 Multiple monitors in the Settings tab of the Display Properties dialog box

3. Click the number of the monitor that will act as your additional display. Then select the Extend My Windows Desktop onto This Monitor check box. Repeat this step for each additional monitor you wish to configure.

You can arrange the order in which the displays are arranged by dragging and dropping the monitor icons in the Settings tab of the Display Properties dialog box.

4. When you are finished configuring the monitors, click OK to close the dialog box.

Troubleshooting Multiple-Display Support

If you are having problems with multiple-display support, use the following troubleshooting guidelines:

The Extend My Windows Desktop onto This Monitor option does not appear in the Settings tab of the Display Properties dialog box	Confirm that your secondary adapter is supported for multiple-display support. Confirm that Windows 2000 is able to detect the secondary video adapter. Try selecting the secondary adapter rather than the primary adapter in the Display Properties dialog box.
No output appears on the secondary display	Confirm that your secondary adapter is supported for multiple-display support, especially if you are using the built-in motherboard video adapter. Confirm that the correct video driver has been installed for the secondary display. Restart the computer to see if the secondary video driver is initialized. Check the status of the video adapter in Device Manager. Try switching the order of the video adapters in the computers slots. See if the system will recognize the device as the primary display.
An application is not properly displayed	Disable the secondary display to determine if the problem is specific to multiple-display support. Run the application on the primary display. If you are running MS-DOS applications, try running the application in full-screen mode. For Windows applications, try running the application in a maximized window.

Managing Mobile Computer Hardware

Windows 2000 Professional includes several features that are particularly useful for laptop computers. For example, through Power Options, you can set power schemes and enable Advanced Power Management (APM) support. Windows 2000 also supports hot-swapping of PC Cards.

Microsoft ✓ *Exam* *Objective*	**Implement, manage, and troubleshoot mobile computer hardware.** • Configure Advanced Power Management (APM). • Configure and manage card services.

The following sections describe the power management and card service options.

Managing Power Options

You can configure power options through the Power Options Properties dialog box, as shown in Figure 4.35. To access this dialog box, select the Power Options icon in Control Panel.

FIGURE 4.35 The Power Options Properties dialog box

This dialog box has five tabs: Power Schemes, Advanced, Hibernate, APM, and UPS. The options on these tabs are described in the following sections.

Configuring Power Schemes

The Power Schemes tab (see Figure 4.35) allows you to select the most appropriate power scheme for your computer. Power schemes control when the monitor and hard disks will be turned off automatically, based on the specified period of no activity. This feature allows you to conserve your laptop's battery during periods of inactivity. From the drop-down list, you can select one of the preconfigured power schemes listed in Table 4.4. Alternatively, you can create a custom power scheme by clicking the Save As button, giving the power scheme a new name, and selecting power scheme options.

TABLE 4.4 Windows 2000 Power Schemes

Power Scheme	Turn off Monitor	Turn off Hard Disks
Home/Office Desk	After 20 minutes	Never
Portable/Laptop	After 15 minutes	After 30 minutes
Presentation	Never	Never
Always On	After 20 minutes	Never
Minimal Power Management	After 15 minutes	Never
Max. Battery	After 15 minutes	Never

Configuring Advanced Options

One option on the Advanced tab of the Power Options Properties dialog box allows you to show the Power Options icon on the Taskbar. The other options on the Advanced tab depend on the hardware configuration you are using.

Configuring Hibernation

Hibernation for a computer means that anything that is stored in memory is also stored on your hard disk. This ensures that when your computer is shut down, you do not lose any of the information that is stored in memory. When you take your computer out of hibernation, it returns to the state it was in previously.

You can configure your computer to hibernate through the Hibernate tab of the Power Options Properties dialog box, as shown in Figure 4.36. Simply check the Enable Hibernate Support check box.

FIGURE 4.36 The Hibernate tab of the Power Options Properties dialog box

Configuring Advanced Power Management

Advanced Power Management (*APM*) allows you to reduce the power consumption of your computer, which is especially important for laptops that are running from battery power. You can configure your computer to use APM through the APM tab of the Power Options Properties dialog box, as shown in Figure 4.37. Just check the Enable Advanced Power Management Support check box.

In order to use APM, the BIOS of your computer must support a standard called Advanced Configuration and Power Interface (ACPI). If your BIOS does not support this feature, you may not see the APM tab.

FIGURE 4.37 The APM tab of the Power Options Properties dialog box

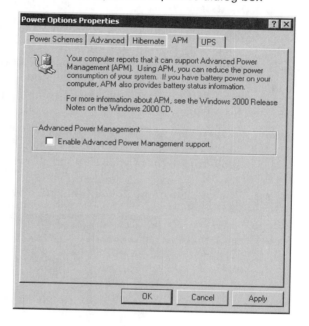

If you have a laptop running Windows 2000 Professional, you can complete the steps in Exercise 4.5 to configure the laptop to support APM.

EXERCISE 4.5

Configuring Advanced Power Management Support

1. Select Start ➤ Settings ➤ Control Panel and double-click the Power Options icon.

2. In the Power Options Properties dialog box, click the APM tab.

EXERCISE 4.5 *(continued)*

3. Check the Enable Advanced Power Management Support check box and click the OK button.

4. Close the Control Panel.

Configuring Your Uninterruptible Power Supply

An *uninterruptible power supply* (UPS) protects your computer by supplying battery power in the event of an electrical power outage. This allows you to shut down the computer properly, so you don't lose any data.

You should follow the UPS manufacturer's instructions for connecting the UPS to your computer and completing any additional steps to start your UPS.

If you have a UPS attached to your computer, you can access the UPS tab of the Power Options Properties dialog box, shown in Figure 4.38. This tab shows the status of your UPS and allows you to configure it.

FIGURE 4.38 The UPS tab of the Power Options Properties dialog box

Managing Card Services

In order to add devices to a laptop computer, you use special credit-card sized devices called *PCMCIA* (Personal Computer Memory Card International Association) cards, or more simply, PC Cards. PC Cards have three different standards:

- Type I cards can be up to 3.3 mm thick. These cards are primarily used for adding memory to a computer.

- Type II cards can be up to 5.5 mm thick. These cards are typically used for modem and network cards.

- Type III cards can be up to 10.5 mm thick. These cards are typically used for portable disk drives.

Windows 2000 Professional allows you to exchange PC Cards on the fly (hot-swapping). However, you should make sure that your laptop supports hot-swap technology before you try to remove a card from or add a card to a running computer.

As with any Plug-and-Play device, when you add a PC Card to a Windows 2000 Professional computer, the card will be recognized automatically. You can view and manage PC Cards through Device Manager.

Managing I/O Devices

Your input/output (I/O) devices are the ones that allow you to get information into and out of your computer. Examples of I/O devices are keyboards, mice, printers, and scanners. Your devices may be connected to your computer by standard cabling, or they may use wireless technology (such as IrDA or RF) or be connected through a USB port.

Microsoft Exam Objective

Implement, manage, and troubleshoot input and output (I/O) devices.

- Monitor, configure, and troubleshoot I/O devices, such as printers, scanners, multimedia devices, mouse, keyboard, and smart card reader.
- Install, configure, and manage Infrared Data Association (IrDA) devices.
- Install, configure, and manage wireless devices.
- Install, configure, and manage USB devices.

The subobjective "Install, configure, and manage modems" for the objective "Implement, manage, and troubleshoot input and output (I/O) devices" is covered in Chapter 13, "Dial-Up Networking and Internet Productivity."

The following sections describe how to manage your keyboard, mouse, wireless devices, and USB devices. Scanners are covered in the next section. You will learn how to install and configure printers in Chapter 12, "Managing Printing."

Configuring the Keyboard

You can configure keyboard options through the Keyboard Properties dialog box, shown in Figure 4.39. To access this dialog box, select the Keyboard icon in Control Panel.

You must have a keyboard attached to your computer before you can install Windows 2000 Professional.

FIGURE 4.39   The Keyboard Properties dialog box

This dialog box has three tabs with options that control your keyboard's behavior:

- The Speed tab lets you how configure how quickly characters are repeated when you hold down a key. You can also specify the cursor blink rate.

- The Input Locales tab allows you to specify the keyboard layout based on your input locale (for example, English United States or United States-Dvorak).

- The Hardware tab specifies the device settings for your keyboard.

Configuring the Mouse

You can configure your mouse through the Mouse Properties dialog box, shown in Figure 4.40. To access this dialog box, select the Mouse icon in Control Panel.

FIGURE 4.40 The Mouse Properties dialog box

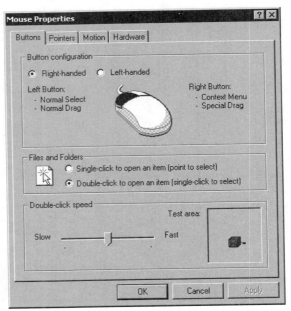

The Mouse Properties dialog box has four tabs with options that control your mouse's behavior:

- The Buttons tab allows you to configure the mouse properties for right-handed or left-handed use and choose whether you use a single-click to open an item (point to select) or double-click to open an item (single-click to select). You can also configure the speed that is used to indicate a double-click.

- The Pointers tab lets you select the pointer scheme that is used by your mouse.

- The Motion tab lets you specify how fast your mouse pointer moves. You can also configure the snap-to-default feature, which automatically moves the pointer to a default button in a dialog box when new dialog boxes are opened.

- The Hardware tab specifies the device settings for your mouse.

In Exercise 4.6, you will configure your keyboard and mouse I/O devices.

EXERCISE 4.6

Configuring I/O Devices

1. Select Start ➢ Settings ➢ Control Panel and double-click the Keyboard icon.

2. In the Speed tab, set the Repeat Delay and Repeat Rate options based on your personal preferences. Also adjust the Cursor Blink Rate if you want to change it. Click the OK button.

3. In Control Panel, double-click the Mouse icon.

4. In the Motion tab, set the Speed, Acceleration, and Snap-to-Default options as you prefer. Click the OK button.

5. Close Control Panel.

Configuring Wireless Devices

Wireless devices are those that use wireless transmission rather than transmitting over cable. The following are two of the technologies used for wireless transmission:

- Infrared Data Association (IrDA), which is a standard for transmitting data through infrared light waves

- RF (Radio Frequency), which is a standard for transmitting data through radio waves

Common examples of wireless devices include keyboards, mice, and network cards. You should follow the vendor's instructions to install wireless devices. Wireless devices are configured in the same manner as other devices on your computer. For example, you can set options for a wireless keyboard through the Keyboard Properties dialog box.

Configuring USB Devices

Universal Serial Bus (USB) is an external bus standard that allows you to connect USB devices through a USB port. USB supports transfer rates up to

12Mbps. A single USB port can support up to 127 devices. Examples of USB devices include modems, printers, and keyboards.

If your computer supports USB, and USB is enabled in the BIOS, you will see Universal Serial Bus Controller listed in Device Manager. Double-click your USB controller to see the dialog box shown in Figure 4.41.

FIGURE 4.41 The USB controller Properties dialog box

The USB controller Properties dialog box has four tabs with options and information for your USB adapter:

- The General tab lists the device type, manufacturer, and location. It also shows the device status, which indicates whether or not the device is working properly. If the device is not working properly, you can click the Troubleshooter button in the lower-right area of the dialog box.

- The Advanced tab allows you to configure how much of the bandwidth each device that is connected to the USB adapter can use.

- The Driver tab shows driver properties and lets you uninstall or update the driver.

- The Resources tab shows all of the resources that are used by the USB adapter.

After the USB adapter is configured, you can attach USB devices to the adapter in a daisy-chain configuration.

Managing Imaging Devices

A scanner is a device that can read text or graphics that are on paper and translate the information to digital data that the computer can understand. Digital cameras take pictures in a digital format that can be read by the computer.

Microsoft ✓ *Exam* *Objective*	**Implement, manage, and troubleshoot input and output (I/O) devices.**
	• Monitor, configure, and troubleshoot I/O devices, such as printers, scanners, multimedia devices, mouse, keyboard, and smart card reader.
	• Monitor, configure, and troubleshoot multimedia hardware, such as cameras.

After you install a scanner or digital camera on a Windows 2000 Professional computer, you can manage the device through the Scanners and Cameras Properties dialog box, shown in Figure 4.42. You access this dialog box by selecting the Cameras and Scanners icon in Control Panel.

FIGURE 4.42 The Scanners and Cameras Properties dialog box

The Scanners and Cameras Properties dialog box lists the devices that are recognized by your computer. You can click the Add button to add a scanner or camera, the Remove button to remove the selected device, or the Troubleshooter button to run a Troubleshooter Wizard. Clicking the Properties button displays a dialog box with additional options, as shown in Figure 4.43.

FIGURE 4.43 A scanner Properties dialog box

The scanner or camera Properties dialog box has three tabs with options and information about the device:

- The General tab lists the manufacturer, description, port, and status of the device. It also contains a button that you can click to test the scanner or camera.

- The Events tab allows you to associate an event with an application. For example, you can specify that when you scan a document, it should be automatically linked to the imaging program, and the imaging program will start and display the document you just scanned.

- The Color Management tab allows you to associate a color profile with the scanner or camera.

If you have a scanner or digital camera installed on your computer, you can complete the steps in Exercise 4.7 to view and configure its properties.

EXERCISE 4.7

Managing and Monitoring Imaging Devices

1. Select Start ➤ Settings ➤ Control Panel and double-click the Scanners and Camera icon.

2. In the Scanners and Cameras Properties dialog box, click the Properties button.

3. In the General tab of the scanner or camera Properties dialog box, click the Test Scanner or Camera button to make sure the device is working properly.

4. Click the Events tab. Set any associations based on your computer's configuration and your personal preferences.

5. Click the Color Management tab. If desired, associate a color profile with the scanner or camera.

6. Click the OK button to close the scanner or camera Properties dialog box.

7. Click the OK button to close the Scanner and Camera Properties dialog box.

8. Close Control Panel.

Managing Processors

Normally, multiple processors are associated with servers. However Windows 2000 Professional can support up to two processors. If your computer is capable of supporting multiple processors, you should follow the computer manufacturer's instructions for installing the second processor. This usually involves updating the processors driver to a driver that supports multiple processors through the Upgrade Device Driver Wizard.

Microsoft ✓ *Exam* *Objective*	**Monitor and configure multiple processing units.**

Once you install your second processor, you can monitor the processors through the System Monitor utility. You can verify that multiple processors are recognized by the operating system, as well as configure multiple processors, through the Task Manager utility. The System Monitor and Task Manager utilities are covered in detail in Chapter 14.

To configure multiple processors, you can associate each processor with specific processes that are running on the computer. This is called *processor affinity*. Once you have two processors installed on your computer, you can set processor affinity through the following steps:

1. Press Ctrl+Alt+Delete to access the Windows Security dialog box. Click the Task Manager button.

2. You see the Task Manager dialog box. Click the Processes tab to list all of the processes that are currently running on your computer, as shown in Figure 4.44.

FIGURE 4.44   The Processes tab of the Task Manager dialog box

3. Right-click the process you want to associate with a specific processor and select Processor Affinity from the pop-up menu.

4. You see the Processor Affinity dialog box, as shown in Figure 4.45. Specify the specific processor that the process will use and click the OK button.

FIGURE 4.45   The Processor Affinity dialog box

If you have two processors installed on your computer, you can complete the steps in Exercise 4.8 to configure processor affinity.

EXERCISE 4.8

Configuring Multiple Processors

1. Press Ctrl+Alt+Delete and click the Task Manager button.

2. In the Task Manager dialog box, click the Processes tab.

3. In the Processes tab, right-click the explorer.exe process and select Processor Affinity.

4. In the Processor Affinity dialog box, check the CPU 1 check box and click the OK button.

5. Close the Task Manager utility.

Configuring Fax Support

Windows 2000 Professional allows you to add and configure fax support. In order to add fax support, you must have a device connected to your computer that can send and receive faxes. The most common example of a fax device is a fax modem.

Microsoft ✓ *Exam* *Objective*	**Configure and troubleshoot fax support.**

You configure fax support through the Fax icon in Control Panel and start the Fax Service through the Computer Management utility, as described in the following sections.

Setting Fax Properties

To configure fax support and set fax properties, take the following steps:

1. Select Start ➢ Settings ➢ Control Panel and double-click the Fax icon.

2. You see the Fax Properties dialog box, as shown in Figure 4.46. In the User Information tab, you can fill in the information you want to appear on your cover page. You can set other cover page options on the Cover Pages tab, and specify notification options on the Status Monitor tab. Click the Advanced Options tab to configure fax support.

FIGURE 4.46 The User Information tab of the Fax Properties dialog box

3. The Advanced Options tab contains options for managing the fax service and adding a fax printer, as shown in Figure 4.47. Click the Add a Fax Printer button.

FIGURE 4.47 The Advanced Options tab of the Fax Properties dialog box

4. If a device that supports faxing capabilities is attached to your computer, you will see a message indicating that the fax printer was created successfully. Click the OK button.

5. You return to the Advanced Options tab. Click the Open Fax Service Management Console button.

6. The Fax Service Management window appears, as shown in Figure 4.48. Click Devices in the right pane to list the fax devices. Double-click the fax device you want to configure.

FIGURE 4.48 The Fax Service Management window

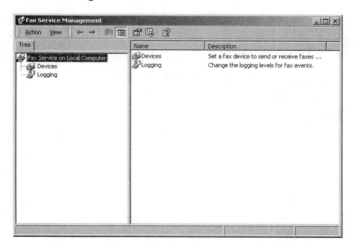

7. The fax device Properties dialog box appears, as shown in Figure 4.49. In this dialog box, you can configure Send and Receive properties. If you want to receive faxes, you can configure their properties through the Received Faxes tab. When you are finished setting the fax device properties, click the OK button.

FIGURE 4.49 The fax device Properties dialog box

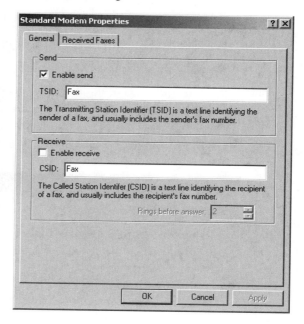

8. Close the Fax Service Management window.

You can also configure the Fax Queue, Fax Service Management, My Faxes, and Send Cover Page Fax options through the Fax Service Management utility. To access this utility, select Start ➢ Programs ➢ Accessories ➢ Communications ➢ Fax.

Starting the Fax Service

After you configure fax support, you need to start the Fax Service in Windows 2000 Professional. To start the service, take the following steps:

1. Right-click My Computer on the Desktop and select Manage from the pop-up menu.

2. Expand Services and Applications, then Services.

3. Double-click Fax Service and click the Start button.

4. Select Automatic as the Startup Type and click the OK button.

5. Close the Computer Management window.

Starting and configuring Windows 2000 Professional services are discussed in more detail in the next section.

If you have a fax device connected to your computer, you can complete the steps in Exercise 4.9 to configure fax support and start the Fax Service.

EXERCISE 4.9

Configuring Fax Support

1. Select Start ➢ Settings ➢ Control Panel and double-click the Fax icon.

2. In the Fax Properties dialog box, click the Advanced Options tab.

3. In the Advanced Options tab, click the Add a Fax Printer icon.

4. You should see a message indicating that the fax printer was created successfully. Click the OK button.

5. In the Advanced Options tab, click the Open Fax Service Management Console button.

6. In the right pane of the Fax Service Management window, click Devices and then double-click your fax device.

7. In the fax device Properties dialog box, check the Enable Receive check box and click the OK button. Close the Fax Service Management window.

EXERCISE 4.9 *(continued)*

8. Right-click My Computer and selecting Manage. Open Services and Applications, then Services.

9. Double-click Fax Service and click the Start button. Select Automatic from the Startup Type drop-down list and click the OK button.

10. Close the Computer Management window.

If you are having trouble with your fax device, you should use the Troubleshooter Wizard available through the Device Manager utility, as described in the next section.

Troubleshooting Devices

When Device Manager does not properly recognize a device, it reports the problem by displaying an exclamation point icon next to the device. To troubleshoot a device that is not working properly, double-click the device to open its Properties dialog box. Figure 4.50 shows an example of the Properties dialog box for a device that does not have the proper driver loaded.

FIGURE 4.50 The device Properties dialog box reports that the device is not configured correctly.

If a device connected to your computer doesn't appear in Device Manager, you can get some hints on troubleshooting through the Troubleshooter Wizard. As an example, if your sound card is not working properly and is not listed in Device Manager, you can use the Troubleshooter Wizard as follows:

1. From the Desktop, right-click My Computer and select Manage. In Computer Management, select System Tools, then Device Manager.

2. In Device Manager, double-click Computer and double-click Standard PC.

3. The computer Properties dialog box appears, as shown in Figure 4.51. Click the Troubleshooter button.

FIGURE 4.51   The Standard PC Properties dialog box

4. The Windows 2000 Help window opens, with the Hardware Troubleshooter section displayed in the right pane, as shown in Figure 4.52. You can select from a wide range of problems. In this example, select the My Sound Card Doesn't Work radio button and click the Next button.

FIGURE 4.52 Selecting a problem to troubleshoot

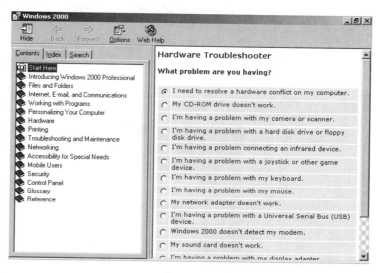

5. The Troubleshooter Wizard window for sound cards appears, as shown in Figure 4.53. Here, you specify whether or not you have a PCI sound card. In this example, select the Yes, I Have a PCI Sound Card option and click the Next button.

FIGURE 4.53 Specifying a sound card type

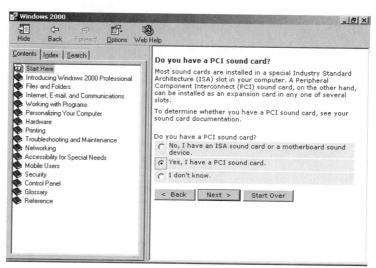

6. The Troubleshooter Wizard asks if your sound card is compatible with Windows 2000, as shown in Figure 4.54. If your sound card is not on the HCL, the Wizard directs you to the card manufacturer for assistance. In this example, select the Yes, Windows 2000 Supports My Sound Card option and click the Next button.

FIGURE 4.54 Checking whether a sound card is on the HCL

7. The Troubleshooter Wizard identifies a possible problem and solution, as shown in Figure 4.55. It suggests that your PCI card might be in a faulty slot. You are advised to move your PCI card to a different slot to see if this corrects the problem. (You may prefer to have this tested at a computer repair center.)

FIGURE 4.55 Checking whether a sound card is in a faulty slot

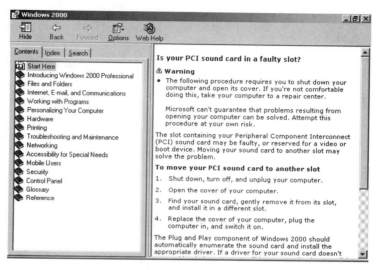

8. After you follow the suggested procedure, the Wizard asks if this fixed your problem. In this example, the problem is fixed. If your device still isn't working, the Troubleshooter Wizard will suggest other possible courses of action.

Managing Windows 2000 Services

A service is a program, routine, or process that performs a specific function within the Windows 2000 operating system. You can manage services through the Services window, shown in Figure 4.56. You can access this window in a variety of ways, including through the Computer Management utility (right-click My Computer, select Manage, expand Services and Applications, and then expand Services), through Administrative Tools, or as an MMC snap-in.

FIGURE 4.56 The Services window

For each service, the Services window listing shows the name, a short description, the startup type, and the logon account that is used to start the service. To configure the properties of a service, double-click it to open its Properties dialog box, as shown in Figure 4.57. This dialog box contains four tabs of options for services, which are described in the following sections.

FIGURE 4.57 The General tab of the service Properties dialog box

Configuring General Service Properties

The General tab of the service Properties dialog box (see Figure 4.57), allows you to view and configure the following options:

- The service display name

- A description of the service

- The path to the service executable

- The startup type, which can be automatic, manual, or disabled

- The current service status

- Startup parameters that can be applied when the service is started

The buttons across the lower part of the dialog box allow you to start, stop, pause, or resume the service.

Configuring Service Log On Properties

The Log On tab of the service Properties dialog box, shown in Figure 4.58, allows you to configure the logon account that will be used to start the service. You can choose to use the local system account or specify another logon account.

FIGURE 4.58 The Log On tab of the service Properties dialog box

At the bottom of the Log On tab, you can select hardware profiles to associate the service with. For each hardware profile, you can set the service as enabled or disabled.

Configuring Service Recovery Properties

The Recovery tab of the service Properties dialog box, shown in Figure 4.59, allows you to configure what action will be taken if the service fails to load. For the first, second, and subsequent failures, you can select from the following actions:

- Take no action

- Restart the service

- Run a file

- Reboot the computer

FIGURE 4.59 The Recovery tab of the service Properties dialog box

If you choose to run a file, you then specify the file and any command-line parameters. If you choose to reboot the computer, you can then configure a message that will be sent to users who are connected to the computer before it is restarted.

Checking Service Dependencies

The Dependencies tab of the service Properties dialog box, shown in Figure 4.60, lists any services that must be running in order for the specified service to start. If a service fails to start, you can use this information to determine what the dependencies are, then make sure that each dependency service is running.

FIGURE 4.60 The Dependencies tab of the service Properties dialog box

At the bottom of the Dependencies tab, you can see if any other services depend on this service. You should verify that there are no services that depend on a service that you are about to stop.

Summary

In this chapter, you learned about configuring the Windows 2000 Professional environment. We covered the following topics:

- Utilities used to manage configuration, which include Control Panel, Computer Management, the Microsoft Management Console (MMC), and the Registry Editor

- Installing hardware, including Plug-and-Play and non-Plug-and-Play devices

- Managing device drivers, including how to update drivers and set options for driver signing

- Managing disk devices, including CD-ROM devices, DVD devices, and removable media

- Managing display devices, including video adapters and multiple displays

- Managing mobile computer hardware, including how to set power options and configure card services

- Managing I/O devices, including keyboards, mice, wireless devices, and USB devices

- Managing imaging devices, including scanners and digital cameras

- Managing processors, including how to setting processor affinity in a multiple-processor computer

- Configuring fax support and starting the Fax Service

- Using the Windows 2000 Troubleshooter Wizard to troubleshoot problems with devices

- Managing Windows 2000 Professional services

Key Terms

Before taking the exam, you should be familiar with the following terms:

Advanced Power Management (APM)

Computer Management

Control Panel

device driver

Device Manager

Disk Defragmenter

Disk Management

driver signing

DVD (Digital Versatile Disc)

Event Viewer

hibernation

Indexing Service

Local Users and Groups

Logical Drives

Microsoft Management Console (MMC)

Performance Logs and Alerts

PCMCIA

Plug-and-Play

processor affinity

REGEDIT

REGEDT32

Registry

Removable Storage

Services

Shared Folders

System Information

System Tools

uninterruptible power supply (UPS)

Universal Serial Bus (USB)

video adapter

WMI (Windows Management Instrumentation) Control

Review Questions

1. Which of the following Windows 2000 configuration utilities allows you to create a customized administrative interface using snap-ins?

   A. Control Panel

   B. Computer Management

   C. Microsoft Management Console

   D. Registry Editor

2. What is the primary utility that supports full editing of the Windows 2000 Registry?

   A. REGEDIT

   B. REDIT

   C. REGEDIT32

   D. REGEDT32

3. What is the process that Microsoft uses with Windows 2000 to ensure that the drivers you install on your computer are properly tested and verified?

   A. Driver confirmation

   B. Driver optimization

   C. Driver signing

   D. Driver verification

4. Which of the following statements is true regarding the configuration of multiple displays? Choose two answers.

   A. You need a special cable that allows you to connect two monitors to a video adapter.

   B. You need to install an adapter for each monitor that you will configure.

   C. You must use PCI or AGP adapters.

   D. Windows 2000 allows you to extend your Desktop across up to eight monitors.

5. Which Windows 2000 feature allows you to conserve power on your computer and is especially important for laptop users whose computers are running on battery power?

   A. APM

   B. UPS

   C. HPS

   D. HPM

6. Which of the following statements regarding USB devices is *not* true?

   A. USB supports transmission speeds up to 20Mbps.

   B. You can connect up to 127 devices through a single USB port.

   C. You can configure your USB adapter properties through Device Manager.

   D. Common examples of USB devices include modems, printers, and keyboards.

7. Which utility can you use to configure keyboard and mouse properties?

   A. Control Panel

   B. Computer Management

   C. Microsoft Management Console

   D. Registry Editor

8. Which utility can you use to install hardware that is not Plug-and-Play compatible?

   A. Device Manager

   B. Computer Manager

   C. Control Panel, Add/Remove Hardware

   D. MMC

9. Which utility can you use to configure power options such as hibernation and APM?

   A. Device Manager

   B. Computer Manager

   C. Control Panel, Power Management

   D. MMC

10. Which utility can you use to configure fax support in Windows 2000?

    A. Device Manager

    B. Computer Manager

    C. Control Panel, Fax

    D. MMC

11. Which of the following steps would you need to take in Windows 2000 Professional if you upgraded your computer from one processor to two processors?

    A. Update the driver to support multiple processors.

    B. Through Device Manager, access the computer's properties and check the Allow Multiple Processors box.

    C. Through Control Panel, access System Properties, Advanced tab and check the Allow Multiple Processors box.

    D. Do nothing; this is enabled by default.

12. Which command-line utility can you use to search for a specific data value in the Windows 2000 Registry?

A. REGEDIT

B. REDIT

C. REGEDIT32

D. REGEDT32

13. In the past, you have had problems with users updating drivers that have caused their computers to not work properly. You want to guarantee that this does not happen in Windows 2000. What can you do?

A. Configure driver signing for Ignore

B. Configure driver signing for Warn

C. Configure driver signing for Block

D. Configure driver signing for Stop

14. You are installing an application that specifies that your monitor should use the screen area 1024 × 768. How can you verify or make this setting?

A. Through Control Panel, Monitor Settings

B. Through Device Manager, Monitor

C. Through Control Panel, Display Properties, Settings

D. Through Device Manager, Display Properties, Settings

15. You have configured your computer for multiple-display support. Everything works properly when you run Windows applications. However, you do not see your MS-DOS application properly displayed. What can you do?

A. Try running the application in full-screen mode.

B. Restart the computer and see if the secondary video adapter is initialized.

C. Increase the screen area on both displays to 1024×768.

D. Set the colors to 256 Colors.

16. Which power option can you configure to store on your hard disk whatever is in memory whenever a user with a laptop puts that computer to sleep?

A. Sleep

B. Hibernate

C. Rest

D. Configure a power scheme for APM

17. Your office, located in Pakistan, frequently experiences power outages. You decide to configure a UPS for each computer running Windows 2000. How do you configure the UPS?

A. Through Control Panel, UPS

B. Through Device Manager, UPS

C. Through Control Panel, Power Options

D. Through Device Manager, Power Options

18. Which of the following options is not something you can configure through the Keyboard icon in Control Panel?

   A. How quickly characters are repeated when you hold down a key

   B. The hot keys that you will use for your applications

   C. Input locales (the input language you are using)

   D. The device driver that is used by your keyboard

19. Which utility can you use to access the Hardware Troubleshooter Wizard if your computer does not recognize your network adapter?

   A. Device Manager

   B. Computer Manager

   C. Control Panel, Network

   D. System Information

20. If you looked in Device Manager and saw a yellow exclamation point next to your sound card, what would that indicate?

   A. The device is not working properly.

   B. The device is disabled.

   C. The device is working properly.

   D. The device has been deleted.

Answers to Review Questions

1. C. The Microsoft Management Console (MMC) is a console framework that uses snap-ins. Administrators can create custom consoles for administrative tasks.

2. D. In Windows 2000, you can edit the Registry with REGEDIT or REGEDT32. REGEDIT includes more advanced search capabilities, but REGEDT32 supports full editing.

3. C. Microsoft uses driver signing to verify that drivers have been properly tested before they are installed on a Windows 2000 computer. If a driver has not been signed, by default, you will see a warning message when you try to install the driver.

4. B, C. If you want to configure multiple displays in Windows 2000, you need a PCI or an AGP video adapter for each monitor that will be connected. Windows 2000 allows you to extend your Desktop across up to 10 monitors.

5. A. APM (Advanced Power Management) is used to reduce the power consumption of your computer.

6. A. USB supports transmission speeds up to 12Mbps.

7. A. You configure keyboard and mouse properties through their respective icons in Control Panel.

8. C. The Add/Remove Hardware icon in Control Panel starts the Add/Remove Hardware Wizard to install hardware that is not Plug-and-Play compatible.

9. C. The Power Management icon in Control Panel can be used to configure options such as power schemes, advanced options, hibernation, APM, and UPS properties.

10. C. You configure fax support in Windows 2000 through the Fax icon in Control Panel.

11. A. When you upgrade your computer from a single processor to a multiple-processor configuration, you need to update the processor's driver to support this configuration.

12. A. In Windows 2000, you can edit the Registry with REGEDIT or REGEDT32. REGEDIT includes more advanced search capabilities, but REGEDT32 supports full editing.

13. C. Driver signing verifies that drivers have been thoroughly tested and verified by Microsoft. If you set driver signing to Block, only signed drivers can be installed.

14. C. Through Control Panel, Display Properties, Settings, you can set your display's colors and screen area.

15. A. If you are running a MS-DOS application with multiple-display support and you do not see the application properly, you should try running the application in full-screen mode. If the problem was with a Windows application, you would try running the application in a maximized window. You could also try disabling the secondary display to determine whether the problem was specific to multiple-display support.

16. B. When you configure your computer for hibernation, anything that is stored in memory is also stored on your hard disk. This ensures that you do not lose any information that is stored in memory when you shut down the computer (or put your laptop in sleep mode). When you take your computer out of hibernation, it returns to the state it was previously in.

17. C. Through Control Panel, Power Options, you can configure your UPS through the UPS tab.

18. B. Through Control Panel, Keyboard, you can configure speed, input locales, and the device driver you will use. You typically configure hot keys for applications through the application that will use the hot keys.

19. A. You can access the Hardware Troubleshooter Wizard through the Device Manager utility. Select your computer and then click the Troubleshooter button to be guided through a series of questions to help you solve your problem.

20. A. When a device is not working properly, you will see a yellow exclamation point next to the device. The problem could be that the device is not recognized because the proper driver is not loaded or that the device is in conflict with another device.

Chapter

5

Managing the Desktop

MICROSOFT EXAM OBJECTIVES COVERED IN THIS CHAPTER

✓ Configure and troubleshoot desktop settings.

✓ Configure support for multiple languages or multiple locations.

- Enable multiple-language support.
- Configure multiple-language support for users.
- Configure local settings.
- Configure Windows 2000 Professional for multiple locations.

✓ Configure and troubleshoot accessibility services.

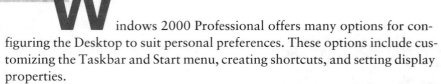

Windows 2000 Professional offers many options for configuring the Desktop to suit personal preferences. These options include customizing the Taskbar and Start menu, creating shortcuts, and setting display properties.

Windows 2000 Professional also includes support for multiple languages and regional settings. The support that comes with localized versions of Windows 2000 Professional allows users to view, edit, and print multilingual documents. You can also specify locale settings for the Desktop to customize items like the date and currency for your geographical location.

Accessibility options are used to support users with limited sight, hearing, or mobility. You can configure the Desktop and use Windows 2000 Professional utilities to provide a higher degree of accessibility.

This chapter describes how to manage Desktop settings, multilanguage support, and accessibility options.

Managing Desktop Settings

The *Desktop*, shown in Figure 5.1, appears after a user has logged on to a Windows 2000 Professional computer. Users can configure their Desktops to suit their personal preferences and to make their work more efficient.

As an administrator, you may need to troubleshoot an improperly configured Desktop.

Microsoft
Exam
Objective

Configure and troubleshoot desktop settings.

By default, the items listed in Table 5.1 appear on the Desktop.

FIGURE 5.1   The Windows 2000 Desktop

TABLE 5.1 Default Desktop Items

Item	Description
My Documents	By default, stores the documents that are created. Each user has a unique *My Documents* folder, so even if multiple users share the same computer, they will each have unique personal folders.
My Computer	Provides access to all local and network drives, as well as Control Panel. *My Computer* is used to view and manage the computer.
My Network Places	Provides access to shared resources. *My Network Places* is used to connect to resources such as local network resources and Web resources.
Recycle Bin	Holds files and folders that have been deleted. Files can be retrieved or cleared (for permanent deletion) from the *Recycle Bin*.
Internet Explorer	Along with an Internet connection, provides an interface for accessing the Internet or a local intranet. *Internet Explorer* is the built-in Web browser.
Taskbar	Contains the Start button to open the *Start menu* and buttons for any programs, documents, or windows that are running on the computer. You can easily switch between open items by clicking the item in the *Taskbar*.
Connect to the Internet	Starts a Wizard to configure your Internet connection.

You can configure the Desktop by customizing the Taskbar and Start menu, adding shortcuts, and setting display properties. These configurations are described in the following sections.

Customizing the Taskbar and Start Menu

Users can customize the Taskbar and Start menu through the Taskbar and Start Menu Properties dialog box, shown in Figure 5.2. The easiest way to access this dialog box is to right-click a blank area in the Taskbar and choose Properties from the pop-up menu.

FIGURE 5.2 The General tab of the Taskbar and Start Menu Properties dialog box

The Taskbar and Start Menu Properties dialog box has two tabs: General and Advanced. The options on these tabs are described in the following sections.

Configuring General Properties

Through the General tab of the Taskbar and Start Menu Properties dialog box (see Figure 5.2), you can specify Taskbar and Start menu features such as whether the Taskbar is always visible and whether small icons are used on the Start menu. Table 5.2 lists the properties on the General tab.

T A B L E   5 . 2   General Taskbar and Start Menu Properties

Property	Description
Always on Top	Specifies that the Taskbar will always be displayed, even if you maximize another window. This option is enabled by default.
Auto Hide	Hides the Taskbar. This option is disabled by default. When it is enabled, you show the Taskbar by clicking the area of the screen where the Taskbar appears.
Show Small Icons in Start Menu	Reduces the size of the icons that are displayed on the Start menu. This option is disabled by default. You might enable it if you have many icons and want to display more options without needing to scroll.
Show Clock	Displays a digital clock in the right corner of the Taskbar. By right-clicking the clock, you can adjust the computer's date and time. This option is enabled by default
Use Personalized Menus	Hides applications that have not been recently used. You can access the hidden applications by clicking the arrow at the bottom of the Programs menu. This option is enabled by default.

Configuring Advanced Properties

The Advanced tab of the Taskbar and Start Menu Properties dialog box, shown in Figure 5.3, allows you to customize your Start menu. You can add or remove items from the Start menu, remove records of recently accessed items, and specify which options are displayed.

FIGURE 5.3   The Advanced tab of the Taskbar and Start Menu Properties dialog box

To add an option to the Start menu, click the Add button in the upper-right corner of the Advanced tab. This starts a Wizard that guides you through the process of creating a shortcut that will be placed on the Start menu. To delete a Start menu option, click the Remove button. If you want to remove the records that Windows 2000 Professional keeps of recently accessed documents, programs, and Web sites, click the Clear button. The Advanced button allows you to add or remove items from the Start menu through Windows Explorer. If you want to return to the defaults for the Program menu, click the Re-sort button.

The Start Menu Settings section of the Advanced tab allows you to configure various Start menu features. These settings are listed in Table 5.3. By default, all of these options are disabled for new users.

TABLE 5.3 The Start Menu Settings

Setting	Description
Display Administrative Tools	Specifies whether Administrative Tools appears on the Programs menu
Display Favorites	Specifies whether the Favorites menu appears on the Start menu.
Display Logoff	Specifies whether the Logoff menu appears on the Start menu
Expand Control Panel	Specifies that you want the contents of Control Panel to be displayed in a menu instead of a window
Expand My Documents	Specifies that you want the contents of My Documents to be displayed in a menu instead of a window
Expand Network and Dial-Up Connections	Specifies that you want the contents of Network and Dial-Up Connections to be displayed in a menu instead of a window
Expand Printers	Specifies that you want the contents of Printers to be displayed in a menu instead of a window
Scroll the Programs Menu	Specifies that you want the contents of Programs to be displayed in a scrolling menu instead of listed in columns

In Exercise 5.1, you will check your current Taskbar and Start menu configuration and then set general and advanced Taskbar and Start menu properties.

EXERCISE 5.1

Configuring Taskbar and Start Menu Options

1. Select Start ➤ Programs. Note the size of the icons in the Start menu. Notice that there is no Programs menu item for Administrative Tools or Windows Explorer.

2. Select Start ➤ Settings ➤ Control Panel. A window with all of the Control Panel contents appears.

3. Right-click an empty space on the Taskbar and choose Properties.

4. In the General tab of the Taskbar and Start Menu Properties dialog box, select the Show Small Icons in Start Menu check box.

5. Click the Advanced tab. Click the Add button. In the Create Shortcut dialog box, type **Explorer** in the Type the Location of the Item text box and click the **Next** button. In the Select Program Folder dialog box, accept the default folder of Programs and click the Next button. In the Select a Title for the Program dialog box, edit the name for the shortcut to **Windows Explorer** and click the Finish button.

6. In the Start Menu Settings section of the Advanced tab, check the Display Administrative Tools and Expand Control Panel check boxes. Click the Apply button, then click the OK button.

7. Select Start ➤ Programs and note the size of the icons in the Start menu. Notice that the Programs menu lists Administrative Tools and Windows Explorer.

8. Select Start ➤ Settings ➤ Control Panel. Notice that the Control Panel contents are displayed in a menu.

9. Edit the Taskbar and Start Menu properties as you like, or return them to their default settings.

Using Shortcuts

Shortcuts are links to items that are accessible from your computer or network. You can use a shortcut to quickly access a file, program, folder, printer, or computer from your Desktop. Shortcuts can exist in various locations, including on the Desktop, on the Start menu, and within folders.

To create a shortcut from Windows Explorer, just right-click the item you want to create a shortcut to and select Create Shortcut from the pop-up menu. Then you can click the shortcut and drag it to where you want it to appear.

In Exercise 5.2, you will create a shortcut and place it on the Desktop.

EXERCISE 5.2

Creating a Shortcut

1. Select Start ➤ Programs ➤ Accessories ➤ Windows Explorer to start Windows Explorer.

2. Expand My Computer, then Local Disk, then WINNT, then System32.

3. Right-click `calc.exe` and select Create Shortcut. You see an icon labeled Shortcut to `calc.exe`.

4. Click the Shortcut to `calc.exe` icon and drag it to the Desktop.

Setting Display Properties

The options in the Display Properties dialog box, shown in Figure 5.4, allow you to customize the appearance of your Desktop. You can access this dialog box by right-clicking an empty area on the Desktop and selecting Properties from the pop-up menu. Alternatively, you can select Start ➤ Settings ➤ Control Panel ➤ Display.

FIGURE 5.4 The Display Properties dialog box

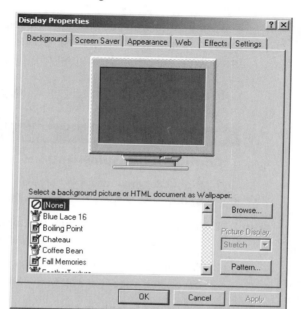

The Display Properties dialog box has six tabs with options that control various aspects of your display:

- The Background tab lets you pick your Desktop background, which uses a picture or an HTML document as wallpaper.

- The Screen Saver tab lets you select a screen saver that will start after the system has been idle for a specified amount of time. You can also specify a password that must be used to reaccess the system after it has been idle. When the idle time has been reached, the computer will be locked, and you must enter the password of the user who is currently logged on to access the computer.

- The Appearance tab has choices for the color scheme used for the Desktop.

- The Web tab lets you select whether or not you want to use the *Active Desktop*, which makes your Desktop look and work like a Web page.

- The Effects tab lets you set special visual effects for the Desktop.

The Settings tab is used to configure display properties, which are not related to user preferences. Configuring the display is covered in Chapter 4, "Configuring the Windows 2000 Environment."

In Exercise 5.3, you will configure display options.

EXERCISE 5.3

Configuring Display Options

1. Right-click an unoccupied area on the Desktop and select Properties to open the Display Properties dialog box.

2. In the Background tab, select Prairie Wind as wallpaper. From the Picture Display drop-down list, select Stretch.

3. Click the Screen Saver tab, select the Starfield Simulation screen saver, and specify a wait of five minutes.

4. Click the Appearance tab, select the Red, White, and Blue (VGA) Scheme. Click the OK button to see your new display settings.

5. Set the display properties to suit your personal preferences, or reset them to their default values.

Through the Mouse and Keyboard icons in Control Panel, you can specify your personal preferences for mouse and keyboard settings. Mouse and keyboard properties are covered in Chapter 4, "Configuring the Windows 2000 Environment."

Managing Multiple Languages and Regional Settings

Windows 2000 Professional supports multiple languages through the use of multilanguage technology. Multilanguage technology is designed to meet the following needs:

- Provide support for multilingual editing of documents
- Provide support for different language interfaces in your environment
- Allow users who speak different languages to share the same computer

---

Microsoft
✓ *Exam*
Objective

Configure support for multiple languages or multiple locations.

- Enable multiple-language support.
- Configure multiple-language support for users.
- Configure local settings.
- Configure Windows 2000 Professional for multiple locations.

Choosing Windows 2000 Multiple-Language Support

Multilanguage support consists of two technologies:

- Multilingual editing and viewing, which supports multiple languages while a user is viewing, editing, and printing documents
- Multilanguage user interfaces, which allow the Windows 2000 Professional user interface to be presented in different languages

Depending on the level of language support that your environment requires, you may use either a localized version of Window 2000 Professional or the Multilanguage version of Windows 2000 Professional. The following sections describe these versions and how to configure multilanguage support.

Using Localized Windows 2000

Microsoft provides localized editions of Windows 2000 Professional. For example, users in the United States will most likely use the English version, and users in Japan will most likely use the Japanese version.

Localized versions of Windows 2000 Professional include fully localized user interfaces for the language that was selected. In addition, localized versions include the ability to view, edit, and print documents in more than 60 different languages. However, localized versions do not support multi-language user interfaces.

Using Windows 2000 Multilanguage Version

Windows 2000 Multilanguage Version provides user interfaces in a number of different languages. This version is useful in multinational corporations where users speak different languages and must share computers. It is also useful in cases where administrators want to deploy a single version of Windows 2000 Professional worldwide. You can manage multiple users who share a single computer and speak different languages through user profiles (covered in Chapter 8, "Using User Profiles and Hardware Profiles") or through group policies (covered in Chapter 7, "Managing Groups").

Two sets of files are necessary to support Windows 2000 Multilanguage Version:

- Language groups, which contain the fonts and files that are required to process and display a specific language

- Windows 2000 Professional Multilanguage Version files, which contain the language content required by the user interface and help files

When you install Windows 2000 Multilanguage Version, you select the initial language that will be installed on the computer. For each language that you wish to use, you must also have the appropriate language group installed. For example, if you want to use the Japanese user interface, you must also install the Japanese language group. If you want to install other language support after installation, you can install and remove Windows 2000 Multilanguage Version files and language groups through Regional Options in Control Panel. Each instance of Multilanguage Version files will use approximately 45MB of disk space. You can edit the default user language interface or add or remove user interface languages through the Muisetup.exe file.

Windows 2000 Multilanguage Version supports the following languages:

Arabic	French	Norwegian
Brazilian	German	Portuguese
Chinese (Simplified)	Greek	Russian
Chinese (Traditional)	Hebrew	Polish
Czech	Hungarian	Spanish
Danish	Italian	Swedish
Dutch	Japanese	Turkish
Finnish	Korean	

Windows 2000 Multilanguage Version is not available through retail stores. You need to order this version of Windows 2000 Professional through Microsoft Volume Licensing Programs. You can get more information about the multilanguage version at www.microsoft.com/licensing.

Enabling and Configuring Multilingual Support

On a localized version of Windows 2000 Professional, you enable and configure multilingual editing and viewing through *Regional Options* in Control Panel. To access the Regional Options dialog box, shown in Figure 5.5, select Start ➢ Settings ➢ Control Panel ➢ Regional Options.

In the list box at the bottom of the Regional Options dialog box, check the language settings that you wish to support on the computer. After you click OK, you may be prompted to insert the Windows 2000 Professional CD to copy the distribution files required for multiple-language support. Then you will need to restart your computer for the new changes to take effect.

FIGURE 5.5 The Regional Options dialog box

After your computer restarts, you will notice a new icon on the Taskbar that shows the current locale and keyboard inputs that are being used. You can switch to another supported language by clicking this icon and selecting the locale input you wish to use.

In Exercise 5.4, you will configure your computer for multilanguage support.

EXERCISE 5.4

Configuring Multiple-Language Support

1. Select Start ➢ Settings ➢ Control Panel ➢ Regional Options.

2. In the Regional Options dialog box, select the language settings that you wish to support on the computer. Then click the OK button.

3. If prompted, insert the Windows 2000 Professional CD to copy the distribution files required for multilanguage support.

4. Restart your computer.

Configuring Locale Settings

You can also configure *locale settings* for numbers, currency, time, date, and input locales (which allows you to select the input language you will use). Like multilingual support, these settings are made through the Regional

Options dialog box (see Figure 5.5). Simply select the locale (location) for the regional settings that you want to use from the drop-down list at the top of the dialog box.

In Exercise 5.5, you will configure the locale settings on your computer.

EXERCISE 5.5

Configuring Locale Settings

1. Select Start ➢ Settings ➢ Control Panel ➢ Regional Options. In the Regional Options dialog box, note your current locale.

2. Click the Numbers, Currency, Time, and Date tabs and note the configurations.

3. Click the General tab and select the Danish locale (location) from the drop-down list at the top of the dialog box. Then click the Apply button.

4. Click the Numbers, Currency, Time, and Date tabs and note the configurations.

5. Click the General tab and reset your locale to the original configuration. Then click the Apply button.

Configuring Accessibility Features

Windows 2000 Professional supports users with limited sight, hearing, or mobility through accessibility options and accessibility utilities. The following sections describe how to use these accessibility features.

Microsoft
✓ **Exam**
Objective

Configure and troubleshoot accessibility services.

Setting Accessibility Options

Through *Accessibility Options* in Control Panel, you can configure keyboard, sound, display, mouse, and general properties of Windows 2000 Professional for users with special needs. To access the Accessibility Options dialog box, shown in Figure 5.6, select Control Panel ➢ Accessibility Options.

FIGURE 5.6 The Accessibility Options dialog box

This dialog box has five tabs with options to configure special behavior for your computer:

- The Keyboard tab allows you to specify whether you want to use StickyKeys, FilterKeys, and ToggleKeys. StickyKeys allows the use of the Shift, Ctrl, or Alt key in conjunction with another key, one key at a time. FilterKeys ignores brief or repeated keystrokes. ToggleKeys makes a noise whenever you press the Caps Lock, Num Lock, or Scroll Lock key.

- The Sound tab allows you specify whether you want to use Sound-Sentry, which generates a visual warning whenever the computer makes a sound, and ShowSounds, which displays captions for speech and sounds on your computer.

- The Display tab allows you to configure high-contrast settings for Windows colors and fonts.

- The Mouse tab allows you to specify whether you want to use MouseKeys, which allows you to control the mouse pointer through the keyboard.

- The General tab allows you to configure several maintenance and administrative options. You can choose to automatically reset accessibility features after these features have been idle for a specified amount of time and to use notification features to notify you when accessibility features are turned on or off. You can also configure SerialKey devices to provide alternative access to keyboard and mouse features. Administrative options allow you to apply accessibility options to the logon Desktop and to defaults for new users.

Using Accessibility Utilities

Windows 2000 provides several accessibility utilities. These utilities include the Accessibility Wizard, Magnifier, Narrator, On-Screen Keyboard, and Utility Manager.

The Accessibility Wizard

The *Accessibility Wizard* configures a computer based on the user's vision, hearing, and mobility needs. The Accessibility Wizard has the user select the text size that is the easiest to read. It also collects input to determine if the user has difficulty with vision, hearing, and mobility.

The Magnifier Utility

The *Magnifier* utility creates a separate window to magnify a portion of your screen, as shown in Figure 5.7. This option is useful for users who have poor vision. To access Magnifier, select Start ➢ Programs ➢ Accessories ➢ Accessibility ➢ Magnifier.

FIGURE 5.7 The Magnifier utility

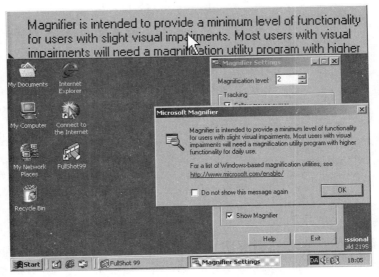

The Narrator Utility

The *Narrator* utility can read aloud on-screen text, dialog boxes, menus, and buttons. This utility requires that you have some type of sound output device installed and configured. To access Narrator, select Start ➢ Programs ➢ Accessories ➢ Accessibility ➢ Narrator. This brings up the dialog box shown in Figure 5.8.

FIGURE 5.8 The Narrator dialog box

The On-Screen Keyboard

The *On-Screen Keyboard* displays a keyboard on the screen, as shown in Figure 5.9. Users can use the On-Screen Keyboard keys through a mouse or another input device as an alternative to the keys on the regular keyboard. To access the On-Screen Keyboard, select Start ➤ Programs ➤ Accessories ➤ Accessibility ➤ On-Screen Keyboard.

FIGURE 5.9   The On-Screen Keyboard

The Utility Manager

The *Utility Manager* allows you to start and stop the Windows 2000 Professional accessibility utilities. You can also specify whether these utilities are automatically started when Windows 2000 Professional starts or when the Utility Manager is started. To access the Utility Manager, select Start ➤ Programs ➤ Accessories ➤ Accessibility ➤ Utility Manager. Figure 5.10 shows the Utility Manager.

FIGURE 5.10   The Utility Manager

In Exercise 5.6, you will use the Windows 2000 Professional accessibility features.

EXERCISE 5.6

Using Accessibility Features

1. Select Start ➤ Programs ➤ Accessories ➤ Accessibility ➤ Magnifier.

2. Experiment with the Magnifier utility. When you are finished, click the Exit button in the Magnifier Settings dialog box.

3. Select Start ➤ Programs ➤ Accessories ➤ Accessibility ➤ On-Screen Keyboard.

4. Select Start ➤ Programs ➤ Accessories ➤ Notepad to open Notepad.

5. Create a text document using the On-Screen Keyboard. When you are finished, close the Notepad document without saving it.

6. Close the On-Screen Keyboard.

Summary

In this chapter, you learned about managing the Windows 2000 Professional Desktop. We covered the following topics:

- Managing Desktop settings, which include customizing the Taskbar and Start menu, using shortcuts, and setting display properties

- Managing multiple languages and regional settings, which include enabling and configuring multilingual support and choosing locale settings

- Configuring accessibility options and using accessibility utilities

Key Terms

Accessibility Options

Accessibility Wizard

Active Desktop

Desktop

Internet Explorer

locale settings

Magnifier

My Computer

My Documents

My Network Places

Narrator

On-Screen Keyboard

Recycle Bin

Regional Options

shortcut

Start menu

Taskbar

Utility Manager

Review Questions

1. What is the purpose of the Desktop setting Use Personalized Menus?

   A. To allow users to create and manage customized menus based on a Wizard called the Personalized Menu Setup Wizard

   B. To keep the Desktop clean by displaying only commonly used applications

   C. To allow users to personalize their menus by choosing colors and fonts

   D. To add the user's name and description at the top of each menu

2. Which of the following methods can be used to configure the Taskbar and Start menu in Windows 2000 Professional?

   A. Right-click an empty space on the Taskbar and choose Properties from the pop-up menu.

   B. Select Control Panel ➢ Menu Settings.

   C. Right-click My Computer and choose Manage from the pop-up menu.

   D. Right-click My Computer and choose Properties from the pop-up menu.

3. Which of the following locations can contain a shortcut? Choose all that apply.

   A. Start menu

   B. MMC

   C. Desktop

   D. Folder

4. Which Desktop option is used to make your Desktop look like a Web page and is able to show Web content?

A. Web Enabler

B. Web Desktop

C. Active Web

D. Active Desktop

5. Which method would you use to configure a Windows 2000 Professional English version to display the user interface in Spanish?

A. Configure Regional Options to add Spanish language support.

B. Through Control Panel, Add/Remove Software icon, add Spanish language support.

C. Configure Regional Options to add Spanish language support, then set the locale settings for Mexico.

D. None of the above.

6. Which accessibility utility is used to enlarge a portion of the screen to support users with poor vision?

A. Enlarger

B. Expander

C. Magnifier

D. Microscope

7. Which of the following options can be configured through the Taskbar and Start Menu Properties dialog box? Choose all that apply.

A. Display Administrative Tools

B. Expand Control Panel

C. Expand Administrative Tools

D. Display Computer Management

8. Which of the following options appear on a Windows 2000 Professional Desktop by default? Choose all that apply.

A. Network Neighborhood

B. Recycle Bin

C. My Computer

D. My Documents

9. Which of the following options are considered locale settings? Choose all that apply.

A. How the date is displayed

B. The language that is used to display the GUI

C. The type of currency that is used

D. How the time is displayed

10. You have just accidentally deleted your `C:\Documents\Timesheet.xls` file. What is the easiest way to recover this file?

A. In Folder Options, click the Show Deleted Files option

B. In Folder Options, click the Undo Deleted Files option

C. Click the Recycle Bin icon on the Desktop and restore the deleted file

D. Restore the file from your most recent tape backup

11. You work in a workgroup environment of computers running Windows 2000 Professional. You log on as a user named Kasia who is a member of the Administrators group. When you select Start ➢ Programs, you do not see Administrative Tools. How do you correct this problem?

   A. Log on as the user Administrator

   B. Add Administrative Tools through the Taskbar and Start Menu Properties dialog box, General tab

   C. Add Administrative Tools through the Taskbar and Start Menu Properties dialog box, Advanced tab

   D. Add Administrative Tools through the Taskbar and Start Menu Properties dialog box, Management tab

12. Which of the following options are *not* set through the Display Properties dialog box?

   A. Desktop background

   B. Screen saver

   C. Special visual effects for your Desktop

   D. Contrast and brightness of the monitor

13. You sit in a busy area of the office. Sometimes, when you leave your desk, you forget to log off or lock your computer. How can you configure your computer so that it will become password-protected if it is idle for more than 10 minutes?

   A. Through Control Panel, Logon/Logoff icon

   B. Through Display Properties, Screen Saver tab

   C. Through Control Panel, Security icon

   D. Through Local Users and Groups, Security properties

14. Brett is using a laptop computer that has Windows 2000 Multi-language Version. The computer is configured for English and Spanish. The default language is configured as English. Brett has been assigned to work in Mexico City for a year and now wants his default user interface to be in Spanish. Through which file can you edit the default language interface?

   A. `Muisetup.exe`

   B. `MLsetup.exe`

   C. `Langsetup.exe`

   D. `Muiconfig.exe`

15. You are planning on installing Windows 2000 Multilanguage Version in your environment. Maria has requested that you install user interfaces on her computer for Russian, Polish, and English. When determining the amount of resources that will be required for this configuration, how much disk space should be allocated for each language?

   A. 10MB

   B. 20MB

   C. 45MB

   D. 85MB

16. Cindy has just installed Windows 2000 Professional on her home computer. The Windows 2000 version she is using is a localized English version. Cindy would also like to be able to create documents using Simplified Chinese to send to her friends in Taiwan. How can she configure the computer to support Simplified Chinese language settings?

   A. Through the Control Panel, Language icon

   B. Through the Control Panel, Regional Options icon

   C. Through the Control Panel, Multilanguage Support icon

   D. Only by upgrading to Windows 2000 Multilanguage Version

17. Bent has configured his computer with English and Danish locale settings. He is currently using English locale settings. He needs to write a letter to a distributor in Denmark. What is the easiest way for Bent to change his locale settings?

   A. Log off and log on again. As a part of the logon process, he will see a menu asking which locale settings he will use.

   B. Restart the computer. As a part of the startup process, he will see a menu asking which locale settings he will use.

   C. Select the Danish locale settings through the Control Panel, Language icon.

   D. When multiple locale settings are configured, he can switch between locales through icons on the Taskbar.

18. Ken configured his computer with the accessibility options StickyKeys and ToggleKeys. Everything was working properly. Then Ken went to a meeting. When he returned after 30 minutes, his accessibility options were no longer working. What is the most likely problem?

   A. The accessibility options were configured to be automatically reset if the computer was idle for a specified amount of time.

   B. Ken needs to log on again to enable the accessibility features.

   C. Ken needs to restart his computer to enable the accessibility features.

   D. The accessibility feature settings have become corrupt and need to be reset.

19. Meredith is a user with limited accessibility. She wants to use an alternative pointing device instead of a regular mouse pointer. You install the device and load the appropriate driver. What additional step should you take?

    A. Configure SerialKey Devices through Accessibility Options

    B. Configure Disable Serial Devices through Accessibility Options

    C. Configure Alternative Serial Devices through Accessibility Options

    D. Configure ParallelKey Devices through Accessibility Options

20. Mike sometimes has problems where he presses keyboard keys too long, which accidentally repeats keystrokes within his documents. What accessibility feature should you configure so that these accidental keystrokes are ignored?

    A. StickyKeys

    B. FilterKeys

    C. SerialKeys

    D. ToggleKeys

Answers to Review Questions

1. B. Over time, as users add more programs, the Desktop can become very cluttered. To avoid this clutter, you can select the Use Personalized Menus option in the General tab of the Taskbar and Start Menu Properties dialog box. Then any programs that you don't use will be hidden. The hidden programs can still be accessed by clicking the small arrow at the bottom of the menu.

2. A. The easiest way to configure the Taskbar and Start menu properties is by right-clicking an open area of the Taskbar and choosing Properties. There is no Menu Settings option in Control Panel.

3. A, C, D. You can put shortcuts in the Start menu, on the Desktop, or in a folder. You can't put a shortcut in the Microsoft Management Console (MMC).

4. D. The Active Desktop configures your Desktop like a Web page and allows your computer to display Web content. The other options do not exist.

5. D. Localized versions of Windows 2000 Professional do not support multilanguage user interfaces. Localized versions support only the ability to view, edit, and print documents in other languages. Language support for the GUI is provided in Windows 2000 Multilanguage Version.

6. C. The Magnifier utility is used to create a separate window that magnifies the portion of the screen that is being used.

7. A, B. The Start menu options that can be configured include Display Administrative Tools, Display Favorites, Display Logoff, Expand Control Panel, Expand My Documents, Expand Network and Dial-Up Connections, Expand Printers, and Scroll the Programs Menu.

8. B, C, D. In Windows 2000 Professional, you see My Network Places instead of Network Neighborhood, which was used in Windows NT 4.

9. A, C, D. Locale settings are used to configure regional settings for numbers, currency, time, date, and input locales.

10. C. The easiest way to recover a deleted file is to restore it from the Recycle Bin. The Recycle Bin holds all of the files and folders that have been deleted. From this utility, you can retrieve or permanently delete files.

11. C. You can specify options such as Display Administrative Tools, Display Logoff, and Display Favorites through the Advanced tab of the Taskbar and Start Menu Properties dialog box.

12. D. Through the Display Properties dialog box, you can set your Desktop background, the screen saver that will be used by your computer, and any special visual effects for your Desktop. You typically set the contrast and brightness of the monitor through controls on the monitor.

13. B. The Screen Saver tab of the Display Properties dialog box allows you to select a screen saver that will start after the computer has been idle for a specified amount of time. When the password is invoked, the computer will be locked. To access the computer, you need to enter the password of the user who is currently logged on.

14. A. You can edit the default user language interface or add or remove user interface languages through the Muisetup.exe file.

15. C. Each instance of Multilanguage Version files will use approximately 45MB of disk space.

16. B. Localized versions of Windows 2000 Professional include fully localized user interfaces for the language that was selected. In addition, localized versions include the ability to view, edit, and print documents in more than 60 different languages. On a localized version of Windows 2000 Professional, you enable and configure multilingual editing and viewing through the Regional Options icon in Control Panel.

17. D. After you configure your computer to use multiple locale settings, you will notice a new icon on the Taskbar that shows the current locale and keyboard inputs that are being used. You can switch to another supported language by clicking this icon and selecting the locale input you wish to use.

18. A. Through the Accessibility Options icon of Control Panel, you can control how long the accessibility options will be active if the computer is idle. A setting on the General tab allows you to turn off accessibility options if the computer has been idle for a specified number of minutes. You should check this setting if the accessibility options were working, but now they are disabled.

19. A. In the General tab of the Accessibility Options dialog box, you can select the Support SerialKey Devices option to allow alternative access to keyboard and mouse features.

20. B. FilterKeys is the feature you should use to ignore brief or repeated keystrokes. The StickyKeys feature allows you to press Shift, Ctrl, or Alt key combinations by using one key at a time. The ToggleKeys feature sounds tones when you press the Cap Lock, Num Lock, or Scroll Lock key.

Chapter 6

Managing Users

MICROSOFT EXAM OBJECTIVES COVERED IN THIS CHAPTER

✓ **Implement, configure, manage, and troubleshoot local user accounts.**

- Implement, configure, manage, and troubleshoot auditing.
- Implement, configure, manage, and troubleshoot account settings.
- Implement, configure, manage, and troubleshoot account policy.
- Create and manage local users and groups.
- Implement, configure, manage, and troubleshoot user rights.

✓ **Implement, configure, manage, and troubleshoot local user authentication.**

- Configure and troubleshoot local user accounts.
- Configure and troubleshoot domain user accounts.

✓ **Implement, configure, manage, and troubleshoot a security configuration.**

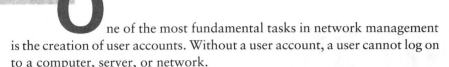

One of the most fundamental tasks in network management is the creation of user accounts. Without a user account, a user cannot log on to a computer, server, or network.

When users log on, they supply a username and password. Then their user accounts are validated by some security mechanism. In Windows 2000 Professional, users can log on to a computer locally, or they can log on through the Active Directory.

When you first create users, you assign them usernames, passwords, and password settings. After a user is created, you can change these settings and select other options for that user through the user Properties dialog box.

You can also set up policies to help manage user accounts. Account policies are used to control the logon environment for the computer, such as password and logon restrictions. Local policies specify what users are able to do once they log on and include auditing, user rights, and security options.

In this chapter, you will learn about user management at the local level. This chapter covers how to create user accounts, manage user properties, set account and local policies, and troubleshoot user account authentication. We'll begin with an overview of the types of Windows 2000 user accounts and how the logon process works.

Reviewing Windows 2000 User Accounts

When you install Windows 2000 Professional, several user accounts are created automatically. You can then create new user accounts. On Windows 2000 Professional computers, you can create local user accounts. If your network has a Windows 2000 Server domain controller, your network can have domain user accounts.

Built-In Accounts

By default, a computer that is installed with Windows 2000 Professional in a workgroup has three users:

Administrator   The *Administrator* account is a special account that has full control over the computer. You provide a password for this account during Windows 2000 Professional installation. The Administrator account can perform all tasks, such as creating users and groups, managing the file system, and setting up printing.

Guest   The *Guest* account allows users to access the computer even if they do not have a unique username and password. Because of the inherent security risks associated with this type of user, this account is disabled by default. When this account is enabled, it is usually given very limited privileges.

Initial user   The *initial user* account uses the name of the registered user. This account is created only if the computer is installed as a member of a workgroup, rather than as part of a domain. By default, the initial user is a member of the Administrators group.

By default, the name Administrator is given to the account with full control over the computer. You can increase the computer's security by renaming the Administrator account and then creating an account named Administrator without any permissions. This way, even if a hacker is able to log on as Administrator, the intruder won't be able to access any system resources.

Local and Domain User Accounts

Windows 2000 supports two kinds of users: local users and domain users. A computer that is running Windows 2000 Professional has the ability to store its own user accounts database. The users that are stored at the local computer are known as *local user accounts*.

Microsoft ✓ ***Exam*** ***Objective***

Implement, configure, manage, and troubleshoot local user authentication.

- Configure and troubleshoot local user accounts.
- Configure and troubleshoot domain user accounts.

The *Active Directory* is a directory service that is available with the Windows 2000 Server platform. It stores information in a central database that allows users to have a single user account for the network. The users that are stored in the Active Directory's central database are called *domain user accounts*.

If you use local user accounts, they are required on each computer that the user needs access to within the network. For this reason, domain user accounts are commonly used to manage users on large networks.

On Windows 2000 Professional computers and Windows 2000 member servers, you create local users through the Local Users and Groups utility, as described in the "Working with User Accounts" section later in the chapter. On Windows 2000 Server domain controllers, you manage users with the Microsoft Active Directory Users and Computers utility.

The Active Directory is covered in detail in *MCSE: Windows 2000 Directory Services Administration Study Guide*, by Anil Desai with James Chellis (Sybex, 2000).

Logging On and Logging Off

U̲sers must log on to a Windows 2000 Professional computer before they can use that computer. When you create user accounts, you set up the computer to accept the *logon* information provided by the user.

When users are ready to stop working on a Windows 2000 Professional computer, they should log off. Logging off is accomplished through the Windows Security dialog box.

The following sections describe the *logon* and logoff processes and the options in the Windows Security dialog box.

Local User Logon Authentication

When you log on to a Windows 2000 Professional computer locally, you must present a valid username and password (ones that exist within the local accounts database). As part of a successful *authentication*, the following steps take place:

1. At system startup, the user is prompted to press Ctrl+Alt+Delete to access the logon dialog box. The user types in a valid logon name and password, and then clicks the OK button.

The Ctrl+Alt+Delete sequence was originally used for security purposes. Security violations occurred when programs were written to mimic the logon process, but were actually copying out the username and password. If a rogue password program were running and you pressed Ctrl+Alt+Delete, it would cause the computer to reboot or the Windows Security dialog box to appear.

2. The local computer compares the user's logon credentials with the information in the local security database.

3. If the information presented matches the account database, an *access token* is created. Access tokens are used to identify the user and the groups that the user is a member of.

Access tokens are created only when you log on. If you change group memberships, you need to log off and log on again to update the access token.

Figure 6.1 illustrates the three main steps in the logon process.

FIGURE 6.1 The logon process

Other actions that take place as part of the logon process include the following:

- The system reads the part of the Registry that contains user configuration information.

- The user's profile is loaded. (User profiles are discussed briefly in the "Setting Up User Profiles, Logon Scripts, and Home Folders" section later in this chapter and in more detail in Chapter 8, "Using User Profiles and Hardware Profiles.")

- Any policies that have been assigned to the user through a user or group policy are enforced. (Policies for users are discussed later in this chapter, in the "Using Account Policies" and "Using Local Policies" sections. Group policies are covered in Chapter 7, "Managing Groups.")

- Any logon scripts that have been assigned are executed. (Assigning logon scripts to users is discussed in the "Setting Up User Profiles, Logon Scripts, and Home Folders" section.)

- Persistent network and printer connections are restored. (Network connections are discussed in Chapter 11, "Managing Network Connections," and printer connections are covered in Chapter 12, "Managing Printing.")

Through the logon process, you can control what resources a user can access by assigning permissions. Permissions are granted to either users or groups. Permissions also determine what actions a user can perform on a computer. In Chapter 10, "Accessing Files and Folders," you will learn more about assigning resource permissions.

Logging Off Windows 2000 Professional

You normally log off Windows 2000 Professional via the Windows Security dialog box, shown in Figure 6.2. (Another way to log off is to use Start ➢ Shutdown ➢ Logoff.) You access the Windows Security dialog box by pressing Ctrl+Alt+Delete.

FIGURE 6.2 The Windows Security dialog box

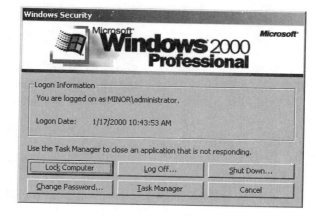

The Windows Security dialog box shows which user is currently logged on, as well as the logon date and time. From this dialog box, you can just log off the current user (and leave the computer running) or you can log off and shut down the computer. In addition, there are a few other tasks you can perform using the Windows Security dialog box. Table 6.1 lists the options in the Windows Security dialog box.

TABLE 6.1 The Windows Security Dialog Box Options

Option	Description
Lock Computer	Leaves the current user logged on while securing the computer from other access. You type in the password of the user who locked the computer to unlock it.
Change Password	Allows users to change their own password. The user must enter the old password and then type in and confirm the new password.
Log Off	Logs off the active user but leaves the Windows 2000 Professional computer running. This allows other users to access services and shares that have been created on that computer.
Task Manager	Brings up the Task Manager utility.
Shut Down	Forces all files to be closed, saves all changes that have been made to the operating system, and prepares the computer to be shut down.
Cancel	Closes the Windows Security dialog box without making any changes.

In Exercise 6.1, you will use the options in the Windows Security dialog box. You should already be logged on as Administrator before you begin this exercise.

EXERCISE 6.1

Using the Windows Security Dialog Box

1. Press Ctrl+Alt+Delete to access the Windows Security dialog box.

2. Click the Lock Computer button to lock the computer.

EXERCISE 6.1 *(continued)*

3. Press Ctrl+Alt+Delete. Supply the Administrator password to unlock the computer.

4. Click the Change Password button to access the Change Password dialog box. You can change the password or click the Cancel button to keep your current password.

5. Click the Task Manager button. Click each tab in the Task Manager window to get a general idea of the features that Task Manager offers. (See Chapter 14, "Optimizing Windows 2000," for details on using the Task Manager.)

6. When you're finished exploring, close the Task Manager window. You return to the Desktop.

Working with User Accounts

To set up and manage users, you use the *Local Users and Groups* utility. With Local Users and Groups, you can create, delete, and rename user accounts, as well as change passwords.

Microsoft Exam Objective

Implement, configure, manage, and troubleshoot local user accounts.

- Implement, configure, manage, and troubleshoot account settings.
- Create and manage local users and groups.

The procedures for many basic user management tasks—such as creating, disabling, deleting, and renaming user accounts—are the same for both Windows 2000 Professional and Server.

Using the Local Users and Groups Utility

The first step to working with Windows 2000 Professional user accounts is to access the Local Users and Groups utility. There are two common methods for accessing this utility:

- You can load Local Users and Groups as a Microsoft Management Console (MMC) snap-in. (See Chapter 4, "Configuring the Windows 2000 Environment," for details on the MMC and the purpose of snap-ins.)

- You can access the Local Users and Groups utility through the Computer Management utility.

The following steps are used to add the Local Users and Groups snap-in to the MMC:

1. Select Start ≻ Run, type **MMC** in the Run dialog box, and press Enter to open the MMC window, as shown in Figure 6.3.

FIGURE 6.3 The MMC window

2. Select Console ≻ Add/Remove Snap-in to open the Add/Remove Snap-in dialog box.

3. Click the Add button to open the Add Standalone Snap-in dialog box.

4. Select Local Users and Groups and click the Add button.

5. The Choose Target Machine dialog box appears, with Local Computer selected. Click the Finish button. You return to the Add Standalone Snap-in dialog box.

6. Click the Close button. You return to the Add/Remove Snap-in dialog box.

7. Click the OK button. You will see that the Local Users and Groups snap-in has been added to the MMC, as shown in Figure 6.4.

FIGURE 6.4   The Local Users and Groups snap-in added to the MMC

8. Save the console by selecting Console ➢ Save. Specify the path and filename for your console. For easy access to the MMC, you might want to save the console to your Desktop.

If your computer doesn't have the MMC configured, the quickest way to access the Local Users and Groups utility is through the Computer Management utility. Right-click My Computer and select Manage from the pop-up menu to open the Computer Management window. In the System Tools folder, you will see the Local Users and Groups folder. Expand that folder to access the Users and Groups folders in the utility, as shown in Figure 6.5.

FIGURE 6.5 The Local Users and Groups folder in Computer Management

In Exercise 6.2, you will use both methods for accessing the Local Users and Groups utility.

EXERCISE 6.2

Accessing the Local Users and Groups Utility

In this exercise, you will first add the Local Users and Groups snap-in to the MMC. Next, you will add a shortcut to your Desktop that will take you to the MMC. Finally, you will use the other access technique of opening the Local Users and Groups utility from the Computer Management utility.

Adding the Local Users and Groups Snap-in to the MMC

1. Select Start ➢ Run. In the Run dialog box, type **MMC** and press Enter.

2. Select Console ➢ Add/Remove Snap-in.

3. In the Add/Remove Snap-in dialog box, click the Add button.

4. In the Add Standalone Snap-in dialog box, select Local Users and Groups and click the Add button.

5. In the Choose Target Machine dialog box, click the Finish button to accept the default selection of Local Computer.

6. Click the Close button in the Add Standalone Snap-in dialog box. Then click the OK button in the Add/Remove Snap-in dialog box.

7. In the MMC window, expand the Local Users and Groups folder to see the Users and Groups folders.

Adding the MMC to Your Desktop

1. Select Console ➢ Save. Click the folder with the up arrow icon until you are at the root of the computer.

2. Select the Desktop option and specify **Admin Console** as the filename. The default extension is .msc. Click the Save button.

Accessing Local Users and Groups through Computer Management

1. Right-click My Computer and select Manage.

2. In the Computer Management window, expand the System Tools folder, then expand the Local Users and Groups folder.

Creating New Users

To create users on a Windows 2000 Professional computer, you must be logged on as a user with permissions to create a new user, and you must be a member of the Administrators group or Power Users group. (Groups are covered in Chapter 7.)

Username Rules and Conventions

The only real requirement for creating a new user is that you must provide a valid username. "Valid" means that the name must follow the Windows 2000 rules for usernames. However, it's also a good idea to have your own rules for usernames, which form your naming convention.

The following are the Windows 2000 rules for usernames:

- A username must be between 1 and 20 characters.

- The username must be unique to all other user and group names stored on the specified computer.

- The username cannot contain the following characters:

  * / \ [ ] : ; | = , + * ? < > "

- A username cannot consist exclusively of periods or spaces.

Keeping these rules in mind, you should choose a naming convention, which is a consistent naming format. For example, consider a user named Kevin Donald. One naming convention might use the last name and first initial, for the username DonaldK. Another naming convention might use the first initial and last name, for the username KDonald. Other user-naming conventions are based on the naming convention defined for e-mail names, so that the logon name and e-mail name match. You should also provide a mechanism that would accommodate duplicate names. For example, if you had a user named Kevin Donald and a user named Kate Donald, you might use a middle initial, for the usernames such as KLDonald and KMDonald.

Naming conventions should also be applied to objects such as groups, printers, and computers.

Usernames and Security Identifiers

When you create a new user, a *security identifier*, or *SID*, is automatically created on the computer for the user account. The username is a property of the SID. For example, a user SID might look like this:

    S-1-5-21-823518204-746137067-120266-629-500

It's apparent that using SIDs would make administration a nightmare. Fortunately, for your administrative tasks, you see and use the username instead of the SID.

SIDs have several advantages. Because Windows 2000 uses the SID as the user object, you can easily rename a user while still retaining all the properties of that user. SIDs also ensure that if you delete and recreate a user using the same username, the new user account will not have any of the properties of the old account, because it is based on a new, unique SID. Renaming and deleting user accounts are discussed later in this chapter.

Options for New User Accounts

To create a new user, you open the Local Users and Groups utility, highlight the Users folder, and select Action ➢ New User. This opens the New User dialog box, as shown in Figure 6.6.

FIGURE 6.6 The New User dialog box

In this dialog box, you must fill in the User Name field. All of the other settings in the New User dialog box are optional. Table 6.2 describes the options in the New User dialog box.

TABLE 6.2 The New User Dialog Box Options

Option	Description
User Name	Defines the username for the new account. Choose a name that is consistent with your naming convention (e.g., WSmith). This is the only required field. Usernames are not case-sensitive.
Full Name	Allows you to provide more detailed information about this user. This is typically the user's first and last name (e.g., Wendy Smith). By default, this field is the same as the entry in the User Name field.

TABLE 6.2 The New User Dialog Box Options *(continued)*

Option	Description
Description	Allows you to provide additional information. This is typically used to specify a title and/or location (e.g., Sales-Texas), but it can be used for any purpose.
Password	Assigns the initial password for the user. For security purposes, it is not advisable to use readily available information about the user. Passwords can be up to 14 characters and are case-sensitive.
Confirm Password	Confirms that you typed the password the same way two times to verify that you entered the password correctly.
User Must Change Password at Next Logon	If selected, forces the user to change the password the first time that user logs on. This is done to increase security. By default, this option is selected.
User Cannot Change Password	If selected, prevents a user from changing the password. It is useful for accounts like Guest and those that are shared by more than one user. By default, this option is not selected.
Password Never Expires	If selected, specifies that the password will never expire, even if a password policy has been specified. For example, you might select this option if this is a service account and you did not want the administrative overhead of managing changing passwords. By default, this option is not selected.
Account Is Disabled	If selected, specifies that this account cannot be used for logon purposes. For example, you might select this option for template accounts or if an account is not currently being used. It helps keep inactive accounts from posing security threats. By default, this option is not selected.

Make sure that your users know that usernames are not case-sensitive, but passwords are.

In Exercise 6.3, you will create several new local user accounts. We will use these users for the subsequent exercises in this chapter. Before you start this exercise, make sure that you are logged on as user with permissions to create new users and have already added the Local Users and Groups snap-in to the MMC (see Exercise 6.2).

EXERCISE 6.3

Creating New Local Users

1. Open the MMC and expand the Local Users and Groups snap-in.

2. Highlight the Users folder and select Action ➤ New User. The New User dialog box appears.

3. In the User Name text box, type **Cam**.

4. In the Full Name text box, type **Cam Presely**.

5. In the Description text box, type **Sales Vice President**.

6. Click the Create button to add the user. (Leave the Password and Confirm Password text boxes empty and the defaults for the check boxes.)

7. Use the New User dialog box to create six more users, filling out the fields as follows:

    Name: **Dick**; Full Name: **Dick Jones**; Description: **Sales-Florida**; Password: (blank)

    Name: **Terry**; Full Name: **Terry Belle**; Description: **Marketing**; Password: (blank)

    Name: **Ron**; Full Name: **Ron Klein**; Description: **PR**; Password: **superman**

    Name: **Wendy**; Full Name: **Wendy Smith**; Description: **Sales-Texas**; Password: **supergirl**

EXERCISE 6.3 *(continued)*

Name: **Emily**; Full Name: **Emily Buras**; Description: **President**; Password: **peach**

Name: **Michael**; Full Name: **Michael Phillips**; Description: **Tech Support**; Password: **apple**

8. After you've finished creating all of the users, click the Close button to exit the New User dialog box.

You can also create users through the command-line utility NET USER. For more information about this command, type *NET USER /?* from a command prompt.

Disabling User Accounts

When a user account is no longer needed, the account should be disabled or deleted. If you choose to disable an account, you can later enable that account to restore it with all of its associated user properties. An account that is deleted can never be recovered.

User accounts that are not in use pose a security threat because an intruder could access your network though an inactive account. For example, after inheriting a network, I ran a network security diagnostic and noticed several accounts for users who no longer worked for the company. These accounts had Administrative rights, including dial-in permissions. This was not a good situation, and the accounts were deleted on the spot.

You might disable an account because a user will not be using it for a period of time, perhaps because that employee is going on vacation or taking a leave of absence. Another reason to disable an account is if you're planning on putting another user in that some function. For example, suppose that Rick, the engineering manager, quit. If you disable his account, when your company hires a new engineering manager, you can simply rename the user account (from Rick to the username for the new manager) and enable that account. This ensures that the user who takes over Rick's position will have all of the user properties and own all of the resources that original user Rick had.

Disabling accounts also provides a security mechanism for special situations. For example, if your company were laying off a group of people, a security measure would be to disable their accounts at the same time as these employees get their layoff notices. This prevents the users from inflicting any damage to the company's files on their way out. (Yes, this does seem cold-hearted, and other employees are bound to fear for their jobs any time the servers go down and they aren't able to log on, but it does serve the purpose.)

You disable a user account by checking the Account Is Disabled check box in the user's Properties dialog box, shown in Figure 6.7. To access this dialog box, double-click the user account in the Users folder in the Local Users and Groups utility.

FIGURE 6.7   A user Properties dialog box

In Exercise 6.4, you will disable a user account. Before you follow this exercise, you should have already created new users (see Exercise 6.3).

EXERCISE 6.4

Disabling a User

1. Open the MMC and expand the Local Users and Groups snap-in.

2. Open the Users folder. Double-click user Dick to open his Properties dialog box.

3. In the General tab, check the Account Is Disabled box. Click the OK button.

4. Log off as Administrator and attempt to log on as Dick. This should fail, since the account is now disabled.

5. Log on as Administrator.

You can also access a user's Properties dialog box by highlighting the user and right-clicking (clicking the secondary mouse button).

Deleting User Accounts

As noted in the previous section, you should delete a user account if you are sure that the account will never be needed again.

To delete a user, open the Local Users and Groups utility, highlight the user account you wish to delete, and click Action to bring up the menu shown in Figure 6.8. Then select Delete.

FIGURE 6.8   Choosing to delete a user

Because user deletion is a permanent action, you will see the dialog box shown in Figure 6.9, asking you to confirm that you really wish to delete the account. After you click the Yes button here, you will not be able to recreate or reaccess the account (unless you restore your local user accounts database from a backup).

FIGURE 6.9   Confirming user deletion

In Exercise 6.5, you will delete a user account. This exercise assumes that you have completed the previous exercises in this chapter.

EXERCISE 6.5

Deleting a User

1. Open the MMC and expand the Local Users and Groups snap-in.

2. Open the Users folder and highlight user Dick.

3. Select Action ➤ Delete. The dialog box for confirming user deletion appears.

4. Click the Yes button.

The Administrator and Guest accounts cannot be deleted. The *initial user* account can be deleted.

Renaming Users

Once an account has been created, you can rename the account at any time. Renaming a user account allows the user to retain all of the associated user properties of the previous username. As noted earlier in the chapter, the name is a property of the SID.

You might want to rename a user account because the user's name has changed (for example, the user got married) or because the name was spelled incorrectly. Also, as explained in the "Disabling User Accounts" section, you can rename an existing user's account for a new user who you want to have the same properties, such as someone hired to take an ex-employee's position.

To rename a user, open the Local Users and Groups utility, highlight the user account you wish to rename, and select Action ➤ Rename. Edit the username and press Enter to complete the action.

In Exercise 6.6, you will rename a user account. This exercise assumes that you have completed all of the previous exercises in this chapter.

EXERCISE 6.6

Renaming a User

1. Open the MMC and expand the Local Users and Groups snap-in.

2. Open the Users folder and highlight user Terry.

3. Select Action ➤ Rename.

4. Type in the username **Taralyn** and press Enter. Notice that the Full Name retained the original property of Terry in the Local Users and Groups utility.

Renaming a user does not change any "hard-coded" names, such as the user's home folder. If you want to change these names as well, you need to modify them manually.

Changing a User's Password

What do you do if user Terry forgot her password and can't log on? You can't just open a dialog box and see her old password. However, as the Administrator, you can change Terry's password, and then she can use the new one.

To change a user's password, open the Local Users and Groups utility, highlight the user account, and select Action ➤ Set Password. Type in the new password to set it and then again to confirm it.

In Exercise 6.7, you will change a user's password. This exercise assumes that you have completed all of the previous exercises in this chapter.

EXERCISE 6.7

Changing a User's Password

1. Open the MMC and expand the Local Users and Groups snap-in.

2. Open the Users folder and highlight user Ron.

3. Select Action ➤ Set Password. The Set Password dialog box appears.

4. Type in the new password and then confirm the password. Click the OK button.

Managing User Properties

For more control over user accounts, you can configure user properties. Through the user Properties dialog box, you can change the original password options, add the users to existing groups, and specify user profile information.

Microsoft ✓ *Exam* *Objective*

Implement, configure, manage, and troubleshoot local user accounts.

- Implement, configure, manage, and troubleshoot account settings.
- Create and manage local users and groups.

To open the user Properties dialog box, access the Local Users and Groups utility, open the Users folder, and double-click the user account. The user Properties dialog box has tabs for the three main categories of properties: General, Member Of, and Profile.

The General tab (see Figure 6.7 earlier in the chapter) contains the information that you supplied when you set up the new user account, including any Full Name and Description information you entered, the password options you selected, and whether or not the account is disabled (see the "Creating a New User" section earlier in this chapter). If you want to modify any of these properties after you've created the user, simply open the user Properties dialog box and make the changes on the General tab.

The Member Of tab is used to manage the user's membership in groups. The Profile tab lets you set properties to customize the user's environment. These properties are discussed in detail in the following sections.

Managing User Group Membership

The Member Of tab of the user Properties dialog box displays all the groups that the user belongs to, as shown in Figure 6.10. From this tab, you can add the user to an existing group or remove that user from a group. To add a user to a group, click the Add button and select the group that the user should belong to. If you want to remove the user from a group, highlight the group and click the Remove button.

FIGURE 6.10 The Member Of tab of the user Properties dialog box

Groups are used to logically group users who have similar resource access requirements. Managing groups is much easier than managing individual users. Creating and managing groups are covered in detail in Chapter 7.

The steps used to add a user to an existing group are shown in Exercise 6.8. This exercise assumes that you have completed all of the previous exercises in this chapter.

EXERCISE 6.8

Adding a User to a Group

1. Open the MMC and expand the Local Users and Groups snap-in.

2. Open the Users folder and double-click user Wendy. The user Properties dialog box appears.

3. Select the Member Of tab and click the Add button. The Select Groups dialog box appears.

4. Highlight the Power Users group and click the Add button. Then click the OK button.

5. Click the OK button to close the user Properties dialog box.

Setting Up User Profiles, Logon Scripts, and Home Folders

The Profile tab of the user Properties dialog box, shown in Figure 6.11, allows you to customize the user's environment. Here, you can specify the following items for the user:

- User profile path
- Logon script
- Home folder

The following sections describe how these properties work and when you might want to use them.

FIGURE 6.11 The Profile tab of the user Properties dialog box

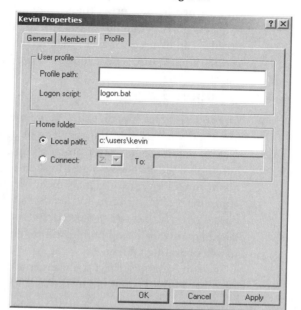

Setting a Profile Path

User profiles contain information about the Windows 2000 environment for a specific user. For example, profile settings include the Desktop arrangement, program groups, and screen colors that users see when they log on.

By default, when a user logs on, a profile is opened for a user. Any changes that the user makes to the Desktop are stored on the local computer when the user logs off. For example, suppose that user Rick logs on, picks his wallpaper, creates shortcuts, and customizes the Desktop to his personal preference. When he logs off, his profile is stored locally. If another user logs on at the same computer, that user's profile—not Rick's—is loaded.

Profiles are covered in detail in Chapter 8, "Using User Profiles and Hardware Profiles."

The Profile Path option in the Profile tab is used to point to another location for profile files other than the default local location. This allows users to access profiles that have been stored in a shared network folder. This way, profiles can be used for an individual user or shared by a group of users. To specify a path, just type it in the Profile Path text box.

Using Logon Scripts

Logon scripts are files that run every time a user logs on to the network. They are usually batch files, but they can be any type of executable file.

You might use logon scripts to set up drive mappings or to run a specific executable file each time a user logs on to the computer. For example, you could run an inventory management file that collects information about the computer's configuration and sends that data to a central management database. Logon scripts are also useful for compatibility with non-Windows 2000 clients that want to log on but still maintain consistent settings with their native operating system.

To run a logon script for a user, enter the script name in the Logon Script text box in the Profile tab of the user Properties dialog box.

Logon scripts are not commonly used in Windows 2000 networks. Windows 2000 automates much of the user's configuration. In older NetWare environments, for example, this isn't the case, and administrators use logon scripts to configure the users' environment.

Setting Up Home Folders

Users normally store their personal files and information is a private folder called a *home folder*. In the Profile tab of the user Properties dialog box, you can specify the location of a home folder as a local folder or a network folder.

To specify a local path folder, choose the Local Path option and type the path in the text box next to that option. To specify a network path for a folder, choose the Connect option and specify a network path using a UNC (Universal Naming Convention) path. In this case, a network folder should already be created and shared.

In Exercise 6.9, you will assign a home folder to a user. This exercise assumes that you have completed all of the previous exercises in this chapter.

EXERCISE 6.9

Assigning a Home Folder to a User

1. Open the MMC and expand the Local Users and Groups snap-in.

2. Open the Users folder and double-click user Wendy. The user Properties dialog box appears.

3. Select the Profile tab and click the Local Path radio button to select it.

4. Specify the home folder path by typing **C:\Users\Wendy** in the text box for the Local Path option. Then click the OK button.

5. Use Windows Explorer to verify that this folder was created.

Using Account Policies

Account policies are used to specify the user account properties that relate to the logon process. They allow you to configure computer security settings for passwords and account lockout specifications.

Microsoft ✓ *Exam Objective*	**Implement, configure, manage, and troubleshoot local user accounts.** • Implement, configure, manage, and troubleshoot account policy.

Microsoft ✓ *Exam Objective*	**Implement, configure, manage, and troubleshoot a security configuration.**

If security is not an issue—perhaps because you are using your Windows 2000 Professional computer at home—then you don't need to bother with account policies. On the other hand, if security is important—for example, because your computer provides access to payroll information—then you should set very restrictive account policies.

Loading the Local Computer Policy Snap-In

To implement account policies, you first need to add the *Local Computer Policy* snap-in to the MMC. Exercise 6.10 shows the steps for adding the Local Computer Policy snap-in.

You can also access the account policies and local policies by opening Control Panel and selecting Administrative Tools ➤ Local Security Policy.

EXERCISE 6.10

Adding the Local Computer Policy Snap-in to the MMC

1. Open the MMC by double-clicking the Admin Console icon on your Desktop (which you created in Exercise 6.2).

2. From the main menu, select Console ➤ Add/Remove Snap-in.

3. In the Add/Remove Snap-in dialog box, click the Add button.

4. Highlight the Group Policy option and click the Add button.

5. The Group Policy object specifies Local Computer by default. Click the Finish button.

6. Click the Close button.

7. In the Add/Remove Snap-in dialog box, click the OK button.

From the MMC, follow this path of folders to access the Account Policies folders: Local Computer Policy, Computer Configuration, Windows Settings, Security Settings, Account Policies. Figure 6.12 shows the Account Policies folders.

FIGURE 6.12 Accessing the Account Policies folders

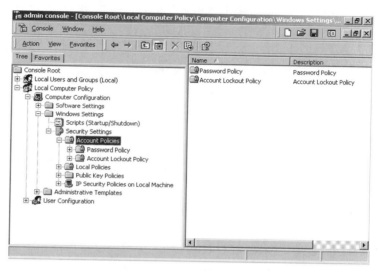

Here, you see two folders: Password Policy and Account Lockout Policy. These represent the two types of account policies, which are covered in the following sections.

Setting Password Policies

Password policies ensure that security requirements are enforced on the computer. It is important to note that the password policy is set on a per-computer basis; it cannot be configured for specific users.

Figure 6.13 shows the password policies, which are described in Table 6.3.

FIGURE 6.13 The password policies

TABLE 6.3 Password Policy Options

Policy	Description	Default	Minimum	Maximum
Enforce Password History	Keeps track of user's password history	Remember 0 passwords	Same as default	Remember 24 passwords
Maximum Password Age	Determines maximum number of days user can keep valid password	Keep password for 42 days	Keep password for 1 day	Keep password for up to 999 days

TABLE 6.3 Password Policy Options *(continued)*

Policy	Description	Default	Minimum	Maximum
Minimum Password Age	Specifies how long password must be kept before it can be changed	0 days (password can be changed immediately)	Same as default	999 days
Minimum Password Length	Specifies minimum number of characters password must contain	0 characters (no password required)	Same as default	14 characters
Passwords Must Meet the Complexity Requirements of the Installed Password Filters	Allows you to install password filter	Disabled	Same as default	Enabled
Store Password Using Reversible Encryption for All Users in the Domain	Specifies higher level of encryption for stored user passwords	Disabled	Same as default	Enabled

The password policies are used as follows:

- The Enforce Password History option is used so that users cannot use the same password. Users must create a new password when their password expires or is changed.

- The Maximum Password Age option is used so that after the maximum password age is exceeded, users are forced to change their password.

- The Minimum Password Age option is used to prevent users from changing their password several times in rapid succession in order to defeat the purpose of the Enforce Password History policy.

- The Minimum Password Length option is used to ensure that users create a password, as well as to specify that it meets the length requirement. If this option isn't set, users are not required to create a password.

- The Passwords Must Meet the Complexity Requirements of the Installed Password Filters option is used to prevent users from using as passwords items found in a dictionary of common names.

- The Store Password Using Reversible Encryption for All Users in the Domain option is used to provide a higher level of security for user passwords.

In Exercise 6.11, you will configure password policies for your computer. This exercise assumes that you have added the Local Computer Policy snap-in to the MMC (see Exercise 6.10).

EXERCISE 6.11

Setting Password Policies

1. Open the MMC and expand the Local Computer Policy Snap-in.

2. Expand the folders as follows: Computer Configuration, Windows Settings, Security Settings, Account Policies, Password Policy.

3. Open the Enforce Password History policy. In the Effective Policy Setting field, specify **5** passwords remembered. Click the OK button.

4. Open the Maximum Password Age policy. In the Local Policy Setting field, specify that the password expires in **60** days. Click the OK button.

Setting Account Lockout Policies

The *account lockout policies* are used to specify how many invalid logon attempts should be tolerated. You configure the account lockout policies so that after *x* number of unsuccessful logon attempts within *y* number of minutes, the account will be locked for a specified amount of time or until the Administrator unlocks the account.

The account lockout policies are similar to how banks handle ATM access code security. You have a certain amount of chances to enter the correct access code. That way, if someone stole your card, they would not be able to keep guessing you access code until they got it right. Typically, after three unsuccessful attempts at your access code, the ATM machine takes the card. Then you need to request a new card from the bank.

Figure 6.14 shows the account lockout policies, which are described in Table 6.4.

FIGURE 6.14 The account lockout policies

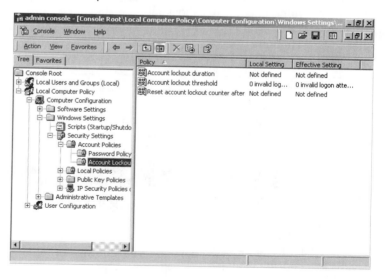

TABLE 6.4 Account Lockout Policy Options

Policy	Description	Default	Minimum	Maximum	Suggested
Account Lockout Threshold	Specifies number of invalid attempts allowed before account is locked out	0 (disabled, account will not be locked out)	Same as default	999 attempts	5 attempts
Account Lockout Duration	Specifies how long account will remain locked if Account Lockout Threshold is exceeded	0; but if Account Lockout Threshold is enabled, 30 minutes	Same as default	99,999 minutes	5 minutes
Reset Account Lockout Counter After	Specifies how long counter will remember unsuccessful logon attempts	0, but if Account Lockout Threshold is enabled, 5 minutes	Same as default	99,999 minutes	5 minutes

In Exercise 6.12, you will configure account lockout policies and test their effects. This exercise assumes that you have completed all of the previous exercises in this chapter.

EXERCISE 6.12

Setting Account Lockout Policies

1. Open the MMC and expand the Local Computer Policy snap-in.

2. Expand the folders as follows: Computer Configuration, Windows Settings, Security Settings, Account Policies, Account Lockout Policy.

EXERCISE 6.12 *(continued)*

3. Open the Account Lockout Threshold policy. In the Local Policy Setting field, specify that the account will lock after **3** invalid logon attempts. Click the OK button.

4. Open the Account Lockout Duration policy. In the Local Policy Setting field, specify that the account will remain locked for **5** minutes. Click the OK button.

5. Log off as Administrator. Try to log on as Emily with an incorrect password three times.

6. After you see the error message stating that account lockout has been enabled, log on as Administrator.

7. To unlock Emily's account, open the Local Users and Groups snap-in in the MMC, expand the Users folder, and double-click user Emily.

8. In the General tab of Emily's Properties dialog box, click to remove the check from the Account Is Locked Out check box. Then click OK.

Using Local Policies

As you learned in the previous section, account policies are used to control logon procedures. When you want to control what a user can do after logging on, you use *local policies*. With local policies, you can implement auditing, specify user rights, and set security options.

Microsoft
✓ *Exam*
Objective

Implement, configure, manage, and troubleshoot local user accounts.

- Implement, configure, manage, and troubleshoot auditing.
- Implement, configure, manage, and troubleshoot user rights.

To use local policies, first add the Local Computer Policy snap-in to the MMC (see Exercise 6.10). Then, from the MMC, follow this path of folders to access the Local Policies folders: Local Computer Policy, Computer Configuration, Windows Settings, Security Settings, Local Policies. Figure 6.15 shows the Local Policies folders.

FIGURE 6.15   Accessing the Local Policies folders

There are three folders in Local Policies: Audit Policy, User Rights Assignment, and Security Options. These policies are covered in the following sections.

Setting Audit Policies

My mother once told me to trust no one. The *audit policies* reinforce this thinking. By implementing auditing, you can watch what your users are doing.

You audit events that pertain to user management through the audit policies. By tracking certain events, you can create a history of specific tasks, such as user creation and successful or unsuccessful logon attempts. You can also identify security violations that arise when users attempt to access system management tasks that they do not have permission to access.

WARNING Users who try to go to areas that they do not have permission to go to usually fall into two categories: those who are hackers and those who are just curious to see what they can do. Both are very dangerous.

When you define an audit policy, you can choose to audit success or failure of specific events. The success of an event means that the task was successfully accomplished. The failure of an event means that the task was not successfully accomplished.

By default, auditing is not enabled, and it must be manually configured. Once auditing has been configured, you can see the results of the audit through the Event Viewer utility, Security log. (The Event Viewer utility is covered in Chapter 15.)

WARNING Auditing too many events can degrade system performance due to its high processing requirements. Auditing can also use excessive disk space to store the audit log. You should use this utility judiciously.

Figure 6.16 shows the audit policies, which are described in Table 6.5.

FIGURE 6.16 The audit policies

TABLE 6.5 Audit Policy Options

Policy	Description
Audit Account Logon Events	Tracks when a user logs on, logs off, or makes a network connection
Audit Account Management	Tracks user and group account creation, deletion, and management actions
Audit Directory Service Access	Tracks directory service accesses
Audit Logon Events	Audits events related to logon, such as running a logon script or accessing a roaming profile
Audit Object Access	Enables auditing of access to files, folders, and printers
Audit Policy Change	Tracks any changes to the audit policy
Audit Privilege Use	Tracks any changes to who can or cannot define or see the results of auditing
Audit Process Tracking	Tracks events such as activating a program, accessing an object, and exiting a process
Audit System Events	Tracks system events such as shutting down or restarting the computer, as well as events that relate to the Security log in Event Viewer

After you set the Audit Object Access policy to enable auditing of object access, you must enable file auditing through NTFS security or print auditing through printer security.

In Exercise 6.13, you will configure audit policies and view their results. This exercise assumes that you have completed all previous exercises in this chapter.

EXERCISE 6.13

Setting Audit Policies

1. Open the MMC and expand the Local Computer Policy snap-in.

2. Expand the folders as follows: Computer Configuration, Windows Settings, Security Settings, Local Policies, Audit Policy.

3. Open the Audit Account Logon Events policy. In the Local Policy Setting field, specify Audit These Attempts. Check the boxes for Success and Failure. Click the OK button.

4. Open the Audit Account Management policy. In the Local Policy Setting field, specify Audit These Attempts. Check the boxes for Success and Failure. Click the OK button.

5. Log off as Administrator. Attempt to log on as Kevin. The logon should fail (because there is no user account with the username Kevin).

6. Log on as Administrator. Select Start ➢ Settings ➢ Control Panel ➢ Administrative Tools ➢ Event Viewer to open Event Viewer.

7. From Event Viewer, open the Security log. You should see the audited events listed in this log.

Assigning User Rights

The user right policies determine what rights a user or group has on the computer. *User rights* apply to the system. They are not the same as permissions, which apply to a specific object (permissions are covered in Chapter 10).

An example of a user right is the Back Up Files and Directories right. This right allows a user to back up files and folders, even if the user does not have permissions through the file system. The other user rights are similar in that they deal with system access as opposed to resource access.

Figure 6.17 shows the user right policies, which are described in Table 6.6.

FIGURE 6.17 The user right policies

TABLE 6.6 User Rights Assignment Policy Options

Right	Description
Access This Computer from the Network	Allows a user to access the computer from the network
Act as Part of the Operating System	Allows low-level authentication services to authenticate as any user
Add Workstations to the Domain	Allows a user to create a computer account on the domain
Back Up Files and Directories	Allows a user to back up all files and directories, regardless of how the file and directory permissions have been set
Bypass Traverse Checking	Allows a user to pass through and traverse the directory structure, even if that user does not have permissions to list the contents of the directory

TABLE 6.6 User Rights Assignment Policy Options *(continued)*

Right	Description
Change the System Time	Allows a user to change the internal time of the computer
Create a Pagefile	Allows a user to create or change the size of a page file
Create a Token Object	Allows a process to create a token if the process uses the NtCreateToken API
Create Permanent Shared Objects	Allows a process to create directory objects through the Windows 2000 Object Manager
Debug Programs	Allows a user to attach a debugging program to any process
Deny Access to This Computer from the Network	Allows you to deny specific users or groups access to this computer from the network
Deny Logon as a Batch File	Allows you to prevent specific users or groups from logging on as a batch file
Deny Logon as a Service	Allows you to prevent specific users or groups from logging on as a service
Deny Logon Locally	Allows you to deny specific users or groups access to the computer locally
Enable Computer and User Accounts to Be Trusted by Delegation	Allows a user or group to set the Trusted for Delegation setting for a user or computer object
Force Shutdown from a Remote System	Allows the system to be shut down by a user at a remote location on the network
Generate Security Audits	Allows a user, group, or process to make entries in the Security log
Increase Quotas	Allows a user to manipulate how processes are served by manipulating the processor quota

TABLE 6.6 User Rights Assignment Policy Options *(continued)*

Right	Description
Increase Scheduling Priority	Specifies that a process can increase or decrease the priority that is assigned to another process
Load and Unload Device Drivers	Allows a user to dynamically unload and load Plug-and-Play device drivers
Lock Pages in Memory	No longer used in Windows 2000 (it was originally intended to force data to be kept in physical memory and not allow the data to be paged to the page file)
Log On as a Batch Job	Allows a process to log on to the system and run a file that contains one or more operating system commands
Log On as a Service	Allows a service to log on in order to run the specific service
Log On Locally	Allows a user to log on at the computer where the user account has been defined
Manage Auditing and Security Log	Allows a user to manage the Security log
Modify Firmware Environment Variables	Allows a user or process to modify the system environment variables
Profile Single Process	Allows a user to monitor nonsystem processes through tools such as the Performance Logs and Alerts utility
Profile System Performance	Allows a user to monitor system processes through tools such as the Performance Logs and Alerts utility
Remove Computer from Docking Station	Allows a user to undock a laptop through the Windows 2000 user interface

TABLE 6.6 User Rights Assignment Policy Options *(continued)*

Right	Description
Replace a Process Level Token	Allows a process to replace the default token that is created by the subprocess with the token that the process specifies
Restore Files and Directories	Allows a user to restore files and directories, regardless of file and directory permissions
Shut Down the System	Allows a user to shut down the local Windows 2000 computer
Synchronize Directory Service Data	Allows a user to synchronize data associated with a directory service
Take Ownership of Files or Other Objects	Allows a user to take ownership of system objects

In Exercise 6.14, you will apply a user right policy. This exercise assumes that you have completed all of the previous exercises in this chapter.

EXERCISE 6.14

Setting User Rights

1. Open the MMC and expand the Local Computer Policy snap-in.

2. Expand folders as follows: Computer Configuration, Windows Settings, Security Settings, Local Policies, User Rights Assignment.

3. Open the Log On as a Service user right. The Local Security Policy Setting dialog box appears.

4. Click the Add button. The Select Users or Groups dialog box appears.

5. Select user Emily. Click the Add button. Then click the OK button.

6. In the Local Security Policy Setting dialog box, click the OK button.

Defining Security Options

Security option policies are used to configure security for the computer. Unlike user right policies, which are applied to a user or group, security option policies apply to the computer.

Microsoft ✓ *Exam Objective*

Implement, configure, manage, and troubleshoot a security configuration.

Figure 6.18 shows the security option policies, which are described briefly in Table 6.7.

FIGURE 6.18 The security option policies

TABLE 6.7 Security Options

Option	Description	Default
Additional Restrictions for Anonymous Users	Allows you to impose additional restrictions on anonymous connections	None (rely on default permissions)
Allow Server Operators to Schedule Tasks (domain controllers only)	Allows server operators to schedule specific tasks to occur at specific times or intervals	Not defined
Allow System to Be Shut Down Without Having to Log On	Allows the user to shut down the system without logging on	Enabled (but the local policy settings are overridden if the domain-level policy settings are defined)
Allowed to Eject Removable NTFS Media	Allows removable NTFS media to be ejected	Administrators
Amount of Time Idle Before Disconnecting Session	Allows sessions to be disconnected when they are idle	15 minutes
Audit the Access of Global System Objects	Allows access of global system objects to be audited	Disabled
Audit Use of All User Rights including Backup and Restore Privilege	Allows all user rights, including backup and restore, to be audited	Disabled

TABLE 6.7 Security Options *(continued)*

Option	Description	Default
Automatically Log Off Users When Logon Time Expires	Automatically logs off users if they have limited logon hours and their logon time has expired	Enabled
Clear Virtual Memory Pagefile When System Shuts Down	Specifies that the page file should be cleared when the system is shut down	Disabled
Digitally Sign Client Communication (always)	Specifies that the server should always digitally sign client communication	Disabled
Digitally Sign Client Communication (when possible)	Specifies that the server should digitally sign client communication when possible	Enabled
Digitally Sign Server Communication (always)	Ensures that server communications will always be digitally signed	Disabled
Digitally Sign Server Communication (when possible)	Specifies that server communications should be signed when possible	Disabled
Disable CTRL+ALT+DEL Requirement for Logon	Allows the Ctrl+Alt+Delete requirement for logon to be disabled	Not defined

TABLE 6.7 Security Options *(continued)*

Option	Description	Default
Do Not Display Last User Name in Logon Screen	Prevents the last user-name in the logon screen from being displayed	Disabled
LAN Manager Authentication Level	Specifies the LAN Manager Authentication Level	Send LAN Manager and NTLM (NT LAN Manager) responses
Message Text for Users Attempting to Log On	Displays message text for users trying to log on	Text space is blank
Message Title for Users Attempting to Log On	Displays a message title for users trying to log on	Title space is blank
Number of Previous Logon Attempts to Cache (in case domain controller is not available)	Specifies the number of previous logon attempts stored in the cache	10
Prevent System Maintenance of Computer Account Password	Prevents the system maintenance of computer account passwords	Disabled
Prevent Users from Installing Print Drivers	Prevents users from installing print drivers	Disabled
Prompt User to Change Password Before Expiration	Prompts the user to change the password before expiration	14 days before password expiration

TABLE 6.7 Security Options *(continued)*

Option	Description	Default
Recovery Console: Allow Automatic Administrative Logon	Specifies that when the Recovery Console is loaded, Administrative logon should be automatic, as opposed to a manual process	Disabled
Recovery Console: Allow Floppy Copy and Access to All Drives and Folders	Allows you to copy files from all drives and folders when the Recovery Console is loaded	Disabled
Rename Administrator Account	Allows the Administrator account to be renamed	Not defined
Rename Guest Account	Allows the Guest account to be renamed	Not defined
Restrict CD-ROM Access to Locally Logged-On Users Only	Restricts CD-ROM access to users who are logged on locally	Disabled
Restrict Floppy Access to Locally Logged-On Users Only	Restricts floppy disk drive access to users who are logged on locally	Disabled
Secure Channel: Digitally Encrypt or Sign Secure Channel Data (always)	Specifies that secure channel data is always digitally encrypted or signed	Disabled
Secure Channel: Digitally Encrypt Secure Channel Data (when possible)	Specifies that secure channel data is digitally encrypted when possible	Disabled

TABLE 6.7 Security Options *(continued)*

Option	Description	Default
Secure Channel: Digitally Sign Secure Channel Data (when possible)	Specifies that secure channel data is digitally signed when possible	Enabled
Secure Channel: Require Strong (Windows 2000 or later) Session Key	Provides a secure channel and requires a strong (Windows 2000 or later) session key	Disabled
Send Unencrypted Passwords to Connect to Third-Party SMB Servers	Allows unencrypted passwords to connect to third-party SMB servers	Disabled
Shut Down System Immediately If Unable to Log Security Audits	Specifies that the system shuts down immediately if it is unable to log security audits	Disabled
Smart Card Removal Behavior	Changes the smart card removal behavior	No action
Strengthen Default Permissions of Global System Objects (e.g. Symbolic Links)	Strengthens the default permissions of global system objects	Enabled
Unsigned Driver Installation Behavior	Controls the behavior of the unsigned driver installation	Warn but allow installation
Unsigned Non-Driver Installation Behavior	Controls the behavior of the unsigned non-driver installation	Silently succeed

In Exercise 6.15, you will define some security option policies and see how they work. This exercise assumes that you have completed all of the previous exercises in this chapter.

EXERCISE 6.15

Defining Security Options

1. Open the MMC and expand the Local Computer Policy snap-in.

2. Expand folders as follows: Computer Configuration, Windows Settings, Security Settings, Local Policies, Security Options.

3. Open the policy Message Text for Users Attempting to Log On. In the Local Policy Setting field, type **Welcome to all authorized users**. Click the OK button.

4. Open the policy Prompt User to Change Password Before Expiration. In the Local Policy Setting field, specify **3** days. Click the OK button.

5. Log off as Administrator and log on as Michael (with the password **apple**).

6. Log off as Michael and log on as Administrator.

Troubleshooting User Accounts Authentication

When a user attempts to log on through Windows 2000 and is unable to be authenticated, you will need to track down the reason for the problem. The following sections offer some suggestions that can help you troubleshoot logon authentication errors for local and domain user accounts.

Microsoft ✓ ***Exam Objective***

Implement, configure, manage, and troubleshoot local user authentication

- Configure and troubleshoot local user accounts.
- Configure and troubleshoot domain user accounts.

Troubleshooting Local User Account Authentication

If a local user is having trouble logging on, the problem may be with the username, password, or the user account itself.

The following are some common cause of local logon errors:

Incorrect username	You can verify that the username is correct by checking the Local Users and Groups utility. Verify that the name was spelled correctly.
Incorrect password	Remember that passwords are case-sensitive. Is the Caps Lock key on? If you see any messages relating to an expired password or locked-out account, the reason for the problem is obvious. If necessary, you can assign a new password through the Local Users and Groups utility.
Prohibitive user rights	Does the user have permission to log on locally at the computer? By default, the Log On Locally user right is granted to the user's group, so all users can log on to Windows 2000 Professional computers. However, if this user right was modified, you will see an error message stating that the local policy of this computer does not allow interactive logon. The terms *interactive logon* and *local logon* are synonymous and mean that the user is logging on at the computer where the user account is stored on the computer's local database.
A disabled or deleted account	You can verify whether an account has been disabled or deleted by checking the account properties through the Local Users and Groups utility.
A domain account logon at the local computer	If a computer is a part of a domain, the logon dialog box has options for logging on to the domain or to the local computer. Make sure that the user has chosen the correct option.

Domain User Accounts Authentication

Troubleshooting a logon problem for a user with a domain account involves checking the same areas as you do for local account logon problems, as well as a few others.

The following are some common causes of domain logon errors:

Incorrect username	You can verify that the username is correct by checking the Microsoft Active Directory Users and Computers utility to verify that the name was spelled correctly.
Incorrect password	As with local accounts, check that the password was entered in the proper case (and the Caps Lock key isn't on), the password hasn't expired, and the account has not been locked out. If the password still doesn't work, you can assign a new password through the Local Users and Groups utility.
Prohibitive user rights	Does the user have permission to log on locally at the computer? This assumes that the user is attempting to log on to the domain controller. Regular users do not have permission to log on locally at the domain controller. The assumption is that users will log on to the domain from network workstations. If the user has a legitimate reason to log on locally at the domain controller, that user should be assigned the Log On Locally user right.
A disabled or deleted account	You can verify whether an account has been disabled or deleted by checking the account properties through the Microsoft Active Directory Users and Computers utility.
A local account logon at a domain computer	Is the user trying to log on with a local user account name instead of a domain account? Make sure that the user has selected to log on to a domain in the logon dialog box.

The computer is not part of the domain	Is the computer that the user sitting at a part of the domain that user is trying to log on to? If the Windows 2000 Professional computer is not a part of the domain that contains the user account or does not have a trust relationship defined with the domain that contains the user account, the user will not be able to log on.
Unavailable domain controller	Is the domain controller available to authenticate the user's request? If the domain controller is down for some reason, the user will not be able to log on until it comes back up (unless the user logs on using a local user account).

Using the Microsoft Active Directory Users and Computers utility is covered in *MCSE: Windows 2000 Directory Services Administration Study Guide,* by Anil Desai with James Chellis (Sybex, 2000).

In Exercise 6.16, you will propose solutions to user authentication problems.

EXERCISE 6.16

Troubleshooting User Authentication

1. Log on as user Emily with the password **peach** (all lowercase). You should see a message indicating that the system could not log you on. The problem is that Emily's password is Peach, and passwords are case-sensitive.

2. Log on as user Bryan with the password **apple**. You should see the same error message that you saw in step 1. The problem is that the user Bryan does not exist.

3. Log on as Administrator. Right-click My Computer and select Manage. Double-click Local Users and Groups.

EXERCISE 6.16 *(continued)*

4. Right-click Users and select New User. Create a user named **Gus**. Type in and confirm the password **abcde**. Deselect the User Must Change Password at Next Logon option and check the Account Is Disabled option.

5. Log off as Administrator and log on as Gus with no password. You will see a message indicating that the system could not log you on because the username or password was incorrect.

6. Log on as Gus with the password **abcde**. You will see a different message indicating that your account has been disabled.

7. Log on as Administrator.

Summary

In this chapter, you learned about user management features in Windows 2000 Professional. We covered the following topics:

- The different types of accounts supported by Windows 2000 Professional. You can set up local user accounts and domain user accounts. Windows 2000 also comes with three built-in system accounts: Administrator, Guest, and *initial user*.

- The user logon and logoff processes. To log on to a Windows 2000 Professional computer, the user must supply a username and password, which the system uses to authenticate the user. The Log Off option is in the Windows Security dialog box.

- The procedures for creating and managing user accounts. You create user accounts and manage them through the Local Users and Groups utility.

- The user properties, which you can set to manage user accounts. Through the Member Of tab of the user Properties dialog box, you can add users to groups or remove them from group membership. Through the Profile tab, you can set a profile path, logon script, and home folder for users.

- Account policies, which control the logon process. The two types of account policies are password and account lockout policies.

- Local policies, which control what a user can do at the computer. The three types of local policies are audit, user rights, and security options policies.

- Troubleshooting user logon and authentication problems. Some of the problems you may encounter are incorrect usernames or passwords, prohibitive user rights, and disabled or deleted accounts.

Key Terms

Before you take the exam, be sure you're familiar with the following key terms:

access token

account lockout policies

account policies

Active Directory

Administrator account

audit policies

authentication

domain user account

Guest account

home folder

interactive logon

Local Computer Policy

local policies

local user account

Local Users and Groups

logon

logon script

password policies

security identifier (SID)

security option policies

user profile

user rights

Review Questions

1. What policies are used to keep a hacker from repeatedly attempting to log on as a user with different passwords?

   A. Account lockout policies

   B. Local policies

   C. Security policies

   D. Password policies

2. Which MMC snap-in is used to create, delete, and manage users?

   A. User Manager

   B. User Manager for Professional

   C. Local Users and Groups

   D. Professional Users and Groups

3. Which of the following statements are true regarding the creation of a user? Choose all that apply.

   A. The username can be up to 20 characters.

   B. The username must be unique to all other users, but can be the same as a group that resides on the computer.

   C. The username can contain spaces, but cannot consist solely of spaces.

   D. The username cannot contain any periods.

4. Which password policy would you implement if you did not want your users to use passwords consisting of simple words?

   A. Passwords Must Be Advanced

   B. Passwords Must Contain Non-alphanumeric Characters

   C. Passwords Must Be Unique

   D. Passwords Must Meet the Complexity Requirements of the Installed Password Filters

5. Which of the following statements are true regarding the built-in accounts? Choose all that apply.

   A. By default, the Administrator account cannot be deleted.

   B. By default, the Guest account can be deleted.

   C. By default, the Administrator account is enabled.

   D. By default, the Guest account is enabled.

6. Which of the following options are configured through the Profile tab of the user Properties dialog box for a local user account? Choose all that apply.

   A. The user profile path

   B. Logon scripts

   C. Home folders

   D. Logon hours

7. Which option would you select if you wanted to create a home folder that was located on a network path?

   A. Connect

   B. Local path

   C. Network path

   D. Connect path

8. Which of the following can users use to change their password on a Windows 2000 Professional computer?

A. The Change Password button in the Windows Security dialog box

B. The NET PASS command-line utility

C. The SETPASS utility

D. The Local Users and Groups utility

9. Which policy group is used to specify guidelines for secure user passwords?

A. Group policies

B. Local policies

C. Security policies

D. Password policy

10. Which of the following are considered local policies? Choose all that apply.

A. Audit policy

B. Password policy

C. User rights assignment

D. Security options

11. Which of the following users is not created by default on a Windows 2000 Professional computer that is installed into a workgroup?

A. Administrator

B. IUSR_Anonymous

C. Guest

D. *Initial user*

12. You are creating user accounts on your Windows 2000 Professional computer. Which of the following usernames is *not* valid?

    A. Beth Johnson

    B. Anthony Johnson-Smith

    C. Beth123

    D. BSmith (Beth)

13. You want to configure auditing so that you are notified of anytime a user logs on to the computer or logs off of the computer. Which of the following auditing policies must be enabled?

    A. Audit Account Logon Events

    B. Audit Process Tracking

    C. Audit Logon Events

    D. Audit System Events

14. You have recently hired Bill as an assistant for network administration. You have not decided how much responsibility you want Bill to have. While you are deciding, you want Bill to be able to update drivers on the Windows 2000 Professional computers in your network. What is the minimum assignment that will allow Bill to complete this task?

    A. Add Bill to the Administrators group.

    B. Add Bill to the Server Operators group.

    C. Add Bill to the Manage Devices group.

    D. Grant Bill the user right Load and Unload Device Drivers on each computer he will manage.

15. You have just decided to install the XYZ Virus Scanner application. The scanner runs as a service. You create a user account called VirScan that will be used to run the service. What user right does this account need to be granted?

   A. Log On as a Batch Job

   B. Log On as a Service

   C. Process Service Requests

   D. Manage Services and Security

16. You have a computer that is shared by many users. You want to ensure that when users press Ctrl+Alt+Delete to log on, they do not see the name of the last user. What do you configure?

   A. Set the security option Clear User Settings When Users Log Off

   B. Set the security option Do Not Display Last User Name in Logon Screen

   C. Set the security option Prevent Users from Seeing Last User Name

   D. Configure nothing; this is the default setting

17. You have configured auditing so that you can track events such as account management tasks and system events. Where can you view the results of the audit?

   A. Audit Manager

   B. *Windir*\audit.log

   C. Event Viewer, System log

   D. Event Viewer, Security log

18. You have recently hired Al as an assistant for network administration. You have not decided how much responsibility you want Al to have. While you are deciding, you want Al to be able to restore files on Windows 2000 Professional computers in your network, but you do not want Al to be able to run the backups. What is the minimum assignment that will allow Al to complete this task?

    A. Add Al to the Administrators group.

    B. Grant Al the Read right to the root of each volume he will back up.

    C. Add Al to the Backup Operators group.

    D. Grant Al the user right Restore Files and Directories.

19. Which password policy would you implement if you did not want users to reuse passwords that they had previously used?

    A. Passwords Must Be Advanced

    B. Enforce Password History

    C. Passwords Must Be Unique

    D. Passwords Must Meet the Complexity Requirements of the Installed Password Filters

20. What is the default account lockout policy that is configured on Windows 2000 computers?

    A. Account Lockout Threshold = 3, Account Lockout Duration = 15 minutes

    B. Account Lockout Threshold = 5, Account Lockout Duration = 30 minutes

    C. Account Lockout Threshold = 7, Account Lockout Duration = 45 minutes

    D. Account lockout policy is not set by default

Answers to Review Questions

1. A. Account lockout policies, a subset of account policies, are used to specify options that prevent a user from attempting multiple failed logon attempts. If the Account Lockout Threshold value is exceeded, the account can be locked.

2. C. User Manager was the utility used in Windows NT 4. Local Users and Groups is the utility used by Windows 2000 Professional.

3. A, C. The username can be up to 20 characters. It must be unique to all users and groups within the local database. The name can contain spaces and periods, but it cannot consist solely of spaces or periods.

4. D. While all of the options sound plausible, the only valid password policy is Passwords Must Meet the Complexity Requirements of the Installed Password Filters.

5. A, C. By default, the Administrator and Guest accounts cannot be deleted, although they can both be renamed. The Administrator account is enabled by default, but the Guest account is disabled by default for security reasons. It is strongly recommended that you use a complex password for the Administrator account during the system installation.

6. A, B, C. Logon hours are only defined for domain users. This option does not appear in the Profile tab of the user Properties dialog box.

7. A. While all of the options seem plausible, the only option that appears on the Profile tab of the user Properties dialog box is Connect.

8. A. The only way for the users to change their passwords is through the Windows Security dialog box. There is no command-line option. An Administrator can change a user's password through the Local Users and Groups utility.

9. D. Sometimes the answer is actually the obvious choice.

10. A, C, D. Password policies are part of the account policies.

11. B. When you install Windows 2000 Professional, there are three users created by default: Administrator, Guest (which is disabled by default), and *initial user* (which is the name of the registered user).

12. B. Anthony Johnson-Smith is not a valid username because it is more than 20 characters. The other names that include spaces and parentheses are valid. The characters that are not valid include * / \ [ ] : ; | = , + * ? < > ". A username that consist solely of periods or spaces is also not valid.

13. A. Audit Account Logon Events is used to track when a user logs on, logs off, or makes a network connection.

14. D. The Load and Unload Device Drivers user right allows a user to dynamically unload and load Plug-and-Play device drivers.

15. B. The Log On as a Service user right allows a service to log on in order to run the specific service.

16. B. The security option Do Not Display Last User Name is used to prevent the last username in the logon screen from being displayed in the logon dialog box.

17. D. Once auditing has been configured, you can see the results of the audit through the Security log in the Event Viewer utility.

18. D. The Restore Files and Directories user right allows a user to restore files and directories, regardless of file and directory permissions.

19. B. The Enforce Password History policy allows the system to keep track of a user's password history for up to 24 passwords.

20. D. By default, account lockout policy is not enabled.

Chapter

7

Managing Groups

MICROSOFT EXAM OBJECTIVES COVERED IN THIS CHAPTER

✓ **Implement, configure, manage, and troubleshoot local user accounts.**

- Implement, configure, manage, and troubleshoot account settings.
- Create and manage local users and groups.

✓ **Implement, configure, manage, and troubleshoot local Group Policy.**

Groups are an important part of network management. Many administrators are able to accomplish the majority of their management tasks through the use of groups; they rarely assign permissions to individual users.

Windows 2000 Professional includes built-in local groups, such as Administrators and Backup Operators. These groups already have all of the permissions needed to accomplish specific tasks. Windows 2000 Professional also uses default special groups, which are managed by the system. Users become members of special groups based on computer and network access.

You create and manage local groups through the Local Users and Groups utility. Through this utility, you can add groups, change group membership, rename groups, and delete groups.

Local group policies allow you to set computer configuration and user configuration options that apply to every user of the computer. Group policies are typically used with the Active Directory. Local group policies may be useful for computers that are not part of a network or in networks that don't have a domain controller.

In this chapter, you will learn about all the built-in groups. Then you will learn how to create and manage groups. The final sections in this chapter cover local group policies.

Using Built-In Groups

On a Windows 2000 Professional computer, default local groups have already been created and assigned all of the permissions to accomplish basic tasks. There are also built-in special groups that the Windows 2000 system handles automatically. These groups are described in the following sections.

Windows 2000 Professional and Windows 2000 Servers that are installed as member servers have the same default groups.

Default Local Groups

A *local group* is a group that is stored on the local computer's accounts database. These are the groups that you can add users to and manage directly on a Windows 2000 Professional computer.

By default, the following local groups are created on Windows 2000 Professional computers:

- Administrators
- Backup Operators
- Guests
- Power Users
- Replicator
- Users

The following sections briefly describe each group, its default permissions, and the users assigned to the group by default.

If possible, you should add users to the built-in local groups rather than creating new groups from scratch. This makes your job easier, because the built-in groups already have the appropriate permissions. All you need to do is add the users you want to be members of the group.

The Administrators Group

The *Administrators group* has full permissions and privileges. Its members can grant themselves any permissions they do not have by default, to manage all the objects on the computer. (Objects include the file system, printers, and account management.)

You should assign users to the Administrators group with caution.

Members of the Administrators group can perform the following tasks:

- Install the operating system.
- Install and configure hardware device drivers.
- Install system services.
- Install service packs, hot fixes, and Windows updates.
- Upgrade the operating system.
- Repair the operating system.
- Install applications that modify the Windows system files.
- Configure password policies.
- Configure audit policies.
- Manage security logs.
- Create administrative shares.
- Create administrative accounts.
- Modify groups and accounts that have been created by other users.
- Remotely access the Registry.
- Stop or start any service.
- Configure services.
- Increase and manage disk quotas.
- Increase and manage execution priorities.
- Remotely shut down the system.
- Assign and manage user rights.
- Reenable locked-out and disabled accounts.
- Manage disk properties, including formatting hard drives.
- Modify system-wide environment variables.
- Access any data on the computer.
- Back up and restore all data.

By default, the Administrator and *initial user* account are members of the Administrators local group.

The Backup Operators Group

The members of the *Backup Operators group* have permissions to back up and restore the file system, even if the file system is NTFS and they have not been assigned permissions to the file system. However, the members of Backup Operators can only access the file system through the Backup utility. To be able to access the file system directly, they must have explicit permissions assigned. By default, there are no members of the Backup Operators local group.

The Guests Group

The *Guests group* has limited access to the computer. This group is provided so that you can let people who are not regular users access specific network resources. As a general rule, most administrators do not allow Guest access because it poses a potential security risk. By default, the Guest user account is a member of the Guests local group.

The Power Users Group

The *Power Users group* has fewer rights than the Administrators group, but more rights than the Users group.

You should assign users to the Power Users group with caution.

Members of the Power Users group can perform the following tasks:

- Create local users and groups.
- Modify the users and groups that they have created.
- Create and delete network shares (except administrative shares).
- Create, manage, and delete local printers.
- Modify the system clock.
- Stop or start services (except services that are configured to start automatically).
- Modify the program files directory.

By default, there are no members of the Power Users local group.

Members of the Power Users group cannot access any NTFS resources that they have not been given permission to.

The Replicator Group

The *Replicator group* is intended to support directory replication, which is a feature used by domain servers. Only domain users who will start the replication service should be assigned to this group. By default, there are no members of the Replicator local group.

The Users Group

The *Users group* is used by end users who should have very limited system access. If you have installed a fresh copy of Windows 2000 Professional, the default settings for this group prohibit users from compromising the operating system or program files. By default, all users who have been created on the computer, except Guest, are members of the Users local group.

An efficient use of the Users group is to allow users to run but not modify installed applications. Users should not be allowed general access to the file system.

Special Groups

Special groups are used by the system. Membership in these groups is automatic if certain criteria are met. You cannot manage special groups through the Local Users and Groups utility. The special groups that are built into Windows 2000 Professional are described in Table 7.1.

TABLE 7.1 Windows 2000 Professional Special Groups

Group	Description
Creator Owner	The account that created or took ownership of the object. This is usually a user account. Each object (such as files, folders, printers, and print jobs) has an owner. Members of the *Creator Owner group* are able to have special permissions to resources. For example, if you are a regular user who has submitted 12 print jobs to a printer, you can manipulate your print jobs as Creator Owner, but you can't manage any print jobs submitted by other users.

TABLE 7.1 Windows 2000 Professional Special Groups *(continued)*

Group	Description
Creator Group	The group that created or took ownership of the object (rather than an individual user). When a regular user creates an object or takes ownership of an object, the username becomes the Creator Owner. When a member of the Administrators group creates or takes ownership of an object, the group Administrators becomes the *Creator Group*.
Everyone	The group that includes anyone who could possibly access the computer. *Everyone* includes all of the users who have been defined on the computer (including Guest), and if your computer is a part of a domain, all of the users within the domain. If the domain has trust relationships with other domains, all of the users in the trusted domains are part of the Everyone group.
Interactive	The group that includes all the users who use the computer's resources locally. Local users belong to the *Interactive group*.
Network	The group that includes the users who access the computer's resources over a network connection. Network users belong to the *Network group*.
Authenticated Users	The group that includes users who access the Windows 2000 operating system through a valid username and password. Users who can log on belong to the *Authenticated Users group*.
Anonymous Logon	The group that includes users who access the computer through anonymous logons. When users gain access through special accounts created for anonymous access to Windows 2000 services, they become members of the *Anonymous Logon group*.
Batch	The group that includes users who log on as a user account that is only used to run a batch job. Batch job accounts are members of the *Batch group*.

TABLE 7.1 Windows 2000 Professional Special Groups *(continued)*

Group	Description
Dialup	The group that includes users who log on to the network from a dial-up connection. Dial-up users are members of the *Dialup group*. (Dialup connections are covered in Chapter 13, "Dial-Up Networking and Internet Productivity.")
Service	The group that includes users who log on as a user account that is only used to run a service. You can configure the use of user accounts for log on through the Services program (discussed in Chapter 4, "Configuring the Windows 2000 Environment"), and these accounts become members of the *Service group*.
System	When the system accesses specific functions as a user, that process becomes a member of the *System group*.
Terminal Server User	The group that includes users who log on through Terminal Services. These users become members of the *Terminal Server User group*.

You can learn more about domains and trust relationships in *MCSE: Windows 2000 Directory Services Administration Study Guide*, by Anil Desai with James Chellis (Sybex, 2000). Terminal Services are covered in *MCSE: Windows 2000 Server Study Guide*, by Lisa Donald with James Chellis (Sybex, 2000).

Working with Groups

Groups are used to logically organize users with similar rights requirements. Groups simplify administration because you can manage a few groups rather than many user accounts. For the same reason, groups simplify troubleshooting. Users can belong to as many groups as needed, so it's not difficult put users into groups that make sense for your organization.

For example, suppose that Jane is hired as a data analyst, to join the four other data analysts that work for your company. You sit down with Jane and create an account for her and assign her the network permissions for the access you think she needs. But then you later find that the four other data analysts, who have similar job functions, sometimes have network access Jane doesn't have, and sometimes she has access they don't have. This happened because all of their permissions were assigned individually, months apart. To avoid such problems and reduce your workload, you can assign all the data analysts to a group and then assign the group the appropriate permissions. Then, as users join or leave the department, you can simply add them to or remove them from the group.

> ## Microsoft ✓ Exam Objective
>
> **Implement, configure, manage, and troubleshoot local user accounts.**
>
> - Implement, configure, manage, and troubleshoot account settings.
> - Create and manage local users and groups.

This chapter covers the group-related material for the "Implement, configure, and troubleshoot local user accounts" objective. All of the subobjectives for this objective are covered in Chapter 6, "Managing Users."

You can create new groups for your users, as well as use the Windows 2000 Professional default local built-in groups, which were described in the previous section. When you plan your groups, you should check to see if an existing local group meets your requirements before you decide to create a new group. For example, if all of the users need to access a particular application, it makes sense to use the default Users group instead of creating a new group and adding all of the users to that group.

To work with groups, you use the Local Users and Groups utility. In Chapter 6, "Managing Users," you learned how to load and use the Local Users and Groups MMC snap-in to create and manage users. In the following sections, you will learn how to use this snap-in to create and manage groups.

The procedures for many basic group management tasks—creating, deleting, and renaming groups—are the same for both Windows 2000 Professional and Server.

Creating Groups

In order to create a group, you must be logged on as a member of the Administrators group or the Power Users group. The Administrators group has full permissions to manage users and groups. The members of the Power Users group can manage only the users and groups that they create.

When you create a local group, you should use the following guidelines:

- The group name should be descriptive (for example, Accounting Data Users).

- The group name must be unique to the computer, different from all of the other group names and usernames that exist on that computer.

- Group names can be up to 256 characters. It is best to use alphanumeric characters for ease of administration. The backslash (\) character is not allowed.

As when you choose usernames, you should consider your naming conventions when assigning names to groups.

Creating groups is similar to creating users, and it is a fairly easy process. After you've added the Local Users and Groups snap-in to the MMC, you expand it to see the Users and Groups folders. Right-click the Groups folder and select New Group from the pop-up menu. This brings up the New Group dialog box, as shown in Figure 7.1.

If your computer doesn't have MMC configured, you can access the Local Users and Groups utility through the Computer Management utility. Right-click My Computer and select Manage from the pop-up menu to open the Computer Management utility. In the System Tools folder, you will see the Local Users and Groups folder. Expand that folder to access the Users and Groups folders in the utility.

FIGURE 7.1   The New Group dialog box

The only required entry in the New Group dialog box is the group name. Optionally, you can enter a description for the group and add (or remove) group members. When you're ready to create the new group, click the Create button.

In Exercise 7.1, you will create two new local groups. This exercise assumes that you have added the Local Users and Groups snap-in to the MMC (see Exercise 6.2 in Chapter 6).

EXERCISE 7.1

Creating Local Groups

1. Open the MMC and expand the Local Users and Groups snap-in.

2. Right-click the Groups folder and select New Group.

3. In the New Group dialog box, type **Data Users** in the Group Name text box. Click the Create button.

4. Right-click the Groups folder and select New Group.

5. In the New Group dialog box, type **Application Users** in the Group Name text box. Click the Create button.

Managing Group Membership

After you've created a group, you can add members to it. As mentioned earlier, you can put the same user in multiple groups.

You can easily add and remove users through the group Properties dialog box, shown in Figure 7.2. To access this dialog box from the Groups folder in the Local Users and Groups utility, double-click the group you want to manage.

FIGURE 7.2 The group Properties dialog box

From the group Properties dialog box, you can change the group's description and add or remove group members. When you click the Add button to add members, the Select Users or Groups dialog box appears, as shown in Figure 7.3. In this dialog box, you select the user accounts you wish to add and click the Add button. Click the OK button to add the users to the group. (Although the special groups that were covered earlier in the chapter are listed in this dialog box, you cannot manage the membership of these special groups.)

FIGURE 7.3 The Select Users or Groups dialog box

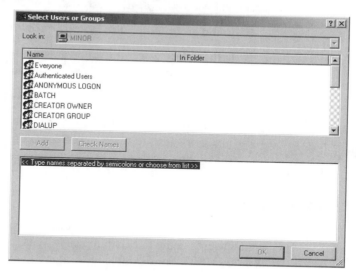

To remove a member from the group, select the member in the Members list and click the Remove button.

You can select multiple contiguous users to add to or remove from a group by Shift+clicking the first and last ones to add. To select multiple noncontiguous users to a group, Ctrl+click each one.

In Exercise 7.2, you will create new user accounts and then add these users to one of the groups you created in Exercise 7.1.

EXERCISE 7.2

Adding Users to a Local Group

1. Open the MMC and expand the Local Users and Groups snap-in.

2. Create four new users: **Bent**, **Claire**, **Patrick**, and **Trina**. (See Chapter 6 for details on creating user accounts.) Deselect the User Must Change Password at Next Logon option for each user.

3. Expand the Groups folder.

4. Double-click the Data Users group (created in Exercise 7.1).

EXERCISE 7.2 *(continued)*

5. In the group Properties dialog box, click the Add button.

6. In the Select Users or Groups dialog box, select Bent, Claire, Patrick, and Trina (hold down the Ctrl key as you click each member).

7. Click the Add button. Then click the OK button.

8. In the group Properties dialog box, you will see that the users have all been added to the group. Click OK to close the group Properties dialog box.

Renaming Groups

Windows 2000 Professional provides an easy-to-use mechanism for changing a group's name (a capability that was never offered in any versions of Windows NT). For example, you might want to rename a group because its current name does not conform to existing naming conventions.

As when you rename a user account, a renamed group keeps of all its properties, including its members and permissions.

To rename a group, right-click the group and choose the Rename option from the pop-up menu. Rename the group and press Enter.

In Exercise 7.3, you will rename one of the groups you created in Exercise 7.1.

EXERCISE 7.3

Renaming a Local Group

1. Open the MMC and expand the Local Users and Groups snap-in.

2. Expand the Groups folder.

3. Right-click the Application Users group (created in Exercise 7.1) and select Rename.

4. Rename the group to **App Users** and press Enter.

Deleting Groups

If you are sure that you will never want to use a group again, you can delete it. Once a group is deleted, you lose all permissions assignments that have been specified for the group.

To delete a group, right-click the group and choose Delete from the pop-up menu. You will see the dialog box shown in Figure 7.4, which warns you that once a group is deleted, it is gone for good. Click the Yes button to delete the group.

If you delete a group and give another group the same name, it won't be created with the same properties as the deleted group.

FIGURE 7.4 Confirming group deletion

In Exercise 7.4, you will delete one of the groups that you created in Exercise 7.1 and renamed in Exercise 7.3.

EXERCISE 7.4

Deleting a Local Group

1. Open the MMC and expand the Local Users and Groups snap-in.

2. Expand the Groups folder.

3. Right-click the App Users group and choose Delete.

4. In the dialog box that appears, click Yes to confirm that you want to delete the group.

Using Local Group Policies

Group policies allow you to manage various computer and user configuration settings, ranging from IP security to connection sharing. Administrators typically use group policies to manage users' Desktops, controlling which options users see and are able to change.

Microsoft
Exam
Objective

Implement, configure, manage, and troubleshoot local Group Policy.

When you use the Active Directory, group policies are inherited. The order of inheritance is local, site, domain, and then Organizational Unit. Using this order, the Group Policy object of the Organizational Unit that the user or computer is a member of contains the final group policy settings.

However, when you use *local group policies*, there is only one Group Policy object, which applies to all of the computer's users. Any policies that have been linked though the Active Directory will take precedence over any local group policies that have been set. Local group policies are typically applied to computers that are not part of a network or in networks that do not have a domain controller, and thus do not use the Active Directory.

Managing group policies in the Active Directory is covered in *MCSE: Windows 2000 Directory Services Administration Study Guide,* by Anil Desai with James Chellis (Sybex, 2000).

You administer local group policies through the *Local Group Policy* snap-in in the MMC. Group policy settings are organized into two main categories:

- Computer configuration policies, which relate to all users of a particular computer.

- User configuration policies, which typically deal with options that are specific to users or groups.

The following sections provide an overview of the local group policies available in these two main categories.

WARNING Use caution in setting local group policies. Any policies you set will be applied to all of the users of the computer, including the Administrator.

Setting Computer Configuration Policies

Computer configuration policies apply to every user of a computer, no matter what username a user uses to log on. As shown in Figure 7.5, there are three folders stored under Computer Configuration: Software Settings, Windows Settings, and Administrative Templates.

FIGURE 7.5 The computer configuration policies folders

NOTE When you add the snap-in through the Add/Remove Snap-in dialog box, it is listed as Group Policy. However, in the MMC window, it is shown as Local Computer Policy.

Computer Configuration Software Settings

Software settings policies can be used by independent software vendors to apply settings for specific applications. For example, if an application required a specific local configuration but was accessed over the network, a policy could be used to configure the local computer.

Software settings are not commonly used as a local group policy because it is easier to configure the application on the computer than to configure the local group policy. With the Active Directory, this policy is useful for configuring multiple computers in a network.

Computer Configuration Windows Settings

Through the Windows settings policies, you can configure options for scripts and for security settings.

There are two options for scripts policies: You can configure scripts to run whenever the computer is started or whenever the computer is shut down.

The security settings policies allow you to configure account policies, local policies, public key policies, and IP security policies on the local machine. Account policies are used to control the logon environment for the computer. Local policies specify what users are able to do once they log on. Account policies and local policies are covered in detail in Chapter 6. You can use public key policies to manage security through the use of public\ private key technology and certificates. IP security policies allow you to configure Windows Internet Protocol Security (IPSec). IPSec provides an internal security mechanism for encrypting data between two computers on a local network.

Computer Configuration Administrative Templates

Administrative templates are used to configure options that are normally found in the HKEY_CURRENT_USER and HKEY_LOCAL_MACHINE portions of the Registry. These policies are grouped in four folders: System, Network, Printers, and Windows Components.

System Policies

System policies allow you to configure options for the areas listed in Table 7.2.

TABLE 7.2 Computer Configuration System Policy Options

Policy Category	Policy	Description
Logon	Run Logon Scripts Synchronously	Specifies that the logon scripts should finish running before the Windows Explorer interface is run. Configuring this option can cause a delay in the Desktop appearing.
Logon	Run Startup Scripts Asynchronously	Allows the system to run startup scripts simultaneously. Otherwise, if you have multiple startup scripts, a startup script can't run until the previous script has finished running.
Logon	Run Startup Scripts Visible	Displays the startup script instructions as they are run.
Logon	Run Shutdown Scripts Visible	Displays the shutdown script instructions as they are run.
Logon	Maximum Wait Time for Group Policy Scripts	Specifies the maximum amount of time that the system will wait for scripts (logon, startup, and shutdown) to be applied before scripts stop processing and an error is recorded. This value is 600 seconds (10 minutes) by default.
Logon	Delete Cached Copies of Roaming Profiles	Specifies that a local copy of the roaming profile should not be saved to the local computer. Normally, you want to save a local copy of a roaming profile, because loading a copy locally is faster than loading from a network drive.
Logon	Do Not Detect Slow Network Connections	By default, the system will try to detect slow links and respond to slow links differently than it does to faster links. Setting this policy disables the detection of slow links.
Logon	Slow Network Connection Timeout for User Profiles	Allows you to specify what a slow network connection is.
Logon	Wait for Remote User Profile	Specifies that if a roaming profile is used, the roaming (network) copy of the profile should be used rather than a locally cached copy of the profile.
Logon	Prompt User When Slow Link Is Detected	Notifies users of a slow link and prompts users to select whether they will use a locally cached copy of a user profile or the roaming (network) copy.

TABLE 7.2 Computer Configuration System Policy Options *(continued)*

Policy Category	Policy	Description
Logon	Timeout for Dialog Boxes	Allows you to configure the default timeout value that will be used to display dialog boxes.
Logon	Log Users Off When Roaming Profile Fails	Specifies that if a roaming profile is not available, the user should be logged off. If you do not enable this option and a roaming profile fails to load, the user will use a locally cached copy or the default user profile.
Logon	Maximum Retries to Unload and Update User Profile	Determines the number of retries the system will take if it tries to update the portions of the Registry that store user profile information and the update is not successful.
Disk Quotas	Enable Disk Quotas	Forces the system to enable disk quota management on all NTFS volumes for the computer.
Disk Quotas	Enforce Disk Quota Limit	Specifies that if disk quotas are configured, they should be enforced.
Disk Quotas	Default Quota Limit and Warning Level	Allows you to configure the default quota limit for quota management and the value for disk use before users see a warning message.
Disk Quotas	Log Event when Quota Limit Exceeded	Specifies that if users reach their quota limit, an entry will be added to the Event Viewer Application log.
Disk Quotas	Log Event when Quota Warning Level Exceeded	Specifies that if users reach their warning limit, an entry will be added to the Event Viewer Application log.
Disk Quotas	Apply Policy to Removable Media	Extends the disk quota policies that are applied to fixed disks to removable media that are formatted as NTFS.
DNS Client	Primary DNS Suffix	Specifies the primary DNS suffix that will be used for DNS name registration and DNS name resolution.
Group Policy	Disable Background Refresh of Group Policy	Prevents group policies from being updated if the computer is currently in use.

TABLE 7.2   Computer Configuration System Policy Options *(continued)*

Policy Category	Policy	Description
Group Policy	Apply Group Policy for Computers Asynchronously during Startup	Specifies that the computer can display the logon dialog box before it finishes updating the computer's Group Policy.
Group Policy	Apply Group Policy for Users Asynchronously during Startup	Specifies that the computer can display the Windows Desktop before it finishes updating the computer's Group Policy.
Group Policy	Group Policy Refresh Intervals for Computers	Specifies the interval rate that will be used to update the computer's Group Policy. By default, this background operation occurs every 90 minutes.
Group Policy	Group Policy Refresh Intervals for Domain Controllers	Specifies the interval rate that will be used to update the domain controller's Group Policy. By default, this background operation occurs every 5 minutes.
Group Policy	User Group Policy Loopback Processing Mode	Specifies how group policies are applied when a user logs on to a computer with this option configured. You can specify that the group policy is replaced or merged with other policy settings.
Group Policy	Group Policy Slow Link Detection	Defines what a slow link is for the purpose of applying and updating group policies.
Group Policy	Registry Policy Processing	Specifies how Registry policies are processed, such as whether Registry policies can be applied during periodic background processing.
Group Policy	Internet Explorer Maintenance Policy Processing	Determines when Internet Explorer Maintenance polices can be applied.
Group Policy	Software Installation Policy Processing	Determines how often software installation policies are updated. This option does not apply to local policies.

TABLE 7.2 Computer Configuration System Policy Options *(continued)*

Policy Category	Policy	Description
Group Policy	Folder Redirection Policy Processing	Specifies how folder redirection policies are updated.
Group Policy	Scripts Policy Processing	Specifies how shared script policies are updated.
Group Policy	Security Policy Processing	Specifies how security policies are updated.
Group Policy	IP Security Policy Processing	Specifies how IP security policies are updated.
Group Policy	EFS Recovery Policy Processing	Specifies how encryption policies are updated.
Group Policy	Disk Quota Policy Processing	Specifies how disk quota policies are updated.
Windows File Protection	Set Windows File Protection Scanning	Determines the frequency of Windows File Protection scans.
Windows File Protection	Hide the File Scan Progress Window	Suppresses the display of the file-scan progress window.
Windows File Protection	Limit Windows File Protection Cache Size	Specifies the maximum amount of disk space that can be used by Windows File Protection.
Windows File Protection	Specify Windows File Protection Cache Location	Specifies an alternate location to be used by the Windows File Protection cache.

Network

Through the network policies, you can configure options for offline files and folders, as well as for network and dial-up connections.

Offline files and folders are a Windows 2000 feature that allows network folders and files to be stored on Windows 2000 clients. The network policies for offline files and folders include options such as whether or not offline files and folders can be enabled and whether or not users can configure offline files and folders. Offline files and folders are covered in detail in Chapter 10, "Accessing Files and Folders."

Network and dial-up connections options allow you to configure whether or not connection sharing is allowed. Network and dial-up connections are covered in Chapter 13, "Dial-Up Networking and Internet Productivity."

Printers

Printers policies allow you to configure options for the computer's printers. Examples of options that can be configured include whether or not printer browsing is allowed, whether printers are published to the network, and whether printers can be created.

Windows Components

Windows components policies allow you to configure options for the areas listed in Table 7.3.

TABLE 7.3 Computer Configuration Windows Components Policy Options

Policy Category	Description
Task Scheduler	Allows you to configure options that relate to the Task Scheduler (the Task Scheduler is covered in Chapter 14, "Optimizing Windows 2000 Professional")
Windows Installer	Allows you to configure options associated with the Windows Installer service (this service is covered in Chapter 2, "Automating Windows 2000 Professional Installation")
Internet Explorer	Allows you to configure options that relate to Internet Explorer, such as security settings and whether or not the automatic installation of Internet Explorer components is enabled
NetMeeting	Allows you to configure whether or not remote Desktop sharing is allowed

Setting User Configuration Policies

When used as local group policies, user configuration policies apply to all of the users of the computer. Like the computer configuration policies, user configuration policies are stored in Software Settings, Windows Settings, and Administrative Templates folders, as shown in Figure 7.6.

FIGURE 7.6 The user configuration policies folders

User configuration policies are typically applied through the Active Directory, where they provide a great deal of control over what network users can do.

User Configuration Software Settings

Software settings policies allow independent software vendors to configure settings for specific applications. These policies are similar to the computer configuration software settings policies.

User Configuration Windows Settings

Through the Windows settings policies, you can configure options for Internet Explorer maintenance, scripts, and security settings.

Internet Explorer maintenance policies allow you to configure options for the areas listed in Table 7.4.

TABLE 7.4 Internet Explorer Maintenance Policy Options

Policy Category	Description
Browser User Interface	Allows you to configure browser settings such as browser title settings and browser toolbar settings
Connection	Allows you to configure connection settings such as automatic browser configuration and proxy settings
URLs	Allows you to configure options such as Favorites and Links and Important URLs
Security	Allows you to configure security options for your browser
Programs	Allows you to customize default programs that Windows 2000 will use for each Internet service

The two options for scripts policies allow you to configure scripts to run whenever a user logs on to Windows 2000 Professional or whenever a user logs off.

The security settings policies allow administrators to configure customized security options that can be applied as group policies.

User Configuration Administrative Templates

Like the administrative templates policies for computer configuration, the administrative templates for user configuration configure settings that are normally found in the HKEY_CURRENT_USER and HKEY_LOCAL_MACHINE portions of the Registry. These policies are grouped in six folders: Start Menu & Taskbar, Desktop, Control Panel, Network, System, and Windows Components.

Start Menu and Taskbar

Through Start menu and Taskbar policies, you can configure users' Start menu and Taskbar options. For example, you can specify whether or not users see common program groups and whether or not Logoff is an option on the Start menu. (The Start menu and Taskbar are covered in Chapter 5, "Managing the Desktop.")

Desktop

Desktop policies allow you to configure options for the Active Desktop. For example, you can set whether or not the Active Desktop is enabled and whether or not changes can be made.

The Desktop policies also include an Active Directory folder. However, you can't configure Active Directory options if you are using local group policies.

Control Panel

Control Panel policies allow you to configure options for the areas listed in Table 7.5.

TABLE 7.5 Control Panel Policy Options

Policy Category	Description
Add/Remove Programs	Allows you to specify options such as whether or not the Add/Remove Programs icon is displayed in Control Panel and whether or not the Add New Programs page should be hidden
Display	Allows you to configure options such as whether or not users see options on the Appearance tab and Settings tab of the Display Properties dialog box (the Display Properties dialog box is covered in Chapter 5)
Printers	Allows you to configure printing options such as whether or not users can add printers and whether or not users can browse a common Web site to find printers (printing is covered in Chapter 12, "Managing Printing)
Regional Options	Allows you to restrict the selection of Windows 2000 menus and dialog box languages (using multiple languages with Windows 2000 is covered in Chapter 5)

Network

Through network policies, you can configure options for offline files and folders and network and dial-up connections. These policies are similar to the computer configuration network policies.

System

System policies allow you to configure options for logons and how group policies are processed. These policies are similar to the computer configuration system policies.

Windows Components

Windows components policies allow you to configure options for the areas listed in Table 7.6.

TABLE 7.6 User Configuration Windows Components Policy Options

Policy Category	Description
Windows Explorer	Allows you to configure options for Windows Explorer, such as removing the File menu and preventing access to drives from My Computer.
Microsoft Management Console	Allows you to configure options for the MMC, such as restricting users from using authoring mode and restricting users to explicitly permitted snap-ins.
Task Scheduler	Allows you to configure options that relate to the Task Scheduler (the Task Scheduler is covered in Chapter 14)
Windows Installer	Allows you to configure options associated with the Windows Installer service (this service is covered in Chapter 2)
Internet Explorer	Allows you to configure options that relate to Internet Explorer, such as specifying search options and disabling external branding of Internet Explorer
NetMeeting	Allows you to configure options such as whether or not users can send files and whether or not Chat is enabled

In Exercise 7.5, you will configure local group policies for your computer. This exercise assumes that you have added the Local Computer Policy snap-in to the MMC (see Exercise 6.10 in Chapter 6).

EXERCISE 7.5

Applying Local Group Policy

1. Open the MMC and expand the Local Computer Policy snap-in.

2. Expand the Computer Configuration, then Administrative Templates, then System folders.

3. Double-click the Disable Autoplay option. In the Disable Autoplay Properties dialog box, click the Disabled radio button. Then click the OK button.

4. In the Local Computer Policy snap-in, expand User Configuration, then Administrative Templates, then System.

5. Double-click the Don't Display Welcome Screen at Logon option. In the dialog box that appears, click the Disabled radio button. Then click the OK button.

6. You can test that the group policy setting is working by inserting the Windows 2000 Professional CD. Because you selected the Disable Autoplay option, the computer will not automatically start the CD.

Summary

In this chapter, you learned about group management with Windows 2000 Professional. We covered the following topics:

- The Windows 2000 Professional built-in groups, which include default local groups, like Administrators and Power Users, and default special groups, like Everyone and Network. You can manage the default local groups, but the special groups are managed by the system.

- The procedure for creating groups. You create groups through Local Users and Groups utility.

- The procedure for adding users to groups and removing users from groups. You perform these tasks through the group Properties dialog box.

- How to rename and delete groups. Both of these tasks are performed by right-clicking the group in the Groups folder of the Local Users and Groups utility and selecting the appropriate option from the pop-up menu.

- The purpose of group policies and the options that you can configure for local group policies

Key Terms

Before you take the exam, be sure you're familiar with the following key terms:

Administrators group

Anonymous Logon group

Authenticated Users group

Backup Operators group

Batch group

Creator group

Creator Owner group

Dialup group

Everyone group

Guests group

Interactive group

local group

Local Group Policy

Network group

Power Users group

Replicator group

Service group

special group

System group

Terminal Server User group

Users group

Review Questions

1. Which built-in group would you add a user to if you wanted the user to be able to create users and groups, but not manage properties of users and groups that user did not create?

   A. Administrators

   B. Power Users

   C. Server Operators

   D. Power Operators

2. Which of the following groups are default built-in local groups that can be managed through the Local Users and Groups utility? Choose all that apply.

   A. Backup Operators

   B. Everyone

   C. Replicator

   D. Dialup

3. Which of the following statements about the Backup Operators group is true?

   A. By default, only Administrators and Power Users are members of the Backup Operators group.

   B. Backup Operators do not require any permissions to NTFS file systems in order to back up and restore the file system.

   C. Backup Operators have full access to the NTFS file system.

   D. Backup Operators can modify any services that relate to system backup.

4. Which types of groups can exist on a Windows 2000 Professional computer?

   A. Security group

   B. Distribution group

   C. Source group

   D. Local group

5. Which default local group has the most limited access to the computer by default?

    A. Users

    B. Guests

    C. Replicator

    D. Peons

6. What is the primary purpose of the Replicator group?

    A. To replicate user accounts to the domain controller

    B. For replication if you have configured DFS on the network

    C. To replicate and manage concurrent time across the network

    D. To support directory replication, which is set up on domain controllers

7. Which of the following tasks can be completed by a member of the Power Users group? Choose all that apply.

    A. Create local users and groups.

    B. Create and delete all network shares.

    C. Stop and start all network services.

    D. Create, manage, and delete local printers.

8. If you logged on as user Brad to a Windows 2000 Professional computer that contained the user account Brad, which of the following groups would you belong to by default? Choose all that apply.

    A. Users

    B. Authenticated Users

    C. Everyone

    D. Interactive

9. Which of following statements regarding local groups is true?

    A. You cannot rename a group.

    B. You can add users and other local groups to an existing local group.

    C. The local group's properties can contain a description.

    D. You manage groups through the User Manager utility.

10. Which of the following are considered to be special groups in Windows 2000 Professional? Choose all that apply.

    A. Creator Owner

    B. Creator Group

    C. Dialup

    D. Local User

11. You have a logon script that is used to partially configure the Windows Explorer interface. You want to ensure that the entire script is processed before the Windows Explorer interface is run. What group policy setting should you use?

    A. Run Logon Scripts Synchronously

    B. Run Startup Scripts Asynchronously

    C. Minimum Wait Time for Group Policy Scripts

    D. Wait for Logon Scripts to Complete

12. You log on to multiple network environments. It takes a long time for your logon scripts to be processed. What group policy setting can be used to process your multiple logon scripts more quickly?

    A. Run Logon Scripts Synchronously

    B. Run Startup Scripts Asynchronously

    C. Process Logon Scripts High Priority

    D. Run Logon Scripts Simultaneously

13. You want to configure your computer so that `test.samplecorp.com` is the primary DNS suffix that will be used for DNS name registration and DNS name resolution. What group policy setting can be used to configure this option?

    A. Set DNS Suffix

    B. Enable DNS Name Resolution

    C. Apply DNS Configuration

    D. Primary DNS Suffix

14. You want to configure a Windows 2000 computer so that all users see an option for logoff on the Start menu. Which of the following options can be used to set this configuration?

    A. Create custom logon scripts

    B. Create a custom local group policy

    C. Set this option in the Profile tab of the user Properties dialog box

    D. Create a custom local group object that is configured with this attribute

15. Rick has been added to the Administrators group. You suspect that Rick may be abusing his administrative privileges. All he really needs to do is create and manage local user accounts. You do not want Rick to be able to look at any NTFS folders or files that he has not been granted explicit permissions to access. Which group should you add Rick to so that he can do his job, with the minimum level of administrative rights?

    A. Administrators

    B. Power Users

    C. Account Operators

    D. Server Operators

16. You are logged on as John, who is a member of the Power Users group. When John accesses the Printers folder, he does not see an Add Printer option. What is the most likely cause of this?

   A. There are no Plug-and-Play printers attached to the computer.

   B. There are no LPT ports defined in the computer's BIOS.

   C. The group policy settings have disabled the addition of printers.

   D. Members of the Power Users group do not have permissions to create new printers.

17. Which of the following options can be used to configure group policies?

   A. Administrative Tools ➤ Group Policy Editor

   B. Administrative Tools ➤ System Policy Editor

   C. The MMC snap-in Group Policy (local)

   D. The MMC snap-in System Policy (local)

18. When you create a local group policy on a Windows 2000 Professional computer, which users are *not* affected by the policies by default?

   A. Users

   B. Everyone

   C. Administrators

   D. All users are affected by default

19. What are the two major areas of configuration for group policies? Choose two answers.

   A. User configuration

   B. Group configuration

   C. Computer configuration

   D. Registry configuration

20. Which configuration option is modified when you set group policies?

   A. The Registry

   B. `.ini` files

   C. `.inf` files

   D. `.cfg` files

Answers to Review Questions

1. B. Members of the Power Users group can create users and groups, but can only manage the users and groups that they have created. Administrators can manage all users and groups. The Server Operators group only exists on Windows 2000 domain controllers. The Power Operators group does not exist by default on Windows 2000 computers.

2. A, C. You can manage the Backup Operators and Replicator local groups through the Local Users and Groups utility. The Everyone and Dialup groups are considered special groups, and their membership is determined by computer and network access.

3. B. There are no members of the Backup Operators group by default. Members of the Backup Operators group have access to the file system during the backup process, but not normal file access. Backup Operators group members have no special permissions to modify system services.

4. D. The only type of group that can exist on a Windows 2000 Professional computer is a local group.

5. B. The Guests group has the most limited access to computer resources.

6. D. The Replicator group is used to support directory replication, which is a feature used by domain controllers. If this feature is not used, there should be no members of the Replicator group.

7. A, D. Members of the Power Users group can create local users and groups, but they can only manage the users and groups that they have created. Power Users can create and delete network shares, *except* administrative shares. Power Users can stop and start network services, *except* services that are configured to start automatically. Power Users can create, manage, and delete local printers.

8. A, B, C, D. By default, all users who exist on a Windows 2000 Professional computer are added to the computer's Users group. Users who log on with a valid username and password automatically become a member of the Authenticated Users special group. By default, anyone who can use the computer becomes a member of the special group Everyone. Because Brad is using the computer where his user account resides, he automatically becomes a member of the special group Interactive.

9. C. In Windows NT, you cannot rename groups. In Windows 2000, you can rename groups. You cannot add a local group to another local group. Local group properties can contain a description. Windows NT used the User Manager utility. Windows 2000 uses the Local Users and Groups utility for user and group management.

10. A, B, C. Creator Owner, Creator Group, and Dialup are all special groups in Windows 2000. There is no Local User group, but there is a special group called Interactive, which has local users as members.

11. A. Run Logon Scripts Synchronously is the computer configuration system policy option that specifies that logon scripts should finish running before the Windows Explorer interface is run. Configuring this option can cause a delay in the Desktop appearance.

12. B. Run Startup Scripts Asynchronously is the computer configuration system policy option that allows the system to run startup scripts simultaneously. If you don't enable this policy, a startup script can't run until the previous script is complete.

13. D. Primary DNS Suffix is the local group policy that is used to specify the primary Domain Name Service (DNS) suffix that will be used for DNS name registration and DNS name resolution.

14. B. Start menu and Taskbar local group policies allow you to configure options such as whether users see a Logoff option on the Start menu.

15. B. The members of the Power Users group have the rights to create and manage the local users and groups that they create without being able to look at NTFS folders and files that they have not been given access to. Account Operators and Server Operators are not built-in groups on Windows 2000 Professional computers.

16. C. You do not need a Plug-and-Play printer attached to the computer or to have LPT ports configured to create a printer. Members of the Power Users group can create new printers. The most likely problem is that the group policy settings have disabled the option to add new printers.

17. C. You administer local group policies through the Group Policy MMC snap-in. As a part of the configuration, you specify that you will manage the local computer.

18. D. By default, all users are affected by local group policies. By using group policies in conjunction with the Active Directory, you have greater control over how group policies are applied.

19. A, C. When you load the Local Group Policy MMC snap-in, you see the Local Computer Policy option in the main MMC window. When you expand this option, the two main areas of configuration for group policy are listed: User Configuration and Computer Configuration.

20. A. When you edit group policies, you edit the configuration settings that are stored in the Windows 2000 Registry.

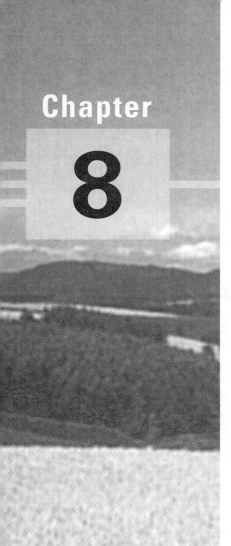

Chapter 8

Using User Profiles and Hardware Profiles

MICROSOFT EXAM OBJECTIVES COVERED IN THIS CHAPTER

✓ Configure and manage user profiles.

✓ Manage hardware profiles.

User profiles store users' Desktop configurations. A user profile can contain a user's Desktop arrangement, program items, personal program groups, network and printer connections, screen colors, mouse settings, and other personal preferences.

User profiles are stored locally by default, but they can be accessed through the network if you configure roaming profiles. If you don't want users to be able to change their user profiles, you can configure mandatory profiles.

Hardware profiles store different hardware configurations for a computer. Hardware profiles are useful when a single computer has multiple hardware configurations.

This chapter covers how to create and manage user profiles and hardware profiles. We will begin with an overview of the configuration information stored in user profiles.

Reviewing User Profile Configuration Options

*U**ser profiles* store many of the personal configuration options for Windows 2000 Professional. For example, say user Kevin has logged on and customized his Desktop by changing the wallpaper, adding shortcuts, adding items to the Startup folder, and changing the mouse pointer. All of this information will be saved in Kevin's user profile when he logs off. The next time he logs on, his Desktop customizations will be restored.

If the configuration option is a personal preference, it is most likely a part of the user profile. Configuration options that relate to the computer are not a part of the user profile. For example, the mouse driver is not a part of a user profile. However, the properties of the mouse configuration—such as the speed, pointer, and mouse button settings—reflect the user's personal preferences and are a part of a user profile.

Table 8.1 lists some of the settings that are saved by user profiles.

TABLE 8.1 User Preferences Saved in User Profiles

Settings From	Items Stored in User Profile
Windows Explorer	View of Windows Explorer, mapped network drives, types of files that are displayed
Control Panel	Screen appearance, accessibility options, and mouse and keyboard preferences
Printer settings	Network printer connections
Taskbar	All settings, including program items and their properties
Accessories	Preference settings for programs, such as Calculator, Command Prompt, and Notepad
Online Help bookmarks	Any bookmarks that the user has set in the Windows 2000 Help program
Windows 2000–based applications	User configuration settings for applications that support such settings

Creating and Managing User Profiles

User profiles are particularly useful when multiple users share the same computer. If each user has a profile, his or her Desktop preferences will be maintained and loaded when that user logs on to the computer.

Microsoft ✓ Exam Objective	**Configure and manage user profiles.**

User profiles can be used by a single user or by a group of users. If you assign a user profile to a group of users, you can ensure that all users in the group maintain a consistent Desktop. This makes it easier to train users and to troubleshoot problems.

By default, user profiles are created locally on the computer that the user account logs on to, but you can create roaming profiles that are available from the network. Roaming profiles allow users to access their customized Desktop from any computer they log on to within the network.

By default, users can change their own profiles, but Administrators can create and assign mandatory, or read-only, profiles. Users cannot modify mandatory profiles.

The following sections describe how to create local, roaming, and mandatory user profiles.

Using Local User Profiles

Each time you log on to a Windows 2000 Professional computer, the system checks to see if you have a *local user profile* in the Documents and Settings folder, which was created on the boot partition when you installed Windows 2000 Professional.

The first time users log on, they receive a default user profile. A folder that matches the user's logon name is created for the user in the Documents and Settings folder. The user profile folder that is created holds a file called *NTUSER.DAT*, as well as subfolders that contain directory links to the user's Desktop items.

In Exercise 8.1, you will create new users and set up local user profiles.

EXERCISE 8.1

Using Local Profiles

1. Using the Local Users and Groups utility, create two new users: **Liz** and **Tracy**. (See Chapter 6, "Managing Users," for details on creating user accounts.) Deselect the User Must Change Password at Next Logon option for each user.

2. Select Start ➢ Programs ➢ Accessories ➢ Windows Explorer. Expand My Computer, then Local Disk (C:), then Documents and Settings. Notice that this folder does not contain user profile folders for the new users.

3. Log off as Administrator and log on as Liz. When the Getting Started with Windows 2000 dialog box appears, deselect the Show This Screen at Startup option and then click the Exit button.

4. Right-click an open area on the Desktop and select Properties. In the Display Properties dialog box, click the Appearance tab. Select the color scheme Red, White, and Blue (VGA), click the Apply button, and then click the OK button.

5. Right-click an open area on the Desktop and select New ➢ Shortcut. In the Create Shortcut dialog box, type **CALC**. Accept CALC as the name for the shortcut and click the Finish button.

6. Log off as Liz and log on as Tracy. Notice that user Tracy sees the Desktop configuration stored in the default user profile.

7. Log off as Tracy and log on as Liz. Notice that Liz sees the Desktop configuration you set up in steps 3, 4, and 5.

8. Log off as Liz and log on as Administrator. Select Start ➢ Programs ➢ Accessories ➢ Windows Explorer. Expand My Computer, then Local Disk (C:), then Documents and Settings. Notice that this folder now contains user profile folders for Liz and Tracy.

The drawback of local user profiles is that they are available only on the computer where they were created. For example, suppose that all of your Windows 2000 Professional computers are a part of a domain and you use only local user profiles. User Rick logs on at Computer A and creates a customized user profile. When he logs on to Computer B for the first time, he will receive the default user profile, rather than the customized user profile he created on Computer A. For users to be able to access their user profile from any computer they log on to, you need to use roaming profiles, as described in the next section.

Using Roaming Profiles

A *roaming profile* is stored on a network server and allows users to access their user profile, regardless of the client computer that they have logged on to. Roaming profiles provide users who move around with a consistent Desktop, no matter which computer they access. If the server that stores the roaming profile is unavailable, the user can log on using a local profile.

To create a roaming profile, take the following steps:

1. Create the profile that will be used as the roaming profile.

2. Create a folder on a network server and share the folder. (Creating shared folders is covered in Chapter 10, "Accessing Files and Folders.")

3. Copy the profile to the network share. To copy a profile, use the Copy To button in the User Profiles tab of the System Properties dialog box, shown in Figure 8.1. To access this dialog box, select Control Panel ➤ System and click the User Profiles tab. (You can also access the System Properties dialog box by right-clicking My Computer and selecting Properties.) Click the Copy To button and specify the share folder and profile name in the Copy To dialog box.

When you go through the Copy To button in the User Profiles tab of the System Properties dialog box, the process copies the NTUSER.DAT file, as well as all of the folders associated with the profile. You should always use this method to copy a profile to a network share, rather than using other file-copy options.

4. Open the Local Users and Groups utility and access the properties of the user who will be assigned the roaming profile. Click the Profile tab in the user Properties dialog box. In the Profile Path text box, specify

the UNC (Universal Naming Convention) path for the roaming profile, as shown in Figure 8.2.

FIGURE 8.1   The User Profiles tab of the System Properties dialog box

FIGURE 8.2   The Profile tab of the user Properties dialog box

If you need to reapply the default user profile for a user, you can delete the user's profile through the System icon in Control Panel, User Profiles tab.

In Exercise 8.2, you will simulate the process of creating a roaming profile. This is just a simulation because, in order for roaming profiles to work on a Windows 2000 Professional computer, roaming profiles must be configured on a Windows 2000 Server computer.

EXERCISE 8.2

Using Roaming Profiles

In this exercise, you will set up a roaming profile, which is a four-part process. Then you will test the profile.

Creating a Profile

1. Using the Local Users and Groups utility, create a user named **Tester**. Deselect the User Must Change Password at Next Logon option.

2. Log on as Tester. Right-click an open area on the Desktop and select New ➤ Shortcut. In the Create Shortcut dialog box, type **EXPLORER**. Accept EXPLORER as the name for the shortcut and click the Finish button.

3. Right-click an open area on the Desktop and select Properties. In the Display Properties dialog box, click the Appearance tab. Select the color scheme Maple, click the Apply button, and then click the OK button.

Creating a Network Share for User Profiles

1. Log off as Tester and log on as Administrator.

2. Select Start ➤ Programs ➤ Accessories ➤ Windows Explorer. Expand My Computer, then Local Disk (C:).

3. Select File ➤ New ➤ Folder. Name the new folder **Profiles**.

4. Right-click the Profiles folder and select Sharing. In the Sharing dialog box, click the Share This Folder radio button and leave all of the other values at their default settings. Click the OK button.

EXERCISE 8.2 *(continued)*

Copying the User Profile to the Network Share Folder

1. Select Start ➢ Settings ➢ Control Panel ➢ System and click the User Profiles tab.

2. In the User Profiles tab of the System Properties dialog box, highlight the *computername*\Tester profile and click the Copy To button.

3. In the Copy To dialog box, specify `C:\Profiles\Tester` and click the OK button. Click the OK button to close the System Properties dialog box.

Configuring the User Properties to Use a Roaming Profile

1. Open the Local Users and Groups utility and expand the Users folder.

2. Double-click user Tester to open the user Properties dialog box and click the Profile tab.

3. In the Profile Path text box, type `\\`*computername*`\Profiles\Tester`, replacing *computername* with the unique name of your computer. Click the Apply button and then click the Close button.

Testing the Roaming Profile

1. Log off as Administrator and log on as Tester. You should see the profile that was created for Tester.

2. Log off as Tester and log on as Administrator.

Using Mandatory Profiles

A *mandatory profile* is a profile that can't be modified by the user. Only members of the Administrators group can manage mandatory profiles. You might consider creating mandatory profiles for users who should maintain consistent Desktops. For example, suppose that you have a group of 20 salespeople, who know enough about system configuration to make changes, but not enough to fix any problems they create. For ease of support, you could use mandatory profiles. This way, all of the salespeople will always have the same profile and will not be able to change their profiles.

You can create mandatory profiles for a single user or a group of users. A mandatory profile is stored in a file named *NTUSER.MAN*. A user with a mandatory profile can set different Desktop preferences while logged on, but those settings will not be saved when the user logs off.

To create a mandatory profile, take the following steps:

1. Rename the user profile from NTUSER.DAT to **NTUSER.MAN**.

2. Copy the profile to a network share. As with roaming profiles, you should use the Copy To button in the User Profiles tab of the System Properties dialog box to copy the appropriate files.

3. In the Local Users and Groups utility, access the properties of the user who will be assigned the roaming profile and specify the location of the mandatory profile. This path must be a UNC path for the mandatory profile to work.

Only roaming profiles can be used as mandatory profiles. Mandatory profiles do not work for local user profiles.

In Exercise 8.3, you will simulate the process of creating a mandatory profile. As with the sample roaming profile you created in Exercise 8.2, the mandatory profile will not actually work. This is because you must first configure roaming profiles on a Windows 2000 Server computer.

EXERCISE 8.3

Using Mandatory Profiles

In this exercise, you will set up a mandatory profile, which is a four-part process. Then you will test the profile.

Creating a Profile

1. Using the Local Users and Groups utility, create a user named **Sales User**. Deselect the User Must Change Password at Next Logon option.

2. Log off as Administrator and log on as Sales User.

3. Select Start ➢ Settings ➢ Control Panel ➢ Mouse. Click the Pointers tab and select Conductor from the Scheme drop-down list. Click the Apply button, then click the OK button.

EXERCISE 8.3 *(continued)*

4. In Control Panel, select Sounds and Multimedia. In the Sounds tab, select Utopia from the Scheme drop-down list, then click the OK button.

5. Right-click an open area on the Desktop and select Properties. In the Display Properties dialog box, click the Effects tab. Under Visual Effects, select the Use Large Icons option. Click the Apply button, then click the OK button.

Renaming the NTUSER.DAT File

1. Log off as Sales User and log on as Administrator.

2. Select Start ➢ Programs ➢ Accessories ➢ Windows Explorer.

3. In Windows Explorer, select Tools ➢ Folder Options and click the View tab. Click the Show Hidden Files and Folders radio button and uncheck the Hide File Extensions for Known File Types check box. Click the Apply button, then click the OK button.

4. In Windows Explorer, expand My Computer, then Local Disk (C:), then Documents and Settings, then Sales User.

5. Right-click the NTUSER.DAT file and rename the file to NTUSER.MAN. Close Windows Explorer.

Copying the User Profile to the Network Share Folder

1. Select Start ➢ Settings ➢ Control Panel ➢ System and click the User Profiles tab in the System Properties dialog box.

2. Highlight the *computername*\Sales User profile and click the Copy To button.

3. In the Copy To dialog box, specify **C:\Profiles\Sales User** and click the OK button. Click the OK button to close the System Properties dialog box.

Configuring the User Properties to Use a Mandatory Profile

1. Open the Local Users and Groups utility and expand the Users folder.

EXERCISE 8.3 *(continued)*

2. Double-click user Sales User to open the user Properties dialog box and click the Profile tab.

3. In the Profile Path text box, type ***computername*\\Profiles\\Sales User**, replacing *computername* with the unique name of your computer. Click the Apply button, then click the Close button.

Testing the Mandatory Profile

1. Log off as Administrator and log on as Sales User.

2. Select Start ➤ Settings ➤ Control Panel ➤ Mouse. Click the Pointers tab and choose Dinosaur from the Scheme drop-down list. Click the Apply button, then click the OK button.

3. Log off as Sales User and log on again as Sales User.

4. Log off as Sales User and log on as Administrator.

 If the client that is accessing the mandatory profile is a Windows NT 4 or Windows 2000 computer, you do not need to include the user profile name in the Profile Path setting in the user Properties dialog box. For example, you could specify \\Server1\Profiles\Tester. However, if the client is a Windows NT 3.*x* computer, you must include the user profile name in the Profile Path setting. For example, you could specify \\Server\Profiles\Tester\NTUSER.MAN.

Creating and Managing Hardware Profiles

*H*ardware profiles store hardware configurations for a computer. Using hardware profiles allows you to manage multiple hardware configurations for a single computer. For example, suppose that you have a laptop computer that can be used with a docking station that attaches to the network. If the computer is configured for network connectivity and the computer is not docked, you will see error messages at startup. To avoid this, you can create hardware profiles for this laptop computer: one hardware profile (with network settings) to load when the computer is docked and another hardware profile (without network settings) to load when the computer is undocked.

Microsoft ✓ *Exam* *Objective*

Manage hardware profiles.

When you set up hardware profiles, you specify different hardware configurations that can be accessed when Windows 2000 Professional is started. You manage hardware profiles through the Hardware Profiles dialog box, shown in Figure 8.3. To access this dialog box, select Start ➢ Settings ➢ Control Panel ➢ System. (You can also access the System Properties dialog box by right-clicking My Computer and selecting Properties.) In the System Properties dialog box, click the Hardware tab and then click the Hardware Profiles button. The options in the Hardware Profiles dialog box are described in Table 8.2.

FIGURE 8.3 The Hardware Profiles dialog box

TABLE 8.2 Hardware Profile Options

Option	Description
Available Hardware Profiles	Lists all of the hardware profiles that have been created. If only one profile is listed, you will not see hardware profile selection options when Windows 2000 is started. If there is only one profile, it can't be deleted. You can change the order of the profiles in the Available Hardware Profiles list by selecting a profile and clicking the up or down arrow button to the right of the list.
Properties	Opens a dialog box where you can specify whether or not the computer is portable. A portable computer usually has two profiles: one for when the computer is docked and another for when the computer is undocked. You can also specify whether the profile will appear in the hardware profile selection options when Windows 2000 is started.
Copy	Opens a dialog box that lets you copy an existing hardware profile. You can then edit the copied profile.
Rename	Allows you to give your hardware profile a different name. For example, you might rename Profile 1 to Docked Portable.
Delete	Deletes the hardware profile that is currently highlighted. This option is not active if only one hardware profile is listed.
Hardware Profiles Selection	Specifies how the hardware profile selection options should be configured for Windows 2000 startup. You can specify that the computer boot process stop until a selection is made, or you can configure the computer to select the first profile that is listed (the list is in the order shown in the Available Hardware Profiles list box) if no choice has been made within x number of seconds.

Every computer has at least one hardware profile. The default profile that is created when you install Windows 2000 Professional is called Profile 1.

To configure the properties of a hardware profile, click the Properties button in the Hardware Profiles dialog box. This brings up the hardware profile Properties dialog box, as shown in Figure 8.4. Through this dialog box, you specify whether or not the computer is portable and if you want the hardware profile to be displayed as an option when Windows 2000 Professional starts.

FIGURE 8.4   The hardware profile Properties dialog box

In Exercise 8.4, you will configure two hardware profiles for your computer.

EXERCISE 8.4

Managing Hardware Profiles

1. Select Start ➢ Settings ➢ Control Panel ➢ System, click the Hardware tab, and click the Hardware Profiles button.

2. Click the Copy button to copy Profile 1. Name the copy **Undocked** and click the OK button.

3. Highlight Undocked and click the Properties button. Select the This Is a Portable Computer check box and The Computer Is Undocked radio button. Click the OK button.

EXERCISE 8.4 *(continued)*

4. Highlight Profile 1 (Current) and click the Rename button. Rename the profile to **Docked** and click the OK button.

5. Highlight Docked and click the Properties button. Select the The Computer Is Docked radio button. Click the OK button.

6. Click the OK button to close the Hardware Profiles dialog box. Close any other dialog boxes that are open.

7. Shut down and restart your computer. When the computer restarts, you will see the hardware profile selection options. Select a profile to load it.

Summary

This chapter described how to create and manage user profiles and hardware profiles. We covered the following topics:

- The configurations stored in user profiles, which include most user preference settings

- How to create local user profiles, roaming profiles, and mandatory profiles

- How to configure hardware profiles, which are used to manage a single computer that has more than one hardware configuration

Key Terms

Before taking the exam, you should be familiar with the following terms:

hardware profile

local user profile

mandatory profile

NTUSER.DAT

NTUSER.MAN

roaming profile

user profile

Review Questions

1. Where are user profiles stored by default on a Windows 2000 Professional computer?

   A. \WINNT\Profiles

   B. \Documents and Settings

   C. \WINNT\User Profiles

   D. \User Profiles

2. What is the default filename for user profiles in Windows 2000 Professional?

   A. NTUSER.PRO

   B. NTUSER.DAT

   C. PROFILE.DAT

   D. PROFILE.USR

3. Which of the following steps would you need to take in order to specify that a user profile is available over the network for a Windows 2000 client?

   A. In Control Panel, in the User Profiles tab of the System Properties dialog box, specify that the profile is a roaming profile.

   B. Rename the user profile to NTUSER.NET.

   C. Use Windows Explorer to copy the user profile to a network share.

   D. In the Local Users and Groups utility, in the Profile tab of the user Properties dialog box, specify a UNC path for the roaming profile.

4. Which of the following options would be stored within a user profile? Choose all that apply.

   A. The mouse driver that the user will use

   B. The mouse pointer that the user will use

   C. The keyboard layout that the user will use

   D. The screen saver that the user will use

5. What steps would you take to create a mandatory profile in Windows 2000 Professional? Choose all that apply.

   A. In Control Panel, in the User Profiles tab of the System Properties dialog box, specify that the profile is a mandatory profile.

   B. Rename the user profile to NTUSER.MAN.

   C. Copy the profile to a network share using the User Profiles tab of the System Properties dialog box in Control Panel.

   D. In the Local Users and Groups utility, in the Profile tab of the user Properties dialog box, specify a UNC path for the roaming profile.

6. Which of the following options can be configured when you edit hardware profile properties? Choose all that apply.

   A. Whether or not the computer is portable

   B. Whether or not the computer uses different displays

   C. Whether or not the computer uses different hot-plug devices

   D. Whether or not the hardware profile is included in the hardware profile selection options when Windows 2000 is booted

7. Which utility is used to specify that a user will use a roaming profile?

   A. Local Users and Groups

   B. Control Panel, System, User Profiles tab

   C. User Profile Editor

   D. User Manager

8. When you look at the Profile tab of the Properties dialog box for user Liz, you see the following:

What user profile will Liz use based on this information?

A. Since Liz has no user profile specified, she will access the default profile each time she logs on.

B. The Profile Path box is blank since Liz has never logged on to the computer.

C. Because the Profile Path box is blank, Liz will use her locally stored profile.

D. Because the Profile Path box is blank, Liz will use a roaming profile by default.

9. You have decided to store the roaming profile for user Rick on the domain SALES, computer SERVER, share PROFILES, subfolder RICK. What path should you specify for Rick's profile path?

A. \\SALES\SERVER\PROFILES\RICK

B. \\SERVER\PROFILES\RICK

C. \\SALES\PROFILES\RICK

D. \\SERVER\PROFILES

10. You are trying to create a mandatory profile for user Brett. When you look in Brett's profile folder, you see the following:

What is the most likely explanation?

A. Brett has never logged on to the computer, so his profile has not been created.

B. You are not in the correct folder for user Brett.

C. Brett is using a roaming profile.

D. By default, the NTUSER.DAT file is hidden, and you need to configure Folder Options to allow you to view hidden files.

11. Everything has been working properly on your computer. You have just edited your hardware profiles for docked (which is on the network) and undocked (which is not on the network). You reboot your computer and take a coffee break. When you return, you realize you can't access any network resources. What is the most likely problem?

A. Your IP configuration is not properly set.

B. You pulled the network cable from your computer.

C. Your network card is failing.

D. The hardware profile for undocked has been set as the default profile.

12. You have created two hardware profiles for your laptop, named Docked and Undocked. How do you specify which of the hardware profiles will be used?

    A. Press F8 during the computer startup and select the profile that will be used.

    B. Press F6 during the computer startup and select the profile that will be used.

    C. Select the profile that will be used by clicking the profile icon that appears on the Taskbar.

    D. Select the profile from that menu that appears during the computer startup by default.

13. Which of the following user profile types must be stored on a Windows 2000 Server computer? Choose all that apply.

    A. Local profiles

    B. Roaming profiles

    C. Mandatory profiles

    D. Hardware profiles

14. When Kalea logs on to the Windows 2000 Professional computer W2KSales1, she sees her normal Desktop. When Kalea logs on to the Windows 2000 Professional computer W2KSales2, she does not see her normal Desktop. What is the most likely cause?

    A. A roaming user profile is not configured for Kalea.

    B. Kalea does not have permissions to access her user profile from W2KSales2.

    C. Kalea has a mandatory profile configured in W2KSales2.

    D. The computer that Kalea is logging on from is a Windows NT 4 computer.

15. How many hardware profiles are created on a Windows 2000 Professional computer by default?

    A. 0

    B. 1

    C. 2

    D. 3

16. Which of the following computers would most likely use a hardware profile in Windows 2000?

    A. A computer that dual-boots

    B. A computer that was upgraded from Windows 95

    C. A computer without Plug-and-Play hardware

    D. A laptop computer that uses a docking station

17. Which of the following groups are able to manage mandatory user profiles?

    A. The user who the profile is assigned to

    B. The Administrators group

    C. The Power Users group

    D. The Server Operators group

18. Nicky and Jaime share the same Windows 2000 Professional computer. Nicky has configured a Desktop that Jaime would like to use. How can you configure Jaime's user profile so that it will initially match Nicky's settings?

    A. Copy the NTUSER.DAT file from Nicky's folder to Jaime's folder.

    B. Configure a roaming profile that will be used by both users.

    C. Copy Nicky's user profile to Jaime's folder in the Documents and Settings folder using Control Panel, System, User Profiles tab. Configure the profile so that Jaime is permitted to use the copied profile.

    D. Copy Nicky's user profile to Jaime's folder in the Profiles folder using Control Panel, System, User Profiles tab.

19. Which of the following steps is *not* required to configure a mandatory profile?

A. Create the profile that will be used.

B. Rename the NTUSER.DAT file to NTUSER.MAN.

C. Specify that the user will use a mandatory profile in Control Panel, System, User Profiles tab.

D. Configure the profile as a roaming profile.

20. Bette has completely mucked up her user profile. What is the easiest way to restore her Desktop to the original configuration?

A. Copy the default user profile to Bette's folder in the Documents and Settings folder.

B. Delete Bette's user profile through Control Panel, System, User Profiles tab.

C. Delete user Bette and recreate user Bette.

D. Create a new user, then copy the new user's user profile to Bette's folder in the Profiles folder.

Answers to Review Questions

1. B. The default location for user profiles is the \Documents and Settings folder in Windows 2000. In Windows NT 4, the default location for user profiles was \WINNT\Profiles.

2. B. By default, user profiles are named NTUSER.DAT in Windows 2000 Professional. This is the same default filename that was used in Windows NT 4.

3. D. After you create the profile that will be used as the roaming profile, you create a folder and share on the network location where the roaming profile will be stored. You use the User Profiles tab of the System Properties dialog box in Control Panel to copy the local profile to the network share. Finally, you specify that the user is using a roaming profile by configuring the user's properties through the Local Users and Groups utility. In the Profile tab, you specify a UNC path for the roaming profile.

4. B, C, D. User profiles generally contain user preference items, which include mouse pointers, keyboard layout, and screen saver settings. User profiles do not contain computer configuration settings such as mouse drivers.

5. B, C, D. Creating a mandatory profile involves three main steps. First, rename the user profile from NTUSER.DAT to NTUSER.MAN. Second, copy the profile to a network share using the User Profiles tab of the System Properties dialog box in Control Panel. Third, in the Local Users and Groups utility, access the properties of the user who will be assigned the roaming profile, and specify the location of the mandatory profile. This path must be a UNC path for the mandatory profile to work.

6. A, D. The only options that can be configured when you set hardware profile properties are whether or not the computer is portable and whether or not the hardware profile will be included in the hardware profile selection options when Windows 2000 Professional is booted.

7. A. You specify the location of a user profile through the Local Users and Groups utility.

8. C. If the Profile Path box is blank, then the user will use a locally stored profile by default.

9. B. You use a UNC path to specify the location of roaming profiles. UNC paths always start with two backslashes \\, followed by the computer name, followed by the share name. If there are any subfolders under the share, then they can be a part of the UNC path. In this example, the correct UNC path to find Rick's profile is \\SERVER\PROFILES\RICK.

10. D. If Brett had never logged on to the computer, he would not have a folder. You can assume that you are in the correct folder since the window shows the folders associated with user profiles. If Brett has a folder, he is using a local profile, or at some point he had a local profile. The most logical explanation is that since the NTUSER.DAT file is hidden, you need to configure Folder Options to display hidden files.

11. D. When you configured your two hardware profiles, it is possible that the undocked profile was set as the default selection if no choice was made within a set amount of seconds.

12. D. When you have multiple hardware profiles, by default, you see a menu during the computer startup that allows you to select the hardware profile that will be used. Through this menu, you can select from the docked or undocked profile.

13. B, C. In order to use roaming and mandatory profiles, you must store the profiles on a Windows 2000 Server computer.

14. A. By default, profiles are only configured to be used locally. In this case, it is likely that Kalea has not had a roaming profile configured.

15. B. By default, there is one hardware profile created, called Profile 1.

16. D. Hardware profiles are used with laptop computers that use docking stations. The hardware profile specifies whether or not the computer is attached to a network.

17. B. Only members of the Administrators group can create and assign mandatory user profiles.

18. C. You can copy Nicky's user profile so that Jaime can use it initially by copying Nicky's user profile to Jaime's folder in the Document and Settings folder. You can perform this copy operation through Control Panel, System, User Profiles tab.

19. C. You specify the profile, in this case mandatory, that the user will use through the user's properties in the Local Users and Groups utility.

20. B. You can replace an existing user profile with the default user profile by deleting the user profile through Control Panel, System, User Profiles tab.

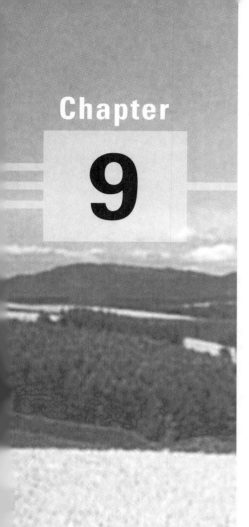

Chapter

9

Managing Disks

MICROSOFT EXAM OBJECTIVES COVERED IN THIS CHAPTER

✓ **Monitor, manage, and troubleshoot access to files and folders.**

- Configure, manage, and troubleshoot file compression.
- Control access to files and folders by using permissions.
- Optimize access to files and folders.

✓ **Configure and manage file systems.**

- Convert from one file system to another file system.
- Configure file systems by using NTFS, FAT32, or FAT.

✓ **Implement, manage, and troubleshoot disk devices.**

- Install, configure, and manage DVD and CD-ROM devices.
- Monitor and configure disks.
- Monitor, configure, and troubleshoot volumes.
- Monitor and configure removable media, such as tape devices.

✓ **Encrypt data on a hard disk by using Encrypting File System (EFS).**

When you install Windows 2000 Professional, you choose how your disks are initially configured. Through Windows 2000 Professional's utilities and features, you can change your configuration and perform disk-management tasks.

For your file system configuration, you can choose FAT, FAT32, or NTFS. You can also update a FAT or FAT32 partition to NTFS. This chapter covers the features of each file system and how to use the CONVERT utility to upgrade to NTFS.

Another factor in disk management is choosing how your physical drives are configured. Windows 2000 supports basic storage and dynamic storage. When you install Windows 2000 Professional or upgrade from Windows NT, the drives are configured as basic storage. Dynamic storage is new to Windows 2000 and allows you to create simple volumes, spanned volumes, and striped volumes.

Once you decide on how your disks should be configured, you implement the disk configurations through the Disk Management utility. This utility allows you to view and manage your physical disks and volumes. In this chapter, you will learn how to manage both types of storage and upgrade from basic storage to dynamic storage.

The other disk-management features covered in this chapter are data compression, disk quotas, data encryption, disk defragmentation, disk cleanup, and disk error checking.

The procedures for many disk-management tasks are the same for both Windows 2000 Professional and Server. The main difference is that Windows 2000 Server also supports mirrored and RAID 5 volumes.

Configuring File Systems

Each partition (logical drive that is created on your hard drive) you create under Windows 2000 Professional must have a file system associated with it.

Microsoft *Exam* *Objective*

Configure and manage file systems.

- Convert from one file system to another file system.
- Configure file systems by using NTFS, FAT32, or FAT.

You configure file systems by using NTFS, FAT32, or FAT. You choose the file system you will use when you create and format the partition. If you have a FAT or FAT32 partition and want to update it to NTFS, you can use the CONVERT utility. The features of each file system and the procedure for converting file systems are covered in the following sections.

File System Selection

Your file system is used to store and retrieve the files stored on your hard drive. One of the most fundamental choices associated with file management is how your file system is configured.

As explained in Chapter 1, "Getting Started with Windows Professional," Windows 2000 Professional supports the FAT16, FAT32, and NTFS file systems. You should choose FAT16 or FAT32 if you want to dual-boot your computer, because these file systems are backward compatible with other operating systems. You should choose NTFS if you want to take advantage of features such as local security, file compression, and file encryption.

Table 9.1 summarizes the capabilities of each file system, and they are described in more detail in the following sections.

TABLE 9.1 File System Capabilities

Feature	FAT16	FAT32	NTFS
Supporting operating systems	Most	Windows 95 OSR2, Windows 98, and Windows 2000	Windows NT and Windows 2000

TABLE 9.1 File System Capabilities *(continued)*

Feature	FAT16	FAT32	NTFS
Long filename support?	Yes	Yes	Yes
Efficient use of disk space?	No	Yes	Yes
Compression support?	No	No	Yes
Quota support?	No	No	Yes
Encryption support?	No	No	Yes
Support for local security?	No	No	Yes
Support for network security?	Yes	Yes	Yes
Maximum volume size	2GB	32GB	2TB

Windows 2000 Professional also supports *CDFS* (*Compact Disk File System*). However, CDFS cannot be managed. It is only used to mount and read CDs.

FAT16

FAT16 was first used with DOS (Disk Operating System) in 1981. With FAT16, the directory-entry table keeps track of the location of the file's first block, the filename and extension, the date and time stamps on the file, and any attributes associated with the file. It is similar in nature to a card catalog at a library. When the operating system needs a file, the FAT listing is consulted.

The main advantage of FAT16 is that almost all operating systems support this file system. This makes FAT16 a good choice if the computer will dual-boot with other operating systems (see Chapter 1 for more information about dual-booting). FAT16 is also a good choice for small partitions (FAT16 partitions can be up to 2GB). Because FAT16 is a very simple file system, the overhead associated with storing files is much smaller than with NTFS.

The problem with using FAT16 is that it was designed to be used as a single-user file system, and thus it does not support any kind of security. It also does not support long filenames. Other file systems, such as NTFS, offer many more features, including local security, file compression, and encrypting capabilities.

FAT32

FAT32 is an updated version of FAT. FAT32 was first shipped with Windows 95 OSR2 (Operating System Release 2), and it currently ships with Windows 98. It is supported by Windows 2000.

One of the main advantages of FAT32 is its support for smaller cluster sizes, which results in more efficient space allocation than was possible with FAT16. Files stored on a FAT32 partition can use 20 to 30 percent less disk space than those stored on a FAT16 partition. FAT32 partitions can be up to 32GB.

The main disadvantage of FAT32 is that it is not compatible with previous versions of Windows NT, including NT 4.

NTFS

NTFS, which was first used with the NT operating system, now offers the highest level of service and features for Windows 2000 computers. NTFS partitions can be up to 2TB.

NTFS offers comprehensive folder and file-level security. This allows you to set an additional level of security for users who access the files and folders locally or through the network. For example, two users who share the same Windows 2000 Professional computer can be assigned different NTFS permissions, so that one user has access to a folder, but the other user is denied access to that folder.

NTFS also offers disk-management features—such as compression, disk quotas, and encryption services—and data-recovery features. The disk-management features are covered later in this chapter. The data-recovery features are covered in Chapter 15, "Performing System Recovery Functions."

The main drawback of using NTFS is that only the Windows NT and Windows 2000 operating systems recognize the NTFS file system. If your computer dual-boots with other operating systems, such as Windows 98, the NTFS partition will not be recognized.

File System Conversion

In Windows 2000, you can convert both FAT16 and FAT32 partitions to NTFS. File system conversion is the process of converting one file system to another without the loss of data. If you format a drive as another file system, as opposed to converting that drive, all the data on that drive will be lost.

In order to convert a partition, you use the *CONVERT* command-line utility. The syntax for the CONVERT command is:

    CONVERT [*drive:*] /fs:ntfs

For example, if you wanted to convert your D: drive to NTFS, you would type the following from a command prompt:

    CONVERT D: /fs:ntfs

When the conversion process begins, it will attempt to lock the partition. If the partition cannot be locked—perhaps because the partition contains the Windows 2000 operating system files or the system's page file—the conversion will not take place until the computer is restarted.

You can use the /v switch with the CONVERT command. This switch specifies that you want to use verbose mode, and all messages will be displayed during the conversion process.

In Exercise 9.1, you will convert your D: drive from FAT16 to NTFS.

EXERCISE 9.1

Converting a FAT16 Partition to NTFS

1. Copy some folders to the D: drive.

2. Select Start ➢ Programs ➢ Accessories ➢ Command Prompt.

EXERCISE 9.1 *(continued)*

3. In the Command Prompt dialog box, type **CONVERT D: /fs:ntfs** and press Enter.

4. After the conversion process is complete, close the Command Prompt dialog box.

5. Verify that the folders you copied in step 1 still exist on the partition.

Configuring Disk Storage

Windows 2000 Professional supports two types of disk storage: basic storage and dynamic storage. Basic storage is backward compatible with other operating systems and can be configured to support up to four partitions. Dynamic storage is a new system that is configured as volumes. The following sections describe the basic storage and dynamic storage configurations.

Basic Storage

Basic storage consists of primary and extended partitions. The first partition that is created on a hard drive is called a *primary partition*. The primary partition uses all of the space that is allocated to the partition. Each physical drive can have up to four partitions. You can set up four primary partitions, or you can have three primary partitions and one extended partition. With *extended partitions*, you can allocate the space however you like. For example, a 500MB extended partition could have a 250MB D: partition and a 250MB E: partition.

At the highest level of disk organization, you have a physical hard drive. You cannot use space on the physical drive until you have logically partitioned the physical drive. A *partition* is a logical definition of hard drive space.

An advantage of using a single partition on a single physical disk is that you can allocate the space however you want. For example, if you had a 1GB physical drive and you created a single primary partition, you could allocate the space on the drive as needed. On the other hand, if you created two 500MB partitions called C: and D:, and C: was full and D: had space left, you could not take space from the D: drive without deleting the partition first.

One of the advantages of using multiple partitions on a single physical hard drive is that each partition can have a different file system. For example, the C: drive might be FAT32 and the D: drive might be NTFS. Multiple partitions also make it easier to manage security requirements.

Laptop computers support only basic storage.

Dynamic Storage

Dynamic storage is a new Windows 2000 feature that consists of a *dynamic disk* divided into dynamic *volumes*. Dynamic volumes cannot contain partitions or logical drives, and they are not accessible through DOS.

Dynamic storage supports three dynamic volume types: simple volumes, spanned volumes, and striped volumes. These are similar to disk configurations that were used with Windows NT 4. However, if you've upgraded from NT 4, you are using basic storage, and you can't add volume sets. Fortunately, you can upgrade from basic storage to dynamic storage, as explained in the "Upgrading a Basic Disk to a Dynamic Disk" section later in this chapter.

To set up dynamic storage, you create or upgrade a disk to a dynamic disk. Then you create dynamic volumes within the dynamic disk. You create dynamic storage with the Windows 2000 Disk Management utility, which is covered after the descriptions of the dynamic volume types.

Simple Volumes

A *simple volume* contains space from a single dynamic drive. The space from the single drive can be contiguous or noncontiguous. Simple volumes are used when you have enough disk space on a single drive to hold your entire volume. Figure 9.1 illustrates two simple volumes on a physical disk.

FIGURE 9.1 Two simple volumes

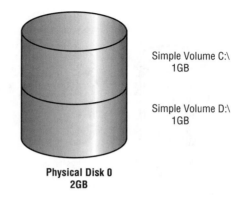

Simple Volume C:\
1GB

Simple Volume D:\
1GB

Physical Disk 0
2GB

Spanned Volumes

A *spanned volume* consists of disk space on two or more dynamic drives; up to 32 dynamic drives can be used in a spanned volume configuration. Spanned volume sets are used to dynamically increase the size of a dynamic volume. When you create spanned volumes, the data is written sequentially, filling space on one physical drive before writing to space on the next physical drive in the spanned volume set. Typically, administrators use spanned volumes when they are running out of disk space on a volume and want to dynamically extend the volume with space from another hard drive.

You do not need to allocate the same amount of space to the volume set on each physical drive. This means that you could combine a 500MB partition on one physical drive with two 750MB partitions on other dynamic drives, as shown in Figure 9.2.

Because data is written sequentially, you do not see any performance enhancements with spanned volumes, as you do with striped volumes (discussed next). The main disadvantage of spanned volumes is that if any drive in the spanned volume set fails, you lose access to all of the data in the spanned set.

FIGURE 9.2 A spanned volume set

Data written
sequentially

Physical Disk 0
1GB

Physical Disk 1
500MB

Physical Disk 2
750MB

Physical Disk 3
750MB

Spanned Volume Set D:\

Striped Volumes

A *striped volume* stores data in equal stripes between two or more (up to 32) dynamic drives, as illustrated in Figure 9.3. Since the data is written sequentially in the stripes, you can take advantage of multiple I/O performance and increase the speed at which data reads and writes take place. Typically, administrators use striped volumes when they want to combine the space of several physical drives into a single logical volume and increase disk performance.

FIGURE 9.3 A striped volume set

Physical Disk 1

Physical Disk 2

Physical Disk 3

Striped Volume Set D:\

The main disadvantage of striped volumes is that if any drive in the striped volume set fails, you lose access to all of the data in the striped set.

Mirrored volumes and RAID 5 volumes are fault-tolerant dynamic disk configurations. These options are available only with Windows 2000 Server and are covered in detail in *MCSE: Windows 2000 Server Study Guide*, by Lisa Donald with James Chellis (Sybex, 2000).

Using the Disk Management Utility

The *Disk Management utility* is a graphical tool for managing disks and volumes within the Windows 2000 environment. In this section, you will learn how to access the Disk Management utility and use it to manage basic tasks, basic storage, and dynamic storage.

Microsoft ✓ Exam Objective	**Implement, manage, and troubleshoot disk devices.** • Monitor and configure disks. • Monitor, configure, and troubleshoot volumes.

This chapter covers the material related to managing disks and volumes, for the "Implement, manage, and troubleshoot disk devices" objective. The subobjectives for managing DVD devices, CD-ROM devices, and removable media are covered in Chapter 4, "Configuring the Windows 2000 Environment."

In order to have full permissions to use the Disk Management utility, you should be logged on with Administrative privileges. To access the utility, open Control Panel, select Administrative Tools, then Computer Management. Expand the Storage folder to see the Disk Management utility. The Disk Management utility opening window is shown in Figure 9.4.

FIGURE 9.4 The Disk Management window

The main window shows the following information:

- The volumes that are recognized by the computer

- The type of partition, either basic or dynamic

- The type of file system used by each partition

- The status of the partition and whether or not the partition contains the system or boot partition

- The capacity, or amount of space, that is allocated to the partition

- The amount of free space remaining on the partition

- The amount of overhead associated with the partition

You can also add Disk Management as a Microsoft Management Console (MMC) snap-in. Adding MMC snap-ins is covered in Chapter 4.

Managing Basic Tasks

With the Disk Management utility, you can perform a variety of basic tasks:

- View disk and volume properties.
- Add a new disk.
- Create partitions and volumes.
- Upgrade a basic disk to a dynamic disk.
- Change a drive letter and path.
- Delete partitions and volumes.

These tasks are covered in detail in the following sections.

Viewing Disk Properties

To view the properties of a disk, right-click the drive in the lower half of the Disk Management main window (see Figure 9.4) and choose Properties from the pop-up menu. This brings up the Disk Properties dialog box, as shown in Figure 9.5.

FIGURE 9.5   The Disk Properties dialog box

This dialog box displays the following disk properties:

- The disk number
- The type of disk (basic, dynamic, CD-ROM, removable, DVD, or unknown)
- The status of the disk (online or offline)
- The capacity of the disk
- The amount of unallocated space on the disk
- The hardware device type
- The hardware vendor who produced the drive
- The adapter name
- The logical volumes that have been defined on the physical drive

Viewing Volume and Local Disk Properties

On a dynamic disk, you manage volume properties. On a basic disk, you manage local disk properties. Volumes and local disks perform the same function, and the options discussed in the following sections apply to both. The examples are based on a dynamic disk using a simple volume. If you are using basic storage, you will view the local disk properties rather than the volume properties.

To view the properties of a volume, right-click the volume in the upper half of the Disk Management main window and choose Properties. This brings up the volume Properties dialog box, as shown in Figure 9.6.

In the dialog box, the volume properties are organized on six tabs (four for FAT volumes): General, Tools, Hardware, Sharing, Security, and Quota. The Security and Quota tabs appear only for NTFS volumes. These tabs are covered in detail in the following sections.

FIGURE 9.6   The volume Properties dialog box

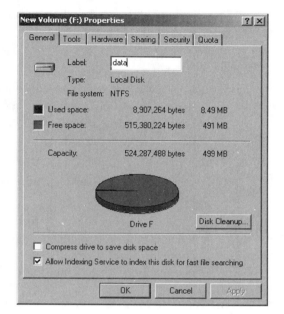

General

The information on the General tab of the volume Properties dialog box (see Figure 9.6) gives you a general idea of how the volume is configured. This dialog box shows the label, type, file system, used and free space, and capacity of the volume. The label is shown in an editable text box, and you can change it if desired. The space allocated to the volume is shown in a graphical representation as well as in text form.

The volume or local disk label is for informational purposes only. For example, depending on its use, you might give a volume a label like APPS or ACCTDB.

The Disk Cleanup button starts the Disk Cleanup utility, which allows you to delete unnecessary files and free disk space. This utility is covered in more detail later in this chapter in the "Using the Disk Cleanup Utility" section.

Tools

The Tools tab of the volume Properties dialog box, shown in Figure 9.7, provides access to three tools:

- Click the Check Now button to run the Check Disk utility. You would check the volume for errors if you were experiencing problems accessing the volume, or if the volume had been open during a system restart that had not gone through a proper shutdown sequence. This utility is covered in more detail later in this chapter in the "Troubleshooting Disk Devices and Volumes" section.

- Click the Backup Now button to run the Backup Wizard. This Wizard steps you through backing up the files on the volume. Backup procedures are covered in Chapter 15, "Performing System Recovery Functions."

- Click the Defragment Now button to run the Disk Defragmenter utility. This utility defragments files on the volume by storing files in a contiguous manner on the hard drive. Defragmentation is covered in detail later in this chapter in the "Defragmenting Disks" section.

FIGURE 9.7 The Tools tab of the volume Properties dialog box

Hardware

The Hardware tab of the volume Properties dialog box, shown in Figure 9.8, lists the hardware associated with the disk drives that are recognized by the Windows 2000 operating system. The bottom half of the dialog box shows the properties of the device that is highlighted in the top half of the dialog box.

FIGURE 9.8   The Hardware tab of the volume Properties dialog box

For more details about a hardware item, highlight it and click the Properties button in the lower-right corner of the dialog box. This brings up a Properties dialog box for the item. Figure 9.9 shows an example of the disk drive Properties dialog box. With luck, your device status will report that "This device is working properly." If the device is not working properly, you can click the Troubleshooter button to bring up a troubleshooting Wizard to help you discover what the problem is.

FIGURE 9.9 A disk drive Properties dialog box accessed through the Hardware tab of the volume Properties dialog box

Sharing

The Sharing tab of the volume Properties dialog box, shown in Figure 9.10, allows you to specify whether or not the volume is shared. By default, all volumes are shared. The share name is the drive letter followed by a $ (dollar sign). The $ indicates that the share is hidden. From this dialog box, you can set the user limit, permissions, and caching for the share. Sharing is covered in Chapter 10, "Accessing Files and Folders."

Security

The Security tab of the volume Properties dialog box, shown in Figure 9.11, appears only if the volume is NTFS. The Security tab is used to set the NTFS permissions for the volume. Notice that the default permissions allow the Everyone group Full Control permissions at the root of the volume. This could cause major security problems if any user decides to manipulate or delete the data within the volume. Managing security is covered in Chapter 10.

FIGURE 9.10   The Sharing tab of the volume Properties dialog box

FIGURE 9.11   The Security tab of the volume Properties dialog box

Quota

Like the Security tab, the Quota tab of the volume Properties dialog box appears only if the volume is NTFS. Through this tab, you can limit the amount of space users can use within the volume. Quotas are covered in detail later in this chapter in the "Setting Disk Quotas" section.

Adding a New Disk

To increase the amount of disk storage you have, you can add a new disk. This is a fairly common task that you will need to perform as your application programs and files grow larger. How you add a disk depends on whether your computer supports hot swapping of drives. *Hot swapping* is the ability to add new hard drives while the computer is turned on. Most computers do not support this capability.

Computer Doesn't Support Hot Swap

If your computer does not support hot swapping, you need to first shut down the computer before you add a new disk. Then add the drive according to the manufacturer's directions. When you're finished, restart the computer. The new drive should now be listed in the Disk Management utility.

Computer Supports Hot Swap

If your computer does support hot swapping, you don't need to turn off your computer first. Just add the drive according to the manufacturer's directions. Then, open the Disk Management utility and select Action ➢ Rescan Disks. The new drive should appear in the Disk Management utility.

Creating Partitions and Volumes

Once you add a new disk, the next step is to create a partition (on a basic disk) or a volume (on a dynamic disk). The purpose of partitions and volumes and the process for creating them are similar, as described in the following sections.

Creating a Volume

The Create Volume Wizard guides you through the process of creating a new volume, as follows:

1. Right-click an area of free storage space and choose Create Volume.

2. The Welcome to the Create Volume Wizard dialog box appears, as shown in Figure 9.12. Click the Next button to continue.

FIGURE 9.12   The Welcome to the Create Volume Wizard dialog box

3. The Select Volume Type dialog box appears, as shown in Figure 9.13. In this dialog box, select the type of volume you want to create: simple, spanned, or striped. Only the options supported by your computer's hardware configuration are available. Click the radio button for the type, then click the Next button.

FIGURE 9.13   The Select Volume Type dialog box

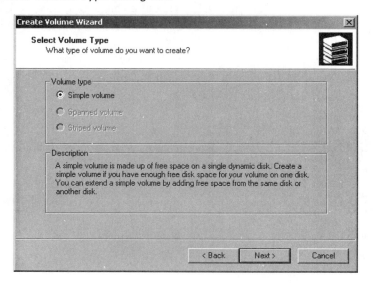

4. The Select Disks dialog box appears, as shown in Figure 9.14. Here, you select the disks and specify the maximum volume size, up to the amount of free disk space that is recognized. Choose the disk that you want the volume to be created on and click the Next button.

FIGURE 9.14 The Select Disks dialog box

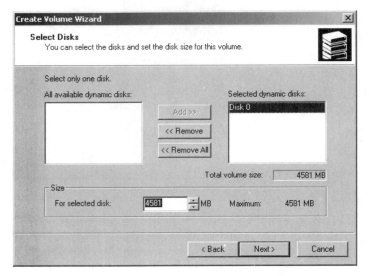

5. The Assign Drive Letter or Path dialog box appears, as shown in Figure 9.15. Through this dialog box, you can specify a drive letter, mount the volume as an empty folder, or choose not to assign a drive letter or drive path. If you choose to mount the volume as an empty folder, you can have an unlimited number of volumes, negating the drive-letter limitation. Make your selections, then click the Next button.

If you choose not to assign a drive letter or path, users will not be able to access the volume.

FIGURE 9.15 The Assign Drive Letter or Path dialog box

6. The Format Volume dialog box appears, as shown in Figure 9.16. This dialog box allows you to choose whether or not you will format the volume. If you choose to format the volume, you can format it as FAT, FAT32, or NTFS. You can also select the allocation block size, enter a volume label (for informative purposes), specify a quick format, or choose to enable file and folder compression. Specifying a quick format is risky, because it will not scan the disk for bad sectors (which is done in a normal format operation). After you've made your choices, click the Next button.

7. The Completing the Create Volume Wizard dialog box appears, as shown in Figure 9.17. Verify your selections. If you need to change any of them, click the Back button to reach the appropriate dialog box. Otherwise, click the Finish button.

FIGURE 9.16 The Format Volume dialog box

FIGURE 9.17 The Completing the Create Volume Wizard dialog box

Creating a Partition

When you right-click an area of free space and select the Create Logical Drive option, the Create Partition Wizard starts. This Wizard displays a series of dialog boxes to guide you through the process of creating a partition:

- The Select Partition Type dialog box allows you to select the type of partition you want to create. You can choose to create a primary partition, an extended partition, or a logical drive.

- The Specify Partition Size dialog box allows you to specify the maximum partition size, up to the amount of free disk space that is recognized.

- The Assign Drive Letter or Path dialog box allows you to assign a drive letter or a drive path. There is also an option to not assign a drive letter or path, but if you choose this option, users will not be able to access the volume.

- The Format Partition dialog box lets you specify whether or not you want to format the partition. If you choose to format the partition, you can select the file system, allocation unit size, and the volume label. You can also choose to perform a quick format and to enable file and folder compression.

The steps to create a logical drive are similar to the steps for creating a volume, which were covered in the previous section. In Exercise 9.2, you will create a partition from the free space that was left on your drive when you installed Windows 2000 Professional (in Exercise 1.1), as specified in Chapter 1.

EXERCISE 9.2

Creating a New Partition

1. Select Start ➤ Settings ➤ Control Panel ➤ Administrative Tools. Expand Computer Management, then Storage, then Disk Management.

2. Right-click an area of free storage and select the Create Partition option.

3. The Create Partition Wizard starts. Click the Next button to continue.

EXERCISE 9.2 *(continued)*

4. The Select Partition Type dialog box appears. Choose Primary Partition and click the Next button.

5. The Specify Partition Size dialog box appears. Specify a partition size of 250MB and click the Next button.

6. The Assign Drive Letter or Path dialog box appears. Click Next to assign the default drive letter shown in this dialog box. If you are using the recommended configuration, C: and D: are assigned as drive letters, E: should be your CD-ROM drive, and the next available drive will be F:.

7. In the Format Partition dialog box, choose to format the drive as NTFS and leave the other settings at their default values. Click the Next button.

8. The Completing the Create Partition Wizard dialog box appears. Click the Finish button.

Upgrading a Basic Disk to a Dynamic Disk

When you install Windows 2000 or upgrade your computer from Windows NT 4 to Windows 2000, your drives are configured as basic disks. To take advantage of the features offered by Windows 2000 dynamic disks, you must upgrade your basic disks to dynamic disks.

WARNING

Upgrading basic disks to dynamic disks is a one-way process. If you decide to revert back to a basic disk, you must first delete all volumes associated with the drive. Also, this is a potentially dangerous operation. Before you do this (or make any major change to your drives or volumes), create a new backup of the drive or volume and verify that you can successfully restore the backup.

The following steps are involved in the disk-upgrade process:

1. In the Disk Management utility, right-click the drive you want to convert and select the Upgrade to Dynamic Disk option.

2. The Upgrade to Dynamic Disk dialog box appears, as shown in Figure 9.18. Check the disk that you want to upgrade and click the OK button.

FIGURE 9.18   The Upgrade to Dynamic Disk dialog box

3. The Disks to Upgrade dialog box appears, as shown in Figure 9.19.
    Click the Upgrade button.

FIGURE 9.19   The Disks to Upgrade dialog box

4. A confirmation dialog box warns you that you will no longer be able to boot previous versions of Windows from this disk, as shown in Figure 9.20. Click the Yes button to continue.

FIGURE 9.20 The warning that you will not be able to boot to other operating systems

5. Another confirmation dialog box warns you that any file systems mounted on the disk will be dismounted, as shown in Figure 9.21. Click the Yes button to continue.

FIGURE 9.21 The warning about dismounting file systems

6. An information dialog box tells you that a reboot is required to complete the upgrade, as shown in Figure 9.22. Click the OK button. Your computer will restart, and the disk-upgrade process is complete.

FIGURE 9.22   The dialog box indicating a reboot will take place

Changing the Drive Letter and Path

Suppose that you have drive C: assigned as your first partition and drive D: assigned as your CD drive. You add a new drive and partition it as a new volume. By default, the new partition is assigned as drive E:. If you want your logical drives to appear before the CD drive, you can use the Disk Management utility's Change Drive Letter and Path option to rearrange your drive letters.

When you need to reassign drive letters, right-click the volume you want to change the drive letter on and choose the Change Drive Letter and Path option. This brings up the Change Drive Letter and Paths for *drive* dialog box, shown in Figure 9.23. Click the Edit button to access the Edit Drive Letter or Path dialog box, as shown in Figure 9.24. Use the drop-down list next to the Assign a Drive Letter option to select the drive letter you want to assign to the volume.

FIGURE 9.23   The Change Drive Letter and Paths for (F:) dialog box

FIGURE 9.24   The Edit Drive Letter or Path dialog box

In Exercise 9.3, you will edit the drive letter of the partition you created in Exercise 9.2.

EXERCISE 9.3

Editing a Drive Letter

1. Select Start ➢ Settings ➢ Control Panel ➢ Administrative Tools. Expand Computer Management, then Storage, then Disk Management.

2. Right-click the drive you created in Exercise 9.2 and select Change Drive Letter and Path.

3. In the Change Drive Letter and Paths dialog box, click the Edit button.

4. In the Edit Drive Letter or Path dialog box, select a new drive letter and click the OK button.

5. In the dialog box that appears, click the Yes button to confirm that you want to change the drive letter.

Deleting Partitions and Volumes

You would delete a partition or volume if you wanted to reorganize your disk or make sure that data would not be accessed. Once you delete a partition or volume, it is gone forever.

To delete a partition or volume, in the Disk Management window, right-click the partition or volume and choose the Delete Volume (or Delete Partition) option. You will see a dialog box warning you that all the data on the partition or volume will be lost, as shown in Figure 9.25. Click Yes to confirm that you want to delete the volume or partition.

FIGURE 9.25   Confirming volume deletion

Managing Basic Storage

The Disk Management utility offers limited support for managing basic storage. You can create, delete, and format partitions on basic drives. You also can delete volume sets and stripe sets that were created under Windows NT. Most other disk-management tasks require that you upgrade your drive to dynamic disks. (The upgrade process was described earlier in this chapter in the "Upgrading a Basic Disk to a Dynamic Disk" section.)

Managing Dynamic Storage

As noted earlier in this chapter, a dynamic disk can contain simple, spanned, or striped volumes. Through the Disk Management utility, you can create volumes of each type. You can also create an extended volume, which is the process of adding disk space to a single simple volume. The following sections describe these disk-management tasks.

Creating Simple, Spanned, and Striped Volumes

As explained earlier in the chapter in the "Creating Partitions and Volumes" section, you use the Create Volume Wizard to create a new volume. To start the Wizard, right-click an area of free space where you want to create the volume and choose Create Volume. When the Wizard displays the Select Volume Type dialog box (see Figure 9.13 earlier in the chapter), select the type of volume you want to create.

When you choose to create a spanned volume, you are creating a new volume from scratch that includes space from 2 or more physical drives, up to a maximum of 32 drives. You can create spanned volumes that are formatted as FAT, FAT32, or NTFS.

When you choose to create a striped volume, you are creating a new volume that combines free space on 2 to 32 drives into a single logical partition. The free space on all drives must be equal in size. Data in the striped volume is written across all drives in 64KB stripes. (Data in spanned and extended volumes is written sequentially.)

Creating Extended Volumes

When you create an extended volume, you are taking a single simple volume (maybe one that is almost out of disk space) and adding more disk space to the volume from free space that exists on the same physical hard drive. When the volume is extended, it is seen as a single drive letter. In order to extend a volume, the simple volume must be formatted as NTFS. You cannot extend a system or boot partition.

An extended volume assumes that you are only using one physical drive. A spanned volume assumes that you are using two or more physical drives.

The following steps are used to create an extended volume:

1. In the Disk Management utility, right-click the volume you want to extend and choose the Extend Volume option.

2. The Extend Volume Wizard starts. Click the Next button.

3. The Select Disks dialog box appears, as shown in Figure 9.26. You can specify the maximum size of the extended volume. The maximum size you can specify is determined by the amount of free space that exists in all of the dynamic drives on your computer.

FIGURE 9.26   The Select Disks dialog box

4. The Completing the Extend Volume Wizard dialog box appears. Click the Finish button.

Once a volume is extended, no portion of the volume can be deleted without losing data on the entire set.

Managing Data Compression

*D*ata compression is the process of storing data in a form that takes less space than uncompressed data does. If you have ever "zipped" or "packed" a file, you have used data compression. With Windows 2000, data compression is only available on NTFS partitions.

Microsoft
✓ *Exam*
Objective

Monitor, manage, and troubleshoot access to files and folders.

▪ Configure, manage, and troubleshoot file compression.

This chapter covers material related to file compression and optimizing access to files and folders, for the "Monitor, manage, and troubleshoot access to files and folders" objective. Controlling access to files and folders by using permissions, a third subobjective, is covered in Chapter 10, "Accessing Files and Folders." That chapter also provides more information about optimizing access to files and folders.

Both files and folders in the NTFS file system can be compressed or uncompressed. Files and folders are managed independently, which means that a compressed folder can contain uncompressed files, and an uncompressed folder can contain compressed files.

Access to compressed files by DOS or Windows applications is transparent. For example, if you access a compressed file through Microsoft Word, the file will be uncompressed automatically when it is opened, and then automatically compressed again when it is closed.

Data compression is only available on NTFS partitions. If you copy or move a compressed folder or file to a FAT partition (or a floppy disk), Windows 2000 will automatically uncompress the folder or file.

You cannot have a folder or file compressed and encrypted at the same time. Encryption is discussed in the "Managing Data Encryption with EFS" section later in this chapter.

You implement compression through the Windows Explorer utility. Compression is an advanced attribute of a folder's or file's properties. Use the following procedure to compress a folder or file:

1. Open Windows Explorer by selecting Start ➢ Programs ➢ Accessories ➢ Windows Explorer.

2. In Windows Explorer, navigate to the folder or file you wish to compress and select it.

3. Right-click the folder or file you wish to compress and select Properties from the pop-up menu.

4. In the Properties dialog box, click the Advanced button on the General tab.

5. The Advanced Attributes dialog box appears, as shown in Figure 9.27. Check the Compress Contents to Save Disk Space check box. Then click the OK button.

FIGURE 9.27 The Advanced Attributes dialog box accessed from the folder Properties dialog box

6. If you are compressing a folder and it contains any files, the Confirm Attribute Changes dialog box appears, as shown in Figure 9.28. Specify whether you want to compress only this folder (Apply Changes to This Folder Only) or if you want to compress the subfolder and files in the folder as well (Apply Changes to This Folder, Subfolder, and Files). Then click the OK button.

To uncompress folders and files, repeat the steps above, but uncheck the Compress Contents to Save Disk Space option in the Advanced Attributes dialog box.

FIGURE 9.28 The Confirm Attribute Changes dialog box that appears after you change a folder's properties

You will compress folders and files in Exercise 9.4. This exercise assumes that you have completed Exercise 9.1.

EXERCISE 9.4

Compressing Folders and Files

1. Select Start ➢ Programs ➢ Accessories ➢ Windows Explorer.

2. In Windows Explorer, find and select a folder on the D: drive. The folder you select should contain files.

3. Right-click the folder and select Properties. In the General tab of the folder Properties dialog box, note the value listed for Size on Disk. Then click the Advanced button.

4. In the Advanced Attributes dialog box, check the Compress Contents to Save Disk Space option. Then click the OK button.

5. In the Confirm Attribute Changes dialog box, select Apply Changes to This Folder, Subfolder, and Files (if this dialog box does not appear, click the Apply button in the Properties dialog box to display it). Then click the OK button.

6. In the General tab of the folder Properties dialog box, note the value that now appears for Size on Disk. This size should have decreased because you compressed the folder.

You can specify that compressed files be displayed in a different color than the uncompressed files. To do so, in Windows Explorer, select Tools ➢ Folder Options ➢ Views. Under Files and Folders, check the Display Compressed Files and Folders with an Alternate Color option.

Setting Disk Quotas

Suppose that you have a server with an 18GB drive, which is mainly used for users' home folders, and you start getting "out of disk space" error messages. On closer inspection, you find that a single user has taken up 10GB of space by storing multimedia files that she has downloaded from the Internet. This type of problem can be avoided through the use of disk quotas.

Microsoft Exam Objective

Implement, manage, and troubleshoot disk devices.

- Monitor and configure disks.

Disk quotas are used to specify how much disk space a user is allowed on specific NTFS volumes. You can specify disk quotas for all users, or you can limit disk space on a per-user basis.

Before you administer disk quotas, you should be aware of the following aspects of disk quotas:

- Disk quotas can be specified only for NTFS volumes.

- Disk quotas apply only at the volume level, even if the NTFS partitions reside on the same physical hard drive.

- Disk usage is calculated on file and folder ownership. When a user creates, copies, or takes ownership of a file, that user is the owner of the file.

- When a user installs an application, the free space that the application will see is based on the disk quota availability, not the actual amount of free space on the volume.

- Disk quota space used is based on actual file size. There is no mechanism to support or recognize file compression.

 Disk quotas are not applied to the Administrator account or members of the Administrators group.

The following sections describe how to set up and monitor disk quotas.

Configuring Disk Quotas

You configure disk quotas through the NTFS volume Properties dialog box. This dialog box was discussed in detail earlier in the chapter in the "Managing Basic Tasks" section. You learned that you can access the volume Properties dialog box in the Disk Management utility by right-clicking the drive letter and selecting Properties from the pop-up menu. Another way to access this dialog box is from Windows Explorer—just right-click the drive letter in the listing and select Properties. In the volume Properties dialog box, click the Quota tab to see the dialog box shown in Figure 9.29. When you open the Quota tab, you will see that disk quotas are disabled by default.

FIGURE 9.29   The Quota tab of the volume Properties dialog box

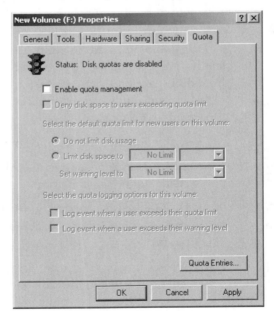

The options that can be configured through the Quota tab are described in Table 9.2.

TABLE 9.2 Disk Quota Configuration Options

Option	Description
Enable Quota Management	Specifies whether quota management is enabled for the volume.
Deny Disk Space to Users Exceeding the Quota Limit	Specifies that users who exceed their disk quota will not be able to override their disk allocation. Those users will receive "out of disk space" error messages.
Select the Default Quota Limit for New Users on This Volume	Allows you to define quota limits for new users. Options include not limiting disk space, limiting disk space, and specifying warning levels.
Select the Quota Logging Options for This Volume	Specifies whether log events that relate to quotas will be recorded. You can enable log events for users exceeding quota limits or users exceeding warning limits.

Notice the traffic light icon in the upper-left corner of the Quota tab. The traffic light indicates the status of disk quotas, as follows:

- A red light specifies that disk quotas are disabled.
- A yellow light specifies that Windows 2000 is rebuilding disk quota information.
- A green light specifies that the disk quota system is enabled and active.

The next sections cover how to set quotas for all new users as default quotas and how to set quotas for a specific user.

Setting Default Quotas

When you set default quota limits for new users on a volume, the quotas apply only to users who have not yet created files on that volume. This means that users who already own files or folders on the volume will be exempt from the quota policy. Users who have not created a file on the volume will be bound by the quota policy.

To set the default quota limit for new users, access the Quota tab of the volume Properties dialog box and check the Enable Quota Management box. Click the Limit Disk Space To radio button and enter a number in the first box next to the option. In the drop-down list in the second box, specify whether disk space is limited by KB (kilobytes), MB (megabytes), GB (gigabytes), TB (terabytes), PB (petabytes), or EB (exabytes). If you choose to limit disk space, you can also set a warning level, so that users will be warned if they come close to reaching their limit.

If you want to apply disk quotas for all users, you should apply the quota when the volume is first created. That way, no users can already have files on the volume and thus be exempt from the quota limit.

In Exercise 9.5, you will set a default quota limit on your D: drive. This exercise assumes that you have completed Exercise 9.1.

EXERCISE 9.5

Applying Default Quota Limits

1. Use the Local Users and Groups utility to create three new users: **Shannon**, **Dana**, and **Michelle**. (See Chapter 6, "Managing Users," for details on creating user accounts.) Deselect the User Must Change Password at Next Logon option for each user.

2. Log off as Administrator and log on as Shannon. Drop and drag some folders to drive D:.

3. Log on as Administrator. Select Start ➢ Programs ➢ Accessories ➢ Windows Explorer.

4. In Windows Explorer, expand My Computer. Right-click Local Disk (D:) and select Properties.

5. In the Local Disk Properties dialog box, select the Quota tab.

6. Check the Enable Quota Management check box.

EXERCISE 9.5 *(continued)*

7. Click the Limit Disk Space To radio button. Specify **5**MB as the limit. Specify the Set Warning Level To value as 4MB.

8. Click the Apply button, then click the OK button.

9. Log off as Administrator and log on as Dana. Drop and drag some folders to drive D:.

10. Log off as Dana and log on as Administrator.

Setting an Individual Quota

You can also set quotas for individual users. There are several reasons for setting quotas this way:

- You can allow a user who routinely updates your applications to have unlimited disk space, while restricting other users.

- You can set warnings at lower levels for a user who routinely exceeds disk space.

- You can apply the quota to users who already had files on the volume before the quota was implemented and thus have been granted unlimited disk space.

To set an individual quota, click the Quota Entries button in the bottom-right corner of the Quota tab. This brings up the dialog box shown in Figure 9.30.

FIGURE 9.30 The Quota Entries for volume dialog box

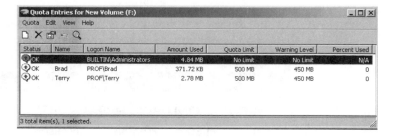

To modify a user's quota, double-click that user. This brings up a dialog box similar to the one shown in Figure 9.31. Here, you can specify whether or not the user's disk space should be limited, the limit, and the warning level.

FIGURE 9.31 The Quota Settings for user dialog box

 You can also modify the quotas of several users at once by Ctrl+clicking to highlight several users and selecting Quota ➢ Properties.

In Exercise 9.6, you will configure the quotas for individual users. This exercise assumes that you have completed Exercise 9.5.

EXERCISE 9.6

Applying Individual Quota Limits

1. Select Start ➢ Programs ➢ Accessories ➢ Windows Explorer.

2. In Windows Explorer, expand My Computer. Right-click Local Disk (D:) and select Properties.

EXERCISE 9.6 *(continued)*

3. In the Local Disk Properties dialog box, select the Quota tab. Then click the Quota Entries button.

4. Double-click user Dana to bring up his Quota Settings dialog box. Notice that Dana has limited disk space (because he did not create files on the volume before disk quotas were applied). Click the Do Not Limit Disk Usage radio button. Click the Apply button and then click the OK button.

5. Double-click user Shannon to bring up his Quota Settings dialog box. Notice that Shannon does not have his disk space limited (because he created files on the volume before disk quotas were applied). Click the Limit Disk Space To radio button and specify the limit as 100MB. Set the warning level to 95MB. Click the Apply button and then click the OK button.

Monitoring Disk Quotas

If you implement disk quotas, you will want to monitor disk quotas on a regular basis. This allows you to check the disk usage by all the users who own files on the volume with the quotas applied.

It is especially important to monitor quotas if you have specified that disk space should be denied to users who exceeded their quota limit. Otherwise, some users may not be able to get their work done. For example, suppose that you have set a limit for all users on a specific volume. Your boss tries to save a file she has been working on all afternoon, but she gets an "out of disk space" error message because she has exceeded her disk quota. While your intentions of setting up and using disk quotas were good, the boss is still cranky.

You monitor disk quotas through the Quota Entries dialog box (see Figure 9.30), which appears when you click the Quota Entries button in the Quota tab of the volume Properties dialog box. The dialog box shows the following information:

- The status of the user's disk quota. Status icons include:

  - A green arrow in a dialog bubble indicating the status is OK.

  - An exclamation point in a yellow triangle indicating the warning threshold has been exceeded.

- An exclamation point in a red circle indicating the user threshold has been exceeded.

- The name and logon name of the user who has stored files on the volume

- The amount of disk space the user has used on the volume

- The user's quota limit

- The user's warning level

- The percent of disk space the user has used in relation to their disk quota

Managing Data Encryption with EFS

*D*ata encryption is a way to increase data security. Encryption is the process of translating data into code that is not easily accessible. Once data has been encrypted, you must have a password or key to decrypt the data. Unencrypted data is known as plain text, and encrypted data is known as *cipher text*.

Microsoft ✓ *Exam Objective*	**Encrypt data on a hard disk by using Encrypting File System (EFS).**

The *Encrypting File System (EFS)* is the Windows 2000 technology that is used to store encrypted files on NTFS partitions. Encrypted files add an extra layer of security to your file system. A user with the proper key can transparently access encrypted files. A user without the proper key is denied access. There is a recovery agent that can be used by the Administrator if the owner is unavailable to provide the proper key to decrypt folders or files.

You can encrypt and decrypt files through the volume Properties dialog box or by using the CIPHER utility, as explained in the following sections.

Encrypting and Decrypting Folders and Files

To use EFS, a user specifies that a folder or file on an NTFS partition should be encrypted. The encryption is transparent to that user, who has access to the file. However, when other users try to access the file, they will not be able to unencrypt the file—even if those users have Full Control NTFS permissions. Instead, they will receive an error message.

To encrypt a folder or a file, take the following steps.

1. Open Windows Explorer by selecting Start ➢ Programs ➢ Accessories ➢ Windows Explorer.

2. In Windows Explorer, find and select the folder or file you wish to encrypt.

3. Right-click the folder or file and select Properties from the pop-up menu.

4. In the General tab of the folder or file Properties dialog box, click the Advanced button.

5. The Advanced Attributes dialog box appears (see Figure 9.27 earlier in this chapter). Check the Encrypt Contents to Secure Data check box. Then click the OK button.

6. The Confirm Attribute Changes dialog box appears (see Figure 9.28 earlier in this chapter). Specify whether you want to apply encryption to only this folder (Apply Changes to This Folder Only) or if you want to apply encryption to the subfolders and files in the folder as well (Apply Changes to this Folder, Subfolder, and Files). Then click the OK button.

To decrypt folders and files, repeat the steps above, but uncheck the Encrypt Contents to Secure Data option in the Advanced Attributes dialog box.

In Exercise 9.7, you will use EFS to encrypt a folder. This exercise assumes that you have completed Exercise 9.1.

EXERCISE 9.7

Using EFS to Manage Data Encryption

1. Use the Local Users and Groups utility to create the new user **Lauren**. (See Chapter 6 for details on creating user accounts.) Deselect the User Must Change Password at Next Logon option for this user.

EXERCISE 9.7 *(continued)*

2. Select Start ➢ Programs ➢ Accessories ➢ Windows Explorer.

3. In Windows Explorer, find and select a folder on the D: drive. The folder you select should contain files. Right-click the folder and select Properties.

4. In the General tab of the folder Properties dialog box, click the Advanced button.

5. In the Advanced Attributes dialog box, check the Encrypt Contents to Secure Data option. Then click the OK button.

6. In the Confirm Attribute Changes dialog box (if this dialog box does not appear, click the Apply button in the Properties dialog box to display it), select Apply Changes to This Folder, Subfolder, and Files. Then click the OK button.

7. Log off as Administrator and log on as Lauren.

8. Open Windows Explorer and attempt to access one of the files in the folder you encrypted. You should receive an error message stating that the file is not accessible.

9. Log off as Lauren and log on as Administrator.

Using the *CIPHER* Utility

CIPHER is a command-line utility that can be used to encrypt files on NTFS volumes. The syntax for the CIPHER command is:

CIPHER /[*command parameter*] [*filename*]

Table 9.3 lists the command parameters associated with the CIPHER command.

TABLE 9.3 CIPHER Command Parameters

Parameter	Description
/e	Specifies that files or folders should be encrypted.
/d	Specifies that files or folders should be decrypted.

TABLE 9.3 CIPHER Command Parameters *(continued)*

Parameter	Description
/s:dir	Specifies that subfolders of the target folder should also be encrypted or decrypted based on the option specified.
/I	Causes any errors that occur to be ignored. By default, the CIPHER utility stops whenever an error occurs.
/f	Forces all files and folders to be encrypted or decrypted, regardless of their current state. Normally, if a file is already in the specified state, it is skipped.
/q	Runs in a quiet mode and only displays the most important information.

In Exercise 9.8, you will use the CIPHER utility to encrypt and decrypt files. This exercise assumes that you have completed Exercise 9.7.

EXERCISE 9.8

Using the CIPHER **Utility**

1. Select Start ➢ Programs ➢ Accessories ➢ Command Prompt.

2. In the Command Prompt dialog box, type **D:** and press Enter to access the D: drive.

3. From the D:\> prompt, type **cipher**. You will see a list of folders and files and the state of encryption. The folder you encrypted in Exercise 9.7 should be indicated by an E.

4. Type **MD TEST** and press Enter to create a new folder named Test.

5. Type **cipher /e test** and press Enter. You will see a message verifying that the folder was encrypted.

Recovering Encrypted Files

If the user who encrypted the folders or files is unavailable to decrypt the folders or files, you can use the recovery agent to access the encrypted files. On Windows 2000 Professional computers that are not a part of a domain, the default recovery agent is the Administrator.

The following steps are used to recover decrypted files:

1. Back up the encrypted files using the Windows Backup utility. (Backing up and restoring files are covered in Chapter 15, "Performing System Recovery Functions.")

2. Restore the backup of the encrypted files on the computer where the recovery agent is located.

3. In Windows Explorer, access the folder or file Properties dialog box. In the General tab, click the Advanced button.

4. In the Advanced tab, clear the Encrypt Contents to Secure Data check box.

Because this procedure decrypts the backup copy of the folder or file, the original folder or file should remain encrypted.

Using the Disk Defragmenter Utility

Data is normally stored sequentially on the disk as space is available. Fragmentation naturally occurs as users create, delete, and modify files. The access of noncontiguous data is transparent to the user. However, when data is stored in this manner, the operating system must search through the disk drive to access all of the pieces of a file. This slows down data access.

Microsoft ✓ *Exam* *Objective*

Monitor, manage, and troubleshoot access to files and folders.

- Optimize access to files and folders.

Disk defragmentation rearranges the existing files so that they are stored contiguously, which optimizes access to those files. In Windows 2000, you use the *Disk Defragmenter utility* to defragment your disk.

To access the Disk Defragmenter utility, select Start ➢ Programs ➢ Accessories ➢ System Tools ➢ Disk Defragmenter. The main Disk Defragmenter window, shown in Figure 9.32, lists each volume, the file system used, capacity, free space, and the percent of free space.

FIGURE 9.32 The main Disk Defragmenter window

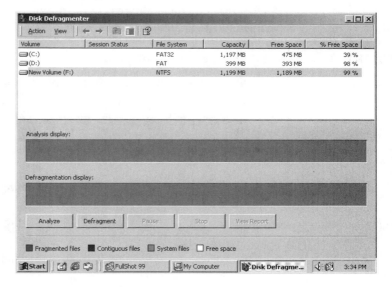

Along with defragmenting disks, this utility can analyze your disk and report on the current file arrangement. Analyzing and defragmenting disks are covered in the following sections.

Analyzing Disks

To analyze a disk, open the Disk Defragmenter utility, select the drive to be analyzed, and click the Analyze button on the bottom-left side of the window. When you analyze a disk, the Disk Defragmenter utility checks for fragmented files, contiguous files, system files, and free space. The results of the analysis are shown in the Analysis display bar that is color-coded as follows:

Fragmented file	Red
Contiguous files	Blue
System files	Green
Free space	White

Even though you can't see the colors, you can get an idea of what this Analysis bar looks like in Figure 9.33.

FIGURE 9.33 The Disk Defragmenter Analysis bar

The disk analysis also produces a report, which is displayed when you click the View Report button. The report contains the following information:

- Whether or not the volume needs defragmenting

- Volume information that includes general volume statistics, volume fragmentation, file fragmentation, page file fragmentation, directory fragmentation, and master file table (MFT) fragmentation

- A list of the most fragmented files

Defragmenting Disks

To defragment a disk, open the Disk Defragmenter utility, select the drive to be defragmented, and click the Defragment button (to the right of the Analyze button at the bottom of the window). Defragmenting causes all files to be stored more efficiently in contiguous space. When defragmentation is complete, you can view a report of the defragmentation process.

You will use the Disk Defragmenter utility in Exercise 9.9 to analyze and defragment a disk.

EXERCISE 9.9

Analyzing and Defragmenting Disks

1. Select Start ➢ Programs ➢ Accessories ➢ System Tools ➢ Disk Defragmenter.

2. Highlight the C: drive and click the Analyze button.

3. When the analysis is complete, click the View Report button to see the analysis report. Record the following information:

    a. Volume size: _____

    b. Cluster size: _____

    c. Used space: _____

    d. Free space: _____

    e. Volume fragmentation-Total fragmentation: _____

    f. Most fragmented file: _____

4. Click the Defragment button.

5. When the defragmentation process is complete, click the Close button.

Using the Disk Cleanup Utility

The *Disk Cleanup utility* identifies areas of disk space that can be deleted to free hard disk space. Disk Cleanup works by identifying temporary files, Internet cache files, and unnecessary program files.

Monitor, manage, and troubleshoot access to files and folders.

- Optimize access to files and folders.

To access this utility, select Start ➣ Programs ➣ Accessories ➣ System Tools ➣ Disk Cleanup. The first dialog box you see, shown in Figure 9.34, asks you to select the drive you want to clean up.

FIGURE 9.34 The Disk Cleanup Select Drive dialog box

The Disk Cleanup utility will run and calculate the amount of disk space you can free. After the analysis is complete, the Disk Cleanup dialog box appears, as shown in Figure 9.35. This dialog box lists files that are suggested for deletion and shows how much space will be gained by deleting those files. You can select and deselect files in the list. After you select the files to be deleted and click the OK button, you will be asked to confirm the deletions. If you click Yes, the Disk Cleanup utility will delete the files and automatically close the Disk Cleanup dialog box.

In Exercise 9.10, you will use the Disk Cleanup utility.

EXERCISE 9.10

Using the Disk Cleanup Utility

1. Select Start ➣ Programs ➣ Accessories ➣ System Tools ➣ Disk Cleanup.

2. Highlight the C: drive and click the OK button.

3. In the Disk Cleanup dialog box, leave all of the boxes checked and click the OK button.

4. When you are asked to confirm that you want to delete the files, click the Yes button.

FIGURE 9.35 The main Disk Cleanup dialog box

Troubleshooting Disk Devices and Volumes

If you are having trouble with your disk devices or volumes, you can use the Windows 2000 *Check Disk utility*. This utility detects bad sectors, attempts to fix file system errors, and scans for and attempts to recover bad sectors.

Microsoft
✓ *Exam*
Objective

Implement, manage, and troubleshoot disk devices.

- Monitor and configure disks.

- Monitor, configure, and troubleshoot volumes.

File system errors can be caused by a corrupt file system or by hardware errors. There is no way to fix hardware errors through software. If you have software errors, the Check Disk utility may help you find them. If you have excessive hardware errors, you should replace your disk drive.

To access the Check Disk utility, open the Control Panel, select Administrative Tools, then select Computer Management. Expand the Storage folder to see the Disk Management utility. In the Disk Management utility, right-click the partition or volume you want to check and choose Properties. Click the Tools tab of the volume Properties dialog box, then click the Check Now button. This brings up the Check Disk dialog box, shown in Figure 9.36. Here, you can choose the Automatically Fix File System Errors and Scan for and Attempt Recovery of Bad Sectors options. Check the options you want and click the Start button.

FIGURE 9.36 The Check Disk dialog box

If the system cannot gain exclusive access to the partition, the disk will be checked the next time the system is restarted. You cannot gain exclusive access to partitions or volumes that contain the system or boot partition.

In Exercise 9.11, you will run the Check Disk utility.

Using the Check Disk Utility

1. Select Start ➤ Settings ➤ Control Panel ➤ Administrative Tools. Expand Computer Management, then Storage, then Disk Management.

2. Right-click the D: drive and choose Properties.

3. Click the Tools tab, then click the Check Now button.

4. In the Check Disk dialog box, check both of the disk options check boxes. Then click the Start button.

Summary

In this chapter, you learned about disk management with Windows 2000 Professional. We covered the following topics:

- File system configuration, which can be FAT16, FAT32, or NTFS. You also learned how to convert a FAT or FAT32 partition to NTFS by using the CONVERT command-line utility.

- Disk storage configuration, which can be basic storage or dynamic storage. Dynamic storage is used to create simple volumes, spanned volumes, and striped volumes.

- The Disk Management utility, which is used to manage routine tasks, basic storage, and dynamic storage.

- Data compression, which is used to store files in a compressed format that uses less disk space.

- Disk quotas, which are used to limit the amount of disk space that users can have on an NTFS partition.

- Data encryption, which is implemented through the Encrypting File System (EFS) and provides increased security for files and folders.

- Disk defragmentation, which is accomplished through the Disk Defragmenter utility and allows you to store files contiguously on your hard drive for improved access speeds.

- The Disk Cleanup utility, which is used to free disk space by removing unnecessary files.

- The Check Disk utility, which can be used to troubleshoot disk errors.

Key Terms

Before you take the exam, be sure you're familiar with the following key terms:

basic storage

CDFS (Compact Disk File System)

Check Disk utility

CIPHER

cipher text

CONVERT

data compression

data encryption

Disk Cleanup utility

disk defragmentation

Disk Defragmenter utility

Disk Management utility

disk quotas

dynamic disk

dynamic storage

Encrypting File System (EFS)

extended partition

FAT16

FAT32

hot swapping

NTFS

partition

primary partition

simple volume

spanned volume

striped volume

volume

Review Questions

1. Which of the following file systems are supported by Windows 2000 Professional? Choose all that apply.

   A. FAT16

   B. FAT32

   C. FAT64

   D. NTFS

2. Which of the following statements is true about file system conversion using the CONVERT utility?

   A. You can convert from FAT8 or FAT16 to NTFS.

   B. You can convert from FAT16 or FAT 32 to NTFS.

   C. You can convert from FAT16, FAT32, or HPFS to NTFS.

   D. You can convert from NTFS back to FAT16 or FAT32.

3. What are the two types of disk storage supported by Windows 2000 Professional?

   A. Basic storage

   B. Advanced storage

   C. Dynamic storage

   D. Extended storage

4. What types of dynamic storage are supported by Windows 2000 Professional? Choose all that apply.

   A. Simple volumes

   B. Spanned volumes

   C. Mirrored volumes

   D. Striped volumes

5. Which utility is used to graphically manage your disks and volumes in Windows 2000 Professional?

   A. Disk Management utility

   B. Disk Manager utility

   C. Disk Administrator utility

   D. Disk and File Management utility

6. Which of the following volume Property dialog box tabs do you see for FAT32 partitions in the Disk Management utility? Choose all that apply.

   A. General

   B. Sharing

   C. Security

   D. Quota

7. Which of the following statements is true of dynamic disks in Windows 2000 Professional? Choose all that apply.

   A. Dynamic disks can be recognized by Windows NT 4 or Windows 2000.

   B. Dynamic disks are only supported by Windows 2000.

   C. Dynamic disks support features such as simple volumes, extended volumes, spanned volumes, and striped volumes.

   D. Dynamic disks support features such as simple volumes, extended volumes, spanned volumes, mirrored volumes, and striped volumes.

8. What utility can be used to identify areas of disk space that can be deleted to free additional disk space?

   A. Disk Cleanup

   B. Disk Manager

   C. Disk Administrator

   D. Disk Defragmenter

9. Which of the following options allows you to compress files in Windows 2000 Professional?

    A. COMPRESS.EXE

    B. CIPHER.EXE

    C. PACKER.EXE

    D. Windows Explorer

10. Which of the following statements is true for disk quota management in Windows 2000 Professional?

    A. Quotas can only be set for all users of a volume.

    B. Quotas can only be set for specific users or groups of a volume.

    C. Quotas can be set for all new users of a volume or set individually for users of a volume.

    D. Quotas are only set for all users at the computer level through a group policy.

11. Which command-line utility is used to manage data encryption?

    A. ENCRYPT

    B. CIPHER

    C. CRYPTO

    D. EFS

12. You have compressed a 4MB file into 2MB. You are copying the file to another computer that has a FAT32 partition. How can you ensure that the file will remain compressed?

    A. When you copy the file, use the XCOPY command with the /Comp switch.

    B. When you copy the file, use the Windows Explorer utility and specify Keep Existing Attributes.

    C. On the destination folder, make sure that the folder's properties are configured to Compress Contents Save Disk Space.

    D. You can't maintain disk compression on a non-NTFS partition.

13. Julie is trying to save a file that is 2MB in size. When she tries to save the file, she gets an error message that the disk is out of space. When the administrator checks available disk space, it is determined that there is more than 4GB of free disk space. What is the most likely cause?

   A. The disk needs to be defragmented.

   B. Julie does not have the NTFS permissions she needs to access the folder where she is trying to save the file.

   C. Julie has exceeded her disk quota.

   D. The folder is encrypted and Julie does not have the key required to write to the folder.

14. Cindy is the payroll manager of your company. She is concerned that members of the Administrators group will be able to easily view the contents of the payroll files. What is the highest level of security that can be applied to the payroll files?

   A. Apply NTFS permissions to the files

   B. Encrypt the files with EFS

   C. Secure the files with the `Secure.exe` command

   D. Encrypt the files with HSP

15. Scott frequently accesses and updates a large number of files. He is noticing that the larger the files get, the longer it takes to access the files. He suspects that the problem is related to the files being spread over the disk. What utility can be used to store the files sequentially on the disk?

   A. Disk Cleanup

   B. Disk Manager

   C. Disk Administrator

   D. Disk Defragmenter

16. What steps would you take to access the Disk Defragmenter utility?

   A. Use Disk Administrator

   B. Use Disk Manager

   C. Through Programs ➤ Accessories ➤ System Tools

   D. Through Programs ➤ Administrative Tools ➤ System Tools

17. Cindy is the payroll manager at your company. The day before the payroll is processed, Cindy is involved in a minor car accident and ends up in the hospital for two days. She has encrypted the payroll files with EFS. How can these files be accessed?

   A. The Administrator can access the files by backing up the files, restoring the files on the computer where the recovery agent is located, and disabling the Encrypt the Contents to Secure Data option.

   B. The Administrator can access the files by using the unencrypt command-line utility.

   C. The Administrator can access the files by using the encrypt -d command-line utility.

   D. The Administrator can access the files by using the access command-line utility.

18. You have an extremely large database that needs to be stored on a single partition. Your boss asks you what the maximum capacity is for an NTFS partition. What is the correct answer?

   A. 32GB

   B. 64GB

   C. 132GB

   D. 2TB

19. You have just added a new disk to your computer that supports hot-swapping capabilities. You do not see the new disk in Disk Management. What is the fastest way to see the new disk?

A. Restart the computer

B. In Disk Manager, select Action ➤ Rescan Disk

C. In Disk Management, select Action ➤ Rescan Disk

D. In System Tools, select Update Disks

20. Which of the following utilities can be used to configure Windows 2000 disk compression?

A. Disk Manager

B. Disk Management

C. Disk Compressor

D. Windows Explorer

Answers to Review Questions

1. A, B, D. The only file systems that are supported by Windows 2000 are FAT16, FAT32, and NTFS.

2. B. You can convert from FAT16 or FAT32 to NTFS, but it is a one-way process. You cannot convert from NTFS back to FAT16 or FAT32.

3. A, C. Windows 2000 supports basic storage, which is what is installed for backward compatibility, and dynamic storage, which supports Windows 2000 disk configurations.

4. A, B, D. Windows 2000 Professional supports simple, spanned, and striped volumes. Mirrored volumes are available with Windows 2000 Server.

5. A. Only the Disk Management utility exists in Windows 2000.

6. A, B. The Security and Quota tabs are only available for NTFS partitions.

7. B, C. Dynamic disks can only be accessed through Windows 2000. They do not support mirrored volumes in the Professional version of Windows 2000.

8. A. The Disk Cleanup utility is used to identify areas of space that may be reclaimed through the deletion of temporary files or Recycle Bin files.

9. D. There are no programs in Windows 2000 called COMPRESS or PACKER. CIPHER is used to encrypt or decrypt files. In Windows 2000, one way you can compress files is through Windows Explorer.

10. C. You cannot specify a quota for a group. Quotas are set for all new users of a volume or for individual users of a volume.

11. B. There are no programs in Windows 2000 called ENCRYPT, CRYPTO, or EFS. You encrypt or decrypt files with the CIPHER utility.

12. D. Windows 2000 data compression is only supported on NTFS partitions.

13. C. If Julie is getting "out of space" errors and the disk has free space, it is likely that the disk has disk quotas applied and Julie has exceeded her quota limitation.

14. B. You can apply a higher level of security to folders and files on an NTFS partition by using Encrypting File System (EFS). Only a user with the correct key can access this data.

15. D. The Disk Defragmenter utility is used to rearrange files so that they are stored contiguously on the disk. This optimizes access to those files.

16. C. You access the Disk Defragmenter utility through Start ➢ Programs ➢ Accessories ➢ System Tools ➢ Defragmenter.

17. A. By default, the Administrator is automatically designated as the recovery agent with the ability to access files that have been encrypted. The Administrator is able to access the files by backing up the files, restoring the files on the computer where the recovery agent is located, and disabling the Encrypt the Contents to Secure Data option.

18. D. You can have NTFS partitions that are up to 2TB in size.

19. C. If your computer supports hot-swapping capabilities, all you need to do after you add a new disk is select Action ➢ Rescan Disk in the Disk Management utility.

20. D. You can implement disk compression through Windows Explorer by managing a folder's or file's disk properties.

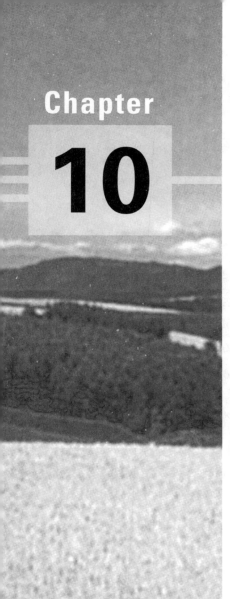

Chapter

10

Accessing Files and Folders

MICROSOFT EXAM OBJECTIVES COVERED IN THIS CHAPTER

✓ **Monitor, manage, and troubleshoot access to files and folders.**

- Configure, manage, and troubleshoot file compression
- Control access to files and folders by using permissions.
- Optimize access to files and folders.

✓ **Manage and troubleshoot access to shared folders.**

- Create and remove shared folders.
- Control access to shared folders by using permissions.

✓ **Connect to shared resources on a Microsoft network.**

✓ **Manage and troubleshoot the use and synchronization of offline files.**

Administrators must have basic file management skills, including the ability to create a well-defined, logically organized directory structure and maintain that structure. Windows 2000 Professional Folder Options allow you to configure many properties associated with files and folders, such as what you see when you access folders, file type associations, and the use of offline files and folders. Finally, you should know how to search for files and folders.

Local access defines what access a user has to local resources. You can limit local access by applying security for folders and files on NTFS partitions. You should know what NTFS permissions are and how they are applied. You can also optimize local access through the use of the Indexing Service.

A powerful feature of networking is the ability to allow network access to local folders. In Windows 2000 Professional, it is very easy to share folders. You can also apply security to shared folders in a manner that is similar to applying NTFS permissions. Once you share a folder, users with appropriate access rights can access the folders through a variety of methods.

To effectively manage both local and network resource access and troubleshoot related problems, you should understand the resource-access process. Windows 2000 Professional uses access tokens, access control lists, and access control entries to handle resource access.

This chapter covers file and folder management tasks, beginning with the basics of planning and creating a directory structure.

File and Folder Management Basics

Before you perform tasks such as managing NTFS security and network shares, you need to understand how to perform basic file and folder management tasks. The first step in file and folder management is organizing your files and folders. After you have created the structure, you can manage folder options. Another common task is searching for files and folders. These tasks are covered in the following sections.

Organizing Files and Folders

When your files and folders are well organized, you can easily access the information that is stored on your computer. Organizing your files and folders is similar to storing your papers. If you don't have very many papers, the task is easy. The more papers you have, the more c hallenging the task becomes.

The key to organization is good planning. For example, you might decide to store all of your applications on your C: drive and all of your data on your D: drive. You might organize data by function or by type. Figure 10.1 shows an example of a directory structure that has been logically organized.

FIGURE 10.1 A sample directory structure

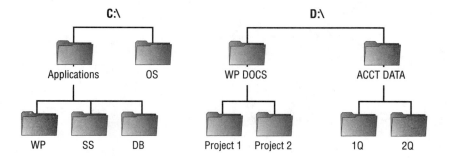

Once you plan your directory structure, you are ready to create the structure on your computer. This involves creating files and folders and may also require you to rename, delete, move, and copy files and folders. These tasks are described in the following sections.

Creating Folders

You can create folders in several ways, such as through Windows Explorer, the DOS MD command, and My Computer. The examples in this chapter will use Windows Explorer for file management.

You take the following steps to create a folder:

1. Select Start ➢ Programs ➢ Accessories ➢ Windows Explorer to open Windows Explorer.

2. Open My Computer and select the drive where the folder will be created.

3. Select File ➢ New ➢ Folder, as shown in Figure 10.2.

FIGURE 10.2 Creating a new folder

4. A folder icon labeled New Folder appears in the Windows Explorer window, as shown in Figure 10.3. Replace the label by typing in the name of the new folder.

FIGURE 10.3   Naming a new folder

New Folder

Creating Files

There are many ways to create files. The most common way is through applications, including the Windows 2000 Professional WordPad and Notepad utilities. You take the following steps to create a file with Notepad:

1. Select Start ➤ Programs ➤ Accessories ➤ Windows Explorer to open Windows Explorer.

2. Open My Computer and select the drive where the file will be created.

3. Select File ➤ New ➤ Text Document.

4. A new file icon appears in the Windows Explorer window. Type in the name of the new file under the file icon.

5. Double-click the new file to open it in Notepad. Add text to the file, as shown in Figure 10.4.

FIGURE 10.4   Editing a text document with Notepad

6. Save the file by selecting File ➢ Exit. You will see a dialog box indicating that the contents of the file have changed. Save the changes by clicking the Yes button.

In Exercise 10.1, you will create a simple directory structure and add folders and files. This structure will be used in the other exercises in this chapter.

EXERCISE 10.1

Creating a Directory and File Structure

1. Select Start ➢ Programs ➢ Accessories ➢ Windows Explorer to start Windows Explorer.

2. Expand My Computer, then Local Disk (D:). Select File ➢ New ➢ Folder and name the new folder **DATA**.

3. Double-click the DATA folder to open the folder. Select File ➢ New ➢ Folder and name the new folder **WP DOCS**.

4. Double-click the Data folder, select File ➢ New ➢ Folder, and name the new folder **SS DOCS** folder.

5. Confirm that you are still in the DATA folder. Select File ➢ New ➢ Text Document. Name the file **DOC1.TXT**.

6. Double-click the WP DOCS folder. Select File ➢ New ➢ Text Document. Name the file **DOC2.TXT**.

7. Double-click the SS DOCS folder. Select File ➢ New ➢ Text Document. Name the file **DOC3.TXT**. Your structure should look like the one shown below.

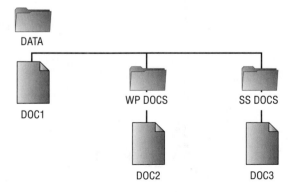

Renaming and Deleting Folders and Files

If you need to rename a folder or a file, right-click the folder or file that you want to rename and select Rename from the pop-up menu. The name will be selected and boxed. Start typing to replace the existing name with your entry, or position the cursor and edit the existing folder name or filename.

To delete a folder or file, right-click the folder or file that you want to remove and select Delete from the pop-up menu. When prompted, click the Yes button to confirm the deletion.

Deleted files or folders are moved to the Recycle Bin, which you can clear periodically to delete files or folders permanently. If you delete a folder or file by accident, you can usually restore the folder or file through the Recycle Bin.

Copying and Moving Folders and Files

You can easily reorganize your directory structure by copying and moving folders and files. When you move a folder or file from its original location (called the source) to a new location (called the destination), it no longer exists in the source location. When you copy a folder or file, it will exist in both the source and destination locations.

To copy or move a folder or file, right-click the folder or file that you want to copy or move and drag and drop it to its destination location. You will see a pop-up menu that includes the options Copy Here and Move Here, as shown in Figure 10.5. Make the appropriate selection.

FIGURE 10.5 Choosing to move a folder

Managing Folder Options

Through the Folder Options dialog box, you can configure options such as the Desktop view and what you see when you open folders. To open the Folder Options dialog box, start Windows Explorer and select Tools ➢ Folder Options. Folder Options also appears as an icon in Control Panel.

The Folder Options dialog box has four tabs: General, View, File Types, and Offline Files. The options on each of these tabs are described in the following sections.

General Folder Options

The General tab of the Folder Options dialog box, shown in Figure 10.6, includes the following options:

- Whether the computer is configured to use the Windows classic Desktop or to use the Active Desktop, which enables Web content on the Desktop

- Whether the computer is configured to use Windows classic folders or to enable Web content in folders

- Whether folders are opened in the same window or each folder is opened in a separate window when a user is browsing folders

- Whether a user opens items with a single-click or a double-click

FIGURE 10.6   The General tab of the Folder Options dialog box

Folder View Options

The options on the View tab of the Folder Options dialog box, shown in Figure 10.7, are used to configure what users see when they open files and folders. For example, you can change the default setting so that hidden files and folders are shown in Windows Explorer and other file lists. The View tab options are described in Table 10.1.

FIGURE 10.7   The View tab of the Folder Options dialog box

TABLE 10.1   Folder View Options

Option	Description
Display Compressed Files and Folders with an Alternate Color	By default, compressed files and folders are displayed in the same color as uncompressed files and folders. Enabling this option displays compressed files and folders in an alternate color so that they can be easily identified.
Display the Full Path in the Address Bar	By default, the address bar in the Windows Explorer window shows an abbreviated path of your location, such as Chapter 10 (from the Word Documents folder). Enabling this option displays the full path, such as `C:\Word Documents\Sybex\Prof Book\Chapter 10`.

TABLE 10.1 Folder View Options *(continued)*

Option	Description
Display the Full Path in the Title Bar	By default, the title bar at the top of the Windows Explorer window shows an abbreviated path of your location. Enabling this option displays the full path.
Hidden Files and Folders	By default, Do Not Show Hidden Files and Folders is selected, so that files and folders with the Hidden attribute are not listed. Choosing Show Hidden Files and Folders displays these items.
Hide File Extensions for Known File Types	By default, filename extensions, which identify the file type (for example, .DOC for Word files and .XLS for Excel files), are not shown. Disabling this option displays all filename extensions.
Hide Protected Operating System Files (Recommended)	By default, operating system files are not shown, which protects operating system files from being modified or deleted by a user. Disabling this option displays the operating system files.
Launch Folder Windows in a Separate Process	By default, when you open a folder, it shares memory with the previous folders that were opened. Enabling this option opens folders in separate parts of memory, which increases the stability of Windows 2000 but can slightly decrease the performance of the computer.
Remember Each Folder's View Settings	By default, any folder display settings you make are retained each time the folder is reopened. Disabling this option resets the folder display settings to their defaults each time the folder is opened.
Show My Documents on the Desktop	By default, My Documents (a folder created by Windows 2000 for each user who accesses the computer and used as the default location for storing user files) appears on the Desktop. Disabling this option removes My Computer from the Desktop.
Show Pop-Up Description for Folder and Desktop Options	By default, any summary information configured through file properties (such as title, subject, and author) appears when you click a file. Disabling this option suppresses the display of the summary information.

File Type Options

The File Types tab of the Folder Options dialog box, shown in Figure 10.8, is used to associate filename extensions with application file types. When an extension is associated with a file type, users can double-click the filename in Windows Explorer to open the file in its application. For example, if you have associated .PDF with Adobe Acrobat Reader and you double-click the Presentation.PDF file, Acrobat Reader will start and that file will be opened in it.

FIGURE 10.8 The File Types tab of the Folder Options dialog box

Through the File Types tab, you can add, delete, and change file type associations. New file extensions also may be added automatically when you install new applications on your computer.

Offline Folder Options

Through the Offline Files tab of the Folder Options dialog box, shown in Figure 10.9, you can configure the computer to use *offline files and folders*. This is a new Windows 2000 Professional feature that allows network folders and files to be stored on Windows 2000 clients. Then if the network location is not available, users can still access network files.

Manage and troubleshoot the use and synchronization of offline files.

FIGURE 10.9 The Offline Files tab of the Folder Options dialog box

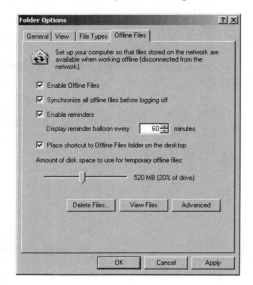

Offline files and folders are particularly useful for mobile users who use the same set of files when they are attached to the network and when they are traveling. Offline files and folders are also useful on networks where users require specific files to perform their jobs, because they will be able to access those files even if the network server goes down (for scheduled maintenance or because of a power outage or another problem). Offline files and folders also increase performance even if the network is available, because users can use the local copy of the file instead of accessing files over the network.

Configuring offline files and folders requires a minimum of two computers:

- The network computer that contains the network version of the folders and files

- The Windows 2000 client computer that will access the network files while they are online or offline

The network computer does not need to be running Windows 2000, but it must use the file and print sharing protocol SMB (Server Message Blocks). All Microsoft operating systems use SMB, but some other operating systems do not use SMB. For example, if you were connected to a Novell NetWare share, you would not be able to use offline files and folders, because NetWare uses a protocol called NCP (NetWare Core Protocol) for file and print sharing.

In order to use offline files and folders, you must complete the following tasks:

1. Attach to the shared file or folder that you want to access offline.

2. Configure your computer to use offline files and folders.

3. Make files and folders available for offline access.

4. Specify how offline files and folders will respond to network disconnection.

These tasks are covered in the following sections.

Attaching to the Share

In order to use a file or folder offline, the file or folder must first be made available online. Someone at the server must share the file or folder, and the user must have proper permissions to access the file or folder. Then the user can attach to the shared file or folder. The procedure for sharing files and folders is described in the "Managing Network Access" section later in this chapter.

Configuring Your Computer

You configure your computer to use offline files and folders through the Offline Files tab of the Folder Options dialog box (see Figure 10.9). In this tab, verify that the Enable Offline Files box is checked (this option is enabled by default). To configure automatic synchronization between the offline and online files, make sure that the Synchronize All Offline Files before Logging Off option is checked (this option is also enabled by default).

If you don't configure offline files and folders to be synchronized automatically when you log on or log off from your computer, you will need to perform the synchronization manually. To manually synchronize a file or folder, right-click the file or folder that has been configured for offline use and select Synchronize from the pop-up menu, as shown in Figure 10.10.

FIGURE 10.10 Manually synchronizing an offline folder

Making Folders or Files Available

To make a file or folder available for offline access, take the following steps:

1. Access the shared file or folder that you wish to use offline. Right-click the file or folder and select Make Available Offline from the pop-up menu (see Figure 10.10).

2. The Welcome to the Offline Files Wizard starts (this Wizard will run only the first time you create an offline file or folder). Click the Next button.

3. You see a dialog box asking you how to synchronize offline files, as shown in Figure 10.11. By default, the Automatically Synchronize the Offline Files When I Log On and Log Off My Computer option is selected. If you would prefer to manually synchronize files, deselect this option. Click the Next button to continue.

4. The next dialog box, shown in Figure 10.12, allows you to configure reminders and to create a shortcut to the Offline Files folder. Reminders periodically remind you that you are not connected to the network and are working offline. The Offline Files shortcut is an easy way to access folders that have been configured for offline use. If you are online when you access this folder, you are working online. You can select or deselect either of these options. Then click the Finish button.

FIGURE 10.11   Configuring the synchronization of offline files and folders

FIGURE 10.12   Configuring Reminders and the Offline Files shortcut

5. If the folder you have selected contains subfolders, you will see the Confirm Offline Subfolders dialog box, shown in Figure 10.13. This dialog box allows you to choose whether the subfolders should also be made available offline. Make your selection and click the OK button.

FIGURE 10.13 Configuring offline subfolder availability

The offline files will be copied (synchronized) to the local computer. You can tell that a folder has been configured for offline access by the icon that appears under the folder, as shown in Figure 10.14.

FIGURE 10.14 The icon for offline folders

test

Configuring Your Computer's Behavior after Losing the Network Connection

Through the Offline Files tab of the Folder Options dialog box, you can specify whether or not your computer will begin working offline when a network connection is lost. To configure your computer's behavior after a network connection is lost, click the Advanced button in the bottom-right corner of the dialog box. This brings up the Offline Files - Advanced Settings dialog box, as shown in Figure 10.15. In this dialog box, you can specify Notify Me and Begin Working Offline (the default selection) or you can select Never Allow My Computer to Go Offline. If you have created offline files and folders for multiple servers, you can use the Exception List portion of the dialog box to specify different behavior for each one.

FIGURE 10.15 The Offline Files - Advanced Settings dialog box

In Exercise 10.2, you will set up your computer to use and synchronize offline files and folders.

If your Windows 2000 Professional computer is attached to a network that has another computer with a shared file or folder, you can also attach to the shared file or folder that you want to access offline, make folders or files available for offline access, and configure how offline files will respond to network disconnection, as described in the previous sections.

EXERCISE 10.2

Configuring Offline Files and Folders

1. Select Start ➤ Programs ➤ Accessories ➤ Windows Explorer.

2. In Windows Explorer, select Tools ➤ Folder Options and click the Offline Files tab.

3. In the Offline Files tab of the Folder Options dialog box, make sure that the following options are selected:

   Enable Offline Files

EXERCISE 10.2 *(continued)*

Synchronize All Offline Files before Logging Off

Enable Reminders; Display Message Balloon Every 60 Minutes

Place Shortcut to Offline Files Folder on the Desktop

4. Click the OK button to close the dialog box.

Troubleshooting Offline Files

If you are trying to configure offline files and folders, and you don't see the Make Available Offline option as a folder property, check the following:

- Are you connected to a network share on a computer that uses SMB? Offline files and folders won't work from a network computer that does not use SMB.

- Have you configured your computer to use offline files and folders? Before you can make a file or folder available offline, this feature must be enabled through the Offline Files tab of the Folder Options dialog box (accessed by selected Tools ➢ Folder Options in Windows Explorer).

- Has the folder that you want to access been shared and do you have proper permissions to access the folder? If you don't see a folder that you want to configure for offline use, it may not be shared or you may not have proper share (and NTFS) permissions to the folder.

Searching for Files and Folders

Windows 2000 Professional offers powerful search capabilities that allow you to find a file or folder based on the filename or folder name and also through the text that is contained in the file. This is an extremely useful feature when you know that you have saved a specific file on your computer but you can't find it.

Windows Explorer has a Search button on its toolbar. Clicking this button brings up the Search dialog box, as shown in Figure 10.16.

FIGURE 10.16   The Search dialog box

In this dialog box, you can specify the following options for your search:

- The filename or folder name (the name can contain wildcard characters, such as *)

- The text that you are looking for

- The location that you want to look in

Depending on what you are looking for, you might specify the filename or folder name you are looking for and/or the text that you are looking for. Only one of these fields must be filled in for a search. The location that you want to look in must be specified. This can be as broad as My Computer, or you can specify a specific drive or folder.

Once you have specified your search criteria, click the Search Now button to start the search. The results of the search are displayed in the right side of the window, as shown in Figure 10.17.

The Search Options at the bottom of the Search dialog box allow you to configure more advanced searches by date, type, and size. For even more complex searches, you can select Advanced Options and specify subfolders, case sensitivity, and search slow files (files that reside on removable storage media, such as tape or optical drives).

FIGURE 10.17 Search results

Managing Local Access

The two common types of file systems used by local partitions are FAT (which includes FAT16 and FAT32) and NTFS. (File systems are covered in detail in Chapter 9, "Managing Disks.") FAT partitions do not support local security; NTFS partitions do support local security. This means that if the file system on the partition that users access is configured as a FAT partition, you cannot specify any security for the file system once a user has logged on. However, if the partition is NTFS, you can specify the access each user has to specific folders on the partition, based on the user's logon name and group associations.

Microsoft
✓ *Exam*
Objective

Monitor, manage, and troubleshoot access to files and folders.

- Control access to files and folders by using permissions.
- Optimize access to files and folders.

This chapter covers material related to optimizing access to files and folders and using permissions to control access to files and folders, for the "Monitor, manage, and troubleshoot access to files and folders" objective. Using file compression, another subobjective for this objective, is covered in Chapter 9, "Managing Disks." That chapter also provides more information about optimizing access to files and folders.

The following sections describe how to apply NTFS permissions and some techniques for optimizing local access.

Applying NTFS Permissions

NTFS permissions control access to NTFS folders and files. You configure access by allowing or denying NTFS permissions to users and groups. Normally, NTFS permissions are cumulative, based on group memberships if the user has been allowed access. However, if the user had been denied access through user or group membership, those permissions override allowed permissions.

Windows 2000 Professional offers five levels of NTFS permissions:

- The Full Control permission allows the following rights:
    - Traverse folders and execute files (programs) in the folders
    - List the contents of a folder and read the data in a folder's files
    - See a folder's or file's attributes
    - Change a folder's or file's attributes
    - Create new files and write data to the files
    - Create new folders and append data to files
    - Delete subfolders and files
    - Delete files
    - Change permissions for files and folders
    - Take ownership of files and folders
- The Modify permission allows the following rights:
    - Traverse folders and execute files in the folders
    - List the contents of a folder and read the data in a folder's files

- See a folder's or file's attributes
- Change a folder's or file's attributes
- Create new files and write data to the files
- Create new folders and append data to files
- Delete files

- The Read & Execute permission allows the following rights:
  - Traverse folders and execute files in the folders
  - List the contents of a folder and read the data in a folder's files
  - See a folder's or file's attributes

- The List Folder Contents permission allows the following rights:
  - Traverse folders and execute files in the folders
  - List the contents of a folder and read the data in a folder's files
  - See a folder's or file's attributes

- The Read permission allows the following rights:
  - List the contents of a folder and read the data in a folder's files
  - See a folder's or file's attributes

- The Write permission allows the following rights:
  - Change a folder's or file's attributes
  - Create new files and write data to the files
  - Create new folders and append data to files

Any user with Full Control access can manage the security of a folder. By default, the Everyone group has Full Control permission for the entire NTFS partition. However, in order to access folders, a user must have physical access to the computer as well as a valid logon name and password. By default, regular users can't access folders over the network unless the folders have been shared. Sharing folders is covered in the "Managing Network Access" section later in this chapter.

You apply NTFS permissions through Windows Explorer. Right-click the file or folder that you want to control access to and select Properties from the pop-up menu. This brings up the folder or file Properties dialog box. Figure 10.18 shows a folder Properties dialog box.

The process for configuring NTFS permissions for folders and files is the same. The examples in this chapter use a folder, since NTFS permissions are most commonly applied at the folder level.

FIGURE 10.18   The folder Properties dialog box

The tabs in the file or folder Properties dialog box depend on the options that have been configured for your computer. For files and folders on NTFS partitions, the dialog box will contain a Security tab, which is where you configure NTFS permissions. (The Security tab is not present in the Properties dialog box for files or folders on FAT partitions, because FAT partitions do not support local security.) The Security tab lists the users and groups that have been assigned permissions to the folder or file. When you click a user or group in the top half of the dialog box, you see the permissions that have been allowed or denied for that user or group in the lower half of the dialog box, as shown in Figure 10.19.

FIGURE 10.19 The Security tab of the folder Properties dialog box

Adding and Removing User and Group NTFS Permissions

To manage NTFS permissions, take the following steps:

1. In Windows Explorer, right-click the file or folder that you want to control access to, select Properties from the pop-up menu, and click the Security tab of the Properties dialog box.

2. Click the Add button to open the Select Users, Computers, or Groups dialog box, as shown in Figure 10.20. You can select users from the computer's local database or from the domain you are in (or trusted domains) from the list box at the top of the dialog box. The list box at the bottom of the dialog box lists all of the groups and users for the location that was specified in the top list box.

3. Click the user, computer, or group that you wish to add and click the Add button. The user, computer, or group appears in the bottom list box. Use Ctrl+click to select noncontiguous users, computers, or groups or Shift+click to select contiguous users, computers, or groups.

FIGURE 10.20 The Select Users, Computers, or Groups dialog box

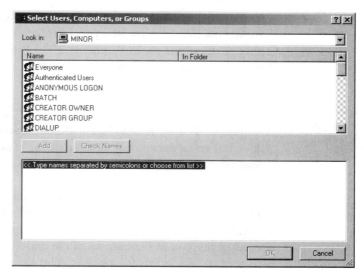

4. You return to the Security tab of the folder Properties dialog box. Highlight each user, computer, or group in the top list box individually and specify the NTFS permissions that should be applied. When you are finished, click the OK button.

Through the Advanced button of the Security tab, you can configure more granular NTFS permissions, such as Traverse Folder/ Execute File and Read Attributes permissions.

To remove the NTFS permissions for a user, computer, or group, highlight the user, computer, or group you wish to remove in the Security tab and click the Remove button.

Be careful when you remove NTFS permissions. Unlike when you delete most other types of items in Windows 2000 Professional, you won't be asked to confirm the removal of NTFS permissions.

Controlling Permission Inheritance

Normally, the directory structure is organized in a hierarchical manner. This means that you are likely to have subfolders in the folders that you apply permissions to. In Windows 2000 Professional, by default, parent folder permissions are applied to any files or subfolders in that folder. These are called *inherited permissions*.

In Windows NT 4, by default, files in a folder inherit permissions from the parent folder, but subfolders do not inherit parent permissions. In Windows 2000 Professional, the default is for the permissions to be inherited by subfolders.

You can specify that permissions should not be inherited by subfolders and files through the Security tab of the folder Properties dialog box. If you deselect the Allow Inheritable Permissions from Parent to Propagate to This Object check box at the bottom of the dialog box, you have disabled inherited permissions at this folder level. You are then given a choice of either copying the permissions or removing the permissions from the parent folder.

If an Allow or a Deny check box in the Permission list in the Security tab has a shaded check mark, this indicates that the permission was inherited from an upper-level folder. If the check mark is not shaded, it indicates that the permission was applied at the selected folder. This is known as an explicitly assigned permission. Knowing which permissions are inherited and which are explicitly assigned is useful when you need to troubleshoot permissions.

Determining Effective Permissions

To determine a user's *effective rights* (the rights the user actually has to a file or folder), add all of the permissions that have been allowed through the user's assignments based on that user's username and group associations. After you determine what the user is allowed, you subtract any permissions that have been denied the user through the username or group associations.

As an example, suppose that user Marilyn is a member of the Accounting and Execs groups. The following assignments have been made to the Accounting Group Permissions:

Permission	Allow	Deny
Full Control		
Modify	✓	

Permission	Allow	Deny
Read & Execute	✓	
List Folder Contents		
Read		
Write		

The following assignments have been made to the Execs Group Permissions:

Permission	Allow	Deny
Full Control		
Modify		
Read & Execute		
List Folder Contents		
Read	✓	
Write		

To determine Marilyn's effective rights, you combine the permissions that have been assigned. The result is that Marilyn's effective rights are Modify, Read & Execute, and Read.

As another example, suppose that user Dan is a member of the Sales and Temps groups. The following assignments have been made to the Sales Group Permissions:

Permission	Allow	Deny
Full Control		
Modify	✓	
Read & Execute	✓	
List Folder Contents	✓	
Read	✓	
Write	✓	

The following assignments have been made to the Temps Group Permissions:

Permission	Allow	Deny
Full Control		
Modify		✓
Read & Execute		
List Folder Contents		
Read		
Write		✓

To determine Dan's effective rights, you start by seeing what Dan has been allowed: Modify, Read & Execute, List Folder Contents, Read, and Write permissions. You then remove anything that he is denied: Modify and Write permissions. In this case, Dan's effective rights are Read & Execute, List Folder Contents, and Read.

In Exercise 10.3, you will configure NTFS permissions based on the preceding examples. This exercise assumes that you have completed Exercise 10.1.

EXERCISE 10.3

Configuring NTFS Permissions

1. Using the Local Users and Groups utility, create two users: **Marilyn** and **Dan**. (See Chapter 6, "Managing Users," for details on creating user accounts.) Deselect the User Must Change Password at Next Logon option.

2. Using the Local Users and Groups utility, create four groups: **Accounting**, **Execs**, **Sales**, and **Temps**. (See Chapter 7, "Managing Groups," for details on creating groups.) Add Marilyn to the Accounting and Execs groups. Add Dan to the Sales and Temps groups.

3. Select Start ➤ Programs ➤ Accessories ➤ Windows Explorer to open Windows Explorer. Expand the DATA folder (on drive D:) you created in Exercise 10.1.

4. Right-click DATA, select Properties, and click the Security tab.

5. In the Security tab of the folder Properties dialog box, highlight the Everyone group and click the Remove button. You see a dialog box telling you that you cannot remove Everyone because this group is inheriting permissions from a higher level. Click the OK button.

6. In the Security tab, deselect the Allow Inheritable Permissions from Parent to Propagate to This Object. In the dialog box that appears, click the Remove button.

7. Configure NTFS permissions for the Accounting, Execs, Sales, and Temps groups by clicking the Add button. In the Select Users, Computers, or Groups dialog box, highlight the Accounting, Execs, Sales, and Temps groups and click the Add button. Then click OK.

8. In the Security tab, highlight each group and check the Allow or Deny check boxes to add permissions as follows:

   For Accounting, allow Read & Execute (List Folder Contents and Read will automatically be allowed) and Write.

   For Execs, allow Read.

   For Sales, allow Modify (Read & Execute, List Folder Contents, Read, and Write will automatically be allowed).

   For Temps, deny Write.

9. Click the OK button to close the folder Properties dialog box.

10. Log off as Administrator and log on as Marilyn. Access the D:\DATA\ DOC1 file, make changes, and then save the changes. Marilyn's permissions should allow these actions.

11. Log off as Marilyn and log on as Dan. Access the D:\DATA\DOC1 file, make changes, and then save the changes. Dan's permissions should allow you to open the file but not to save any changes.

12. Log off as Dan and log on as Administrator.

Determining NTFS Permissions for Copied or Moved Files

When you copy or move NTFS files, the permissions that have been set for those files might change. The following guidelines can be used to predict what will happen:

- If you move a file from one folder to another folder on the same volume, the file will retain the original NTFS permissions.

- If you move a file from one folder to another folder between different NTFS volumes, the file is treated as a copy and will have the same permissions as the destination folder.

- If you copy a file from one folder to another folder (on the same volume or on a different volume), the file will have the same permissions as the destination folder.

- If you copy or move a folder or file to a FAT partition, it will not retain any NTFS permissions.

Optimizing Local Access

In order for the data that you store on your computer to be useful, users must be able to access that data easily. One way to optimize local access is to logically organize your directory structure so that it is intuitive for users to find files. Planning and creating your directory structure were discussed in the "Organizing Files and Folders" section earlier in this chapter.

Another way to optimize local access is to configure the *Indexing Service* to index folders. By default, the Indexing Service is not started on Windows 2000 Professional computers. You can speed up searches by starting and configuring the Indexing Service.

You can find the Indexing Service under Services and Applications in the Computer Management utility (right-click My Computer, select Manage, and expand Services and Applications). To start the service and have it run automatically, double-click the Indexing Service to open the Indexing Service Properties dialog box, as shown in Figure 10.21. Select Automatic from the Startup Type drop-down list, click the Start button, and then click the OK button.

After you start the Indexing Service, you need to configure the folder that you want to be indexed. Enabling indexing for a folder is an advanced attribute, which you access through the folder Properties dialog box. On the General tab, click the Advanced button in the bottom-right corner of the dialog box to open the Advanced Attributes dialog box, as shown in Figure 10.22. The For Fast Searching, Allow Indexing Service to Index This Folder option should be enabled by default.

FIGURE 10.21 The Indexing Service Properties dialog box

FIGURE 10.22 The Advanced Attributes dialog box

In Exercise 10.4, you will optimize access to folders and files by starting and configuring the Indexing Service.

EXERCISE 10.4

Starting and Configuring the Indexing Service

1. Right-click My Computer and select Manage.

2. Expand Services and Applications, select Services, and double-click Indexing Service.

3. In the Indexing Service Properties dialog box, select Automatic from the Startup Type drop-down list. Click the Start button to start the Indexing Service. Click the OK button.

4. Select Start ➢ Programs ➢ Accessories ➢ Windows Explorer to open Windows Explorer. Access the DATA folder (on drive D:).

5. Right-click the folder and select Properties. On the General tab, click the Advanced button at the bottom of the dialog box.

6. In the Advanced Attributes dialog box, verify that the For Fast Searching, Allow Indexing Service to Index This Folder option is enabled. Then click the OK button.

7. Click the OK button to close the folder Properties dialog box.

Managing Network Access

Sharing is the process of allowing network users to access a folder located on a Windows 2000 Professional computer. A network share provides a single location to manage shared data used by many users. Sharing also allows an administrator to install an application once, as opposed to installing it locally at each computer, and to manage the application from a single location.

Microsoft ✓ *Exam Objective*

Manage and troubleshoot access to shared folders.

- Create and remove shared folders.
- Control access to shared folders by using permissions.

This chapter covers material related to managing shared folders, for the "Manage and troubleshoot access to shared folders" objective. Managing Web server resources, a third subobjective for this objective, is covered in Chapter 13, "Dial-Up Networking and Internet Productivity."

The following sections describe how to create and manage *shared folders*, configure *share permissions*, and provide access to shared resources.

Creating Shared Folders

To share a folder, you must be logged on as a member of the Administrators or Power Users group. You enable and configure sharing through the Sharing tab of the folder Properties dialog box, as shown in Figure 10.23.

FIGURE 10.23   The Sharing tab of the folder Properties dialog box

When you share a folder, you can configure the options listed in Table 10.2.

TABLE 10.2   Share Folder Options

Option	Description
Do Not Share This Folder	Specifies that the folder is only available through local access

TABLE 10.2 Share Folder Options *(continued)*

Option	Description
Share This Folder	Specifies that the folder is available through local access and network access
Share Name	Specifies a descriptive name by which users will access the folder
Comment	Allows you to enter more descriptive information about the share (optional)
User Limit	Allows you to specify the maximum number of connections to the share at any one time (the default is to allow up to 10 users access to a share on a Windows 2000 Professional computer)
Permissions	Allows you to configure how users will access the folder over the network
Caching	Specifies how folders are cached when the folder is offline

If you share a folder and then decide that you do not want to share it, just select the Do Not Share This Folder radio button in the Sharing tab of the folder Properties dialog box.

In Windows Explorer, you can easily tell that a folder has been shared by the hand icon under the folder.

In Exercise 10.5, you will create a shared folder.

EXERCISE 10.5

Creating a Shared Folder

1. Select Start ➤ Programs ➤ Accessories ➤ Windows Explorer. Expand My Computer, then expand Local Disk (D:).

2. Select File ➤ New ➤ Folder and name the new folder **Share Me**.

EXERCISE 10.5 *(continued)*

3. Right-click the Share Me folder, select Properties, and click the Sharing tab.

4. In the Sharing tab of the folder Properties dialog box, click the Share This Folder radio button.

5. Type **Test Shared Folder** in the Share Name text box.

6. Type **This is a comment for a shared folder** in the Comment text box.

7. Under User Limit, click the Allow radio button and specify 5 Users.

8. Click the OK button to close the dialog box.

Configuring Share Permissions

You can control users' access to shared folders by assigning share permissions. Share permissions are less complex than NTFS permissions and can be applied only to folders (unlike NTFS permissions, which can be applied to folders and files).

To assign share permissions, click the Permissions button in the Sharing tab of the folder Properties dialog box. This brings up the Share Permissions dialog box, as shown in Figure 10.24.

FIGURE 10.24   The Share Permissions dialog box

You can assign three types of share permissions:

- The Full Control share permission allows full access to the shared folder.

- The Change share permission allows users to change data within a file or to delete files.

- The Read share permission allows a user to view and execute files in the shared folder.

Full Control is the default permission on shared folders for the Everyone group.

 Shared folders do not use the same concept of inheritance as NTFS folders. If you share a folder, there is no way to block access to lower-level resources through share permissions.

In Exercise 10.6, you will apply share permissions to a folder. This exercise assumes that you have completed Exercises 10.3 and 10.5.

EXERCISE 10.6

Applying Share Permissions

1. Select Start ➤ Programs ➤ Accessories ➤ Windows Explorer. Expand My Computer, then expand Local Disk (D:).

2. Right-click the Share Me folder, select Sharing, and click the Permissions button.

3. In the Share Permissions dialog box, highlight the Everyone group and click the Remove button. Then click the Add button.

4. In the Select Users, Computers, and Groups dialog box, select users Dan and Marilyn, click the Add button, and then click the OK button.

5. Click user Marilyn and check the Allow box for the Full Control permission.

6. Click user Dan and check the Allow box for the Read permission.

7. Click the OK button to close the dialog box.

Managing Shares with the Shared Folders Utility

Shared Folders is a Computer Management utility for creating and managing shared folders on the computer. The Shared Folders window displays all of the shares that have been created on the computer, the user sessions that are open on each share, and the files that are currently open, listed by user.

To access Shared Folders, right-click My Computer on the Desktop and select Manage from the pop-up menu. In Computer Management, expand System Tools and then expand Shared Folders.

You can add the Shared Folders utility as an MMC snap-in. See Chapter 4, "Configuring the Windows 2000 Environment," for information about adding snap-ins to the MMC.

Viewing Shares

When you select Shares in the Shared Folders utility, you see all of the shares that have been configured on the computer. Figure 10.25 shows an example of a Shares listing.

FIGURE 10.25 The Shares listing in the Shared Folders window

Along with the shares that you have specifically configured, you will also see the Windows 2000 special shares, which are shares created by the system automatically to facilitate system administration. A share that is followed by a dollar sign ($) indicates that the share is hidden from view when users access utilities such as My Network Places and browse network resources. The following special shares may appear on your Windows 2000 Professional computer, depending on how the computer is configured:

- The *drive_letter*$ share is the share for the root of the drive. By default, the root of every drive is shared. For example, the C: drive is shared as C$.

On Windows 2000 Professional computers and Windows 2000 member servers, only members of the Administrators and Backup Operators group can access the *drive_letter*$ share. On Windows 2000 domain controllers, members of the Administrators, Backup Operators, and Server Operators group can access this share.

- The ADMIN$ share points to the Windows 2000 system root (for example, C:\WINNT).

- The IPC$ share allows remote administration of a computer and is used to view a computer's shared resources. (IPC stands for interprocess communication.)

- The PRINT$ share is used for remote printer administration.

- The FAX$ share is used by fax clients to cache fax cover sheets and documents that are in the process of being faxed.

Creating New Shares

In Shared Folders, you can create new shares through the following steps:

1. Right-click the Shares folder and select New File Share from the pop-up menu.

2. The Create Shared Folder Wizard starts, as shown in Figure 10.26. Specify the folder that will be shared (you can use the Browse button to select the folder) and provide a share name and description. Click the Next button.

FIGURE 10.26   The Create Shared Folder Wizard dialog box

3. The Create Shared Folder Wizard dialog box for assigning share permissions appears, as shown in Figure 10.27. You can select from one of the predefined permissions assignments or customize the share permissions. After you specify the permissions that will be assigned, click the Finish button.

FIGURE 10.27   Assigning share permissions

4. The Create Shared Folder dialog box appears, as shown in Figure 10.28. This dialog box verifies that the folder has been shared successfully. Click the Yes button to create another shared folder or the No button if you are finished creating shared folders.

FIGURE 10.28 Verifying shared folder creation

You can stop sharing a folder by right-clicking the share and selecting Stop Sharing from the pop-up menu. You will be asked to confirm that you want to stop sharing the folder.

Viewing Share Sessions

When you select Sessions in the Shared Folders utility, you see all of the users who are currently accessing shared folders on the computer. Figure 10.29 shows an example of a Sessions listing in Shared Folders.

FIGURE 10.29 The Sessions listing in the Shared Folders window

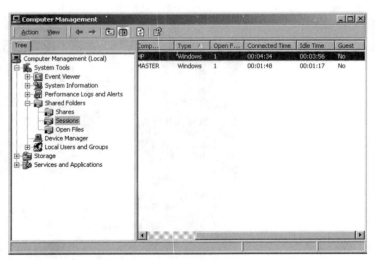

The Sessions listing includes the following information:

- The username that has connected to the share
- The computer name that the user has connected from
- The client operating system that is used by the connecting computer
- The number of files that the user has open
- The amount of time that the user has been connected
- The amount of idle time for the connection
- Whether or not the user has connected through Guest access

Viewing Open Files in Shared Folders

When you select Open Files in the Shared Folders utility, you see all of the files that are currently open from shared folders. Figure 10.30 shows an example of an Open Files listing in Shared Folders.

FIGURE 10.30   The Open Files listing in the Shared Folders window

The Open Files listing includes the following information:

- The path and files that are currently open
- The username that is accessing the file
- The operating system that the user who is accessing the file is using

- Whether or not any file locks have been applied (file locks are used to prevent two users from opening the same file and editing it at the same time)

- The open mode that is being used (such as read or write)

Providing Access to Shared Resources

There are many ways that a user can access a shared resource. Here, we will look at three common methods:

- Through My Network Places

- By mapping a network drive in Windows Explorer

- Through the NET USE command-line utility

Microsoft ✓ ***Exam*** ***Objective***   **Connect to shared resources on a Microsoft network.**

Accessing a Shared Resource through My Network Places

The advantage of mapping a network location through *My Network Places* is that you do not use a drive letter. This is useful if you have already exceeded the limit of 26 drive letters.

To access a shared resource through My Network Places, take the following steps:

1. Double-click the My Network Places icon on the Desktop.

2. Double-click Add Network Place.

3. The Add Network Place Wizard starts, as shown in Figure 10.31. Type in the location of the Network Place. This can be a UNC path to a shared network folder, an HTTP path to a Web folder, or an FTP path to an FTP site. If you are unsure of the path, you can use the Browse button to search for the path. After specifying the path, click the Next button.

FIGURE 10.31   The Add Network Place Wizard dialog box

4. Enter the name that you want to use for the network location. This name will appear in the computer's My Network Places listing.

 iNetwork Places are unique for each user and are part of the user's profile. User profiles are covered in Chapter 8, "Using User Profiles and Hardware Profiles."

Mapping a Network Drive through Windows Explorer

Through Windows Explorer, you can map a network drive to a drive letter that appears to the user as a local connection on their computer. Once you create a *mapped drive*, it can be accessed through a drive letter using My Computer.

The following steps are used to map a network drive:

1. Select Start ➢ Programs ➢ Accessories ➢ Windows Explorer to open Windows Explorer.

2. Select Tools ➢ Map Network Drive.

3. The Map Network Drive dialog box appears, as shown in Figure 10.32. Choose the drive letter that will be associated with the network drive.

FIGURE 10.32   The Map Network Drive dialog box

4. Choose the shared network folder that you will map the drive to from the Folder drop-down list.

5. If you want this connection to be persistent (you want to save the connection and use it every time you log on), make sure that the Reconnect at Logon check box is checked.

6. If you will connect to the share using a different username, click the underlined part of Connect Using a Different User Name. This brings up the Connect As dialog box, shown in Figure 10.33. Fill in the User Name and Password text boxes, then click OK.

FIGURE 10.33   The Connect As dialog box

7. If you want to create a shortcut to a Web folder, click the underlined part of Create a Shortcut to a Web Folder or FTP Site. This starts the Add Network Place Wizard, which was described in the previous section.

Using the NET USE **Command-Line Utility**

The *NET USE* command-line utility provides a quick and easy way to map a network drive. This command has the following syntax:

    NET USE x: \\computername\sharename

For example, the following command maps drive G to a share called App-Data on a computer named AppServer:

    NET USE G: \\AppServer\AppData

You can get more information about the NET USE command by typing **NET USE** /? from a command prompt.

In Exercise 10.7, you will access shared resources through My Network Places and map a drive in Windows Explorer. This exercise assumes that you have completed Exercise 10.6.

EXERCISE 10.7

Accessing Network Resources

1. Log on as user Marilyn. Double-click the My Network Places icon on the Desktop.

2. Double-click Add Network Place. When the Add Network Place Wizard starts, click the Browse button.

3. Select the workgroup or domain that your computer is installed in. Click your computer name. Select Test Shared Folder and click the OK button. Click the Next button.

4. Enter the name that you want to use for the network location. This name will appear in the computer's My Network Places listing.

5. Accept the default name for the Network Place and click the Finish button.

6. The folder opens automatically. Close the folder. You will see the new folder in My Network Places.

7. Log off as Marilyn and log on as Dan.

8. Double-click My Network Places. You will not see the Network Place that you created as user Marilyn.

9. Open Windows Explorer and select Tools ➤ Map Network Drive.

10. In the Map Network Drives dialog box, accept the default drive letter and click the Browse button to select the folder. Select the workgroup or domain that your computer is installed in. Click your computer name. Select Test Shared Folder and click the Finish button.

Reviewing the Flow of Resource Access

Understanding the resource-flow process will help you to troubleshoot access problems. As you've learned, a user account must have appropriate permissions to access a resource. Resource access is determined through the following steps:

1. At logon, an *access token* is created for the logon account.

2. When a resource is accessed, Windows 2000 Professional checks the *access control list (ACL)* to see if the user should be granted access.

3. If the user is on the list, the ACL checks the *access control entries (ACEs)* to see what type of access the user should be given.

Access tokens, ACLs, and ACEs are covered in the following sections.

Access Token Creation

Each time a user account logs on, an access token is created. The access token contains the security identifier (SID) of the currently logged on user. It also contains the SIDs for any groups the user is associated with. Once an access token is created, it is not updated until the next logon.

Let's assume that user Kevin needs to access the Sales database and that SALESDB is the name of the shared folder that contains the database. Kevin logs on, but he is not able to access the database. You do some detective work and find that Kevin has not been added to the Sales group, which is necessary in order for anyone to have proper access to SALESDB. You add Kevin to the Sales group and let him know that everything is working. Kevin tries to access SALESDB, but he is still unable to do so. Kevin logs off and logs on again, and now he can access the database. This is because Kevin's access token was not updated to reflect his new group membership until he logged off and logged back on. When he logged on, a new access token was created, identifying Kevin as a member of the Sales group.

Access tokens are only updated during the logon sequence. They are not updated on the fly. This means that if you add a user to a group, that user needs to log off and log on for their access token to be updated.

ACLs and ACEs

Each object in Windows 2000 Professional has an ACL. An object is defined as a set of data that can be used by the system or as a set of actions that can be used to manipulate system data. Examples of objects include folders, files, network shares, and printers. The ACL is a list of user accounts and groups that are allowed to access the resource. Figure 10.34 shows how ACLs are associated with each object.

FIGURE 10.34 Access control lists (ACLs) for network shares

For each ACL, there is an ACE that defines what a user or a group can actually do at the resource. Deny permissions are always listed first. This means that if users have Deny permissions through user or group membership, they

will not be allowed to access the object, even if they have explicit Allow permissions through other user or group permissions. Figure 10.35 illustrates the interaction between the ACL and the ACE.

FIGURE 10.35 Access control entries (ACEs) associated with an ACL

ACL	ACE
Users	Read
Administrators	Full Control
Sales	Change

Local and Network Resource Access

Local and network security work together. The most restrictive access will determine what a user can do. For example, if the local folder is NTFS and the default permissions have not been changed, the Everyone group has the Full Control permission. On the other hand, if that local folder is shared and the permissions are set so that only the Sales group had been assigned the Read permission, then only the Sales group can access that shared folder.

Conversely, if the local NTFS permissions allow only the Managers group the Read permission to a local folder, and that folder has been shared with default permissions allowing the Everyone group Full Control permission, only the Managers group can access the folder with Read permissions, because Read is the more restrictive permission.

For example, suppose that you have set up the NTFS and share permissions for the DATA folder as shown in Figure 10.36, and Jose is a member of the Sales group and wants to access the DATA folder. If he accesses the folder locally, he will be governed by only the NTFS security, so he will have the Modify permission. However, if Jose accesses the folder from another workstation through the network share, he also will be governed by the more restrictive share permission, Read.

As another example, suppose that Chandler is a member of the Everyone group. He wants to access the DATA folder. If he accesses the folder locally, he will have Read permission. If he accesses the folder remotely via the network share, he will still have Read permission. Even though the share permission allows the Everyone group the Change permission to the folder, the more restrictive permission (in this case, the NTFS permission Read) will be applied.

FIGURE 10.36 Local and network security govern access

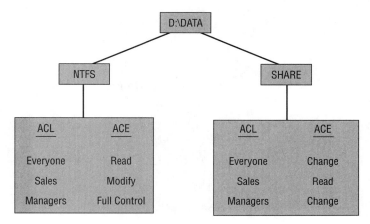

Summary

In this chapter, you learned about managing access to files and folders. We covered the following topics:

- Basic file management, which includes organizing files and folders, creating files and folders, managing folder options, and searching for files and folders

- Local access management, which includes assigning NTFS permissions and optimizing local access

- Network access management, which includes creating shared folders, assigning share permissions, and accessing network resources

- How resources are accessed when local NTFS permissions and network share permissions have been applied

- The flow of resource access, which includes access token creation and accessing objects by checking the ACL and ACEs

Key Terms

Before you take the exam, be sure you're familiar with the following key terms:

access control list (ACL)

access control entry (ACE)

access token

effective rights

Indexing Service

inherited permissions

mapped drive

My Network Places

NET USE

NTFS permissions

offline files and folders

share permissions

shared folders

Review Questions

1. Who is able to manage NTFS permissions on NTFS folders? Choose all that apply.

   A. Administrators

   B. Power Users

   C. Any user with the Manage NTFS permission

   D. Any user with the Full Control NTFS permission

2. What is the main purpose of the File Types tab in the Folder Options dialog box?

   A. To configure your file associations

   B. To configure what types of files can be used on Windows 2000 computers

   C. To specify what file types you see when you open a folder in Windows Explorer

   D. To configure offline files and folders

3. Who is able to create a shared network folder? Choose all that apply.

   A. Administrators

   B. Power Users

   C. Any user with the Manage NTFS permission

   D. Any user with the Full Control NTFS permission

4. On which tab of the Folder Options dialog box can a user configure folder views, such as whether or not hidden files are displayed when a folder is opened?

   A. The File Types tab

   B. The View tab

   C. The Display tab

   D. The Advanced tab

5. What is the default permission that is applied to the Everyone group for NTFS partitions?

   A. No permissions are assigned

   B. Read

   C. Read & Execute

   D. Full Control

6. Which of the following NTFS permissions can be applied in Windows 2000 Professional? Choose all that apply.

   A. Read & Execute

   B. List Folder Contents

   C. No Access

   D. Change

7. Which of the following options best describes which shares can be used for offline files and folders?

   A. You can use offline files and folders only from shares on Windows 2000 computers.

   B. You can use offline files and folders only from shares on Windows 2000 or Windows 98 clients.

   C. You can use offline files and folders from any share on a computer that uses the SMB protocol.

   D. You can use offline files and folders from any share that is local to your network.

8. Which of the following statements is true regarding indexing files on Windows 2000 Professional computers?

   A. By default, the Indexing Service is started, and NTFS folders are configured to allow the Indexing Service to index this folder.

   B. By default, the Indexing Service is not started, and NTFS folders are not configured to allow the Indexing Service to index this folder.

   C. By default, the Indexing Service is started, and NTFS folders are not configured to allow the Indexing Service to index this folder.

   D. By default, the Indexing Service is not started, and NTFS folders are configured to allow the Indexing Service to index this folder.

9. Which command-line utility can be used to map to shared network folders?

A. MAP

B. NET SHARE

C. NET USE

D. NET ACCESS

10. Which of the following options can be used to access shared network folders from a Windows 2000 Professional computer? Choose all that apply.

A. Network Neighborhood

B. My Network Places

C. Map a drive in Windows Explorer

D. Control Panel, Network

11. You have decided to implement compressed folders and files on your D: drive. How can you easily tell which folders and files are compressed?

A. The folders and files are displayed in an alternate color by default.

B. Run the showcomp command to display folders and files in an alternate color.

C. In Windows Explorer, access Folder Options, View tab and select the Display Compressed Files and Folders with an Alternate Color option.

D. In Windows Explorer, access Tools, Advanced Options and select the Display Compressed Files and Folders with an Alternate Color option.

12. Which utility can you use to quickly see a list of all of the shares that have been configured on your Windows 2000 Professional computer?

A. Windows Explorer

B. Shared Folders

C. Share Manager

D. Disk Management

13. Which option can you use to prevent a shared folder from being displayed in users' browse lists?

   A. $

   B. %

   C. *

   D. #

14. Linda has a folder that she would like to share on the network. This folder contains the `salesdata.txt` file. She wants to allow only one user at a time to edit the file, so that one user can't overwrite another user's changes if they open the file at the same time. How should Linda configure this share?

   A. She should set the user limit to allow 1 user.

   B. She should configure the file attribute on the `salesdata.txt` file as non-shared.

   C. She should set a schedule so that users access the file at different times.

   D. In Windows Explorer, she should configure the shared folder so that users are not allowed offline access to the folder.

15. Greg has configured his share for the Marketing folder for the maximum allowed on his Windows 2000 Professional computer. What is the maximum number of users that can access this share at the same time?

   A. 5

   B. 10

   C. 12

   D. 15

16. Rick has configured his D:\TEST folder so that the Everyone group has Read access to the folder. What will the Everyone group's permissions be for D:\TEST\DATA by default?

   A. No permissions

   B. Full Control permissions

   C. Read permissions

   D. Full Access permissions

17. Which of the following options is used to identify a user who is attempting to access an NTFS object or network share?

   A. Access token

   B. Access control list

   C. Access control entry

   D. Access identifier

18. Which of the following options is used to define what permissions a user or group has to an NTFS object or a network share?

   A. Access token

   B. Access control list

   C. Access control entry

   D. Access identifier

19. Which of the following options is used to define which users and groups have permissions to access an NTFS object or a network share?

   A. Access token

   B. Access control list

   C. Access control entry

   D. Access identifier

20. Which of the following statements best describes how share permissions and NTFS permissions work together if they have been applied to the same folder?

   A. The NTFS permissions will always take precedence.

   B. The share permissions will always take precedence.

   C. The most restrictive permission within all of the share and NTFS permissions will take precedence.

   D. The system will look at the cumulative share permissions and the cumulative NTFS permissions. Whichever set is more restrictive will be applied.

Answer to Review Questions

1. A, D. Only members of the Administrators group and users with Full Control NTFS permissions can manage NTFS permissions on NTFS folders. Members of the Power Users group do not have any special access to NTFS folders. There is no Manage NTFS permission.

2. A. The File Types tab is used to configure file associations, which associate a file extension with an application that has been installed on the computer.

3. A, B. Only members of the Administrators and Power Users groups can create network shares.

4. B. The folder views are configured through the View tab of the Folder Options dialog box. The File Types tab is used for file associations. There is no Display or Advanced tab.

5. D. By default, the Everyone group is assigned Full Control permission for NTFS volumes.

6. A, B. Read & Execute and List Folder Contents are Windows 2000 NTFS permissions. No Access was a permission in Windows NT 4. Change is a share permission.

7. C. You can use offline files and folders from any share on a computer that uses the SMB protocol, which is essentially any Microsoft computer with a share.

8. D. By default, the Indexing Service is not started on Windows 2000 Professional computers. However, NTFS folders are configured to allow the Indexing Service to index this folder.

9. C. The NET USE command is used to map shared network folders.

10. B, C. You can access network shares through My Network Places or by mapping a drive in Windows Explorer. Network Neighborhood was in Windows NT 4, and is not in Windows 2000. The Network icon in Control Panel is used to configure network settings, not map network drives.

11. C. In Windows Explorer, you can set the options for viewing folders and files through the View tab of the Folder Options dialog box. This tab includes the Display Compressed Files and Folders with an Alternate Color option.

12. B. The quickest way to see all of the folders that have been shared on a Windows 2000 Professional computer is to open the Shared Folders utility and select the Shares folder.

13. A. If you do not want a folder to be displayed in users' browse lists, you can hide the share by placing a $ at the beginning of the share name.

14. A. When you configure a share, you can specify a user limit. The Sharing tab of the folder Properties dialog box includes a User Limit option, which you can set to limit access to the folder to one user at a time.

15. B. In Windows 2000 Professional, you can have a maximum of 10 users connected to a share at any one time.

16. C. In Windows 2000 Professional, the default is for the permissions to be inherited by subfolders. This is different from the default in Windows NT 4, where files in a folder inherited permissions from the parent folder, but subfolders did not inherit parent permissions.

17. A. The access token contains the security identifier (SID) of the currently logged on user. It also contains the SIDs for any groups the user is associated with. Once an access token is created, it is not updated until the next logon.

18. C. Access control entries (ACEs) define what a user or a group can actually do at the resource. Deny permissions are always listed first.

19. B. The access control list (ACL) is a list of user accounts and groups that are allowed to access the resource.

20. D. When share and NTFS permissions have been applied, the system looks at the effective rights for NTFS and share permissions and then applies the most restrictive of the cumulative permissions.

Chapter

11

Managing Network Connections

MICROSOFT EXAM OBJECTIVES COVERED IN THIS CHAPTER

✓ Install, configure, and troubleshoot network adapters.

✓ Configure and troubleshoot the TCP/IP protocol.

For successful network connection management, you need to understand how network protocols work. The OSI model helps you gain this understanding by showing how network protocols are modular in nature.

Network adapters are hardware used to connect your computer to the network. You also need a driver for the network adapter installed on your computer.

Managing network connections also involves configuring your network protocols. The three protocols supported by Windows 2000 Professional are TCP/IP, NWLink IPX/SPX/NetBIOS, and NetBEUI.

This chapter begins with an overview of network protocols, including a discussion of network data flow and the OSI model. Then you will learn how to install and configure network adapters and network protocols.

Reviewing Networking Protocols

Communications over a network are accomplished through the use of networking protocols. To understand the purpose of networking protocols, you should have a basic knowledge of the *OSI (Open Systems Interconnection) model*. The OSI model is not an actual product. It is a theoretical model that describes how networks work.

There are several advantages to using the OSI model as a framework for understanding network protocols:

- Breaking down a large concept, such as a network, makes it easier to understand.

- Modularizing network functions allows you to apply specific technologies or protocols at specific layers in a mix-and-match manner.

- Understanding how one network system works and applying it to the OSI model allows you to easily apply that knowledge to other operating systems.

We'll start by looking at an example of how data flows through a network. Then we'll examine how the seven layers of the OSI model work to move data through a network.

Network Data Flow

Figure 11.1 illustrates an example of how data flows from Computer A on one network segment to Computer B on a separate network segment.

FIGURE 11.1   Data flows from Computer A on one network segment to Computer B on another network segment.

Computer A
Send "Hello"

Router

Router

Computer B
Receive "Hello"

In this example, the following steps are involved in moving the data from Computer A to Computer B:

1. Starting at Computer A, you create a message (file) using some type of program that offers file services. In this example, the message says "Hello."

2. The computer doesn't understand the characters in "Hello," but does understand ones and zeros. The message must be translated into ones and zeros through a protocol such as ASCII.

3. At the higher levels of communication, a connection (or session) is established. The connection determines when requests are made so that appropriate responses can be made. Just like human conversations, computer communications are usually a series of requests and responses that must be answered sequentially.

4. You next need to determine if you want the connection to be reliable, called a connection-oriented service, or if you want the connection to use less overhead and assume that the connection is reliable, called a connectionless service. An analogy for the reliability of the two services is that you can communicate by making a telephone call, which is like using a connection-oriented service, or you can communicate by mailing a letter, which is like using a connectionless service.

5. Because Computer A and Computer B are on separate network segments, you must figure out how to route the message across an internetwork based on the best possible path available.

6. Once the message gets to the correct network segment, it must be delivered to the correct computer on the segment.

7. The message needs to travel over the physical connection that actually exists between Computer A and Computer B, which is at the lowest level of communication. The data moves through the cabling and network cards that connect the network. At this level, you are sending ones and zeros over the physical network.

The steps in this data-flow example correlate to the seven layers of the OSI model, which are covered in the next section.

The OSI Model Layers

Each of the OSI model layers has a specific function in providing networking capabilities. The seven layers of the OSI model are Application, Presentation, Session, Transport, Network, Data Link, and Physical. Table 11.1 lists a couple of mnemonics to help you remember the order of the layers.

TABLE 11.1 Mnemonics for the OSI Model Layers

Layer	Memory Trick Top to Bottom	Memory Trick Bottom to Top
Application	All	Albert
Presentation	People	Prince
Session	Seem	See

TABLE 11.1   Mnemonics for the OSI Model Layers *(continued)*

Layer	Memory Trick Top to Bottom	Memory Trick Bottom to Top
Transport	To	To
Network	Need	Need
Data Link	Data	Don't
Physical	Processing	People

The Application Layer

The *Application layer* is used to support the following services:

File services	Used to store, move, control access to, and retrieve files
Print services	Used to send data to local or network printers
Message services	Used to transfer text, graphics, audio, and video over a network
Application services	Used to process applications locally or through distributed processing
Database services	Used to allow a local computer to access network services for database storage and retrieval

In addition, the Application layer advertises any services that are being offered and determines whether requests that are made by the client should be processed locally or remotely (through another network resource).

The Presentation Layer

The *Presentation layer* is used for four main processes:

Character-code translation	The process of converting symbolic characters like the letter h into ones and zeros like 01101000, which is the ASCII code equivalent
Data encryption	The process of coding data so that it is protected from unauthorized access

| Data compression | The process of making data take less space at the sending end for transport |
| Data expansion | The process of restoring compressed data to its original format at the receiver's end |

The Session Layer

The *Session layer* is responsible for managing communication between a sender and a receiver. The following are some of the communication tasks that are performed at this layer:

- Establishing connections
- Maintaining connections
- Synchronizing communications
- Controlling dialogues
- Terminating connections

When you create a connection, you authenticate the user account at the sending and receiving computers. Connection creation also involves determining the type of communication that will take place and the protocols that will be used by the lower layers.

Data transfer and dialogue control are used to determine which computer is making requests and which computer is making responses. This also determines if acknowledgments are required for data transmission.

The Transport Layer

The *Transport layer* is associated with reliable data delivery. With reliable delivery, the sender and receiver establish a connection, and the receiver acknowledges the receipt of data by sending acknowledgment packets to the sender.

Depending on the protocol used, you can send data through the Transport layer using a *connection-oriented service* or a *connectionless service*. A connection-oriented service is like a telephone conversation, where the connection is established and acknowledgments are sent. This type of communication has a high overhead. A connectionless service does not establish a connection and is similar to communicating through the mail. You assume that your letter will arrive, but this form of communication is not as reliable as a telephone conversation (a connection-oriented service).

The Network Layer

The primary responsibility of the *Network layer* is to move data over an *internetwork*. An internetwork is made up of multiple network segments that are connected with some device, such as a router. Each network segment is assigned a network address. Network layer protocols build routing tables that are used to route packets through the network in the most efficient manner.

The Data Link Layer

The *Data Link layer* is responsible for establishing and maintaining the communication channel, identifying computers on network segments by their physical address, and organizing data into a logical group called a frame. There are two main sublayers at the Data Link layer: the *Logical Link Control (LLC) sublayer*, which defines flow control, and the *Media Access Control (MAC) sublayer*, which is used for physical addressing.

The communication channel that is established at the Data Link layer is a low-level channel that manages whether or not a communication channel exists. All higher-level communication is handled at the Session layer. Computers are identified by their physical address, which is called the *MAC address*. Ethernet and Token Ring cards have their MAC address assigned through a chip on the network card. *Frames* are logical groupings of the bits from the Physical layer. Frames contain information about the destination physical address and the source physical address, as well as all of the data that has been used at the upper layers of the OSI model.

The Physical Layer

When you get down to the details of sending ones and zeros across a cable, you are dealing with the *Physical layer*. The Physical layer is responsible for determining the following information:

- The physical network structure you are using

- The mechanical and electrical specifications of the transmission media that will be used

- How the data will be encoded and transmitted

Installing and Configuring Network Adapters

*N*etwork adapters are hardware used to connect computers (or other devices) to the network. They function at the Physical and Data Link layers of the OSI model, as shown in Figure 11.2.

Microsoft ✓ *Exam* *Objective*	**Install, configure, and troubleshoot network adapters.**

FIGURE 11.2 Network adapters function at the Physical and Data Link layers of the OSI model.

Network adapters are responsible for providing the physical connection to the network and the physical address of the computer. Network adapters (and all other hardware devices) need a *driver* in order to communicate with the Windows 2000 operating system.

In the following sections, you will learn how to install and configure network adapters, as well as how to troubleshoot network adapters that are not working.

Installing a Network Adapter

Before you physically install you network adapter, you should read the instructions that came with your hardware. If your network adapter is new, it should be self-configuring, with Plug-and-Play capabilities. After you install a network adapter that supports Plug-and-Play, it should work the next time you start up the computer.

New devices will auto-detect settings and be self-configuring. Older devices rely on hardware setup programs to configure hardware. Really old devices require you to manually configure the adapter through switches or jumpers.

If the network adapter is not Plug-and-Play, after you install it, the operating system should detect that you have a new piece of hardware and start a Wizard that leads you through the process of loading the adapter's driver. You take the following steps to install a driver for a network adapter that is not Plug-and-Play:

1. If the Add/Remove Hardware Wizard doesn't start automatically, select Start ➢ Settings ➢ Control Panel ➢ Add/Remove Hardware.

2. The Welcome to the Add/Remove Hardware Wizard dialog box appears, as shown in Figure 11.3. Click the Next button to continue.

FIGURE 11.3 The Welcome to Add/Remove Hardware Wizard dialog box

3. The Choose a Hardware Task dialog box appears, as shown in Figure 11.4. Select the Add/Troubleshoot a Device radio button and click the Next button.

FIGURE 11.4 The Choose a Hardware Task dialog box

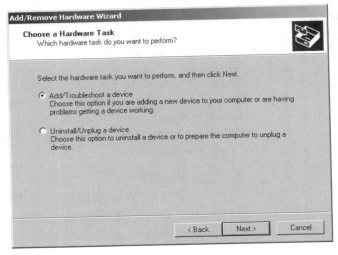

4. Windows 2000 runs the process to detect new hardware and then displays the Choose a Hardware Device dialog box, as shown in Figure 11.5. Choose the Add a New Device option, which is at the top of the Devices list box. Then click the Next button.

FIGURE 11.5 The Choose a Hardware Device dialog box

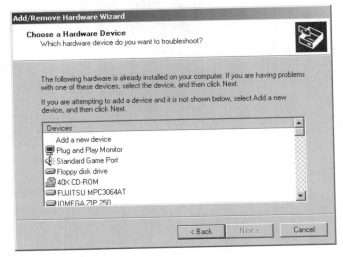

5. The Find New Hardware dialog box appears, as shown in Figure 11.6. Select the Yes, Search for New Hardware option to let Windows 2000 attempt to detect your hardware. If the operating system detects the new network adapter, click Next and then skip to step 9. If Windows 2000 cannot detect your hardware, select the No, I Want to Select the Hardware from a List radio button, click the Next button and continue with step 6.

FIGURE 11.6 The Find New Hardware dialog box

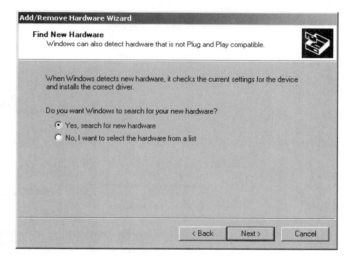

6. The Hardware Type dialog box appears, as shown in Figure 11.7. In the Hardware Type list box, select Network Adapters. Then click the Next button.

7. The Select Network Adapter dialog box appears, as shown in Figure 11.8. If your manufacturer and network adapter model are listed in this dialog box, select them. If your manufacturer and model do not appear, click the Have Disk button and specify the location of the driver's distribution files.

FIGURE 11.7 The Hardware Type dialog box

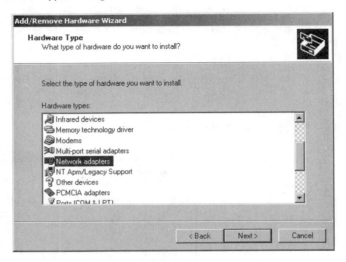

FIGURE 11.8 The Select Network Adapter dialog box

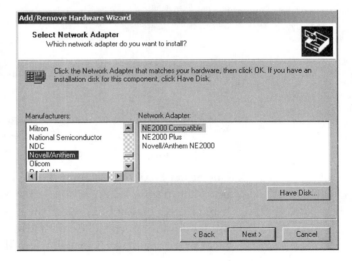

8. In the case that Windows 2000 cannot detect the settings of the device, you will see a warning message. At this point, you will need to refer to the manufacturer's documentation on how to set up the network card. After you configure your device, click the OK button.

9. The Start Hardware Installation dialog box appears, as shown in Figure 11.9. If the driver shown in this dialog box is correct, click the Next button.

FIGURE 11.9   The Start Hardware Installation dialog box

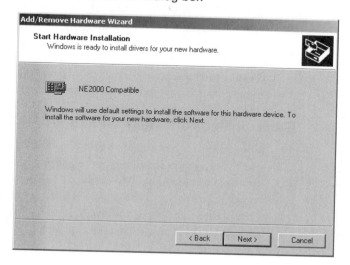

10. The Completing the Add/Remove Hardware Wizard dialog box appears, as shown in Figure 11.10. Click the Finish button.

FIGURE 11.10   The Completing the Add/Remove Hardware Wizard dialog box

Configuring a Network Adapter

Once the network adapter has been installed, you can configure your network adapter through its Properties dialog box. To access this dialog box, select Start ➤ Settings ➤ Control Panel ➤ Network and Dial-up Connections ➤ Local Area Connection ➤ Properties and click the Configure button. Alternatively, right-click My Network Places and choose Properties, then right-click Local Area Connection, choose Properties, and click the Configure button.

In the network adapter Properties dialog box, the properties are grouped on four tabs: General, Advanced, Driver, and Resources. The properties on these tabs are covered in the following sections.

General Network Adapter Properties

The General tab of the network adapter Properties dialog box, shown in Figure 11.11, shows the name of the adapter, the device type, the manufacturer, and the location. The Device Status box reports whether or not the device is working properly. If the device is not working properly, you can click the Troubleshooter button to have Windows 2000 display some general trouble-shooting tips. You can also enable or disable the device through the Device Usage drop-down list options.

FIGURE 11.11 The General tab of the network adapter Properties dialog box

Advanced Network Adapter Properties

The contents of the Advanced tab of the network adapter Properties dialog box vary depending on the network adapter and driver that you are using. Figure 11.12 shows an example of the Advanced tab for a Fast Ethernet adapter. To configure options in this dialog box, choose the property you want to modify in the Property list box on the left and specify the value for the property in the Value box on the right.

FIGURE 11.12 The Advanced tab of the network adapter Properties dialog box

You should not need to change the settings on the Advanced tab of the network adapter Properties dialog box unless you have been instructed to do so by the manufacturer.

Driver Properties

The Driver tab of the network adapter Properties dialog box, shown in Figure 11.13, provides the following information about your driver:

- The driver provider, which is usually Microsoft or the network adapter manufacturer

- The date that the driver was released

- The driver version, which is useful in determining if you have the latest driver installed

- The digital signer, which is the company that provides the digital signature for driver signing (driver signing is covered in Chapter 4, "Configuring the Windows 2000 Environment")

FIGURE 11.13 The Driver tab of the network adapter Properties dialog box

Clicking the Driver Details button at the bottom of the Driver tab brings up the Driver File Details dialog box, as shown in Figure 11.14. This dialog box lists the following details about the driver:

- The location of the driver file, which is useful for troubleshooting
- The original provider of the driver, which is usually the manufacturer
- The file version, which is useful for troubleshooting
- Copyright information about the driver

FIGURE 11.14   The Driver File Details dialog box

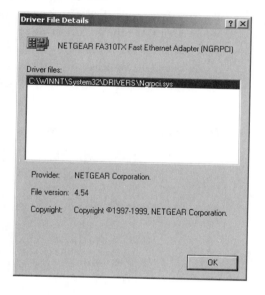

The Uninstall button at the bottom of the Driver tab removes the driver from your computer. You would uninstall the driver if you were going to replace the driver with a completely new driver. Normally, you update the driver rather than uninstalling it.

To update a driver, click the Update Driver button at the bottom of the Driver tab. This starts the Upgrade Device Driver Wizard, which steps you through upgrading the driver for an existing device.

If you cannot find the driver for your network card or the configuration instructions, check the vendor's Web site. Usually, you will be able to find the latest drivers. You also should be able to locate a list of Frequently Asked Questions (FAQs) about your hardware.

Resource Properties

Each device installed on a computer uses computer resources. Resources include interrupt request (IRQ), memory, and I/O (input/output) settings. The Resources tab of the network adapter Properties dialog box lists the resource settings for your network adapter, as shown in Figure 11.15. This information is important for troubleshooting, because if other devices are trying to use the same resource settings, your devices will not work properly. The Conflicting Device List box at the bottom of the Resources tab shows if any conflicts exist.

FIGURE 11.15 The Resources tab of the network adapter Properties dialog box

In Exercise 11.1, you will view the properties of your network adapter. This exercise assumes that you have a network adapter installed in your computer.

EXERCISE 11.1

Viewing Network Adapter Properties

1. Select Start ➢ Settings ➢ Control Panel ➢ Network and Dial-up Connections ➢ Local Area Connection ➢ Properties and click the Configure button.

2. In the General tab of the connection Properties dialog box, click the Configure button under Connect Using.

3. In the General tab of the network adapter Properties dialog box, verify that the Device Status box shows "This device is working properly."

4. Click the Advanced tab. Note the properties that are available for your driver.

5. Click the Driver tab. Note the driver date and version information. Click the Driver Details button to see the location of your network adapter's driver file. Click OK to close the Driver File Details dialog box.

6. Click the Resources tab. Note the resources that are being used by your network adapter. Verify that the Conflicting Device List box shows "No conflicts."

Troubleshooting Network Adapters

If your network adapter is not working, the problem may be with the hardware, the driver software, or the network protocols. The following are some common causes for network adapter problems:

Network adapter not on the HCL	If the device is not on the HCL, you should contact the adapter vendor for advice.
Outdated driver	Make sure that you have the most up-to-date driver for your adapter. You can check for the latest driver on your hardware vendor's Web site.

Network adapter not recognized by Windows 2000	Check Device Manager to see if Windows 2000 recognizes your device. If you do not see your adapter, you will need to manually install it (see the "Installing a Network Adapter" section earlier in the chapter). You should also verify that the adapter's resource settings do not conflict with the resource settings of other devices (check the Resources tab of the network adapter Properties dialog box).
Hardware that is not working properly	Verify that your hardware is working properly. Run any diagnostics that came with the adapter. If everything seems to work properly, make sure that the cable is good and that all of the applicable network hardware is installed properly and is working. This is where it pays off to have spare hardware (such as cables and extra network adapters) that you know works properly.
Improperly configured network protocols	Make sure that your network protocols have been configured properly. Network protocols are covered in detail in the next section of this chapter.

 Check Event Viewer to see if there are any messages that give you a hint about what is causing a network adapter error. See Chapter 15. "Performing System Recovery Functions," for details on using Event Viewer.

Installing and Configuring Network Protocols

Network protocols function at the Network and Transport layers of the OSI model. They are responsible for transporting data across an internetwork. You can mix and match the network protocols you use with Windows 2000 Professional, which supports three protocols: TCP/IP, NWLink IPX/SPX/NetBIOS, and NetBEUI. The following sections describe how to install and configure these protocols.

Using TCP/IP

TCP/IP (Transmission Control Protocol/Internet Protocol) is one of the most commonly used network protocols. TCP/IP was originally developed in the 1970s for the Department of Defense (DoD) as a way of connecting dissimilar networks. Since then, TCP/IP has become an industry standard.

Microsoft ✓ *Exam* *Objective*	**Configure and troubleshoot the TCP/IP protocol.**

On a clean installation of Windows 2000 Professional, TCP/IP is installed by default. TCP/IP has the following benefits:

- It is the most commonly used protocol and is supported by almost all network operating systems. It is the required protocol for Internet access.

- TCP/IP is scalable for use in small and large networks. In large networks, TCP/IP provides routing services.

- TCP/IP is designed to be fault tolerant and is able to dynamically reroute packets if network links become unavailable (assuming alternate paths exist).

- Protocol companions like DHCP (Dynamic Host Configuration Protocol) and DNS (Domain Name System) offer advanced functionality.

In the next sections, you will learn the basics of using TCP/IP, and then how to configure and test TCP/IP.

Reviewing TCP/IP Basics

TCP/IP requires an IP address and a subnet mask. You can also configure many other optional parameters, including the default gateway, DNS server settings, and WINS server settings.

IP Address

The *IP address* uniquely identifies your computer on the network. The IP address is a four-field, 32-bit address, separated by periods. Part of the address is used to identify your network address, and part of the address is used to identify the host (or local) computer's address.

If you use the Internet, then you should register your IP addresses with one of the Internet registration sites. There are three main classes of IP addresses. Depending on the class you use, different parts of the address show the network portion of the address and the host address, as illustrated in Figure 11.16.

FIGURE 11.16   IP class network and host addresses

 You can find more information about Internet registration at InterNIC's Web site, www.internic.net.

Table 11.2 shows the three classes of network addresses and the number of networks and hosts that are available for each network class.

TABLE 11.2 IP Class Assignments

Network Class	Address Range of First Field	Number of Networks Available	Number of Host Nodes Supported
A	1-126	126	16,777,214
B	128-191	16,384	65,534
C	192-223	2,097,152	254

Subnet Mask

The *subnet mask* is used to specify which part of the IP address is the network address and which part of the address is the host address. By default, the following subnet masks are applied:

Class A	255.0.0.0
Class B	255.255.0.0
Class C	255.255.255.0

By using 255, you are selecting the octet or octets (or in some cases, a piece of an octet) used to identify the network address. For example, in the class B network address 191.200.2.1, if the subnet mask is 255.255.0.0, then 191.200 is the network address and 2.1 is the host address.

Default Gateway

You configure a *default gateway* if the network contains routers. A router is a device that connects two or more network segments together. Routers function at the Network layer of the OSI model.

You can configure a Windows 2000 server to act as a router by installing two or more network cards in the server, attaching each network card to a different network segment, and then configuring each network card for the segment that it will attach to. You can also use third-party routers, which typically offer more features than Windows 2000 servers configured as routers.

As an example, suppose that your network is configured as shown in Figure 11.17. Network A uses the IP network address 131.1.0.0. Network B uses the IP network address 131.2.0.0. In this case, each network card in the router should be configured with an IP address from the segment that the network card is addressed to.

You configure the computers on each segment to point to the IP address of the network card on the router that is attached to their network segment. For example, in Figure 11.17, the computer W2K1 is attached to Network A. The default gateway that would be configured for this computer is 131.1.0.10. The computer W2K2 is attached to Network B. The default gateway that would be configured for this computer is 131.2.0.10.

FIGURE 11.17 Configuring default gateways

DNS Servers

DNS servers are used to resolve host names to IP addresses. This makes it easier for people to access domain hosts.

Do you know what the IP address is for the White House? It's 198.137.240.91. Do you know the domain host name of the White House? It's www.whitehouse.gov. You can understand why many people might not know the IP address but would know the domain host name.

When you access the Internet and type in www.whitehouse.gov, there are DNS servers that resolve the host name to the proper IP address. If you did not have access to a properly configured DNS server, you could configure a HOSTS file for your computer that contains the mappings of IP addresses to the domain hosts that you need to access.

WINS Servers

WINS servers are used to resolve NetBIOS names to IP addresses. Windows 2000 uses NetBIOS names in addition to host names to identify network computers. This is mainly for backward compatibility with

Windows NT 4, which used this addressing scheme extensively. When you attempt to access a computer using the NetBIOS name, the NetBIOS name must be able to be resolved to an IP address. This address resolution can be accomplished by using one of the following methods:

- Through a broadcast (if the computer you are trying to reach is on the same network segment)

- Through a WINS server

- Through an LMHOSTS file, which is a static mapping of IP addresses to NetBIOS computer names

Configuring TCP/IP

Depending on your network setup, TCP/IP configuration is done either manually or dynamically. You can also use advanced TCP/IP options to configure DNS and WINS settings.

Manual IP Configuration

You can manually configure IP if you know your IP address and subnet mask. If you are using optional components such as a default gateway or a DNS server, you need to know the IP addresses of the computers that host these services as well.

To manually configure IP, take the following steps:

1. From the Desktop, right-click My Network Places and choose Properties.

2. Right-click Local Area Connection and choose Properties.

3. In the Local Area Connection Properties dialog box, highlight Internet Protocol (TCP/IP) and click the Properties button.

4. The Internet Protocol (TCP/IP) Properties dialog box appears, as shown in Figure 11.18. Choose the Use the Following IP Address radio button.

5. In the appropriate text boxes, specify the IP address, subnet mask, and default gateway (optional) that you want to use.

FIGURE 11.18   The Internet Protocol (TCP/IP) Properties dialog box

   6. Optionally, select the Use the Following DNS Server Addresses radio
   button and specify a preferred and alternate DNS server in the corresponding text boxes.

   7. Click the OK button to save your settings and close the dialog box.

In Exercise 11.2, you will manually configure TCP/IP. This exercise
assumes that you have a network adapter installed in your computer.

If you are on a working network, consult your network administrator before
you make any changes to your TCP/IP configuration.

EXERCISE 11.2

Manually Configuring TCP/IP

1. From the Desktop, right-click My Network Places and choose Properties.

2. Right-click Local Area Connection and choose Properties.

EXERCISE 11.2 *(continued)*

3. In the Local Area Connection Properties dialog box, highlight Internet Protocol (TCP/IP) and click the Properties button.

4. In the Internet Protocol (TCP/IP) Properties dialog box, click the Use the Following IP Address radio button to select it.

5. In the IP Address text box, type **131.200.2.1**.

6. In the Subnet Mask text box, type **255.255.0.0**.

7. Click the OK button.

Advanced Configuration

Clicking the Advanced button in the Internet Protocol (TCP/IP) dialog box (see Figure 11.18) opens the Advanced TCP/IP Settings dialog box, shown in Figure 11.19. From this dialog box, you can configure advanced DNS and WINS settings.

FIGURE 11.19 The Advanced TCP/IP Settings dialog box

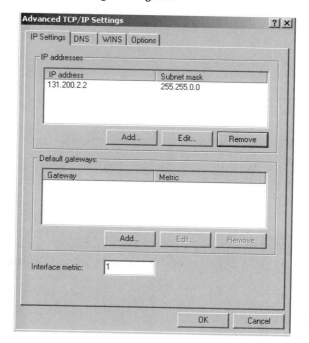

Advanced DNS Settings

You can configure additional DNS servers that can be used for name resolution and other advanced DNS settings through the DNS tab of the Advanced TCP/IP Settings dialog box, shown in Figure 11.20. The options in this dialog box are described in Table 11.3.

FIGURE 11.20 The DNS tab of the Advanced TCP/IP Settings dialog box

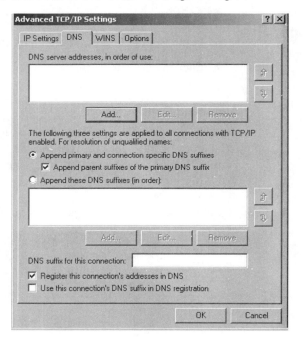

TABLE 11.3 Advanced DNS TCP/IP Settings Options

Option	Description
DNS Server Addresses, in Order of Use	Specifies the DNS servers that are used to resolve DNS queries. You can use the arrow buttons on the right side of the list box to move the servers up or down in the list.

TABLE 11.3 Advanced DNS TCP/IP Settings Options *(continued)*

Option	Description
Append Primary and Connection Specific DNS Suffixes	Specifies how unqualified domain names are resolved by DNS. For example, if your primary DNS suffix is TestCorp.com and you type ping lala, DNS will try to resolve the address as lala.TestCorp.com.
Append Parent Suffixes of the Primary DNS Suffix	Specifies whether name resolution includes the parent suffix for the primary domain DNS suffix, up to the second level of the domain name. For example, if your primary DNS suffix is SanJose.TestCorp.com and you type ping lala, DNS will try to resolve the address as lala.SanJose.TestCorp.com. If this doesn't work, DNS will try to resolve the address as lala.TestCorp.com.
Append These DNS Suffixes (in order)	Specifies the DNS suffixes that will be used to attempt to resolve unqualified name resolution. For example, if your primary DNS suffix is TestCorp.com and you type ping lala, DNS will try to resolve the address as lala.TestCorp.com. If you append the additional DNS suffix MyCorp.com and type ping lala, DNS will try to resolve the address as lala.TestCorp.com and lala.MyCorp.com.
DNS Suffix for This Connection	Specifies the DNS suffix for the computer. If this value is configured by a DHCP server and you specify a DNS suffix, it will override the value set by DHCP.
Register This Connection's Address in DNS	Specifies that the connection will try to register its address dynamically using the computer name that was specified through the Network Identification tab of the System Properties dialog box (accessed through the System icon in Control Panel).

TABLE 11.3 Advanced DNS TCP/IP Settings Options *(continued)*

Option	Description
Use This Connection's DNS Suffix in DNS Registration	Specifies that when the computer registers automatically with the DNS server, it should use the combination of the computer name and the DNS suffix.

Advanced WINS Settings

You can configure advanced WINS options through the WINS tab in the Advanced TCP/IP Settings dialog box, shown in Figure 11.21. The options in this dialog box are described in Table 11.4.

FIGURE 11.21 The WINS tab of the Advanced TCP/IP Settings dialog box

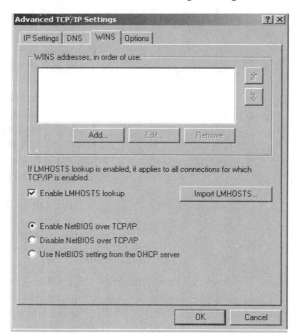

TABLE 11.4 Advanced WINS TCP/IP Settings Options

Option	Description
WINS Addresses, in Order of Use	Specifies the WINS servers that are used to re-solve WINS queries. You can use the arrow buttons on the right side of the list box to move the servers up or down in the list.
Enable LMHOSTS Lookup	Specifies whether an LMHOSTS file can be used for name resolution. If you configure this option, you can use the Import LMHOSTS button to import an LMHOSTS file to the computer.
Enable NetBIOS over TCP/IP	Allows you to use statically configured IP addresses so that the computer is able to communicate with pre-Windows 2000 computers.
Disable NetBIOS over TCP/IP	Allows you to disable NetBIOS over TCP/IP. Use this option only if your network includes only Windows 2000 clients or DNS-enabled clients.
Use NetBIOS Settings from the DHCP Server	Specifies that the computer should obtain its NetBIOS and WINS settings from the DHCP server.

Dynamic IP Configuration

Dynamic IP configuration assumes that you have a DHCP server on your network. DHCP servers are configured to provide DHCP clients with all of their IP configuration information automatically. By default, when TCP/IP is installed on a Windows 2000 Professional computer, the computer is configured for dynamic IP configuration.

The DHCP process is covered in detail in *MCSE: Windows 2000 Server Study Guide,* by Lisa Donald with James Chellis (Sybex, 2000).

If your computer is configured for manual IP configuration and you want to use dynamic IP configuration, take the following steps:

1. From the Desktop, right-click My Network Places and choose Properties.

2. Right-click Local Area Connection and choose Properties.

3. In the Local Area Connection Properties dialog box, highlight Internet Protocol (TCP/IP) and click the Properties button.

4. The Internet Protocol (TCP/IP) Properties dialog box appears (see Figure 11.18). Choose the Obtain an IP Address Automatically radio button. Then click the OK button.

Testing IP Configuration

After you have configured IP, you can test the IP configuration by using the IPCONFIG and PING commands.

The IPCONFIG Command

The *IPCONFIG* command displays your IP configuration. Table 11.5 lists the command switches that can be used with the IPCONFIG command.

TABLE 11.5   IPCONFIG Switches

Switch	Description
/all	Shows verbose information about your IP configuration, including your computer's physical address, the DNS server you are using, and whether you are using DHCP
/release	Releases an address that has been assigned through DHCP
/renew	Renews an address through DHCP

In Exercise 11.3, you will verify your configuration with the IPCONFIG command. This exercise assumes that you have a network adapter installed in your computer and have completed Exercise 11.2.

EXERCISE 11.3

Using the IPCONFIG Command

1. Select Start ➢ Programs ➢ Accessories ➢ Command Prompt.

2. In the Command Prompt dialog box, type **IPCONFIG** and press Enter. Note the IP address, which should be the address that you configured in Exercise 11.2.

3. In the Command Prompt dialog box, type **IPCONFIG /all** and press Enter. You now see more information.

The PING Command

The *PING* command is used to send an ICMP (Internet Control Message Protocol) echo request and echo reply to verify if the remote computer is available. The PING command has the following syntax:

```
PING IP address
```

For example, if your IP address is 131.200.2.30, type the following command:

```
PING 131.200.2.30
```

PING is useful for verifying connectivity between two hosts. For example, if you were having trouble connecting to a host on another network, you would use PING to verify that a valid communication path existed by pinging the following addresses:

- The loopback address, 127.0.0.1
- The local computer's IP address (you can verify this with IPCONFIG)
- The local router's (default gateway's) IP address
- The remote computer's IP address

If PING failed to get a reply from any of these addresses, you would have a starting point for troubleshooting the connection error.

Using NWLink IPX/SPX/NetBIOS

NWLink IPX/SPX/NetBIOS Compatible Transport is Microsoft's implementation of the Novell IPX/SPX (Internetwork Packet Exchange/Sequenced Packet Exchange) protocol stack. The Windows 2000 implementation of the IPX/SPX protocol stack adds NetBIOS support.

The main function of NWLink is to act as a transport protocol to route packets through internetworks. By itself, the NWLink protocol does not allow you to access NetWare File and Print Services. However, it does provide a method of transporting the data across the network. If you want to access NetWare File and Print Services, you need to install NWLink and Client Services for NetWare (software that works at the upper layers of the OSI model to allow access to File and Print Services).

One advantage of using NWLink is that it is easy to install and configure. The following sections describe how to install and configure this protocol.

Installing NWLink IPX/SPX/NetBIOS

To install NWLink, take the following steps:

1. From the Desktop, right-click My Network Places and choose Properties.

2. Right-click Local Area Connection and choose Properties.

3. In the Local Area Connection Properties dialog box, click the Install button.

4. The Select Network Component Type dialog box appears, as shown in Figure 11.22. Highlight Protocol and click the Add button.

FIGURE 11.22 The Select Network Component Type dialog box

5. The Select Network Protocol dialog box appears, as shown in Figure 11.23. Select NWLink IPX/SPX/NetBIOS Compatible Transport Protocol from the list. Then click the OK button.

FIGURE 11.23   The Select Network Protocol dialog box

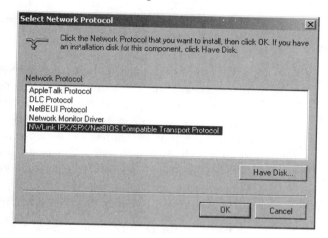

In Exercise 11.4, you will install the NWLink IPX/SPX protocol. This exercise assumes that you have a network adapter installed in your computer.

EXERCISE 11.4

Installing the NWLink IPX/SPX Protocol

1. From the Desktop, right-click My Network Places and choose Properties.

2. Right-click Local Area Connection and choose Properties.

3. In the Local Area Connection Properties dialog box, click the Install button.

4. In the Select Network Component Type dialog box, highlight Protocol and click the Add button.

5. In the Select Network Protocol dialog box, select NWLink IPX/SPX/ NetBIOS Compatible Transport Protocol and click the OK button.

Configuring NWLink IPX/SPX

The only options that you need to configure for NWLink are the *internal network number* and the *frame type*. Normally, you leave both settings at their default values.

The internal network number is usually used to identify NetWare file servers. It is also used if you are running File and Print Services for NetWare or are using IPX routing. Normally, you leave the internal network number at the default setting.

The frame type specifies how the data is packaged for transmission over the network. If the computers that are using NWLink use different frame types, they are not able to communicate with each other. By default, the frame type is set to Auto Detect, which will attempt to automatically choose a compatible frame type for your network. If you need to connect to servers that use different frame types, you should configure Manual Frame Type Detection, which will allow you to use a different frame type for each network.

To configure NWLink IPX/SPX, take the following steps:

1. From the Desktop, right-click My Network Places and select Properties.

2. Right-click Local Area Connection and select Properties.

3. In the Local Area Connection Properties dialog box, highlight NWLink IPX/SPX/NetBIOS Compatible Transport Protocol and click the Properties button.

4. The NWLink IPX/SPX/NetBIOS Compatible Transport Protocol Properties dialog box appears, as shown in Figure 11.24. In this dialog box, you can configure your internal network number and frame type.

FIGURE 11.24   The NWLink IPX/SPX/NetBIOS Compatible Transport Protocol Properties dialog box

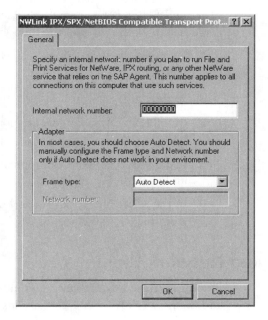

Using NetBEUI

NetBEUI stands for NetBIOS Extended User Interface. It was developed in the mid-1980s to connect workgroups that were running the OS/2 and LAN Manager operating systems.

The NetBEUI protocol offers the following advantages:

- It is easy to install.

- There are no configuration requirements.

- NetBEUI has self-tuning capabilities.

- NetBEUI has less overhead than TCP/IP and IPX/SPX and thus offers better performance.

- NetBEUI uses less memory than TCP/IP and IPX/SPX.

The main disadvantage of the NetBEUI protocol is that it is not routable, so you cannot use it in networks that have more than one network segment. Also, NetBEUI is not as commonly accepted as the TCP/IP protocol.

To install NetBEUI, take the following steps:

1. From the Desktop, right-click My Network Places and select Properties.

2. Right-click Local Area Connection and select Properties.

3. In the Local Area Connection Properties dialog box, click the Install button.

4. In the Select Network Component Type dialog box, highlight Protocol and click the Add button.

5. In the Select Network Protocol dialog box, select NetBEUI Protocol from the list and click the OK button.

Managing Network Bindings

Bindings are used to enable communication between your network adapter and the network protocols that are installed. If you have multiple network protocols installed on your computer, you can improve performance by binding the most commonly used protocols higher in the binding order.

To configure network bindings, access the Network and Dial-up Connections window and then select Advanced ➢ Advanced Settings from the main menu bar. The Adapters and Binding tab of the Advanced Settings dialog box appears, as shown in Figure 11.25. For each local area connection, if there are multiple protocols listed, you can use the arrow buttons on the right side of the dialog box to move the protocols to the top or bottom of the binding order.

FIGURE 11.25 The Adapters and Bindings tab of the Advanced Settings dialog box

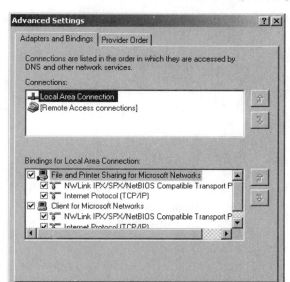

Summary

The chapter described how to manage network connections. We covered the following topics:

- How network protocols are used for network communications, including how data moves through a network and an overview of the OSI model.

- How to install, configure, and troubleshoot network adapters. You install adapters that are not Plug-and-Play through the Add/Remove Hardware Wizard. You configure a network adapter through its Properties dialog box.

- How to install, configure, and test network protocols. The default protocol installed with Windows 2000 Professional is TCP/IP. You can also install the NWLink IPX/SPX/NetBIOS and NetBEUI protocols.

Key Terms

Before you take the exam, be sure you're familiar with the following key terms:

Application layer

connection-oriented service

connectionless service

Data Link layer

default gateway

DNS (Domain Name System) server

driver

frame

frame type

internal network number

internetwork

IP address

IPCONFIG

Logical Link Control (LLC) sublayer

MAC address

Media Access Control (MAC) sublayer

NetBEUI

network adapter

Network layer

NWLink IPX/SPX/NetBIOS Compatible Transport

OSI (Open Systems Interconnection) model

Physical layer

PING

Presentation layer

Session layer

subnet mask

TCP/IP (Transmission Control Protocol/Internet Protocol)

Transport layer

WINS (Windows Internet Name Service) server

Review Questions

1. Which protocols are installed by default on a Windows 2000 Professional computer in a clean installation?

   A. TCP/IP

   B. NWLink IPX/SPX/NetBIOS

   C. NetBEUI

   D. NetBIOS

2. Which two options can be configured for the NWLink IPX/SPX/NetBIOS protocol on a Windows 2000 computer?

   A. NetBIOS address

   B. IPX address

   C. Internal network number

   D. Frame type

3. Which two options must be configured for TCP/IP in a manual configuration?

   A. IP address

   B. Default gateway

   C. Frame type

   D. Subnet mask

4. Which protocol would you use on your Windows 2000 Professional computer if you wanted the fastest service and did not need any routing services?

   A. TCP/IP

   B. NWLink IPX/SPX/NetBIOS

   C. NetBIOS

   D. NetBEUI

5. Which service must be installed on a Windows 2000 Server in order to use dynamic IP configuration on a Windows 2000 Professional computer?

    A. DHCP

    B. DNS

    C. WINS

    D. DLC

6. What is the name of the reference model that is used to define common networking concepts?

    A. ISO (International Standards Organization) model

    B. OSI (Open System Interconnection) model

    C. Networking reference model (NRM)

    D. Basic networking reference model (BNRM)

7. If you had a network adapter installed, and wanted to update the driver it was using, which tab would you use in the network adapter Properties dialog box?

    A. General

    B. Advanced

    C. Driver

    D. Resources

8. Which command would you use to test communications with another computer based on its IP address?

    A. IPCONFIG

    B. TESTIP

    C. PING

    D. GROPE

9. What is the primary function of an IP subnet mask?

   A. To specify which part of the IP address is the network address and which part of the IP address is the host address

   B. To specify how packets should be routed through an internetwork

   C. To determine the preferred DNS and WINS servers that exist on a network

   D. To specify whether you are using a dynamic or static configuration

10. What IP configuration would you set if you wanted to point your Windows 2000 Professional computer to a server that resolved NetBIOS computer names to IP addresses?

    A. DHCP

    B. WINS

    C. DNS

    D. NetBIOS

11. Julie is sitting at computer W2KP1. She wants to be able to access resources on W2KP2. Based on the following diagram, how should Julie configure her default gateway?

Network segment 131.1.1.0   Network segment 131.1.2.0

131.1.1.10   131.1.2.10

131.1.1.101   Router   131.1.2.101
W2KP1   W2KP2

    A. 131.1.1.0

    B. 131.1.1.10

    C. 131.1.2.0

    D. 131.1.2.10

12. Your primary DNS suffix is configured as acmetest.com. You want to access resources on the acmecorp.com domain without using fully qualified domain names. Which option should you use?

    A. Append Primary and Connection Specific DNS Suffixes

    B. Append These DNS Suffixes (in order)

    C. Configure This as a HOSTS File

    D. Configure This as an LMHOSTS File

13. When you try to access the sales.acmecorp.com server, you can access the server using the server's IP address, but not the fully qualified domain name. Which configuration file can you use to alleviate this problem?

    A. HOSTS

    B. LMHOSTS

    C. dns.txt

    D. wins.txt

14. Your domain suffix is configured as sanjose.acmecorp.com. Normally, you access resources from within your domain. Occasionally, you access resources in the acmecorp.com domain. You want to be able to access resources in either domain without specifying a fully qualified domain name. Which option should you use?

    A. Append Parent Suffixes of the Primary DNS Suffix

    B. Append Secondary DNS Suffix

    C. Append Child Suffixes of the Primary DNS Suffix

    D. Append Upstream Suffixes of the Primary DNS Suffix

15. Your network consists of Windows 2000 Professional computers and Windows NT 4 Workstation computers. You want to be able to access the Windows NT 4 Workstation computers by using their NetBIOS names. Your network does not have WINS servers configured. Which file should you configure and use?

    A. HOSTS

    B. LMHOSTS

    C. wins.cfg

    D. wins.txt

16. Your network consists of a variety of NetWare servers of many different versions. You have configured your Windows 2000 Professional computer with the NWLink IPX/SPX/NetBIOS Compatible Transport protocol and Client Services for NetWare. You only see some of the NetWare servers, but not the servers you need to access. What should you verify is configured for the NWLink IPX/SPX/NetBIOS Compatible Transport protocol?

    A. Make sure that you have configured the proper internal network number.

    B. Make sure that you use automatic frame type detection.

    C. Make sure that you use manual frame types and that you have configured your computer to use the same frame type as the NetWare server you are trying to access.

    D. Make sure that you have configured your default gateway properly.

17. You have two DHCP servers on your network. Your computer accidentally received the wrong IP configuration from a DHCP server that was misconfigured. The DHCP server with the incorrect configuration has been disabled. What command would you use to release and renew your computer's DHCP configuration?

    A. IPCONFIG

    B. DHCPRECON

    C. RELEASE

    D. IPADJUST

18. You are considering using the NetBEUI protocol on your Windows 2000 Professional computer. Which of the following options is *not* an advantage of NetBEUI?

A. It is easy to install.

B. It is a routable protocol.

C. It is self-configuring.

D. It uses less memory than TCP/IP and IPX/SPX.

19. You are considering using the TCP/IP protocol on your Windows 2000 Professional computer. Which of the following options is *not* an advantage of TCP/IP?

A. It is the most commonly used and widely supported network protocol.

B. It is designed to be a fault-tolerant network protocol.

C. It is scalable to small and large networks.

D. It uses less overhead than protocols such as NetBEUI and IPX/SPX.

20. Your Windows 2000 Professional computer is configured with TCP/IP, NWLink IPX/SPX/NetBIOS Compatible Transport, and NetBEUI. TCP/IP is your most commonly used network protocol. You want to configure your network bindings so that the TCP/IP protocol is listed first. How do you configure network bindings in Windows 2000?

A. In the Network and Dial-up Connections window, select Advanced, then Advanced Settings.

B. In the network adapter Properties dialog box, click the Bindings tab.

C. In the network adapter Properties dialog box, click the Advanced tab, then the Bindings button.

D. This is only configurable through the Registry.

Answers to Review Questions

1. A. The only protocol that is installed by default on a Windows 2000 Professional computer during a clean installation is TCP/IP.

2. C, D. The only options that can be configured for NWLink IPX/SPX/ NetBIOS are the internal network number and frame type. You normally leave these configurations at their default settings.

3. A, D. In a manual IP configuration, you must specify the IP address and subnet mask. The IP configuration only requires a default gateway if you will be routing packets between two or more network segments. Frame type is not an option that is used by IP (it is used by NWLink IPX/SPX/NetBIOS).

4. D. NetBEUI is the fastest and most efficient protocol if you do not require routing services.

5. A. DHCP (Dynamic Host Configuration Protocol) is used to dynamically assign and configure IP. DNS (Domain Name Service) is used to resolve domain names to IP addresses. WINS (Windows Internet Name Service) is used to resolve NetBIOS names to IP addresses. The DLC (Data Link Control) protocol is most commonly used to communicate between a host and a printer.

6. B. The OSI model is a theoretical model of networking that is used to make networking easier to understand and modularize. The ISO specified the OSI model.

7. C. You use the Driver tab to uninstall or update a device driver.

8. C. The PING command is used to send an ICMP echo request and echo reply between two IP hosts to test whether or not a valid communication path exits.

9. A. The subnet mask is used to specify which part of the address is the network address and which part of the address is the host or client address.

10. B. You use WINS servers to resolve NetBIOS computer names to IP addresses. DHCP servers are used to dynamically assign the IP configuration. DNS servers are used to resolve domain names to IP addresses. Windows 2000 does not use anything called a NetBIOS server.

11. B. Julie needs to configure the default gateway with the IP address of the router connection that is attached to her subnet, 131.1.1.10.

12. B. The Append These DNS Suffixes (in order) option (in the DNS tab of the Advanced TCP/IP Settings dialog box) specifies the DNS suffixes that will be used for unqualified name resolution. For example, if your primary DNS suffix is TestCorp.com and you type ping lala, DNS will try to resolve the address as lala.TestCorp.com. If you append the additional DNS suffix MyCorp.com and type ping lala, DNS will try to resolve the address as lala.TestCorp.com and lala.MyCorp.com.

13. A. If you do not have access to a properly configured DNS server, you can use a HOSTS file to map IP addresses to domain host names.

14. A. If you use the Append Primary and Connection Specific DNS Suffixes option (in the DNS tab of the Advanced TCP/IP Settings dialog box), you can also configure the Append Parent Suffixes of the Primary DNS Suffix option. This option specifies whether name resolution includes the parent suffix for the primary domain DNS suffix, up to the second level of the domain name.

15. B. If your network does not use a WINS server, you can configure an LMHOSTS file to map IP addresses to NetBIOS computer names.

16. C. The NetWare server you need to connect to may be configured with different frame type. You should find out what frame type the server is using and configure the Windows 2000 computer with the same frame type.

17. A. You can release your DHCP configuration with the IPCONFIG /release command and renew your DHCP configuration with the IPCONFIG /renew command.

18. B. NetBEUI is not a routable protocol.

19. D. The TCP/IP protocol uses more overhead than the NetBEUI protocol.

20. A. To configure network bindings, you open the Network and Dial-up Connections window and select Advanced ≻ Advanced Settings. You can specify the binding order in the Adapters and Bindings tab of the Advanced Settings dialog box.

Chapter 12

Managing Printing

MICROSOFT EXAM OBJECTIVES COVERED IN THIS CHAPTER

✓ **Connect to local and network print devices.**

- Manage printers and print jobs.
- Control access to printers by using permissions.
- Connect to a local print device.

One common network management task is setting up and using printers. To manage printing, you need an understanding of the printing process and the terminology associated with the process.

The process of creating, managing, and deleting printers is fairly easy. When you create printers, you use a Wizard, which leads you through each step of the configuration. Anything that is not configured through the Add Printer Wizard can be configured through the printer's properties. You can also manage printing options such as pausing and deleting print jobs for the entire printer or for specific print documents.

In this chapter, you will learn the basics of Windows 2000 Professional printing, how to set up and configure printers, and how to manage printers and print jobs.

The printing processes used by Windows 2000 Server and Windows 2000 Professional are the same.

Reviewing Printing Basics

Before you learn about the specifics of Windows 2000 printing, you should have an understanding of basic network printing principles. Table 12.1 defines the terms that relate to network printing, and the following sections describe the printing process and the roles of print devices and printers.

TABLE 12.1 Windows 2000 Printing Terminology

Term	Definition
Printer	The software interface between the *physical printer* (the print device) and the operating system. You can create printers through the Printers folder. This is also referred to as a *logical printer*.
Print device	The actual physical printer or hardware device that produces the printed output.
Print server	The computer on which the printer has been defined. When you send a job to a network printer, you are actually sending it to the print server first.
Print spooler	A directory or folder on the print server that stores the print jobs until they can be printed. Your print server and print spooler must have enough hard disk space to hold all of the print jobs that could be pending at any given time. This is also referred to as a *print queue*.
Print processor	The process that determines whether or not a print job needs further processing once that job has been sent to the spooler. The processing (also called *rendering*) is used to format the print job so that it can print correctly at the print device.
Printer pool	*A configuration that allows you to use* one printer for multiple print devices. A printer pool is useful when you have multiple printers that use the same print driver and are in the same location. By using printer pools, users can send their print jobs to the first available printer.
Print driver	The specific software that understands your print device. Each print device has its own command set, and each print device has an associated print driver.
Physical port	The port through which a printer is directly connected to a computer, either a serial (COM) or parallel (LPT) port.

TABLE 12.1 Windows 2000 Printing Terminology *(continued)*

Term	Definition
Logical port	The port through which a printer with a network card is attached to a network. *Logical ports* are much faster than *physical ports*. They also are not restricted by parallel and serial cable distance limitations, which apply to printers connected to a PC's parallel or serial port.
Local printer	A printer that uses a physical port and that has not been shared. If a printer is defined as local, the only users who can use the printer are the local users of the computer that the printer is attached to.
Network printer	A *printer* that is available to local and network users. A network printer can use either a physical or logical port.

Reviewing the Windows 2000 Printing Process

Printing is a common problem area in many networks. To troubleshoot the problems related to the Windows 2000 printing process, you need to understand the steps involved in the process. A simple overview of the printing process is illustrated in Figure 12.1.

FIGURE 12.1 A simple overview of the Windows 2000 printing process

Print Server
Logical Printer
Print Driver

Print Device

Client

1. Client creates document.
2. Client connects to network printer (downloads print driver).
3. Print job is sent to spooler.
4. Job is sent to print device.

The following steps are involved in the printing process:

1. From the client, the user chooses to print. On any Windows platform, the print request is passed to the *Graphics Device Interface (GDI)*. The GDI calls the *print driver*. If the user is accessing the printer for the first time, the print driver is loaded into the client's memory from the *print server*. The print driver will stay in memory until the computer is turned off or a newer print driver is detected on the print server. The GDI is also responsible for processing print jobs for the appropriate *print device*.

2. The print job is sent to the computer's local *print spooler*, which in turn sends the job over the network to the print server.

3. The router at the print server receives the print job.

4. The router passes the print job to the print spooler on the print server, which spools the print job to a disk.

5. The *print processor* on the spooler analyzes the print job. If the job needs any further processing, the print processor processes the job so that the job will print correctly.

6. If specified, the separator page processor adds a *separator page* to the front of the print job.

7. The print job is passed to the print manager, which determines when the job should print and directs the print job to the correct port.

8. The print job goes to the print device, and the job prints.

In order to print to a printer, you must have that printer's driver to tell the application how to send the print job. Windows 2000 Professional clients automatically download the print driver from the print server each time they send a print job. If the print driver is updated on the print server, the next time the user sends a job to the printer, the driver is automatically updated.

With Windows 2000 Professional, you can also specify drivers for automatic download for other Windows clients. See the "Sharing Properties" section later in this chapter for details.

Understanding the Roles of Print Devices and Printers

A *print device* is the actual physical printer or hardware device that does the printing. In Windows 2000 terminology, a *printer* is the software interface between the print device and the operating system.

When you set up your computer or your network, you can determine how many print devices you have by counting the devices you can see and touch. Printers are a bit trickier to enumerate, because you can configure them in several ways:

- One printer per print device

- One printer for multiple print devices, called *printer pooling*

- Multiple printers for a single print device, a configuration usually set up to allow print scheduling

You'll learn how to configure printer pools and set up print scheduling (by configuring the printer's availability) in the "Managing Printer Properties" section later in this chapter.

Setting Up Printers

Before you can access your physical print device under Windows 2000 Professional, you must first create a logical printer. To create a printer, you use the Add Printer Wizard, which guides you through all of the steps. In order to create a new printer in Windows 2000 Professional, you must be logged on as a member of the Administrators or Power Users group.

Microsoft
✓ *Exam*
Objective

Connect to local and network print devices.

- Manage printers and print jobs.

This chapter covers the material related to managing printing for the "Connect to local and network print devices" objective. The subobjective for connecting to an Internet printer is covered in Chapter 13, "Dial-Up Networking and Internet Productivity."

The computer on which you run the Add Printer Wizard and create the printer automatically becomes the print server for that printer. As the print server, the computer must have enough processing power to support incoming print jobs and enough disk space to hold all of the print jobs that will be queued.

To create a new *local printer* or *network printer*, take the following steps:

1. Select Start ➤ Settings ➤ Printers to open the Printers folder, as shown in Figure 12.2. Then double-click the Add Printer icon.

FIGURE 12.2   The Printers folder with the Add Printer icon

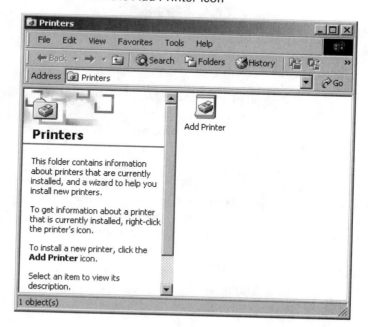

2. The Add Printer Wizard starts, as shown in Figure 12.3. Click the Next button to continue.

FIGURE 12.3 The Welcome to the Add Printer Wizard dialog box

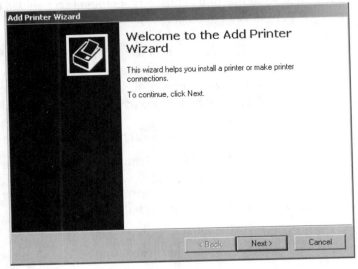

3. The Local or Network Printer dialog box appears, as shown in Figure 12.4. Choose Local Printer if you have a printer directly attached to computer, or choose Network Printer if you have a printer attached to a network. Then click the Next button. If you have a Plug-and-Play print device attached to your computer, it should be automatically detected, and you can skip to step 6. If your print device is not attached or recognized, deselect the Automatically Detect and Install My Plug and Play Printer option and continue with the following steps to manually specify the print device configuration.

FIGURE 12.4   The Local or Network Printer dialog box

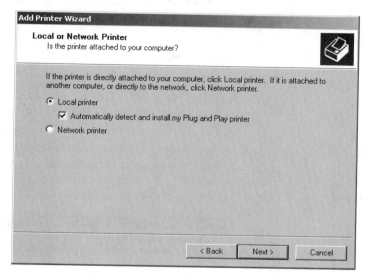

4. If you chose to manually configure a print device, the Select the Printer Port dialog box appears, as shown in Figure 12.5. Specify the port the print device will use and then click the Next button.

FIGURE 12.5   The Select the Printer Port dialog box

NOTE

If you have already installed this driver on your computer, the dialog box that lists the printer manufacturers and models will also include a Windows Update button next to the Have Disk button.

5. A dialog box that lists printer manufacturers and models appears, as shown in Figure 12.6. Specify the print device manufacturer and model and then click the Next button. If the print device is not listed, click the Have Disk button and insert the disk that contains the driver that came with your print device.

FIGURE 12.6 Selecting the printer manufacturer and model

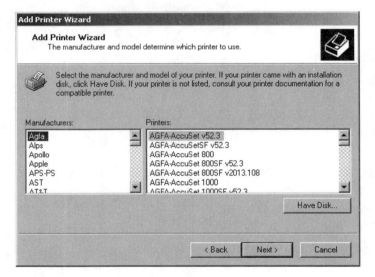

6. The Name Your Printer dialog box appears, as shown in Figure 12.7. Accept the default name or enter another name for your printer and click the Next button.

FIGURE 12.7   The Name Your Printer dialog box

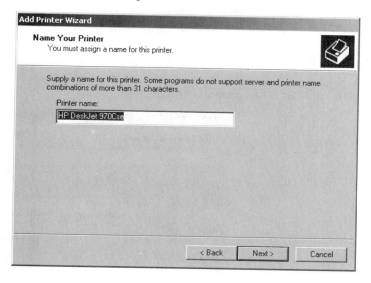

7. The Printer Sharing dialog box appears, as shown in Figure 12.8. You can choose to not share the printer or to share the printer. If you choose to share the printer, specify a share name to be used by the printer. Then click the Next button.

FIGURE 12.8   The Printer Sharing dialog box

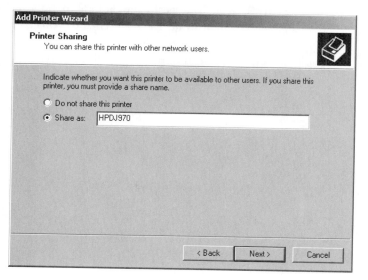

8. If you chose to share the printer, the Location and Comment dialog box appears, as shown in Figure 12.9. In this dialog box, specify location information and a comment. Network users can use this information to search for a description of the printer's location, configuration, and capabilities. Click the Next button.

FIGURE 12.9 The Location and Comment dialog box

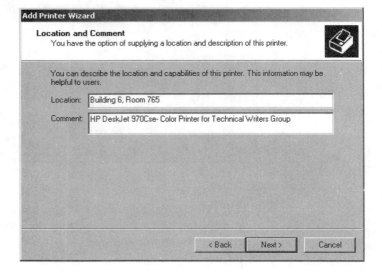

9. The Print Test Page dialog box appears, as shown in Figure 12.10. If the print device is attached to your computer, you should print a test page to verify that everything is configured properly. Otherwise, you should skip this step. Click the Next button to continue.

FIGURE 12.10   The Print Test Page dialog box

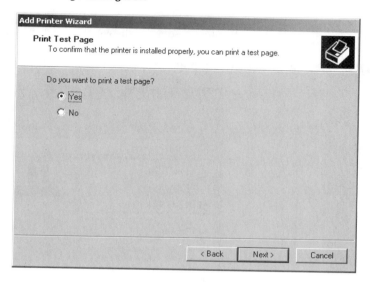

10. The Completing the Add Printer Wizard dialog box appears, as shown
     in Figure 12.11. This gives you a chance to verify that all of the printer
     settings have been set correctly. If there are any problems, click the
     Back button to make corrections. If everything is configured properly,
     click the Finish button.

FIGURE 12.11   The Completing the Add Printer Wizard dialog box

To complete the setup process, the Add Printer Wizard will copy files (if necessary) and create your printer. An icon for your new printer will appear in the Printers folder, as shown in Figure 12.12.

FIGURE 12.12 An icon for a printer in the Printers folder

 If you are creating a printer that is attached to a computer that is running Windows 2000 Professional, you will most likely be configuring a printer for personal use or limited network access.

In Exercise 12.1, you will create printers using the Add Printer Wizard.

EXERCISE 12.1

Creating Printers

In this exercise, you will create two local printers—one to share and one that will not be shared. You will manually specify their print device configuration.

Adding the First Printer

1. Select Start ➤ Settings ➤ Printers to open the Printers folder. Then double-click the Add Printer icon.

2. The Add Printer Wizard starts. Click the Next button to continue.

3. In the Local or Network Printer dialog box, select the Local Printer radio button. Make sure that the Automatically Detect and Install My Plug and Play Printer check box is not checked (unless you have a print device attached to your computer) and click the Next button.

4. In the Select the Printer Port dialog box, select the Use the Following Port radio button, select LPT1 in the list box, and click the Next button.

5. In the next dialog box, choose HP in the Manufacturers list box and HP DeskJet 970Cse in the Printers list box. Then click the Next button.

6. In the Name Your Printer dialog box, leave the default name of HP DeskJet 970Cse and click the Next button.

7. In the Printer Sharing dialog box, select the Share As radio button and type **HPDJ970** in the text box. Then click the Next button.

8. In the Location and Comment dialog box, type **Training Room** in the Location text box and **Color Printer** in the Comment text box. Click the Next button.

9. In the next dialog box, select the No radio button to skip printing a test page and click the Next button.

10. In the Completing the Add Printer Wizard dialog box, click the Finish button.

Adding the Second Printer

1. In the Printers folder, double-click the Add Printer icon.

2. When the Add Printer Wizard starts, click the Next button to continue.

3. In the Local or Network Printer dialog box, select the Local Printer radio button. Make sure that Automatically Detect and Install My Plug and Play Printer is not checked (unless you have a print device attached to your computer) and click the Next button.

4. In the Select the Printer Port dialog box, select the Use the Following Port radio button, select LPT2 in the list box, and click the Next button.

5. In next dialog box, choose HP in the Manufacturers list box and HP LaserJet 4 in the Printers list box. Then click the Next button.

6. In the Name Your Printer dialog box, leave the default name of HP LaserJet 4 and click the Next button.

7. In the Printer Sharing dialog box, select the Do Not Share This Printer radio button and click the Next button.

8. In the Print Test Page dialog box, select No to skip printing a test page and click the Next button.

9. In the Completing the Add Printer Wizard dialog box, click the Finish button.

Managing Printer Properties

Printer properties allow you to configure options such as the printer name, whether or not the printer is shared, and printer security. To access the printer Properties dialog box, open the Printers folder, right-click the printer you want to manage, and choose Properties from the pop-up menu.

Microsoft
Exam
Objective

Connect to local and network print devices.

- Manage printers and print jobs.

- Control access to printers by using permissions.

The printer Properties dialog box has six tabs: General, Sharing, Ports, Advanced, Security, and Device Settings. The following sections describe the properties on these tabs.

> **NOTE** The Properties dialog boxes for some printers will contain additional tabs to allow advanced configuration of the printer. For example, if you install an HP DeskJet 970Cse printer, its Properties dialog box will have additional tabs for Color Management and Services.

Configuring General Properties

The General tab of the printer Properties dialog box, shown in Figure 12.13, contains information about the printer. It also lets you set printing preferences and print test pages.

FIGURE 12.13 The General tab of the printer Properties dialog box

The name of the printer, the location of the printer, and comments about the printer shown here reflect your entries when you set up the printer (as described in the previous section). You can add or change this information in the text boxes.

Beneath the Comment box, you see the model of the printer. The items listed in the Features section of the dialog box depend on the model and driver you are using. The following are some examples of printer features:

- Color printing support

- Double-sided printing support

- Stapling support

- The maximum number of pages that can be printed per minute (ppm)

- The maximum resolution for the printer, in dots per inch (dpi)

At the bottom of the dialog box, you see the Printing Preferences and Print Test Page buttons. Their functions are described in the following sections.

Setting Printing Preferences

Clicking the Printing Preferences button brings up the Printing Preferences dialog box, which allows you to specify the layout of the paper, page order, and paper source. This dialog box has Layout and Paper Quality tabs, as well as an Advanced button that allows you to configure more printer options.

Layout Settings

The Layout tab of the Printing Preferences dialog box, shown in Figure 12.14, allows you to specify the orientation and page order. Your choices for the Orientation setting are Portrait (vertical) or Landscape (horizontal).

FIGURE 12.14 The Layout tab of the Printing Preferences dialog box

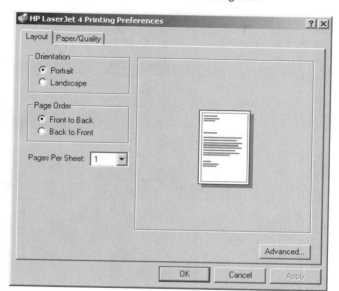

The Page Order setting is new to Windows 2000. It specifies whether you want page 1 of the document to be on the top of the stack (Front to Back) or page 1 of the document to be on the bottom of the stack (Back to Front).

In Windows NT 4, your documents always printed back to front, meaning page 1 printed first. At the end of the print job, you needed to reorder your pages.

The Pages Per Sheet setting determines how many pages should be printed on a single page. You might use this feature if you were printing a book and wanted two pages to be printed side by side on a single page.

Paper/Quality Settings

The Paper/Quality tab of the Printing Preferences dialog box allows you to configure properties that relate to the paper and quality of a print job. The options that are available depend on the features of your printer. For example, a printer may have only one option, such as Paper Source. For an HP DeskJet

970Cse printer, you can configure Paper Source, Media, Quality Settings, and Color options, as shown in Figure 12.15.

FIGURE 12.15 The Paper/Quality tab of the Printing Preferences dialog box

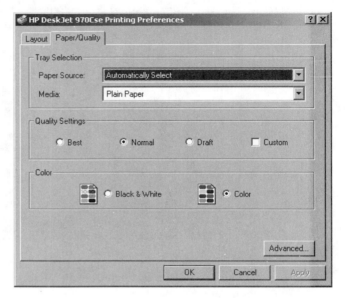

Advanced Settings

Clicking the Advanced button in the lower-right corner of the Printing Preferences dialog box brings up the Advanced Options dialog box, as shown in Figure 12.16. Here, you can configure printer options such as Paper/Output, Graphic, Document Options, and Printer Features. The availability of these options depends on the specific print driver you are using.

FIGURE 12.16 The Advanced Options dialog box

Printing a Test Page

The Print Test Page button at the bottom of the General tab of the printer Properties tab allows you to print a test page. This option is especially useful in troubleshooting printing problems. For example, you might use the Print Test Page option in a situation where no print driver is available for a print device and you want to try to use a compatible print driver. If the print job doesn't print or doesn't print correctly (it might print just one character per page, for example), you will know that the print driver isn't compatible.

Configuring Sharing Properties

The Sharing tab of the printer Properties dialog box, shown in Figure 12.17, allows you to specify whether the computer will be configured as a local printer or as a shared network printer. If you choose to share the printer, you also need to specify a share name, which will be seen by the network users.

FIGURE 12.17 The Sharing tab of the printer Properties dialog box

The other option that can be configured through the Sharing tab is driver support for print clients other than Windows 2000 clients. This is a significant feature of Windows 2000 Professional print support, because it allows you to specify print drivers for other clients to automatically download. By default, the only driver that is loaded is the Intel driver for Windows 2000. To provide the additional drivers for the clients, click the Additional Drivers button at the bottom of the Sharing tab. This brings up the Additional Drivers dialog box, as shown in Figure 12.18.

FIGURE 12.18 The Additional Drivers dialog box

Windows 2000 Professional supports adding print drivers for the following platforms:

- Windows 95 or Windows 98 Intel

- Windows NT 3.1 Alpha, Intel, and MIPS

- Windows NT 3.5 or 3.51 Alpha, Intel, MIPS, and PowerPC

- Windows NT 4.0 Alpha, Intel, MIPS, and PowerPC

In Exercise 12.2, you will share an existing printer. This exercise assumes that you have completed Exercise 12.1.

EXERCISE 12.2

Sharing an Existing Printer

1. Select Start ➢ Settings ➢ Printers to open the Printers folder.

2. Right-click HP LaserJet 4, choose Properties, and click the Sharing tab.

3. Click the Shared As radio button. Type **HPLJ4** in the text box.

4. Click the Apply button, then click the OK button to close the dialog box.

Configuring Port Properties

A port is defined as the interface, which allows the computer to communicate with the print device.

Windows 2000 Professional supports local ports (physical ports) and standard *TCP/IP ports* (logical ports). Local ports are used when the printer attaches directly to the computer. In the case where you are running Windows 2000 Professional in a small workgroup, you would likely run printers attached to the local port LPT1.

Standard TCP/IP ports are used when the printer is attached to the network by installing a network card in the printer. The advantage of network printers is that they are faster than local printers and can be located anywhere on the network. When you specify a TCP/IP port, you must know the IP address of the network printer.

The Ports tab, shown in Figure 12.19, allows you to configure all of the ports that have been defined for printer use. Along with deleting and configuring existing ports, you can also set up printer pooling and redirect print jobs to another printer, as described in the next sections.

The Enable Bidirectional Support option on the Ports tab will be available if your printer supports this feature. It allows the printer to communicate with the computer. For example, your printer may be able to send more informative printer errors.

FIGURE 12.19 The Ports tab of the printer Properties dialog box

Printer Pooling

Printer pools are used to associate multiple physical print devices with a single logical printer, as illustrated in Figure 12.20. You would use a printer pool if you had multiple physical printers in the same location that were the same type and could use a single print driver. The advantage of using a printer pool is that the first available print device will print your job. This is useful in situations where there is a group of print devices shared by a group of users, such as a secretarial pool.

FIGURE 12.20 Printer pooling

Print Server
Printer - Sales

To configure a printer pool, click the Enable Printer Pooling check box at the bottom of the Ports tab and then check all of the ports that the print devices in the printer pool will attach to. If you do not select the Enable Printer Pooling option, you can select only one port per printer.

All of the print devices in a printer pool must be able to use the same print driver.

Redirecting Print Jobs to Another Printer

If your print device fails, you can redirect all of the jobs that are scheduled to be printed to that print device to another print device that has been configured as a printer. For this redirection to work, the new print device must be able to use the same print driver as the old print device.

To redirect print jobs, click the Add Port button in the Ports tab, highlight New Port, and choose New Port Type. In the Port Name dialog box, type the UNC name of the printer that you want to redirect the jobs to, in the format *computername**printer*.

Configuring Advanced Properties

The Advanced tab of the printer Properties dialog box, shown in Figure 12.21, allows you to control many characteristics of the printer. You can configure the following options:

- The availability of the printer
- The priority of the printer
- The driver the printer will use
- Spooling properties
- How documents are printed
- Printing defaults
- The print processor that will be used
- The separator page

FIGURE 12.21   The Advanced tab of the printer Properties dialog box

These options are covered in the following sections.

In Windows NT 4, the options that are in the Windows 2000 Professional Advanced tab of the printer Properties dialog box were located in the General tab and the Scheduling tab of the printer Properties dialog box.

Printer Availability

Availability, or scheduling, specifies when a printer will service jobs. Usually, you control availability when you have multiple printers that use a single print device. For example, you might use this option if you have large jobs that tie up the print device for extended periods of time. You could schedule the large jobs to print only during a specified time, say between 10:00 P.M. and 4:00 A.M. To set this up, you could create two printers on the same port, such as printers named LASER and REPORTS on the LPT1 port. (Both printers are on the same port since the same physical print device services them.) Configure LASER to always be available. Configure REPORTS to be available only from 10:00 P.M. to 4:00 A.M. You would then instruct your users to send short jobs to LASER and long jobs to REPORTS, with the understanding that print jobs sent to REPORTS print only during the specified hours.

By default, the Always Available radio button in the Advanced tab is selected, so that users can use the printer 24 hours a day. To limit the printer's availability, select the Available From radio button and specify the range of time when the printer should be available.

Printer Priority

Priority is another option that you might configure if you have multiple printers that use a single print device. When you set priority, you specify how jobs are directed to the print device. For example, you might use this option when two groups share a printer and you need to control the priority in which print jobs are serviced by the print device. In the Advanced tab of the printer Properties dialog box, you can set the Priority value to a number from 1 to 99, with 1 as the lowest priority and 99 as the highest priority.

As an example, suppose that a single print device is used by the accounting department. The managers in the accounting department always want their print jobs to print before the jobs created by the other workers in the accounting department. To configure this arrangement, you could create a printer called MANAGERS on port LPT1 with a priority of 99. You would then create a printer on port LPT1 called WORKERS with a priority of 1. Through the Security tab of the printer Properties dialog box, you would allow only managers to use the MANAGERS printer and allow the other accounting users to use the WORKERS printer (Security tab options are covered later in this chapter). When the print manager polled for print jobs, it would always poll the higher-priority printer for print jobs before the lower-priority printer.

 The print manager is responsible for polling the print queue for print jobs and directing the print jobs to the correct port.

Print Driver

The Driver setting in the Advanced tab shows the driver that is associated with your printer. If you have configured multiple printers on the computer, you can select to use any of the installed drivers. Clicking the New Driver button starts the Add Printer Driver Wizard, which allows you to update or add new print drivers.

Spooling

When you configure spooling options, you specify whether print jobs are spooled or sent directly to the printer. Spooling means that print jobs are saved to disk in a queue before they are sent to the printer. Consider spooling as the traffic controller of printing—it keeps all of the print jobs from trying to print at the same time.

By default, spooling is enabled, with printing beginning immediately. Your other option is to wait until the last page is spooled before printing. An analogy for these choices is the actions you can take in a grocery store cashier line. Let's say you have an entire cart full of groceries and the guy behind you has only a few things. Even if you've started loading your groceries onto the belt, as long as the cashier hasn't started with your items, you can choose to let the person with fewer items go before you, or you can make him wait. If the cashier has already started totaling your groceries, then you don't have that choice. Windows 2000 Professional spooling options allow you to configure your print environment for similar situations.

In the Advanced tab, you can leave the Start Printing Immediately option selected, or you can choose the Start Printing After Last Page Is Spooled option. If you choose the latter option, a smaller print job that finishes spooling first will print before your print job, even if your job started spooling before it did. If you specify Start Printing Immediately, the smaller job will need to wait until your print job is complete.

The other main option is to Print Directly to the Printer, which bypasses spooling altogether. This option doesn't work well in a multiuser environment, where multiple print jobs are sent to the same device. However, it is useful in troubleshooting printer problems. If you can print to a print device directly, but you can't print through the spooler, then you know that your spooler is corrupt or has other problems.

Print Options

The Advanced tab contains check boxes for four print options:

- The Hold Mismatched Documents option is useful when you're using multiple forms with a printer. By default, this feature is disabled, and jobs are printed on a first-in-first-out (FIFO) basis. For example, you might enable this option if you need to print on both plain paper and certificate forms. Then all the jobs with the same form will print first.

- The Print Spooled Documents First option specifies that the spooler print jobs that have completed spooling before large jobs that are still spooling, even if the large print job that is still spooling has a higher priority. By default, this option is enabled, which increases printer efficiency.

- The Keep Printed Documents option specifies that print jobs should not be deleted from the print spooler (queue) when they are finished printing. You normally want to delete the print jobs as they print, because saving print jobs can take up a lot of disk space. By default, this option is disabled.

- The Enable Advanced Printing Features option specifies that any advanced features that your printer supports, such as Page Order and Pages Per Sheet, should be enabled. By default, this option is enabled. You would disable these features if there were compatibility problems. For example, if you are using the driver for a similar print device that does not support all of the features of the print device that the driver was written for, you should disable the advanced printing features.

Enabling the Keep Printed Documents option can be useful if you need to identify the source or other attributes of a finished print job. For example, this option helped track down a person who had been sending nasty notes to a co-worker. The workers knew that the notes were being printed on the company laser printer. Since the print queue was on an NTFS volume, the administrator enabled the Keep Printed Documents option and was able to identify the offender through the owner attribute of the file.

Printing Defaults

The Printing Defaults button in the lower-left corner of the Advanced tab calls up the Printing Preferences dialog box (see Figure 12.14, earlier in the chapter). This is the same dialog box that appears when you click the Printing Preferences button in the General tab of the printer Properties dialog box, and its options were covered in the "Configuring General Properties" section earlier in this chapter.

Print Processor

Print processors are used to specify whether Windows 2000 Professional needs to do additional processing to print jobs. The five print processors supported by Windows 2000 Professional are listed in Table 12.2.

TABLE 12.2 Print Processors supported by Windows 2000

RAW	Makes no changes to the print document
RAW (FF appended)	Makes no changes to the print document except to always add a form-feed character
RAW (FF Auto)	Makes no changes to the print document except to try to detect if a form-feed character needs to be added

TABLE 12.2 Print Processors supported by Windows 2000 *(continued)*

NT EMF	Generally spools documents that are sent from other Windows 2000 clients
TEXT	Interprets all of the data as plain text, and the printer will print the data using standard text commands

To modify your Print Processor settings, click the Print Processor button at the bottom of the Advanced tab to open the Print Processor dialog box, shown in Figure 12.22. You would generally leave the default settings in this dialog box, unless otherwise directed by the print device manufacturer.

FIGURE 12.22 The Print Processor dialog box

Separator Pages

Separator pages are used at the beginning of each document to identify the user who submitted the print job. If your printer is not shared, a separator page is generally a waste of paper. If the printer is shared by many users, the separator page can be useful for distributing finished print jobs.

To add a separator page, click the Separator Page button in the lower-right corner of the Advanced tab of the printer Properties dialog box. This brings up the Separator Page dialog box, shown in Figure 12.23. Click the Browse button to locate and select the separator page file that you want to use. Windows 2000 Professional supplies the Separator files listed in Table 12.3, which are stored in *Windir*\System32.

FIGURE 12.23   The Separator Page dialog box

TABLE 12.3   Separator Page Files

Separator Page File	Description
pcl.sep	Used to send a separator page on a dual-language HP printer after switching the printer to PCL (Printer Control Language), which is a common printing standard
pscript.sep	Does not send a separator page, but switches the computer to PostScript printing mode
sysprint.sep	Used by PostScript printers to send a separator page
sysprintj.sep	Same as sysprint.sep, but with support for Japanese characters

You can also create custom separator pages. For more information about creating separator pages, refer to the Windows 2000 Resource Kit.

In Exercise 12.3, you will configure some advanced printer properties. This exercise assumes you have completed Exercise 12.2.

EXERCISE 12.3

Managing Advanced Printer Properties

1. Select Start ➢ Settings ➢ Printers to open the Printers folder.

2. Right-click HP LaserJet 4, choose Properties, and click the Advanced tab.

3. Click the Available From radio button and specify that the printer is available from 12:00 A.M. to 6:00 A.M.

4. Click the Start Printing After Last Page Is Spooled radio button.

5. Click the Separator Page button. In the Separator Page dialog box, click the Browse button and choose the sysprint.sep file. Click the Open button, then click the OK button in the Separator Page dialog box.

6. Click the OK button to close the printer Properties dialog box.

Security Properties

You can control which users and groups can access Windows 2000 printers by configuring the print permissions. In Windows 2000 Professional, you can allow or deny access to a printer. If you deny access, the user or group will not be able to use the printer, even if their user or group permissions allow such access.

You assign print permissions to users and groups through the Security tab of the printer Properties dialog box, as shown in Figure 12.24. The print permissions that can be assigned are defined in Table 12.4.

FIGURE 12.24 The Security tab of the printer Properties dialog box

TABLE 12.4 Print Permissions

Print Permission	Description
Print	Allows a user or group to connect to a printer and can send print jobs to the printer.
Manage Printers	Allows administrative control of the printer. With this permission, a user or group can pause and re-start the printer, change the spooler settings, share or unshare a printer, change print permissions, and manage printer properties.
Manage Documents	Allows users to manage documents by pausing, restarting, resuming, and deleting queued documents. Users cannot control the status of the printer.

By default, whenever a printer is created, default print permissions are assigned. The default permissions are normally appropriate for most network environments. Table 12.5 shows the default print permissions that are assigned.

TABLE 12.5 Default Print Permissions

Group	Print	Manage Printers	Manage Documents
Administrators	✓	✓	✓
Power Users	✓	✓	✓
Creator Owner			✓
Everyone	✓		

Print Permission Assignment

Usually, you can accept the default print permissions, but you might need to modify them for special situations. For example, if your company bought an expensive color laser printer for the marketing department, you probably wouldn't want to allow general access to that printer. In this case, you would deselect the Allow check box for the Everyone group, add the Marketing group to the Security tab list, and then allow the Marketing group the Print permission.

To add print permissions, take the following steps:

1. In the Security tab of the printer Properties dialog box, click the Add button.

2. The Select Users, Computers, or Groups dialog box appears. Click the user, computer, or group that you want to assign print permissions to and click the Add button. After you specify all of the users you want to assign permissions to, click the OK button.

3. Highlight the user, computer, or group and select Allow or Deny access for the Print, Manage Printers, and Manage Documents permissions. Click the OK button when you are finished assigning permissions.

To remove an existing group from the permissions list, highlight the group and click the Remove button. That group will no longer be listed in the Security tab and cannot be assigned permissions.

In Exercise 12.4, you will assign print permissions. This exercise assumes that you have completed Exercise 12.1.

EXERCISE 12.4

Assigning Print Permissions

1. Using the Local Users and Groups utility, create two users: **Kim** and **Jennifer**. (See Chapter 6, "Managing Users," for details on creating user accounts.) Deselect the User Must Change Password at Next Logon option.

2. Using the Local Users and Groups utility, create a new group named **Executivess**. (See Chapter 7, "Managing Groups," for details on creating groups.) Place Kim in the Execs group.

3. Select Start ➤ Settings ➤ Printers to open the Printers folder.

4. Right-click HP LaserJet 4, select Properties, and click the Security tab. Click the Add button.

5. In the Select Users, Computers, or Groups dialog box, click Execs and click the Add button. Click the OK button to continue.

6. In the Security tab, highlight the Execs group. By default, the Allow check box should be selected for the Print permission. Leave the default setting. Highlight the Everyone group and click the Remove button. Click OK to close the Printer Properties dialog box.

7. Log off as Administrator and log on as Kim.

8. Open the Printers folder and select HP LaserJet 4. Kim should be able to connect to this printer based on her membership in the Execs group.

9. Log off as Kim and log on as Jennifer.

10. Open the Printers folder and select HP LaserJet 4. At the top of the dialog box, you should see the message "HP LaserJet 4 Access denied, unable to connect."

11. Log off as Jennifer and log on as Administrator.

Advanced Settings

The advanced settings accessed from the Security tab allow you to configure permissions, auditing, and owner properties. Clicking the Advanced button in the lower-left corner of the Security tab brings up the Access Control Settings dialog box, shown in Figure 12.25. This dialog box has three tabs that you can use to add, remove, or edit print permissions:

- The Permissions tab lists all of the users, computers, and groups that have been given permission to the printer, the permission that has been granted, and whether the permission applies to documents or to the printer.

- The Auditing tab allows you to keep track of who is using the printer and what type of access is being used. You can track the success or failure of the six events: Print, Manage Printers, Manage Documents, Read Permissions, Change Permissions, and Take Ownership.

- The Owner tab shows the owner of the printer (the user or group who created the printer), which you can change if you have the proper permissions. For example, if the print permissions excluded the Administrator from using or managing the printer, and the print permissions needed to be reassigned, an Administrator could take ownership of the printer and then reapply print permissions.

FIGURE 12.25   The Access Control Settings dialog box

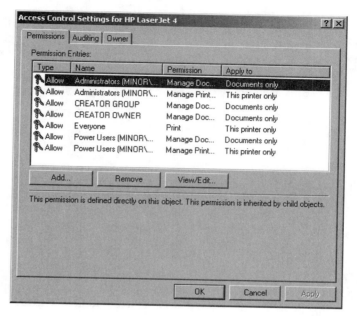

Device Settings Properties

The properties that you see on the Device Settings tab of the printer Properties dialog box depend on the printer and print driver that you have installed. You might configure these properties if you want to manage which forms are associated with tray assignments. For example, you could configure the upper tray to use letterhead and the lower tray to use regular paper. An example of the Device Settings tab for an HP LaserJet 6P printer is shown in Figure 12.26.

FIGURE 12.26 The Device Settings tab of the printer Properties dialog box

Managing Printers and Print Documents

Administrators or users with the Manage Printers permission can manage how the printer services print jobs and the print documents in a print queue. When you manage a printer, you manage all of the documents in a queue. When you manage print documents, you manage specific documents.

Microsoft
✓ *Exam*
Objective

Connect to local and network print devices.

▪ Manage printers and print jobs.

As you would expect, you manage printers and print documents from the Printers folder (select Start ➤ Settings ➤ Printers). The following sections describe the printer management and print document management options.

Managing Printers

To manage a printer, right-click the printer you want to manage. From the pop-up menu, shown in Figure 12.27, select the appropriate option for the area you want to manage. Table 12.6 describes these options.

FIGURE 12.27 The printer management options

Managing Print Documents

As an Administrator or a user with the Manage Printers or Manage Documents permission, you can manage print documents within a print queue. For example, if a user has sent the same job multiple times, you might need to delete the duplicate print jobs.

To manage print documents, in the Printers folder double-click the printer that contains the documents to open a dialog box with information about the documents in its print queue. Select Document from the menu bar to access the pull-down menu of options that you can use to manage documents, as shown in Figure 12.28. These menu options are described in Table 12.7.

TABLE 12.6 Printer Management Options

Option	Description
Set as Default Printer	Allows you to specify the default printer that will be used when the user does not send a job to an explicit printer (if the computer is configured to access multiple printers).
Printing Preferences	Brings up the Printing Preferences dialog box (see Figure 12.14), which allows you to configure printer settings for page layout and paper quality. You can also access this dialog box through the General tab of the printer Properties dialog box, as described earlier in this chapter.
Pause Printing	Pauses the printer. Print jobs can be submitted to the printer, but they will not be forwarded to the print device until you resume printing (by unchecking this option). You might use this option if you need to troubleshoot the printer or maintain the print device.
Cancel All Documents	Specifies that any jobs that are currently in the queue will be deleted. You might use this option if the print queue contains jobs that are no longer needed.
Sharing	Allows the printer to be shared or not shared.
Use Printer Offline	Pauses the printer. Print documents will remain in the print queue, even if you restart the computer.
Delete	Removes the printer. You might use this option if you no longer need the printer, if you want to move the printer to another print server, or if you suspect the printer is corrupt and you want to delete and recreate it.
Rename	Allows you to rename the printer. You might use this option to give a printer a more descriptive name or a name that follows naming conventions.

FIGURE 12.28   The Document menu options

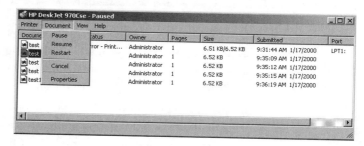

TABLE 12.7   Document Management Options

Option	Description
Pause	Places the printing of this document on hold
Resume	Allows the document to print normally (after it has been paused)
Restart	Resends the job from the beginning, even if it has already partially printed
Cancel	Deletes the job from the print spooler
Properties	Brings up the document Properties dialog box, which allows you to set options such as user notification when a print job is complete, document priority, document printing time, page layout, and paper quality

In Exercise 12.5, you will manage printers and print documents.

EXERCISE 12.5

Managing Printers and Print Documents

1. Select Start ≻ Settings ≻ Printers to open the Printers folder.

2. Right-click HP LaserJet 4 and select Pause Printing.

EXERCISE 12.5 *(continued)*

3. Select Start ➤ Programs ➤ Accessories ➤ Notepad.

4. Create a new text file and then select File ➤ Save As. In the Save As dialog box, save the file in the default location, My Documents, as **PrintMe.txt**. Click the Save button.

5. While still in Notepad, select File ➤ Print. Select HP LaserJet 4 and click the Print button. Repeat this step two more times so that you have sent a total of three print jobs. Close Notepad.

6. In the Printers folder, double-click HP LaserJet 4. At the top of the window, you will see that the status of the printer is Paused.

7. Right-click one of the print jobs in the print queue and select Cancel. The print job will be deleted.

8. Right-click one of the print jobs in the print queue and select Properties. The print job Properties dialog box appears. Change Notify from Administrator to Emily. Set the Priority from 1 to 99. For Schedule, select Only from 12:00 AM to 4:00 AM. Then click the OK button.

9. Close all of the dialog boxes.

Connecting to Printers

Users can access a local printer or a shared printer. Once a printer has been shared, users with the Print permission can connect to the network printer through their network connection.

Microsoft ✓ *Exam Objective*

Connect to local and network print devices.

▪ Connect to a local print device.

To connect to a network printer, from the Desktop, open My Network Places, expand Entire Network, and click View Entire Contents. Expand Microsoft Windows Network, then Workgroup, then *computername*. Finally, double-click the printer to connect to it.

In Exercise 12.6, you will connect to a local network printer.

EXERCISE 12.6

Connecting to a Local Network Printer

1. Double-click My Network Places and then double-click the Entire Network icon.

2. Click View Entire Contents and then double-click Microsoft Windows Network.

3. Double-click Workgroup and then double-click your computer's name. You should see HPDJ970 and HPLJ4. These are the share names for the printers you created in earlier exercises in this chapter.

4. Double-click HPDJ970. At this point, you have a network connection to the HP DeskJet 970Cse printer.

Summary

This chapter explained how to manage printing with Windows 2000 Professional. We covered the following topics:

- Basic printing principles, which included printing terminology, an overview of the Windows 2000 Professional printing process, and how printers and print devices work together

- How to create local and network printers

- Printer properties, which include general properties, sharing properties, port properties, advanced properties, security properties, and device settings

- Print management tasks, such as setting default printers and canceling all print documents

- Document management tasks, such as pausing, resuming, and canceling print documents

- Connecting to shared printers

Key Terms

Before taking the exam, you should be familiar with the following terms:

Graphics Device Interface (GDI)

local printer

logical port

logical printer

network printer

physical port

print device

print driver

print processor

print queue

print server

print spooler

printer

printer pool

rendering

separator page

TCP/IP port

Review Questions

1. Which of the following options allow you to create a new printer on a Windows 2000 Professional computer? Choose all that apply.

   A. Be a member of the Print Operators group

   B. Be a member of the Power Users group

   C. Be a member of the Administrators group

   D. Be a member of the Print Managers group

2. You have shared a network printer on a Windows 2000 Professional computer. Which of the following clients can you support drivers for on the print server? Choose all that apply.

   A. Windows 3.1

   B. Windows 95

   C. Windows 98

   D. Windows NT 3.1

3. Which of the following print permissions are applied to the Everyone group by default on shared Windows 2000 printers?

   A. No permissions are granted

   B. Print

   C. Manage Printers

   D. Manage Documents

4. Meredith is a member of Everyone, Print Managers, Power Users, and Accounting. The following print permissions have been applied:

Group	Print	Manage Printers	Manage Documents
Everyone	Allow		
Print Managers		Allow	Allow
Accounting	Allow		Deny
Power Users	Allow	Allow	Allow

Based on these assignments, which of the following are Meredith's effective rights?

A. Print

B. Print and Manage Printers

C. Print and Manage Documents

D. Print, Manage Printers, and Manage Documents

5. What printing feature allows you to track printer usage and the type of access in Windows 2000 Professional?

A. Accounting

B. Auditing

C. Print Management Tracking

D. Print Usage Tracking

6. You have five print devices that are all used by a pool of administrative assistants. You want to configure the printing environment so that print jobs are sent to the first print device that is available. What requirement must be met if you want to use a printer pool?

A. You must use the same print manufacturer and model for all print devices within the printer pool.

B. All of your print devices must be network printers.

C. All of your print devices must be configured to use the same port.

D. All of your print devices must be able to use the same print driver.

7. What is the main purpose of the print processor?

A. It determines if print jobs need additional processing, and if so processes the print job.

B. It takes print jobs from the print spooler and redirects the print job to the appropriate print device.

C. It provides the software so that the operating system can communicate with the print device.

D. It is the service that adds print jobs to the print spooler and logically organizes the print jobs so that they do not print at the same time.

8. Which printer Properties dialog box tab would you use to update your print driver on a Windows 2000 Professional computer?

A. General

B. Driver

C. Advanced

D. Device Settings

9. Which settings are required when you create a new printer in Windows 2000 Professional? Choose all that apply.

   A. Printer name

   B. Share name

   C. Port printer is attached to

   D. Location and comment

10. Which of the following options can be managed by a user who has the Manage Documents permission?

    A. Connect and send jobs to a printer

    B. Pause a printer

    C. Pause a print job

    D. Manage the status of a printer

11. You have an Acme laser printer called Acme1. There are 20 network Sales users who use this printer. The printer has failed and has been sent out for servicing. It is estimated that the printer will be out of service for one week. In the meantime, you want the users to have all of their print jobs connected to another Acme laser printer called Acme2, which is used by the Marketing users. What is the easiest way to have the users send their jobs to Acme2 until the Acme1 printer is back in service?

    A. Have the users create a printer for Acme2 and set this printer as their default printer. When Acme1 is back in service, have them reconfigure their default printer as Acme1.

    B. Create a new port that will redirect all of the print jobs that are sent to Acme1 to Acme2. After the print device is returned, disable the redirection.

    C. Rename the Acme2 printer to Acme1.

    D. Rename the Acme1 printer to Acme2.

12. You have 10 users who send their print jobs to a Windows 2000 printer called MISLaser. You want to have a custom separator page that identifies the user and the date and time that the job is printed. You have a separator page created called `custom.sep`. Where should this file be stored?

   A. *Windir*\Printers

   B. *Windir*\Queues

   C. *Windir*\System32

   D. *Windir*\System32\Printers

13. You have a Windows 2000 printer called ABCLaser that is associated with the ABC laser device. This printer keeps jamming. Jim sits close to the print device and is able to unjam the printer. Jim needs to be able to pause and restart the printer when he performs the maintenance. What is the minimum amount of permissions that Jim needs to perform this task?

   A. Grant Jim the Manage Documents print permission for the ABCLaser printer.

   B. Grant Jim the Manage Printers print permission for the ABCLaser printer.

   C. Grant Jim the Full Control print permission for the ABCLaser printer.

   D. Make Jim a Printer Operator.

14. Your Windows 2000 Professional computer has an ABC laser printer attached. Five other users in your workgroup want to use your printer. These clients are also running the Windows 2000 Professional operating system. You create a printer called ABCLP and share the printer. All of the users can attach to the share and use the printer. Six months later, you update the print driver. What do the other users in your group need to do to update the print driver on their computers?

    A. Use the Upgrade Driver Wizard to update the driver on their computers.

    B. Upgrade the print driver through the Printers utility.

    C. Use the Device Manager Wizard to update the driver on their computers.

    D. Do nothing; the next time they attach to the printer, the new print driver will be loaded automatically.

15. You have configured your network printer to be shared. When you configured the printer, you specified that the printer uses a Windows 2000 print driver. Which of the following clients can use the printer?

    A. Only Windows 2000 clients

    B. Windows NT 4 clients and Windows 2000 clients

    C. Windows 98 clients, Windows NT 4 clients, and Windows 2000 clients

    D. Windows 95 clients, Windows 98 clients, Windows NT 4 clients, and Windows 2000 clients

16. You have a printer device that is attached to the network through a network card that uses the TCP/IP protocol. What do you need to configure for this printer?

    A. A local port

    B. A network port

    C. A TCP/IP port

    D. A URL port

17. You have configured a network printer called Test. You want to make sure that the printer is properly configured. Which option can you use?

   A. Verify printer configuration

   B. Test printer configuration

   C. Print test page

   D. Confirm printer settings

18. You have set up the Accounting and Sales groups to share the same printer device. You want the Sales group's documents to print first. You create an Accounting printer and a Sales printer and assign the respective groups permissions to their printers. Both printers point to the shared print device. How should you configure the printer priority? Choose two answers.

   A. Configure Accounting priority 1

   B. Configure Accounting priority 99

   C. Configure Sales priority 1

   D. Configure Sales priority 99

19. You have been having problems with the HR printer. You are not sure if the problem is with the print device or with the shared printer configuration. Which of the following steps can you take to bypass network spooling?

   A. In the Advanced tab of the printer Properties dialog box, configure the Print Directly to the Printer option.

   B. In the General tab of the printer Properties dialog box, configure the Print Directly to the Printer option.

   C. In the Advanced tab of the printer Properties dialog box, configure the Bypass Network Printing option.

   D. In the General tab of the printer Properties dialog box, configure the Bypass Network Printing option.

20. You want your network printer to service print jobs from 8:00 A.M. to 5:00 P.M. Which tab in the printer Properties dialog box can you use to specify this configuration?

A. Scheduling

B. Availability

C. General

D. Advanced

Answers to Review Questions

1. B, C. In order to create a new printer on a Windows 2000 Professional computer, you must be logged on as a member of the Power Users or Administrators group. By default, Print Operators and Print Managers groups do not exist on Windows 2000 Professional computers.

2. B, C, D. You can't provide drivers for Windows 3.1 clients. You can provide drivers for the following clients: Windows 95 and Windows 98, Windows NT 3.1 (Alpha, Intel, MIPS, and PowerPC platforms), Windows 3.5 or 3.51 (Alpha, Intel, MIPS, and PowerPC platforms), and Windows NT 4 (Alpha, Intel, MIPS, and PowerPC platforms).

3. B. By default, the Everyone group has Print permission to shared printers. Users also have the Manage Documents permission if they are the Creator Owner of a document, but they can't manage other users' documents.

4. B. Normally, your print permissions are combined based on group membership, but in this case, Meredith is a member of a group that has been explicitly denied the Manage Documents permission. In this case, Meredith's effective rights are Print and Manage Printers.

5. B. You would use auditing to track printer usage and the type of access in Windows 2000. There are no options for Accounting, Print Management Tracking, or Print Usage Tracking.

6. D. In order to use a printer pool, all of your print devices must be able to use the same print driver. If they can use the same print driver, the print devices do not necessarily have to be from the same manufacturer or the same model. Print devices in a pool can be a mixture of local and network printers. They are not configured to use the same port. When you enable printer pooling through the Ports tab of the printer Properties dialog box, you can check multiple ports. You would check each port that a print device was attached to.

7. A. The print processor looks at print jobs and determines if they need additional processing (also called rendering) before the print job is sent to the print device.

8. C. You can update a print driver through the Advanced tab of the printer Properties dialog box. The General tab is used to set options such as printer name, location, and comment. There is no Driver tab. The Device Settings tab is used to set options such as assigning forms to trays.

9. A, C. You must specify a printer name and the port that the printer is attached to. Sharing the printer and providing a location and comment are optional configuration options.

10. C. The Manage Documents permission allows a user to manage print documents, including pausing, resuming, and deleting queued documents. A user must have Print permission to connect and send jobs to a printer. In order to pause a printer or manage the status of a printer, a user must have the Manage Printers permission.

11. B. If your print device fails, you can redirect all of the jobs that are scheduled to be printed to that print device to another print device that has been configured as a printer. For this redirection to work, the new print device must be able to use the same print driver as the old print device. To redirect print jobs, click the Add Port button in the Ports tab, highlight New Port, and choose New Port Type. In the Port Name dialog box, type the UNC name of the printer that you want to redirect the jobs to, in the format *computername**printer*.

12. C. By default, Windows 2000 separator page files are stored in the *Windir*\System32 folder.

13. B. A person or group with the Manage Printers print permission has administrative control of the printer. With this permission, a user or group can pause and restart the printer, change the spooler settings, share and unshare the printer, change print permissions, and manage printer properties.

14. D. Windows 2000 clients automatically download the print driver for a print device when they connect to a network printer. If the print driver is updated on the print server, the driver is automatically updated on the clients the next time they send a print job.

15. A. If you load only Windows 2000 drivers, the other client platforms will not be able to use the printer. In Windows 2000, you can also specify (and provide) print drivers for Windows 95/98 clients, Windows NT 3.1 clients (Alpha, Intel, or MIPS), Windows NT 3.5 and 3.51 clients (Alpha, Intel, MIPS, or PowerPC), and Windows NT 4 clients (Alpha, Intel, MIPS, or PowerPC).

16. C. If you have a print device that attaches to the network with a network card using the TCP/IP protocol, you must configure a TCP/IP port for the printer's use.

17. C. By printing a test page, you can confirm whether the printer has been properly configured.

18. A, D. You can set printer priority from 1 to 99, with 1 as the lowest priority and 99 as the highest priority.

19. A. The Print Directly to the Printer option, in the Advanced tab of the printer Properties dialog box, bypasses spooling altogether. You can use this option to troubleshoot printer problems. If you can print to a print device directly, but you can't print through the spooler, then you know that your spooler is corrupt or has other problems.

20. D. The Advanced tab of the printer Properties dialog box includes options for configuring a printer's availability.

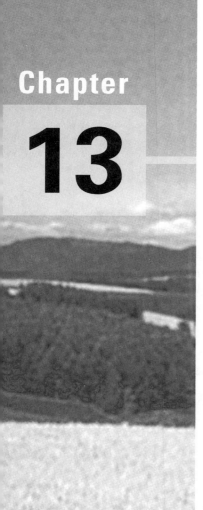

Chapter

13

Dial-Up Networking and Internet Productivity

MICROSOFT EXAM OBJECTIVES COVERED IN THIS CHAPTER

✓ **Implement, manage, and troubleshoot input and output (I/O) devices.**

- Install, configure, and manage modems.

✓ **Connect to computers by using dial-up networking.**

- Connect to computers by using a virtual private network (VPN) connection.
- Create a dial-up connection to connect to a remote access server.
- Connect to the Internet by using dial-up networking.
- Configure and troubleshoot Internet Connection Sharing.

✓ **Manage and troubleshoot access to shared folders.**

- Manage and troubleshoot Web server resources.

✓ **Connect to local and network print devices.**

- Connect to an Internet printer.

When you want to connect to a remote network or the Internet, you use dial-up networking. To use dial-up networking, you need a modem and connections to the remote server or the Internet. You can dial into a Remote Access Service server, the Internet, or access a virtual private network server on your network via a connection (for example, through the Internet).

With Windows 2000 Professional, you can also configure Internet connection sharing. This feature allows you to connect a single computer to the network and let other users on the same, small network share the Internet connection.

Another Internet feature of Windows 2000 Professional is Peer Web Services (PWS), which is a program that acts as a small-scale Web server. Once you have PWS installed, you can manage your Web site through Personal Web Manager and Internet Services Manager. You can also configure printers to be used through the Internet, or local clients can access the printer through a Web browser.

In this chapter, you will learn how to configure dial-up networking and create dial-up connections on a Windows 2000 Professional client. You will also learn how to use PWS and configure Internet printing.

The server side of dial-up networking is covered in detail in *MCSE: Windows 2000 Server Study Guide,* by Lisa Donald with James Chellis (Sybex, 2000).

Setting Up a Modem

*D*ial-up networking allows remote users (for example, a person working from home or someone with a laptop on a business trip) to dial into the network or the Internet. Before you can use dial-up networking, you must have your computer configured to dial out. This requires that you have a modem installed and properly configured.

Microsoft Exam Objective

Implement, manage, and troubleshoot input and output (I/O) devices.

- Install, configure, and manage modems.

The other subobjectives for the "Implement, manage, and troubleshoot input and output (I/O) devices" objective are covered in Chapter 4, "Configuring the Windows 2000 Environment."

If you install a Plug-and-Play modem on your Windows 2000 computer, it should be recognized automatically, and an appropriate driver should be loaded.

You can configure and manage the modems installed on your computer through Device Manager. To access Device Manager, right-click My Computer and select Manage from the pop-up menu. Select System Tools, then Device Manager. In the Device Manager window, select Modems and then double-click the modem you want to manage. This brings up the modem Properties dialog box, as shown in Figure 13.1. This dialog box has six tabs: General, Modem, Diagnostics, Advanced, Driver, and Resources. The options on these tabs are covered in the following sections.

FIGURE   13.1   The General tab of the modem Properties dialog box

 You should not change the default modem properties unless your modem manufacturer or the entity you are connecting to (for example, your Internet service provider) recommends the change. If you make incorrect changes to the modem configuration, your modem may not work.

Configuring General Modem Properties

The General tab of the modem Properties dialog box (see Figure 13.1) displays the device type, manufacturer, and location. It also shows the device status.

If the modem is not working properly, you can click the Troubleshooter button to start a Troubleshooting Wizard that can help you determine the cause of the problem. See Chapter 4, "Configuring the Windows 2000 Environment," for more information about troubleshooting devices.

Configuring Modem Properties

The Modem tab, shown in Figure 13.2, shows the port that the modem is attached to. From this tab, you can set the following options:

- The speaker volume for the modem
- The maximum port speed (specified in bits per second)
- Dial control to wait for a dial tone before dialing

FIGURE 13.2   The Modem tab of the modem Properties dialog box

Running Modem Diagnostics

Through the Diagnostics tab, shown in Figure 13.3, you can query the modem. This process can be used in troubleshooting to ensure that the modem is properly responding to requests.

FIGURE 13.3 The Diagnostics tab of the modem Properties dialog box

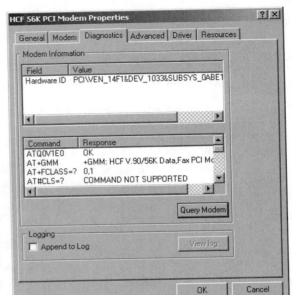

When you click the Query Modem button, Device Manager will test the modem by issuing a series of modem commands. The commands and the responses sent back from the modem are listed in the dialog box.

Configuring Advanced Modem Properties

The Advanced tab, shown in Figure 13.4, allows you to specify additional initialization commands. You can also configure advanced port settings and change default preferences, as explained in the following sections.

FIGURE 13.4 The Advanced tab of the modem Properties dialog box

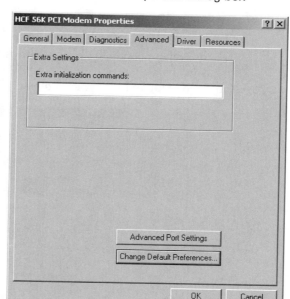

Advanced Port Settings

Clicking the Advanced Port Settings button brings up the Advanced Settings dialog box for your communications (COM) port, as shown in Figure 13.5. Through this dialog box, you can specify whether the port will use first in, first out (FIFO) buffers and the settings that will be used for the receive and transmit buffers. Lower settings can be used to correct connection problems. Higher settings can increase performance.

FIGURE 13.5 The Advanced Settings for COM port dialog box

Default Preferences

Clicking the Change Default Preferences button brings up the modem Default Preferences dialog box, as shown in Figure 13.6.

FIGURE 13.6 The General tab of the modem Default Preferences dialog box

In the General tab, you can set call and data connection preferences. The call preferences options include settings for how long the connection will last if a call is idle for more than the specified time and how long to wait for a connection before canceling a call. The data connection preferences options include settings for the port speed, the data protocol, compression (enabled or disabled), and flow control (hardware or software).

Through the Advanced tab, you can specify the hardware settings for the port, as shown in Figure 13.7. The options for hardware settings include data bits, parity, stop bits, and modulation.

FIGURE 13.7   The Advanced tab of the modem Default Preferences dialog box

Viewing Driver Details and Updating Drivers

The Driver tab of the modem Properties dialog box, shown in Figure 13.8, displays information about the modem driver that is currently loaded. Clicking the Driver Details button brings up a dialog box with additional information about the modem driver.

FIGURE 13.8   The Driver tab of the modem Properties dialog box

To uninstall the driver, click the Uninstall button. To update the driver, click the Update Driver button. See Chapter 4 for details on updating drivers.

Viewing Modem Resources

The Resources tab, shown in Figure 13.9, lists the resources that are used by your modem. Resources include memory, I/O memory, and interrupt request (IRQ) settings. You can use this information to detect resource conflicts, which may arise if you have non-Plug-and-Play hardware installed on your computer.

FIGURE 13.9 The Resources tab of the modem Properties dialog box

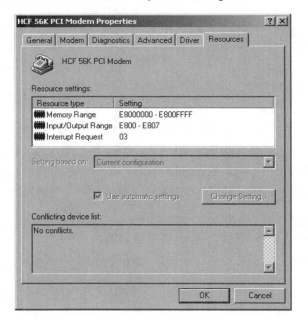

Using Dial-Up Connections

You can use dial-up connections to dial into Remote Access Service servers or into the Internet. Windows 2000 also supports virtual private network connections and Internet connection sharing. You will learn how to create these connections in the following sections.

Microsoft ✓ Exam Objective

Connect to computers by using dial-up networking.

- Connect to computers by using a virtual private network (VPN) connection.

- Create a dial-up connection to connect to a remote access server.

- Connect to the Internet by using dial-up networking.

- Configure and troubleshoot Internet Connection Sharing.

Dialing into a Remote Access Server

When you dial into a *Remote Access Service (RAS)* server, you are making a direct connection to an existing RAS server, as illustrated in Figure 13.10. You can connect to the RAS server through a modem connection, an Integrated Services Digital Network (ISDN) connection, or a null-modem cable. The RAS server and the RAS client must use the same connectivity option. They must also use the same protocols and use compatible security protocols.

FIGURE 13.10 Connecting to a Remote Access Service (RAS) server

Remote Computer

Connect through:
- Modem
- ISDN
- Null-modem cable

Windows 2000
RAS Server

Creating a RAS Connection

To configure an RAS client, take the following steps:

1. Select Start ➢ Settings ➢ Control Panel and double-click the Network and Dial-up Connections icon.

2. The Network and Dial-up Connections window appears, as shown in Figure 13.11. Double-click the Make New Connection icon.

FIGURE 13.11 The Network and Dial-up Connections window

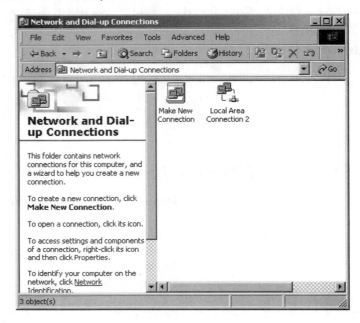

3. The Network Connection Wizard starts, as shown in Figure 13.12. Click the Next button.

FIGURE 13.12 The Welcome to the Network Connection Wizard dialog box

4. The Network Connection Type dialog box appears, as shown in Figure 13.13. Select the Dial-up to Private Network option and click the Next button.

FIGURE 13.13   The Network Connection Type dialog box

5. The Phone Number to Dial dialog box appears, as shown in Figure 13.14. Check the Use Dialing Rules check box (if you don't select this option, you won't be able to access the area code field). Enter the telephone number you wish to dial. If the telephone number is in a different country, enter the associated country code in the Country/Region Code field (for example, Czech Republic has a country code of 420 that must be dialed when calling internationally.) After you enter the information, click the Next button.

FIGURE 13.14 The Phone Number to Dial dialog box

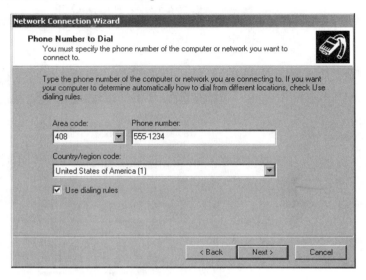

6. The Connection Availability dialog box appears, as shown in Figure 13.15. You can specify that the connection is for all users or only for the current user. Make your selection and click the Next button.

FIGURE 13.15 The Connection Availability dialog box

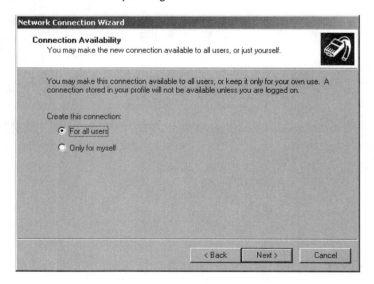

7. The Completing the Network Connection Wizard dialog box appears, as shown in Figure 13.16. You can specify the name that will be used for this connection in this dialog box. To save the network connection, click the Finish button.

FIGURE 13.16 The Completing the Network Connection Wizard dialog box

8. The Connect Dial-up Connection dialog box appears, as shown in Figure 13.17. This dialog box allows you to specify the username and password that will be used to dial into the remote location. You can also specify the number that you will dial and the location you are dialing from. Enter the information and then click the Dial button.

FIGURE 13.17 The Connect Dial-up Connection dialog box

9. When the connection is established, you will see the Connection Complete dialog box, as shown in Figure 13.18. Click the OK button. You are now connected to the RAS server and can use the remote network.

FIGURE 13.18 The Connection Complete dialog box

 Configuring an RAS server is covered in *MCSE: Windows 2000 Server Study Guide,* by Lisa Donald with James Chellis (Sybex, 2000).

If you have a modem installed, you can follow the steps in Exercise 13.1 to set up a connection to an RAS server.

EXERCISE 13.1

Creating a Dial-Up Connection to an RAS Server

1. Select Start ➢ Settings ➢ Control Panel and double-click the Network and Dial-up Connections icon.

2. In the Network and Dial-up Connections window, double-click the Make New Connection icon.

3. When the Welcome to the Network Connection Wizard starts, click the Next button.

4. In the Network Connection Type dialog box, select the Dial-up to Private Network option and click the Next button.

5. In the Phone Number to Dial dialog box, enter a telephone number (since you will not actually dial into an RAS server, specify any telephone number you wish). If you want to enter an area code, first check the Use Dialing Rules check box. After you enter the number, click the Next button.

EXERCISE 13.1 *(continued)*

6. In the Connection Availability dialog box, select the Only for Myself option and click the Next button.

7. In the Completing the Network Connection Wizard dialog box, click the Finish button.

8. When the Connect Dial-up Connection dialog box appears, click the Cancel button.

Managing the Properties of an RAS Connection

To manage the properties of an RAS connection, open the Network and Dial-up Connections window, right-click the RAS connection, and select Properties from the pop-up menu. This brings up the Dial-up Connection Properties dialog box, as shown in Figure 13.19. This dialog box has five tabs: General, Options, Security, Networking, and Sharing. The options on these tabs are covered in the following sections.

FIGURE 13.19 The General tab of the Dial-up Connection Properties dialog box

Configuring General RAS Connection Properties

The General tab (see Figure 13.19) includes options for configuring the connection you will use and the telephone number you are dialing. You can also specify whether an icon will be displayed on the Taskbar when a connection is in use.

The Connect Using option specifies the device that will be used to create the connection. For example, the device may be a modem or an ISDN adapter. To configure specific properties of the connection device, click the Configure button.

The Phone Number section has text boxes for the area code and telephone number for the connection. To specify alternate telephone numbers that can be used to make a connection, click the Alternates button. If you choose to use dialing rules, you can click the Rules button and configure the connection to access an outside line, disable call waiting, or use a calling card.

Configuring RAS Connection Options

The Options tab, shown in Figure 13.20, contains dialing options and redialing options.

FIGURE 13.20 The Options tab of the Dial-up Connection Properties dialog box

You can configure the following options for dialing:

- The Display Progress while Connecting option displays the progress of the connection attempt.

- The Prompt for Name and Password, Certificate, etc. option specifies that before a connection is attempted, the user will be prompted for a username, password, or a certificate (if smart card authentication is being used).

- The Include Windows Logon Domain option works in conjunction with the Prompt for Name and Password, Certificate, etc. option. This option specifies that Windows 2000 logon domain information should be requested prior to initiating a connection.

- The Prompt for Phone Number option allows the telephone number to be viewed, selected, or modified prior to initiating a connection.

The options for redialing let you specify the number of redial attempts if the connection is not established and the time between the redial attempts. You can also set how long a connection will remain idle before the computer hangs up. If you want the computer to redial the connection number if the connection is dropped, check the Redial If Line Is Dropped check box.

Configuring RAS Connection Security

One of the most important options that should be configured for dial-up connections is security. You can set typical or advanced security options in the Security tab of the Dial-up Connection Properties dialog box, as shown in Figure 13.21. This tab also has options for interactive logon and scripting.

FIGURE 13.21   The Security tab of the Dial-up Connection Properties dialog box

More secure connections require more overhead and are usually slower. Less secure connections require less overhead and are typically faster.

Typical Security Settings

You generally will configure typical security settings, unless you need to use specific security protocols. When you select the Typical radio button, you can then choose to validate the user's identity, automatically use the Windows logon name and password (and domain if specified), and specify whether data encryption is required. When you validate the user's identity you can select from the following options:

- The Allow Unsecured Password option specifies that the password can be transmitted without any encryption.

- The Require Secured Password option specifies that the password must be encrypted prior to transmission.

- The Use Smart Card option specifies that you must use a smart card (a special piece of hardware that is used to store public and private keys, passwords, and other personal information securely).

Advanced Security Settings

If you need to configure specific security protocols, select the Advanced radio button in the Security tab and then click the Settings button. This brings up the Advanced Security Settings dialog box, as shown in Figure 13.22.

FIGURE 13.22 The Advanced Security Settings dialog box

This dialog box allows you to configure the type of data encryption that will be used and whether logon security will use the Extensible Authentication Protocol (EAP), which is used in conjunction with other security devices, including smart cards and certificates. It also lets you select from the following protocols for logon security:

- Unencrypted password (PAP), which uses a plain text password and is the least secure authentication.

- Shiva Password Authentication Password (SPAP), which is used to dial into and be authenticated by Shiva servers.

- Challenge Handshake Authentication Protocol (CHAP), which negotiates a secure form of encrypted authentication.

- Microsoft CHAP (MS-CHAP), which uses the one-way encryption with challenge-response method. This protocol was designed for Windows NT and Windows 2000, but it can also be used by Windows 9x.

- Microsoft CHAP Version 2 (MS-CHAP v2), which is a more secure form of MS-CHAP.

Interactive Logon and Scripting

The Interactive Logon and Scripting options on the Security tab are provided for users who use terminal services for remote access. These options allow you to display a terminal window after dialing and run a script after dialing.

Scripting features are only supported for serial modems. These features are not available for ISDN devices.

Configuring Networking Options for RAS Connections

The Networking tab, shown in Figure 13.23, contains networking options for the dial-up connection. You can configure the wide area network (WAN) protocol you will use and the network components that will be used by the network connection.

FIGURE 13.23   The Networking tab of the Dial-up Connection Properties dialog box

Your choices for the WAN protocol are the Point-to-Point Protocol (PPP) or Serial Line Internet Protocol (SLIP). PPP offers more features and is the WAN protocol used by Windows 9*x*, Windows NT, Windows 2000, and most Internet servers. SLIP is an older protocol that is used with some Unix servers.

The network components that will be used by the connection might include the protocols (such as NWLink IPX/SPX/NetBIOS Compatible Transport Protocol and TCP/IP) and client software (such as File and Printer Sharing for Microsoft Networks and Client for Microsoft Networks).

Sharing

The Sharing tab of the Dial-up Connection Properties dialog box is used to configure Internet connection sharing. These options are covered in the "Using Internet Connection Sharing" section later in this chapter.

Dialing into the Internet

When you dial into the Internet, you use an Internet account, as illustrated in Figure 13.24. The Internet account is through a valid *Internet service provider (ISP)*. There are many ISPs to choose from, and they usually supply software to facilitate your Internet connection through their service.

FIGURE 13.24 Making an Internet connection

Remote Computer   Internet Service Provider   Internet

   If you do not have software from your ISP, you can set up an Internet connection the first time you click the Internet Explorer icon or the Connect to the Internet icon on the Desktop.

   The following steps are used to create a dial-up Internet connection for a new Internet account:

1. Select Start ➤ Settings and double-click the Network and Dial-up Connections icon.

2. The Network and Dial-up Connections window appears (see Figure 13.11). Double-click the Make New Connection icon.

3. The Network Connection Wizard starts (see Figure 13.12). Click the Next button.

4. The Network Connection Type dialog box appears (see Figure 13.13). Select the Dial-up to the Internet option and click the Next button.

5. The Internet Connection Wizard starts, as shown in Figure 13.25. You can choose from the following options:

   - The I Want to Sign Up for a New Internet Account option guides you through selecting an ISP and setting up a new account. You can use this option if you do not already have an ISP.

   - The I Want to Transfer My Existing Internet Account to This Computer option lets you set up a connection to your ISP. You can use this option if you already have an account with an ISP, but you do not have any software configured on your computer to make a connection to the ISP.

   - The I Want to Set Up My Internet Account Manually, or I Want to Connect through a Local Area Network (LAN) option allows you greater control over how your Internet connection is set up.

6. In this example, select the I Want to Sign Up for a New Internet Account option. Then click the Next button.

FIGURE 13.25 The Welcome to the Internet Connection Wizard dialog box

7. The Wizard connects to a referral service and downloads a list of ISPs in your area, as shown in Figure 13.26. By highlighting each ISP, you can see their billing rate, services, and modem support. Select the ISP you wish to use and click the Next button.

FIGURE 13.26 The Selecting an Internet Service Provider dialog box

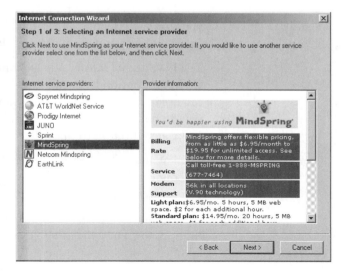

8. You are asked to provide information that is used to sign up with an ISP, as shown in Figure 13.27. After you fill in this information, click the Next button.

FIGURE 13.27 The Signing Up with an Internet Service Provider dialog box

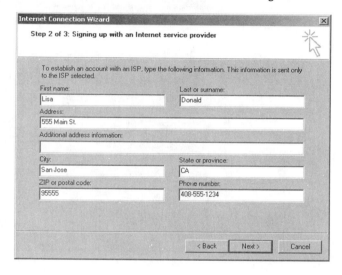

9. You are asked to select the billing option you will use, as shown in Figure 13.28. Select an option and click the Next button.

FIGURE 13.28 Choosing a billing option

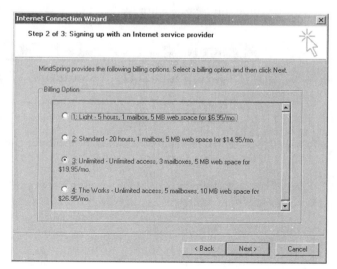

10. You are asked to provide payment information, as shown in Figure 13.29. Fill in the information and click the Next button.

FIGURE 13.29 Providing customer payment information

11. You are connected to the ISP, which will prompt you to accept the ISP's service agreement and select a username and password. Complete the signup procedure.

In Exercise 13.2, you will create a new dial-up Internet connection for a new Internet account.

EXERCISE 13.2

Creating a Dial-Up Connection to the Internet

1. Select Start ➢ Settings and double-click the Network and Dial-up Connections icon.

2. In the Network and Dial-up Connections window, double-click the Make New Connection icon.

3. When the Welcome to the Network Connection Wizard starts, click the Next button.

4. In the Network Connection Type dialog box, select the Dial-up to the Internet option and click the Next button.

5. In the Welcome to the Internet Connection Wizard dialog box, select the I Want to Sign Up for a New Internet Account option and click the Next button.

6. When the list of ISPs in your area appears, select an ISP and click the Next button.

7. Fill in the next dialog box to provide the information for signing up with an ISP. Then click the Next button.

8. Select the billing option you will use and click the Next button.

9. Complete the payment information and click the Next button.

10. When you are connected to the ISP, accept the ISP's service agreement and select a username and password.

Using Virtual Private Network Connections

A *virtual private network (VPN)* is a private network that uses links across private or public networks (such as the Internet). When data is sent over the remote link, it is encapsulated, encrypted, and requires authentication services. In order to have a VPN, you must have a Windows 2000 Server computer that has been configured as a VPN server. A sample VPN is illustrated in Figure 13.30.

FIGURE 13.30 Making a virtual private network (VPN) connection

The main advantage of using a VPN rather than an RAS connection is that with an RAS connection, a long-distance call might be required to dial into the RAS server. With a VPN connection, all you need is access to a network such as the Internet.

To configure a VPN client, take the following steps:

1. Select Start ➢ Settings ➢ Control Panel and double-click the Network and Dial-up Connections icon.

2. The Network and Dial-up Connections window appears (see Figure 13.11). Double-click the Make New Connection icon.

3. The Network Connection Wizard starts (see Figure 13.12). Click the Next button.

4. The Network Connection Type dialog box appears (see Figure 13.13). Select the Connect to a Private Network through the Internet option and click the Next button.

5. The Public Network dialog box appears, as shown in Figure 13.31. You can choose whether or not Windows should automatically dial the initial connection. In this example, Windows will automatically dial the initial connection. Click the Next button.

FIGURE 13.31   The Public Network dialog box

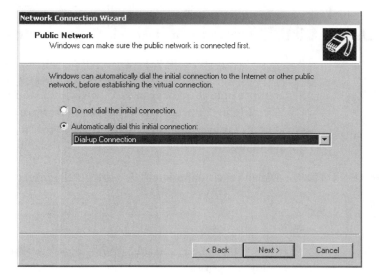

6. The Destination Address dialog box appears, as shown in Figure 13.32. Enter the host name or the IP address of the computer that you will connect to and click the Next button.

FIGURE 13.32 The Destination Address dialog box

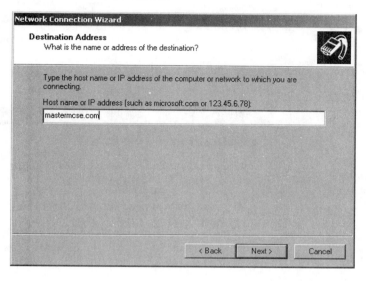

7. The Connection Availability dialog box appears (see Figure 13.15). You can configure the connection to be available for all users or only the current user. Make your selection and click the Next button.

8. The Completing the Network Connection Wizard dialog box appears. Specify the name that you want to use for the connection and click the Finish button.

9. The Initial Connection dialog box appears. Click the Yes button to continue.

10. The Connect Dial-up Connection dialog box appears. Specify the username and password that will be used to log on to the VPN server and the telephone number of the network that you will dial into. Then click the Dial button.

11. When the connection is established, you will see the Connection Complete dialog box. Click the OK button. You are now connected to the VPN server and can use the remote network.

Configuring a VPN server is covered in *MCSE: Windows 2000 Server Study Guide,* by Lisa Donald with James Chellis (Sybex, 2000).

In Exercise 13.3, you will configure the client for a VPN connection.

EXERCISE 13.3

Configuring a VPN Client

1. Select Start ➢ Settings ➢ Control Panel and double-click the Network and Dial-up Connections icon.

2. In the Network and Dial-up Connections window, double-click the Make New Connection icon.

3. When the Welcome to the Network Connection Wizard starts, click the Next button.

4. In the Network Connection Type dialog box, select the Connect to a Private Network through the Internet option and click the Next button.

5. In the Public Network dialog box, select the Automatically Dial This Initial Connection radio button, make sure Dial-Up Connection is selected in the box below, and click the Next button.

6. In the Destination Address dialog box, enter the host name or the IP address of the computer that you will connect to. Then click the Next button.

7. In the Connection Availability dialog box, select the For All Users option and click the Next button.

8. In the Completing the Network Connection Wizard dialog box, specify the name that you want to use for the connection and click the Finish button.

9. In the Initial Connection dialog box, click the Yes button to continue.

10. In the Connect Dial-up Connection dialog box, specify the username and password that will be used to log on to the VPN server, and the telephone number of the network that you will dial into. Then click the Dial button.

11. In the dialog box that appears after the connection is established, click the OK button.

Using Internet Connection Sharing

Internet connection sharing allows you to connect a small network to the Internet through a single connection, as illustrated in Figure 13.33. The computer that dials into the Internet provides network address translation, addressing, and name resolution services for all of the computers on the network. Through Internet connection sharing, the other computers on the network can use Internet applications, such as Internet Explorer and Outlook Express, as well as access Internet resources.

FIGURE 13.33   Internet connection sharing

In order to use Internet connection sharing, the following conditions must be met:

- All of the network clients must get their IP addresses automatically through DHCP.

- The host computer must be configured to support Internet connection sharing.

- The client computers must be configured to use Internet connection sharing.

In order to configure Internet connection sharing, you must be a member of the Administrators group.

Configuring Internet Connection Sharing on the Host Computer

To configure Internet connection sharing on the host computer, take the following steps:

1. Create an Internet connection or a VPN connection.

2. Verify that the host computer is configured as a DHCP client and that there is a DHCP server properly configured.

3. Select Start ➤ Settings and double-click the Network and Dial-up Connections icon.

4. Right-click the connection you want to share and select Properties from the pop-up menu.

5. The Virtual Private Connections Properties dialog box appears. Click the Sharing tab and check the Enable Internet Connection Sharing for This Connection check box, as shown in Figure 13.34. You can also select the Enable On-Demand Dialing check box. When on-demand dialing is enabled, if the Internet connection is not active and another computer tries to access Internet resources, a connection will be automatically established. Click the OK button.

FIGURE 13.34 The Sharing tab of the Virtual Private Connection Properties dialog box

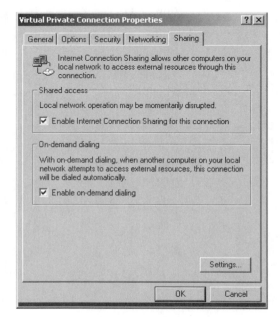

Configuring Internet Connection Sharing on the Network Computers

To configure Internet connection sharing on the network computers, take the following steps:

1. Right-click the Internet Explorer icon on the Desktop and select Properties from the pop-up menu.

2. The Internet Properties dialog box appears. Click the Connections tab, shown in Figure 13.35. Click the Setup button.

FIGURE 13.35 The Connections tab of the Internet Properties dialog box

3. The Internet Connection Wizard starts. Select the I Want to Set Up My Internet Connection Manually, or I Want to Connect through a Local Area Network (LAN) option and click the Next button.

4. The Setting Up Your Internet Connection dialog box appears, as shown in Figure 13.36. Select the I Connect through a Local Area Network (LAN) option and click the Next button.

FIGURE 13.36 The Setting Up Your Internet Connection dialog box

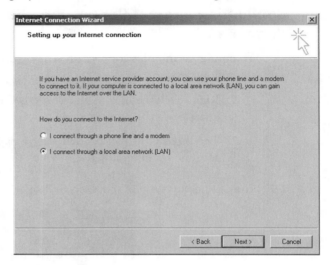

5. The Local Area Network Internet Configuration dialog box appears, as shown in Figure 13.37. You can choose the Automatic Discovery of Proxy Server option to automatically configure proxy settings or the Manual Proxy Server option to configure these settings manually. Make your selection and click the Next button.

FIGURE 13.37 The Local Area Network Internet Configuration dialog box

6. The Set Up Your Internet Mail Account dialog box appears, as shown in Figure 13.38. If desired, you can set up an Internet mail account. In this example, a mail account is not set up. Click the Next button.

FIGURE 13.38   The Set Up Your Internet Mail Account dialog box

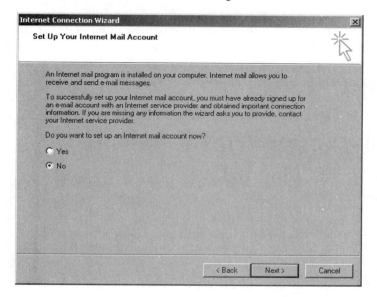

7. The Completing the Internet Connection Wizard dialog box appears. Click the Finish button.

In Exercise 13.4, you will configure the VPN connection you created in Exercise 13.3 to support Internet connection sharing.

EXERCISE 13.4

Configuring Internet Connection Sharing

1. Select Start ➢ Settings and double-click the Network and Dial-up Connections icon.

2. In the Network and Dial-up Connections window, right-click the connection you want to share and select Properties from the pop-up menu.

EXERCISE 13.4 *(continued)*

3. In the Virtual Private Connections Properties dialog box, click the Sharing tab. Check the Enable Internet Connection Sharing for This Connection check box. If desired, click the Enable On-Demand Dialing check box. Click the OK button.

4. Since your computer is not configured as a DHCP client, you will see a message warning you that the IP address that is assigned to the computer may be lost. Click the Yes button to enable Internet connection sharing.

Using Peer Web Services

Windows 2000 uses *Internet Information Services (IIS)* and *Peer Web Services (PWS)* to publish resources on the Internet or a private intranet. The IIS software that is installed on a Windows 2000 Server computer is fully functional and is designed to support heavy Internet usage. When you install IIS on a Windows 2000 Professional computer, you are actually installing PWS. PWS is designed to act as a small-scale Web server for a small intranet or a small Internet site with limited traffic.

Microsoft ✓ *Exam* *Objective*

Manage and troubleshoot access to shared folders.

- Manage and troubleshoot Web server resources.

This chapter covers material related to managing Web server resources for the "Manage and troubleshoot access to shared folders" objective. Creating shared folders and controlling access to shared folders, two other subobjectives for this objective, are covered in Chapter 10, "Accessing Files and Folders."

When you install IIS (PWS) on a Windows 2000 Professional computer, the following services are installed:

- File Transfer Protocol (FTP), which is used to transfer files between two computers using the TCP/IP protocol

- Hypertext Transfer Protocol (HTTP), which is used to create content for Web sites as well as to navigate Web sites

- Simple Mail Transfer Protocol (SMTP), which is used to transfer mail between two SMTP mail systems

In order to install IIS or PWS, the Windows 2000 computer must be running the TCP/IP protocol.

Installing Peer Web Services

To install PWS, take the following steps:

1. Select Start ➢ Settings ➢ Control Panel and double-click the Add/Remove Programs icon.

2. The Add/Remove Programs window appears, as shown in Figure 13.39. Click the Add/Remove Windows Components option.

FIGURE 13.39 The Add/Remove Programs window

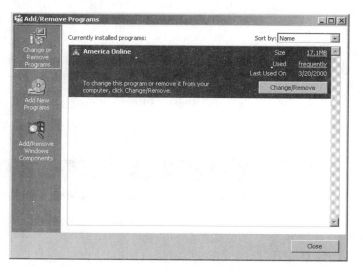

3. The Windows Components Wizard starts, as shown in Figure 13.40. Check the Internet Information Services (IIS) box and click the Next button.

FIGURE 13.40 The Windows Components Wizard

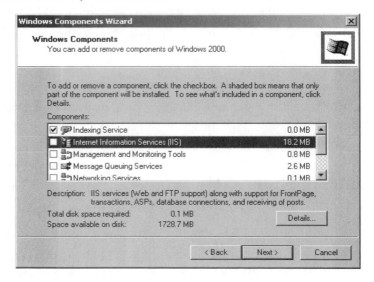

4. When prompted, insert the Windows 2000 Professional CD and click the OK button. If you see the Files Needed dialog box, you will need to specify the location of your CD drive (you can use the Browse button) and the I386 folder. Click the OK button.

5. After all of the files have been copied, you will see the Completing the Windows Components Wizard. Click the Finish button.

6. Close the Add/Remove Programs window.

In Exercise 13.5, you will install PWS.

EXERCISE 13.5

Installing Peer Web Services

1. Select Start ➢ Settings ➢ Control Panel and double-click the Add/Remove Programs icon.

2. In the Add/Remove Programs window, select the Add/Remove Windows Components option.

3. In the Windows Components Wizard dialog box, check the Internet Information Services (IIS) box and click the Next button.

EXERCISE 13.5 *(continued)*

4. When prompted, insert the Windows 2000 Professional CD and click the OK button. If you see the Files Needed dialog box, specify the location of your CD drive (you can use the Browse button) and the I386 folder. Click the OK button.

5. When the Completing the Windows Components Wizard appears, click the Finish button.

6. Close the Add/Remove Programs window.

Configuring and Managing Peer Web Services

Once you have PWS installed, you will see new program items in Administrative Tools called Personal Web Manager and Internet Services Manager. These utilities are used to configure and manage PWS.

Using Personal Web Manager

The main Personal Web Manager window is shown in Figure 13.41. Through this window, you can configure the location of your home page and choose to stop your Web site. The bottom of the window shows some statistics for monitoring your Web site.

FIGURE 13.41   The Personal Web Manager window

Two other windows are available:

- Click the Tour option on the left side of the window to see basic information about the configuration of PWS.

- Click the Advanced option on the left side of the window to configure virtual directories for PWS. A virtual directory can be on the local computer or on a remote computer.

A virtual directory is a directory, other than the default home directory, that is used to publish Web content.

Using Internet Services Manager

When you choose the *Internet Services Manager* in Administrative Tools, you see the Internet Information Services window, as shown in Figure 13.42.

FIGURE 13.42 The Internet Services Manager window

This utility allows you to configure the protocols that are used by IIS and PWS. The following options are installed by default:

- Default FTP site

- Default Web site

- Default SMTP server

You can manage any of these options by right-clicking the option and selecting Properties from the pop-up menu.

The Internet Services Manager is covered in greater detail in *MCSE: Windows 2000 Server Study Guide,* by Lisa Donald with James Chellis (Sybex, 2000).

Managing Internet Printers

A new feature in Windows 2000 is *Internet printing*, which allows you to send documents to be printed through the Internet. For example, you could send a new company catalog directly to your publisher's printer through the Internet. A new protocol, called *Internet Print Protocol (IPP)*, allows users to print directly to a URL. Printer and job-related information are generated in HTML format.

Microsoft **Exam** *Objective*	**Connect to local and network print devices.** ▪ Connect to an Internet printer.

This chapter covers the material related to Internet printing for the "Connect to local and network print devices" objective. The other subobjectives for this objective are covered in Chapter 12, "Managing Printing."

To install a printer from the Internet or an intranet, use the printer's URL as the name of the printer. For Windows 2000 Professional to process print jobs that contain URLs, PWS must be running. Print server security is handled by PWS (IIS if the print server is a Windows 2000 Server computer). To support all browsers, an administrator must choose basic authentication. Internet Explorer supports LAN Manager Challenge/Response and Kerberos version 5 authentication.

Adding an Internet Printer

To install an Internet printer on a Windows 2000 computer, first set up a shared printer (see Chapter 12, "Managing Printing" for details on setting up a shared printer). Then complete the following steps:

1. Select Start ➢ Settings ➢ Printers.

2. In the Printers folder, double-click Add Printer and click the Next button.

3. The Add Printer Wizard starts. Click the Next button.

4. The Local or Network Printer dialog box appears, as shown in Figure 13.43. Select Network Printer and click the Next button.

FIGURE 13.43   The Local or Network Printer dialog box

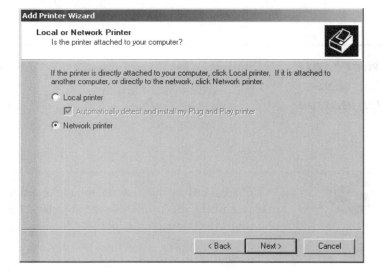

5. The Locate Your Printer dialog box appears, as shown in Figure 13.44. Click the Connect to a Printer on the Internet or on Your Intranet option. In the URL box, type **http://**_computername_**/printers/** _share_name_**/.printer** and click the Next button.

FIGURE 13.44 The Locate Your Printer dialog box

Connecting to an Internet Printer Using a Web Browser

You can manage printers from any browser, but you must use Internet Explorer 4 or later to be able to connect to a printer using a browser (the browser must support frames).

To connect to an Internet printer using a Web browser, take the following steps:

1. Open the Web browser, type **http://print_server/printers** in the address bar, and press Enter. If prompted, type your username, domain name, and password.

2. Click the link for the printer you want to connect to.

3. Under Printer Actions, click Connect.

Summary

In this chapter, you learned about dial-up networking and Internet connectivity. We covered the following topics:

- How to configure and manage the modems installed on your computer through Device Manager.

- Using dial-up networking, including creating dial-up connections to RAS servers and to the Internet. You also learned how to configure a VPN connection and how to configure Internet connection sharing.

- Using Peer Web Services (PWS), which installs a small-scale Web server on a Windows 2000 Professional computer. You can use PWS to publish files and to provide print resources over the Internet.

Key Terms

Before taking the exam, you should be familiar with the following terms:

dial-up networking

Internet connection sharing

Internet Information Services (IIS)

Internet Print Protocol (IPP)

Internet printer

Internet service provider (ISP)

Internet Services Manager

Peer Web Services (PWS)

Personal Web Manager

Remote Access Service (RAS)

virtual private network (VPN)

Review Questions

1. Which of the following options *cannot* be used by an RAS client to dial into an RAS server?

   A. Modem

   B. ISDN

   C. Null-modem cable

   D. Infrared connection

2. What type of connection would you create if you wanted to dial into your Windows 2000 network through the Internet?

   A. Internet connection

   B. RAS connection

   C. ISP connection

   D. VPN connection

3. Which of the following requirements must be met in order to use Internet connection sharing?

   A. You must have a VPN connection.

   B. The network clients must be configured to use WINS.

   C. The network clients must be configured to use DHCP.

   D. The network clients must have the ICS service installed.

4. Which of the following services is *not* associated with PWS?

   A. FTP

   B. HTTP

   C. SMTP

   D. SNMP

5. How do you install PWS?

   A. As an MMC snap-in

   B. Through Control Panel, Add/Remove Programs

   C. Through Programs ➢ Administrative Tools ➢ Component Services

   D. As an ActiveX Control

6. What protocol is used to allow users to send print jobs to a URL?

   A. IPP

   B. PIP

   C. LIP

   D. POP

7. If you want to use a URL to attach to a printer that is defined on a Windows 2000 Professional print server, what service must be running?

   A. Peer Web Services

   B. Print Web Manager

   C. Internet Print Manager

   D. URL Print Manager

8. You decide to create a new network or dial-up connection. Which of the following items *cannot* be created from the Network Connection Wizard?

   A. Dial-up to private network

   B. Dial-up to a VPN server

   C. Dial-up to the Internet

   D. Connect directly to another computer

9. You decide to create a new network or dial-up connection to connect to an RAS server using an ISDN connection. Which of the following items would you select in the Network Connection Type dialog box of the Network Connection Wizard?

   A. Dial-up to Private Network

   B. Dial-up to an RAS Server

   C. Dial-up to the Internet

   D. Connect Directly to Another Computer

10. How do you configure Internet connection sharing on the computer that will act as the host connection?

    A. On the computer that will act as the host, install the ICS service.

    B. On the computer that will act as the host, install the ISC service.

    C. This option is configured as a part of the Network Connection Wizard when you create an Internet connection.

    D. Access the Internet Connections Properties dialog box, click the Sharing tab, and check the Enable Internet Connection Sharing option.

11. You are using a modem to dial into a VPN server. When you attempt to dial into the VPN server, the connection can't be established. When you listen to the connection, you don't hear anything—not even a dial tone. You are sure that your sound card works properly. What option should you check so that you can hear what is happening when you try to establish the connection?

    A. In the Modem tab of the modem Properties dialog box, set the Speaker Volume option using the High setting.

    B. In the Advanced tab of the modem Properties dialog box, set the speaker volume using the High setting.

    C. In the modem adapter Properties dialog box, select the Audible Connection option.

    D. Use the `volume` command-line utility to adjust the volume.

12. You are having trouble connecting to the Internet. You are not sure if the problem is with your modem or with your configuration. How can you determine if your modem is working properly?

    A. Use the `moddiag` command-line utility to run a series of modem diagnostics.

    B. Check the modem diagnostics log that is created in *Windir*\System32\Moddiag.

    C. Use the `testcomm` command-line utility to run a series of modem diagnostics.

    D. In the Diagnostics tab of the modem Properties dialog box, click the Query Modem button.

13. You are configuring a dial-up connection on your Windows 2000 Professional computer. You want the connection to be available only for the user Martha. What should you configure?

    A. Log on as Administrator and create the connection. Grant Martha Full Control permission to the dial-up connection.

    B. In the user profile, configure the dial-up connection as nonshared. Specify that only Martha can use the dial-up connection.

    C. Log on as Martha and create the connection. For Connection Availability, specify that the connection is only available for the current user.

    D. In the user profile, configure the dial-up connection as private. Specify that only Martha can use the dial-up connection.

14. You are using a dial-up connection to connect to your company's RAS server. You want to use your company calling card for the connection. How do you configure this?

    A. In the Dial-up Connection Properties dialog box, General tab, select Rules to configure the calling card.

    B. In the modem Properties dialog box, General tab, select Dialing Properties to configure the calling card.

    C. In the modem Properties dialog box, use the Configure Calling Cards tab to configure the calling card.

    D. This option can't be configured.

15. Which dial-up connection security protocol should you configure if your laptop will use a security device such as a smart card?

    A. EAP

    B. CHAP

    C. PAP

    D. RAP

16. You are configuring a dial-up connection to dial into your company's RAS server. You are using a Windows 2000 Professional computer to access a Windows 2000 RAS server. Which of the following dial-in security protocols offers the highest level of security?

    A. PAP

    B. CHAP

    C. MS-CHAP

    D. MS-CHAP v2

17. You are configuring the networking properties of your dial-up connection. When would you configure a SLIP connection?

    A. When you are dialing into a Windows 95 computer

    B. When you are dialing into a Windows NT 4 computer

    C. When you are dialing into a Windows 2000 computer

    D. When you are dialing into a Unix server that does not use PPP connections

18. You are considering using a VPN network connection. Which of the following options are offered through VPN connections. Choose three answers.

    A. The data will be encapsulated.

    B. The data will be encrypted.

    C. A username and password will be required.

    D. The data will require certificate services.

19. You have a workgroup with five computers. You have only one telephone line that is dedicated to remote communications. All five users require Internet access to send and receive e-mail. Which option should be configured to support this environment?

A. Dial-up connection sharing

B. Internet connection sharing

C. SLIP connection sharing

D. PPP connection sharing

20. Which of the following options can be configured through a dial-up connection's dialing rules? Choose three answers.

A. The area code you are dialing

B. Whether you need to use a rule to access an outside line for long-distance connections

C. Whether the telephone uses tone or pulse dialing

D. How many times the computer will retry to create the connection if a busy signal is reached

Answers to Review Questions

1. D. RAS clients can access the RAS server through a modem, an ISDN connection, or a null-modem cable.

2. D. You would use a VPN connection to connect to a VPN server on your local network. Using a VPN connection allows you to use a link across a private or public network such as the Internet.

3. C. In order to use Internet connection sharing, the network clients must be able to get their IP addresses automatically (through DHCP). The host computer and the client computers must be configured to use Internet connection sharing.

4. D. When you install Peer Web Services (PWS), the File Transfer Protocol (FTP), Hypertext Transfer Protocol (HTTP), and Simple Mail Transfer Protocol (SMTP) services are installed.

5. B. You install PWS through Control Panel ➤ Add/Remove Programs and then select Add/Remove Windows Components.

6. A. The Internet Printing Protocol (IPP) is used to support Internet printing.

7. A. If you want to use Internet printing on a Window 2000 Professional print server, you must have PWS installed.

8. B. There is no option to dial-up to a VPN server. If you want to create a VPN connection, you select the Connect to a Private Network through the Internet option.

9. A. To configure an RAS client to dial into an RAS server, you use the Dial-up to Private Network option in the Network Connection Type dialog box.

10. D. To configure Internet connection sharing on the computer that will act as the host connection, you create an Internet connection, then access the Internet connections properties, click the Sharing tab, and check the Enable Internet Connection Sharing option.

11. A. In the Modem tab of the modem Properties dialog box, you can set the speaker volume by adjusting a slider between Off and High.

12. D. The Diagnostics tab of the modem Properties dialog box contains a Query Modem button. Click this button to run a series of modem commands and see how the modem responds.

13. C. To create a dial-up connection, you use the Network Connection Wizard. One of the Wizard's dialog boxes asks you to specify the connection's availability. You can specify that the connection is to be used for all users or only for the current user.

14. A. To configure a connection to use a calling card, access the Dial-up Connection Properties dialog box, General tab, and click the Rules button.

15. A. The Extensible Authentication Protocol (EAP) is used in conjunction with other security devices, including smart cards and certificates.

16. D. The MS-CHAP v2 protocol is the most secure form of the Challenge Handshake Authentication Protocol. The PAP protocol uses an unencrypted password.

17. D. Windows 9*x*, Windows NT, and Windows 2000 use the PPP protocol. You use the SLIP protocol with some Unix servers.

18. A, B, C. When you use virtual private network (VPN) connections, data is encapsulated, encrypted, and requires authentication services.

19. B. Internet connection sharing allows you to connect a small network to the Internet through a single connection.

20. A, B, C. With dialing rules, you can configure the area code you are calling, whether there is anything you need to do to access an outside line for long-distance calls, and whether the telephone uses tone or pulse dialing. You configure the retries through the Options tab of the Dial-up Connection Properties dialog box.

Chapter 14

Optimizing Windows 2000

MICROSOFT EXAM OBJECTIVES COVERED IN THIS CHAPTER

✓ **Deploy service packs.**

✓ **Optimize and troubleshoot performance of the Windows 2000 Professional desktop.**

- Optimize and troubleshoot memory performance.
- Optimize and troubleshoot processor utilization.
- Optimize and troubleshoot disk performance.
- Optimize and troubleshoot network performance.
- Optimize and troubleshoot application performance.

✓ **Configure, manage, and troubleshoot the Task Scheduler.**

To have an optimized system, you must monitor its performance. The two tools for monitoring Windows 2000 Professional are System Monitor and Performance Logs and Alerts. With these tools, you can track memory, processor activity, the disk subsystem, the network subsystem, and other computer subsystems.

You can make your administrative tasks easier by automating some of them. You can schedule system tasks by using the Scheduled Task Wizard.

This chapter begins with discussions of the Windows Update utility and service packs. Then you will learn how to monitor and optimize Windows 2000 Professional using the System Monitor, Performance Logs and Alerts, and Task Manager utilities. You will also learn how to optimize application performance.

Keeping Windows 2000 Up-to-Date

An optimal operating system is one that is running the most up-to-date software and has had the most recent service pack installed. Microsoft provides the Windows Update utility to help you obtain updated Windows 2000 software. Microsoft issues service packs as necessary to update the operating system with bug fixes and new features.

Using the Windows Update Utility

The *Windows Update* utility connects your computer to Microsoft's Web site and checks your files to make sure that you have all of the latest and greatest updates.

To use Windows Update, you must first have a valid Internet connection. Then simply choose Start ➤ Windows Update to go to the correct URL for updates.

For product updates, click the Product Updates option on the home page and follow the directions to choose which files you want to update. The files in the update section are arranged by the following categories:

- Critical updates

- Picks of the month

- Recommended updates

- Additional Windows features

- Device drivers

Within each category, you will see the available updates, along with a description, file size, and download time estimate for each update. Just check the files you want to update and click the Download icon to download your selections.

Using Windows Service Packs

Service packs are used to deliver bug fixes (and sometimes new features) to Windows operating systems. Windows 2000 offers a new technology for service packs called *slipstream*. With slipstream technology, service packs are applied once, and they are not overwritten as new services are added to the computer. This means that you should not need to reapply service packs after new services are added, which sometimes was required when Windows NT 4 service packs were applied.

Microsoft
✓ *Exam*
Objective

Deploy service packs.

You can determine if any service packs have been installed on your computer by using the WINVER command. To issue this command, select Start ➤ Programs ➤ Accessories ➤ Command Prompt. In the Command Prompt dialog box, type **WINVER** and press Enter. You will see a dialog box that shows which service packs are currently installed.

Using System Monitoring Tools

Before you can optimize the performance of Windows 2000 Professional, you must monitor critical subsystems to determine how your system is currently performing and what (if anything) is causing system bottlenecks. Windows 2000 Professional ships with two tools that you can use to track and monitor system performance: the System Monitor utility and the Performance Logs and Alerts utility.

Microsoft
✓ *Exam*
Objective

Optimize and troubleshoot performance of the Windows 2000 Professional desktop.

- Optimize and troubleshoot memory performance.
- Optimize and troubleshoot processor utilization.
- Optimize and troubleshoot disk performance.
- Optimize and troubleshoot network performance.

You can access the monitoring tools by adding the System Monitor snap-in and the Performance Logs and Alerts snap-in to the MMC. The System Monitor snap-in is added as an ActiveX control.

In Exercise 14.1, you will create a management console for monitoring system performance.

EXERCISE 14.1

Creating a Management Console for Monitoring System Performance

1. Select Start ➢ Run, type MMC in the Run dialog box, and click the OK button.

2. Select Console ➢ Add/Remove Snap-in.

3. In the Add/Remove Snap-in dialog box, click the Add button. In the Add Standalone Snap-in dialog box, select ActiveX Control and click the Add button.

4. In the Insert ActiveX Control dialog box, click the Next button.

EXERCISE 14.1 *(continued)*

5. In the Insert ActiveX Control dialog box, select System Monitor Control and click the Next button. Click the Finish button.

6. In the Add Standalone Snap-in dialog box, click the Close button.

7. In the Add/Remove Snap-in dialog box, click the Add button. In the Add Standalone Snap-in dialog box, select Performance Logs and Alerts and click the Add button, then click the Close button.

8. In the Add/Remove Snap-in dialog box, click the OK button.

9. Select Console ➢ Save As.

10. In the Save As dialog box, select Save in Administrative Tools (the default selection) and save the file as **Monitor**.

You can now access this console by selecting Start ➢ Programs ➢ Administrative Tools ➢ Monitor.

In Windows NT 4, the functions of the System Monitor utility and the Performance Logs and Alerts utility were implemented in the Performance Monitor utility.

Now that you've added the monitoring tools to the MMC, you can use them to monitor and optimize Windows 2000. The following sections describe how to evaluate your system's current performance; how to use System Monitor and Performance Logs and Alerts; and how to monitor and optimize the system memory, processor, disk subsystem, and network subsystem.

Determining System Performance

The monitoring tools allow you to assess your server's current health and determine what it requires to improve its present condition. With System Monitor and Performance Logs and Alerts, you can perform the following tasks:

- Create baselines.
- Identify system bottlenecks.

- Determine trends.
- Create alert thresholds.

Each of these tasks is discussed in the following sections.

Creating Baselines

A *baseline* is a snapshot of how your system is currently performing. Suppose that your computer's hardware has not changed over the last six months, but the computer seems to be performing more slowly now than it did six months ago. If you have been using the Performance Logs and Alerts utility and taking baseline logs, as well as noting the changes in your workload, you can more easily determine what resources are causing the system to slow down.

You should create baselines at the following times:

- When the system is first configured without any load
- At regular intervals of typical usage
- Whenever any changes are made to the system's hardware or software configuration

Baselines are particularly useful for determining the effect of changes that you make to your computer. For example, if you are adding more memory to your computer, you should take baselines before and after you install the memory to determine the effect of the change. Along with hardware changes, system configuration modifications also can affect your computer's performance, so you should create baselines before and after you make any changes to your Windows 2000 Professional configuration.

For the most part, Windows 2000 Professional is a self-tuning operating system. If you decide to tweak the operating system, you should take baselines before and after each change. If you do not notice a performance gain after the tweak, you should consider returning the computer to its original configuration, because some tweaks may cause more problems than they solve.

You create baselines by using the Performance Logs and Alerts utility to create a baseline counters log file. This process is described in the "Creating Baseline Reports" section later in this chapter.

Identifying System Bottlenecks

A *bottleneck* is a system resource that is inefficient compared with the rest of the computer system as a whole. The bottleneck can cause the rest of the system to run slowly.

You need to pinpoint the cause of a bottleneck in order to correct it. Consider a system that has a Pentium 166 processor with 64MB of RAM. If your applications are memory-intensive, and lack of memory is your bottleneck, then upgrading your processor will not eliminate the bottleneck.

By using System Monitor, you can measure the performance of the various parts of your system, which allows you to identify system bottlenecks in a scientific manner. You will learn how to set counters to monitor your network and spot bottlenecks in the "Using System Monitor" section later in this chapter.

Determining Trends

Many of us tend to manage situations reactively instead of proactively. With reactive management, you focus on a problem when it occurs. With proactive management, you take steps to avoid the problem before it happens. In a perfect world, all management would be proactive.

System Monitor and Performance Logs and Alerts are great tools for proactive network management. If you are creating baselines on a regular basis, you can identify system trends. For example, if you notice average CPU utilization increasing 5 percent every month, you can assume that within the next six months, you're going to have a problem. Before performance becomes so slow that your system is not responding, you can upgrade the hardware.

Using Alerts for Problem Notification

The Performance Logs and Alerts utility provides another tool for proactive management in the form of *alerts*. Through Performance Logs and Alerts, you can specify alert thresholds (when a counter reaches a specified value) and have the utility notify you when these thresholds are reached.

For example, you could specify that if your logical disk has less than 10 percent of free space, you want to be notified. Once alerted, you can add more disk space or delete unneeded files before you run out of disk space. You will learn how to create alerts in the "Using Performance Logs and Alerts" section later in this chapter.

Using System Monitor

Through *System Monitor*, you can view current data or data from a log file. When you view current activity, you are monitoring real-time activity. When you view data from a log file, you are importing a log file from a previous session.

After you've added the System Monitor snap-in to the MMC (see Exercise 14.1), you can open it by selecting Start ➢ Programs ➢ Administrative Tools ➢ Monitor. Figure 14.1 shows the main System Monitor window when you first open it.

FIGURE 14.1 The main System Monitor window

The System Monitor toolbar, shown below, provides access to all of the System Monitor functions.

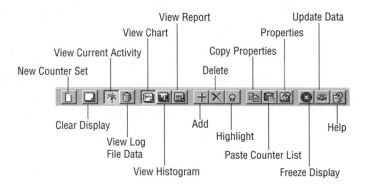

When you first start System Monitor, you will notice that nothing is tracked by default. In order for System Monitor to be useful, you must configure it to track some type of system activity, which is done by adding counters, as described shortly. After you've added counters, they will be listed at the bottom of the System Monitor window. The fields just above the counter list will contain data, based on the counter that is highlighted in the list, as follows:

- The Last field displays the most current data.

- The Average field shows the average of the counter.

- The Minimum field shows the lowest value that has been recorded for the counter.

- The Maximum field shows the highest value that has been recorded for the counter.

- The Duration field shows how long the counter has been tracking data.

The following sections describe the three System Monitor views, how to add counters to track data, and how to configure System Monitor properties.

Selecting the Appropriate View

By clicking the appropriate button on the System Monitor toolbar, you can see your data in three views:

Chart view   The chart view, shown in Figure 14.2, is the default view used with System Monitor. This view is useful for viewing a small number of counters in a graphical format. The main advantage of chart view is that you can see how the data has been tracked during the defined time period. When you start to track a large number of counters, it can be difficult to view the data in chart form.

Histogram view   The histogram view, shown in Figure 14.3, shows System Monitor data in bar graph form. This view is useful for viewing large amounts of data. However, it only shows performance for the current period. You do not see a record of performance over time, as you do with the chart view.

Report view   The report view, shown in Figure 14.4, is used to list all of the counters that are being tracked through System Monitor in a logical report. The data that is displayed is for the current session. Watching these numbers in real time is like watching someone on a pogo stick, because the numbers are constantly jumping up and down. The advantage of this view is that it allows you to easily track large numbers of counters in a real-time manner.

FIGURE 14.2 The chart view in System Monitor

FIGURE 14.3 The histogram view in System Monitor

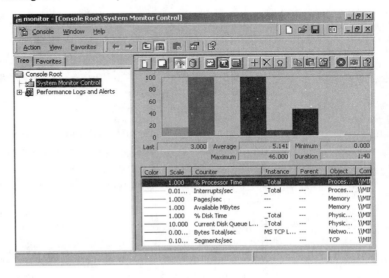

FIGURE 14.4 The report view in System Monitor

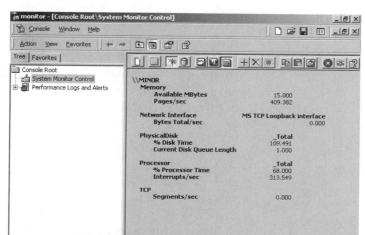

Adding Counters

To use System Monitor, you must add *counters*. To add counters, use the following steps:

1. In System Monitor, click the Add button on the toolbar. This brings up the Add Counters dialog box, as shown in Figure 14.5.

To see information about a specific counter, select it and click the Explain button in the upper-right corner of the Add Counters dialog box. System Monitor will display text regarding the highlighted counter.

FIGURE 14.5 The Add Counters dialog box

2. In the Add Counters dialog box, select the Use Local Computer Counters (the default) radio button to monitor the local computer. Alternatively, select the Select Counters from Computer radio button and choose a computer from the drop-down list to select counters from a specific computer. You can monitor remote computers if you have Administrative permissions. This option is useful when you do not want the overhead of System Monitor running on the computer you are trying to monitor.

3. Select the performance object from the drop-down list. All Windows 2000 system resources are tracked as performance objects, such as Cache, Memory, Paging File, Process, and Processor. The sum of all objects represents your total system. Some performance objects exist on all Windows 2000 computers; other objects appear only if specific processes or services are running. For example, if you want to track how busy the physical disk is, choose the Physical Disk performance object.

4. Select the All Counters radio button to track all the associated counters, or select the Select Counters from List radio button and choose specific counters from the list box below. Each performance object has an associated set of counters. Counters are used to track specific information regarding a performance object. For example, for the PhysicalDisk performance object, there is a %Disk Time counter, which will tell you how busy a disk has been servicing read and write requests. PhysicalDisk also has %Disk Read Time and %Disk Write Time counters, which will show you what percentage of disk requests are read requests and what percentage of disk requests are write requests, respectively.

You can select multiple counters of the same performance object by Shift+clicking contiguous counters or Ctrl+clicking noncontiguous counters.

5. Select the All Instances radio button to track all the associated instances, or select the Select Instances from List radio button and choose specific instances from the list box below. An instance is a mechanism that allows you to track how a specific object is performing if you have more than one item associated with a specific performance object. For example, suppose that your computer has two

physical drives. When you track the PhysicalDisk performance object, you can track both of your drives, or you could track drive 0 and drive 1 separately.

6. Click the Add button to add the counters for the performance object.

7. Repeat steps 2 through 6 to specify any additional counters you want to track. When you are finished, click the Close button.

After you've added counters, you can select a specific counter by highlighting it in System Monitor. To highlight a counter, click it and then click the Highlight button on the System Monitor toolbar. Alternatively, you can highlight a counter by selecting it and pressing Ctrl+H.

To remove a counter, highlight the counter in System Monitor and click the Delete button on the System Monitor toolbar.

Managing System Monitor Properties

To configure the System Monitor properties, click the Properties button on the System Monitor toolbar. This brings up the System Monitor Properties dialog box, as shown in Figure 14.6. This dialog box has six tabs: General, Source, Data, Graph, Colors, and Fonts. The properties you can configure on each of these tabs are described in the following sections.

FIGURE 14.6   The General tab of the System Monitor Properties dialog box

General Properties

The General tab of the System Monitor Properties dialog box (see Figure 14.6) contains the following options:

- The view that will be displayed: graph, histogram, or report
- The display elements that will be used: legend, value bar, and/or toolbar
- The data that will be displayed: default (for reports or histograms this is current data; for logs, this is average data), current, average, minimum, or maximum
- The appearance, either flat or 3D
- The border, either none or fixed single
- How often the data is updated, in seconds
- Whether duplicate counter instances are allowed

Source Properties

The Source tab, shown in Figure 14.7, allows you to specify the data source. This can be current activity, or it can be data that has been collected in a log file. If you import data from a log file, you can specify the time range that you wish to view.

FIGURE 14.7 The Source tab of the System Monitor Properties dialog box

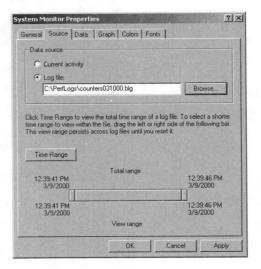

Data Properties

The Data tab, shown in Figure 14.8, lets you specify the counters that you wish to track. You can add and remove counters by clicking the Add and Remove buttons. You can also select a specific counter and define the color, scale, width, and style that is used to represent the counter in the graph.

FIGURE 14.8   The Data tab of the System Monitor Properties dialog box

Graph Properties

The Graph tab, shown in Figure 14.9, contains the following options, which can be applied to the chart or histogram view:

- A title

- A vertical axis label

- Whether you will show a vertical grid, a horizontal grid, and/or vertical scale numbers

- The minimum and maximum numbers for the vertical scale

FIGURE 14.9 **FIGURE 14.9** The Graph tab of the System Monitor Properties dialog box

Color and Font Properties

The Colors and Fonts tabs of the System Monitor Properties dialog box have options for customizing the appearance of the System Monitor display. In the Colors tab, you can choose the colors that will be used by System Monitor. In the Fonts, tab, you can choose the fonts that System Monitor will use.

Using Performance Logs and Alerts

Through *Performance Logs and Alerts*, you can create counter logs and trace logs, and you can define alerts. After you've created logs, you can view the log files with the System Monitor, as described in the previous section.

After you've added the Performance Logs and Alerts snap-in to the MMC (see Exercise 14.1), you can open it by selecting Start ➢ Programs ➢ Administrative Tools ➢ Monitor and clicking Performance Logs and Alerts. Figure 14.10 shows the expanded Performance Logs and Alerts snap-in. From here, you can define new counter logs, trace logs, and alerts, as described in the following sections.

FIGURE 14.10   The expanded Performance Logs and Alerts snap-in

Creating a Counter Log

Counter logs record data about hardware usage and the activity of system services. You can configure logging to occur manually or on a predefined schedule.

To create a counter log, take the following steps:

1. Expand Performance Logs and Alerts, right-click Counter Logs, and select New Log Settings from the pop-up menu.

2. The New Log Settings dialog box appears, as shown in Figure 14.11. Type in a name for the log file. For example, you might give the log a name that indicates its type and the date (Counter*mmddyy*). Then click the OK button.

FIGURE 14.11   The New Log Settings dialog box

3. The counter log file Properties dialog box appears. You can configure counter log properties as follows:

- In the General tab, shown in Figure 14.12, you can specify the counters you want to track in the log and the interval for sampling data. Click the Add button to add counters.

FIGURE 14.12 The General tab of the counter log file Properties dialog box

- In the Log Files tab, shown in Figure 14.13, you can configure the location of the log file, the filename, the log file type, and the log file size.

FIGURE 14.13 The Log Files tab of the counter log Properties dialog box

- In the Schedule tab, shown in Figure 14.14, you can specify when the log file will start, when the log file will stop, and what action should be taken, if any, when the log file is closed.

FIGURE 14.14 The Schedule tab of the counter log Properties dialog box

4. When you are finished configuring the counter log file properties, click the OK button. The log will be created and will record the activity for the counters you specified.

Creating a Trace Log

Trace logs measure data continuously as opposed to measuring data through periodic samples. Trace logs are also used to track data that is collected by the operating system or programs. For example, you could specify that you want to trace the creation or deletion of processes or threads.

To create a trace log, take the following steps:

1. Expand Performance Logs and Alerts, right-click Trace Logs, and select New Log Settings from the pop-up menu.

2. The New Log Settings dialog box appears. Type in a name for the log file, such as the type of log and the date (Trace*mmddyy*), and click the OK button.

3. The trace log file Properties dialog box appears. You can configure trace log properties as follows:

- In the General tab, shown in Figure 14.15, you can select which system events you want to track. For example, you can check the Process Creations/Deletions and Thread Creations/Deletions check boxes. You can also specify which system providers you want to track.

FIGURE 14.15 The General tab of the trace log file Properties dialog box

- In the Log Files tab, shown in Figure 14.16, you can configure the location, filename, log file type, and log file size.

FIGURE 14.16 The Log Files tab of the trace log file Properties dialog box

- In the Schedule tab, shown in Figure 14.17, you can configure when the log file will start, when the log file will stop, and what action should be taken, if any, when the log file is closed.

FIGURE 14.17 The Schedule tab of the trace log file Properties dialog box

- In the Advanced tab, shown in Figure 14.18, you can configure the buffer settings for the log file. By default, the log service will save the trace file to memory and then transfer the data to the log file.

FIGURE 14.18 The Advanced tab of the trace log file Properties dialog box

4. When you are finished configuring the trace file properties, click the OK button. The log will be created and will record the activity for the system events you specified.

Creating an Alert

Alerts can be generated when a specific counter exceeds or falls below a specified value. You can configure alerts so that a message is sent, a program is run, or a more detailed log file is generated.

To create an alert, take the following steps:

1. Expand Performance Logs and Alerts, right-click Alerts, and select New Alert Settings from the pop-up menu.

2. The New Alert Settings dialog box appears. Type in a name for the alert file and click the OK button.

3. The alert file Properties dialog box appears. You can configure alert properties as follows:

   - In the General tab, shown in Figure 14.19, you can select which counters you want to track. When you add a counter, you must specify that the alert be generated when the counter is under or over a certain value. You can also set the interval for sampling data.

FIGURE 14.19   The General tab of the alert Properties dialog box

- In the Action tab, shown in Figure 14.20, specify what action should be taken if an alert is triggered. You can select to log an entry in the application event log, send a network message, start another performance data log, and/or run a specific program.

FIGURE 14.20 The Action tab of the alert Properties dialog box

- In the Schedule tab, shown in Figure 14.21, you can configure when scans of the counters you have defined will start and stop.

FIGURE 14.21 The Schedule tab of the alert Properties dialog box

> **4.** When you are finished configuring the alert properties, click the OK button.

Monitoring and Optimizing Memory

When a program or process is required by the operating system, the first place it looks is physical memory. If the program or process is not in physical memory, the system will look in logical memory (the page file). If the program or process is not in logical memory, the system will need to retrieve the program or process from the hard disk. It has been estimated that it can take up to 1,000 times longer to access information from the hard disk than to access it from physical RAM.

Memory is the most likely cause of system bottlenecks. If you have no idea what is causing a system bottleneck, memory is usually a good place to start checking. To determine how memory is being used, there are two areas you need to examine:

- Physical memory, which is the physical RAM you have installed on your computer. You can't have too much memory. It's actually a good idea to have more memory than you think you will need just to be on the safe side. As you've probably noticed, each time you add or upgrade applications, you require more system memory.

- The *page file*, which is logical memory that exists on the hard drive. If you are using excessive paging (swapping between the page file and physical RAM), it's a clear sign that you need to add more memory.

For example, suppose that the accounting department has just started using a new accounting application that runs on the accounting manager's local computer. The accounting manager complains that this application is slow, and he says that he needs a new computer. You decide to use System Monitor to determine why the computer is responding so slowly. You see that the processor utilization is low, and that the system is using excessive paging. Based on this information, you determine that the account manager's computer will work with the application, but it needs a memory upgrade.

NOTE   In this book, we use the format *performance object > counter*. For example, Memory > Available MBytes denotes the Memory performance object and the Available MBytes counter.

The following are the three most important counters for monitoring memory:

- Memory > Available MBytes measures the amount of physical memory that is available to run processes on the computer. If this number is less than 4MB, you should consider adding more memory.

- Memory > Pages/Sec shows the number of times that the requested information was not in memory and the request had to be retrieved from disk. This counter's value should be below 20. For optimal performance, this counter's value should be 4 to 5.

- Paging File > %Usage indicates how much of the allocated page file is currently in use. If this number is consistently over 99%, you may need to add more memory.

These counters work together to show what is happening on your system, so you should use the Paging File > % Usage counter value in conjunction with the Memory > Available MBytes and Memory > Pages/Sec counters to determine how much paging is occurring on your computer.

Some documentation suggests that you can optimize memory by manipulating the page file. This generally applies to servers that use more sophisticated disk subsystems. On a regular workstation running Windows 2000 Professional, the best way to optimize memory is to add more physical memory.

In Exercise 14.2, you will monitor your computer's memory subsystem. This exercise assumes that you have completed Exercise 14.1.

EXERCISE 14.2

Monitoring System Memory

1. Select Start ➢ Programs ➢ Administrative Tools ➢ Monitor.

2. In the System Monitor window, click the Add button on the toolbar.

3. In the Add Counters dialog box, select the following performance objects and counters:

   - Select Memory from the performance object drop-down list, select Available MBytes in the counter list box, and click the Add button.

- Select Memory from the performance object drop-down list, select Pages/Sec in the counter list box, and click the Add button.

- Select Paging File from the performance object drop-down list, select %Usage in the counter list box, and click the Add button.

4. Click the Close button. You should see a chart showing how your computer's memory is being used.

5. To generate some activity, select Start ➤ Help. Close Help. Open Help again and then close Help. You should have seen that the first time you opened Help, your Memory > Pages/Sec counter spiked, and the second time you accessed Help, the spike was much lower. This is because the first time you accessed the program, it needed to be retrieved from disk; the second time you accessed this program, it was already in memory.

6. Note the Paging > %Usage counter. If this counter is below 99%, you are not using excessive paging.

7. Note the Memory > Available MBytes counter. If this counter is above 4MB, you should have sufficient RAM.

Leave System Monitor open, because you will use this utility again in Exercise 14.3.

Monitoring and Optimizing the Processor

Although processors are usually not the source of bottlenecks, you should still monitor this subsystem to make sure that processor utilization is at an efficient level.

The following are the two most important counters for monitoring the system processor:

- Processor > %Processor Time measures the time that the processor spends responding to system requests. If this value is consistently above an average of 80%, you may have a processor bottleneck.

- Processor > Interrupts/Sec shows the average number of hardware interrupts the processor receives each second. If this value is more than 3,500 on a Pentium computer, you might have a problem with a program or hardware that is generating spurious interrupts.

If you suspect that you have a processor bottleneck, you can try the following solutions:

- Use less processor-intensive applications.

- Upgrade your processor.

- If your computer supports multiple processors, add a processor. Windows 2000 Professional can support up to two processors, which will help if you use multithreaded applications.

Beware of running 3-D screen savers on your computer. As you will see in Exercise 14.3, they can use quite a bit of the processor's time.

In Exercise 14.3, you will monitor your computer's processor. This exercise assumes that you have completed the other exercises in this chapter.

EXERCISE 14.3

Monitoring the System Processor

1. If System Monitor is not already open, select Start ➢ Programs ➢ Administrative Tools ➢ Monitor.

2. In the System Monitor window, click the Add button on the toolbar.

3. In the Add Counters dialog box, select the following performance objects and counters:

   - Select Processor from the performance object drop-down list, select %Processor Time in the counter list box, and click the Add button.

   - Select Processor from the performance object drop-down list, select Interrupts/Sec in the counter list box, and click the Add button.

4. Click the Close button. You should see these counters added to your chart.

5. To generate some activity, select Start ➢ Settings ➢ Control Panel ➢ Display. Click the Screen Saver tab. Select 3D FlowerBox (OpenGL) and click the Preview button. Let this process run for about 5 seconds. Close all of the dialog boxes you opened in this step. You should see that the %Processor Time counter spiked during this process.

6. Note the Processor > %Processor Time counter. If this counter's average is below 80%, you do not have a processor bottleneck.

7. Note the Processor > Interrupts/Sec counter. If this counter is below 3,500 on a Pentium computer, you do not have any processes or hardware that are generating excessive interrupts.

Leave System Monitor open, because you will use this utility again in Exercise 14.4.

Monitoring and Optimizing the Disk Subsystem

Disk access is the amount of time it takes your disk subsystem to retrieve data that is requested by the operating system. The two factors that determine how quickly your disk subsystem will respond to system requests are the average disk access time on your hard drive and the speed of your disk controller.

You can monitor the PhysicalDisk object, which is the sum of all logical drives on a single physical drive, or you can monitor the LogicalDisk object, which represents a specific logical disk. The following are the most important counters for monitoring the disk subsystem:

- PhysicalDisk > %Disk Time shows the amount of time the physical disk is busy because it is servicing read or write requests. If the disk is busy more than 90% of the time, you will improve performance by adding another disk channel and splitting the disk I/O requests between the channels.

- PhysicalDisk > %Current Disk Queue Length indicates the number of outstanding disk requests that are waiting to be processed. This value should be less than 2.

These counters can be tracked for both the PhysicalDisk object and the LogicalDisk object.

If you suspect that you have a disk subsystem bottleneck, the first thing you should check is your memory subsystem. If you do not have enough physical memory, it can cause excessive paging, which in turn affects the disk subsystem. If you do not have a memory problem, you can try the following solutions to improve disk performance:

- Use faster disks and controllers.
- Use disk striping to take advantage of multiple I/O channels.
- Balance heavily used files on multiple I/O channels.
- Add another disk controller for load balancing.

In Windows NT 4, you enabled all disk counters through the DISKPERF -Y command. Physical disk counters are automatically enabled in Windows 2000 Professional. However, you must enable DISKPERF to track the logical disk object and counters.

In Exercise 14.4, you will monitor your disk subsystem. This exercise assumes that you have completed the other exercises in this chapter.

EXERCISE 14.4

Monitoring the Disk Subsystem

1. If System Monitor is not already open, select Start ➤ Programs ➤ Administrative Tools ➤ Monitor.

2. In the System Monitor window, click the Add button on the toolbar.

3. Notice that there is a performance object for PhysicalDisk, but but not LogicalDisk.

4. Select Start ➤ Programs ➤ Accessories ➤ Command Prompt.

5. At the command prompt, type **DISKPERF -Y** and press Enter. You see a message stating that both the logical and physical disk performance counters are set to start when the computer boots. Close the Command Prompt dialog box and restart your computer.

6. Select Start ➤ Programs ➤ Administrative Tools ➤ Monitor.

7. In the System Monitor window, click the Add button on the toolbar.

EXERCISE 14.4 *(continued)*

8. In the Add Counters dialog box, select the following performance objects and counters:

   - Select PhysicalDisk from the performance object drop-down list, select %Disk Time from the counter list box, and click the Add button.

   - Select PhysicalDisk from the performance object drop-down list, select Current Disk Queue Length from the counter list box, and click the Add button.

   - Select LogicalDisk from the performance object drop-down list, select %Idle Time from the counter list box, and click the Add button.

9. Click the Close button. You should see these counters added to your chart.

10. To generate some activity, open and close some applications and copy some files between your C: drive and D: drive.

11. Note the PhysicalDisk > %Disk Time counter. If this counter's average is below 90%, you are not generating excessive requests to this disk.

12. Note the PhysicalDisk > %Current Disk Queue Length counter. If this counter's average is below 2, you are not generating excessive requests to this disk.

Leave System Monitor open, because you will use this utility again in Exercise 14.5.

You can monitor your logical disk's amount of free disk space through the LogicalDisk > %Free Space counter. This counter can also be used as an alert. For example, you might set an alert to notify you when LogicalDisk > %Free Space on your C: drive is under 10%.

Monitoring and Optimizing the Network Subsystem

Windows 2000 Professional does not have a built-in mechanism for monitoring the entire network. However, you can monitor and optimize the traffic that is generated on the specific Windows 2000 computer. You can monitor the network interface (your network card), and you can monitor the network protocols that have been installed on your computer.

The following are two of the counters that are useful for monitoring the network subsystem:

- Network Interface > Bytes Total/Sec measures the total number of bytes that are sent or received from the network interface and includes all network protocols.

- TCP > Segments/Sec measures the number of bytes that are sent or received from the network interface and includes only the TCP protocol.

Normally, you monitor and optimize the network subsystem from a network perspective rather than from a single computer. For example, you can use a network protocol analyzer to monitor all of the traffic on the network to determine if the network bandwidth is acceptable for your requirements or if the network bandwidth is saturated.

The following suggestions can help to optimize and minimize network traffic:

- Use only the network protocols you need. For example, use TCP/IP and don't use NWLink and NetBEUI.

- If you need to use multiple network protocols, place the most commonly used protocols higher in the binding order.

- Use network cards that take full advantage of your bus width. For example, use 32-bit cards instead of 16-bit cards.

- Use faster network cards. For example, use 100Mbps Ethernet instead of 10Mbps Ethernet.

In Exercise 14.5, you will monitor your network subsystem. This exercise assumes that you have completed the other exercises in this chapter.

EXERCISE 14.5

Monitoring the Network Subsystem

1. If System Monitor is not already open, select Start ➢ Programs ➢ Administrative Tools ➢ Monitor.

2. In the System Monitor window, click the Add button on the toolbar.

3. In the Add Counters dialog box, select the following performance objects and counters:

   - Select Network Interface from the performance object drop-down list, select Bytes Total/Sec in the counter list box, and click the Add button.

   - Select TCP from the performance object drop-down list, select Segments/Sec from the counter list box, and click the Add button.

4. Click the Close button. You should see these counters added to your chart.

5. To generate some activity, copy some files between your C: drive and D: drive.

6. Note the Network Interface > Bytes Total/Sec and TCP > Segments/ Sec counters. These numbers are cumulative. Use them in your baselines to determine network activity.

Leave your Monitor console open, because you will use it again in Exercise 14.6.

Creating Baseline Reports

As explained earlier in this chapter, baselines show how your server is performing at a certain time. By taking baselines at regular intervals and also whenever you make any changes to the system's configuration, you can monitor your server's performance over time.

You can create baselines by setting up a counter log file in the Performance Logs and Alerts utility. After you've created the baseline log file, you can view it in System Monitor, as shown in Figure 14.22.

FIGURE 14.22   Viewing a baseline in System Monitor

In Exercise 14.6, you will create a baseline report for your computer.

EXERCISE 14.6

Creating a Baseline Report

1. If the Monitor console is not already open, select Start ➢ Programs ➢ Administrative Tools ➢ Monitor.

2. Double-click Performance Logs and Alerts.

3. Right-click Counter Logs and select New Log Settings.

EXERCISE 14.6 *(continued)*

4. In the New Log Settings dialog box, type **Counter***mmddyy* (replace *mmddyy* with the current month, date, and year) as the log name. The log file should be stored in the C:\PerfLogs folder by default. Click the OK button.

5. In the General tab of the counter log Properties dialog box, click the Add button and add the following counters:

   - Memory > Available MBytes

   - Memory > Pages/Sec

   - Paging File > %Usage

   - Processor > %Processor Time

   - Processor > Interrupts/Sec

   - PhysicalDisk > %Disk Time

   - PhysicalDisk > Current Disk Queue Length

   - Network Interface > Bytes Total/Sec

   - TCP > Segments/Sec

6. Set the interval for sampling data to 5 seconds.

7. Click the Log Files tab. Uncheck the End File Names With check box. This will prevent the filename from being appended with *mmddhh* (month/day/hour). Click the OK button to close the Properties dialog box and start the log file.

8. To generate system activity, start and stop some applications, copy a few files, and run a screen saver for 1 to 2 minutes.

9. To view your log file, open System Monitor. Click the View Log File Data button on the toolbar.

10. In the open file dialog box, select C:\PerfLogs\Counter*mmddyy* and click the Open button.

11. Add the counters from the log file you created to see the data that was collected in your log.

Using Task Manager

The *Task Manager* utility shows the applications and processes that are currently running on your computer, as well as CPU and memory usage information. To access Task Manager, press Ctrl+Alt+Delete and click the Task Manager button. Alternatively, right-click an empty area in the Taskbar and select Task Manager from the pop-up menu.

Managing Application Tasks

The Applications tab of the Task Manager dialog box, shown in Figure 14.23, lists all of the applications that are currently running on the computer. For each task, you will see the name of the task and the current status (running, not responding, or stopped).

FIGURE 14.23 The Applications tab of the Task Manager dialog box

To close an application, select it and click the End Task button at the bottom of the dialog box. To make the application window active, select it and click the Switch To button. If you want to start an application that isn't running, click the New Task button and specify the location and name of the program you wish to start.

Managing Process Tasks

The Processes tab of the Task Manager dialog box, shown in Figure 14.24, lists all of the processes that are currently running on the computer. This is a convenient way to get a quick look at how your system is performing. Unlike with System Monitor, you don't need to first configure the collection of this data; it's gathered automatically.

FIGURE 14.24   The Processes tab of the Task Manager dialog box

For each process, you will see a unique process ID (PID) that changes each time a process is started, the amount of CPU utilization that the process is using, and the amount of time the processor spent running the process.

From the Processes tab, you can organize the listing and control processes as follows:

- To organize the processes based on usage, click the column headings. For example, if you click the CPU column, the listing will start with the processes that use the most CPU resources. If you click the CPU column a second time, the listing will be reversed.

- To manage a process, right-click it and choose an option from the pop-up menu. You can choose to end the process, end the process tree, or set the priority of the process (to real time, high, above normal, normal, below normal, or low). If your computer has multiple processors installed, you can also set processor affinity (the process of associating a specific process with a specific processor) for a process. See Chapter 4, "Configuring the Windows 2000 Environment," for details on setting processor affinity.

- To customize the counters that are listed, select View ➢ Select Columns. This brings up the Select Columns dialog box, shown in Figure 14.25, where you can select the information that you want to see listed on the Processes tab.

FIGURE 14.25   The Select Columns dialog box

Managing Performance Tasks

The Performance tab of the Task Manager dialog box, shown in Figure 14.26, provides an overview of your computer's CPU and memory usage. This is similar to the information that System Monitor tracks, and you don't need to configure it first as you do with System Monitor.

FIGURE 14.26 The Performance tab of the Task Manager dialog box

Microsoft ✓ Exam Objective	**Optimize and troubleshoot performance of the Windows 2000 Professional desktop.** • Optimize and troubleshoot memory performance

The Performance tab shows the following information:

- CPU usage, real-time and history graph
- Memory usage, real-time and history graph
- Totals for handles, threads, and processes
- Physical memory statistics
- Commit charge memory statistics
- Kernel memory statistics

Configuring Application Performance

If you run multiple applications concurrently on your Windows 2000 Professional computer, the foreground application is given higher priority when the applications are processed. As noted in the previous section, you can dynamically change an application's priority through the Processes tab of the Task Manager dialog box. The options for foreground and background application processing are accessed through the System icon in Control Panel.

To configure application performance, open Control Panel, double-click the System icon, select the Advanced tab, and click the Performance Options button. You will see the Performance Options dialog box, as shown in Figure 14.27.

FIGURE 14.27 The Performance Options dialog box

This dialog box allows you to configure application response as follows:

- If you select the Applications radio button, foreground applications are always processed at a higher priority than background applications.

- If you select the Background Services radio button, foreground and background applications are processed at the same priority.

In Exercise 14.7, you will configure your computer so that foreground and background applications are processed at the same priority.

EXERCISE 14.7

Optimizing Applications

1. Select Start ➤ Settings ➤ Control Panel and double-click the System icon.

EXERCISE 14.7 *(continued)*

2. In the System Properties dialog box, click the Advanced tab.

3. Click the Performance Options button.

4. In the Performance Options dialog box, click the Background Services radio button. Then click the OK button.

5. In the System Properties dialog box, click the OK button.

Scheduling Tasks

Windows 2000 Professional includes a *Task Scheduler* utility that allows you to schedule tasks to occur at specified intervals. You can have any of your Windows programs run automatically at a specific time and at a set interval, such as daily, weekly, or monthly. For example, you might schedule your Windows Backup program to run daily at 2:00 A.M.

Microsoft ✓ *Exam Objective*   **Configure, manage, and troubleshoot the Task Scheduler.**

Creating a New Task

To set up scheduled tasks, take the following steps:

1. Select Start ➢ Settings ➢ Control Panel and double-click the Scheduled Tasks icon.

2. The Scheduled Tasks window appears, as shown in Figure 14.28. Double-click the Add Scheduled Task icon.

FIGURE 14.28 The Scheduled Tasks window

3. The Scheduled Task Wizard starts, as shown in Figure 14.29. Click the Next button.

FIGURE 14.29 Starting the Scheduled Task Wizard

> **4.** The first Scheduled Task Wizard dialog box lists applications you can run, as shown in Figure 14.30. You can select an application from the list or click the Browse button to locate any application or program that your computer has access to. After you select an application, click the Next button.

FIGURE 14.30 Selecting an application

> **5.** The next Scheduled Task Wizard dialog box, shown in Figure 14.31, prompts you to select a name for the task and specify when the task will be performed. Your choices are Daily, Weekly, Monthly, One Time Only, When My Computer Starts, or When I Log On. Make your selection and click the Next button.

FIGURE 14.31 Specifying a name and schedule

6. Depending on the selection you made for the task's schedule, you may see another dialog box for setting the specific schedule. For example, if you chose to run the task weekly, the next dialog box lets you select the start time for the task, run the task every *x* weeks, and choose the day of the week that the task should be run, as shown in Figure 14.32. Make your selection and click the Next button.

FIGURE 14.32 Setting a daily schedule

7. The next Scheduled Task Wizard dialog box prompts you to enter the username and password that will be used to start the task, as shown in Figure 14.33. After you enter this information, click the Next button.

FIGURE 14.33 Entering a username and password for running a scheduled task

8. The final dialog box shows your selections for the scheduled task, as shown in Figure 14.34. If this information is correct, click the Finish button.

FIGURE 14.34   Confirming the scheduled task configuration

In Exercise 14.8, you will create a scheduled task.

EXERCISE 14.8

Creating a Scheduled Task

1. Select Start ➢ Settings ➢ Control Panel and double-click the Scheduled Tasks icon.

2. In the Scheduled Tasks window, double-click the Add Scheduled Task icon.

3. In the opening Scheduled Task Wizard dialog box, click the Next button.

4. In the next dialog box, highlight Disk Cleanup and click the Next button.

5. In the next dialog box, leave the default name for the task and make sure that the Weekly radio button is selected. Click the Next button.

EXERCISE 14.8 *(continued)*

6. In the Start Time and Day field, select the time that is 2 minutes from your current time, select every one week, and select the current day of the week. Click the Next button.

7. Enter the Administrator name and password and click the Next button.

8. In the final dialog box, click the Finish button.

9. Wait for your scheduled task to run.

Managing Scheduled Task Properties

You can manage a scheduled task through its properties dialog box, as shown in Figure 14.35. To access this dialog box, open the Scheduled Tasks window (by selecting Start ➤ Settings ➤ Control Panel and double-clicking the Scheduled Tasks icon), right-click the task you wish to manage, and select Properties from the pop-up menu.

FIGURE 14.35   The Disk Cleanup task properties

The scheduled task dialog box has four tabs with options for managing how and when the task is run and who can manage it. These options are described in the following sections.

Task Properties

Through the Task tab (see Figure 14.35), you can configure the following options:

- The command-line program that is used to run the task
- The folders that contain related files that might be required to run the specified task (the Start In option)
- Any comments that you want to include for informational purposes
- The username and password that should be used to run the specified task (the Run As option)
- Whether the scheduled task is enabled

Schedule Properties

The Schedule tab, shown in Figure 14.36, shows the schedule configured for the task. You can change any of the options on this tab to reschedule the task.

FIGURE 14.36 The Schedule tab of the scheduled task dialog box

Settings Properties

Through the Settings tab, shown in Figure 14.37, you can configure several settings for the scheduled task:

- The options in the Scheduled Task Completed section allow you to delete the task if it will not be run again and specify how long the task should be allowed to run before it is stopped.

- The options in the Idle Time section are useful if the computer must be idle when the task is run. You can specify how long the computer must be idle before the task begins and whether the task should be stopped if the computer ceases to be idle.

- The options in the Power Management section are useful if the computer on which the task runs may be battery-powered. You can specify that the task should not start if the computer is running from batteries and choose to stop the task if battery mode begins.

FIGURE 14.37 The Settings tab of the scheduled task dialog box

Security Properties

The Security tab, shown in Figure 14.38, allows you to configure the security settings for the scheduled task object. Normally, only Administrators can manage scheduled tasks. However, you might want to assign this task to other users, who will need the appropriate permissions to manage scheduled tasks. To assign permissions for a task, click the Add button, select the user or group, and then check the Allow or Deny check boxes for the permissions. (See Chapter 10, "Accessing Files and Folders," for more information about assigning permissions to users and groups.)

FIGURE 14.38 The Security tab of the scheduled task dialog box

Summary

In this chapter, you learned about Windows 2000 Professional optimization and reliability. We covered the following topics:

- How to keep your operating system up to date by using the Windows Update utility and applying Windows 2000 service packs

- How to use the System Monitor utility and the Performance Logs and Alerts utility to track and monitor your system's performance

- How to monitor and optimize memory, the processor, the disk subsystem, and the network subsystem and how to create a system baseline

- How to use the Task Manager utility to view and manage running applications and processes, and to get an overview of CPU and memory usage

- How to use the System icon in the Control Panel to optimize application performance

- How to automate tasks through the Task Scheduler utility

Key Terms

Before taking the exam, you should be familiar with the following terms:

alert

baseline

bottleneck

counter

page file

Performance Logs and Alerts

service pack

slipstream technology

System Monitor

Task Manager

Task Scheduler

Windows Update

Review Questions

1. Which of the following options is *not* a valid view in Windows 2000 System Monitor?

   A. Chart

   B. Histogram

   C. Report

   D. Graph

2. Which of the following options *cannot* be configured through Performance Logs and Alerts?

   A. Report logs

   B. Counter logs

   C. Trace logs

   D. Alerts

3. You are monitoring the Memory > Available MBytes counter and see that it is at 12MB. What should you do?

   A. Add RAM

   B. Increase the size of the page file

   C. Split the page file over two physical disk channels

   D. Take no action

4. You are monitoring your Window 2000 Professional computer for a processor bottleneck. When monitoring the Processor > %Processor Time counter, what number would indicate a potential bottleneck?

   A. 5%

   B. 50%

   C. 60%

   D. 85%

5. You notice that your disk subsystem has a high load of activity. What other subsystem should you monitor before determining you have a disk subsystem bottleneck?

A. Memory

B. Processor

C. Network

D. Application

6. Which of the following two subsystems can be easily monitored for performance through the Task Manager utility?

A. Memory

B. Processor

C. Network

D. Disk

7. Which Windows 2000 utility would you use if you wanted to automate a specific application to run every day at 5:00 P.M.?

A. Scheduled Tasks

B. Automated Scheduler

C. Task Manager

D. Task Automater

8. Which Windows 2000 mechanism allows you to deliver bug fixes to the Windows 2000 operating system?

A. Windows Update

B. Service packs

C. Service fixes

D. Windows Upgrade

9. Which Windows 2000 mechanism allows you to connect to Microsoft's Web site to update operating system files?

A. Windows Update

B. Service packs

C. Service fixes

D. Windows Upgrade

10. What needs to be done in order to enable physical disk counters in System Monitor?

A. Run DISKPERF -y

B. Run DISKCOUNT -y

C. Run PERFMON -y

D. The counters are enabled by default

11. You are troubleshooting a Windows 2000 Professional computer in your company. Which command can you use to determine whether any service packs have been applied to the computer?

A. SERVPACK

B. WINVER

C. CURRENTVER

D. CONFIG

12. You suspect that you have a memory bottleneck on your computer. You decide to run System Monitor. You want to track five memory-related counters and see how the data is tracked over a specified time period. Which view should you use in System Monitor?

A. Chart

B. Histogram

C. Trace

D. Report

13. Which of the following counters are added to System Monitor by default?

    A. Memory > Pages/Sec

    B. Processor > %Processor Time

    C. Paging File > %Usage

    D. None

14. You want to configure alerts to be generated when a specific counter exceeds a specific value. Which of the following actions can be generated when an alert is generated? Choose three answers.

    A. Run a specific program

    B. Page a specific person with a predefined code

    C. Send a text message

    D. Generate a more detailed log file

15. You are monitoring the Processor > Interrupts/Sec counter through System Monitor. You should suspect that you have a program or piece of hardware that is generating spurious interrupts when this counter reaches which of the following values on a Pentium computer?

    A. 250

    B. 500

    C. 1,000

    D. 3,500

16. You are monitoring the PhysicalDisk > Current Disk Queue Length counter through System Monitor. You might have a disk subsystem bottleneck when this counter is over which of the following values?

    A. 1

    B. 2

    C. 10

    D. 12

17. You have an application that seems to have hung. Which utility can you use to see the current status of the application?

A. Application Manager

B. Service Manager

C. Task Manager

D. Control Panel, Add/Remove Programs

18. When you schedule a task to be run, which of the following task properties *cannot* be configured?

A. The username and password of the user who will run the task

B. Power management, so that if the computer is battery-operated, the task will not run if the computer is running on batteries

C. Whether the task will be run once or will be a recurring task

D. Whether another task will be run if specific conditions trigger the secondary task

19. You want to track system performance for a baseline over a period of two days. You want the data to be collected every five minutes. What type of log would you create through Performance Logs and Alerts?

A. Counter log

B. Trace log

C. Monitoring log

D. Baseline log

20. You are monitoring the Memory > Pages/Sec counter through System Monitor. Which of the following statements reflects what is considered optimal performance for this counter?

A. This counter's value should be around 4 to 5.

B. This counter's value should be around 30 to 40.

C. This counter's value should be around 40 to 50.

D. This counter's value should be around 50 to 60.

Answers to Review Questions

1. D. There is no graph view in System Monitor. The three views that are supported are chart, histogram, and report.

2. A. Through Performance Logs and Alerts, you can configure counter logs, trace logs, and alerts.

3. D. As long as the Memory > Available MBytes counter shows more than 4MB of memory, no bottleneck is indicated, so you would not need to take any action.

4. D. If the average Processor > %Processor Time counter is consistently above 80%, a processor bottleneck may be indicated.

5. A. You should check the memory. If your computer does not have enough memory, it can cause excessive paging, which may be perceived as a disk subsystem bottleneck.

6. A, B. Through the Performance tab of Task Manager, you can easily monitor your computer's current processor and memory utilization.

7. A. To automate scheduled tasks, you use the Scheduled Tasks utility.

8. B. Service packs are used to deliver bug fixes (and some new features) to the Windows 2000 operating system.

9. A. The Windows Update utility connects you to the Microsoft Web site to make sure you have the most current files.

10. D. In Windows 2000, physical disk counters are enabled by default. In order to view Logical Disk counters, you must run `DISKPERF -y`.

11. B. The `WINVER` command is used to display the current operating system that is loaded, any service packs that are loaded, and the amount of physical memory that is installed on the computer.

12. A. The chart view is used to display a small number of counters in a graphical format. With this view, you can easily track information over a specified time period.

13. D. No counters are tracked by System Monitor by default.

14. A, C, D. When you create an alert, you can configure the following actions when an alert is generated: log an entry to the Application event log, send a network message to a specified user, start a performance data log, or run a specified program.

15. D. The Processor > Interrupts/Sec counter shows the average number of hardware interrupts the processor receives each second. If this value is more than 3,500 on a Pentium computer, you might have a problem with a program or hardware that is generating spurious interrupts.

16. B. The PhysicalDisk > Current Disk Queue Length counter indicates the number of outstanding disk requests that are waiting to be processed. This value should be less than 2.

17. C. The Applications tab of the Task Manager dialog box lists all of the applications that are currently running on the computer. For each task, you will see the name of the task and the current status (running, not responding, or stopped).

18. D. There are no options to trigger secondary conditional tasks.

19. A. Counter logs record data about hardware usage and the activity of system services. You can configure logging to occur manually or on a predefined schedule.

20. A. The Memory > Pages/Sec counter shows the number of times that the requested information was not in memory and the information needed to be retrieved from disk. This counter's value should be below 20. For optimal performance, this counter's value should be 4 to 5.

Chapter

15

Performing System Recovery Functions

MICROSOFT EXAM OBJECTIVES COVERED IN THIS CHAPTER

✓ **Recover systems and user data.**

- Recover systems and user data by using Windows Backup.
- Troubleshoot system restoration by using Safe Mode.
- Recover systems and user data by using the Recovery Console.

System recovery is the process of making your computer work again in the event of failure. In this chapter, you will learn how to safeguard your computer and how to recover from a disaster. The benefit of having a disaster recovery plan is that when you expect the worst to happen and are prepared for it, you can easily recover from most system failures.

One utility that you can use to diagnose system problems is Event Viewer. Through the Event Viewer utility, you can see logs that list events related to your operating system and applications.

If your computer will not boot, an understanding of the Window 2000 boot process will help you identify the area of failure and correct the problem. You should know the steps in each stage of the boot process, the function of each boot file, and how to edit the `BOOT.INI` file.

When you have problems starting Windows 2000, you can press F8 when prompted during the boot sequence. This calls up the Windows 2000 Advanced Options menu, which is new to Windows 2000. This menu includes several special boot options, such as Safe Mode and Last Known Good Configuration, which are useful for getting your system started so you can track down and correct problems.

Startup and Recovery options are used to specify how the operating system will react in the event of system failure. For example, you can specify whether or not the system should automatically reboot and whether or not administrative alerts should be sent.

You can use the Dr. Watson utility, which ships with Windows 2000 Professional, to diagnose application errors. When an application error occurs, Dr. Watson starts automatically, displaying information about the error.

If you cannot boot the operating system and your CD-ROM is not accessible, you can recover by using the Windows 2000 Professional Setup Boot

Disks. After you've created these setup disks, you can use them to reinstall Windows 2000, start the Recovery Console or access your Emergency Repair Disk.

Backups are the best protection you can have against system failure. You can create backups through the Windows Backup utility. The Windows Backup utility offers options to run the Backup Wizard, run the Restore Wizard, and create an Emergency Repair Disk.

Another option that experienced administrators can use to recover from a system failure is the Recovery Console. The Recovery Console boots your computer so that you have limited access to FAT16, FAT32, and NTFS volumes.

In this chapter, you will learn how to use the Windows 2000 Professional system recovery functions. We'll begin with an overview of the techniques you can use to protect your computer and recover from disasters.

Safeguarding Your Computer and Recovering from Disaster

One of the worst events you will experience is a computer that won't boot. An even worse experience is discovering that there is no recent backup for that computer.

Microsoft ✓ *Exam Objective*

Recover systems and user data.

- Recover systems and user data by using Windows Backup.
- Troubleshoot system restoration by using Safe Mode.
- Recover systems and user data by using the Recovery Console.

The first step in preparing for disaster recovery is to expect that a disaster will occur at some point and take proactive steps before the failure to plan your recovery. The following are some of the preparations you can make:

- Perform regular system backups.

- Use virus-scanning software.

- Perform regular administrative functions, such as monitoring the logs in the Event Viewer utility.

In the event that the dreaded day arrives and your system fails, there are several processes you can analyze and Windows 2000 utilities that you can use to help you get up and running. These options are summarized in Table 15.1.

TABLE 15.1 Windows 2000 Professional Recovery Techniques

Recovery Technique	When to Use
Event Viewer	If the Windows 2000 operating system can be loaded through normal or Safe Mode, one of the first places to look for hints about the problem is Event Viewer. Event Viewer displays System, Security, and Application logs.
Safe Mode	This is generally your starting point for system recovery. Safe Mode loads the absolute minimum of services and drivers that are needed to boot Windows 2000. If you can load Safe Mode, you may be able to troubleshoot devices or services that keep Windows 2000 from loading normally.
Last Known Good Configuration	You can use this option if you made changes to your computer and are now having problems. Last Known Good Configuration is an Advanced Options menu item that you can select during startup. It loads the configuration that was used the last time the computer booted successfully. This option will not help if you have hardware errors.

TABLE 15.1 Windows 2000 Professional Recovery Techniques *(continued)*

Recovery Technique	When to Use
Windows 2000 Professional Setup Boot Disks	You can use this option if you suspect that Windows 2000 is not loading due to missing or corrupt boot files. This option allows you to load all the Windows 2000 boot files. If you can boot from a boot disk, you can restore the necessary files from the Emergency Repair Disk.
Emergency Repair Disk (ERD)	You can use this option if you need to correct configuration errors or to repair system files. The ERD can be used to repair problems that prevent your computer from starting. The ERD stores portions of the Registry, the system files, a copy of your partition boot sector, and information that relates to the startup environment.
Dr. Watson	You can use this utility if you are experiencing problems with an application. Dr. Watson is used to diagnose and troubleshoot application errors.
Windows Backup	You should use this utility to safeguard your computer. Through the Backup utility, you can create an ERD, back up the system or parts of the system, and restore data from backups that you have made.
Recovery Console	You can use this option if none of the other options or utilities works. The Recovery Console starts Windows 2000 without the graphical interface and allows the administrator limited capabilities, such as adding or replacing files and enable and disable services.

All of these Windows 2000 Professional recovery techniques are covered in detail in this chapter.

Using Event Viewer

Y̲ou can use the *Event Viewer* utility to track information about your computer's hardware and software, as well as to monitor security events. All of the information that is tracked is stored in three types of log files:

- The *System log* tracks events that relate to the Windows 2000 operating system.

- The *Security log* tracks events that are related to Windows 2000 auditing.

- *Application logs* track events that are related to applications that are running on your computer.

You can access Event Viewer by selecting Start ➤ Settings ➤ Control Panel ➤ Administrative Tools ➤ Event Viewer. Alternatively, right-click My Computer, select Manage from the pop-up menu, and access Event Viewer under System Tools. From Event Viewer, select the log you want to view. Figure 15.1 shows Event Viewer with the System log displayed.

FIGURE 15.1   A System log in Event Viewer

You can also add Event Viewer as a Microsoft Management Console (MMC) snap-in. Adding MMC snap-ins is covered in Chapter 4, "Configuring the Windows 2000 Environment."

In the log file, you will see all of the events that have been recorded. By default, you see the oldest events at the bottom of the screen and the newest events at the top of the screen. This can be misleading in troubleshooting, since one error can precipitate other errors. You should always resolve the oldest errors first. To change the default listing order, click one of the three logs and select View ➤ Oldest First.

The following sections describe how to view events and manage logs.

Reviewing Event Types

The Event Viewer logs display five event types, denoted by their icons. Table 15.2 describes each event type.

TABLE 15.2   Event Viewer Log Events

Event Type	Icon	Description
Information	White dialog bubble with blue *I*	Informs you of the occurrence of a specific action, such as a system shutting down or starting. *Information events* are logged for informative purposes.
Warning	Yellow triangle with black exclamation point	Indicates that you should be concerned with the event. *Warning events* may not be critical in nature but may be indicative of future errors.
Error	Red circle with white *X*	Indicates the occurrence of an error, such as a driver failing to load. You should be very concerned with *Error events*.

TABLE 15.2 Event Viewer Log Events *(continued)*

Event Type	Icon	Description
Success Audit	Yellow key	Indicates the occurrence of an event that has been audited for success. For example, a *Success Audit event* is a successful logon when system logons are being audited.
Failure Audit	Yellow lock	Indicates the occurrence of an event that has been audited for failure. For example, a *Failure Audit event* is a failed logon due to an invalid username and/or password when system logons are being audited.

Getting Event Details

Clicking an event in an Event Viewer log file brings up the Event Properties dialog box, which shows details about the event. An example of the Event Properties dialog box for an Information event is shown in Figure 15.2. Table 15.3 describes the information that appears in this dialog box.

FIGURE 15.2 The Event Properties dialog box

TABLE 15.3 Event Properties Dialog Box Items

Item	Description
Date	The date that the event was generated
Time	The time that the event was generated
Type	The type of event that was generated: Information, Warning, Error, Success Audit, or Failure Audit
User	The name of the user that the event is attributed to, if applicable (not all events are attributed to a user)
Computer	The name of the computer on which the event occurred
Source	The software that generated the event (e.g., operating system components or drivers)
Category	The source that logged the event (this field will say None until this feature has been fully implemented in Windows 2000)
Event ID	The event number specific to the type of event that was generated (e.g., a print error event has the event ID 45)
Description	A detailed description of the event
Data	The binary data generated by the event (if any; some events do not generate binary data) in hexadecimal bytes or DWORD format (programmers can use this information to interpret the event)

Managing Log Files

Over time, your log files will grow, and you will need to decide how to manage them. You can clear a log file for a fresh start. You may want to save the existing log file before you clear it, to keep that log file available for reference or future analysis.

To clear all log file events, right-click the log you wish to clear and choose Clear All Events from the pop-up menu. Then specify whether or not you want to save the log before it is cleared.

If you just want to save an existing log file, right-click that log and choose Save Log File As. Then specify the location and name of the file.

To open an existing log file, right-click the log you wish to open and choose Open Log File. Then specify the name and location of the log file and click the Open button.

Setting Log File Properties

Each Event Viewer log has two sets of properties associated with it:

- General properties control items such as the log filename, its maximum size, and the action to take when the log file reaches its maximum size.

- Filter properties specify which events are displayed.

To access the log Properties dialog box, right-click the log you want to manage and select Properties from the pop-up menu. The following sections describe the properties available on the General and Filter tabs of this dialog box.

General Properties

The General tab of the log Properties dialog box, shown in Figure 15.3, displays information about the log file and includes options to control its size. Table 15.4 describes the properties on the General tab.

FIGURE 15.3   The General tab of the log Properties dialog box

TABLE 15.4   General Log Properties

Property	Description
Display Name	Allows you to change the name of the log file. For example, if you are managing multiple computers and want to distinguish the logs for each computer, you can make the names more descriptive (e.g., DATA-Application and ROVER-Application).
Log Name	Displays the path and filename of the log file.
Size	Displays the current size of the log file.
Created	Specifies the date and time that the log file was created.
Modified	Specifies the date and time that the log file was last modified.

TABLE 15.4 General Log Properties *(continued)*

Property	Description
Accessed	Specifies the date and time that the log file was last accessed.
Maximum Log Size	Allows you to specify the maximum size that the log file can grow to. You can use this option to prevent the log file from taking up excessive disk space.
When Maximum Log Size Is Reached	Allows you to specify what action will be taken when the log file reaches the maximum size (if a maximum size is specified). You can choose to overwrite events as needed (on a first-in-first-out basis), overwrite events that are over a certain age, or specify that events should not be overwritten (which means that you would need to clear log events manually).
Using a Low-Speed Connection	Specifies that you are monitoring the log file of a remote computer and that you connect to that computer through a low-speed connection.

The Clear Log button in the General tab of the log Properties dialog box clears all log events.

Filter Properties

The Filter tab of the log Properties dialog box, shown in Figure 15.4, allows you to control which events are listed in the log. For example, if your system generates a large amount of log events, you might want to set the Filter properties so that you can track specific events. You can filter log events based on the event type, source, category, ID, users, computer, or specific time period. Table 15.5 describes the properties on the Filter tab.

FIGURE 15.4   The Filter tab of the log Properties dialog box

TABLE 15.5   Filter Properties for Logs

Property	Description
Event Type	Allows you to list only the specified event types (Warning, Error, Success Audit, or Failure Audit). By default, all event types are listed.
Event Source	Allows you to filter events based on the source of the event. The drop-down box lists the software that might generate events, such as Application Popup and DHCP. By default, events triggered by all sources are listed.
Category	Allows you to filter events based on the category that generated the event. The drop-down box lists the event categories. By default, events in all categories are listed.

TABLE 15.5 Filter Properties for Logs *(continued)*

Property	Description
Event ID	Allows you to filter events based on a specific event number.
User	Allows you to filter events based on the user who caused the event to be triggered.
Computer	Allows you to filter events based on the name of the computer that generated the event.
From-To	Allows you to filter events based on the date and time that the events were generated. By default, events are listed from the first event to the last event. To specify specific dates and times, select Events On from the drop-down list and select dates and times.

In Exercise 15.1, you will view events in Event Viewer and set log properties.

EXERCISE 15.1

Using the Event Viewer Utility

1. Select Start ➢ Settings ➢ Control Panel ➢ Administrative Tools ➢ Event Viewer.

2. Click System Log in the left pane of the Event Viewer window to display the System log events.

3. Double-click the first event in the right pane of the Event Viewer window to see its Event Properties dialog box. Click the Cancel button to close the dialog box.

4. Right-click System Log in the left pane of the Event Viewer window and select Properties.

EXERCISE 15.1 *(continued)*

5. Click the Filter tab. Clear all the check marks under Event Types except those in the Warning and Error check boxes, then click the OK button. You should see only Warning and Error events listed in the System log.

6. To remove the filter, return to the Filter tab of the log Properties dialog box, click the Restore Defaults button at the bottom of the dialog box, and click the OK button. You should see all of the event types listed again.

7. Right-click System Log and select Clear All Events.

8. You see a dialog box asking if you want to save the System log before clearing it. Click the Yes button. Specify the path and filename for the log file, then click the Save button. All the events should be cleared from the System log.

Understanding the Windows 2000 Boot Process

Some of the problems that cause system failure are related to the Windows 2000 boot process. The boot process starts when you turn on your computer and ends when you log on to Windows 2000.

To identify problems related to the boot process, you need to understand the steps involved in the process, as well as how the BOOT.INI file controls the process. Also, you should create a Windows 2000 boot disk that you can use to boot the operating system if your computer suffers a boot failure. These topics are covered in the following sections.

Reviewing the Normal Boot Process

The Windows 2000 boot process consists of five major stages: the preboot sequence, the boot sequence, kernel load, kernel initialization, and logon. Many files are used during these stages of the boot process. The following sections describe the steps in each boot process stage, the files used, and the errors that might occur.

Finding the Boot Process Files

Most of the boot process files reside in the root of the system partition. In the Windows 2000 Professional documentation, you will see the terms *system partition* and *boot partition*. The system partition is the computer's active partition where the files needed to boot the operating system are stored. This is typically the C: drive. The boot partition refers to the partition where the system files are stored. You can place the system files anywhere. The default folder for the system files is \WINNT and is referred to as the variable *Windir*. The system partition and boot partition can be on the same partition or on different partitions.

File attributes are used to specify the properties of a file. Examples of file attributes are System (S), Hidden (H), and Read-only (R). This is important to know because, by default, System and Hidden files are not listed in Windows Explorer or through a standard DIR command. If you look for these files but don't see them, they may just be hidden. You can turn on the display of System and Hidden files in Windows Explorer by selecting Tools ➤ Folder Options and clicking the View tab. In this dialog box, select the Show Hidden Files and Folders option, and uncheck the Hide File Extensions for Known File Types and Hide Protected Operating System Files options.

The Preboot Sequence

A normal boot process begins with the preboot sequence, in which your computer starts up and prepares for booting the operating system.

File Accessed in the Preboot Sequence

During the preboot sequence, your computer accesses the *NTLDR* file. This file is used to control the Windows 2000 boot process until control is passed to the NTOSKRNL file for the boot sequence stage. The NTLDR file is located in the root of the system partition. It has the file attributes of System, Hidden, and Read-only.

Steps in the Preboot Sequence

The preboot sequence consists of the following steps:

1. When the computer is powered on, it runs a *Power On Self Test* (*POST*) routine. The POST detects the processor you are using, how much memory is present, what hardware is recognized, and whether the BIOS (Basic Input/Output System) is standard or has Plug-and-Play capabilities. The system also enumerates and configures hardware devices at this point.

2. The BIOS points to the boot device, and the *Master Boot Record* (*MBR*) is loaded.

3. The MBR points to the active partition. The active partition is used to specify the partition that should be used to boot the operating system. This is normally the C: drive. Once the MBR locates the active partition, the boot sector is loaded into memory and executed.

4. As part of the Windows 2000 installation process, the NTLDR file is copied to the active partition. The boot sector points to the NTLDR file, and this file executes. The NTLDR file is used to initialize and start the Windows 2000 boot process.

Possible Errors during the Preboot Sequence

If you see errors during the preboot sequence they are probably not related to Windows 2000, since the operating system has not yet been loaded. The following are some common causes for errors during the preboot stage:

Improperly configured hardware	If the POST cannot recognize your hard drive, the preboot stage will fail. This error is most likely to occur in a computer that is still being initially configured. If everything has been working properly and you have not made any changes to your configuration, a hardware error is unlikely.
Corrupt MBR	Viruses that are specifically designed to infect the MBR can corrupt it. You can protect your system from this type of error by using virus-scanning software. Also, most virus-scanning programs can correct an infected MBR.

No partition is marked as active	This can happen if you used the FDISK utility and did not create a partition from all of the free space. If the partition is FAT16 or FAT32 and on a basic disk, you can boot the computer to DOS or Windows 9*x* with a boot disk, run FDISK, and mark a partition as active. If you created your partitions as a part of the Windows 2000 installation and have dynamic disks, marking an active partition is done for you during installation.
Corrupt or missing NTLDR file	If the NTLDR file does not execute, it may have been corrupted or deleted (by a virus or malicious intent). You can restore this file through the ERD, which is covered later in this chapter.
SYS program run from DOS or Windows 9*x* after Windows 2000 installation	The NTLDR file may not execute because the SYS program was run from DOS or Windows 9*x* after Windows 2000 was installed. If you have done this, the only solution is to reinstall Windows 2000.

The Boot Sequence

When the preboot sequence is completed, the boot sequence begins. The phases in this stage include the initial boot loader phase, the operating system selection phase, and the hardware detection phase.

Files Accessed in the Boot Sequence

Along with the NTLDR file, which was described in the previous section, the following files are used during the boot sequence:

- *BOOT.INI* is used to build the operating system menu choices that are displayed during the boot process. It is also used to specify the location of the boot partition. This file is located in the root of the system partition. It has the file attributes of System and Hidden.

- *BOOTSECT.DOS* is an optional file that is loaded if you choose to load an operating system other than Windows 2000. It is only used in dual-boot or multi-boot computers. This file is located in the root of the system partition. It has the file attributes of System and Hidden.

- *NTDETECT.COM* is used to detect any hardware that is installed and add information about the hardware to the Registry. This file is located in the root of the system partition. It has the file attributes of System, Hidden, and Read-only.

- *NTBOOTDD.SYS* is an optional file that is used when you have a SCSI (Small Computer Standard Interface) adapter with the onboard BIOS disabled. (This option is not commonly implemented.) This file is located in the root of the system partition. It has the file attributes of System and Hidden.

- *NTOSKRNL.EXE* is used to load the Windows 2000 operating system. This file is located in Windir\System32 and has no file attributes.

Steps in the Boot Sequence

The boot sequence consists of the following steps:

1. For the initial boot loader phase, NTLDR switches the processor from real mode to 32-bit flat memory mode and starts the appropriate mini file system drivers. Mini file system drivers are used to support your computer's file systems and include FAT16, FAT32, and NTFS.

2. For the operating system selection phase, the computer reads the BOOT.INI file. If you have configured your computer to dual-boot or multi-boot and Windows 2000 recognizes that you have choices, a menu of operating systems that can be loaded is built. If you choose an operating system other than Windows 2000, the BOOTSECT.DOS file is used to load the alternate operating system, and the Windows 2000 boot process terminates. If you choose a Windows 2000 operating system, the Windows 2000 boot process continues.

3. If you choose a Windows 2000 operating system, the NTDETECT.COM file is used to perform hardware detection. Any hardware that is detected is added to the Registry, in the HKEY_LOCAL_MACHINE key. Some of the hardware that NTDETECT.COM will recognize includes communication and parallel ports, keyboard, floppy disk drive, mouse, SCSI adapter, and video adapter.

4. Control is passed to NTOSKRNL.EXE to start the kernel load process.

Possible Errors during the Boot Sequence

The following are some common causes for errors during the boot stage:

Missing or corrupt boot files	If NTLDR, BOOT.INI, BOOTSECT.DOS, NTDETECT.COM, or NTOSKRNL.EXE is corrupt or missing (by a virus or malicious intent), the boot sequence will fail. You will see an error message that indicates which file is missing or corrupt. You can restore these files through the ERD, which is covered later in this chapter.
Improperly configured BOOT.INI file	If you have made any changes to your disk configuration and your computer will not restart, chances are your BOOT.INI file is configured incorrectly. The BOOT.INI file is covered after the next sections about the boot process stages.
Unrecognizable or improperly configured hardware	If you have serious errors that cause NTDETECT.COM to fail, you should resolve the hardware problems. If your computer has a lot of hardware, remove all of the hardware that is not required to boot the computer. Add each piece of hardware one at a time and boot the computer. This will help you identify which piece of hardware is bad or is conflicting for a resource with another device.

The Kernel Load Sequence

In the kernel load sequence, the Hardware Abstraction Layer (HAL), computer control set, and low-level device drivers are loaded. The NTOSKRNL.EXE file, which was described in the previous section, is used during this stage.

The kernel load sequence consists of the following steps:

1. The NTOSKRNL.EXE file is loaded and initialized.

2. The HAL is loaded. The HAL is what makes Windows 2000 portable to support platforms such as Intel and Alpha.

3. The control set that the operating system will use is loaded. The control set is used to control system configuration information, such as a list of device drivers that should be loaded.

4. Low-level device drivers, such as disk drivers, are loaded.

If you have problems loading the Windows 2000 kernel, and other recovery options do not solve the problem, you will most likely need to reinstall the operating system.

The Kernel Initialization Sequence

In the kernel initialization sequence, the HKEY_LOCAL_MACHINE\HARDWARE Registry and Clone Control set are created, device drivers are initialized, and high-order subsystems and services are loaded.

The kernel initialization sequence consists of the following steps:

1. Once the kernel has been successfully loaded, the Registry key HKEY_ LOCAL_MACHINE\HARDWARE is created. This Registry key is used to specify the hardware configuration of hardware components when the computer is started.

2. The Clone Control set is created. The Clone Control set is an exact copy of the data that is used to configure the computer and does not include changes made by the startup process.

3. The device drivers that were loaded during the kernel load phase are initialized.

4. Higher-order subsystems and services are loaded.

If you have problems during the kernel initialization sequence, you might try to boot to the Last Known Good Configuration, which is covered in the "Using Advanced Startup Options" section later in this chapter.

The Logon Sequence

In the logon sequence, the user logs on to Windows 2000 and any remaining services are loaded.

The logon sequence consists of the following steps:

1. After the kernel initialization is complete, the Log On to Windows dialog box appears. At this point, you type in a valid Windows 2000 username and password.

2. The service controller executes and performs a final scan of HKEY_LOCAL_MACHINE\SYSTEM\CurrentControlSet\Services to see if there are any remaining services that need to be loaded.

If logon errors occur, they are usually due to an incorrect username or password, or the unavailability of a domain controller to authenticate the request (if the computer is a part of a domain). See Chapter 6, "Managing Users," for more information about troubleshooting user authentication problems.

Errors can also occur if a service cannot be loaded. If a service fails to load, you will see a message in Event Viewer. Using the Event Viewer utility is covered earlier in this chapter.

Editing the BOOT.INI File

The BOOT.INI file is located in the active partition and is used to build the boot loader menu and to specify the location of the Windows 2000 boot partition. It also specifies the default operating system that should be loaded if no selection is made within the default time allotment. You can open and edit this file to add switches or options that allow you to control how the operating system is loaded. Figure 15.5 shows a fairly common example of a BOOT.INI file, opened in Notepad.

FIGURE 15.5 A sample BOOT.INI file

The following sections describe the BOOT.INI ARC (Advanced RISC Computing; RISC stands for Reduced Instruction Set Computing) naming conventions and how to edit the BOOT.INI file.

WARNING If you make changes to your disk configuration, you may see a message stating the number of the BOOT.INI file needs to be changed. This is the ARC number that points to the boot partition. If you try to restart your computer before you edit this file, you will find that the computer will not start.

ARC Naming Conventions

In the BOOT.INI file, the ARC path is used to specify the location of the boot partition within the disk channel. ARC names are made up of the information shown in Table 15.6.

TABLE 15.6 ARC Naming Conventions

ARC Path Option	Description
multi (w) or scsi (w)	Identifies the type of disk controller that is being used by the system. The multi option is used by IDE controllers and SCSI adapters that use the SCSI BIOS. The scsi option is used by SCSI adapters that do not use the SCSI BIOS. The number (w) represents the number of the hardware adapter you are booting from.
disk (x)	Indicates which SCSI adapter you are booting from if you use the scsi option. If you use multi, this setting is always 0.
rdisk (y)	Specifies the number of the physical disk to be used. In an IDE environment, it is the ordinal of the disk attached to the controller and will always be a 0 or a 1. On a SCSI system, this is the ordinal number of the SCSI drive.
partition (z)	Specifies the partition number that contains the operating system files. The first partition is always 1.

As an example, the BOOT.INI file shown in Figure 15.5 contains the following line:

```
multi(0)disk(0)rdisk(0)partition(1)\WINNT.PRO= "Microsoft
Windows 2000 Professional"
```

This indicates that the boot partition is in the following location:

- multi(0) is an IDE controller or a SCSI controller with the BIOS enabled.

- disk(0) is 0 since the multi option was used.

- rdisk(0) specifies that first disk on the controller is being used.

- partition(1) specifies that the system partition is on the first partition.

- \WINNT.PRO indicates the folder that is used to store the system files.

- "Microsoft Windows 2000 Professional" is what the user sees in the boot menu.

BOOT.INI Switches

When you edit your BOOT.INI file, you can add switches or options that allow you to control how the operating system is loaded. Table 15.7 defines the BOOT.INI switches.

TABLE 15.7   BOOT.INI Switches

Switch	Description
/basevideo	Boots the computer using a standard VGA video driver. This option is used when you change your video driver and then cannot use the new driver.
/fastdetect=comx	Keeps the computer from auto-detecting a serial mouse attached to a serial port.

TABLE 15.7   BOOT.INI Switches *(continued)*

Switch	Description
/maxmem:n	Specifies the maximum amount of RAM that is recognized. This option is sometimes used in test environments where you want to analyze performance using different amounts of memory.
/noguiboot	Boots Windows 2000 without loading the GUI. With this option, a command prompt appears after the boot process ends.

BOOT.INI File Access

Because the BOOT.INI file is marked with the System and Hidden attributes, it is not normally seen through Windows Explorer or the DOS DIR command. The following sections explain how to modify the attributes of the BOOT.INI through Windows Explorer and the DOS ATTRIB command.

Changing Attributes through Windows Explorer

To access and change the BOOT.INI attributes through Windows Explorer, take the following steps:

1. Select Start ➢ Programs ➢ Accessories ➢ Windows Explorer.

2. In Windows Explorer, expand My Computer and right-click Local Disk (C:).

3. Select Tools ➢ Folder Options and click the View tab.

4. In the View dialog box, click the Show Hidden Files and Folders radio button, and uncheck the Hide File Extensions for Known File Types and Hide Protected Operating System Files (Recommended) check boxes, as shown in Figure 15.6.

FIGURE 15.6 The View tab of the Folder Options dialog box

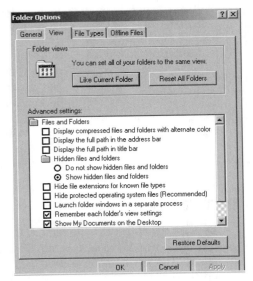

5. You see a dialog box with a warning about displaying protected operating system files. Click the Yes button to display these files. Then click the OK button.

6. You should now see the BOOT.INI file in the root of the C: drive. To change the file attributes, right-click the BOOT.INI file and select Properties.

7. The boot.ini Properties dialog box appears, as shown in Figure 15.7. Uncheck the Read-only attribute at the bottom of the dialog box and click the OK button.

FIGURE 15.7   The boot.ini Properties dialog box

8. Open the BOOT.INI file by double-clicking the file in Windows Explorer.

9. When you're finished editing the BOOT.INI file, you should reset its file attributes by selecting Tools ➢ Folder Options ➢ View ➢ Restore Defaults.

Changing Attributes through the ATTRIB Command

The DOS ATTRIB command provides a quick way to access the BOOT.INI file. To use the ATTRIB command, take the following steps:

1. Select Start ➢ Programs ➢ Accessories ➢ Command Prompt.

2. In the Command Prompt dialog box, type **ATTRIB** and press Enter. You should see all of the files that reside at the root of C: and their current file attributes.

3. Type **ATTRIB BOOT.INI −S −H** and press Enter to remove the System and Hidden file attributes.

4. Type **EDIT BOOT.INI** and press Enter to execute the EDIT program and open the BOOT.INI file for editing.

5. When you're finished editing the BOOT.INI file, choose File ➤ Save to save the file and File ➤ Exit to exit the EDIT program.

6. Reset the file attributes by typing **ATTRIB BOOT.INI +S +H** and pressing Enter.

Creating the Windows 2000 Boot Disk

After you create a *Windows 2000 boot disk*, you can use it to boot to the Windows 2000 Professional operating system in the event of a Windows 2000 Professional boot failure. You create a Windows 2000 boot disk through the following process:

1. Format a floppy disk through the Windows 2000 Professional operating system.

2. Copy the following files from the Windows 2000 Professional system partition:

   NTLDR

   NTDETECT.COM

   NTBOOTDD.SYS (if you use SCSI controllers with the BIOS disabled)

   BOOT.INI

3. Test the boot disk by using it to boot to Windows 2000 Professional.

If the BOOT.INI file for the computer has been edited, you will need to update the BOOT.INI file on your Windows 2000 boot disk.

The BOOT.INI file on the Windows 2000 Professional boot disk contains a specific configuration that points to the computer's boot partition. This might keep a Windows 2000 boot disk that was made on one computer from working on another computer.

In Exercise 15.2, you will create a Windows 2000 boot disk.

EXERCISE 15.2

Creating a Windows 2000 Boot Disk

1. Put a blank floppy diskette in your floppy drive.

2. Select Start ➢ Programs ➢ Accessories ➢ Windows Explorer.

3. In Windows Explorer, expand My Computer, right-click 3½ Floppy (A:), and select Format. Accept all of the default options and click the Start button.

4. You see a dialog box warning you that all the data will be lost. Click the OK button.

5. When you see the Format Complete dialog box, click the OK button, then click the Close button to close the Format dialog box.

6. Select Start ➢ Programs ➢ Accessories ➢ Command Prompt.

7. In the Command Prompt dialog box, type **ATTRIB** and press Enter. You see all of the files at the root of the C: drive. Note the file attributes of the NTLDR, NTDETECT.COM, and BOOT.INI files.

8. Type **ATTRIB NTLDR -S -H -R** and press Enter.

9. Type **COPY NTLDR A:** and press Enter.

10. Type **ATTRIB NTLDR +S +H +R** and press Enter.

11. Repeat steps 8 through 10 for the NTDETECT.COM and BOOT.INI files, to remove the file attributes, copy the file, and replace the file attributes. If you have a SCSI adapter with the BIOS disabled, you will also need to copy the NTBOOTDD.SYS file.

12. Verify that all of the files are on the boot disk by typing **DIR A:**.

13. Type **EXIT** to close the Command Prompt dialog box.

14. To test your Windows 2000 boot disk, select Start ➢ Shut Down ➢ Restart and click the OK button.

15. Label your Windows 2000 boot disk and put it in a safe place.

Using Advanced Startup Options

The Windows 2000 advanced startup options can be used to troubleshoot errors that keep Windows 2000 Professional from successfully booting.

Microsoft ✓ *Exam* *Objective*

Recover systems and user data.

▪ Troubleshoot system restoration by using Safe Mode.

To access the Windows 2000 advanced startup options, press the F8 key when prompted during the beginning of the Windows 2000 Professional boot process. This will bring up the Windows 2000 Advanced Options menu, which allows you to boot Windows 2000 with the following options:

- Safe Mode
- Safe Mode with Networking
- Safe Mode with Command Prompt
- Enable Boot Logging
- Enable VGA Mode
- Last Known Good Configuration
- Debugging Mode
- Boot Normally

Each of these advanced startup options is covered in the following sections.

Starting in Safe Mode

When your computer will not start, one of the basic troubleshooting techniques is to simplify the configuration as much as possible. This is especially important when you do not know the cause of your problem and you have a complex configuration. After you have simplified your configuration, you determine whether the problem is in the basic configuration or is a result of your more complex configuration. If the problem is in the basic configuration, you have a starting point for troubleshooting. If the problem is not in the basic configuration, you proceed to restore each configuration option you removed, one at a time. This helps you to identify what is causing the error.

If Windows 2000 Professional will not load, you can attempt to load the operating system through *Safe Mode*. When you run Windows 2000 in Safe Mode, you are simplifying your Windows configuration as much as possible. Safe Mode loads only the drivers needed to get the computer up and running. The drivers that are loaded with Safe Mode include basic files and drivers for the mouse (unless you have a serial mouse), monitor, keyboard, hard drive, standard video driver, and default system services. Safe Mode is considered a diagnostic mode, so you do not have access to all of the features and devices in Windows 2000 Professional that you have access to when you boot normally, including networking capabilities.

A computer booted to Safe Mode will show *Safe Mode* in the four corners of your Desktop, as shown in Figure 15.8.

FIGURE 15.8   A computer running in Safe Mode shows Safe Mode in each corner of the Desktop.

If you boot to Safe Mode, you should check all of your hardware and software settings in Control Panel to try to determine why Windows 2000 Professional will not boot properly. After you take steps to fix the problem, attempt to boot to Windows 2000 Professional normally.

In Exercise 15.3, you will boot your computer to Safe Mode.

EXERCISE 15.3

Booting Your Computer to Safe Mode

1. If your computer is currently running, select Start ➢ Shutdown ➢ Restart.

2. During the boot process, press the F8 key to access the Windows 2000 Advanced Options menu.

3. Highlight Safe Mode and press Enter. Then log on as Administrator.

4. When you see the Desktop dialog box letting you know that Windows 2000 is running in Safe Mode, click the OK button.

5. Select My Network Places ➢ Entire Network, then click Microsoft Windows Network. You should get an error message stating that you are unable to browse the network (because you are in Safe Mode). Click OK to close the error dialog box.

6. Select Start ➢ Settings ➢ Control Panel ➢ System ➢ Hardware ➢ Device Manager. Look in Device Manager to see if any devices are not working properly.

Don't restart your computer yet; you will do this as a part of the next exercise.

Enabling Boot Logging

Boot logging creates a log file that tracks the loading of drivers and services. When you choose the *Enable Boot Logging* option from the Advanced Options menu, Windows 2000 Professional loads normally, not in Safe Mode. This allows you to log all of the processes that take place during a normal boot sequence.

This log file can be used to troubleshoot the boot process. When logging is enabled, the log file is written to *Windir*\ntbtlog.txt. A sample of the ntbtlog.txt file is shown in Figure 15.9.

FIGURE 15.9   The Windows 2000 boot log file

In Exercise 15.4, you will create and access a boot log file.

EXERCISE 15.4

Using Boot Logging

1. Start your computer. (If your computer is currently running, select Start ➢ Shutdown ➢ Restart.)

2. During the boot process, press the F8 key to access the Windows 2000 Advanced Options menu.

3. Highlight Enable Boot Logging and press Enter. Then log on as Administrator.

4. Select Start ➢ Programs ➢ Accessories ➢ Windows Explorer.

EXERCISE 15.4 *(continued)*

5. In Windows Explorer, expand My Computer, then C:. Open the WINNT folder and double-click ntbtlog.txt.

6. Examine the contents of your boot log file.

7. Shut down your computer and restart in normal mode.

The boot log file is cumulative. Each time you boot to any Advanced Options menu mode (except Last Known Good Configuration), you are writing to this file. This allows you to make changes, reboot, and see if you have fixed any problems. If you want to start from scratch, you should manually delete this file and reboot to an Advanced Options menu selection that supports logging.

Using Other Advanced Options Menu Modes

The other selections on the Advanced Options menu work as follows:

- The *Safe Mode with Networking* option is the same as the Safe Mode option, but it adds networking features. You might use this mode if you need networking capabilities in order to download drivers or service packs from a network location.

- The *Safe Mode with Command Prompt* option starts the computer in Safe Mode, but instead of loading the Windows 2000 graphical interface, it loads a command prompt. Experienced troubleshooters use this mode.

- The *Enable VGA Mode* option loads a standard VGA driver without starting the computer in Safe Mode. You might use this mode if you changed your video driver, did not test it, and tried to boot to Windows 2000 with a bad driver that would not allow you to access video. Enable VGA Mode bails you out by loading a default driver, providing access to video so that you can properly install (and test!) the correct driver for your computer.

When you boot to any Safe Mode, you automatically use VGA Mode.

- The *Last Known Good Configuration* option boots Windows 2000 using the Registry information that was saved the last time the computer was successfully booted. You would use this option to restore configuration information if you have improperly configured the computer and have not successfully rebooted the computer. When you use the Last Known Good Configuration option, you lose any system configuration changes that were made since the computer last successfully booted.

- The *Debugging Mode* option runs the Kernel Debugger, if that utility is installed. The Kernel Debugger is an advanced troubleshooting utility.

- The *Boot Normally* option boots to Windows 2000 in the default manner. This option is on the Advanced Options menu in case you got trigger happy and hit F8 during the boot process, but really wanted to boot Windows 2000 normally.

Windows 2000 handles startup options in a slightly different way than Windows NT 4 does. In Windows NT 4, the boot loader menu shows an option to load VGA mode, which appears each time you restart the computer. In Windows 2000, this has been moved to the Advanced Options menu to present the user with a cleaner boot process. Also, in Windows NT 4, you need to press the spacebar as a part of the boot process to access the Last Known Good Configuration option.

Using Startup and Recovery Options

The Startup and Recovery options are used to specify the default operating system that is loaded and specify which action should be taken in the event of system failure. You can access the Startup and Recovery options from your Desktop by right-clicking My Computer, selecting Properties from the pop-up menu, clicking the Advanced tab, and then clicking the Startup and Recovery button. Alternatively, select Start ➢ Settings ➢ Control Panel ➢ System ➢ Advanced ➢ Startup and Recovery. You will see the dialog box shown in Figure 15.10.

FIGURE 15.10 The Startup and Recovery dialog box

The options that can be specified through the Startup and Recovery dialog box are described in Table 15.8.

TABLE 15.8 Startup and Recovery Options

Option	Description
Default Operating System	Specifies the operating system that is loaded by default if no selection is made from the operating system selection menu (if your computer dual-boots or multi-boots and an operating system selection menu appears during bootup). By default, this option is set to Microsoft Windows 2000 Professional.
Display List of Operating Systems for *x* Seconds	Specifies how long the operating system selection menu is available before the default selection is loaded (if your computer dual-boots or multi-boots and an operating system selection menu appears during bootup). By default, this option is set to 30 seconds.

TABLE 15.8 Startup and Recovery Options *(continued)*

Option	Description
Write an Event to the System Log	Specifies that an entry is made in the System log any time a system failure occurs. By default, this option is enabled, which allows you to track system failures.
Send an Administrative Alert	Specifies that a pop-up alert message will be sent to the Administrator any time a system failure occurs. By default, this option is enabled, so the Administrator is notified of system failures.
Automatically Reboot	Specifies that the computer will automatically re-boot in the event of a system failure. By default, this option is enabled, so the system restarts after a fail-ure without intervention. You would disable this option if you wanted to see the blue screen for analysis.
Write Debugging Information	Specifies that debugging information (a memory dump) is written to a file. You can choose not to cre-ate a dump file or to create a small memory dump (64KB) file, a kernel memory dump file, or a com-plete memory dump file. Complete memory dump files require free disk space equivalent to your memory and a page file that is at least as large as your memory with an extra 2MB. The default set-ting is to write debugging information to a small memory dump file.
Overwrite Any Existing File	If you create dump files, allows you to create a new dump file that overwrites the old dump file or to keep all dump files each time a system failure occurs.

In Exercise 15.5, you will access the Startup and Recovery options and make changes to the settings.

Using Startup and Recovery Options

1. From your Desktop, right-click My Computer and choose Properties. Click the Advanced tab and then click the Startup and Recovery button.

2. Change the Display List of Operating Systems option from 30 seconds to 10 seconds.

3. In the Write Debugging Information section, choose (None) from the drop-down list.

4. Click the OK button to close the Startup and Recovery dialog box.

Using the Dr. Watson Utility

The *Dr. Watson* utility detects and displays information about system and program failures. When an application error occurs, Dr. Watson will be executed automatically and you will see a pop-up message letting you know that an application error has occurred. You also can access Dr. Watson by invoking the *DRWTSN32* command. Application developers can use the Dr. Watson utility to debug their programs. When an application encounters an error or crashes, Dr. Watson can display the application error and dump the contents of memory into a file.

While average users will not be able to determine what is wrong with an application by looking at a memory dump file, they might be asked to configure a memory dump so that it can be sent to an application developer for analysis. The information that is collected by Dr. Watson is stored in a log file that can be viewed at any time.

To access Dr. Watson, select Start ➢ Run and type **DRWTSN32**. The main dialog box for Dr. Watson is shown in Figure 15.11.

FIGURE 15.11 The Dr. Watson for Windows 2000 dialog box

The Application Errors box at the bottom of the dialog box displays any program errors that Dr. Watson encountered. Above this portion are the options that can be configured through Dr. Watson, which are described in Table 15.9.

TABLE 15.9 Dr. Watson Configuration Options

Option	Description
Log File Path	Specifies the location of the log file that contains application error information.
Crash Dump	Specifies the location of the memory dump file that is created when an application crashes (If you choose to create a crash dump file).
Wave File	Specifies the WAV sound file to execute when an error occurs.

TABLE 15.9 Dr. Watson Configuration Options *(continued)*

Option	Description *(continued)*
Number of Instructions	Specifies the maximum number of instructions, or threads, that Dr. Watson can track.
Number of Errors to Save	Specifies the maximum number of errors that Dr. Watson can store within the dump file.
Dump Symbol Table	Specifies that the symbol table should be included in the dump file. Symbol files provide more verbose information, which can be used to diagnose system failures. The drawback of this option is that it can cause the log file to grow very quickly.
Dump All Thread Contexts	Specifies whether Dr. Watson will dump all threads to the state dump, or dump only the thread that caused the application failure.
Append to Existing Log File	Specifies whether Dr. Watson will create a new log file for new program errors or append log information to the existing log file.
Visual Notification	Shows a message box with a program error notification.
Sound Notification	Sounds two beeps when an error occurs. You can also configure a wave file to be used for sound notification.
Create Crash Dump File	Specifies whether you want to create a crash dump file in the event of application failure. If you choose to create a crash dump file, you must also specify a crash dump location.

The difference between Startup and Recovery options and the Dr. Watson utility is that Startup and Recovery options are used to diagnose operating system problems and the Dr. Watson utility is used to diagnose application errors.

Creating Windows 2000 Professional Setup Boot Disks

You can create floppy disks that can be used to boot to the Windows 2000 Professional operating system in case your computer will not boot and will not read the CD-ROM drive. These disks are called the *Windows 2000 Professional Setup Boot Disks*.

From these diskettes, you can perform the following tasks:

- Reinstall the Windows 2000 operating system if you do not have access to the CD-ROM drive.
- Use the Recovery Console.
- Use an ERD.

NOTE

Using the Windows 2000 Professional Setup Boot Disks to install Windows 2000 is described in Chapter 1, "Getting Started with Windows 2000 Professional." The Recovery Console and ERD are covered later in this chapter.

Microsoft
Exam
Objective

Recover systems and user data.

- Recover systems and user data by using the Recovery Console.

The Windows 2000 Professional Setup Boot Disks are not specific to a computer. They are general Windows 2000 Professional disks, which can be used by any computer running Windows 2000 Professional.

To create the Windows 2000 Professional Setup Boot Disks, you need four high-density floppy disks, labeled as follows:

- Windows 2000 Professional Setup Boot Disk
- Windows 2000 Professional Setup Disk #2

- Windows 2000 Professional Setup Disk #3

- Windows 2000 Professional Setup Disk #4

The 32-bit command to create boot disks from Windows 2000 or Windows 9*x* is *MAKEBT32.EXE*. The command to make boot disks from a 16-bit operating system is MAKEBOOT.EXE.

Setup disks created for Windows 2000 Professional will not work with Windows 2000 Server. Setup disks created for Windows 2000 Server will not work with Windows 2000 Professional.

Once you have formatted and labeled your floppy disks, take the following steps to create the Windows 2000 Professional Setup Boot Disks:

1. Insert the Windows 2000 Professional CD into your CD-ROM drive.

2. Select Start ➢ Run ➢ Browse. Select your CD-ROM drive in the dialog box that appears. Select BOOTDISK, then MAKEBT32. Then click the OK button.

3. A dialog box appears, prompting you to specify the floppy drive to copy the image to. This is normally your A: drive.

4. Insert the disk labeled Windows 2000 Professional Setup Boot Disk. The files will be copied.

5. When prompted, insert Windows 2000 Professional Setup Disks #2, #3, and #4.

6. When you are finished, place your disks in a safe location.

In Exercise 15.6, you will create Windows 2000 Professional Setup Boot Disks. This exercise requires four high-density floppy disks. You also need the Windows 2000 Professional CD.

EXERCISE 15.6

Creating Windows 2000 Professional Setup Boot Disks

1. Label each of your high-density floppy disks as follows:

Windows 2000 Professional Setup Boot Disk

Windows 2000 Professional Setup Disk #2

Windows 2000 Professional Setup Disk #3

Windows 2000 Professional Setup Disk #4

2. Insert the Windows 2000 Professional CD into your CD-ROM drive.

3. Select Start ➢ Run ➢ Browse. Select your CD-ROM drive, then select BOOTDISK, and then select MAKEBT32. Click the OK button.

4. In the command-prompt dialog box, specify the floppy drive to copy the image to. This is normally your A: drive.

5. Insert the disk labeled Windows 2000 Professional Setup Boot Disk. The files will be copied.

6. When prompted, insert Windows 2000 Professional Setup Disks #2, #3, and #4 pressing Enter after you insert each one.

7. After the disks have been created, put them in an easily accessible place. You will use them in Exercise 15.8.

Using the Backup Utility

The *Windows 2000 Backup* utility allows you to create and restore backups, and create an *Emergency Repair Disk (ERD)*. Backups protect your data in the event of system failure by storing the data on another medium, such as another hard disk or a tape. If your original data is lost due to corruption, deletion, or media failure, you can restore the data using your backup. The ERD is a subset of a backup that you can use to restore configuration information quickly.

Microsoft
✓ *Exam*
Objective

Recover systems and user data.

- Recover systems and user data by using Windows Backup.

To access the Backup utility, select Start ➢ Programs ➢ Accessories ➢ System Tools ➢ Backup. This brings up the Backup window, as shown in Figure 15.12.

FIGURE 15.12 The Backup window

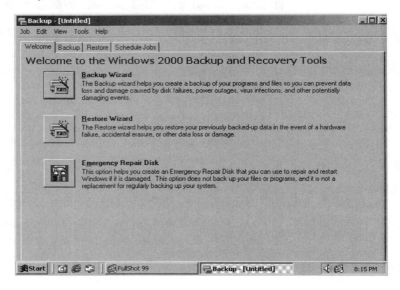

From this window, you can start the Backup Wizard, start the Restore Wizard, or create an ERD. These options are all covered in the following sections.

External tape drives, which attach to your parallel port, are not supported by the Windows 2000 Professional operating system when using the Windows Backup utility. However, you can use third-party backup software to support this configuration.

Creating and Using an ERD

You can use the ERD to repair and restart Windows 2000 in the event that your computer will not start or if the system files have been damaged. You should create an ERD when the computer is installed and then update the ERD after making any changes to the configuration of your computer. This option does not back up any system data.

You can repair the following items with the ERD:

- The basic system
- System files
- The partition boot sector
- The startup environment
- The Registry (return the Registry to its original configuration)

In the next sections, you will learn how to create and use an ERD.

Preparing an ERD

To create an ERD, click the Emergency Repair Disk button in the opening Backup utility window. This brings up the Emergency Repair Disk dialog box, which asks you to insert a blank, formatted floppy disk into drive A:. At this point, you can also specify whether you want to back up the Registry to the ERD. If the Registry will fit onto your ERD, you should select this option. When you click OK, the system data will be copied to the ERD.

You should update your ERD after you make any major configuration changes to your computer.

You will create an ERD in Exercise 15.7. You will need a blank, formatted, high-density floppy disk for this exercise.

EXERCISE 15.7

Creating an Emergency Repair Disk

1. Select Start ➤ Programs ➤ Accessories ➤ System Tools ➤ Backup.

2. Click the Emergency Repair Disk button.

3. The Emergency Repair Disk dialog box appears. Insert a blank, formatted floppy disk into drive A:.

4. Select the Also Back Up the Registry to the Repair Directory option.

5. Click OK. The system data will be copied to the ERD.

6. A confirmation dialog box appears. Click the OK button to close this dialog box.

Using an ERD

The ERD is not a bootable disk and can only be accessed by using the Windows 2000 Professional Setup CD or setup diskettes that are created from the CD. Take the following steps to use an ERD:

1. Restart your computer using the Windows 2000 Professional Setup Boot Disk.

2. When prompted, insert Windows 2000 Professional Setup Disk #2, #3, and #4, pressing Enter after you insert each one.

3. The Welcome to Setup dialog box appears. To repair a Windows 2000 installation, press the R key.

4. The Windows 2000 Repair Options menu appears. To repair Windows 2000 using the ERD, press the R key.

5. Press the M key to choose Manual Repair or the F key to choose Fast Repair. The Manual Repair option lets you select to inspect the startup environment, verify the Windows 2000 system files, and inspect the boot sector. The Fast Repair option doesn't require any user input. It attempts to correct problems that relate to system files, the partition boot sector on the system disk, and the startup environment on dual-boot systems.

6. Insert your Windows 2000 ERD and press Enter. You see one more dialog box indicating that you should insert your ERD. Press Enter again.

7. You see a dialog box asking you whether or not you want to examine your computer's drives. If you press Enter, your drives will be examined. If you want to skip the drive examination, press Escape.

8. If you chose to examine your computer's drives, you will be asked to insert the Windows 2000 Professional CD into your CD-ROM drive and press Enter. The emergency repair process will examine the files on your hard disk.

9. When the repair process is complete, you are prompted to remove any floppies from your computer. Then your computer will restart automatically.

In Windows NT, you create ERDs through the RDISK command. This command is not available in Windows 2000.

In Exercise 15.8, you will restore your system using the ERD. You will need the four Windows Professional Setup Boot Disks you created in Exercise 15.6 and the ERD you created in Exercise 15.7. You will also need the Windows 2000 Professional CD.

EXERCISE 15.8

Restoring Your System with an Emergency Repair Disk

1. Restart your computer using the Windows 2000 Professional Setup Boot Disk.

2. When prompted, insert Windows 2000 Professional Setup Disk #2, #3, and #4, pressing Enter after you insert each one.

3. From the Welcome to Setup dialog box, press the R key to choose to repair a Windows 2000 installation.

4. From the Windows 2000 Repair Options dialog box, press R to repair the Windows 2000 installation using the emergency repair process.

5. Press the F key to choose Fast Repair.

6. Insert your ERD and press Enter. Then press Enter again in the next dialog box.

7. Press Enter to indicate that you want the Setup program to examine your computer's drives.

8. Insert the Windows 2000 Professional CD into your CD-ROM drive and press Enter. The emergency repair process will examine the files on your drive.

9. When prompted, remove any floppies from your floppy drives and the Windows 2000 Professional CD from the CD-ROM drive. Your computer will restart automatically.

Using the Backup Wizard

The *Backup Wizard* takes you through all of the steps that are required for a successful backup. Before you start the Backup Wizard, you should be logged on as an Administrator or a member of the Backup Operators group. To use the Backup Wizard, take the following steps:

1. Start the Backup program and click the Backup Wizard button.

2. The Welcome to the Windows 2000 Backup and Recovery Tools dialog box appears, as shown in Figure 15.13. Click the Next button.

FIGURE 15.13   The Welcome to the Windows 2000 Backup and Recovery Tools dialog box

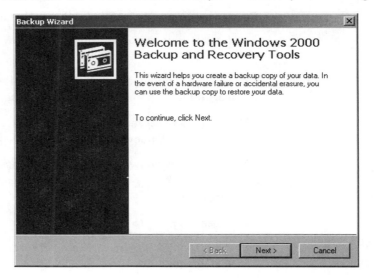

3. The What to Back Up dialog box appears, as shown in Figure 15.14. This dialog box allows you to select what you will back up. You can choose to back up everything; back up just selected files, drives, or network data; or back up only the system state data. System state data includes the Registry, the COM+ registration database, and the system boot files. For this example, select the Back Up Selected Files, Drives, or Network Data radio button, then click the Next button.

FIGURE 15.14   The What to Back Up dialog box

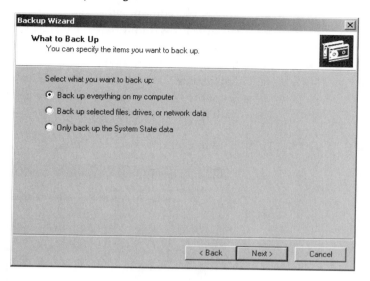

4. The Items to Back Up dialog box appears, as shown in Figure 15.15. Check the items that you want to back up and click the Next button.

FIGURE 15.15   The Items to Back Up dialog box

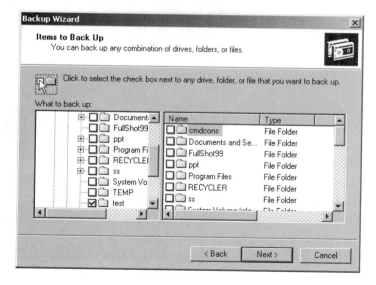

5. The Where to Store the Backup dialog box appears, as shown in Figure 15.16. You can either type in the backup media or filename or click the Browse button to locate it. Clicking the Browse button brings up the Open dialog box, as shown in Figure 15.17. Select the drive, give your backup a filename (for example, you might use the date as the filename), and click the Open button. You return to the Where to Store the Backup dialog box. When your backup media or filename path is correct, click the Next button.

FIGURE 15.16 The Where to Store the Backup dialog box

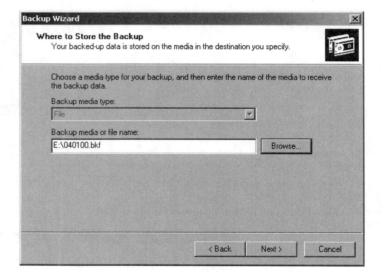

FIGURE 15.17 The Open dialog box

6. The Completing the Backup Wizard dialog box appears, as shown in Figure 15.18. If all of the information is correct, click the Finish button.

Clicking the Advanced button in the Completing the Backup Wizard dialog box brings up a dialog box that allows you to specify the type of backup: Normal, Copy, Incremental, Differential, or Daily.

FIGURE 15.18   The Completing the Backup Wizard dialog box

7. During the backup process, the Wizard displays the Backup Progress dialog box, as shown in Figure 15.19. Once the backup process is complete, you can click the Report button in this dialog box to see details of the backup session. Figure 15.20 shows an example of a backup report.

FIGURE 15.19 The Backup Progress dialog box

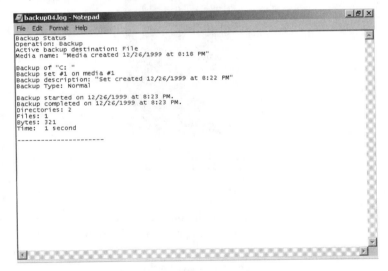

FIGURE 15.20 An example of a backup report

In Exercise 15.9, you will use the Backup Wizard. You will need a blank, formatted, high-density floppy disk for this exercise.

EXERCISE 15.9

Using the Backup Wizard

1. Create a folder on your D: drive called **DATA**. Create some small text files in this folder. The size of all of the files combined should not exceed 1MB.

2. Select Start ➢ Programs ➢ Accessories ➢ System Tools ➢ Backup.

3. In the opening Backup window, click the Backup Wizard button.

4. In the Welcome to the Windows 2000 Backup and Recovery Tools dialog box, click the Next button.

5. In the What to Back Up dialog box, click the Back Up Selected Files, Drives, or Network Data radio button. Then click the Next button.

6. In the Items to Back Up dialog box, select My Computer, expand D:, and check the DATA folder. Click the Next button.

7. In the Where to Store the Backup dialog box, click the Browse button. In the Open dialog box, select 3½ Floppy (A:). For the file-name, enter the date (in the *mmddyy* format). Then click the Open button.

8. In the Where to Store the Backup dialog box, click the Next button.

9. Verify your selections in the Completing the Backup Wizard dialog box. Then click the Finish button.

10. When the Backup Wizard completes, click the Report button in the Backup Progress dialog box. This will show the backup log in a Notepad window. Close this window when you are finished viewing the report.

11. Close all of the Backup Wizard dialog boxes.

Configuring Backup Options

You can configure more specific backup configurations by selecting backup options. To access the backup options, start the Backup program and select Tools ➢ Options. This brings up the Options dialog box, shown in Figure 15.21.

This dialog box has five tabs with options for controlling the backup and restore processes: General, Restore, Backup Type, Backup Log, and Exclude Files. The options of these tabs are covered in the following sections.

FIGURE 15.21 The General tab of the Options dialog box

Configuring General Backup Options

The General tab (see Figure 15.21) contains options for configuring backup sessions. Table 15.10 describes these options.

TABLE 15.10 General Backup Options

Option	Description
Compute Selection Information before Backup and Restore Operations	Estimates the number of files and bytes that will be backed up or restored during the current operation and displays this information prior to the backup or restore operation
Use the Catalogs on the Media to Speed Up Building Restore Catalogs on Disk	Specifies that you want to use an on-media catalog to build an on-disk catalog that can be used to select which folders and files will be restored during a restore operation

TABLE 15.10   General Backup Options *(continued)*

Option	Description
Verify Data after the Backup Completes	Makes sure that all data has been backed up properly
Back Up the Contents of Mounted Drives	Specifies that the data should be backed up on mounted drives; otherwise, only path information on mounted drives is backed up
Show Alert Message when I Start Backup and Removable Storage Is Not Running	Notifies you if Removable Storage is not running (when you are backing up to tape or other removable media)
Show Alert Message when I Start Backup and There Is Compatible Import Media Available	Notifies you when you start Backup if new media have been added to the Removable Storage import pool.
Show Alert Message when New Media Is Inserted into Removable Storage	Notifies you when new media are detected by Removable Storage.
Always Move New Import Media to the Backup Media Pool	Specifies that if new media are detected by Removable Storage, that media should be directed to the Backup media pool.

Configuring Restore Options

The Restore tab of the Options dialog box, shown in Figure 15.22, contains three options that relate to how files are restored when the file already exists on the computer:

- Do Not Replace the File on My Computer (Recommended)
- Replace the File on Disk Only If the File on the Disk Is Older
- Always Replace the File on My Computer

FIGURE 15.22 The Restore tab of the Options dialog box

Selecting a Backup Type

The Backup Type tab, shown in Figure 15.23, allows you to specify the default backup type that will be used. You should select the type of backup based on the following:

- How much data you are backing up
- How quickly you wanted to be able to perform the backup
- The number of tapes you are willing to use in the event that you need to perform a restore operation

Table 15.11 describes the backup type options.

FIGURE 15.23 The Backup Type tab of the Options dialog box

TABLE 15.11 Backup Type Options

Option	Description
Normal	Backs up all files and sets the archive bit as marked for each file that is backed up. Requires only one tape for the restore process.
Copy	Backs up all files and does not set the archive bit as marked for each file that is backed up. Requires only one tape for the restore process.

TABLE 15.11 Backup Type Options *(continued)*

Option	Description
Differential	Backs up only the files that have not been marked as archived and does not set the archive bit for each file that is backed up. Requires the last normal backup and the last differential tape for the restore process.
Incremental	Backs up only the files that have not been marked as archived and sets the archive bit for each file that is backed up. Requires the last normal backup and all of the incremental tapes that have been created since the last normal backup for the restore process.
Daily	Backs up only the files that have been changed today and does not set the archive bit for each file that is backed up. Requires each daily backup and the last normal backup for the restore process.

Setting Backup Log Options

The Backup Log tab, shown in Figure 15.24, allows you to specify the amount of information that is logged during the backup process. You can select from the following options:

- Detailed, which logs all information, including the names of the folders and files that are backed up

- Summary, which logs only key backup operations, such as starting the backup

- None, which specifies that a log file will not be created

FIGURE 15.24   The Backup Log tab of the Options dialog box

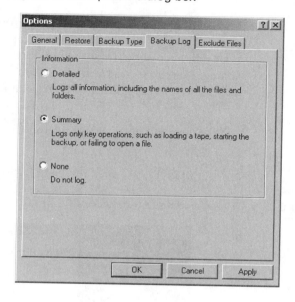

Excluding Files

The Exclude Files tab of the Options dialog box, shown in Figure 15.25, allows you to explicitly exclude specific files during the backup process. For example, you might choose to exclude the page file or application files.

FIGURE 15.25   The Exclude Files tab of the Options dialog box

Using the Restore Wizard

Having a complete backup won't help you if your system should fail unless you can successfully restore that backup. To be sure that you can restore your data, you should test the restoration process before anything goes wrong. You can use the *Restore Wizard* for testing purposes, as well as when you actually need to restore your backup.

To use the Restore Wizard, take the following steps:

1. Start the Backup program and click the Restore Wizard button.

2. The Welcome to the Restore Wizard dialog box appears, as shown in Figure 15.26. Click the Next button.

FIGURE 15.26 The Welcome to the Restore Wizard dialog box

3. The What to Restore dialog box appears, as shown in Figure 15.27. Click the filename of the backup session that you want to restore and click the Next button. After you select the backup you want to restore, you can choose to restore the entire session, or you can selectively restore drives, folders, or files from the backup session.

FIGURE 15.27   The What to Restore dialog box

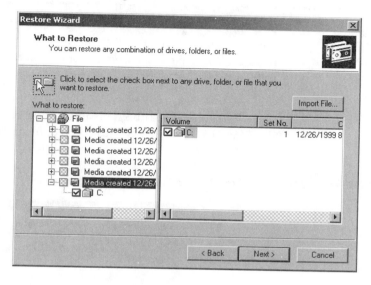

4. The Completing the Restore Wizard dialog box appears, as shown in Figure 15.28. If all of the configuration information is correct, click the Finish button.

FIGURE 15.28   The Completing the Restore Wizard dialog box

Clicking the Advanced button in the Completing the Restore Wizard dialog box brings up a dialog box that allows you to select where files will be restored. You can choose from the original location, an alternate location, or a single folder.

5. The Enter Backup File Name dialog box appears, as shown in Figure 15.29. Verify that the correct filename is specified and click the OK button.

FIGURE 15.29 The Enter Backup File Name dialog box

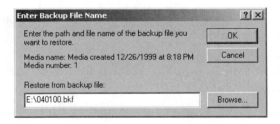

6. During the restoration process, the Wizard displays the Restore Progress dialog box, as shown in Figure 15.30. Once the restoration process is complete, you can click the Report button in this dialog box to see details of the restore session. Figure 15.31 shows an example of a restore report.

FIGURE 15.30 The Restore Progress dialog box

FIGURE 15.31 An example of a restore report

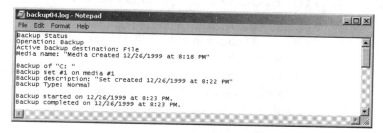

In Exercise 15.10, you will use the Restore Wizard. You will need the floppy disk that you created in Exercise 15.9 for this exercise.

EXERCISE 15.10

Using the Restore Wizard

1. Select Start ➢ Programs ➢ Accessories ➢ System Tools ➢ Backup.

2. In the opening Backup window, click the Restore Wizard button.

3. In the Welcome to the Restore Wizard dialog box, click the Next button.

4. In the What to Restore dialog box, click the filename of the backup session that you created in Exercise 15.9. Click the D: drive to put a check mark in the box. Click the Next button.

5. In the Completing the Restore Wizard dialog box, verify that everything is configured properly. Then click the Finish button.

6. In the Enter Backup File Name dialog box, verify that the filename for the backup session is the same file you specified in Exercise 15.9. Then click the OK button.

7. When the Restore Wizard completes, click the Report button in the Restore Progress dialog box. Close the Notepad window when you are finished viewing the report.

8. Close all of the Restore and Backup dialog boxes.

Using the Recovery Console

If your computer will not start, and you have tried to boot to Safe Mode with no luck, there's one more option you can try. The *Recovery Console* is an option designed for administrators and advanced users. It allows you limited access to FAT16, FAT32, and NTFS volumes without starting the Windows 2000 Professional graphical interface.

Microsoft **Recover systems and user data.**
✓ *Exam*
Objective ▪ Recover systems and user data by using the Recovery Console.

Through the Recovery Console, you can perform the following tasks:

- Copy, replace, or rename operating system files and folders. You might do this if your boot failure may be caused by missing or corrupt files.

- Enable or disable the loading of services when the computer is restarted. If a particular service may be keeping the operating system from booting, you could disable the service. If a particular service is required for successful booting, you want to make sure that service loading was enabled.

- Repair the file system boot sector or the MBR. You might use this option if a virus may have damaged the system boot sector or the MBR.

- Create and format partitions on the drives. You might use this option if your disk utilities will not delete or create Windows 2000 partitions. Normally, you use a disk-partitioning utility for these functions.

In the following sections, you will learn how to access and use the Recovery Console.

Starting the Recovery Console

If you have created the Windows 2000 Professional Setup Disks, you can start the Recovery Console from them. Alternatively, you can add the Recovery Console to the Windows 2000 startup options, but you need to configure this prior to the failure. Each of these options is covered in the following sections.

Starting the Recovery Console with the Windows 2000 Professional Setup Disks

To use the Recovery Console from the Windows 2000 Professional Setup Disks, take the following steps:

1. Restart your computer using the Windows 2000 Professional Setup Boot Disk.

2. Insert each of the other Windows Professional Setup Disks in turn, as prompted.

3. In the Welcome to Setup dialog box, press the R key to repair a Windows 2000 installation.

4. From the Windows 2000 Repair Options menu, press the C key to repair Windows 2000 using the Recovery Console. The Windows 2000 Recovery Console will start.

See the section "Using the Recovery Console" after the next section for details on how to use the Recovery Console.

Adding the Recovery Console to Windows 2000 Startup

You can add the Recovery Console to the Windows 2000 Professional startup options so it will be available in the event of a system failure. This configuration takes about 7MB of disk space to hold the CMDCONS folder and files. To set up this configuration, take the following steps:

1. Insert the Windows 2000 Professional CD into your CD-ROM drive. You can disable auto-play by pressing the Shift key as the CD is read. From a command prompt, type **WINNT32 /CMDCONS**.

2. The Windows 2000 Setup dialog box appears, asking you to confirm that you want to install the Recovery Console, as shown in Figure 15.32. Click the Yes button.

FIGURE 15.32 The Windows 2000 Setup dialog box

3. The installation files will be copied to your computer. Then you will see a dialog box letting you know that the Recovery Console has been successfully installed. Click the OK button to continue.

The next time you restart your computer, you will see an option for the Microsoft Windows 2000 Recovery Console. You will learn how to use the Recovery Console in the next section.

In Exercise 15.11, you will add the Recovery Console to the Windows 2000 startup options. You will need the Windows 2000 Professional CD for this exercise.

EXERCISE 15.11

Adding the Recovery Console to the Windows 2000 Setup

1. Insert the Windows 2000 Professional CD in your CD-ROM drive. Hold down the Shift key as the CD is read to prevent auto-play.

2. Select Start ➢ Programs ➢ Accessories ➢ Command Prompt.

3. Change the drive letter to your CD-ROM drive.

4. From the CD drive letter prompt (*x*:\>), type **CD I386** and press Enter.

5. From *x*:\I386>, type **WINNT32 /CMDCONS**.

EXERCISE 15.11 *(continued)*

6. In the Windows 2000 Setup dialog box, click the Yes button to confirm that you want to install the Recovery Console.

7. After the installation files are copied to your computer, a dialog box appears to let you know that the Recovery Console has been successfully installed. Click the OK button.

8. Shut down and restart your computer. In the startup selection screen, select the option for Microsoft Windows 2000 Recovery Console.

9. At the command prompt, type **EXIT** to close the Recovery Console. You return to the Windows Desktop.

Using the Recovery Console

After you add the Recovery Console, you can access it by restarting your computer. In the operating system selection menu, you will see an option for Microsoft Windows 2000 Recovery Console. Select this option to start the Recovery Console.

The Recovery Console presents you with a command prompt and very limited access to system resources. This keeps unauthorized users from using the Recovery Console to access sensitive data. The following are the only folders you can access through the Recovery Console:

- The root folder
- The *Windir* folder and the subfolders of the Windows 2000 Professional installation
- The CMDCONS folder
- Removable media drives such as CD-ROM drives

If you try to access any other folders besides the ones listed above, you will receive an "access denied" error message.

In the Recovery Console, you cannot copy files from a local hard disk to a floppy disk. You can only copy files from a floppy disk or CD to a hard disk, or from one hard disk to another hard disk. This is for security purposes.

You should use the Recovery Console with extreme caution. Improper use may cause even more damage than the problems you are trying to fix.

The first option you must specify is which Windows 2000 operating system you will log on to. Next, you must specify the Administrator password for the system you are logging on to.

When the Recovery Console starts, you can use the following commands:

ATTRIB	BATCH	CD	CHDIR
CHKDSK	CLS	COPY	DEL
DELETE	DIR	DISABLE	DISKPART
ENABLE	EXIT	EXPAND	FIXBOOT
FIXMBR	FORMAT	HELP	LISTSVC
LOGON	MAP	MD	MKDIR
MORE	RD	REN	RENAME
RMDIR	SYSTEMROOT	TYPE	

These commands are covered in more detail in *MSCE: Windows 2000 Server Study Guide*, by Lisa Donald with James Chellis (Sybex, 2000).

Summary

In this chapter, you learned about the Windows 2000 Professional system recovery options and utilities. We covered the following topics:

- Basic techniques that you can use to safeguard your computer and plan for disaster recovery
- The Event Viewer utility, including how to view the details of an event and manage log files

- The Windows 2000 boot process, including the steps in a normal boot, the BOOT.INI file, and how to create a Windows 2000 boot disk

- Advanced startup options, including Safe Mode, Enable Boot Logging, Last Known Good Configuration, and other options for booting in special modes

- Startup and Recovery options, which are used to specify what action Windows 2000 should take in the event of system failure

- The Dr. Watson utility, which is used to diagnose application errors

- Windows 2000 Professional Setup Boot Disks, which are used to start Windows 2000 in the event of system failure and to access the Recovery Console, and the ERD (Emergency Repair Disk), which can be used to repair problems that prevent your computer from starting

- The Windows Backup utility, which includes a Backup Wizard, a Restore Wizard, and an option for creating an ERD

- The Recovery Console, which is a special boot process that allows you limited access to your file system for replacement of files or specifying which services should be started the next time the computer is booted

Key Terms

Before you take the exam, be sure you're familiar with the following key terms:

Application log

Backup Wizard

Boot Normally

BOOT.INI

BOOTSECT.DOS

Debugging Mode

Dr. Watson

DRWTSN32

Emergency Repair Disk (ERD)

Enable Boot Logging

Enable VGA Mode

Error event

Event Viewer

Failure Audit event

Information event

Last Known Good Configuration

MAKEBT32.EXE

Master Boot Record (MBR)

NTBOOTDD.SYS

NTDETECT.COM

NTLDR

NTOSKRNL.EXE

POST (Power On Self Test)

Recovery Console

Restore Wizard

Safe Mode

Safe Mode with Command Prompt

Safe Mode with Networking

Security log

Success Audit event

System log

Warning event

Windows 2000 Backup

Windows 2000 boot disk

Windows 2000 Professional Setup Boot Disks

Review Questions

1. Which of the following options is *not* an event type logged in the Windows 2000 Professional Event Viewer utility?

   A. Information

   B. Critical

   C. Warning

   D. Error

2. Which of the following files are required to boot the Windows 2000 Professional operating system? Choose all that apply.

   A. NTLDR

   B. BOOT.INI

   C. NTOS.EXE

   D. NTDETECT.COM

3. Which of the following files loads the Windows 2000 Professional operating system?

   A. NTLDR

   B. NTOSKRNL.EXE

   C. BOOTNT.EXE

   D. NTOS.EXE

4. Which of the following options are configured through the BOOT.INI file? Choose all that apply.

   A. The location of the boot partition

   B. The location of the system partition

   C. The Windows 2000 boot menu

   D. The default operating system that should be loaded

5. Which Windows 2000 Advanced Options menu item would you use if you wanted to load Windows 2000 Professional without the GUI?

A. Safe Mode

B. Safe Mode with No GUI

C. Safe Mode Limited

D. Safe Mode with Command Prompt

6. Which utility is used to diagnose application errors?

A. Dr. Watson

B. Sherlock

C. Application Manager

D. Application Event Viewer

7. Which command is used to create the Windows 2000 Professional Setup Boot Disks through the Windows 2000 Professional operating system?

A. MAKEBT32

B. BOOTPRO

C. BOOT32

D. WINNT32 /BOOT

8. Which of the following commands or utilities can be used to create an Emergency Repair Disk?

A. ERD

B. RDISK

C. RDISK32

D. The Backup utility

9. What process do you use to restore an ERD?

   A. Boot with the ERD

   B. Use the Windows Backup utility

   C. Use the Windows 2000 boot disk

   D. Use the Windows 2000 Professional Setup Disks

10. Which command is used to install the Recovery Console?

    A. RECCON

    B. RECCON32

    C. WINNT32 /RC

    D. WINNT32 /CMDCONS

11. Which recovery option can you use to correct configuration errors or to repair system files that might be keeping your computer from starting, and stores portions of the Registry, the system files, a copy of your partition boot sector, and information that relates to the startup environment?

    A. Last Known Good

    B. Windows Safe Mode

    C. Emergency Repair Disk

    D. Recovery Console

12. When you booted Windows 2000 Professional you noticed that an error appeared during the startup sequence. You need the exact error code that was generated, but can't remember what the error code was. Where can you find this information?

    A. *Windir*\error.log file

    B. *Windir*\System32\error.log file

    C. *Windir*\System32\startup.log file

    D. Event Viewer System log

13. Which of the following files is used to initialize and start the Windows 2000 boot process?

A. NTLDR

B. NTOSKRNL.EXE

C. STARTNT

D. NTBOOT.EXE

14. Which of the following files is used to build the operating system menu choices that are displayed during the boot process?

A. NTLDR

B. NTOSKRNL.EXE

C. STARTNT

D. BOOT.INI

15. You are not able to boot your Windows 2000 Professional computer, so you decide to boot the computer to Safe Mode. Which of the following statements regarding Safe Mode is false?

A. When the computer is booted to Safe Mode, there is no network access.

B. Safe Mode will load all of the drivers for the hardware that is installed on the computer.

C. When you run Safe Mode, boot logging is automatically enabled.

D. When you run Safe Mode, the Enable VGA Mode is automatically enabled.

16. You have been having problems with your Windows 2000 Professional computer. You decide to start the computer using the Enable Boot Logging option on the Advanced Options menu. Where can you find the log file that is created?

    A. *Windir*\ntbtlog.txt

    B. *Windir*\System32\ntbtlog.txt

    C. *Windir*\ntboot.log

    D. *Windir*\System32\ntboot.log

17. Which Advanced Options menu item would you use during the system boot to enable and run the Kernel Debugger utility if the utility is installed on your computer?

    A. Run Kernel Debugger

    B. Run Advanced Troubleshooting

    C. Debugging Mode

    D. Boot to Troubleshooting Mode

18. Your computer is configured to dual-boot between Windows 98 and Windows 2000. How would you configure the computer so that Windows 98 would be the default selection if the user did not make a choice within the specified amount of time?

    A. Through the STARTUP.INI file

    B. Through the SYSTEM.INI file

    C. Through Control Panel, Startup Options

    D. Through Control Panel, System, Startup and Recovery

19. You are using the Windows 2000 Backup utility and have decided to back up the system state data. Which of the following items is not backed up when you choose this option?

A. Registry

B. COM+ registration database

C. Windows 2000 OLE database

D. System boot files

20. Which backup types clear the archive bit as the files are backed up? Choose two answers.

A. Normal

B. Copy

C. Differential

D. Incremental

Answers to Review Questions

1. B. The event types logged in Event Viewer are Information, Warning, and Error. Success Audit and Failure Audit events are also logged when events have been audited for success or failure. There is no event called Critical.

2. A, B, D. The files that are required to boot Windows 2000 are NTLDR, BOOT.INI, NTDETECT.COM, and NTOSKRNL.EXE. There is no boot file called NTOS.EXE.

3. B. The NTOSKRNL.EXE file is used to load the Windows 2000 Professional operating system. NTLDR is used to control the Windows 2000 boot process. There is no boot file called BOOTNT.EXE or NTOS.EXE.

4. A, C, D. The BOOT.INI file specifies the location of the boot partition, the boot menu, and the default operating system that should be loaded. The system partition is specified by the active partition.

5. D. Safe Mode with Command Prompt loads the operating system without the graphical interface. Safe Mode uses a graphical interface. There is no startup option called Safe Mode Limited or Safe Mode with No GUI.

6. A. The Dr. Watson utility is used to diagnose application errors. Windows 2000 Professional does not ship with a utility called Sherlock, Application Manager, or Application Event Viewer.

7. A. You use the command-line utility MAKEBT32 to create Windows 2000 Professional boot disks. The BOOTPRO and BOOT32 commands do not exist. There is no switch for WINNT32 called /BOOT.

8. D. The only utility that can be used to create an Emergency Repair Disk (ERD) is the Backup utility. ERD, RDISK, and RDISK32 do not exist in Windows 2000 Professional.

9. D. In order to restore the system using an ERD, you must use the Windows 2000 Professional Setup Disks.

10. D. Options A, B, and C do not exist. You use WINNT32 /CMDCONS to install the Recovery Console.

11. C. The Emergency Repair Disk (ERD) contains the files that can be used to correct configuration errors or repair system files.

12. D. The Event Viewer utility is used to track information about your computer's hardware and software. The System log includes any error messages that have been generated.

13. A. When you install Windows 2000, the NTLDR file is copied to the active partition. This file executes when you choose to load the Windows 2000 operating system and is used to initialize the Windows 2000 boot process.

14. D. The BOOT.INI file is used to build the operating system menu choices that are displayed during the boot process. It is also used to specify the location of the boot partition.

15. B. When you run your computer in Safe Mode, you simplify your Windows 2000 configuration. Only the drivers that are needed to get the computer up and running are loaded.

16. A. When you enable boot logging, the file created is \Windir\ntbtlog.txt. This log file is used to troubleshoot the boot process.

17. C. If you select Debugging Mode and have the Kernel Debugger installed, the Kernel Debugger can be used for advanced troubleshooting.

18. D. Through the System icon in Control Panel, you can access Startup and Recovery options. The Default Operating System option lets you specify which operating system will load if no user selection is made.

19. C. When you back up system state data, you back up the Registry, the COM+ registration database, and the system boot files.

20. A, D. A normal backup includes all files and sets the archive bit for each file that is backed up. An incremental backup includes only the files that have not been marked as archived and sets the archive bit for each file that is backed up. A copy backup includes all files but does not set the archive bit. A differential backup includes only the files that have not been marked as archived and does not set the archive bit for each file that is backed up.

Appendix A

Practice Exam

1. Kate has an older computer that she would like to install Windows 2000 Professional on and use as a practice computer. This computer has a 133MHz Pentium processor, 32MB of RAM, 650MB of free disk space, and a 16-bit network card. What needs to be upgraded?

   A. The processor

   B. The memory

   C. The amount of free disk space

   D. The network card

2. Gina has Windows 98 installed on her computer. She wants to learn how to use Windows 2000, including how to manage local security and disk compression. She is not sure that the applications that she uses will work with Windows 2000 Professional. She decides to configure the computer so that it will dual-boot between the two operating systems. The computer is configured with a single hard drive that has been configured as partition C: and partition D:. Which of the following configurations should Gina use?

   A. She should install Windows 2000 Professional on drive C: and format the partition as NTFS. She should install Windows 98 on drive D: and format the partition as FAT32. The disk should be configured as a basic disk.

   B. She should install Windows 2000 Professional on drive D: and format the partition as NTFS. She should install Windows 98 on drive C: and format the partition as FAT32. The disk should be configured as a basic disk.

   C. She should install Windows 2000 Professional on drive C: and format the partition as NTFS. She should install Windows 98 on drive D: and format the partition as FAT32. The disk should be configured as a dynamic disk.

   D. She should install Windows 2000 Professional on drive D: and format the partition as NTFS. She should install Windows 98 on drive C: and format the partition as FAT32. The disk should be configured as a dynamic disk.

3. Bart has decided to install Windows 2000 Professional on his computer. He wants to use a clean installation, so he decides to format his computer's partitions. Now when he tries to access the CD-ROM drive, it is not recognized. His computer is on the Microsoft HCL. What should he do?

   A. From his Windows 98 computer, create Windows 2000 Boot Disks using the Windows 2000 Professional CD MAKEBT command.

   B. From his Windows 98 computer, create Windows 2000 Boot Disks using the Windows 2000 Professional CD MAKEBT32 command.

   C. From his Windows 98 computer, create Windows 2000 Boot Disks using the Windows 2000 Professional CD SETUPDISK command.

   D. From his Windows 98 computer, create Windows 2000 Boot Disks using the Windows 2000 Professional CD MAKEDISK command.

4. You have just purchased 150 computers that are able to boot to the network using a PXE-boot ROM. You want to automate the installation of Windows 2000 Professional on these computers. Which of the following automated installation options offers the easiest deployment?

   A. Install the computers using RIS

   B. Install the computers using disk imaging

   C. Install the computers using unattended installation

   D. Install the computers using Sysprep

5. You have decided to automatically deploy Windows 2000 Professional using RIS. You have 500 computers that are configured identically. You are installing the computers in batches of 100. After you install the first 200 computers, you start to have errors and the installations fail. Which network service should you make sure is properly configured?

A. Make sure that the additional computers have been configured in the Active Directory.

B. Make sure that the additional computers have been configured and are able to access the DNS server.

C. Make sure that the additional computers have been configured and are able to access the WINS server.

D. Make sure that you have a large enough scope to accommodate all of the computers in the DHCP configuration.

6. Homer has a Windows 2000 computer that has become severely corrupted. You decide to reinstall Windows 2000 on his computer by using a disk image that you have previously created. You have created an answer file that will be used to automate the installation. After the disk image is copied, what command switch can be used to run the installation without requiring any responses from Homer?

A. quiet

B. nouserinteraction

C. useanswerfile

D. unattended

7. You are the network manager in charge of deploying Windows 2000 Professional in your environment. You have been asked to evaluate which computers in your organization would be able to be directly upgraded to Windows 2000. Which of the following clients could be directly upgraded? Choose all that apply.

A. Windows 95

B. Windows 98

C. Windows NT Workstation 3.5

D. Windows NT Workstation 3.51

8. You have Windows 98 installed on your home computer. You are considering upgrading to Windows 2000 Professional. After some research, you determine that all of your hardware is on the HCL. You are not sure if all of your applications are compatible with Windows 2000. How can you generate a Windows 2000 compatibility report without making any changes to your computer? Choose all that apply.

A. Run the WINNT /checkupgradeonly command

B. Run the WINNT32 /checkupgradeonly command

C. Run the Chkupgrd.exe program

D. Run the Upgrade.exe program

9. Maggie wants to upgrade her Windows 98 computer to Windows 2000 Professional. Before she upgrades her computer, she wants to determine if her computer is using any virtual device drivers. What configuration file can she check to determine if any virtual device drivers have been loaded?

A. vdd.ini

B. vxd.ini

C. System.ini

D. Config.ini

10. Your computer contains a share called \\W2KP1\SalesData. You need to restart your computer, and you want to make sure that no users are currently attached to the share before you do this. Which utility can be used to determine which users are attached to the share?

    A. Windows Explorer

    B. Server Manager

    C. Share Manager

    D. Shared Folders

11. You are exploring the Windows 2000 Registry. Which of the following options is not a default Registry key?

    A. HKEY_LOCAL_USER

    B. HKEY_USERS

    C. HKEY_LOCAL_MACHINE

    D. HKEY_CLASSES_ROOT

12. Kathy has detected a processor bottleneck on her computer. The computer supports multiple processors, so she adds a second processor to her computer. When she loads System Monitor, she realizes that the second processor has not been detected. What should Kathy do?

    A. She should update the processor driver to a driver that supports multiple processors.

    B. She should configure the computer to support multiple processors through Control Panel, System.

    C. She should configure the computer to support multiple processors through the Registry.

    D. She should configure the computer to support multiple processors though the Advanced tab of the processor Properties dialog box in Device Manager.

13. Sally works for a multinational company and speaks fluent English and German. She uses an English version of the Windows 2000 operating system. Which of the following options are supported by Windows 2000 multilingual support?

    A. Sally can translate documents that are written in English to German.

    B. Sally can use a Windows 2000 user interface that is in English or German.

    C. Sally can enable and configure multilingual editing and viewing of documents.

    D. Sally can add and configure multilingual support through the Control Panel, Language Options.

14. Dick is only able to press a single keyboard key at a time. Which accessibility option can he use to allow the use of the Shift, Ctrl, or Alt key in conjunction with another key, one key at a time?

    A. StickyKeys

    B. FilterKeys

    C. ToggleKeys

    D. AccessKeys

15. Kate is a user with poor vision. She needs to have the screen greatly expanded to read the display. Which Windows 2000 Professional accessibility utility should Kate use?

    A. Expander

    B. Magnifier

    C. Enlarger

    D. Expander

16. Peg is configuring the password policies for her Windows 2000 Professional computer. She wants to import a password filter that will keep users from using commonly used passwords. How would she configure this option in password policies?

    A. Confirm Password Complexity Options

    B. Use the Following Password Filter

    C. Passwords Must Meet Complexity Requirements

    D. Store Passwords Using Password Complexity Options

17. Hank has decided to configure auditing on his Windows 2000 computer. He wants to allow Marilyn to manage the auditing logs, but he does not want to add her to the Administrators group. What needs to be done to allow Marilyn to access the auditing logs?

    A. Marilyn needs to be added to the Power Users group.

    B. Marilyn needs to be added to the Server Operators group.

    C. Marilyn needs to be assigned the Manage Auditing and Security Log user right.

    D. Marilyn needs to be assigned the Administer Audit Logs user right.

18. Ed does not want any users to be able to install network printers on his Windows 2000 computer. Which security option should he configure?

    A. Do Not Allow Printer Creation

    B. Prevent Users from Installing Print Drivers

    C. Manage Print Operators

    D. Secure Printer Creation

19. You are designing Windows 2000 Professional naming conventions for your user accounts. Which of the following conventions cannot be applied to service accounts?

    A. #Service_account

    B. %Service account

    C. &Service-account

    D. =Service_account

20. You are considering adding Jose to the Power Users group on your computer. Which of the following tasks cannot be managed by the Power Users group?

    A. Create and delete network shares (except administrative shares)

    B. Manage all NTFS volumes

    C. Stop and start services (except services that are configured to start automatically)

    D. Create local users and groups

21. Pete has logged on to the corporate network using a dial-up connection. Which special group will he belong to by default?

    A. Service

    B. Dialup

    C. RAS

    D. Remote

22. Allie suspects that her startup script is not executing properly. She wants to see the startup script execute so that she can troubleshoot any errors. Which group policy setting should she configure?

    A. Run Startup Scripts Visible

    B. View Logon Scripts

    C. Show Logon Script Commands as They Are Executed

    D. Run Logon Scripts in Verbose Mode

23. When Megan logs on to a Windows 2000 Professional computer, what type of profile is created by default?

    A. Local user profile

    B. Roaming profile

    C. Mandatory profile

    D. Interactive user profile

24. When John logs on to a Windows 2000 Professional computer for the first time, where will his user profile be stored by default?

    A. User Profiles\John

    B. Documents and Settings\John

    C. *Windir*\Profiles\John

    D. *Windir*\System32\Profiles\John

25. Andre has a laptop that can be connected to a docking station. When he is at work, the laptop is attached to the network through the docking station. When he is at home, he does not attach to a network. What type of profile should Andre configure?

    A. Roaming user profile

    B. Network profile

    C. Hardware profile

    D. Managed profile

26. Carole has just upgraded her Windows 98 computer to Windows 2000 Professional. She wants to take advantage of Windows 2000 local security. She realizes that her computer is using FAT32 partitions and wants to upgrade the partition to NTFS without losing any of her current data. Which of the following utilities can she use to accomplish this task?

    A. Disk Administrator

    B. Disk Management

    C. Disk Upgrade

    D. CONVERT command-line utility

27. Monica is configuring her Windows 2000 computer. She has a database that is 8GB in size. She will use eight physical disks. She wants to configure her disk configuration for maximum performance. Which of the following disk configurations should she use?

    A. Basic disks with spanned volumes

    B. Dynamic disks with spanned volumes

    C. Basic disks with striped volumes

    D. Dynamic disks with striped volumes

28. Rich has just upgraded his Windows 98 computer to Windows 2000 Professional. He wants to take advantage of Windows 2000 dynamic disks. He realizes that his computer is using a basic disk and wants to upgrade the basic disk to a dynamic disk without losing any of his current data. Which of the following utilities can he use to accomplish this task?

A. Disk Administrator

B. Disk Management

C. Disk Upgrade

D. CONVERT command-line utility

29. Ginnie has several data files that average 100MB in size. She wants to save disk space by compressing these files. Which of the following utilities can she use to accomplish this task?

A. COMPRESS command-line utility

B. Disk Administrator

C. Disk Management

D. Windows Explorer

30. Julie is trying to find the `sales.txt` file on her computer. The previous user configured the file as hidden. Julie is positive that the file is in the C:\Sales folder. What should she do next?

A. Log on as Administrator; then she will see the file.

B. Access the file from a DOS prompt by using the `DIR` command.

C. With Disk Management, under the C: drive properties, choose the Show Hidden Files option.

D. With Windows Explorer, in the View tab of the Folder Options dialog box, choose the Show Hidden Files and Folders option.

31. Sam has installed a photo-editing application. Whenever he accesses a file with a `.tif` extension, the file opens in his graphics-editing application. How can he configure his computer so that any files with a `.tif` extension automatically open in his photo-editing application?

A. With Windows Explorer, in the File Types tab of the Folder Options dialog box, configure a file association to link the photo-editing application with `.tif` files.

B. With Disk Manager, under the C: drive properties, configure a file association to link the photo-editing application with `.tif` files.

C. Use the FileAssoc utility to associate the photo-editing application with `.tif` files.

D. Use the Associate utility to associate the photo-editing application with `.tif` files.

32. Jim wants to create home folders for five users on his computer. Each user should be able to access a network share where the home folder resides. Each user should have full access to his or her home folder, but not the other user's home folders. Jim wants to minimize the actual number of shares that need to be configured. What should Jim do?

A. Create a folder called Home. Share the folder with Read permission for the Everyone group. Under Home, create a folder for each user. Using NTFS permissions, only assign Full Control permission to each respective user.

B. Create a folder called Home. Share the folder with Full Control permission for the Everyone group. Under Home, create a folder for each user. Using NTFS permissions, only assign Full Control permission to each respective user.

C. Create a folder called Home. Under Home, create a folder for each user. Share the individual home folder for each user and assign the Full Control share permission to each user.

D. Create a folder called Home. Under Home, create a folder for each user. Share the individual home folder for each user and assign the Full Control NTFS permission to each user.

33. Erica wants to access a shared resource on a Windows 2000 server called \\Server1\Data. Which of the following commands can be used to access the network share?

    A. NET USE

    B. NET SHARE

    C. NET ACCESS

    D. MAP

34. Jessica's computer runs the TCP/IP protocol and is located on subnet 1. She wants to access a resource that is located on subnet 2. When she tries to access the resource on subnet 2, she receives a network error. Jessica is not having any problems accessing resources on subnet 1. Which of the following configuration options should she check first?

    A. Subnet mask

    B. Default gateway

    C. DNS server

    D. WINS server

35. Jennifer's computer runs the TCP/IP protocol and is located on subnet 1. She wants to access a resource that is located on subnet 2. When she tries to access the resource on subnet 2, she receives a network error. Jessica is able to access the resource on subnet 2 by using the resource's IP address, but she is not able to access the resource using the host name. Which of the following configuration options should she check first?

    A. Subnet mask

    B. Default gateway

    C. DNS server

    D. WINS server

36. Ian's computer runs the TCP/IP protocol and is located on subnet 1. He wants to access a resource that is located on subnet 2. When he tries to access the resource on subnet 2, he receives a network error. Which command can Ian use to make sure that he can access different computers within the communication channel?

    A. PING

    B. IPCONFIG

    C. IPROUTE

    D. TCPCONFIG

37. Ralph wants to share his printer. Which of the following options cannot be configured for his printer?

    A. The hours that the printer is available

    B. The print priority that will be assigned to specific groups

    C. The print drivers that will be stored on the print server for different client platforms

    D. The separator page

38. Sean is configuring his printer to be shared by other members in his local workgroup. Sean wants to configure the printer so that short print jobs will be printed before long print jobs if a long print job has not finished spooling. Which of the following options should Sean configure?

    A. Start Printing Immediately

    B. Start Printing after Last Page Is Spooled

    C. Print Directly to Printer

    D. Hold Mismatched Print Jobs

39. Martin wants to configure a separator page for his Windows 2000 printer. The print device is a PostScript printer. Which of the following separator page files should he use?

A. `pcl.sep`

B. `pscript.sep`

C. `sysprint.sep`

D. `sysprintj.sep`

40. Frank is dialing into a Windows 2000 RAS server. How should Frank configure the type of dial-up server he is using on his Windows 2000 Professional dial-up client?

A. Use PPP

B. Use SLIP

C. Use TCP/IP

D. Use NetBEUI

41. Sam wants to be able to dial into a Windows 2000 server that is attached to the Internet using a secure Internet connection. Which of the following connection types should he configure?

A. RAS connection

B. Dial-up connection

C. VPN connection

D. Internet connection

42. Linda has configured her computer so that it supports Internet connection sharing. Greg and Linda are on the same network. How should Greg configure his Internet connection so that he can access Linda's shared connection?

A. When he creates his connection, he should specify that he will connect to the Internet using Linda's IP address.

B. When he creates his connection, he should specify that he will connect to the Internet using the NetBIOS name of Linda's computer.

C. When he creates his connection, he should specify that he will connect to the Internet using Linda's host name.

D. When he creates his connection, he should specify that he will connect to the Internet using the I Connect through a Local Area Network (LAN) option.

43. Rudy wants to create a baseline for his Windows 2000 Professional computer that will track counters for the memory subsystem, the processor subsystem, the disk subsystem, and the network subsystem. He wants to create a baseline file every seven days and use it to monitor the computer's performance over time. Which utility should Rudy use?

A. System Monitor

B. Performance Monitor

C. Performance Logs and Alerts

D. ActiveX Baselines

44. Pat has determined that he has a memory bottleneck on his Windows 2000 Professional computer. What is the best way that Pat can correct this problem?

A. Increase the size of his page file

B. Spread the page file over multiple disk I/O channels

C. Make sure that the page file is not on the same partition as the system and boot partitions

D. Add more memory to the computer

45. Peter suspects that he has a disk subsystem bottleneck. He determines that the PhysicalDisk > %DiskTime counter is at 90%. What should Peter do next?

    A. Make sure that he does not have a memory bottleneck

    B. Make sure that he does not have a processor bottleneck

    C. Make sure that he does not have a network bottleneck

    D. Based on this information, no bottleneck is indicated

46. Bob configured his Windows 2000 computer to use auditing. Now he wants to view the results of the audit. Which log should he check in the Event Viewer utility?

    A. Audit

    B. System

    C. Application

    D. Security

47. Alvin has determined that he has corrupt Windows 2000 boot files. What is the fastest way that Alvin can restore his boot files?

    A. He should use the Last Known Good Configuration option.

    B. He should use his ERD.

    C. He should boot the computer to Safe Mode.

    D. He should restore the files through the Recovery Console.

48. When Walt attempts to start his Windows 2000 Professional computer, all he sees is a blue screen. He suspects that his problem is due to a device driver that he just updated. Which system recovery option will allow him to start his computer with a simplified configuration so that he can attempt to fix his computer?

    A. He should use his ERD.

    B. He should boot the computer using the Last Known Good Configuration option.

    C. He should boot the computer using Safe Mode.

    D. He should boot the computer using Simplified Configuration Mode.

49. Lynne has decided that she wants to create an Emergency Repair Disk (ERD) for her Windows 2000 computer. Which utility should she use to create the ERD?

    A. RDISK command-line utility

    B. ERD command-line utility

    C. MAKEERD command-line utility

    D. Windows 2000 Backup utility

50. You are deciding how to handle the use of drivers that have not been extensively tested. One of the vendors you deal with does not always have signed drivers, but the drivers have been extensively tested, and you are willing to load those drivers. You do not want to load drivers from any other companies. Which driver signing option should you configure?

    A. Ignore

    B. Warn

    C. Manage

    D. Block

Answers to Practice Exam

1. B. Windows 2000 Professional requires a minimum of 64MB of RAM, so Kate needs to upgrade the memory on her computer. See Chapter 1 for more information.

2. B. Since the computer will dual-boot, the disk must be configured as a basic disk, because Windows 98 will not recognize a dynamic disk. Since Gina wants to use local security and disk compression, the partition that Windows 2000 Professional will be installed on needs to use NTFS. The partition that Windows 98 will be installed on needs to use FAT32. Since the first partition (C:) is usually the active and bootable partition, it should have Windows 98 installed on it. See Chapter 1 for more information.

3. B. If your computer cannot boot from the CD-ROM drive, you can create floppy disks that can boot to the Windows 2000 Professional operating system. The command to create boot disks from Windows 95/98, Windows NT, or Windows 2000 is MAKEBT32. See Chapter 1 for more information.

4. A. You can easily deploy automated installations of Windows 2000 Professional on computers that are PXE-compliant by using Remote Installation Services (RIS). See Chapter 2 for more information.

5. D. DHCP is required to install Windows 2000 Professional computers using RIS. You should make sure that the DHCP scope has enough available IP addresses to accommodate all of the RIS clients. See Chapter 2 for more information.

6. A. The quiet switch can be used with the Sysprep program to run the installation without any user interaction. See Chapter 2 for more information.

7. A, B, D. Windows 95, Windows 98, Windows NT Workstation 3.51, and Windows NT Workstation 4 can be directly upgraded to Windows 2000 Professional. If you want to upgrade from Windows NT Workstation 3.5, you must first upgrade to Windows NT Workstation 3.51 or Windows NT Workstation 4. See Chapter 3 for more information.

8. B, C. There are two ways to check upgrade compatibility without making any changes to the Windows 98 operating system. You can use the WINNT32 /checkupgradeonly command, or you can run the Chkupgrd program that is available from Microsoft's Web site. See Chapter 3 for more information.

9. C. You can determine if your computer is running any virtual device drivers (VxDs) by checking the [386Enh] section of the System.ini file. See Chapter 3 for more information.

10. D. The Shared Folders utility can be used to display information about all of the shares that have been created on the computer, the user sessions that are open on each share, and the files that are currently open, listed by user. See Chapter 10 for more information.

11. A. The five Registry keys that are created by default include HKEY_CURRENT_USER, HKEY_USERS, HKEY_LOCAL_MACHINE, HKEY_CLASSES_ROOT, and HKEY_CURRENT_CONFIG. See Chapter 4 for more information.

12. A. If Kathy adds a second processor, she will also need to update the processor driver to a driver that supports multiple processors. See Chapter 4 for more information.

13. C. On a localized version of Windows 2000, you can enable and configure multilingual editing and viewing of documents through the Regional Options icon in Control Panel. If you want to have support for multiple-language user interfaces, you need to use Windows 2000 Multilanguage Version. See Chapter 5 for more information.

14. A. The Accessibility Options icon in Control Panel allows you to configure the keyboard for users with special needs. StickyKeys allows you to use the Shift, Ctrl, or Alt key in conjunction with another key, one key at a time. FilterKeys ignores brief or repeated keystrokes. ToggleKeys makes a noise whenever you press the Caps Lock, Num Lock, or Scroll Lock key. The AccessKeys option does not exist. See Chapter 5 for more information.

15. B. The Magnifier utility creates a separate window to magnify a portion of the Windows screen. See Chapter 5 for more information.

16. C. The Passwords Must Meet Complexity Requirements option allows you to install a password filter that will prevent users from using passwords that are contained in the password filter. See Chapter 6 for more information.

17. C. The Manage Auditing and Security Log user right allows a user to manage the auditing and security logs. See Chapter 6 for more information.

18. B. The Prevent Users from Installing Print Drivers security option prevents users from installing network printers. See Chapter 6 for more information.

19. D. You cannot use the equal sign (=) character in Windows 2000 usernames. See Chapter 6 for more information.

20. B. Members of the Power Users groups can create local users and groups; modify users and groups they create; create and delete network shares (except administrative shares); create, manage, and delete local printers; modify the system clock; stop or start services (except services that are configured to start automatically); and modify the program files directory. Members of the Power Users groups cannot access any NTFS resources that they have not been given explicit permission to access. See Chapter 7 for more information.

21. B. The Dialup special group includes any users who log on to the network from a dial-up connection. See Chapter 7 for more information.

22. A. The Run Startup Scripts Visible option displays the startup script instructions as they are run. See Chapter 7 for more information.

23. A. By default, local user profiles are created when a user logs on to a Windows 2000 Professional computer. See Chapter 8 for more information.

24. B. In Windows 2000 Professional, user profiles are stored in the Documents and Settings folder. See Chapter 8 for more information.

25. C. Hardware profiles are used to store hardware configurations for a computer. They are typically used for computers that can be attached to the network or not attached to the network. See Chapter 8 for more information.

26. D. The only utility that can be used to upgrade a FAT16 or FAT32 partition to NTFS is the CONVERT command-line utility. See Chapter 9 for more information.

27. D. You can create striped volumes only on dynamic disks. Striped volumes store and write data in equal stripes between the disks in the stripe set. This allows you to take advantage of multiple I/O channels and increase the speeds at which data reads and writes take place. See Chapter 9 for more information.

28. B. The Disk Management utility is used to convert basic disks to dynamic disks. See Chapter 9 for more information.

29. D. You can use the COMPACT command-line utility or the Windows Explorer utility to compress files in Windows 2000. See Chapter 9 for more information.

30. D. By default, Windows 2000 computers are configured with the Do Not Show Hidden Files and Folders setting. You can set the Show Hidden Files and Folders, as well as other options for viewing files and folders, through Windows Explorer's Folder Options dialog box, View tab. See Chapter 10 for more information.

31. A. With Windows Explorer, in the File Types tab of the Folder Options dialog box, you can configure file associations so that when a user accesses a file with a specific extension, an associated application automatically opens the file. See Chapter 10 for more information.

32. B. Share permissions and NTFS permissions work together. Whichever permission is more restrictive will be applied. This means that if you have Read permission for the share and Full Control for NTFS, you will only be allowed Read permission. If the Everyone group has Full Control permission for the share, but is limited at the subfolder level, then users can only access their respective home folders. See Chapter 10 for more information.

33. A. The NET USE command-line utility provides a quick and easy way to map a network drive in Windows 2000. See Chapter 10 for more information.

34. B. The default gateway option is used with TCP/IP configurations to specify the location of the router that is used to access other network segments. See Chapter 11 for more information.

35. C. DNS servers are used to resolve IP addresses to host names.

36. A. The PING command-line utility is used to send an ICMP (Internet Control Message Protocol) echo request and echo reply to verify if a remote computer is available. See Chapter 11 for more information.

37. B. You can set print priority only for the printer as a whole. You cannot specify print priority for different groups on a single printer. See Chapter 12 for more information.

38. B. If you choose the Start Printing after Last Page Is Spooled print option, a smaller print job that finishes spooling first will be printed before a large print job that is still in the process of being spooled. See Chapter 12 for more information.

39. C. The sysprint.sep separator page file is used by PostScript printers to send a separator page. See Chapter 12 for more information.

40. A. The PPP (Point-to-Point Protocol) is used to connect to a dial-up server that is using Windows 95/98, Windows NT, or Windows 2000. See Chapter 13 for more information.

41. C. A virtual private network (VPN) is a private network that uses links across private or public networks (such as the Internet). See Chapter 13 for more information.

42. D. When the Internet Connection Wizard starts, Greg should select the I Want to Set Up My Internet Connection Manually, or I Want to Connect through a Local Area Network (LAN) option. Then, in the Setting Up Your Internet Connection dialog box, Greg should select the I Connect through a Local Area Network (LAN) option. See Chapter 13 for more information.

43. C. The Performance Logs and Alerts utility is used to create counter logs and trace logs, and to define alerts. You can configure counter logs to create baselines. See Chapter 14 for more information.

44. D. Although you can achieve some performance improvement by manipulating the page file, the best way to optimize the memory subsystem is to actually add more physical memory to the computer. See Chapter 14 for more information.

45. A. A value of 90% or higher for the Physical Disk > %DiskTime counter does indicate a disk subsystem bottleneck. You should verify that you don't have a memory bottleneck before you do anything else. A memory bottleneck can cause excessive paging, which in turn affects the disk subsystem. See Chapter 14 for more information.

46. D. The Security log tracks events that are generated through Windows 2000 auditing. See Chapter 15 for more information.

47. B. Alvin can restore the Windows 2000 boot files from the Emergency Repair Disk (ERD) in conjunction with the Windows 2000 Setup Boot Disks. See Chapter 15 for more information.

48. C. If Windows 2000 will not load, you should attempt to load the operating system through Safe Mode. When you run Windows 2000 in Safe Mode, you are simplifying your Windows 2000 configuration as much as possible. Only the drivers that are required to get the computer up and running are loaded. See Chapter 15 for more information.

49. D. In Windows 2000, you use the Windows 2000 Backup utility to create an ERD. In Windows NT 4, you use the RDISK command-line utility to create an ERD. See Chapter 15 for more information.

50. B. There are three options for driver signing: Ignore, Warn, and Block. The Warn option has Windows 2000 display a warning message before installing an unsigned file. You can choose to install the driver or cancel the installation with this option. See Chapter 4 for more information.

Glossary

A

Advanced Graphics Port (AGP) A type of expansion slot supported by Windows 2000. AGP is used by video cards and supports high-quality video and graphics performance.

access control entry (ACE) An item used by the operating system to determine *resource* access. Each *access control list* (*ACL*) has an associated ACE that lists the permissions that have been granted or denied to the users and groups listed in the ACL.

access control list (ACL) An item used by the operating system to determine *resource* access. Each object (such as a folder, network share, or printer) in Windows 2000 has an ACL. The ACL lists the *security identifiers* (*SIDs*) contained by objects. Only those identified in the list as having the appropriate permission can activate the services of that object.

access token An object containing the *security identifier* (*SID*) of a running *process*. A process started by another process inherits the starting process's access token. The access token is checked against each object's *access control list* (*ACL*) to determine whether or not appropriate permissions are granted to perform any requested service.

Accessibility Options Windows 2000 Professional features used to support users with limited sight, hearing, or mobility. Accessibility Options include special keyboard, sound, display, and mouse configurations.

Accessibility Wizard A Windows 2000 Professional Wizard used to configure a computer based on the user's vision, hearing, and mobility needs.

account lockout policy A Windows 2000 policy used to specify how many invalid *logon* attempts should be tolerated before a user account is locked out. Account lockout policies are set through *account policies*.

account policies Windows 2000 policies used to determine password and *logon* requirements. Account policies are set through the *Microsoft Management Console* (*MMC*) *Local Computer Policy* snap-in.

ACE See *access control entry*.

ACL See *access control list*.

ACPI See *Advanced Configuration and Power Interface*.

Active Desktop A Windows 2000 feature that makes the *Desktop* look and work like a Web page.

Active Directory A directory service available with the Windows 2000 Server platform. The Active Directory stores information in a central database and allows users to have a single user account (called a *domain user account* or *Active Directory user account*) for the network.

Active Directory user account A user account that is stored in the Windows 2000 Server *Active Directory's* central database. An Active Directory user account can provide a user with a single user account for a network. Also called a domain user account.

adapter Any hardware device that allows communications to occur through physically dissimilar systems. This term usually refers to peripheral cards that are permanently mounted inside computers and provide an interface from the computer's bus to another medium such as a hard disk or a network.

Administrator account A Windows 2000 special account that has the ultimate set of security permissions and can assign any permission to any user or group.

Administrators group A Windows 2000 built-in group that consists of *Administrator accounts*.

Advanced Configuration and Power Interface (ACPI) A specification that controls the amount of power given to each device attached to the computer. With ACPI, the operating system can turn off peripheral devices when they are not in use.

Advanced Power Management (APM) A Windows 2000 feature designed to reduce the power consumption of a computer, which is especially important for laptops that are running on battery power.

AGP See *Accelerated Graphics Port*.

alert A system-monitoring feature that is generated when a specific *counter* exceeds or falls below a specified value. Through the *Performance Logs and Alerts* utility, administrators can configure alerts so that a message is sent, a program is run, or a more detailed log file is generated.

Anonymous Logon group A Windows 2000 *special group* that includes users who access the computer through anonymous logons. Anonymous logons occur when users gain access through special accounts, such as the IUSR_*computername* and TsInternetUser user accounts.

answer file An automated installation script used to respond to configuration prompts that normally occur in a Windows 2000 Professional installation. Administrators can create Windows 2000 answer files with the *Setup Manager* utility.

APM See *Advanced Power Management*.

Application layer The seventh (top) layer of the *Open Systems Interconnection (OSI)* model that interfaces with application programs by providing high-level network services based on lower-level network layers.

Application log A log that tracks events that are related to applications that are running on the computer. The Application log can be viewed in the *Event Viewer* utility.

assigned applications Applications installed with *Windows Installer packages*. Assigned applications are automatically installed when the user selects the application on the Programs menu or by document invocation (by the document extension).

audit policy A Windows 2000 policy that tracks the success or failure of specified security events. Audit policies are set through *Local Computer Policy*.

Authenticated Users group A Windows 2000 *special group* that includes users who access the Windows 2000 operating system through a valid username and password.

authentication The process required to log on to a computer locally. Authentication requires a valid username and a password that exists in the local accounts database. An *access token* will be created if the information presented matches the account in the database.

automated installation The process of installing Windows 2000 using an unattended setup method such as *Remote Installation Services (RIS)*, *unattended installation*, or *disk images*.

B

backup The process of writing all the data contained in online mass-storage devices to offline mass-storage devices for the purpose of safekeeping. Backups are usually performed from hard disk drives to tape drives. Also referred to as archiving.

Backup Operators group A Windows 2000 built-in group that includes users who can back up and restore the *file system*, even if the file system is *NTFS* and they have not been assigned permissions to the file system. The members of the Backup Operators group can only access the file system through the *Windows 2000 Backup* utility. To be able to directly access the file system, the user must have explicit permissions assigned.

backup type A *backup* choice that determines which files are backed up during a backup process. Backup types include *normal backup*, *copy backup*, *incremental backup*, *differential backup*, and *daily backup*.

Backup Wizard A Wizard used to perform a backup. The Backup Wizard is accessed through the *Windows 2000 Backup* utility.

baseline A snapshot record of a computer's current performance statistics that can be used for performance analysis and planning purposes.

Basic Input/Output System (BIOS) A set of routines in firmware that provides the most basic software interface drivers for hardware attached to the computer. The BIOS contains the boot routine.

basic storage A disk-storage system supported by Windows 2000 that consists of *primary partitions* and *extended partitions*.

Batch group A Windows 2000 *special group* that includes users who log on as a user account that is only used to run a batch job.

binding The process of linking together software components, such as network *protocols* and *network adapters*.

BIOS See *Basic Input/Output System*.

boot   The process of loading a computer's operating system. Booting usually occurs in multiple phases, each successively more complex until the entire operating system and all its services are running. Also called bootstrap. The computer's *BIOS* must contain the first level of booting.

BOOT.INI   A file accessed during the Windows 2000 *boot* sequence. The BOOT.INI file is used to build the operating system menu choices that are displayed during the boot process. It is also used to specify the location of the *boot partition*.

Boot Normally   A Windows 2000 Advanced Options menu item used to boot Windows 2000 normally.

boot partition   The *partition* that contains the system files. The system files are located in C:\WINNT by default.

BOOTSECT.DOS   An optional file that is loaded if the user chooses to load an operating system other than Windows 2000. This file is only used in *dual-boot* or *multi-boot* computers.

bottleneck   A system *resource* that is inefficient compared with the rest of the computer system as a whole. The bottleneck can cause the rest of the system to run slowly.

C

caching   A speed-optimization technique that keeps a copy of the most recently used data in a fast, high-cost, low-capacity storage device rather than in the device on which the actual data resides. Caching assumes that recently used data is likely to be used again. Fetching data from the cache is faster than fetching data from the slower, larger storage device. Most caching algorithms also copy data that is most likely to be used next and perform *write-back caching* to further increase speed gains.

CD-based image   A type of image configured on a *Remote Installation Services (RIS)* server. A CD-based image contains only the Windows 2000 Professional operating system.

CDFS   See *Compact Disk File System*.

central processing unit (CPU)   The main *processor* in a computer.

Check Disk   A Windows 2000 utility that checks a hard disk for errors. Check Disk (chkdsk) attempts to fix file-system errors and scans for and attempts to recover bad sectors.

CIPHER   A command-line utility that can be used to encrypt files on *NTFS volumes*.

cipher text   Encrypted data. Encryption is the process of translating data into code that is not easily accessible. Once data has been encrypted, a user must have a password or key to decrypt the data. Unencrypted data is known as plain text.

clean install   A method of Windows 2000 Professional installation that puts the operating system into a new folder and uses its default settings the first time the operating system is loaded.

client   A computer on a network that subscribes to the services provided by a server.

COM port   Communications port. A serial hardware interface conforming to the RS-232C standard for low-speed, serial communications.

Compact Disk File System (CDFS)   A *file system* used by Windows 2000 to read the file system on a CD-ROM.

compression   The process of storing data in a form that takes less space than the uncompressed data.

Computer Management   A consolidated tool for performing common Windows 2000 management tasks. The interface is organized into three main areas of management: System Tools, Storage, and Services and Applications.

computer name   A *NetBIOS* name used to uniquely identify a computer on the network. A computer name can be from 1 to 15 characters in length.

connection-oriented service   A type of connection service in which a connection (a path) is established and acknowledgments are sent. This type of communication is reliable but has a high overhead.

connectionless service   A type of connection service that does not establish a connection (path) before transmission. This type of communication is fast, but it is not very reliable.

Control Panel A Windows 2000 utility that allows users to change default settings for operating system services to match their preferences. The *Registry* contains the Control Panel settings.

CONVERT A command-line utility used to convert a *partition* from *FAT16* or *FAT32* to the *NTFS* file system.

copy backup A *backup type* that backs up selected folders and files but does not set the archive bit.

counter A performance-measuring tool used to track specific information regarding a system resource, called a performance object. All Windows 2000 system resources are tracked as performance objects, such as Cache, Memory, Paging File, Process, and Processor. Each performance object has an associated set of counters. Counters are set through the *System Monitor* utility.

CPU See *central processing unit*.

Creator Group The Windows 2000 *special group* that created or took ownership of the object (rather than an individual user). When a regular user creates an object or takes ownership of an object, the username becomes the *Creator Owner*. When a member of the *Administrators group* creates or takes ownership of an object, the Administrators group becomes the Creator Group.

Creator Owner group The Windows 2000 *special group* that includes the account that created or took ownership of an object. The account, usually a user account, has the right to modify the object, but cannot modify any other objects that were not created by the user account.

D

daily backup A *backup type* that backs up all of the files that have been modified on the day that the daily backup is performed. The archive attribute is not set on the files that have been backed up.

data compression The process of storing data in a form that takes less space than the uncompressed data.

data encryption The process of translating data into code that is not easily accessible to increase security. Once data has been encrypted, a user must have a password or key to decrypt the data.

Data Link layer In the *Open Systems Interconnection (OSI) model*, the layer that provides the digital interconnection of network devices and the software that directly operates these devices, such as *network adapters*.

Debugging Mode A Windows 2000 Advanced Option menu item that runs the Kernel Debugger, if that utility is installed. The Kernel Debugger is an advanced troubleshooting utility.

default gateway A *TCP/IP* configuration option that specifies the gateway that will be used if the network contains routers.

Desktop A directory that the background of the Windows Explorer shell represents. By default, the Desktop includes objects that contain the local storage devices and available network *shares*. Also a key operating part of the Windows 2000 graphical interface.

device driver Software that allows a specific piece of hardware to communicate with the Windows 2000 operating system.

Device Manager A Windows 2000 utility used to provide information about the computer's configuration.

DHCP See *Dynamic Host Configuration Protocol*.

DHCP server A server configured to provide *DHCP* clients with all of their *IP* configuration information automatically.

dial-up networking A service that allows remote users to dial into the network or the Internet (such as through a telephone or an ISDN connection).

Dialup group A Windows 2000 *special group* that includes users who log on to the network from a dial-up connection.

differential backup A *backup type* that copies only the files that have been changed since the last *normal* *backup* (full backup) or *incremental backup*. A differential backup backs up only those files that have changed since the last full backup, but does not reset the archive bit.

Digital Versatile Disc (DVD)   A disk standard that supports up to 4.7GB of data. One of DVD's strongest features is backward compatibility with CD-ROM technology, so that a DVD drive can play CD-ROMs. Formerly known as Digital Video Disk.

directory replication   The process of copying a directory structure from an export computer to an import computer(s). Anytime changes are made to the export computer, the import computer(s) is automatically updated with the changes.

Disk Cleanup   A Windows 2000 utility used to identify areas of disk space that can be deleted to free additional hard disk space. Disk Cleanup works by identifying temporary files, Internet cache files, and unnecessary program files.

disk defragmentation   The process of rearranging the existing files on a disk so that they are stored contiguously, which optimizes access to those files.

Disk Defragmenter   A Windows 2000 utility that performs *disk defragmentation*.

disk image   An exact duplicate of a hard disk, used for *automated installation*. The disk image is copied from a reference computer that is configured in the same manner as the computers on which Windows 2000 Professional will be installed.

Disk Management   A Windows 2000 graphical tool for managing disks and *volumes*.

disk partitioning   The process of creating logical *partitions* on the physical hard drive.

disk quotas   A Windows 2000 feature used to specify how much disk space a user is allowed to use on specific *NTFS volumes*. Disk quotas can be applied for all users or for specific users.

distribution server   A network server that contains the Windows 2000 distribution files that have been copied from the distribution CD. Clients can connect to the distribution server and install Windows 2000 over the network.

DNS   See *Domain Name System*.

DNS server   A server that uses *DNS* to resolve domain or host names to *IP addresses*.

domain   In Microsoft networks, an arrangement of client and server computers referenced by a specific name that shares a single security permissions database. On the Internet, a domain is a named collection of hosts and subdomains, registered with a unique name by the InterNIC.

domain name   A name that identifies one or more *IP addresses*, such as sybex.com. Domain names are used in *URLs* to identify particular Web pages.

domain name server   An Internet host dedicated to the function of translating fully qualified domain names into *IP addresses*.

Domain Name Service (DNS)   The *TCP/IP* network service that translates fully qualified domain names (or host names) into *IP addresses*.

domain user account   A user account that is stored in the Windows 2000 Server *Active Directory's* central database. A domain user account can provide a user with a single user account for a network. Also called an Active Directory user account.

drive letter   A single letter assigned as an abbreviation to a mass-storage *volume* available to a computer.

driver   A program that provides a software interface to a hardware device. Drivers are written for the specific devices they control, but they present a common software interface to the computer's operating system, allowing all devices of a similar type to be controlled as if they were the same.

driver signing   A digital imprint that is Microsoft's way of guaranteeing that a driver has been tested and will work with the computer.

Dr. Watson   A Windows 2000 utility used to identify and troubleshoot application errors.

DRWTSN32   The command used to access the *Dr. Watson* utility.

dual-booting   The process of allowing a computer to *boot* more than one operating system.

DVD   See *Digital Versatile Disc*.

dynamic disk   A Windows 2000 disk-storage technique. A dynamic disk is divided into dynamic *volumes*. Dynamic volumes cannot contain *partitions* or *logical drives*, and they are not accessible through DOS. You can size or resize a dynamic disk without restarting Windows 2000. Dynamic disks are accessible only to Windows 2000 systems.

Dynamic Host Configuration Protocol (DHCP) A method of automatically assigning *IP addresses* to client computers on a network.

dynamic storage A Windows 2000 disk-storage system that is configured as *volumes*. Windows 2000 Professional dynamic storage supports *simple volumes*, *spanned volumes*, and *striped volumes*.

E

EB See *exabyte*.

effective rights The rights that a user actually has to a file or folder. To determine a user's effective rights, add all of the permissions that have been allowed through the user's assignments based on that user's username and group associations. Then subtract any permissions that have been denied the user through the username or group associations.

EFS See *Encrypting File System*.

Emergency Repair Disk (ERD) A disk that stores portions of the *Registry*, the system files, a copy of the partition boot sector, and information that relates to the startup environment. The ERD can be used to repair problems that prevent a computer from starting.

Enable Boot Logging A Windows 2000 Professional Advanced Options menu item that is used to create a log file that tracks the loading of *drivers* and *services*.

Enable VGA Mode A Windows 2000 Professional Advanced Options menu item that loads a standard VGA driver without starting the computer in *Safe Mode*.

Encrypting File System (EFS) The Windows 2000 technology used to store encrypted files on *NTFS partitions*. Encrypted files add an extra layer of security to the *file system*.

encryption The process of translating data into code that is not easily accessible to increase security. Once data has been encrypted, a user must have a password or key to decrypt the data.

ERD See *Emergency Repair Disk*.

Error event An *Event Viewer* event type that indicates the occurrence of an error, such as a driver failing to load.

Ethernet The most popular Data Link layer standard for local area networking. Ethernet implements the Carrier Sense Multiple Access with Collision Detection (CSMA/CD) method of arbitrating multiple computer access to the same network. This standard supports the use of Ethernet over any type of media, including wireless broadcast. Standard Ethernet operates as 10Mbps. Fast Ethernet operates at 100Mbps.

Event Viewer A Windows 2000 utility that tracks information about the computer's hardware and software, as well as security events. This information is stored in three log files: the *Application log*, the *Security log*, and the *System log*.

Everyone A Windows 2000 *special group* that includes anyone who could possibly access the computer. The Everyone group includes all of the users (including *Guests*) who have been defined on the computer.

exabyte A computer storage measurement equal to 1,024 *petabytes*.

extended partition In *basic storage*, a *logical drive* that allows you to allocate the logical partitions however you wish. Extended partitions are created after the *primary partition* has been created.

F

Failure Audit event An *Event Viewer* event that indicates the occurrence of an event that has been audited for failure, such a failed logon when someone presents an invalid username and/or password.

FAT16 The 16-bit version of the *File Allocation System (FAT)* system, which was widely used by DOS and Windows 3.*x*. The file system is used to track where files are stored on a disk. Most operating systems support FAT16.

FAT32 The 32-bit version of the *File Allocation System (FAT)* system, which is more efficient and provides more safeguards than *FAT16*. Windows 9*x* and Windows 2000 support FAT32. Windows NT does not support FAT32.

fault tolerance   Any method that prevents system failure by tolerating single faults, usually through hardware redundancy.

fax modem   A special modem that includes hardware to allow the transmission and reception of facsimiles.

File Allocation Table (FAT)   The *file system* used by *MS-DOS* and available to other operating systems such as Windows (all versions) and OS/2. FAT, now known as *FAT16*, has become something of a mass-storage compatibility standard because of its simplicity and wide availability. FAT has fewer fault-tolerance features than the *NTFS* file system and can become corrupted through normal use over time.

file attributes   Bits stored along with the name and location of a file in a directory entry. File attributes show the status of a file, such as archived, hidden, and read-only. Different operating systems use different file attributes to implement services such as *sharing*, *compression*, and *security*.

file system   A software component that manages the storage of files on a mass-storage device by providing services that can create, read, write, and delete files. File systems impose an ordered database of files on the mass-storage device. Storage is arranged in *volumes*. File systems use hierarchies of directories to organize files.

File Transfer Protocol (FTP)   A simple Internet protocol that transfers complete files from an FTP server to a client running the FTP client. FTP provides a simple, low-overhead method of transferring files between computers but cannot perform browsing functions. Users must know the *URL* of the FTP server to which they wish to attach.

frame   A data structure that network hardware devices use to transmit data between computers. Frames consist of the addresses of the sending and receiving computers, size information, and a checksum. Frames are envelopes around packets of data that allow the packets to be addressed to specific computers on a shared media network.

frame type   An option that specifies how data is packaged for transmission over the network. This option must be configured to run the *NWLink IPX/ SPX/NetBIOS Compatible Transport* protocol on a Windows 2000 computer. By default, the frame type is set to Auto Detect, which will attempt to automatically choose a compatible frame type for the network.

FTP   See *File Transfer Protocol*.

G

GB   See *gigabyte*.

GDI   See *Graphic Device Interface*.

gigabyte   A computer storage measurement equal to 1,024 *megabytes*.

Graphics Device Interface (GDI)   The programming interface and graphical services provided to *Win32* for programs to interact with graphical devices such as the screen and printer.

Graphical User Interface (GUI)   A computer shell program that represents mass-storage devices, directories, and files as graphical objects on a screen. A cursor driven by a pointing device such as a mouse manipulates the objects.

groups   Security entities to which users can be assigned membership for the purpose of applying the broad set of group permissions to the user. By managing permissions for groups and assigning users to groups, rather than assigning permissions to users, administrators can more easily manage security.

Guest account   A Windows 2000 user account created to provide a mechanism to allow users to access the computer even if they do not have a unique username and password. This account normally has very limited privileges on the computer. This account is disabled by default.

Guests group   A Windows 2000 built-in group that has limited access to the computer. This group can access only specific areas. Most administrators do not allow Guest account access because it poses a potential security risk.

GUI   See *Graphical User Interface*.

H

HAL   See *Hardware Abstraction Layer*.

hard disk drive   A mass-storage device that reads and writes digital information magnetically on discs that spin under moving heads. Hard disk drives are precisely aligned and cannot normally be removed. Hard disk drives are an inexpensive way to store *gigabytes* of computer data permanently. Hard disk drives also store the software installed on a computer.

Hardware Abstraction Layer (HAL) A Windows 2000 service that provides basic input/output services such as timers, interrupts, and multiprocessor management for computer hardware. The HAL is a *device driver* for the motherboard circuitry that allows different families of computers to be treated the same by the Windows 2000 operating system.

Hardware Compatibility List (HCL) A list of all of the hardware devices supported by Windows 2000. Hardware on the HCL has been tested and verified as being compatible with Windows 2000.

hardware profile A file that stores a hardware configuration for a computer. Hardware profiles are useful when a single computer (a laptop that can be docked or undocked) has multiple hardware configurations.

HCL See *Hardware Compatibility List.*

hibernation The storage of anything that is stored in memory on the computer's hard disk. Hibernation ensures that none of the information stored in memory is lost when the computer is shut down. When the computer is taken out of hibernation, it is returned to its previous state.

home folder A folder where users normally store their personal files and information. A home folder can be a local folder or a network folder.

host An Internet server. A host is a node that is connected to the Internet.

hot swapping The ability of a device to be plugged into or removed from a computer while the computer's power is on.

HTML See *Hypertext Markup Language.*

HTTP See *Hypertext Transfer Protocol.*

hyperlink A link within text or graphics that has a Web address embedded in it. By clicking the link, a user can jump to another Web address.

Hypertext Markup Language (HTML) A textual data format that identifies sections of a document such as headers, lists, hypertext links, and so on. HTML is the data format used on the World Wide Web for the publication of Web pages.

Hypertext Transfer Protocol (HTTP) An Internet protocol that transfers HTML documents over the Internet and responds to context changes that happen when a user clicks a *hyperlink.*

I

IEEE See *Institute of Electrical and Electronic Engineers.*

IIS See *Internet Information Services.*

incremental backup A *backup type* that backs up only the files that have changed since the last normal or incremental backup. It sets the archive attribute on the files that are backed up.

Indexing Service A Windows 2000 service that creates an index based on the contents and properties of files stored on the computer's local hard drive. A user can then use the Windows 2000 Search function to search or query through the index for specific keywords.

Industry Standard Architecture (ISA) The design standard for 16-bit Intel-compatible motherboards and peripheral buses. The 32/64-bit *PCI* bus standard is replacing the ISA standard. Adapters and interface cards must conform to the bus standard(s) used by the motherboard in order to be used in a computer.

Information event An *Event Viewer* event that informs you that a specific action has occurred, such as when a system shuts down or starts.

inherited permissions Parent folder permissions that are applied to (or inherited by) files and subfolders of the parent folder. In Windows 2000 Professional, the default is for parent folder permissions to be applied to any files or subfolders in that folder.

initial user account The account that uses the name of the registered user and is created only if the computer is installed as a member of a workgroup (not into the *Active Directory*). By default, the initial user is a member of the *Administrators group.*

Institute of Electrical and Electronic Engineers (IEEE) A professional organization that defines standards related to networks, communications, and other areas.

Institute of Electrical and Electronic Engineers (IEEE) 1394 standard A standard that supports data transfer at speeds up to 400Mbps. Some of the trademark names for this standard are FireWire, I-link, and Lynx.

Integrated Services Digital Network (ISDN) A direct, digital, dial-up connection that operates at 64KB per channel over regular twisted-pair cable. Up to 24 channels can be multiplexed over two twisted pairs.

Intel architecture A family of microprocessors descended from the Intel 8086, itself descended from the first microprocessor, the Intel 4004. The Intel architecture is the dominant microprocessor family. It was used in the original iBM PC microcomputer adopted by the business market and later adapted for home use.

Interactive group A Windows 2000 *special group* that includes all the users who use the computer's resources locally.

interactive logon A *logon* when the user logs on from the computer where the user account is stored on the computer's local database. Also called a local logon.

interactive user A user who physically logs on to the computer where the user account resides (rather than over the network).

internal network number An identification for *NetWare* file servers. An internal network number is also used if the network is running File and Print Services for NetWare or is using IPX routing. This option must be configured to run the *NWLink IPX/SPX/NetBIOS Compatible Transport* protocol on a Windows 2000 computer. Normally, the internal network number should be left at its default setting.

Internet connection sharing A Windows 2000 feature that allows a small network to be connected to the Internet through a single connection. The computer that dials into the Internet provides network address translation, addressing, and name resolution services for all of the computers on the network. Through Internet connection sharing, the other computers on the network can access Internet resources and use Internet applications, such as Internet Explorer and Outlook Express.

Internet Explorer A World Wide Web browser produced by Microsoft and included with Windows *9x*, Windows NT 4, and now Windows 2000.

Internet Information Services (IIS) Software that serves Internet higher-level protocols like *HTTP* and *FTP* to clients using Web browsers. The IIS software that is installed on a Windows 2000 Server computer is a fully functional Web server and is designed to support heavy Internet usage.

Internet Print Protocol (IPP) A Windows 2000 protocol that allows users to print directly to a *URL*. Printer- and job-related information are generated in *HTML* format.

Internet printer A Windows 2000 feature that allows users to send documents to be printed through the Internet.

Internet Protocol (IP) The Network layer protocol upon which the Internet is based. IP provides a simple connectionless packet exchange. Other protocols such as TCP use IP to perform their *connection-oriented* (or guaranteed delivery) services.

Internet service provider (ISP) A company that provides dial-up connections to the Internet.

Internet Services Manager A Windows 2000 utility used to configure the protocols that are used by *Internet Information Services (IIS)* and *Personal Web Services (PWS)*.

internetwork A network made up of multiple network segments that are connected with some device, such as a router. Each network segment is assigned a network address. *Network layer protocols* build routing tables that are used to route packets through the network in the most efficient manner.

InterNIC The agency that is responsible for assigning *IP addresses*.

interprocess communications (IPC) A generic term describing any manner of client/server communication protocol, specifically those operating in the *Application layer*. IPC mechanisms provide a method for the client and server to trade information.

interrupt request (IRQ)   A hardware signal from a peripheral device to the microcomputer indicating that it has input/output (I/O) traffic to send. If the microprocessor is not running a more important service, it will interrupt its current activity and handle the interrupt request. IBM PCs have 16 levels of interrupt request lines. Under Windows 2000, each device must have a unique interrupt request line.

intranet   A privately owned network based on the *TCP/IP* protocol suite.

IP   See *Internet Protocol.*

IP address   A four-byte number that uniquely identifies a computer on an IP *internetwork.*

IPC   See *interprocess communications.*

IPCONFIG   A command used to display the computer's *IP* configuration.

IPP   See *Internet Print Protocol.*

IRQ   See *interrupt request.*

ISA   See *Industry Standard Architecture.*

ISDN   See *Integrated Services Digital Network.*

ISP   See *Internet service provider.*

K

kernel   The core process of a preemptive operating system, consisting of a multitasking scheduler and the basic security services. Depending on the operating system, other services such as virtual memory drivers may be built into the kernel. The kernel is responsible for managing the scheduling of *threads* and *processes.*

L

Last Known Good Configuration   A Windows 2000 Advanced Options menu item used to load the

control set that was used the last time the computer was successfully booted.

LLC sublayer   See *Logical Link Control sublayer.*

Local Computer Policy   A *Microsoft Management Console (MMC) snap-in* used to implement account policies.

local group   A group that is stored on the local computer's accounts database. These are the groups that administrators can add users to and manage directly on a Windows 2000 Professional computer.

Local Computer Policy   A *Microsoft Management Console (MMC) snap-in* used to implement local group policies, which include computer configuration policies and user configuration policies.

local logon   A *logon* when the user logs on from the computer where the user account is stored on the computer's local database. Also called an interactive logon.

local policies   Policies that allow administrators to control what a user can do after logging on. Local policies include *audit policies*, *security option policies*, and *user rights policies*. These policies are set through *Local Computer Policy.*

local printer   A printer that uses a *physical port* and that has not been shared. If a printer is defined as local, the only users who can use the printer are the local users of the computer that the printer is attached to.

local security   Security that governs a local or interactive user's ability to access locally stored files. Local security can be set through *NTFS permissions.*

local user account   A user account stored locally in the user accounts database of a computer that is running Windows 2000 Professional.

local user profile   A profile created the first time a user logs on, stored in the Documents and Settings folder. The default user profile folder's name matches the user's logon name. This folder contains a file called NTUSER.DAT and subfolders with directory links to the user's *Desktop* items.

Local Users and Groups   A utility that is used to create and manage local user and group accounts on Windows 2000 Professional computers and Windows 2000 member servers.

locale settings   Settings for regional items, including numbers, currency, time, date, and input locales.

logical drive   An allocation of disk space on a hard drive, using a *drive letter*. For example, a 5GB hard drive could be partitioned into two logical drives: a C: drive, which might be 2GB, and a D: drive, which might be 3GB.

Logical Drives   A Windows 2000 utility used to manage the logical drives on the computer.

Logical Link Control (LLC) sublayer   A sublayer in the *Data Link layer* of the *Open Systems Inter-connection (OSI)* model. The LLC sublayer defines flow control.

logical port   A port that connects a device directly to the network. Logical ports are used with printers by installing a network card in the printers.

logical printer   The software interface between the *physical printer* (the *print device*) and the operating system. Also referred to as just a *printer* in Windows 2000 terminology.

logoff   The process of closing an open session with a Windows 2000 computer or network.

logon   The process of opening a session with a Windows 2000 computer or a network by providing a valid authentication consisting of a user account name and a password. After logon, network resources are available to the user according to the user's assigned *permissions*.

logon script   A command file that automates the *logon* process by performing utility functions such as attaching to additional server resources or automatically running different programs based on the user account that established the logon.

M

MAC (media access control) address   The physical address that identifies a computer. *Ethernet* and Token Ring cards have the MAC address assigned through a chip on the network card.

MAC sublayer   See *Media Access Control sublayer*.

Magnifier   A Windows 2000 utility used to create a separate window to magnify a portion of the screen. This option is designed for users who have poor vision.

MAKEBT32.EXE   The command used to create *Windows 2000 Professional Setup Boot Disks*.

mandatory profile   A *user profile* created by an administrator and saved with a special extension (.man) so that the user cannot modify the profile in any way. Mandatory profiles can be assigned to a single user or a group of users.

mapped drive   A shared network folder associated with a drive letter. Mapped drives appear to users as local connections on their computers and can be accessed through a drive letter using My Computer.

Master Boot Record (MBR)   A record used in the Windows 2000 *boot* sequence to point to the active partition, which is the partition that should be used to boot the operating system. This is normally the C: drive. Once the MBR locates the active partition, the boot sector is loaded into memory and executed.

MB   See *megabyte*.

MBR   See *Master Boot Record*.

Media Access Control (MAC) sublayer   A sublayer in the *Data Link layer* of the *Open Systems Intercon-nection (OSI)* model. The MAC sublayer is used for physical addressing.

megabyte   A computer storage measurement equal to 1,024 kilobytes.

member server   A Windows 2000 server that has been installed as a non-domain controller. This allows the server to operate as a file, print, and application server without the overhead of account administration.

memory   Any device capable of storing information. This term is usually used to indicate volatile *random-access memory* (RAM) capable of high-speed access to any portion of the memory space, but incapable of storing information without power.

Microsoft Disk Operating System (MS-DOS)   A 16-bit operating system designed for the 8086 chip that was used in the original IBM PC. MS-DOS is a simple program loader and *file system* that turns over complete control of the computer to the running program and provides very little service beyond file system support and that provided by the *BIOS*.

Microsoft Installer (MSI)   A standard that is used to automatically deploy applications with *Windows Installer packages*.

Microsoft Management Console (MMC)   The Windows 2000 console framework for management applications. The MMC provides a common environment for *snap-ins*.

MMC   See *Microsoft Management Console*.

modem   Modulator/demodulator. A device used to create an analog signal suitable for transmission over telephone lines from a digital data stream. Modern modems also include a command set for negotiating connections and data rates with remote modems and for setting their default behavior.

MS-DOS   See *Microsoft Disk Operating System*.

MSI   See *Microsoft Installer*.

multi-booting   The process of allowing a computer to *boot* multiple operating systems.

My Computer   The folder used to view and manage a computer. My Computer provides access to all local and network drives, as well as *Control Panel*.

My Documents   The default storage location for documents that are created. Each user has a unique My Documents folder.

My Network Places   The folder that provides access to shared resources, such as local network resources and Web resources.

N

Narrator   A Windows 2000 utility used to read aloud on-screen text, dialog boxes, menus, and buttons. This utility requires some type of sound output device.

NetBEUI   See *NetBIOS Extended User Interface*.

NetBIOS   See *Network Basic Input/Output System*.

NetBIOS Extended User Interface (NetBEUI)   A simple *Network layer transport protocol* developed to support *NetBIOS* installations. NetBEUI is not routable, and so it is not appropriate for larger networks. NetBEUI is the fastest transport protocol available for Windows 2000.

NET USE   A command-line utility used to map network drives.

NetWare   A popular network operating system developed by Novell in the early 1980s. NetWare is a cooperative, multitasking, highly optimized, dedicated-server network operating system that has client support for most major operating systems. Recent versions of NetWare include graphical client tools for management from client stations. At one time, NetWare accounted for more than 70 percent of the network operating system market.

network adapter   The hardware used to connect computers (or other devices) to the network. Network adapters function at the *Physical layer* and the *Date Link layer* of the *Open System Interconnection (OSI) model*.

Network Basic Input/Output System (NetBIOS)   A client/server *IPC* service developed by IBM in the early 1980s. NetBIOS presents a relatively primitive mechanism for communication in client/server applications, but its widespread acceptance and availability across most operating systems make it a logical choice for simple network applications. Many of the network *IPC* mechanisms in Windows 2000 are implemented over NetBIOS.

Network group   A Windows 2000 *special group* that includes the users who access a computer's resources over a network connection.

Network layer   The layer of the *Open System Interconnection (OSI) model* that creates a communication path between two computers via routed packets. *Transport protocols* implement both the Network layer and the *Transport layer* of the OSI stack. For example, *IP* is a Network layer service.

network printer   A *printer* that is available to local and network users. A network printer can use a *physical port* or a *logical port*.

New Technology File System (NTFS) A secure, transaction-oriented file system developed for Windows NT and Windows 2000. NTFS offers features such as *local security* on files and folders, *data compression*, *disk quotas*, and *data encryption*.

normal backup A *backup type* that backs up all selected folders and files and then marks each file that has been backed up as archived.

NTBOOTDD.SYS A file accessed in the Windows 2000 *boot* sequence. NTBOOTDD.SYS is an optional file (the *SCSI* driver) that is used when the computer has a SCSI adapter with the on-board *BIOS* disabled.

NTDETECT.COM A file accessed in the Windows 2000 *boot* sequence. NTDETECT.COM is used to detect any hardware that is installed and add information about the hardware to the *Registry*.

NTFS See *New Technology File System*.

NTFS permissions Permissions used to control access to *NTFS* folders and files. Access is configured by allowing or denying NTFS permissions to users and groups.

NTLDR A file used to control the Windows 2000 *boot* process until control is passed to the *NTOSKRNL.EXE* file.

NTOSKRNL.EXE A file accessed in the Windows 2000 *boot* sequence. NTOSKRNL.EXE is used to load the *kernel*.

NTUSER.DAT The file that is created for a *user profile*.

NTUSER.MAN The file that is created for a *mandatory profile*.

NWLINK IPX/SPX/NetBIOS Compatible Transport Microsoft's implementation of the Novell IPX/SPX protocol stack.

O

offline files and folders A Windows 2000 feature that allows network folders and files to be stored on Windows 2000 clients. Users can access network files even if the network location is not available.

On-Screen Keyboard A Windows 2000 utility that displays a keyboard on the screen and allows users to enter keyboard input by using a mouse or other input device.

Open Systems Interconnection (OSI) model A reference model for network component interoperability developed by the International Standards Organization (ISO) to promote cross-vendor compatibility of hardware and software network systems. The OSI model splits the process of networking into seven distinct services, or layers. Each layer uses the services of the layer below to provide its service to the layer above.

optimization Any effort to reduce the workload on a hardware component by eliminating, obviating, or reducing the amount of work required of the hardware component through any means. For instance, file *caching* is an optimization that reduces the workload of a hard disk drive.

OSI model See *Open Systems Interconnection model*.

owner The user associated with an *NTFS* file or folder who is able to control access and grant permissions to other users.

P

page file Logical memory that exists on the hard drive. If a system is experiencing excessive paging (swapping between the page file and physical RAM), it needs more memory.

partition A section of a hard disk that can contain an independent *file system volume*. Partitions can be used to keep multiple operating systems and file systems on the same hard disk.

password policies Windows 2000 policies used to enforce security requirements on the computer. Password policies are set on a per-computer basis, and they cannot be configured for specific users. Password policies are set through *account policies*.

PB See *petabyte*.

PC Card A special, credit-card-sized device used to add devices to a laptop computer. Also called a PCMCIA card.

PCI See *Peripheral Connection Interface.*

PCMCIA card See *Personal Computer Memory Card International Association card.*

Peer Web Services (PWS) Software that acts as a small-scale Web server, for use with a small *intranet* or a small Internet site with limited traffic. Windows 2000 uses PWS to publish resources on the Internet or a private intranet. When you install *Internet Information Services (IIS)* on a Windows 2000 Professional computer, you are actually installing PWS.

Performance Logs and Alerts A Windows 2000 utility used to log performance-related data and generate *alerts* based on performance-related data.

Peripheral Connection Interface (PCI) A high-speed, 32/64-bit bus interface developed by Intel and widely accepted as the successor to the 16-bit *ISA* interface. PCI devices support input/output (I/O) throughput about 40 times faster than the ISA bus.

permissions Security constructs used to regulate access to resources by username or group affiliation. Permissions can be assigned by administrators to allow any level of access, such as read-only, read/write, or delete, by controlling the ability of users to initiate object services. Security is implemented by checking the user's *security identifier (SID)* against each object's *access control list (ACL)*.

Personal Computer Memory Card International Association (PCMCIA) card A special, credit-card-sized device used to add devices to a laptop computer. Also called a PC Card.

Personal Web Manager A Windows 2000 utility used to configure and manage *Peer Web Services (PWS)*. This utility has options for configuring the location of the home page and stopping the Web site, and displays statistics for monitoring the Web site.

petabyte A computer storage measurement that is equal to 1,024 *terabytes.*

Physical layer The first (bottom) layer of the *Open Systems Interconnection (OSI)* model, which represents the cables, connectors, and connection ports of a network. The Physical layer contains the passive physical components required to create a network.

physical port A serial (COM) or parallel (LPT) port that connects a device, such as a printer, directly to a computer.

PING A command used to send an Internet Control Message Protocol (ICMP) echo request and echo reply to verify that a remote computer is available.

Plug and Play A technology that uses a combination of hardware and software to allow the operating system to automatically recognize and configure new hardware without any user intervention.

policies General controls that enhance the *security* of an operating environment. In Windows 2000, policies affect restrictions on password use and rights assignments, and determine which events will be recorded in the *Security log.*

POST See *Power On Self Test.*

Power On Self Test (POST) A part of the Windows 2000 *boot* sequence. The POST detects the computer's *processor*, how much memory is present, what hardware is recognized, and whether or not the *BIOS* is standard or has *Plug-and-Play* capabilities.

Power Users group A Windows 2000 built-in group that has fewer rights than the *Administrators group*, but more rights than the *Users group*. Members of the Power Users group can perform tasks such as creating local users and groups and modifying the users and groups that they have created.

Pre-Boot Execution Environment (PXE) A technology that allows a client computer to remotely boot and connect to a *Remote Installation Service (RIS)* server.

Presentation layer The layer of the *Open Systems Interconnection (OSI) model* that converts and translates (if necessary) information between the *Session layer* and *Application layer.*

primary partition A part of *basic storage* on a disk. The primary partition is the first partition created on a hard drive. The primary partition uses all of the space that is allocated to the partition. This partition is usually marked as active and is the partition that is used to *boot* the computer.

print device The actual physical printer or hardware device that generates printed output.

print driver The specific software that understands a *print device*. Each print device has an associated print driver.

print processor The process that determines whether or not a print job needs further processing once that job has been sent to the *print spooler*. The processing (also called *rendering*) is used to format the print job so that it can print correctly at the *print device*.

print queue A directory or folder on the *print server* that stores the print jobs until they can be printed. Also called a print spooler.

print server The computer on which the printer has been defined. When a user sends a print job to a *network printer*, it goes to the print server first.

print spooler A directory or folder on the *print server* that stores the print jobs until they can be printed. Also called a print queue.

printer In Windows 2000 terminology, the software interface between the physical printer (see *print device*) and the operating system.

printer pool A configuration that allows one printer to be used for multiple *print devices*. A printer pool can be used when multiple printers use the same *print driver* (and are normally in the same location). With a printer pool, users can send their print jobs to the first available printer.

priority A level of execution importance assigned to a *thread*. In combination with other factors, the priority level determines how often that thread will get computer time according to a scheduling algorithm.

process A running program containing one or more *threads*. A process encapsulates the protected memory and environment for its threads.

processor A circuit designed to automatically perform lists of logical and arithmetic operations. Unlike microprocessors, processors may be designed from discrete components rather than be a monolithic integrated circuit.

processor affinity The association of a *processor* with specific *processes* that are running on the computer. Processor affinity is used to configure multiple processors.

protocol An established rule of communication adhered to by the parties operating under it. Protocols provide a context in which to interpret communicated information. Computer protocols are rules used by communicating devices and software services to format data in a way that all participants understand.

PXE See *Pre-Boot Execution Environment.*

published applications Applications installed with *Windows Installer packages*. Users can choose whether or not they will install published applications through the Control Panel Add/Remove Programs icon. Administrators can choose to have published applications installed when the applications are invoked.

PWS See *Peer Web Services.*

R

RAM See *random-access memory.*

random-access memory (RAM) Integrated circuits that store digital bits in massive arrays of logical gates or capacitors. RAM is the primary memory store for modern computers, storing all running software processes and contextual data.

RAS See *Remote Access Service.*

real-time application A *process* that must respond to external events at least as fast as those events can occur. Real-time *threads* must run at very high priorities to ensure their ability to respond in real time.

Recovery Console A Windows 2000 option for recovering from a failed system. The Recovery Console starts Windows 2000 without the graphical interface and allows the administrator limited capabilities, such as adding or replacing files and enabling and disabling services.

Recycle Bin A folder that holds files and folders that have been deleted. Files can be retrieved or cleared (for permanent deletion) from the Recycle Bin.

REGEDIT A Windows program used to edit the *Registry*. It does not support full editing, as does the *REGEDT32* program, but it has better search capabilities than REGEDT32.

REGEDT32 The primary utility for editing the Windows 2000 *Registry.*

Regional Options A *Control Panel* utility used to enable and configure multilingual editing and viewing on a localized version of Windows 2000 Professional,

Registry A database of settings required and maintained by Windows 2000 and its components. The Registry contains all of the configuration information used by the computer. It is stored as a hierarchical structure and is made up of keys, hives, and value entries.

Remote Access Service (RAS) A service that allows network connections to be established over a modem connection, an *Integrated Services Digital Network (ISDN)* connection, or a null-modem cable. The computer initiating the connection is called the RAS client; the answering computer is called the RAS server.

remote installation Installation of Windows 2000 Professional performed remotely through *Remote Installation Services (RIS).*

Remote Installation Preparation (RIPrep) image A type of image configured on a *Remote Installation Services (RIS)* server. An RIPrep image can contain the Windows 2000 operating system and applications. This type of image is based on a preconfigured computer.

Remote Installation Services (RIS) A Windows 2000 technology that allows the remote installation of Windows 2000 Professional. An RIS server installs Windows 2000 Professional on RIS clients. The RIS server can be configured with a *CD-based image* or a *Remote Installation Preparation (RIPrep) image.*

Removable Storage A Windows 2000 utility used to track information on removable storage media, which include CDs, DVDs, tapes, and jukeboxes containing optical discs.

rendering The process that determines whether or not a print job needs further processing once that job has been sent to the spooler. The processing is used to format the print job so that it can print correctly at the *print device.*

Replicator group A Windows 2000 built-in group that supports *directory replication*, which is a feature used by domain servers. Only *domain user accounts* that will be used to start the replication service should be assigned to this group.

Requests for Comments (RFCs) The set of standards defining the Internet protocols as determined by the Internet Engineering Task Force and available in the public domain on the Internet. RFCs define the functions and services provided by each of the many Internet protocols. Compliance with the RFCs guarantees cross-vendor compatibility.

resource Any useful service, such as a *shared folder* or a *printer.*

Restore Wizard A Wizard used to restore data. The Restore Wizard is accessed through the *Windows 2000 Backup* utility.

RFC See *Request For Comments.*

RIPrep image See *Remote Installation Preparation image.*

RIS See *Remote Installation Services.*

roaming profile A *user profile* that is stored and configured to be downloaded from a server. Roaming profiles allow users to access their profiles from any location on the network.

router A *Network layer* device that moves packets between networks. Routers provide *internetwork* connectivity.

S

Safe Mode A Windows 2000 Advanced Options menu item that loads the absolute minimum of *services* and *drivers* that are needed to start Windows 2000. The drivers that are loaded with Safe Mode include basic files and drivers for the mouse (unless a serial mouse is attached to the computer), monitor, keyboard, hard drive, standard video driver, and default system services. Safe Mode is considered a diagnostic mode. It does not include networking capabilities.

Safe Mode with Command Prompt A Windows 2000 Advanced Options menu item that starts Windows 2000 in *Safe Mode*, but instead of loading the graphical interface, it loads a command prompt.

Safe Mode with Networking A Windows 2000 Advanced Options menu item that starts Windows 2000 in *Safe Mode*, but it adds networking features.

SCSI See *Small Computer Systems Interface*.

security The measures taken to secure a system against accidental or intentional loss, usually in the form of accountability procedures and use restriction, for example through *NTFS permissions* and *share permissions*.

security identifier (SID) A unique code that identifies a specific user or group to the Windows 2000 security system. SIDs contain a complete set of *permissions* for that user or group.

Security log A log that tracks events that are related to Windows 2000 auditing. The Security log can be viewed through the *Event Viewer* utility.

security option policies Policies used to configure security for the computer. Security option policies apply to computers rather than to users or groups. These policies are set through *Local Computer Policy*.

separator page A page used at the beginning of each document to identify the user who submitted the print job. When users share a printer, separator pages can be useful for distributing print jobs.

serial A method of communication that transfers data across a medium one bit at a time, usually adding stop, start, and check bits.

service A *process* dedicated to implementing a specific function for another process. Most Windows 2000 components are services used by user-level applications.

Service group A Windows 2000 *special group* that includes users who log on as a user account that is only used to run a *service*.

service pack An update to the Windows 2000 operating system that includes bug fixes and enhancements.

Session layer The layer of the *Open Systems Interconnection (OSI) model* dedicated to maintaining a bi-directional communication connection between two computers. The Session layer uses the services of the *Transport layer* to provide this service.

Services A Windows 2000 utility used to manage the *services* installed on the computer.

Setup Manager (SETUPMGR) A Windows 2000 utility used to create automated installation scripts or unattended *answer files*.

SETUPMGR See *Setup Manager*.

share A *resource* such as a folder or printer shared over a network.

share permissions Permissions used to control access to shared folders. Share permissions can only be applied to folders, as opposed to *NTFS permissions*, which are more complex and can be applied to folders and files.

shared folder A folder on a Windows 2000 computer that network users can access.

Shared Folders A Windows 2000 utility for managing *shared folders* on the computer.

shortcut A quick link to an item that is accessible from a computer or network, such as a file, program, folder, printer, or computer. Shortcuts can exist in various locations including the *Desktop*, the *Start menu*, or within folders.

SID See *security identifier*.

Simple Mail Transfer Protocol (SMTP) An Internet protocol for transferring mail between Internet hosts. SMTP is often used to upload mail directly from the client to an intermediate host, but can only be used to receive mail by computers constantly connected to the Internet.

simple volume A *dynamic disk* volume that contains space from a single disk. The space from the single drive can be contiguous or noncontiguous. Simple volumes are used when the computer has enough disk space on a single drive to hold an entire volume.

slipstream technology A Windows 2000 technology for *service packs*. With slipstream technology, service packs are applied once, and they are not overwritten as new services are added to the computer.

Small Computer Systems Interface (SCSI) A high-speed, parallel-bus interface that connects hard disk drives, CD-ROM drives, tape drives, and many other peripherals to a computer. SCSI is the mass-storage connection standard among all computers except IBM compatibles, which use SCSI or IDE.

SMTP See *Simple Mail Transfer Protocol*.

snap-in An administrative tool developed by Microsoft or a third-party vendor that can be added to the *Microsoft Management Console (MMC)* in Windows 2000.

spanned volume A *dynamic disk* volume that consists of disk space on 2 to 32 dynamic drives. Spanned volume sets are used to dynamically increase the size of a dynamic volume. With spanned volumes, the data is written sequentially, filling space on one physical drive before writing to space on the next physical drive in the spanned volume set.

special group A group used by the system, in which membership is automatic if certain criteria are met. Administrators cannot manage special groups.

spooler A service that buffers output to a low-speed device such as a printer, so the software outputting to the device is not tied up waiting for the device to be ready.

Start menu A Windows 2000 *Desktop* item, located on the *Taskbar*. The Start menu contains a list of options and programs that can be run.

stripe set A single *volume* created across multiple hard disk drives and accessed in parallel for the purpose of optimizing disk-access time. *NTFS* can create stripe sets.

striped volume A *dynamic disk* volume that stores data in equal stripes between 2 to 32 dynamic drives. Typically, administrators use striped volumes when they want to combine the space of several physical drives into a single logical volume and increase disk performance.

subnet mask A number mathematically applied to *IP addresses* to determine which IP addresses are a part of the same subnetwork as the computer applying the subnet mask.

Success Audit event An *Event Viewer* event that indicates the occurrence of an event that has been audited for success, such as a successful logon.

Sysprep See *System Preparation Tool*.

System group A Windows 2000 *special group* that contains system processes that access specific functions as a user.

System Information A Windows 2000 utility used to collect and display information about the computer's current configuration.

System log A log that tracks events that relate to the Windows 2000 operating system. The System log can be viewed through the *Event Viewer* utility.

System Monitor A Windows 2000 utility used to monitor real-time system activity or view data from a log file.

system partition The active *partition* on an Intel-based computer that contains the hardware-specific files used to load the Windows 2000 operating system.

System Preparation Tool (Sysprep) A Windows 2000 utility used to prepare a *disk image* for disk duplication.

System Tools A Computer Management utility grouping that provides access to utilities for managing common system functions. The System Tools utility includes the *Event Viewer*, *System Information*, *Performance Logs and Alerts*, *Shared Folders*, *Device Manager*, and *Local Users and Groups* utilities.

T

Task Manager A Windows 2000 utility that can be used to start, end, or prioritize applications. The Task Manager shows the applications and *processes* that are currently running on the computer, as well as *CPU* and *memory* usage information.

Task Scheduler A Windows 2000 utility used to schedule tasks to occur at specified intervals.

Taskbar A Windows 2000 *Desktop* item, which appears across the bottom of the screen by default. The Taskbar contains the *Start menu* and buttons for any programs, documents, or windows that are currently running on the computer. Users can switch between open items by clicking the item in the Taskbar.

TB See *terabyte*.

TCP See *Transmission Control Protocol*.

TCP/IP See *Transmission Control Protocol/Internet Protocol*.

TCP/IP port A *logical port*, used when a printer is attached to the network by installing a network card in the printer. Configuring a TCP/IP port requires the IP address of the network printer to connect to.

terabyte (TB) A computer storage measurement that equals 1,024 *gigabytes*.

Terminal Server User group A Windows 2000 *special group* that includes users who log on through Terminal Services.

thread A list of instructions running in a computer to perform a certain task. Each thread runs in the context of a *process*, which embodies the protected memory space and the environment of the threads. Multithreaded processes can perform more than one task at the same time.

Transmission Control Protocol (TCP) A *Transport layer* protocol that implements guaranteed packet delivery using the *IP* protocol.

Transmission Control Protocol/Internet Protocol (TCP/IP) A suite of Internet protocols upon which the global Internet is based. TCP/IP is a general term that can refer either to the *TCP* and *IP* protocols used together or to the complete set of Internet protocols. TCP/IP is the default protocol for Windows 2000.

Transport layer The *Open Systems Interconnection (OSI) model* layer responsible for the guaranteed serial delivery of packets between two computers over an *internetwork*. *TCP* is the Transport layer protocol in *TCP/IP*.

transport protocol A service that delivers discreet packets of information between any two computers in a network. Higher-level, *connection-oriented services* are built on transport protocols.

U

unattended installation A method of installing Windows 2000 Professional remotely with little or no user intervention. Unattended installation uses a *distribution server* to install Windows 2000 Professional on a target computer.

UNC See *Universal Naming Convention*.

Uniform Resource Locator (URL) An Internet standard naming convention for identifying resources available via various *TCP/IP* application protocols. For example, http://www.microsoft.com is the URL for Microsoft's World Wide Web server site, and ftp://gateway.dec.com is a popular FTP site. A URL allows easy hypertext references to a particular resource from within a document or mail message.

uninterruptible power supply (UPS) An emergency power source that can provide a limited amount of power to a computer in the event of a power outage.

Universal Naming Convention (UNC) A multivendor, multiplatform convention for identifying shared resources on a network. UNC names follow the naming convention *computername**sharename*.

Universal Serial Bus (USB) An external bus standard that allows USB devices to be connected through a USB port. USB supports transfer rates up to 12Mbps. A single USB port can support up to 127 devices.

upgrade A method for installing Windows 2000 that preserves existing settings and preferences when converting to the newer operating system.

upgrade pack Software in the form of a migration DLL (dynamic link library) used with applications that need to be upgraded to work with Windows 2000.

Upgrade Report A report generated by the Setup program that summarizes any known compatibility issues that you might encounter during the upgrade. The Upgrade Report can be saved as a file or printed.

UPS See *uninterruptible power supply*.

URL See *Uniform Resource Locator*.

USB See *Universal Serial Bus*.

user profile   A profile that stores a user's *Desktop* configuration and other preferences. A user profile can contain a user's Desktop arrangement, program items, personal program groups, network and printer connections, screen colors, mouse settings, and other personal preferences. Administrators can create *mandatory profiles*, which cannot be changed by the users, and *roaming profiles*, which users can access from any computer they log on to.

user rights policies   Policies that control the rights that users and groups have to accomplish network tasks. User rights policies are set through *Local Computer Policy*.

username   A user's account name in a *logon-authenticated* system.

Users group   A Windows 2000 built-in group that includes end users who should have very limited system access. After a *clean installation* of Windows 2000 Professional, the default settings for this group prohibit users from compromising the operating system or program files. By default, all users who have been created on the computer, except *Guest*, are members of the Users group.

Utility Manager   A Windows 2000 utility used to manage the three accessibility utilities: *Magnifier*, *Narrator*, and *On-Screen Keyboard*.

V

video adapter   The hardware device that outputs the display to the monitor.

virtual memory   A *kernel* service that stores memory pages not currently in use on a mass-storage device to free the memory occupied for other uses. Virtual memory hides the memory-swapping process from applications and higher-level services.

virtual private network (VPN)   A private network that uses links across private or public networks (such as the Internet). When data is sent over the remote link, it is encapsulated, encrypted, and requires authentication services.

volume   A storage area on a Windows 2000 *dynamic disk*. Dynamic volumes cannot contain *partitions* or *logical drives*. Windows 2000 Professional

dynamic storage supports three dynamic volume types: *simple volumes*, *spanned volumes*, and *striped volumes*. Dynamic volumes are accessible only to Windows 2000; they are not accessible through DOS, Windows *9x*, or Windows NT.

VPN   See *virtual private network*.

W

Warning event   An *Event Viewer* event that indicates that you should be concerned with the event. The event may not be critical in nature, but it is significant and may be indicative of future errors.

Web browser   An application that makes *HTTP* requests and formats the resultant *HTML* documents for the users. Most Web browsers understand all standard Internet protocols.

Win16   The set of application services provided by the 16-bit versions of Microsoft Windows: Windows 3.1 and Windows for Workgroups 3.11.

Win32   The set of application services provided by the 32-bit versions of Microsoft Windows: Windows 95, Windows 98, Windows NT, and Windows 2000.

Windows 9x   The 32-bit Windows 95 and Windows 98 versions of Microsoft Windows for medium-range, Intel-based personal computers. This system includes peer networking services, Internet support, and strong support for older DOS applications and peripherals.

Windows 2000 Backup   The Windows 2000 utility used to run the *Backup Wizard*, the *Restore Wizard*, and create an *Emergency Repair Disk* (*ERD*).

Windows 2000 boot disk   A disk that can be used to *boot* to the Windows 2000 Professional operating system in the event of a Windows 2000 Professional boot failure.

Windows 2000 Multilanguage Version   The version of Windows 2000 that supports multiple-language user interfaces through a single copy of Windows 2000.

Windows 2000 Professional   The current version of the Windows operating system for high-end desktop environments. Windows 2000 Professional integrates the best features of Windows 98 and Windows

NT Workstation 4, supports a wide range of hardware, makes the operating system easier to use, and reduces the cost of ownership.

Windows 2000 Professional Setup Boot Disks
Floppy disks that can used to boot to the Windows 2000 operating system. With these disks, you can use the *Recovery Console* and the *Emergency Repair Disk (ERD)*.

Windows Installer packages   Special application distribution files used to automate the installation of applications. Windows Installer packages work with applications that are in *Microsoft Installer (MSI)* format or *ZAP file* format. The use of Windows Installer packages requires a Windows 2000 Server computer with the *Active Directory* installed.

Windows Internet Name Service (WINS)   A network service for Microsoft networks that provides Windows computers with the *IP address* for specified *NetBIOS* computer names, facilitating browsing and intercommunication over *TCP/IP* networks.

Windows NT   The predecessor to Windows 2000 that is a 32-bit version of Microsoft Windows for powerful Intel, Alpha, PowerPC, or MIPS-based computers. This operating system includes peer networking services, server networking services, Internet client and server services, and a broad range of utilities.

Windows Update   A utility that connects the computer to Microsoft's Web site and checks the files to make sure that they are the most up-to-date versions.

WINS   See *Windows Internet Name Service.*

WINS server   The server that runs *WINS* and is used to resolve *NetBIOS* names to *IP addresses*.

WMI Control   A Windows 2000 utility that provides an interface for monitoring and controlling system resources. WMI stands for Windows Management Instrumentation.

workgroup   In Microsoft networks, a collection of related computers, such as those used in a department, that do not require the uniform security and coordination of a domain. Workgroups are characterized by decentralized management, as opposed to the centralized management that domains use.

write-back caching   A caching optimization wherein data written to the slow store is cached until the cache is full or until a subsequent write operation overwrites the cached data. Write-back caching can significantly reduce the write operations to a slow store because many write operations are subsequently obviated by new information. Data in the write-back cache is also available for subsequent reads. If something happens to prevent the cache from writing data to the slow store, the cache data will be lost.

write-through caching   A caching optimization wherein data written to a slow store is kept in a cache for subsequent rereading. Unlike *write-back caching*, write-through caching immediately writes the data to the slow store and is therefore less optimal but more secure.

Z

ZAP files   Files that can be used with *Windows Installer packages* instead of *Microsoft Installer (MIS)* format files. ZAP files are used to install applications using their native Setup program.

Index

C

cache files, cleaning up, 421
caching
    defined, 838
    for disks, 18
    for shared folders, 470
Caching option, 470
Cancel option
    for printers, 587
    for Windows Security, 248
Cancel All Documents option, 586
card services, **171**
categories for events, 719, 723
Category property, 723
CD-based images
    defined, 838
    for RIS servers, 58, **62–66**, *62–66*
CD key problems, 26
CD-ROM devices
    installation from, **14–16**
    managing, **157–159**, *157–158*
CDFS (Compact Disc File System), 838
central processing units (CPUs). *See also* processors
    defined, 838
    speed of, 9
Challenge Handshake Authentication Protocol
    (CHAP), 623
Change Default Preferences option, 610
Change Drive Letter and Path for dialog box, 399
Change Password option, 248
Change share permission, 472
Change the System Time right, 283
changing
    drive letters and paths, **399–400**, *399*
    passwords, **263–264**
CHAP (Challenge Handshake Authentication
    Protocol), 623
character-code translation, 499
Chart view, **663**, *664*
Check Disk utility, 424, 838

Check Now button, 386
Chkupgrd.exe program, 102
Choose a Hardware Task dialog box, 503–504, *503*
Choose Target Machine dialog box, 251
cipher text, 414, 838
CIPHER utility, **416–417**, 838
classes of IP addresses, 516–517, *516*
clean installs
    defined, 838
    vs. upgrades, **10, 99**
cleaning up disks, **421–422**, *422–423*
Clear option for Start menu, 213
Clear All Events option, 720
Clear Log option, 722
Clear Virtual Memory Pagefile When System Shuts
    Down policy, 288
clearing log file events, 720
clients
    defined, 838
    RIS server configuration for, **72–73**, *73*
    in upgrading, **100–101**
Clone Control sets, 731
clusters
    in FAT32, 13
    in NTFS, 375
CMDCONS folder, 775, 777
color depth, 161
Color Management tab
    for scanners and cameras, 179
    for video adapters, 162
Color option for printing, 564
color schemes for Desktop, 217
Color tab, **670**
Colors option
    for display, 52
    for video adapters, 161
COM ports
    defined, 838
    for modems, 609
Command Prompt dialog box, 737
Comment option, 470

N

S

T

U

Z